Encyclopedia of the
PEOPLES OF AFRICA AND THE MIDDLE EAST

VOLUME II (L TO Z)

Jamie Stokes, Editor
Anthony Gorman and Andrew Newman,
Historical Consultants

Facts On File
An imprint of Infobase Publishing

Encyclopedia of the Peoples of Africa and the Middle East

Copyright © 2009 Infobase Publishing, Inc.

Copyright © 2000 Diagram Visual Information Limited

Facts On File, Inc.
An imprint of Infobase Publishing
132 West 31st Street
New York NY 10001

Library of Congress Cataloging-in-Publication Data
Encyclopedia of the peoples of Africa and the Middle East /
Jamie Stokes, editor; Anthony Gorman and Andrew Newman,
historical consultants.
p. cm.
Includes bibliographical references and index.
ISBN 978-0-8160-7158-6
1. Ethnology—Africa—Encyclopedias. 2. Ethnology—Middle
East—Encyclopedias. 3. Africa—Social life and customs—Encyclopedias.
4. Middle East—Social life and customs—Encyclopedias. I. Stokes, Jamie.
GN645.E53 2008
305.800956—dc22   2008041256

Facts On File books are available at special discounts when purchased in bulk quantities for businesses, associations, institutions, or sales promotions. Please call our Special Sales Department in New York at (212) 967-8800 or (800) 322-8755.

You can find Facts On File on the World Wide Web at http://www.factsonfile.com

Text design by Mary Susan Ryan-Flynn
Illustrations by Michal Novak with additional illustrations by
Chris Allcott, Darren Bennett, Bob Garwood, Elsa Godfrey,
Brian Hewson, Pavel Kostal, Kyri Kyriacou, Janos Marffy, Kathy McDougall,
Patrick Mulrey, Rob Shone, Graham Rosewarne, Peter Ross
Cover design by Salvatore Luongo

Printed in the United States of America

VB JS 10 9 8 7 6 5 4 3 2 1

This book is printed on acid-free paper and contains
30 percent postconsumer recycled content.

CONTENTS

LIST OF ENTRIES

LIST OF ILLUSTRATIONS, AND MAPS

VOLUME II

MAPS

VOLUME 1

VOLUME II

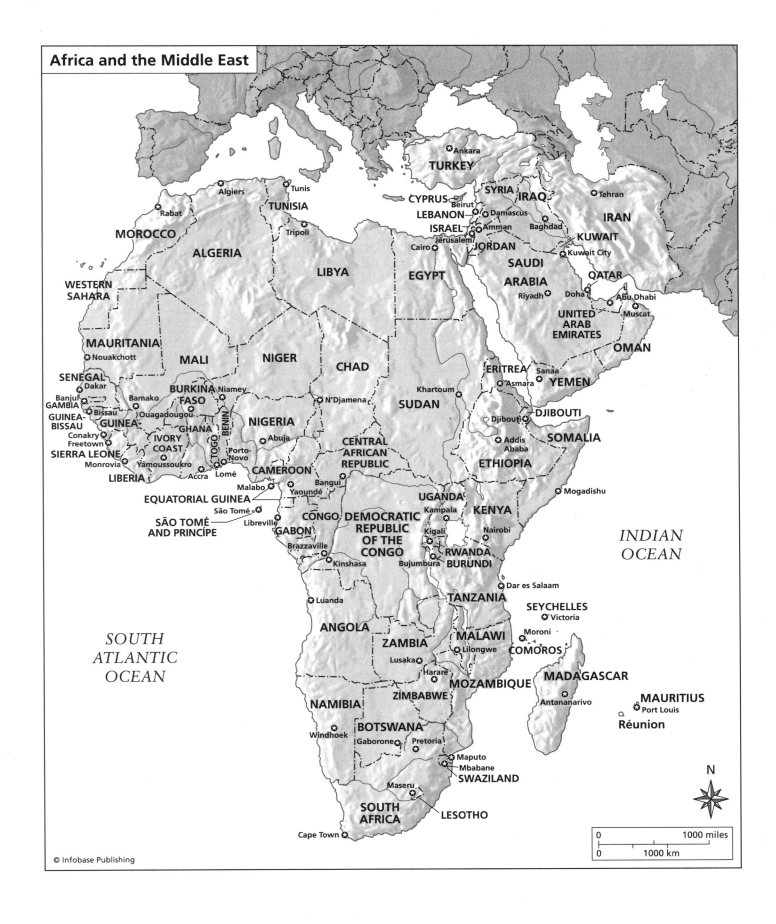

Africa and the Middle East

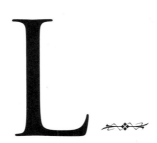

L

Labwor

The Labwor are a small group living among the KARAMOJONG in northeastern Uganda. They speak a LWO language.

Lagoon cluster

"Lagoon cluster" refers to a complex group of largely AKAN-speaking peoples that inhabit the southeastern coastal and lagoon regions of the Ivory Coast. They are related linguistically. The ALLADIAN, ABBE, ABIDJI, ATTIE, and ADJUKRU are part of this cluster.

Lahou *See* AVIKAM.

Laks

The Laks are an ethnic group with a traditional homeland in the mountainous central region of Dagestan (a republic of the Russian Federation). In the period immediately after World War II a number of Laks were relocated to the lowland regions of Dagestan by the Soviet authorities. Their language was traditionally written using the Arabic script, but since 1938 the Cyrillic alphabet has been used.

Lala

The Lala live largely in central Zambia. They are descended from several ethnic groups and make up one of Zambia's larger KONGO subgroups.

Lali

Although they are of TEKE origin, the Lali are part of the KONGO people. They are found in the Republic of the Congo, the Democratic Republic of the Congo, and Angola.

Lamba (Ichilamba)

The Lamba are a people of the Copperbelt (central and northeast Zambia). Many also live in the Democratic Republic of the Congo.

Langi *See* LANGO.

Lango (Langi)

The Lango live in central and northern Uganda. They are perhaps descended from KARAMOJONG ancestors who split away from the main group some 500 years ago. They are the largest non-BANTU population of Uganda.

The Lango are NILOTES, belonging to the so-called River-Lake Nilotes, who originated in a region in the south of present-day Sudan. The ancestors of the Lango, a LWO-speaking people, migrated south probably during the 15th century, traveling along the Nile River to the lakes region of central Uganda. They settled in an area inhabited by Ateker-speaking peoples. The present-day Lango people evolved out of the two cultures.

The Lango have often been in conflict with other Ugandans, such as the GANDA and NYORO. A Lango, Milton Obote, became the first prime minister of independent Uganda in 1962, but he was overthrown and several turbulent decades followed during which the Lango were often active as guerrillas and in opposition movements.

Laz

The Laz are a Caucasian people who live primarily along the southeastern shore of the Black Sea in Turkey and Georgia. The Laz regard themselves as the descendants of the ancient Kingdom of Colchis, which existed from the sixth to the first centuries B.C.E. in the coastal area currently inhabited by the Laz. The Laz language is a South Caucasian language and is closely related to the language spoken by the Mingrelian people who live further north along the Black Sea coast. It is likely that the Laz and Mingrelian languages developed from a common ancestral language spoken by the people of Colchis many centuries ago.

In the Middle Ages the homeland of the Laz was known as Lazistan and was a part of Georgia until it was conquered by the OTTO-MANS in the late 16th century. The majority of Laz, who had been Christian under Georgian rule, converted to Islam under Ottoman rule. Early in the 20th century the homeland of the Laz was divided. The southern portion became part of the modern nation of Turkey while the northern portion lay within Georgia, which was itself part of the Soviet Union until 1991.

Today, the great majority of the Laz live within the borders of Turkey with only small enclaves remaining in southern Georgia.

Lebanese: nationality (people of Lebanon)

GEOGRAPHY

The Republic of Lebanon is a small nation on the eastern shore of the Mediterranean Sea. Its coastline is 140 miles long, and the country has an area of about 3,950 square miles. Lebanon borders two other countries: Syria surrounds Lebanon in the north and east and Israel meets Lebanon's southern border. Israel's border with Lebanon is in dispute following years of conflict between the two nations.

Geographically the nation can be divided into four north-to-south strips. A very narrow coastal plain, only four miles across at its widest point near the city of Tripoli, is the most heavily populated section of the country and the lo-

cation of most of the country's urban centers, including the capital, Beirut. Behind the coastal plain rises a chain of mountain peaks known as the Lebanon Mountains (or the Western Mountain Range of Lebanon). The tallest peak of this range, Qurnat as Sawda, is Lebanon's highest point at approximately 10,130 feet. The entire range is often referred to locally as Mount Lebanon, and its snow-covered peaks are an important symbol of Lebanese nationality. The slopes of Mount Lebanon were historically the source of the Lebanon cedar, a tree prized for thousands of years because of its usefulness as a building material and for its supposed medicinal qualities. An image of the Lebanon cedar is found on the national flag of the Republic of Lebanon in recognition of its importance in the history of the Lebanese people.

East of the Lebanon Mountains lies the Bekaa Valley, the country's most productive agricultural region. On the far side of the Bekaa Valley rise the peaks of the Anti-Lebanon Mountains (or the Eastern Mountain Range of Lebanon), which run along the country's eastern border with Syria. This deep but narrow divide between Lebanon's two mountain ranges is considered to be the northernmost extension of the Great Rift Valley, which extends southward all the way to Mozambique in East Africa. Although the agricultural regions of the country are generally well watered, there are no large navigable rivers; most watercourses are small streams that flow steeply from the mountains down to the coast. The Litani River, which forms from numerous tributaries running into the Bekaa Valley and flows from north to south along the middle of the valley, is too small to be navigable but is a very important source of water for the Bekaa Valley and southern Lebanon.

INCEPTION AS A NATION

The territory of modern Lebanon has been occupied and fought over by dozens of diverse peoples and empires since the beginning of recorded history and was an important center of human habitation for millennia longer. Archaeological evidence of simple dwellings from the sixth millennium B.C.E. in the vicinity of the Lebanese city of Byblos, for example, indicates it is one of the world's oldest continuously inhabited urban centers. Lebanon's position on the coastal route between Africa and southern Europe as well as the route between the ancient civilizations of Mesopotamia and the Mediterranean basin means that it has always been a target for conquest and a busy trading center.

Lebanese: nationality time line

C.E.

1920 France declares the State of Greater Lebanon, including parts of the Lebanon Mountains and the Bekaa Valley traditionally regarded as part of Syria.

1926 Declaration of the Republic of Lebanon (under French administration)

1940 Lebanon comes under the control of the Vichy French government.

1941 Lebanon is occupied by British and Free French forces.

1943 Lebanon becomes independent. An unwritten constitution distributing political power according to the balance of Christians and Muslims in the country is adopted. Christians are guaranteed a small but permanent majority in parliament and the office of the president.

1946 French troops leave Lebanon.

1948 Arab-Israeli War results in an influx of thousands of Palestinians into southern Lebanon.

1958 Lebanon calls on U.S. military intervention to subdue armed rebellions.

1967 Arab-Israeli War (Six-Day War) results in a further influx of Palestinians into Lebanon.

1968 Palestinian militants in southern Lebanon launch attacks against Israel. Israel responds by destroying 13 civilian airliners owned by Arab countries at Beirut airport.

1969 Palestine Liberation Organization (PLO) based in southern Lebanon signs a peace deal with the Lebanese government intended to curb attacks on Israel.

1973 Israelis kill three PLO leaders in Beirut following continued Palestinian attacks across the Lebanese border.

1975 Christian militants ambush a bus carrying Palestinian in Beirut, killing 27. This clash marks the start of civil war.

1975–1990 Civil war in Lebanon

1976 Syrian troops enter Lebanon at the invitation of the government to restore peace.

1978 Israel invades southern Lebanon in response to continuing PLO attacks. The United Nations calls for Israel to withdraw. Israel withdraws but leaves control of the south to a Christian pro-Israeli militia.

1982 Israel launches a second invasion of Lebanon and quickly advances to Beirut. Christian militias carry out massacres at Palestinian refugee camps in West Beirut.

1983 Islamic Jihad militants bomb U.S. and French barracks in Lebanon, killing more than 300.

1985 Israel withdraws to a "security zone" in southern Lebanon.

1988 Two competing governments set up: a mainly Maronite Christian government in East Beirut led by Michel Aoun, and a mainly Muslim government in West Beirut led by Salim al Huss.

1989 Aoun declares war against occupying Syrian forces. Taif Agreement signed.

1990 End of civil war. Government of national reconciliation set up.

1991 All militias apart from Hezbollah in southern Lebanon disarmed.

1992 First elections since 1972 held.

1993 Israel launches a major attack against Hezbollah in southern Lebanon.

1996 U.S.-sponsored peace talks result in an agreement by Hezbollah and the PLO to cease attacks on northern Israel.

2000 Israel withdraws from southern Lebanon.

2005 Syria withdraws from Lebanon.

2006 Israel launches attacks on Hezbollah in Lebanon after two Israeli soldiers are kidnapped.

2008 Dozens are killed in fighting between Hezbollah and pro-government groups; subsequently all parties agree to elect Michel Suleiman as president and a national unity government is formed.

On the other hand, the country's mountainous terrain has allowed its people to retain a degree of isolation and distinctiveness from the numerous conquerors and occupiers that have come and gone over the millennia.

Lebanon's coastal plain was historically the site of a string of trading cities from which the Phoenician maritime empire spread across the Mediterranean in the second and first millennium B.C.E. (see PHOENICIANS). By the fifth century B.C.E. Lebanon had come under the control of the Iranian Achaemenid Empire, although it continued to be a thriving trading center (see ACHAEMENIDS). Subsequently the area was conquered by Alexander the Great, the Seleucid Empire, and then, in the first century B.C.E., the Roman Empire (see ROMANS). It was during Roman rule that Christianity was introduced to and adopted by some Lebanese. Islam came to Lebanon in the seventh century C.E. along with Arab domination. During the Middle Ages Lebanon was the scene of conflict between Christian European Crusaders and Muslim ARABS. In the 12th and 13th centuries it was part of the Christian Crusader states of the Kingdom of Jerusalem in the south and the County of Tripoli in the north. These Crusader kingdoms were finally destroyed by the Egyptian Mamluks in the late 13th century. During the 16th century Lebanon came under the control of the Ottoman Empire and remained under Ottoman rule until the 19th century. The OTTOMANS ruled Lebanon primarily through two local aristocratic families, the Maans and the Shihabs, both of which belonged to the DRUZE sect. The Druze were a minority in Lebanon at the time. The majority of the population during the time of Ottoman rule were Maronite Christians (see MARONITES).

Throughout these centuries of conflict and change the cities of the Lebanese coast continued to act as vital conduits for trade between the Middle East and the Mediterranean basin. Close trading links with southern Europe were established and grew in importance as the civilizations of Europe grew in wealth and importance. During the 19th century the Lebanon Mountains became a center for the production of silk, and most of their exports went to France. This trading relationship with France brought great wealth to the region and a steady growth in the influence of the French in Lebanese affairs. Long-term animosities between the Maronite Christians and the Druze erupted into a series of bloody massacres and wars during the 19th century, with the French,

British, and Ottomans providing support and funding to one or other side as best suited their ambitions in the region. In 1861 French troops partitioned the country, placing the Maronites in control of the bulk of its territory, including Beirut, and reducing the Druze to a series of enclaves around Mount Lebanon and across the Bekaa Valley.

Following the dismantling of the defeated Ottoman Empire at the end of World War I, the territory of Lebanon was mandated to France by the League of Nations (the predecessor of the United Nations) in 1922. France also held the mandate to administer Syria until its independence and unilaterally redrew the border between Syria and Lebanon along the line of the Anti-Lebanon Mountains, greatly increasing Lebanon's territory at the expense of Syria. This radically changed the demographic balance of Lebanon, since it extended Lebanese territory to include many areas that were inhabited by Druze and Muslims. Following the redrawing of the border between Lebanon and Syria, the Maronite Christians, who had previously been a large majority, were now about 50 percent of the population. A constitution promulgated in 1926 under French administration ensured that Christians would retain political power regardless of any change in the Christian, Muslim, or Druze populations. The 1926 constitution required that the country's president should be a Christian and assigned a majority of parliamentary seats to Christian areas.

Following the conquest of France by Germany during World War II, Lebanon and Syria, then still French mandates, came under the influence of the Axis powers through the Vichy French government. The importance of Lebanon's ports as supply routes for Axis operations in the Middle East theater prompted Britain to invade and occupy the country, accompanied by Free French forces, in 1941. In 1943 the Free French government held elections to create a new government for a semi-autonomous Lebanon under a continuation of the French mandate. The new government immediately voted to end the French mandate, and France was forced by international pressure to accept full independence for Lebanon in January 1944. Allied forces continued to be based in Lebanon until the end of the war in 1945, and the last French troops actually left the country in 1946.

CULTURAL IDENTITY

The constitution adopted by Lebanon at independence closely mirrored the constitution imposed by France in 1926. In recognition of the tripartite split in the population's religious affiliations, important political offices were reserved for representatives of those faiths. The post of president was to be filled by a Christian (in practice a Maronite, although there are other Christian groups in the country), the prime minister was to be a Sunni Muslim, and the speaker of the Chamber of Deputies a Shii Muslim. The distribution of seats in the Chamber of Deputies (later known as the National Assembly) was weighted in favor of Christians on a six-to-five ratio. No particular provisions were made for the representation of the Druze or other minority groups. In the decades following independence the nation's demographic balance continued to shift in favor of Muslims as their birth rate exceeded that of the Christians. No census has been taken in Lebanon since 1932, when Christians made up 53 percent of the population, but estimates suggest that by the 1960s Muslims may have made up as much as 60 percent of the population and Christians about 35 percent (the remainder being made up of other smaller sects and denominations). In addition, up to 100,000 PALESTINIANS are believed to have sought refuge in Lebanon during or immediately after the 1948 Arab-Israeli War. Despite this shift in the demographic balance, Christians retained a firm grip on the office of the president and were always able to veto Muslim initiatives in the National Assembly thanks to their fixed majority of seats. Resentment over this state of affairs grew steadily, but Lebanon was enjoying a period of great economic prosperity and the nation remained relatively peaceful throughout until the mid-1960s.

The 1967 Arab-Israeli War (also known as the Six-Day War) bought a second wave of Palestinian refugees into Lebanon. Although Lebanon took no part in the war against Israel, it was to become drawn into the ongoing Palestinian-Israeli conflict largely through its acceptance of large numbers of Palestinian refugees. From 1968 Palestinian militants based in Palestinian refugee camps in southern Lebanon began conducting guerrilla attacks across the Lebanese border into Israel and organizing the hijacking of Israeli civilian aircraft abroad. Israel responded by infiltrating Beirut's international airport and destroying 13 airliners belonging to Arab countries. This Israeli action was intended to galvanize the Lebanese government into stopping Palestinian militant activities within Lebanon. In fact it had the effect of deeply dividing Lebanese society. Those sympathetic to the Palestinians' cause, primarily Lebanese Muslims, hardened their attitude toward Israel, while those who opposed the Palestinians' activities, primarily Lebanese Christians, became more determined to stop them. Sporadic fighting broke out between Palestinian militants and Lebanese government forces. In 1970 Palestinian militants, who had also previously been attacking Israel from Jordanian territory, attempted to overthrow the Jordanian monarchy. They were defeated and expelled from Jordan, many of them ending up in the Palestinian refugee camps of southern Lebanon. By this time the Palestine Liberation Front (PLO) was the leading Palestinian militant group in southern Lebanon, and its leader, Yasir Arafat, established what was effectively an unrecognized Palestinian state there. Division in Lebanese society, a weak government, and a 1969 peace deal with the PLO in which the Lebanese government granted it autonomy over the refugee camps in return for the PLO's recognition of nominal Lebanese sovereignty made it very difficult for Lebanon to eject or curtail the activities of the paramilitaries. From 1970 the PLO stepped up its activities against Israel, and Israel increasingly responded by bombing villages in southern Lebanon it believed were being used as PLO bases.

By 1975 there were approximately 300,000 Palestinians in Lebanon, and conflict between the PLO and Israel continued to intensify. Tension between Muslim and Christian sections of Lebanese society had reached a critical point, partly as a result of the PLO question and partly as a result of growing Arab nationalism in the region and the continued imbalance between Muslim and Christian representation in Lebanon's government. Open hostilities between Muslim militants, Christian militants, and government forces erupted in April 1975. These skirmishes marked the beginning of a civil war that was to devastate Lebanon over the course of the next 15 years. During this war, which left much of Lebanon in ruins and hundreds of thousands dead, Syrian troops were invited by the government to oppose the PLO, Israel invaded twice, dozens of armed militias representing special-interest groups were established, and international troops were deployed on several occasions to try to quell the conflict. The two most important results of the war were the expulsion of the PLO from Lebanon and the reorganization of the National Assembly as a larger body with an equal distribution of seats between Muslims and

Christians. Almost all militia groups were disarmed, with the prominent exception of Hezbollah—a Shii Muslim group that carried out military operations against the Israeli forces that continued to occupy southern Lebanon until 2000. Attacks by Hezbollah into northern Israel and Syria followed the withdrawal of Israeli troops. Israel also attacked targets in southern Lebanon and launched a large-scale assault in the area in 2006.

The years since the end of the civil war in 1990 have seen a gradual rebuilding of Lebanon's economy and a slow return to normality, although sporadic sectarian violence has continued. As a consequence of its geographical position at the crossroads of Africa, Asia, and the Mediterranean, Lebanon is a mosaic of closely interrelated cultures. Although Lebanon is usually referred to as an Arabic country, the Lebanese as a whole are descended from many different peoples who have occupied, invaded, or settled in this corner of the world. This is reflected in the large number of different faiths present in modern Lebanon. Seventeen religions or denominations are officially recognized by the state, including Maronite, Greek Orthodox, Melkite, Armenian, Syrian, Roman Catholic, Chaldean, Assyrian, and Protestant Christians as well as Shii and Sunni Muslims, Druze, Ishmailis, and ALAWIS. For much of Lebanon's history this multitudinous diversity of religious communities has coexisted with little conflict. Unfortunately when political division does arise, as it did in the 1850s and again in the 1960s, the community readily splits along lines of faith, adding religious conviction to matters of primarily socioeconomic conflict. In many day-to-day matters the Lebanese share an almost common culture; the Lebanese dialect of Arabic is spoken almost universally; food, music, and literature are firmly rooted in wider Mediterranean and Levantine norms; and even Western-style dress and popular culture have been widely adopted in urban centers.

FURTHER READING

Latif Abul-Husn. *The Lebanese Conflict: Looking Inward* (Boulder: Lynne Rienner Publishers, 1998).

Carole Dagher. *Bring Down the Walls: Lebanon's Postwar Challenge* (New York: St. Martin's Press, 2000).

Khalid Harub. *Hamas: A Beginner's Guide* (Ann Arbor, Mich: Pluto Press, 2006).

Baruch Kimmerling, Joel S. Migdal, and Baruch Kimmerling. *The Palestinian People: A History* (Cambridge, Mass: Harvard University Press, 2003).

Eyal Zisser. *Lebanon: The Challenge of Independence* (New York: I. B. Tauris, 2000).

Lebou *See* LEBU.

Lebu (Lebou)

The Lebu speak a WOLOF language but are not a Wolof subgroup. Concentrated in the Cape Verde peninsula of western Senegal, where the capital city Dakar is located, the Lebu are the dominant political and economic group in Senegal.

Lega (Kilega; Mwenga; Rega)

The Lega are a BANTU people of the Democratic Republic of the Congo. They live in the east-central region of that country, to the east of the Lualaba River.

A Lega ceremonial mask

Lele (Bashilele; Usilele)

The Lele of the Democratic Republic of the Congo are part of the KUBA group of peoples. They live in the south in the lower Kasai River region.

Lengola

The Lengola are a subgroup of the MONGO of Central Africa. The Lengola live in the central region of the Democratic Republic of the Congo west of the Lokmani River.

Lete

The Lete are a TSWANA people of NGUNI origins. The majority live in the southeast of Botswana.

Lezgins (Lezgi, Lezgis, Lezgs)

The Lezgins are a predominantly Muslim people living in Dagestan and Azerbaijan. They speak a North Caucasian language known as Lezgian.

Lia

The Lia are a subgroup of the MONGO. They live in a region of the Democratic Republic of the Congo that is concentrated between the Tshuapa and Lomami Rivers in the southeast.

Liberians: nationality (people of Liberia)

GEOGRAPHY

Liberia is a nation on the west coast of Africa. It has an area of about 43,000 square miles and is bordered by three other countries. Sierra Leone lies on Liberia's northwestern border, Guinea along its northern border, and Ivory Coast is situated to the east and southeast. Liberia's Atlantic coast stretches for about 360 miles along the country's southwestern side.

Liberia's low-lying coastal strip is about 25 miles wide and is characterized by shallow creeks, lagoons, and mangrove swamps. There are no deepwater harbors, and the river deltas are fronted by wide sand banks that hinder marine navigation. Heavily forested rolling hills with elevations of no more than 500 feet dominate the country inland of the coastal strip. The interior of the country consists of steep mountainous regions and high plateaus, which are generally less heavily forested than the lowland hills. The highest mountains are in the north close to the border with Guinea and are essentially extensions of the Guinea highlands. Mount Wutuvi, with an elevation of over 4,500 feet, is Liberia's highest peak and is situated in this region. Several rivers flow from the highland interior to the coast, but most are narrow and fast flowing and are not navigable for much of their length.

Liberia's capital, Monrovia, is situated on the coast around the mouths of the Saint Paul and Mesuradu Rivers. The city is Liberia's principal port and leading commercial center, and about a third of the population live within its urban area or in outlying settlements. Buchanan, Harper, and Greenville are Liberia's other coastal cities. Much of the interior of the country is sparsely populated, although there are a few sizable towns.

INCEPTION AS A NATION

The majority of the peoples of Liberia are thought to have migrated to their present-day homelands from the north and east in the 12th through 16th centuries. Portuguese explorers reached the coast of present-day Liberia in the 1460s, and Europeans traded with the indigenous peoples of the coastal region for centuries before the establishment of Liberia.

The nation of Liberia was founded by the descendants of freed African slaves who arrived in Africa from the United States in the early 19th century as part of resettlement program. Its name, from the English word *liberty,* was chosen to represent the freedom of these former slaves and their descendants. Although slavery was not abolished in the United States until 1865, there was a significant and growing population of former slaves and their freeborn descendants, particularly in the northern states, by the early 1800s. Some politicians saw this as a potential problem because they did not believe that the United States would thrive as a mixed-race nation. The American Colonization Society (ACS) was founded in 1816 with the aim of establishing settlements outside of the United States for black people. The ACS used private funds to transport volunteer settlers to the west coast of Africa and to purchase land from the native inhabitants. The first settlers arrived in 1822 and established a colony on Providence Island near the site of the present-day capital of Liberia, Monrovia.

Disease and attacks by indigenous peoples almost caused the colony to fail, but a steady stream of settlers continued to arrive and settlement spread to the mainland. The ACS appointed the first governors of the colony, but in 1847 the settlers declared an independent republic. Although the U.S. government did not initially recognize the new nation, Britain and France did, and the U.S. government continued to support the shipment of new settlers. A significant number of these new settlers were black Africans who had been rescued from illegal slave-trading ships. Settlement continued until 1865, by which time almost 15,000 colonists had arrived in Liberia.

LIBERIANS: NATIONALITY

nation:
Liberia; Republic of Liberia

derivation of name:
From the English word *liberty*

government:
Republic

capital:
Monrovia

language:
English is the country's official language but is spoken as a first language by only 20 percent of the population. About 20 other indigenous languages are spoken.

religion:
About 40 percent of the population are Christian, 20 percent are Muslim, and 40 percent follow indigenous faiths.

earlier inhabitants:
Unknown

demographics:
There are 28 indigenous ethnic groups in Liberia. The largest are the Kpelle, Bassa, Gio, Kru, Grebo, Mano, Krahn, Gola, Gbandi, Loma, Kissi, Vai, and Bella. About 2.5 percent of the population are Americo-Liberians (descendents of freed slaves).

Liberians: nationality time line

C.E.

1822 The first group of colonists from the United States arrive in Liberia and found a settlement on Providence Island.

1847 Liberia becomes independent and adopts a constitution based on that of the United States.

1917 During World War I Liberia declares war on Germany.

1926 The Firestone Tire and Rubber Company opens its first rubber plantation on land provided by the Liberian government in exchange for a large development loan. Rubber production quickly becomes the core of Liberia's economy.

1943 William Tubman becomes Liberia's president. He holds the office for 27 years and pursues policies that help to unify Liberia as a nation.

1944 During World War II Liberia declares war on Germany and the Axis powers, providing the Allies with a strategically important South Atlantic harbor.

1951 President Tubman's reforms allow women and indigenous people who are property owners to vote in elections for the first time.

1971 Tubman dies and is replaced by William Tolbert as president.

1979 Public unrest follows proposals to increase the price of basic foods. Dozens are killed in street protests.

1980 A military coup led by Samuel Doe removes Tolbert from power. Tolbert and 13 others are executed. Doe suspends the constitution and assumes dictatorial powers.

1985 Doe is reelected president. Opposition groups protest alleged election fraud.

1989 Charles Taylor leads the National Patriotic Front of Liberia (NPFL) in a violent uprising against Doe's regime.

1990 West African nations send peacekeeping troops to Liberia. Doe is captured and executed by an NPLF faction.

1992 The NPLF launch a major assault against peacekeepers in the capital, Monrovia.

1995 A general peace treaty is signed.

1997 Charles Taylor wins presidential elections with a large majority and his party forms a majority in the National Assembly.

1999–2002 Sporadic border conflicts with Sierra Leone and Guinea displace tens of thousands living in the border regions.

2003 Taylor is forced to leave Liberia as rebels advance on the capital. U.S. and United Nations troops are deployed as peacekeepers.

2006 Ellen Johnson-Sirleaf becomes the first female head of state in Africa after winning presidential elections the previous year.

2007 The United Nations lifts its 2001 ban on the export of diamonds from Liberia. The ban had been introduced to prevent the sale of so-called blood diamonds, which had been a major source of funding for the regions armed conflicts.

2007 Charles Taylor goes on trial in Sierra Leone accused of crimes against humanity. The trial continues throughout 2008.

CULTURAL IDENTITY

The establishment of the colony and, later, the republic of Liberia was not accomplished with the willing participation of the indigenous peoples. The settlers who arrived from the United States formed the kernel of an economic and political elite that continued to dominate Liberia until the late 20th century. For much of the nation's history, the dozens of distinct ethnic groups that make up the overwhelming majority of the population were excluded from political representation and regarded as "uncivilized" by the AMERICO-LIBERIANS who nominally ruled over them. Liberia's indigenous ethnic groups can be categorized under three ethno-linguistic families. Mandé speaking peoples dominate the north and far west, the KRU live in the east and southeast, and the Mel predominate in the northwest. The largest individual groups include the KPELLE, BASSA, Gio, Kru, GREBO, Mano, Krahn, Gola, Gbandi, Loma, KISSI, VAI, and Bella. Americo-Liberians, the descendants of the original settlers, make up only about 2.5 percent of the population today.

In the decades immediately after Liberia's declaration of independence, the survival of the nation was precarious. The Americo-Liberians effectively controlled the coastal region and held a monopoly on international trade, but their influence over the interior of the country was limited. As the major European powers fought to establish spheres of influence over the continent, Liberia's independence came under threat and large portions of the resource-rich interior were annexed by neighboring French and British colonies. The country's economic problems were alleviated somewhat in the 1920s when the U.S. Firestone Tire and Rubber Company extended a substantial loan to the government in exchange for tracts of land on which to establish rubber plantations. The large-scale export of rubber began in the late 1930 and quickly came to dominate Liberia's economy. During World War II the U.S. Navy used Liberia as a base, building an artificial harbor and other infrastructure that greatly aided the Liberian economy after the war.

The 27-year presidency of William Tubman, which began in 1943, is regarded as the period that saw Liberia begin to coalesce as a modern nation in more than name only. Tubman pursued policies to encourage foreign investment and facilitate the unification of the nation by diminishing socioeconomic barriers, particularly between the Americo-Liberians and the indigenous ethnic groups that made up the majority of the population. In 1951 women and indigenous citizens who owned property were allowed to vote in presidential elections for the first time, and in 1958 discrimination on the grounds of ethnic background was outlawed. Despite these positive steps, Tubman remained a representative of the Americo-Liberian elite and upheld a political system in which the Americo-Liberian-dominated True Whigs was the only legal political party. Tubman's successor, William Tolbert, who was also an Americo-Liberian True Whig, ruled for nine years after Tubman's death. The 1970s were a period of economic decline for Liberia, and opposition to more than a century of rule by the True Whigs built steadily.

In 1980 Samuel Doe led a bloody military coup that deposed and executed Tolbert, ended a hundred years of Americo-Liberian political dominance, and ushered in a protracted period of violent insurrection and civil war. Doe was an ethnic Krahn and soon began to appoint people from his own ethnic group to prominent positions in government and the military. An era of interethnic conflict consumed Liberia in the decades that followed. The first five years of Doe's rule saw seven unsuccessful coup attempts, and presidential elections that were described as fraudulent by international observers. In 1989 the National Patriotic Front of Liberia, led by Charles Taylor, launched a long-running and bloody military campaign against Doe's government that essentially pitted the ruling Krahn elite against the Gio and the Mano. Thousands of civilians were deliberately killed in both communities, and hundreds of thousands were forced from their homes. Throughout the early 1990s much of the country was under the control of rebel groups and lawless warlords while the government was besieged in the capital, Monrovia. The war also spilled over into neighboring Sierra Leone. Doe was captured and executed in 1990, but his successor continued to hold Monrovia with the support of a peacekeeping force made up of troops from other West African nations.

The principal combatants in Liberia's civil war agreed a peace settlement in 1996, and Charles Taylor was victorious in presidential elections held the following year. At least 150,000 Liberians are thought to have lost their lives in the conflict, and Liberia's infrastructure was ruined. Although some progress was made in repairing the damage and demobilizing the hundreds of lawless armed gangs that continued to roam the country, these efforts were stalled when violence again flared up as an opposition group called Liberians United for Reconciliation and Democracy made major military gains against government troops. Taylor was forced to leave Liberia in 2003 as rebels closed on the capital and a large United Nations peacekeeping force was installed the same year, bringing an end to much of the fighting. Since 2003 successful multiparty elections have been held, steps have been taken to counter rampant corruption, and foreign investment has helped the Liberian economy to move toward recovery.

For much of Liberia's history its ethnic groups were poorly differentiated and there was little interethnic tension. Prior to the establishment of the colony of Liberia in the 1820s, none of the indigenous peoples had formed structured states or kingdoms, and relationships between groups of the same language family were loose. The coup of 1980 and the subsequent civil war clarified and delineated ethnic differences in a way that had not existed before. Civilians were frequently massacred by all sides because of their perceived ethnic origins and the political affiliations that were assumed to derive from them. There was little or no historical animosity between these groups prior to the polarizations created by the war.

Although the majority of Liberians are Christian, a legacy of the culture of the Americo-Liberian colonists, the country also has a large Muslim community. The MANDING people, who are descendants of the peoples who formed a large Muslim empire in West Africa between the 14th and 17th centuries known as the Mali Empire, live in large numbers in the north and east of the country. Many of the other communities in these regions adopted Islam long before the arrival of the Christian colonists.

FURTHER READING

Adekeye Adebajo. *Building Peace in West Africa: Liberia, Sierra Leone, and Guinea-Bissau* (Boulder, Colo.: Lynne Rienner, 2002).

Emmanuel Dolo. *Democracy Versus Dictatorship: the Quest for Freedom and Justice in Africa's Oldest Republic—Liberia* (Lanham, Md.: University Press of America, 1996).

D. Elwood Dunn. *Historical Dictionary of Liberia* (Lanham, Md.: Scarecrow, 2001).

Libyans: nationality (people of Libya)

GEOGRAPHY

Libya is a large nation on the north coast of Africa. It has an area of about 680,000 square miles and is bordered by six other states. Tunisia and Algeria lie to the west, Chad and Niger to the south, Sudan to the southeast, and Egypt to the east. Libya's coast extends for about 1,100 miles along the southern edge of the Mediterranean Sea.

Almost 90 percent of Libya's territory lies within the Sahara Desert. The south and southeastern portions of the country lie within a wider geographical area known as the Libyan Desert, which extends into Egypt and Sudan and is among the hottest and most arid places on earth.

Traditionally Libya is divided into three distinct regions: Tripolitania, Cyrenaica, and Fezzan. Tripolitania is the western coastal region and its surrounding area, including the capital city of Tripoli; Cyrenaica is the eastern coastal region and its surrounding area; and Fezzan is the desert interior that dominates the south of the country. The coastal areas of Tripolitania and Cyrenaica have a cooler and wetter climate than the interior, and it is in these areas that Libya's major cities and the majority of the population are found. The coastal region of the Gulf of Sirte, which lies between Tripolitania and Cyrenaica, is capable of supporting animal grazing and has traditionally been the home of nomadic peoples. In the largely barren south permanent communities can only exist around the few oases that dot the landscape. There are no permanent watercourses in the country.

Three of Libya's largest cities—Benghazi, Al Bayda, and Darnah—are in Cyrenaica. The capital city, Tripoli, is situated on the coast of Tripolitania and is Libya's economic center. Much of the country is very sparsely inhabited with up to 90 percent of the numerically small population living in less than 10 percent of its area, particularly in its urban centers.

INCEPTION AS A NATION

The concept of Libya as a discrete national entity is a recent development, as is the case with most African nations, but the idea of Libya as a geographically distinct region is of ancient origin. In the classical period "Libya" referred to the entire desert region south of the coastal strip of modern Libya and included territory that now lies within Egypt, Sudan, and Chad.

Archaeological evidence suggests that pastoralists have inhabited the coastal regions of Libya since the seventh millennium B.C.E. and that the interior of the country was well watered and fertile in that period. The BERBERS, who are the ethnic ancestors of most of the inhabitants of North Africa west of Egypt, are thought to have migrated from southwest Asia into North Africa in the third millennium B.C.E. at a time when the region was becoming increasingly arid. The PHOENICIANS, a seafaring people who originated in the eastern Mediterranean, established settlements along the north coast of Africa, including Tripoli, during the first millennium B.C.E.. In the same time period Greek settlers founded colonies along Libya's eastern coast, including Cyrene, which gave its name to the historical and present-day region of Cyrenaica, at a location on the coast about 100 miles

---

LIBYANS: NATIONALITY

nation:
Libya; Great Socialist People's Libyan Arab Jamahiriya

derivation of name:
From the historical name for the desert region that dominates the south of the country

government:
Jamahiriya, meaning "state of the masses"

capital:
Tripoli

language:
Arabic is the country's official language. English and Italian are widely understood in urban centers.

religion:
About 97 percent of the population is Muslim. Of the remaining 3 percent the largest group is Christian.

earlier inhabitants:
Berbers; Ottoman Turks

demographics:
Arab and Berber Libyans make up about 97 percent of the population. The remaining 3 percent is made up of small groups of Greeks, Italians, Egyptians, Maltese, Turks, and Tunisians.

Libyans: nationality time line

B.C.E.

seventh century Phoenician settlers found communities along the coast of Tripolitania in western Libya.

fourth century Greek settlers found communities along the coast of Cyrenaica in eastern Libya.

146–96 Romans conquer Libya after defeating the Carthaginians in the Third Punic War. Libya later becomes a prosperous province of the Roman Empire.

C.E.

643 Arab armies conquer Libya.

16th century Libya is conquered by the Ottoman Turks. Tripolitania, Cyrenaica, and the southern desert region of Fezzan are unified under as a single administrative entity under a local ruler in Tripoli.

1911–12 Italy invades Libya and seizes control of the coastal cities, but resistance in the countryside is not subdued.

1920–34 A second Italian invasion meets strong resistance from Umar al-Mukhtar but eventually succeeds in subduing the entire country.

1942 During World War II Allied forces liberate Libya from Italian control.

1951 Libya becomes independent with King Idris I as head of state.

1956 U.S. oil companies are given permission to locate and exploit oil reserves within Libya.

1961 A new oil pipeline from the oil fields of the interior to the coast allows the large-scale export of Libyan oil to begin.

1969 Idris I is deposed in a military coup led by Muammar Qaddafi.

1973 Qaddafi announces radical plans for a "cultural revolution" and establishes "people's committees" to administer many aspect of Libyan society at a local level. Libyan troops occupy the Anzou Strip in northern Chad.

1977 Qaddafi announces a "people's revolution" and changes the country's name to the Great Socialist People's Libyan Arab Jamahiriyah.

1981 Two Libyan warplanes are shot down over the Gulf of Sirte by U.S. aircraft.

1984 A British police officer is shot dead outside the Libyan embassy in London during anti-Qaddafi demonstrations.

1986 U.S. warplanes bomb targets in Tripoli and Benghazi in response to alleged Libyan involvement in a terrorist bombing that killed U.S. servicemen in Germany.

1992 The United Nations impose economic sanctions on Libya when Qaddafi refuses to surrender two men suspected of involvement in the bombing of Pan American flight 103 in 1988.

1994 Libya withdraws from the Anzou Strip.

2003 United Nations sanctions are suspended after Libya agrees to pay compensation to the families of the victims of Pan American flight 103 and admits responsibility for the attack. Libya also undertakes to abandon its program to develop nuclear weapons.

2005 U.S. oil companies return to Libya.

2006 Libya is accused of abusing the human rights of African migrants.

2008 Libya holds one-month rotating presidency of the United Nations Security Council.

east of the modern city of Benghazi. Cyrene became one of the most important trading cities of the ancient Mediterranean world and was a major source of Greek cultural influence in North Africa (*see* GREEKS).

The second half of the first millennium saw the important Phoenician city of Carthage, in modern Tunisia, come to dominate western Libya, while the Egyptian dynasty of the Ptolemies dominated the east. Throughout this

The partially restored fifth-century B.C.E. Temple of Zeus near the ruins of the ancient Greek colony of Cyrene in modern Libya

period the power of these cities extended little further than the country's narrow, agriculturally productive coastal strip. The indigenous Berber peoples of the interior maintained their independence with ease and posed a constant threat to the prosperous city-states of the coast. A series of conflicts between Carthage and the emerging power of the ROMANS, known as the Punic Wars, ended with the defeat and occupation of Carthage by the Romans in 146 B.C.E. From this time Roman dominance over North Africa grew steadily. By 96 B.C.E. Rome had seized Cyrenaica from the EGYPTIANS and extended its power far south into the desert. Libya became a prosperous and important province of the later Roman Empire.

In the seventh century C.E. the great Arab expansion that conquered much of the Middle East also encompassed Libya and the rest of North Africa, sweeping away the Byzantine rulers who had succeeded the Romans. The ARABS brought Islam and the Arabic language to Libya. In the centuries that followed, successive waves of Arab immigrants and invaders settled across North Africa, intermarrying with the indigenous Berbers and forging a new culture. Today most Libyans refer to themselves as Arabs, and Libya is an integral part of the larger Arab world, although the majority of their ancestors are ethnic Berbers who adopted Arabic culture.

The 16th century brought Ottoman hegemony to Libya, and much of the north coast of Africa and the Ottoman Turks remained in control until the first decades of the 20th century. Italy invaded Libya in 1911 but met determined and effective resistance from the Turks and the indigenous peoples that continued throughout World War I. Italy eventually completed their conquest of the territory in 1934, but Libya became one of the major battlegrounds of World War II and Allied forces had liberated the country by the end of 1942. The British and the French administered Libya until the United Nations voted that the country should become independent in 1949. Libya became an independent state in December of 1951 under King Idris al-Sanusi, known as Idris I.

CULTURAL IDENTITY

During the first decade of Idris's rule, large oil reserves were discovered on Libyan territory, and the country's economy was rapidly transformed as foreign oil companies were granted exploitation rights. The continued presence of a large U.S. military base near Tripoli and another British base at Tobruk also helped boost the economy. The regime of Idris I, however, came under increasing criticism during the same period as the ideas of Pan-Africanism and Pan-Arabism gained prominence among the country's intellectual elite. Pan-Africanism was a broad school of thought that championed the idea of ending foreign rule in Africa and of establishing a unified African state. It was closely linked to Pan-Arabism, which had much the same aims for the Arab world. The free hand that had been given to foreign oil companies and the continued presence of U.S. and British military bases on Libyan soil, particularly after Britain's intervention in Egypt during the Suez

Crises of 1956, was strongly opposed by groups who upheld Pan-Arab and Pan-African ideologies. In 1969 a bloodless military coup deposed Idris I, who was out of the country at the time, and marked the start of a period of radical change for Libya.

Colonel Muammar Qaddafi emerged as the country's leader following the 1969 coup and soon began implementing radical Pan-Arabist policies. The new regime ordered the closure of all U.S. and British military installations in Libya, forcibly deported tens of thousands of Italians from the country, and nationalized their property. In 1973 Qaddafi proclaimed the advent of a "cultural revolution" that sought to establish a new form of socialist "government by the masses" in the nation. Its principles were to be rigidly Islamic in character, and the rule and administration of every institution was to be placed in the hands of hundreds of small "people's committees." Although radical changes were made to Libya's constitution and the administration of daily life, effective power remained firmly in the hands of Qaddafi and his closest advisors.

Qaddafi made numerous attempts to bring the Pan-Arabist goal of a single Arab state to fruition in the 1970s and 1980s. A Federation of Arab Republics that was to merge Libya, Egypt, and Syria into a single entity was approved in a 1971 referendum but failed to materialize. A 1974 agreement to form an Islamic Arab Republic by uniting Libya and Tunisia also failed, and another union between Libya and Syria proposed in 1980 came to nothing.

The Qaddafi regime's social experiments were made possible because of Libya's very substantial oil revenues. This income, coupled with the fact that Libya has a comparatively small population for such a large country, has meant that the nation has for decades consistently achieved one of the highest per capita incomes in Africa. In 1977 Qaddafi announced that a "people's revolution" was in progress. He set up "revolutionary committees" to run all aspects of Libyan society and changed the name of the country to the Great Socialist People's Libyan Arab Jamahiriyah. Once again, however, as the leader of the revolution of 1968, Qaddafi retained almost total power. Libya's political experiments have generally resulted in poor and wasteful administration, the brutal suppression of all opponents of Qaddafi's regime, and steady economic decline. The country's foreign policy proved particularly disastrous for the economy. Evidence that the regime probably supported

Muammar al-Qaddafi: The Colonel ⚬⚬⚬

Muammar al-Qaddafi, popularly known in the West as Colonel Qaddafi, has been the de facto leader of Libya since 1969. Although he has held no official government position since 1979, Qaddafi is referred to by the honorific title Leader and Guide of the Revolution and wields what amounts to dictatorial authority over Libya.

Born in the Surt region of northern Libya in 1942, Qaddafi was the only son of a family of modest means who followed the traditional nomadic Bedouin lifestyle. As a student he was an admirer of Egyptian president Gamal Abdel Nasser and his Arab nationalist and pan-Arabist philosophy. He took part in anti-Israeli demonstrations during the Suez Crisis of 1956 and in 1961 was expelled from school for his political activities. He later received a law degree from the University of Libya and entered the military academy in Benghazi in 1963.

After a period in the United Kingdom in 1965, where he received additional military training, Qaddafi returned to Libya as an officer. Four years later, in 1969, he and a group of fellow Libyan officers staged a bloodless coup that deposed the Libyan king, Idris I. In power Qaddafi based his political philosophy on a combination of elements, including Arab nationalism, popular democracy, socialism, and Islam. Published in a three-volume work called the Green Book, Qaddafi's unique political system came to be known as Islamic socialism. This system permitted the private ownership of small enterprises but required state control of large companies and imposed moral laws such as the banning of alcohol and gambling. Qaddafi coined a new Arabic term for his system, *jamahariyya*, meaning "state of the masses."

During the 1970s and 1980s Qaddafi's approach to politics and international affairs brought him into conflict with neighboring states and Western governments. His government funded armed resistance groups across Africa and the Middle East, including the Palestine Liberation Organization and rebel groups in Liberia and Sierra Leone. By the late-1980s Libya was regarded as a rogue state by the United States and other Western governments and was suspected of having funded terrorist actions, including the Munich massacre at the 1972 Summer Olympics; the Rome and Vienna airport attacks of 1985; the bombing of a Berlin disco frequented by U.S. service personal in 1986; and the bombing of Pan Am flight 103 over Lockerbie, Scotland, in 1988. The United States carried out bombing attacks against Libyan targets in 1986 and imposed strict trade sanctions on the country.

Qaddafi's flamboyant style and his overt support for terrorist groups caused the governments of other Arab states to distance themselves from Libya. His attempts to take on the mantle of Gamal Abdel Nasser as the figurehead of Arab nationalism and pan-Arabism were largely rejected, and other Arab states offered little practical support in his conflicts with the United States. Increasingly he has turned his attention to Africa, where he has gained a reputation as an experienced and trusted statesman.

Since the beginning of the 21st century Qaddafi has undertaken an unexpected program to rehabilitate Libya's image in the international community. In 2003 the Libyan government formally accepted responsibility for the bombing of Pan Am flight 103 and announced that its formerly secret program to build weapons of mass destruction would be dismantled under the scrutiny of international inspectors. Qaddafi was also one of the first Arab leaders to publicly denounce the September 11, 2001, attacks on the United States.

There is no clear mechanism for appointing a successor to Muammar al-Qaddafi since he holds no official government position. His son, Sayf al-Islam Qaddafi, is often cited as a potential future leader, but international observers fear that Qaddafi's eventual death may result in a chaotic and violent period in Libya.

several insurgent groups in Africa, Europe, and the Far East provoked several military strikes carried out by the United States and crippling economic sanctions. United Nations sanctions were imposed on Libya in 1992 and 1993 following the regime's refusal to surrender two men suspected of involvement in the terrorist bombing of a Pan American passenger airline over Lockerbie, Scotland, in 1988. Diplomatic relations with Western nations have slowly been reestablished since the late 1990s as Libya has sought to make reparations for its involvement in terrorism and to open up its economy to foreign investment.

Libyan society is highly culturally homogenous. A large majority of the population identify as Arab, although their ethnic background includes both Arab and Berber elements. Arab Libyans define themselves by the fact that they speak Arabic and profess Sunni Islam as their faith. Berber Libyans are distinguished by their continued use of Berber languages and follow a separate branch of Islam, although their ethnic ancestry is, in many cases, almost identical to that of Arab Libyans. The nation's Berber minority has traditionally been restricted to the poorest and most isolated regions of the country, particularly in the southwest near the border with Algeria. Attempts by Libyan Berbers to establish a degree of autonomy for their region and to have their language and history recognized by the state have met with little success.

Until World War II Libya was home to one of the largest and oldest Jewish communities in North Africa (*see* Jews). It is estimated that there were about 30,000 Jewish people living in Libya's cities in 1945. Many Jewish Libyans migrated to Israel soon after its establishment in 1948 and further migrations occurred after anti-Jewish riots took place in Libya in 1956, 1967, and 1973 until there were fewer than 100 Jewish Libyans remaining. An Italian population of up to 45,000 people was removed almost overnight in 1970 when the revolutionary government nationalized their property and "invited" them to leave the country.

Libya's oil revenues have had a significant impact on the country's culture. Until the late 1950s traditional patterns of agriculture and pastoralism constituted the bulk of the country's economic activity, and the millennia-old ways of life that went with them continued to dominate. A complex system of hierarchies and alliances dominated the political life of the countryside, and most of these rural communities practiced subsistence farming that pro-vided them with their own food and a surplus that could be sold in the urban centers for luxuries and weapons. The inflow of oil revenues that began in the 1960s produced a large migration from the countryside to urban centers. The construction and transport industries, both undergoing substantial growth in response to the growth of the oil industry, absorbed much of this influx of people. Plans to stabilize the rural economy were put into practice in the 1960s and 1970s, forcing many previously nomadic groups to adopt a settled lifestyle.

FURTHER READING

Ali Abdullatif Ahmida. *The Making of Modern Libya: State Formation, Colonization, and Resistance, 1830–1932* (Albany: State University of New York Press, 1994).

Millard Burr. *Africa's Thirty Years War: Libya, Chad, and the Sudan, 1963–1993* (Boulder, Colo.: Westview Press, 1999).

Meghan L O'Sullivan. *Shrewd Sanctions: Statecraft and State Sponsors of Terrorism* (Washington, D.C.: Brookings Institution Press, 2003).

Dirk J. Vandewalle. *A History of Modern Libya* (Cambridge, UK: Cambridge University Press, 2006).

Lima

The Lima are a subgroup of the Bemba. They live largely in central Zambia.

Limba (Yimbe)

The majority of the Limba live in northern Sierra Leone. The remainder live either in Freetown in Sierra Leone or in Guinea.

Lisi

The Lisi are a Nilotic people primarily of northern Chad.

Lobale *See* Lwena.

Lobedu (Lovedu)

The Lobedu live in northern Transvaal in South Africa. They are linguistically related to the Shona and Sotho peoples, but their culture resembles that of the Venda.

Lobi (Lobi-Dagarti; Lodagaa)

The Lobi people live primarily in the southwest of Burkina Faso, northwest Ghana, and northeast Ivory Coast. The Lobi, or Lobi-Dagarti, peoples are a cluster of peoples living in these regions of West Africa and who speak a variety of mostly related languages. The Lobi "proper" of Gaoua in southwestern Burkina Faso speak a language called Lobirifor that is similar to Dogon, although its classification with Dogon has been disputed. The Birifor, or Lobirifor, are another major subgroup that lives to the east of the Lobi proper.

Like the majority of Africans today, the Lobi are mostly farmers, cultivating cereal crops such as sorghum, millet, and maize as well as vegetables such as peppers, beans, and squashes. Historically Lobi women produced gold that was sold to Dyula traders. The Lobi have many expert xylophone players, and differences in xylophone technique are often indications of different ethnic groups within the Lobi cluster.

Lobi-Dagarti *See* Lobi.

Lobirifor *See* Birifor.

Lodagaa *See* Lobi.

Lokko (Loko)
The Lokko live in Sierra Leone and Guinea. In Sierra Leone, they live in around Port Loko. They are closely related to the Mende.

Loko *See* Lokko.

Lokop *See* Samburu.

Lolo *See* Lomwe.

Loma (Toma)
The Loma are a Manding people of Liberia, where the majority live, Guinea-Bissau, and Guinea.

Lomongo *See* Mongo.

Lomwe (Lolo; Ngulu; Mihavane; Nguru)
The Lomwe are a people of southern Malawi, northern Mozambique, and southern Tanzania. They are closely related to the Yao.

A Lobi sculpture

Loumbou (Baloumbou)
The Loumbou live in southwest Gabon and Cameroon. They are a Bantu people.

LOZI

location:
Zambia, Mozambique, and Zimbabwe

time period:
17th century C.E. to present

ancestry:
Bantu

language:
Bantu (Niger-Congo)

Lovale *See* LWENA.

Lovedu *See* LOBEDU.

Lozi (Barotse)

The Lozi live mainly on the floodplains of the Zambezi River in Western (formerly Barotse) Province of Zambia. The Lozi population of Zambia, including the many smaller ethnic groups that have been absorbed by them (such as the Kwanda and the Makoma), is thought to number more than 400,000. There are also smaller groups of Lozi living in Mozambique and Zimbabwe.

Lozi time line

C.E.

ca. 1600s Luyi migrate to Zambezi floodplains.

1700s Emergence of Lozi kingdom

ca. 1780–ca. 1830 Rule of Mulambwa over Lozi: kingdom prospers.

1830s Civil war after Mulambwa dies

ca. 1840–1864 Lozi conquered by Kololo; Kololo ousted by Sipopa.

1890s Lozi come under control of British South Africa (BSA) Company as Barotseland, part of Northern Rhodesia.

1924 Northern Rhodesia taken over by British government. White settlers take much of Lozi land. Africans moved to inadequate "native reserves."

1953 White-minority ruled Central African Federation (CAF) formed including Northern and Southern Rhodesia and Nyasaland (Malawi).

1963 CAF dissolved.

1964 Northern Rhodesia wins independence as Zambia. Litunga Mwanawina Lewanika III signs the Barotseland Agreement incorporating Barotseland into Zambia but retaining a degree of autonomy.

1965 White-minority declare independence of Southern Rhodesia as Rhodesia.

1969 Zambia becomes a one-party state and the Barotseland Agreement is rescinded.

1980 Rhodesia becomes independent with majority rule as Zimbabwe.

1993 Lozi opponents of the Zambian government of Frederick Chiluba threaten to declare Barotseland independent.

1995 Inyambo Yeta, a Lozi, becomes vice president of Zambia.

1996 The Barotse Patriotic Front (BPF) is founded with the aim of achieving independence for Barotseland.

2008 Reinstatement of the Barotseland Agreement becomes a major issue in presidential elections.

See also ZAMBIANS: NATIONALITY *and* ZIMBABWEANS: NATIONALITY

ORIGINS

The Lozi are descended from the Luyi, a people who migrated from the north to the Zambezi floodplains around the 1600s C.E. or earlier.

LANGUAGE

During the years of Kololo rule, the Kololo language displaced Luyana, the original language of the Lozi. Kololo is derived from a dialect of SOTHO, which is a Bantu language from Southern Africa.

HISTORY

The Luyi migrants who arrived in the Zambezi floodplains in the 17th century were led by a woman, Mwambwa, who was succeeded first by her daughter, Mbuywamwambwa, and then by Mbuywamwambwa's son, Mboo, the first *litunga* (king) of the Lozi. During Mboo's reign, the Lozi kingdom expanded by conquering and absorbing neighboring peoples. At that time, the kingdom was not so much a centralized state as a collection of semi-independent chiefdoms ruled by Mboo and his relatives. The unification of these chiefdoms into a single kingdom began in the rule of the fourth *litunga*, Ngalama, in the early 1700s, and was completed by Mulambwa, who ruled from about 1780 to 1830. Mulambwa was able to establish direct rule over the peoples conquered by the Lozi and over the numerous immigrant groups arriving in the kingdom from the north and west.

The most influential of these immigrant groups was the Mbunda, who had been driven from their homes in Angola. Mulambwa allowed them to settle in border areas where they could help to defend the kingdom from raids by neighboring peoples such as the Luvale and the Nkoya. As well as helping the Lozi in this way, the Mbunda played a big part in the military and economic development of the kingdom. They brought with them military innovations—such as the bow and arrow and an improved type of battleax—new crops including cassava, millet, and yam, as well as medical and artistic skills.

The Lozi prospered under Mulambwa's rule, but after his death the country was torn apart by a civil war between the army of his eldest son, Silumelume, and the supporters of a younger son, Mubukwanu. This war was won by Mubukwanu, supported by the Mbunda, but before he could reunite the kingdom it was attacked and conquered by the KOLOLO, a Sotho people from southern Africa. The Kololo ruled the country (and introduced their language) from about 1840 to 1864, when they were defeated by the armies of an exiled Lozi leader, Sipopa. For the next 40 years or so, the kingdom continued to prosper despite a series of leadership disputes, but its power began to wane when treaties agreed with the British in 1890 and 1900 placed it under the control of Cecil Rhodes's British South Africa Company (BSA).

The British ruled the Lozi until the 1960s, incorporating the kingdom (as Barotseland) into the colony of Northern Rhodesia in 1924. In 1958 Northern Rhodesia became part of the white-minority ruled Central African Federation (CAF) along with Nyasaland (Malawi) and Southern Rhodesia (Zimbabwe). CAF dissolved in 1963 and Zambia won independence in 1964.

CULTURE

The life of the Lozi in the rural areas is based on subsistence agriculture, in which people grow crops and raise cattle mainly for their own use rather than for sale. Their main crops are millet, cassava, sorghum, and corn, plus some vegetables and fruit, and their livestock includes sheep, goats, and poultry as well as some cattle. Additional food is obtained by hunting and fishing.

Most of the domestic and light farming work is done by the women, while the men do the heavier farming tasks, tend the livestock, hunt, and fish. Men are also responsible for the skilled ironworking of the Lozi. They dig iron ore from riverbeds and swamps, smelt it into iron, and fashion it into tools, utensils, pots, and other items.

Lozi villages are usually small groups of circular, thatched houses surrounding a central open space, which is often used as a cattle enclosure. On the floodplains of the Zambezi River, the water rises and floods the land every year toward the end of the rainy season, in February and March. When this happens, many villages are temporarily abandoned as the inhabitants and their livestock move to higher ground.

Government and Society

In the Lozi kingdom, the power of the ruler passed downward through a hierarchy of junior kings and chiefs to village-headman level. The *litunga,* based in Lealui in the north of the country, was the overall ruler of the kingdom, but the south was governed by the *mulena mukwae,* or princess chief, who was based in Nalolo. Various councils and offices provided checks and balances to the power of the *litunga.* During the years of British rule, the political power of this hierarchy was gradually replaced by a system of districts and provinces ruled by the state government, but the *litunga,* the *mulena mukwae,* the royal family, and the chiefs retained their titles and ceremonial roles and the respect of the people, though the powers of the *mulena mukwae* were eroded to a greater degree. Since independence, the Zambian government has concentrated on creating a national rather than an ethnic identity and any remnants of political power that the king retained have been lost.

Polygamous marriages, in which men have more than one wife, are common among the Lozi. In such marriages, each of the co-wives usually has her own home, plus a garden and some animals.

Religion

Lozi religion includes belief in a supreme god (Nyambe) and the veneration of the spirits of ancestors. The spirits of former rulers are honored in elaborate public rituals at their burial sites, while those of ordinary people are honored by simpler, more private ceremonies.

The two major festivals of the Lozi are centered on the annual rise and fall of the Zambezi River and the move of the king from his home at Lealui on the floodplain to his capital at Limulunga above the floodplain.

See also ZAMBIANS: NATIONALITY; ZIMBABWEANS: NATIONALITY.

Luba

Luba is the general name for several related ethnic groups living in the southeast of the Democratic Republic of the Congo. There are three main subgroups: the Luba of Katanga Province (previously called Shaba); the Luba Hemba (or Eastern Luba) of northern Katanga and southern Kivu provinces; and the Luba Bambo (or Western Luba) of Kasai Province.

ORIGINS

Archaeological excavations have shown that there has been an uninterrupted culture in the Katanga region from the 700s C.E. onward, though the area has undoubtedly been occupied for longer than that. Some authorities think that the idea of government through chiefs originated in this area as early as the eighth century or before. By the 1300s, there were definitely well-established chieftainships in the region. Increasing population levels as well as

LUBA

location:
Democratic Republic of the Congo

time period:
Eighth century C.E. to present

ancestry:
Bantu

language:
Bantu (Niger-Congo)

A Luba sculpture of a woman. Iconic representations of women are common in Luba art reflecting the important role of females in Luba society.

land shortages set these chieftaincies in conflict with one another, and larger, more military groupings evolved as a result. The most powerful of these was the Luba group, which emerged around the Lake Kisale area.

According to oral traditions, the original rulers of the Luba (then called Kalundwe) were the SONGYE, who had come from the north. The Songye *kongolo* (ruler) married the Kalundwe queen and established a new state, which became the Luba kingdom and covered the lands between the Lualaba and Lubilash Rivers.

LANGUAGE

The Luba language is called Luba (or Tshiluba).

HISTORY

In the 1400s, the Songye rulers of the Luba were displaced by the Kunda from the north. Led by Mbili Kiluhe, the Kunda were at first welcomed by the reigning *kongolo*, Mwana. Kiluhe married two of Mwana's sisters, one of whom gave birth to a son, Kala Ilunga. Kala Ilunga grew up to be a great warrior and he challenged the *kongolo* for the Luba throne, claiming he was the legitimate ruler through matrilineal descent. The *kongolo* was eventually defeated, and Kala Ilunga founded the Kunda dynasty to rule over Luba and took the title of *mulopwe*.

By 1550 the Luba kingdom was powerful, with a strong central government. The *mulopwe* was the head of the government and also the religious leader. He had a group of ministers, *balopwe,* to help him, each with special duties. The *sungu* was a sort of prime minister who mediated between the people and the *mulopwe.* The *nsikala* acted as a temporary ruler when a king died or was unwell. The *inabanza* had charge of ritual matters concerning the *mulopwe*'s sacred role. This included taking care of the king's sacred spears. Finally, the *twite* was the army and police commander. All these ministers, and any other chiefs who ruled sections of the Luba, were themselves descendants of Kala Ilunga. In this way, the Luba kept power in the hands of a small aristocracy.

The Kunda dynasty lasted until the arrival, in the 1880s, of the Belgians, who turned what is now the Democratic Republic of the Congo into a private colony called the Congo Free State, owned and ruled by the Belgian king, Léopold II. His rule was characterized by abuses, brutality, and the committing of atrocities in order to protect the lucrative rubber trade. The Luba were engaged in a war of resistance against colonial rule that lasted from 1907 to 1917. The Belgian government took over the country in 1908, as the Belgian Congo, which became independent in 1960 as the Republic of Congo (renamed Zaire in 1971).

In 1960–63, some people in Katanga (Shaba) and Kasai tried to set up independent states. In 1964 Katangan secessionists again rebelled and soon controlled much of the east and northeast of the Democratic Republic of the Congo before being defeated by the army in 1965. The majority of the Luba opposed the breakaway, which was lead by a member of the Lunda royal family. In fact, the Luba led the wars against the secessionists. Further Katangan rebellions known as the First Katanga War and the Second Katanga War occurred in 1977 and 1978 respectively, and there was another rebellion in 1984.

CULTURE

The Luba country is a mixture of tropical rainforest, wooded savanna (open grasslands), and marshland. The rainy season lasts from October to May. In this environment, the Luba are by tradition hunters and farmers practicing slash-and-burn agriculture. Sections of the forest are cleared for agriculture by cutting and burning the vegetation. These are abandoned when the soil becomes exhausted, and the farmers move on to a fresh patch. This allows the fragile tropical soil time to recover after being cultivated. Cassava and corn are the main cereal crops, and farmers grow millet and sorghum for brewing beer. Other crops include a variety of vegetables, plus bananas, mangoes and tobacco. The Luba raise goats, pigs, poultry, and sheep, and breed hunting dogs. They also fish extensively in the rivers and lakes of the area.

Industrial activities include basket making, blacksmithing, net making, pottery, and woodworking. The Luba also make salt by extracting it from the water in the marshlands. In the past, the Luba were also a caravan-trading people, but rural markets have taken the place of the old trade patterns.

Luba artists are renowned for their sculpture, masks, and jewelry. They make elaborately carved figures out of wood, which are finished carefully and highly polished. Luba masks are probably intended for ceremonial use, particularly in the numerous religious and political societies. The Luba have a well-established core of oral literature.

Government and Society

The different subgroups of the Luba have their own forms of social structure. The Luba Hemba are matrilineal but the Luba of Katanga and Kasai are patrilineal, tracing descent mostly

A modern Luba chief holding his staff of office

through the male line. Families group together to form villages, which vary in size from a hundred people or fewer to several thousand. Although the chiefs still have limited autonomy,

Luba time line

C.E.

700s Shaba region of the modern Democratic Republic of the Congo occupied.

1300s Luba chieftainships well established under Songye

1400s Songye displaced by Kunda.

1550 Luba kingdom a powerful centralized state

1885 Belgian king's Congo Free State is established (Zaire).

1907–17 Luba wage resistance war against Belgian colonizers.

1908 Belgian government takes over Free State as Belgian Congo.

1960 Belgian Congo becomes independent as the Republic of Congo. Katanga Province secedes; some Luba support the breakaway government of Moise Tshombe, others oppose it.

1960–65 Wars to suppress Katangan rebellions

1965 Mobutu Sese Seko seizes power in Congo. Katangans defeated.

1971 Congo renamed Zaire. Katanga is renamed Shaba Province.

1997 Zaire renamed Democratic Republic of Congo; Shaba reverts to its former name, Katanga.

1998–2003 The Second Congo War; millions of Congolese are killed or displaced in the fighting.

2009 Katanga Province is divided into four smaller provinces.

See also CONGOLESE (DEMOCRATIC REPUBLIC OF THE CONGO): NATIONALITY the Luba are more and more coming under central government control, especially those who live and work in urban centers.

Although monogamy is the norm, multiple marriages are still common and a man is expected to give a bride-wealth to his wife's family. Young people go through initiation ceremonies to mark their transition to adulthood; for young men, this involves circumcision.

Religion

The Luba generally still follow the Luba religion. There is a widespread belief in a supreme being, known as the Great Vidye, who is the creator of everything. Spirits known as *mishiki* control the supply of game and fish, while other spirits called *bavide* exert a baleful influence on people, including sorcery. The spirits of the dead, particularly those of ancestors, are thought to exercise a beneficial influence on the living, but some spirits are felt to be malevolent. Specialist witch doctors are called in to combat bad spells. These people also act as medical advisers, because ill health is though to originate with the spirits. The Luba hold special ceremonies for the accession and funerals of their kings. Other ceremonies cover such activities such as mourning, hunting, and harvest time.

See also CONGOLESE (DEMOCRATIC REPUBLIC OF THE CONGO): NATIONALITY.

Luena See LWENA.

Lugbara

The Lugbara live in the region in east-central Africa, where the great rivers of Africa—the Nile and the Congo—begin their journeys to the sea. The majority of the Lugbara live in northwestern Uganda; much of the remainder inhabit the northeast of the Democratic Republic of the Congo. The Lugbara speak a variety of Eastern Sudanic languages, which belong to the Nilo-Saharan family of languages. The Lugbara languages are distantly related to the AZANDE and MANGBETU languages.

In the 1950s the Lugbara numbered around 250,000 people. In the late 1970s and early 1980s the Lugbara suffered near genocide, since they were persecuted under the regime of Milton Obote—after being treated favorably by the country's previous leader, the brutal dictator Idi Amin, who came from the Lugbara region. As a result, the Lugbara number a great many fewer than they did in the mid-20th century.

Lugulu See LUGURU.

Luguru (Lugulu)

The Luguru are a BANTU people who live in and around the Uluguru Mountains of central coastal Tanzania. They are closely related to the ZARAMO.

Luhya See LUYIA.

Lukenyi See SOGA.

Lullubi

The Lullubi were a confederation of tribes who lived in what is now a predominantly Kurdish area of northern in Iraq in the third millennium B.C.E. Little is known about them except that they fought wars with the AKKADIANS.

Lunda

The name "Lunda" covers scores of groups that once lived within the precolonial Lunda Empire of Central Africa. Altogether, these groups total around 1.5 million people. Approximately half of these live in the south of the Democratic Republic of the Congo, around a third in eastern Angola, and the rest in northern and western Zambia.

ORIGINS

The Lunda are descended from BANTU-speaking peoples who settled in Central Africa in the early centuries of the Common Era.

LANGUAGE

People living in the old Lunda Empire heartland speak Lunda. Those who migrated to Angola and Zambia have tended to adopt Angolan or Zambian languages.

HISTORY

By the 1500s the Lunda occupied small separate territories in what is now the south of the Democratic Republic of the Congo. Around 1600 Kibinda Ilunga (probably a relation of a 16th-century Luba king) married the Lunda's senior chief—a woman called Lueji—and became paramount chief. Kibinda's son (by another wife), Lusengi, introduced Luba methods of government. Lusengi's son Naweji began conquering new lands, thus laying the founda-

LUNDA

location:
Democratic Republic of the Congo, Angola, and Zambia

time period:
16th century C.E. to present

ancestry:
Bantu

language:
Bantu (Niger-Congo)

tion of the Lunda Empire. By 1700 the Lunda Empire had a capital, Mussumba; a king bearing the title Mwata Yamvo; and a tax-gathering system run by provincial administrators. These changes coincided with a local growth in trade. Central African commodities such as copper, honey, ivory, and slaves became increasingly sought after by European and Arab traders based on Africa's west and east coasts. Profiting from their own strategic location, the Lunda charged passing merchants transit taxes or bartered food and goods with them for guns and other manufactured goods.

Partly to extend their hold on trade and partly to avoid paying tribute to the Mwata Yamvo, some Lunda groups migrated west, south, and east in the 17th and 18th centuries. These Lunda migrants set up kingdoms in what are now Angola and Zambia. The most powerful of these was the Kazembe Kingdom in present-day Zambia. The building of this kingdom began in the late 17th century when the Mwata Yamvo, Muteba, rewarded the loyalty of one of his citizens by giving the man's son, Ngonda Bilonda, the title Mwata Kazembe and by putting him charge of the eastward expansion. Bilonda's successor, Kanyembo (Kazembe II), became ruler of the lands east of the Lualaba River, and he and his successors completed the expansion into present-day Zambia. Kazembe prospered through trade and tribute, and by 1800 its capital controlled many of trade routes that crossed the continent.

In the 19th century, however, disagreements weakened Lunda rule, and in the 1880s the empire broke up under pressure from the CHOKWE, a people it had once controlled. Then Belgium, Britain, and Portugal colonized Lunda lands. The Portuguese ruled Angola, the British ruled Zambia as Northern Rhodesia (annexing Kazembe in 1899), and Congo came under Belgian domination. Before becoming a Belgian colony, much of the present-day Democratic Republic of the Congo formed the private colony of the Belgian king, Léopold II, as the Congo Free State (1885–1908). His rule was characterized by abuses, brutality, and the committing of atrocities in order to protect and maintain the lucrative rubber trade. Congo became independent in 1960, Zambia in 1964, and Angola gained independence in 1975.

Ethnic tensions in the Democratic Republic of the Congo have led to many rebellions particularly in the north of Katanga (formerly Shaba) Province in the south of the Republic of the Congo, the Lunda heartland. Katanga was only

Lunda time line

C.E.

ca. 1500 Lunda settle in southern Zaire.

1600s Lunda chiefdoms unite.

1700s Centralized Lunda Empire exists; by 1800 Kazembe kingdom is center of transcontinental trade routes.

1880s Lunda Empire breaks up.

1885 Chokwe overthrow Lunda. Belgian king's Congo Free State is established.

1889 Kazembe annexed by British.

1908 Belgian government takes over Free State as Belgian Congo.

1960–63 Belgian Congo independent as Republic of Congo. Katangan rebellion in south (Shaba)

1964 Zambia independent. Katangan rebellion in Congo (Zaire)

1965 Mobutu Sese Seko seizes power and reunites Congo (Zaire).

1971 Former Belgian Congo is renamed Zaire.

1977 First Shaba War in Zaire

1978 Second Shaba War in Zaire

1996–97 First Congo War; Laurent Kabila seizes power and renames the country the Democratic Republic of the Congo.

1998–2003 Second Congo War; millions of Congolese are killed or displaced in the fighting.

See also CONGOLESE (DEMOCRATIC REPUBLIC OF THE CONGO): NATIONALITY

finally defeated by the army in 1965. The secessionist leader Moïse Tshombe, a member of the Lunda royal family, was subsequently made interim prime minister. Despite winning a majority of seats in the elections, a political deadlock ensued that was broken only when Mobutu Sese Seko took power in a military coup. Until 1997 the country was ruled by President Mobutu as a one-party state. Further Katangan rebellions known as the First Katanga War and the Second Katanga War occurred in 1977 and 1978 respectively and there was another in 1984. They were harshly put down by government troops, usually with Western backing. In 1993, the governor, Gabriel Kumwanza, declared the province independent as Katanga. Kumwanza was arrested in 1995 after arms, allegedly for use in a Katangan rebellion, were found at his home. Clashes between his supporters and government troops were defused by his release.

CULTURE

Most Lunda people live in rural villages carved out of the woodland, grassland, or scrub that cover the land. Many villagers practice shifting cultivation—land is cleared and tended for a few years, and then, before overuse exhausts the soil, they move their village and its croplands somewhere else. The main food crops grown are cassava, bananas, corn, and yams. Women grow millet and sorghum, largely for brewing beer. Cassava, corn, pineapples, and sunflower seeds are also grown as cash crops. Most communities keep livestock, chiefly chickens, goats, pigs, and sheep, with smaller numbers of cattle. Trapping forest animals and gathering edible fungi, fruits, and honey adds variety to the diet. Fishing provides another source of protein, and since the mid-1980s, fish farming has become increasingly popular.

During the colonial era, the Lunda's trading activities were widely curtailed and they consequently lost much of their economic wealth. Many Lunda now benefit from cross-border trade that takes advantage of different price structures in Angola, the Democratic Republic of the Congo, and Zambia. Dried fish and meat are exchanged for salt, clothes, sugar, cooking oil, and household utensils.

Government and Society

Each individual fits into a complex system of social relationships. Besides belonging to his or her family and village, a person may be a member of a particular religious group, social club, or political group. In Lunda society, people feel free to marry whom they will, and many marry someone from another culture. Descent is traced through the mother's side, but personal relationships may often be stronger than family ties, although these do provide a network for support if needed. Far-flung maternal relatives meet up at weddings and funerals, and inherited goods and status pass on through the maternal line. The mother supervises her own unmarried daughters and young sons, although there are close bonds between grandparents and their grandchildren. A woman's sons, and their wives and children, typically form the basis of a village.

The Lunda are just one of many peoples under the central control of the governments of the three countries they now inhabit. The Zambian and Democratic Republic of the Congo governments still recognize traditional leaders, who are incorporated into national structures at a local level. Village headmen superintend local affairs and help to settle minor disputes, while senior headmen and chiefs oversee larger areas. Both political and social structures have been disrupted by the civil war in Angola, leaving the Lunda in that country with very little economic stability.

Religion

Many Lunda have converted to Christianity in the 20th century. The Lunda have long held a belief in a supreme creator god called Nzambi, who was reinterpreted as the Christian God by European missionaries. Nevertheless, many Lunda still hold that ancestors' spirits have the power to bless and punish them, and they fear the malign effects of witchcraft.

See also ANGOLANS: NATIONALITY; CONGO-LESE (DEMOCRATIC REPUBLIC OF THE CONGO): NATIONALITY; ZAMBIANS: NATIONALITY.

FURTHER READING

Rafael Marques and Rui Falcão de Campos. *Lundas: The Stones of Death: Angola's Deadly Diamonds, Human Rights Abuses in the Lunda Provinces* ([S.l.]: Apoios [etc.], 2005).

James Anthony Pritchett. *Friends for Life, Friends for Death: Cohorts and Consciousness Among the Lunda-Ndembu* (Charlottesville: University of Virginia Press, 2007).

James Anthony Pritchett. *The Lunda-Ndembu: Style, Change, and Social Transformation in South Central Africa* (Madison: University of Wisconsin Press, 2001).

Luo

More than 3 million Luo people live in the western corner of Kenya, mainly in the Nyanza region. Several hundred thousand live in neighboring parts of Kenya and Tanzania.

The Luo claim descent from a mythical ancestor called Ramogi. The Luo are NILOTES, belonging to the so-called River-Lake Nilotes, who originated in a region in the south of present-day Sudan. The ancestors of the Luo migrated south probably between the 15th and 18th centuries, traveling along the Nile River to the lakes region of Kenya and Tanzania. The Luo arrived in Nyanza in four separate clan groups: The Jok group arrived in the 16th century, the Jokowiny and the Jokomolo in the early 17th century, and the non-Lwo Abasuba in the 18th and 19th centuries. Although the Luo are mainly Christian, elements of the Luo religion still remain.

Lurs (Lors)

The Lurs are an Iranian people from the Zagros Mountains of western Iran (*see* IRANIANS:

NATIONALITY). The modern Iranian province of Luristan (or Lorestan) is regarded as their homeland, although Lurs live throughout the mountainous western provinces of the country. Traditionally the Lurs were nomadic pastoralists. During the 1920s and 1930s some Lurs were forced to settle in urban communities as part of Iran's modernization programs, and many more were persuaded by economic incentives to abandon their traditional way of life in the period from 1940 to 1980. Today, the great majority of the Lur live in towns and villages, but a few nomadic tribes remain.

The Lur are a confederation of tribes with diverse ancestry, although much of their tribal structure has been lost in the transition to a settled lifestyle. They speak a number of closely related dialects of the Luri language.

Lusoga *See* SOGA.

Luvale *See* LWENA.

Luwians

The Luwians were an ancient group of peoples who spoke the Luwian language. The Luwian language was closely related to the language of the ancient HITTITES and was spoken by peoples who lived in Anatolia (present-day Turkey) to the south and west of the centers of Hittite culture during the second millennium B.C.E. It is not clear that Luwian speakers ever represented a single ethnic group, and the language appears to have spread across much of Anatolia during the height of Hittite civilization and following its demise (from about 1200 B.C.E.). In the period after the fall of the Hittite Empire, Luwian was the language of a series of states that developed in Anatolia and northern Syria from about 1800 to 700 B.C.E. The region of Anatolia in which the Luwian language is thought to have originated was later known as Lycia. The LYCIANS are thought to have spoken a language that evolved from Luwian.

Luyana

The Luyana are a subgroup of the LOZI. They live in Botswana, Angola, and Zambia.

Luyia

The Luyia are also known as the Luhya or Abaluyia, the latter especially in Kenya. The Luyia homeland in eastern Uganda and southwestern Kenya is located in the region between the northern shores of Lake Victoria and Mount Elgon to the north. The Luyia region was split in half in 1902 when the British colonial rulers established the boundary between present-day Uganda and Kenya. The Luyia are the second largest ethnic group in Kenya. A smaller, but still substantial number live in Uganda.

The Luyia have a variety of origins. They are descended from KALENJIN, BANTU, and MAASAI ancestors who probably merged sometime in the 17th century. The dominant influence was Bantu, and indeed the Luyia language, Luluyia, is a Bantu language. Luluyia has been spoken in the region for more than 500 years. Different Luyia subnations exist that speak different dialects of Luluyia though most are mutually understandable.

Lwena (Lobale; Lovale; Luena; Luvale)

The Lwena claim descent from the LUNDA of Central Africa. There live in northern and western Zambia. Others, however, live in Angola and the south of the Democratic Republic of the Congo.

Lwo

The Lwo people make up a large family of related ethnic groups largely in East Africa that includes the ALUR, LANGO, LUO, NYORO, and ACHOLI. Lwo is a linguistic and cultural grouping within the larger umbrella group of River-Lake NILOTES. Centuries ago the River-Lake Nilotes migrated south from their cradleland in southern Sudan, along the Nile to the lakes region of Uganda. The Lwo adapted to and absorbed parts of the cultures they met with on their migrations, at the same time transmitting elements of their own—notably their language. Today Lwo languages are widely spoken, both by people of Lwo descent and by those of other origins who adopted the language. The Luo are descended from Lwo people who settled in Kenya and Tanzania. The SHILLUK and the ANUAK of southern Sudan and western Ethiopia are descended from Lwo ancestors who first migrated south then returned north.

Lycians

The Lycians were the traditional inhabitants of Lycia, a region situated on the southwest coast of the Anatolian Peninsula in modern Turkey. According to surviving Ancient Egyptian records the Lycians were allies of the Hittites in the second millennium B.C.E. and Lycia is thought to have been one of the states that emerged after the collapse of the Hittite Empire in about 1200 B.C.E. (known as the Neo-Hittite States). Lycia is mentioned frequently in ancient Greek literature, particularly in Homer's *Illiad* where they are described as allies of the TROJANS.

Lycia came under the control of the Persian Empire in the sixth century B.C.E. along with the rest of the Anatolian Peninsula and remained under Persian domination almost continuously until Alexander the Great conquered the Peninsula in 334–333 B.C.E. In 168 B.C.E. Lycia became independent again for the first time in four centuries following the Romans' defeat of King Perseus of Macedon. The various city-states of the area formed an innovative form of government known as the Lycian League. Under this system an overall leader (or Lyciarch) was elected annually by a senate of representatives from each of the member states. Lycia became a Roman province in 43 C.E. but the Lycian League continued to operate for three centuries until it became subsumed into the structure of the Byzantine Empire.

Lydians

The Lydians were an ancient people of the Anatolian Peninsula (modern-day Turkey). Their origins are obscure, but they may have emerged from the Luwian-speaking peoples (*see* LUWIANS) who were widespread in western and central Anatolia at the time of the Hittite Empire (*see* HITTITES). They established a kingdom centered on the city of Sardis, the ruins of which are situated about 45 miles inland from the modern Turkish city of Izmir, in the period following the disintegration of the Hittite Empire (ca. 1200 B.C.E.).

In the seventh century B.C.E. the Lydian Kingdom entered a period of rapid expansion under Gyges, the first king of the Mermnad dynasty. By the time of the reign of Croesus (560–546 B.C.E.), the fifth king of the dynasty, Lydia had expanded to encompass the entire western half of the Anatolian Peninsula. In 546 B.C.E., however, Lydia was conquered by the Achaemenid ruler Cyrus II and became a satrapy of the Achaemenid Empire. Lydia never regained its independence, subsequently becoming a part of the empire of Alexander the Great, a Roman province (from 133 B.C.E.), a part of the Byzantine Empire, and a province of the Ottoman Empire before being incorporated into the modern Turkish state.

The Lydia and the Lydians feature prominently in ancient Greek mythology and literature. According to the ancient Greek historian Herodotus, the Lydians were the first people to invent coinage; archaeologists have discovered Lydian coins dating from the mid-sixth century B.C.E. that suggest this traditional attribution may be true. Lydia was renowned for its wealth in ancient Persian and Greek literature, and King Croesus has passed into legend as a figure of unparalleled wealth.

Fragments of the Lydian language are known to modern linguists from Lydian coins and from inscriptions on graves. It shares features with other Anatolian languages of the same period but also has many unique features, which has led to speculation that the Lydians may have been recent migrants into Anatolia when they established their kingdom. Lydian became extinct in the first century B.C.E. when it was replaced by Greek.

Ma (Mano)

The Ma are a MANDING-speaking people. The majority of the Ma live in Liberia, but many also live in Guinea-Bissau and Guinea.

Maale

The Maale live in Ethiopia, mostly along the southern fringe of the central Ethiopian Highlands.

Maasai

The Maasai are a collection of ethnically related groups who live primarily in the grasslands of the Great Rift Valley that straddle the border of Kenya and Tanzania. The cattle-herding Maasai, who traditionally follow a semi-nomadic lifestyle, are often regarded as the Maasai "proper." Other Maasai groups include the SAMBURU of Kenya and the ARUSHA of Tanzania.

ORIGINS

The Maasai are Plains NILOTES (people originally from the southwestern fringe of the Ethiopian highlands who migrated to the plains of East Africa). The ancestors of the Maasai initially settled to the east of the Great Rift Valley between Mount Kilimanjaro and Mount Kenya. From the 1600s, the Maasai "proper" migrated southward while the Samburu turned east and settled in the mountains. The Maasai are the most southerly of Africa's Nilotic peoples.

LANGUAGE

The Maasai speak an Eastern Nilotic language called Maa. It is closely related to the language of the Samburu people (known as Samburu) and the Camus people.

HISTORY

The 1700s were a period of increasing power and geographical expansion for the Maasai. Despite their relatively small numbers, by the early 1800s they dominated the region between Mount Elgon and Mount Kenya in the north and Dodoma, now the capital of Tanzania, in the south. As a rule they were not conquerors, but conflict with their neighbors or other Maasai groups began when they raided cattle or defended their own herds.

The 19th century was a period of increasingly frequent civil war among the Maasai. In particular, the Maasai "proper"—united for the first time under one leader, the *laibon* (prophet) Mbatiany—were in conflict with the Laikipiak, an agricultural Maasai group. This was followed by rinderpest (a cattle disease), smallpox, cholera epidemics, and famine during the 1880s and 1890s, which impoverished or killed thousands of Maasai. These disasters sparked further civil wars. This troubled period of Maasai history coincided with the British and German partition of East Africa. Maasai lands in British East Africa were taken over by European settlers and the Maasai were restricted to reserves.

MAASAI

location:
Kenya and Tanzania

time period:
17th century C.E. to present

ancestry:
Nilotic

language:
Nilo-Saharan

Maasai time line

C.E.

1600s Maasai migrate southward from the Rift Valley.

1700–1800 Period of expansion and increasing power

1880s–90s Rinderpest (a cattle disease), cholera, and smallpox epidemics produce famine among the Maasai.

1885–95 Britain and Germany partition East Africa.

1904–08 Maasai lands in British East Africa settled by Europeans.

1961 Tanganyika wins independence.

1963 Kenya wins independence.

1964 Tanganyika and Zanzibar unite to form Tanzania.

2004 One hundred years after losing their lands to the British colonial government Maasai in Kenya begin a campaign to reclaim the Laikipia plateau. Police disperse Maasai protesters in Nairobi.

2005 Maasai protest the release of a white land owner arrested for killing a Maasai game warden.

See also KENYANS: NATIONALITY; TANZANIANS: NATIONALITY

CULTURE

The majority of Maasai are seminomadic pastoralists. A minority, such as the Arusha, are farmers. Boys take the cattle out to graze by day and herd them back inside the village enclosure at night. Each family has its own cattle, but they are managed as part of a larger village herd. During the dry season, the Maasai men drive the cattle to distant water holes, making temporary camps until the rains come.

The Maasai's pastoral way of life is under threat as their right to graze cattle over they land historically dominated is being eroded. This process began under colonialism, when white settlers were given Maasai lands to farm and group ranches were set up to bring the Maasai into the money economy—a process continued after independence under pressure from the World Bank. Under the independent Kenyan government, the Maasai ranches were divided into individual farms, and much of their land was sold to big landowners or allocated to well-connected non-Maasai people. In Tanzania during the socialist era of the 1970s and 1980s, a process called "villagization" placed dispersed populations such as the Maasai into settled villages. Fortunately, however, politicians are beginning to realize the efficiency of traditional herd-management techniques and now try to combine them with new developments—in veterinary care, for instance—instead of trying to eradicate them.

Another threat to Maasai grazing lands has resulted from the loss of wildlife. Widely roaming elephant and giraffe populations once helped maintain grasslands by grazing them, preventing the formation of dense scrub (or bush, dense vegetation of scraggly trees and shrubs). The boom in big-game hunting, which began during the colonial era and was succeeded by poaching, has allowed large tracts of grassland to convert to scrub, which cannot support cattle. One unique solution to this problem, adopted in particular by the Samburu, has been to change to camel herding. Camels are hardy animals that can feed from scrub, they can go for long periods without water, and the milk they produce is more nutritious, more plentiful, and lasts longer than cow's milk. They are also popular with tourists.

Historically, few Maasai engaged in industry. Although some Maasai families have long been blacksmiths, they are despised by others and not allowed to intermarry. As their seminomadic lifestyle is curtailed, however, many Maasai have left the pastoral economy and sought employment in urban areas working in hotels and lodges or as security guards.

The Maasai, who are sought out by visitors, have been greatly affected by tourism; some villages earn a considerable part of their income from sightseeing tours. These tourists expect the Maasai to appear traditionally authentic, however, and this has to be balanced with the need to adapt to the changing economic climate. Much of the revenue earned through tourism does not reach the Maasai; the crafts marketed as Maasai are often in fact neither manufactured nor sold by them. Some Samburu, however, organize camel safaris.

During the dry season, Maasai men live in temporary camps. During the rainy season, they live in homesteads called *enkang*. These are usually built on high ground by women from cattle manure, mud, and grass. They are relatively permanent and are rebuilt every five to 10 years. From time to time, the site of the village is moved. As the Maasai become more settled, however, *enkang* are increasingly being used as year-round homes. To cope with the greater demands on their homes, Maasai women have adopted new building techniques. Houses are often improved by adding a ferrocement coating to the roof (a thin, watertight layer) and gutters to channel off rainwater into a container. Also, changes in the Maasai diet that have entailed more cooking have, in turn, led to the addition of chimneys.

Maasai Homeland

The Maasai diet was once based on milk, which was mixed with cattle blood at times of scarcity. Young men were supposed to stick strictly to a milk, blood, and meat diet; others could eat butter and honey. Only male elders could drink mead made from honey. If cows' milk was scarce, women could drink the milk of goats. Men were supposed to drink only cows' milk. The Maasai diet is now no longer restricted to milk, meat, and blood. In fact, milk with blood is rarely drunk today. Instead, the Maasai supplement their diet with tea, sugar, vegetables, and grains such as corn. Cattle, goats, and sheep are traded for these items.

Until recently, the Maasai usually wore clothes made from calfskin or buffalo hide. Women would wear long skirtlike robes and men shorter tunics. Greased with cow fat, such garments provided protection from both sun and rain, were hard wearing and easily available, and did not need to be washed with wa-ter. As imported fabrics and Western clothes become the norm, however, greater pressure is put on limited water resources, as these textiles need to be washed with water when soiled.

Government and Society

Maasai society is organized into male age-grades. Every man belongs to a particular age-set (a group of males who were initiated at the same time) and moves with this same set up through the various age-grades.

For their initiation into manhood, young men around the age of 16 live away from the village in camps called *manyattas*. Here, they are taught about herd management, religion, politics, and the skills of social life. After they have undergone circumcision they join the youngest age-grade of *moran,* often translated as "warriors." *Moran* did act in the past as the Maasai army, but fighting is not their main function. The *moran* are usually responsible

A young Maasai man with braided hair and traditional jewelry

A young Maasai woman wearing examples of traditional beaded jewelry

for the herds when they are far from the village during the dry season and provide a source of labor for specific tasks. Since the 1960s, many *moran* now complete their education after circumcision. The Maasai trace their history by referring to the time when particular age-sets were serving as *moran*.

After a period of between seven and 15 years, all existing *moran* are promoted to the status of elders as the next generation undergo initiation as *moran*. As elders they have the right to chew tobacco, take snuff, and settle, but at this stage they have little formal influence. The most recent age-set to become elders is called *ilterekeyani*. There are two more grades of elder: senior and retired. Senior elders take decisions on such matters as public disputes, the allocation of pasture, and, in the modern world, development projects. Retired elders are still very influential and can act as patrons of men in younger age-sets.

Each age-set holds council meetings chaired by a nominee known as the *olaiguenani*. At these meetings every man is entitled to have his say and decisions are taken by consensus. If an issue affects other age-sets, then *olaiguenani* from the relevant groups meet. They cannot take decisions without referring back to their age-set, though, and they also consult with the women.

Religion

The Maasai religion is monotheistic. Their god is called Engai (or Enkai) and is described as the husband of the moon. He is thought to dwell above Mount Kilimanjaro, Tanzania—Africa's highest mountain. According to Maasai legend Engai created the world and the Maasai to inhabit it at the beginning of time. He also created all cattle for the benefit of the Maasai. In the past, this legend used to justify raiding a neighbor's cattle. In modern times, disputes over cattle are more likely to be settled by negotiation than raiding.

The Maasai have great respect for their *laibons*, who are prophets, leaders of rituals, and healers. Their major function was once to advise the *moran* on advantageous times for raiding or war, and to bless their ceremonies. *Laibons* would also announce major prophecies from a trancelike state. In the present, *laibons* admit that their prophetic abilities are on the wane, but they claim still to be able to divine the sources of personal misfortune; therefore, they now deal on an individual basis with clients who have problems such as infertility or bad luck rather than advise the whole community or foretell the future.

In a traditional Maasai dance, the performing *moran* would jump up and down, without using their arms, and grunt as they touched the ground. *Moran* would perform this dance in unison, keeping perfect time, and watched by other Maasai.

See also KENYANS: NATIONALITY; TANZANIANS

FURTHER READING

Elizabeth L. Gilbert. *Tribes of the Great Rift Valley* (New York: Abrams, 2007).

Jamie Hetfield. *The Maasai of East Africa* (New York: Rosen Publishing Group, 2005).

Lotte Hughes. *Moving the Maasai: A Colonial Misadventure* (Basingstoke, U.K.: Palgrave Macmillan, 2006).

Robert Wambugu Rukwaro and Sylvester J. M. Maina. *Transformation of Maasai Art and Architecture* (Nairobi, Zimbabwe: ARTS Press, 2006).

Heather Zeppel. *Indigenous Ecotourism: Sustainable Development and Management*. Ecotourism book series, no. 3 (Wallingford, U.K.: CABI Pub, 2006).

Maba

Most of the Maba live in eastern Chad, but around 10 percent of their number live in Sudan. They speak a Nilo-Saharan language called Bora Mabang.

Maban

The Maban are a subgroup of the FUNJ people. The Funj live in southern Sudan.

Mabiha *See* MAVIA

Macedonians

Macedonians of today are citizens of the Republic of Macedonia, a landlocked, mountainous nation that lies in the southern area of the Balkan Peninsula. The country was established in 1991 when it declared its independence from Yugoslavia. It shares a border with Serbia and Kosovo to the north, Bulgaria to the east, Greece to the south, and Albania to the west. Of a population of approximately 2 million, ethnic Macedonians are estimated at 64 percent, with ethnic Albanians making up about 25 percent, and small minorities of TURKS, ROMA, and Serbs accounting for the remainder. The Macedonians are generally Orthodox, while Albanians are Sunni Muslims. Tensions between ethnic Macedonians and ethnic Albanians have been a recurring problem. The Macedonian language belongs to the South Slavic family, related to Bulgarian and written with the Cyrillic alphabet.

People who called themselves Macedonians first appeared around 700 B.C.E. in these northern areas of the Balkan Peninsula. Most historians agree that the ancient Macedonians were a mix of Greek, Illyrian, and Thracian peoples who shared in the religion and culture of the Hellenic world (*see* GREEKS). They came to control the highlands and plains, leaving the coastal areas to the Athenians. Under Philip II, who ruled from 359 to 336 B.C.E., and his son Alexander the Great, the kingdom rose to prominence, and in the centuries that followed, periods of unrest alternated with stability. Macedonia eventually became a Roman province, and in the sixth and seventh centuries C.E. came under rule of the Byzantine Empire. During this period there were large influxes of Slavic peoples into the area. The Ottoman Turks conquered the region in the 15th century and held it until 1912, when Turkey was defeated by an alliance of Balkan countries in the First Balkan War (*see* OTTOMANS). After World War II Macedonia was incorporated into the Socialist Federal Republic of Macedonia, and Macedonian language and culture flourished. Greece, which also contains a region known as Macedonia, has objected to the Republic of Macedonia using that name.

Macha

The Macha are one of the nine main subgroups of the OROMO. They live in Ethiopia.

Machinga

The Machinga are widely considered to be a subgroup of the YAO. They live primarily in Tanzania.

Maconde *See* MAKONDE.

Madagascan Peoples

This entry concentrates on the historical people of Madagascar, *see* MALAGASY: NATIONALITY for information about the modern population of Madagascar.

ORIGINS

The historical peoples of Madagascar can be divided into two main groups: those of Indonesian descent, who live mainly in the central and south-central highlands of the interior, and those of black African descent, who inhabit the coastal regions and are sometimes known collectively as the Côtiers (the coastal people).

Madagascan Peoples time line

C.E.

up to 1000 Indonesians arrive on island of Madagascar.

1400 Muslim trading colonies and kingdoms established.

1500s Sakalava kingdom established.

1600s Tsitambala confederation

1700s Betsimisiraka kingdom emerges from Tsitambala confederation.

1791 Fall of Betsimisiraka kingdom.

1797 Unified Merina kingdom in existence.

1810–28 Reign of Merina king Radama I; island unification and opening up to foreign influences begins.

1822 Sakalava kingdom collapses.

1883–85 Franco-Merina War over control of island

1895 French rule begins.

See also MALAGASY: NATIONALITY

The most numerous of the highland peoples are the MERINA, who make up about 27 percent of the island's population, and the BETSILEO (13 percent of the population). The major coastal peoples include the BETSIMISIRAKA, who represent about 15 percent of the total population; the ANTANDROY (8 percent); and the SAKALAVA (6 percent). The Merina, Betsimisaraka, and Betsileo each number over 1 million people.

LANGUAGE

The official languages of Madagascar are Malagasy and French, but less than 30 percent of the population speak French; outside of the cities, most people speak only Malagasy. The different ethnic groups speak dialects of the Malagasy language, which is a member of the Western Austronesian language family. Standard Malagasy (the "official" form), used to bridge the gap between dialects, is based on the Merina dialect and written in the Roman alphabet.

HISTORY

The first people to settle in Madagascar were of Malayo-Polynesian origin. They arrived on the island from Indonesia between 2,000 and 1,500 years ago, and over the following centuries they were joined by waves of immigrants from Africa, Asia, Arabia, and Europe.

Three Great Kingdoms

Madagascar's history is dominated by three large, powerful kingdoms, formed by the unification of smaller states. The first of these was the Sakalava Kingdom, which was established along the west coast in the late 16th century. By the middle of the 18th century it controlled nearly half the island, but it began to fragment after the death of its last ruler, Queen Ravahiny, in 1808. The second had its origins in the Tsitambala confederation, a 17th-century alliance of chiefdoms along the east coast. This confederation was taken over and expanded in the early 18th century by Ratsimilaho, an English-educated son of an English pirate, who created from it the Betsimisiraka Kingdom. The third great kingdom emerged in the central highlands during the 15th century, when the MERINA settled there and subjugated the original inhabitants, the Vazimba. The Merina Kingdom grew and prospered, and after the fall of the Betsimisiraka Kingdom in 1791 and the Sakalava Kingdom in 1822, it controlled most of the island.

Colonialism

European contact with the island began with the arrival of a Portuguese fleet in 1500. For the next 300 hundred years, the Portuguese, British, Dutch, and French tried to set up colonies on the island. These early colonies were repeatedly destroyed by the islanders, but they tolerated small bases that were set up in the late 17th century by pirates from Europe and the American colonies, who preyed on shipping in the Indian Ocean.

During the first half of the 19th century, the Merina ruler King Radama I opened up Madagascar to outside influences, particularly French and British. In 1817 the British acknowledged him as king of all Madagascar, and British and other European advisors began helping him establish schools, industries, and a professional army and set up Christian churches. These policies were reversed when Radama died in 1828 and was succeeded by his wife, Queen Ranavalona I. She forced most of the Europeans from the country and closed the schools and churches, but the French and British began to return after her death in 1861.

Over the next 30 years, France, Britain, and the Merina argued over which of them should control the island, and there was war between the Merina and the French from 1883 to 1885. In 1890 Britain agreed to let France have Madagascar in return for control of Egypt and Zanzibar, and the country was declared a French protectorate (colony) in 1895. This was opposed by Queen Ranavalona II and by the people, so the French imposed their rule by force. Madagascar remained a French colony until 1960, when it regained its independence under its first president, Philibert Tsiranana.

CULTURE
Agriculture

Outside the main towns and cities, the way of life is mostly agricultural and so is heavily influenced by climate and geography. In the hot and humid tropical climate of the north and east, important crops include coffee, vanilla, cloves, fruit, and sugarcane. The hot coastal plains of the west and southwest are drier than the north and east, and their main products are rice, cotton, tobacco, and cassava. Livestock is raised in the arid south of the country, the temperate highland regions of the interior, and on the coastal plains. Cattle are often regarded as indicators of wealth and not as sources of income. The highlands are important rice-growing areas but have been badly affected by soil erosion and deforestation. Fishing is important in many areas, both along the coast and in the numerous rivers and lakes.

Most farmers practice subsistence agriculture, in which people grow food for their own consumption, but some crops, such as tobacco, coffee, and vanilla, are grown to be sold for cash. The work involved is usually divided between men and women. For example, men typically prepare the ground for planting, build the houses and cattle pens, hunt, and fish. Women usually tend the crops, grow herbs and vegetables, and perform domestic tasks such as cooking and laundry.

Trade and Industry

Only a relatively small proportion of people are involved in industry, and the majority of these work in food-processing plants. Textiles, brewing, and paper and soap production are other important sectors. Sea fishing by coastal fisherman is in the process of being industrialized. The Indian population largely dominates the jewelry and textile trades.

Social Structure

Family and clan relationships are very important in Madagascan society. The members of a clan trace their origins back to a common and revered ancestor. Marriage customs vary from one ethnic group to another. Although most marriages are between one man and one woman, the customs of some people allow a man to

A traditional Malagasy sculpture

have more than one wife, while others allow a woman to have more than one husband.

Religion

About 50 percent of the population of Madagascar follow the Malagasy religion, which is based on reverence for spirits and ancestors. This is expressed in ceremonies centered on the ancestral tombs, which are built and maintained with great care. These ceremonies help people to maintain a feeling of identity with each other and with their past, and, whenever possible, the dead are always buried in their ancestral tombs. Often, aspects of the Malagasy religion (such as ancestor reverence) are practiced in conjunction with Christianity or Islam.

Christianity was brought to Madagascar by European missionaries during the 19th century. The Christians in the interior of the country, where the British had most influence, are mainly Protestant. Those in the coastal regions, where French influence was stronger, are mostly Catholic.

The third major religion of Madagascar is Islam, which is followed by around 10 percent of the population and was brought to the island by Arab, East African, and Comoran traders who began to trade there in the ninth century. These traders, who were mostly Sunni Muslims, also brought with them a tradition of divination, or prophecy, called *sikidy*. Although the majority of Madagascar's Muslims belong to the Sunni branch of Islam, there are also a number of Shii and Ismaili Muslims on the island, most of whom are of Indian or Pakistani origin.

FURTHER READING

Gwyn Campbell. *An Economic History of Imperial Madagascar 1750–1895: The Rise and Fall of an Island Empire* (Cambridge, U.K.: Cambridge University Press, 2005).

Jennifer Cole. *Forget Colonialism?: Sacrifice and the Art of Memory in Madagascar* (Berkeley: University of California Press, 2001).

David Graeber. *Lost People: Magic and the Legacy of Slavery in Madagascar* (Bloomington: Indiana University Press, 2007).

Raymond K. Kent. *The Many Faces of an Anti-Colonial Revolt: Madagascar's Long Journey into 1947* (Albany, Calif.: Foundation for Malagasy Studies, 2007).

Jørgen Ruud. *Gods and Ancestors: Society and Religion Among the Forest Tribes in Madagascar* (Oslo: Solum, 2002).

Madi (Maditi)

The Madi live mostly in northwestern Uganda but some also live in southern Sudan. Most of the Madi live in Uganda. They are sometimes classified as a LUGBARA subgroup.

Maditi See MADI.

Madjigodjia

The Madjigodjia are one the major subgroups of the BUDUMA. They live primarily in southern Chad's lake region.

Madjingaye

The Madjingaye are a subgroup of the SARA of Chad.

Maganga (Chuabo)

The Maganga are a subgroup of the CHEWA of Malawi, Zambia, and Mozambique.

Mahafaly

The Mahafaly are one of Madagascar's ethnic groups. They live in the southwest of the island. (*See* MADAGASCAN PEOPLES.)

Mahi

The Mahi are closely related to the EWE and are a FON subgroup. They live mostly in Togo, but a minority also live in northern Benin.

Maibuloa

The Maibuloa are one of the major BUDUMA subgroups. They live in southern Chad.

Maiombe See MAYOMBE.

Maji

The Maji are thought to be related to the SADAMA. The Maji live in southwest Ethiopia near the border with Sudan.

Majoge

The Majoge are one of the main subdivisions of the GUSII, a large ethnic group of western Kenya.

Makonde (Chimakonde; Konde; Maconde; Matambwe)

The Makonde are a large ethnic group of southeastern Tanzania. They are closely related to the Makua and are sometimes classified as a subgroup of the YAO (*see* MAKUA-LOMWE). The distinctive carvings of the Makonde have been widely copied by artisans throughout the region, largely to supply tourist and foreign markets.

Makua See MAKUA-LOMWE.

Makua-Lomwe

The various ethnic groups that make up the Makua-Lomwe peoples account for roughly 40 percent of Mozambique's total population (see MOZAMBICANS). They are concentrated along the lower Zambezi River Valley in the center of Mozambique, in the northernmost provinces of Niassa and Cabo Delgado, and along parts of the northeast coast of the Indian Ocean. The Makua proper make up the bulk of the Makua-Lomwe peoples, and most live north of the Ligonha River and along the coast. The majority of the Lomwe live south of Ligonha and inland from the coast.

Attempts to balance the power of different ethnic groups have been made in Mozambique. Nevertheless southerners, such as the TSONGA, have tended to benefit from better educational opportunities than northerners, and as a result the government is largely drawn from southern and central groups.

Malagasy: nationality (people of Madagascar)

GEOGRAPHY

Madagascar is a large island nation in the Indian Ocean off the east coast of Africa. The island of Madagascar has an area of about 227,000 square miles and is the fourth largest island in the world. The nation of Madagascar also claims sovereignty over a number of smaller islands that lie off its coast, including the Iles Glorieuses, Bassas da India, Juan de Nova, and Europa, although these are currently administered by France. Together these disputed islands have an area of just 11 square miles. The island of Madagascar is separated from the mainland by the Mozambique Channel. At its closest point it is about 270 miles east of the coast of Mozambique.

The west coast of the island is low lying and indented by numerous natural harbors. Moving east the land rises in a series of escarpments to a central highland plateau that includes many volcanic peaks. Mount Maromokotro is the highest of these at over 9,400 feet. On the east coast the land drops sharply to a narrow low-lying strip that is bounded by a remarkably straight coastline of coral beaches. Behind these beaches a series of interconnected lagoons stretch for 300 miles along the eastern edge of the island. Most of Madagascar's rivers flow westward from the central highlands toward the Mozambique Channel.

Much of Madagascar is covered by relatively arid savanna and poor soil, the result of centuries of land clearance by its inhabitants that has removed much of the original thick forest cover. The only large remnant of this forest is a narrow strip along the eastern edge of the central escarpment. The island's long geographical isolation from the African mainland has resulted in the evolution and survival of many unique animal and plant species. Half of the bird species on the island, 80 percent of its flowering plants, and more than 90 percent of its reptiles are found nowhere else in the world.

The country's capital city, Antananarivo, is located in the center of the island and is connected to the nation's foremost seaport, Toamasina on the east coast, by a railway. About 30 percent of Madagascar's population lives in urban areas. The western half of the island is more sparsely inhabited than the eastern.

INCEPTION AS A NATION

The peoples of Madagascar have African, Arab, Indonesian, and Malayan ancestors. It is thought that the first inhabitants of the island arrived between the first and sixth centuries B.C.E. and that the island had been uninhabited before this time. Some archaeologists hold the view that the Malagasy arrived in Madagascar having already developed as a people with mixed African, Arab, and Asian roots. Others maintain that separate African, Arab, and Asian peoples arrived at different times and eventually merged into the Malagasy of today.

During the 16th and 17th centuries several European nations attempted to establish colonies on Madagascar, but none were successful. The Mozambique Channel was an important sealane at that time as part of the trade route between Europe, India, and Southeast Asia, and became notorious as the haunt of pirates who were based on Madagascar and the smaller islands around its coast.

By the 18th century the island of Madagascar was home to three competing kingdoms. The Kingdom of Merina dominated the central highlands, the Kingdom of Sakalava the west of the island, and the Kingdom of Betsimisaraka the east. Under King Andrianampoinimerina, who reigned from 1787 to 1810, and his son Radama I, who ruled from 1810 to 1828, MERINA became dominant and united the entire island under one rule for the first time. Radama I courted European interest in Madagascar by inviting the British help to set up schools and modernize his armed forces. Britain's interest

---

MALAGASY: NATIONALITY

nation:
Madagascar; Republic of Madagascar

derivation of name:
From the Malagasy word for the island Madagasikara

government:
Republic

capital:
Antananarivo

language:
English, French, and Malagasy are the country's official languages.

religion:
About 52 percent of the population follow indigenous faiths, Christians make up 41 percent of the population, and Muslims 7 percent.

earlier inhabitants:
Uninhabited

demographics:
Malayo-Indonesians (principally Merina and Betsileo) make up about 37 percent of the population. Côtiers (mixed Malayo-Indonesian, African, and Arab ancestry) make up the majority of the remainder. There are also small groups of Creoles, French, Indians, and Comoros.

Malagasy: nationality time line

C.E.

first to sixth centuries Malayo-Indonesian peoples settle on Madagascar.

10th–13th centuries Muslims from East Africa settle the north of the island.

1500 Portuguese explorer Diogo Dias becomes the first European to visit Madagascar.

17th century Foundation of the kingdom of Merina

1643 The French found Fort Dauphin in southern Madagascar.

1671 The French abandon Fort Dauphin.

18th century The Sakalava kingdom dominates Madagascar.

1787–1810 Merina Kingdom wins control of most of Madagascar under King Nampoina.

1817 Britain recognizes Merina King Radama as king of all Madagascar.

1845 Queen Ranavalona I defeats a British and French invasion and expels European missionaries and traders.

1861 Death of Queen Ranavalona; King Radama II gives concessions to a French trading company.

1869 Prime minister Rainilaiarivony imposes Protestant Christianity on the Malagasy.

1883–85 First Franco-Merina war; Merina cedes Diego Suarez to France.

1890 France declares Madagascar a protectorate.

1895 Second Franco-Merina War: France occupies the capital, Antananarivo, after Merina refuses to submit to French rule.

1896 Madagascar is declared a French colony.

1897 France deposes Queen Ranavalona III, the last monarch of Madagascar.

1942 British and South African forces occupy Madagascar.

1943 The British hand Madagascar over to the Free French.

1945 France gives Madagascar the right to elect an assembly.

in Madagascar was focused on preventing it coming under French control because of the threat this could pose to the sea route to India. Britain's influence over Madagascar declined during the 19th century and French ambitions were also frustrated.

In 1883 France launched an invasion that resulted in the establishment of a French protectorate over the entire island in 1885. Britain accepted this situation in 1890 as part of an Anglo-French agreement that promised Britain control over Zanzibar. Local resistance to French rule continued, however, and was not suppressed until 1904. In 1942, during World War II, Madagascar was briefly occupied by British forces but returned to French control in 1943. The island became a French overseas territory in 1946, thereby theoretically bestowing French citizenship on all of its inhabitants. In reality very few Malagasy acquired meaningful rights under the new regime, and a two-tier voting system emerged in which the large majority had little or no political influence while the Europeanized urban elite dominated public life. A major rebellion against continued French dominance broke out in 1947 and was put down only after the loss of tens of thousands of Malagasy lives.

Democratic reforms began in 1956 that led to the abolition of the two-tier voting system and allowed many more Malagasy to take government positions. In a 1958 referendum a large majority of Malagasy voted to become an autonomous republic within the new French Community. The Malagasy Republic, as it was then called, became a fully independent nation in June 1960 with Philibert Tsiranana as its first president. The country was renamed the Republic of Madagascar in 1975.

CULTURAL IDENTITY

Madagascar has suffered from internal disputes and international tensions in the decades since independence. Philibert Tsiranana, the first

1947–48 A pro-independence rebellion breaks out; France crushes the rebellion with the loss of 80,000 lives.

1958 Madagascar gains internal self-government.

1960 Madagascar becomes independent as the Malagasy Republic; Philibert Tsiranana is the first president.

1965 Tsiranana is reelected president.

1972 Mass demonstrations force Tsiranana to resign; the army takes power under Gabriel Ramanantsoa.

1975 President Didier Ratsiraka nationalizes foreign-owned business and changes the country's name to Madagascar.

1982 Ratsiraka is reelected president.

1991 President Ratsiraka places Albert Zafy in control of a transitional government.

1992 A multiparty constitution is approved by voters.

1993 Zafy is elected president

1996 Zafy resigns from the presidency after he is impeached by the National Assembly.

1997 Ratsiraka returns to power after presidential elections.

1998 A new constitution provides for a federal system and increased presidential powers.

2002 Marc Ravalomanana declared president by a constitutional court after disputed elections; Ratsiraka goes into exile in France.

2003 Ratsiraka found guilty of corruption in his absence.

2004 Half of Madagascar's debt to the International Monetary Fund is written off.

2006 Ravalomanana reelected president.

2007 World's largest nickel cobalt mining project opened in Madagascar.

2008 Oil exports recommence for the first time in 60 years.

president, ruled with almost authority until 1972, when public unrest resulted in a handover of power to a military provisional government. The new regime deliberately cut ties with France and turned toward the Soviet bloc for support. A coup in 1975 brought Didier Ratsiraka to power under a new constitution that changed the name of the country to the Republic of Madagascar. Ratsiraka pursued rigorously socialist policies that brought the majority of the economy under state control and strengthened military ties with the Soviet Union and Cuba.

Economic failures and lack of democratic accountability weakened Ratsiraka's regime during the 1980s, and there were several serious riots as unemployment grew and people in the south of the island suffered food shortages. In 1992, following weeks of pro-democracy protests, Ratsiraka agreed to free political opponents from prison and to hold negotiations for a new constitution. The reform process was violent, with widespread social unrest and security forces killing dozens of pro-opposition demonstrators, but a new constitution was finally agreed to and presidential elections were held. Albert Zafy, the leading opposition leader, triumphed in the presidential elections, ending Ratsiraka's 18 years in power. In a remarkable political turnaround Ratsiraka returned to the presidency in the 1996 as the result of a presidential election with a low voter turnout that followed Zafy's impeachment. His second period in office proved no more popular than his first, however, and opposition grew steadily. In the 2001 presidential elections the leading opposition figure Marc Ravalomanana claimed victory and accused Ratsiraka of electoral fraud. A general strike and mass protests followed in which there were violent confrontations between government and opposition supporters. Following a 2002 High Constitutional Court ruling in favor of Ravalomanana, Ratsiraka relinquished power for the second time and went

MALAWIANS: NATIONALITY

nation:
Malawi; Republic of Malawi

derivation of name:
unknown

government:
Multiparty democracy

capital:
Lilongwe

language:
The country's official language, Chichewa, is spoken by 57 percent of the population. Other languages include Chinyanja (13 percent), Chiyao (10 percent), Chitumbuka (10 percent), Chisena (3 percent), Chilomwe (3 percent), and Chitonga (2 percent).

religion:
About 80 percent of the population are Christian (predominantly Church of England, Roman Catholics, and Baptists), another 13 percent are Muslim, and the remainder are Hindus or follow indigenous faiths.

earlier inhabitants:
Fulani; Twa; Bantu peoples

demographics:
Chewa, Nyanja, Tumbuka, Yao, Tonga, Ngoni, Ngonde, Asian, and European (proportions unknown)

into exile in France. Ravalomanana's I Love Madagascar (Tiako I Madagasikara) Party won a convincing majority in parliamentary elections the same year securing his position as president. Ravalomanana went on to win a second presidential term in 2006 and I Love Madagascar became the largest party in the National Assembly after the parliamentary elections of 2007. Ravalomanana government has pursued aggressive free-market reforms in an attempt to reverse the dire poverty of many Malagasy, but these have had a limited impact on the average citizen.

Madagascar is an island nation, and this naturally lends the Malagasy as a whole a strong sense of distinctness from the rest of Africa. The unique flora and fauna of the island coupled with the diverse cultural heritage of its inhabitants, including West African and South Asian elements, contribute to a well-established sense of national identity. Within the nation, however, traditional regional identities continue to divide the Malagasy and have frequently been the source of internal unrest. During the colonial period the Merina Kingdom, originating on the island's central plateau, came to dominate the peoples who lived outside this area. These subjugated peoples came to be known collectively as the Côtiers, although they consisted of numerous distinct and sometimes antagonistic ethnic groups (*see also* MADAGASCAN PEOPLES). Political tensions in Madagascar have often been the result of a perceived lack of representation for the Côtiers in central government. Ethnically the Merinas (and the related BETSILEO people) are described as Malayo-Indonesian, while the Côtiers consist of various groups of mixed Malayo-Indonesian, African, and Arab ancestry. Adding to this already diverse mix are more recent Indian, Chinese, French, and Comoran immigrants.

In the period immediately after independence from France there was a widespread rejection of French culture, most notably in the adoption of a Standard Malagasy language, which was intended to replace the numerous closely related Malagasy dialects that had been in use by the general native population up until that time. Poor educational funding and the extreme isolation of various groups resulted in the failure of this program, and many of the original Malagasy dialects continue to thrive today. Since the 1980s successive governments have gradually encouraged the adoption of western models of commerce and the cultural norms that come with them, particularly from France,

although this has frequently been treated with suspicion by the general population.

FURTHER READING

J. P. Daughton. *An Empire Divided: Religion, Republicanism, and the Making of French Colonialism, 1880–1914* (Oxford: Oxford University Press, 2006).

Richard Huntington. *Gender and Social Structure in Madagascar* (Bloomington: Indiana University Press, 1988).

Ken Preston-Mafham. *Madagascar: A Natural History* (New York: Facts On File, 1991).

Solofo Randrianja and Stephen Ellis. *Madagascar: A Short History* (Chicago: University of Chicago Press, 2009).

Malawians: nationality (people of Malawi)

GEOGRAPHY

The Republic of Malawi is a small landlocked country in southeast Africa. It has an area of approximately 46,000 square miles, about 20 percent of which consists of part of Lake Malawi (also known as Lake Nyasa), the third largest body of fresh water on the African continent, which dominates the eastern half of the country. Malawi has borders with three other nations. Its western border meets Zambia, and Tanzania lies on the eastern shore of Lake Malawi. Mozambique surrounds the southern half of the country, and the Malawi-Mozambique border extends through the middle of the southern half of Lake Malawi. The islands of Likoma and Chisumulu, both situated in the eastern half of Lake Malawi and surrounded by Mozambique's territorial waters, are also part of Malawi.

Lake Malawi lies in the Great Rift Valley, a major geological fault that extends northward through East Africa and continues into Lebanon in the Middle East. The lake drains southward via the Shire River, a tributary of the Zambezi River, which flows into the Indian Ocean. Lake Malawi is approximately 350 miles long and is at an elevation of 1,500 feet above sea level. East and west of the trough of the Great Rift Valley are two elevated plateaus; Malawi occupies the eastern edge of the western plateau, which has an elevation of between 2,500 and 4,400 feet. An upland region known as Mulanje Massif in the north of the country rises from the generally flat landscape of the plateau to elevations of almost 10,000 feet. In the extreme south of the country, close to the

Shire River's confluence with the Zambewi, the land is just 300 feet above sea level.

Malawi is the most densely populated country in sub-Saharan Africa and one of the most densely populated nations in the entire continent. The capital city, Lilongwe, is centrally situated in the country about midway between the western shore of Lake Malawi and the Mo-zambican border. The majority of the population live in the southern third of the country close to the Shire River. The northern third of the country is the least densely populated.

INCEPTION AS A NATION

Forest-forager peoples inhabited Malawi at least 12,000 years ago. In the 13th century C.E.

Malawians: nationality time line

C.E.

15th century Bantu-speaking peoples found the Maravi state around the shores of Lake Malawi extending into present-day Zambia and Mozambique.

18th and 19th centuries Slave traders active in Malawi.

1859 British explorer David Livingstone reaches Lake Malawi (naming it Lake Nyasa), opening the way for Christian missionaries.

1891 Britain establishes the Nyasaland and District Protectorate.

1893 The Nyasaland and District Protectorate is renamed the British Central Africa Protectorate; large-scale commercial exploitation begins.

1907 British Central Africa Protectorate renamed Nyasaland Protectorate.

1944 Nyasaland African Congress party formed.

1953 Nyasaland Protectorate amalgamated with North and South Rhodesian (present-day Zambia and Zimbabwe) despite opposition from Malawian nationalists.

1958 Hastings Kamuzu Banda returns from studies in the United States and Britain to lead the Nyasaland African Congress.

1959 Banda and other nationalist leaders arrested and imprisoned by British authorities; Nyasaland African Congress banned; Malawi Congress Party (MCP) founded.

1961 MCP wins 94 percent of votes in elections to the new Legislative Assembly.

1963 Nyasaland becomes a self-governing state under British authority with Banda as its first prime minister.

1964 Nyasaland declares full independence and adopts the name Malawi.

1966 Banda becomes the first president of the Republic of Malawi; constitution establishes a one-party state.

1971 Banda proclaimed president for life.

1992 Public demonstrations and strikes demanding constitutional reform

1993 Multiparty system adopted after referendum; Banda's presidency for life revoked.

1994 Baklili Muluzi of the United Democratic Front (UDF) voted president in the country's first multiparty elections.

1997 Banda dies.

1999 Muluzi reelected to second five-year term as president.

2002 Serious drought threatens starvation in Malawi.

2004 Bingu wa Mutharika (UDF) wins presidential elections.

2005 Mutharika leaves the UDF to found the Democratic Progressive Party (DPP) claiming anticorruption measures are being blocked by the UDF.

2006 Former president Muluzi arrested for corruption.

2008 Malawi establishes diplomatic relations with China and severs relations with Taiwan.

BANTU-speaking peoples migrated into the area, and by the early 16th century the CHEWA people had consolidated a kingdom along the shores of Lake Malawi that came to be known as the Maravi state. The Chewa suffered depredations at the hands of Arab slave traders and partial conquest by the Gaza Empire, which was established in Mozambique early in the 19th century. European influence in the Lake Malawi area followed soon after the expedition of the British explorer David Livingstone to the lake in 1859. Hoping to establish commercial exploitation of the area, the British declared a protectorate over the Shire River territories of the south in 1889 and extended it to include Lake Malawi (then known as Lake Nyasa) in 1891. Under British administration plantation and mining rights were granted to white settlers, which quickly dispossessed the indigenous population of much of their lands. The name of the territory was changed from the British Central Africa Protectorate to the Nyasaland Protectorate in 1907.

Pressure for independence began to make itself felt in the 1950s, particularly as a growing number of native Malawians became involved in the territory's administration and received an education in Britain or the United States. The Nyasaland African Congress Party (later known as the Malawi Congress Party), founded in 1944, was the focus of this movement. In 1953 Britain amalgamated Nyasaland and Northern and Southern Rhodesia (modern Zambia and Zimbabwe) to form the Federation of Rhodesia and Nyasaland, an act that added strength to ambitions for independence. In 1961 the Malawi Congress Party (MCP) won an overwhelming majority of seats in the newly formed Legislative Council, and its leader, Hastings Banda, was appointed prime minister. Britain remained in control of the territory, however, until a new constitution was adopted in 1963 and the federation with Rhodesia was dissolved. Nyasaland achieved full independence in July 1964 and adopted the name Malawi. Hastings Banda became the country's first president when Malawi became a republic in 1966.

CULTURAL IDENTITY

In the decades after independence Malawi retained many aspects of the culture that had been imported into the territory under British rule. President Banda based the National Assembly on the British parliament (although it only has one chamber, unlike the bicameral British system) and founded the Kamuzu Academy, an exclusive private school for Malawi's elite, modeled on Britain's renowned Eton school. The majority of the population retained their links with the Church of England, although there is also a significant Muslim minority. Malawians also continue to drive on the left side of the road.

Banda's rule, however, did not conform to the democratic principles he claimed to admire. In 1970 the constitution was altered to give Banda the right to rule as president for life, and by this time he had already secured the lifetime presidency of the Malawi Congress Party (MCP), which was the only legal political party in the country. Banda remained in power for 30 years until shortly before his death. His rule was totalitarian and contemptuous of opposition. International observers frequently reported serious human rights abuses in Malawi under his rule, and the leaders of illegal political parties were assassinated or abducted from neighboring counties and sentenced to long prison terms. In foreign policy Banda gained the enmity of many other African nations by maintaining diplomatic and trade links with the white minority government of Rhodesia (modern Zimbabwe), Portuguese-ruled Mozambique, and white-ruled South Africa.

The 1990s brought a weakening of Banda's grip on power as he faced strikes and public demonstrations demanding reform. In 1992 the trade union leader Chakufwa Chihana formed the Alliance for Democracy (AFORD) movement and was immediately imprisoned. Donor nations threatened to suspend aid to Malawi, and Banda agreed to allow a referendum on the adoption of a multiparty system the following year. AFORD and a second opposition group, the United Democratic Front (UDF), campaigned vigorously for a change in the law, and the proposal was accepted by a large majority of voters despite campaigns of intimidation carried out by the MPC's paramilitary wing the Young Pioneers. Clauses guaranteeing Banda's rule and provisions for imprisonment without trial were struck from the constitution, and a provisional National Assembly was inaugurated to oversee the preparation of a new constitution and the country's first multiparty elections. These took place in 1994 and resulted in Banda's removal from office.

Malawi has maintained its commitment to democratic rule since the fall of Banda's government, although allegations of institutionalized corruption have been made against subsequent administrations. The country faced the latest in a series of humanitarian crises in 2002 and 2005 when droughts caused massive crop failures, and tens of thousands of Malawians die every year from AIDS.

Of the several ethnic groups that make up the population of Malawi, the Chewa and the Nyanja are the largest; together they are known as the MARAVI (or Malawi) peoples. The Chewa dominate the central region of the country, while the Nyanja make up the majority of the people of the heavily populated south. The YAO, a predominantly Muslim people, are a significant presence at the southern end of Lake Malawi and form part of a wider transnational community that stretches into neighboring Mozambique and Tanzania. The sparsely populated uplands in the north of Malawi are home to elements of the TUMBUKA and TONGA peoples. Although there is a strong correlation between region and affiliation with the three main political parties, there is little history of interethnic conflict in Malawi. Transnational ethnic affiliations have drawn Malawians into conflicts in Mozambique in the past, and hundreds of thousands of Mozambicans were given refuge in Malawi during that nation's protracted civil wars (see MOZAMBICANS: NATIONALITY), putting great strain on Malawi's economy. Malawi has also been closely tied politically to Mozambique because Malawi's most convenient access to the sea is via the railway link from the south of the country across Mozambique to the India Sea port of Nacala. This vital economic link reopened in 2004 after 20 years during which it was impassable because of conflict within Mozambique.

Malawi has the potential to restructure itself as a self-sustaining nation under a stable political system. Traditionally, the country has produced food surpluses, thanks to its plentiful sources of irrigation, and there is potential for the export of uranium ore recently discovered on Malawian territory. Obstacles include the massive investment necessary to overcome decades of neglect in infrastructure and the need to continue reforming a political system that continues suffer from corruption and mismanagement.

FURTHER READING

Rosemary Argente. *Always with You: A Malawi Legacy* ([S. l.]: Simanyi Books, 2007).
Lisa Gilman. *The Dance of Politics: Gender, Performance, and Democratization in Malawi* (Philadelphia: Temple University Press, 2009).
Markku Hokkanen. *Medicine and Scottish Missionaries in the Northern Malawi Region 1875–1930: Quests for Health in a Colonial Society* (Lewiston, N.Y.: Edwin Mellen Press, 2007).
Owen J. Kalinga and Cynthia A. Crosby. *Historical Dictionary of Malawi* (Lanham, Md.: Scarecrow Press, 2002).
Franklin Simtowe. *Performance and Impact of Microfinance: Evidence from Joint Liability Lending Programs in Malawi*. Development Economics and Policy, 58 (Frankfurt am Main, Germany: Peter Lang, 2008).
Jack Thomson. *Ngoni, Xhosa and Scot: Religious and Cultural Interaction in Malawi* (Zomba, Malawi: Kachere Series, 2007).

Malians: nationality (people of Mali)

GEOGRAPHY

The Republic of Mali is a large landlocked nation in northwest Africa. It has an area of approximately 479,000 square miles and borders seven other countries. Algeria meets Mali's border in the north; Niger in the east; Burkina Faso, Ivory Coast, and Guinea in the south; Senegal and Mauritania to the west.

Much of Mali consists of a flat and arid plateau, particularly in the north of the country, which is dominated by the Sahara Desert and the transitional Sahelian zone. A highland region in the east of the country, known as the Adrar des Iforas, is an extension of neighboring Algeria's Ahaggar Mountains. A second upland region in the southwest is part of the Guinea highlands in which the Niger River has its source. Mali highest point, the peak of Mount Hombori (3,700 feet), is situated in this area. The Niger River is the most prominent geographical feature in Mali, and its course describes a crescent through the south of the nation. The Niger River and its many tributaries create a verdant and fertile zone that contrasts starkly with the aridity of the north.

Three quarters of the population of Mali live in the western quarter of the country, and the majority if these live close to the banks of the Niger River. Mali's capital city, Bamako, is situated on the Niger River in the southwest, close to the border with Guinea. It is one of the largest and most rapidly expanding cities in Africa. Mali has no coastline, but it has a large river port at Koulikoro, which is about 40 miles from Bamako, from which goods can be transported down the Niger to Mali's other large cities and beyond. The cities of Segou, Mopti, Tombouctou, and Gao all lie on the banks of the Niger

---

MALIANS: NATIONALITY

nation:
Mali; Republic of Mali (Republique de Mali)

derivation of name:
From the Mali Empire of the 13th to 17th centuries

government:
Republic

capital:
Bamako

language:
French is the country's official language; Bambara is the lingua franca, spoken by 80 percent of the population. Dozens of other languages are spoken by other ethnic groups.

religion:
About 90 percent of the population are Muslim; indigenous faiths are followed by 9 percent; and Christians constitute 1 percent.

earlier inhabitants:
Unknown

demographics:
Mandé peoples (including the Bambara, Malinke, and Soninke) make up about 50 percent of the population. Other groups include the Peul (17 percent), Voltaic peoples (12 percent), the Songhay (6 percent), and the Berber Tuareg (10 percent).

Malians: nationality time line

C.E.

1898 France defeats Malinke leader Samory Touré and establishes colony of French Sudan.

1959 French Sudan (present-day Mali), Senegal, Dahomey (present-day Benin), and Upper Volta (present-day Burkina Faso) drew up a constitution for the establishment of a unified state to be known as the Mali Federation.

1960 Senegal and French Sudan unite and achieve independence as the Mali Federation; Senegal withdraws; French Sudan becomes independent as the Republic of Mali with Modibo Keita as its first president.

1968 Moussa Traore replaces Keita as president after a military coup.

1977 Keita dies in prison, provoking demonstrations against Traore's regime.

1979 A new constitution provides for elections, but all candidates are from the only legal party, the Democratic Union of the Malian People (UDPM). Traore is elected president by an overwhelming majority.

1985 Border dispute between Mali and Burkina Faso

1991 Traore overthrown in a coup; transitional government established.

1992 Alpha Konaré becomes Mali's first democratically elected president.

1999 Former-president Traore sentenced to death for corruption; later commuted to life imprisonment.

2002 Amadou Toumani Touré wins presidential elections—first peaceful transfer of presidency in Mali's history.

2006 Peace deal signed with northern Tuareg rebels promising greater autonomy.

2007 Touré elected to a second term as president.

2008 Tuareg rebels attack an army base in the northeast of the country.

River. Koulikoro is also the eastern terminus of the Dakar-Niger railway, an important transport link between Mali and the Atlantic coast. The arid north and east of the country are very sparsely populated and are home to the 10 percent of Mali's population who continue to pursue a traditional nomadic lifestyle.

INCEPTION AS A NATION

In the 10th and 11th centuries C.E. the Empire of Ghana, one of the great civilizations of West Africa, controlled territory that included areas of present-day Mali, Senegal, and Mauritania and controlled the flow of trade across the Sahara Desert to the Arab Muslim north of the continent. In the 13th century the Mali Empire established itself as the dominant power in the region as the successor to the disintegrating Empire of Ghana. The Mali Empire achieved its peak in the 14th century under its ruler Mansa Musa (r. ca. 1312–37), and the cities of Tombouctou and Djenné became the centers of West African trade and Muslim culture. By the 17th century, however, BERBERS had taken con-

trol of much of the north of the empire and the SONGHAY Empire, had become established in the east and captured the city of Tombouctou.

The 19th century brought renewed Muslim expansion into West Africa from the north and the beginnings of French colonial interest in the area. The Malinke leader Samory Touré, who had established a large Muslim kingdom in Mali, vigorously opposed the advance of French control into the interior, but he was finally defeated and captured in 1898 after more than 15 years of resistance. The French established a colony known as French Sudan in the area, which was part of the wider federation of French West Africa along with Mauritania, Senegambia and Niger, French Guinea (present-day Guinea), Ivory Coast, Upper Volta (present-day Burkina Faso), and Dahomey (present-day Benin).

In 1946, following World War II, the French government reorganized all its foreign colonies under a new organization known as the French Union. Under the French Union all peoples living within the former French colonies were granted French citizenship, and a greater de-

The Great Mosque in Niono, Mali. Built between 1948 and 1973 the mosque is constructed from traditional sun-baked clay bricks and wooden beams.

gree of local administration was encouraged. In 1958 the French Union was replaced by the French Community, which gave a large degree of autonomy to the former colonies with the understanding that France would not oppose their eventual evolution toward full independence. In 1959 French Sudan (present-day Mali), Senegal, Dahomey (present-day Benin), and Upper Volta (present-day Burkina Faso) drew up a constitution for the establishment of a unified state to be known as the Mali Federation. Although the Mali Federation achieved independence from France as a single nation in June 1960, political differences caused it to break up within two months. French Sudan became a separate independent nation in September 1960 and adopted the name Mali. Modibo Keita was the nation's first president.

CULTURAL IDENTITY

The postindependence leaders of Mali embarked on an ambitious program to shape a national identity for the new republic. The country's borders were a remnant of colonial administration rather than a reflection of natural cultural or geographical division, and a strong image with which all of its diverse peoples could identify was needed. The ancient Mali Empire provided the ideal template. The short-lived Mali Federation was the fullest flowering of this attempt to reanimate a semi-mythical past, but its failure did not discourage the rulers of independent Mali from following the same pattern. Deliberate attempts were made to link the government, and especially the president, with the historical Mali Empire by encouraging the belief that the socialist policies of the new rulers were a continuation of the policies and methods of the indigenous rulers of the region before the intervention of French colonialism. Songs were composed celebrating supposed ancestral links between President Modibo Keita and the legendary founder of the Mali Empire, Sundiata Keita.

A 15th-century sculpture from central Mali.

Discontent with the postindependence government came about largely as a result of its failure to deliver the economic growth it had promised would result from its socialist policies as well as the absence of opportunities for debate in a one-party state. A military coup in 1968 established the Military Committee for National Liberation under the presidency of Moussa Traore, which set out to implement economic reforms, including opening the country up to investment from noncommunist nations. A serious drought across the Sehal and continuous political infighting, however, hampered progress. In 1979 a new constitution was adopted that allowed for general elections, but the country remained a one-party state; all candidates were to be selected from the ranks of the Democratic Union of the Malian People (UDPM). Traore received 99 percent of the votes for the presidency in the country's first elections and was reelected to a second term in 1985. Drought continued to plague Mali throughout this period, as it did other African nations in the Sahel. Severe drought conditions prevailed from 1968 to 1973 and again from 1982 to 1985. A war with Burkina Faso over possession of the mineral-rich Agacher Strip broke out in 1985 but was quickly settled in the International Court of Justice. Student demonstrations against the regime that took place in 1980 were brutally suppressed, and their leader died in detention.

After more than 20 years of oppressive rule, Traore's regime began to lose its grip on power in 1990 when several new political organizations were set up and began demanding democratic reform. A series of bloody confrontations between youth groups supporting change and the security forces occurred in 1990 and 1991. In March 1991 Traore was deposed in a military coup and a National Conference was instituted to discuss oversee the transition to a multiparty state. A series of national polls in 1992 elected representatives to municipal councils, created a new National Assembly, and brought Alpha Oumar Konaré to the office of the presidency. Mali's political history since the transition to multiparty politics has been turbulent but has also remained democratic. In general, Mali's political climate has become far more responsive to the demands of its citizens, and the possibilities for economic growth have become more evident. In 2002 Mali achieved its first peaceful transfer of power when Amadou Toumani Touré became the republic's second democratically elected president.

The democratization of Mali has begun the process of allowing a truly indigenous national culture to emerge. For the first 30 years of its existence Malian national identity was a construct largely fashioned from the political theories, and often the avarice, of its tiny Western-educated elite. Ethnic differences were largely ignored or suppressed under this system. Mali has a long tradition of mutual tolerance and cooperation between its many constituent ethnicities, but this is a very different thing from the disdaining of the differences between these ethnicities. There has been a resurgence of local cultural identities within Mali since the early 1990s, but this has not led to interethnic conflict. The Mandé are the largest ethnic group in Mali. The group is made up of the closely related BAMBARA, Malinke, and Sarakole peoples and forms part of the largest linguistically related ethnic group in West Africa. Other significant groups include the FULANI, the Songhay, and the TUAREG (a BERBER people). The Bambara are found throughout Mali but are concentrated in the center of the country, while the Malinke are found predominately in the southwest. The Fulani and Songhay live chiefly along the eastern half of the course of the Niger River through Mali and also across the arid Sahel region. Almost all of Mali's ethnic groups are predominantly Muslim, a heritage from the ancient Muslim empires of West Africa and the history of incursions by Muslim people from the north. Cities such as Tombouctou and Djenné feature impressive medieval mosques built in the distinctive style of the region. The only significant ethnic conflict in Malian history has been between the nomadic Tuareg of the north and east and the settled peoples of the south and west. The Tuareg have been effectively excluded from Malian society because of their different lifestyles and their remoteness from the urban centers of power. Numerous uprisings and insurgencies have marked attempts to achieve self-rule or increased investment in the region.

FURTHER READING

Marq De Villiers and Sheila Hirtle. *Timbuktu: The Sahara's Fabled City of Gold* (Toronto: McClelland & Stewart, 2007).

Kenny Mann. *Ghana, Mali, Songhay: The Western Sudan* (Parsippany, N.J.: Dillon Press, 1996).

Susanna D. Wing. *Constructing Democracy in Transitioning Societies of Africa: Constitutionalism and Deliberation in Mali* (New York: Palgrave Macmillan, 2008).

Maligo

The Maligo are a KHOISAN people living in the far south of Angola. They are a small ethnic group, numbering only a few thousand.

Malinke *See* BAMBARA.

Mamprusi

The Mamprusi are one of the several ethnic groups that make up the MOSSI people. The Mamprusi inhabit a region in northern Ghana bounded on the north by the White Volta River. The Mamprusi language, Mampruli, is one of many Moré (or Molé) languages spoken in Ghana and Burkina Faso. The Mamprusi people live in northern Ghana where, although they do not make up the majority of that region's population, they are its largest ethnic group.

The Mamprusi probably emerged as a distinct group in the 15th century C.E. when a cavalry group from northern Ghana rode north in search of land. These people established the seven main Mossi kingdoms, one of which was Mamprusi. Historically, the king had an important religious as well as political role, but this role has diminished somewhat at the beginning of the 21st century as more and more Mamprusi convert to Islam.

Mamvu

The Mamvu are concentrated in Mozambique and the Democratic Republic of the Congo. They are a BANTU people.

Manala

The Manala are one of the main NDEBELE groups. The Ndebele live in South Africa and Zimbabwe.

Manasir

The Manasir are descended from Nubian and Arab ancestors (*see* NUBIANS; ARABS). They live mostly in north-central Sudan.

Mandé

The Mandé people make up a large family of related ethnic groups that includes the BAMBARA, DYULA, Malinke, SONINKE, SUSU, and MENDE peoples. The Mandé homeland is centered on the border between present-day Mali and Guinea. Historically, the Mandé were politically important, since Mandé speakers were the founders of two of West Africa's earliest states: the Empire of Ghana, founded by the Soninke, and the Empire of Mali, founded by the Malinke (neither empire should be confused with the present-day countries of the same name). The dominance and large size of these empires is in part responsible for the prevalence of Mandé-speaking societies in West Africa. Furthermore, a wave of Mandé-speaking migrants spread across West Africa in the 15th century C.E. when the Empire of Mali was in decline.

Mandé languages include Manding, which is spoken throughout much of West Africa—in, for example, Guinea, Burkina Faso, Gambia, Senegal, Mali, Ivory Coast, and Guinea-Bissau.

A Manding sword and sheath attached to a belt harness

The Mandé language group belongs to the Niger-Congo subfamily of the Niger-Kordofanian family.

Mandija
The Mandija are a subgroup of the BAYA of the Central African Republic.

Manding (Mandingo; Mandinka)
The Manding are a group of peoples related by language who are spread throughout much of West Africa, in particular in Guinea, Guinea-Bissau, Mali, Senegal, Niger, and Gambia. They are one of the largest ethnic groups in West Africa numbering about 11 million people. The BAMBARA, SUSU, MENDE, KPELLE, DAN, and DYULA are all Manding peoples. Many other West African groups are closely related to the Manding. The Manding languages belong to the wider grouping of MANDÉ languages.

All Manding peoples originated from a mountainous region of the same name that sits astride the border of Mali and Guinea—the core of the great medieval Empire of Mali, which rose to prominence in the 13th century

C.E. All Manding peoples share a common origin forged by the Islamic Empire of Mali, and the majority have been Muslim for centuries.

Mandingo   See MANDING.

Mandinka   See MANDING.

Mandyako   See MANJACO.

Manga
The Manga of Niger, Nigeria, and Chad speak a KANURI language.

Mangbetu
The Mangbetu live in the northeast of the Democratic Republic of the Congo. The Mangbetu language is known as Mangebtu or Kere, and it belongs to the Central Sudanic subfamily of the Nilo-Saharan family. Mangbetu is distantly related to the LUGBARA language.

The Mangbetu are unique in having created one of the few centralized political systems in Central Africa. The Mangbetu Kingdom was founded in the first half of the 19th century by a leader called Nabiembali, who extended Mangbetu control over non-Mangbetu speakers for the first time. By the second half of the 19th century, the court of the Mangbetu king, Mbunza, was famed as a center for the arts and performance. Mbunza was probably the most powerful of a number of Mangbetu kingdoms.

It is a custom for Mangbetu villagers to decorate the outside of their houses with murals, and the beautiful Mangbetu villages were much visited and photographed by Western travelers in the early years of the 20th century.

Mangutu

The Mangutu are closely related to the MAMVU. They majority of the Mangutu live in the northeast of the Democratic Republic of the Congo, some also live in Uganda and southern Sudan.

Manhica (Manyica)

The Manhica are a subgroup of the SHONA. They live in Mozambique and Zimbabwe.

Manicheans

Manicheans were followers of Mani who was born in southern Iraq in the third century C.E. He proclaimed his message of a universal religion and himself as the final prophet in a line that included Adam, Buddha, Zoroaster, and Jesus. Mani was martyred in about 276, and the religion subsequently spread rapidly across the Roman Empire to the west and east into Asia. The religion is a dualist faith, seeing human existence as a struggle between good and evil, light and darkness. Life on earth is seen as evil, with inner illumination the only way to know God and the only path to salvation. Followers were ardent missionaries, and they carried the religion to Egypt and across North Africa, where Saint Augustine became a convert.

Manichanism attained its zenith in the fourth century, having reached Rome, as well as Gaul and Spain. The religion was fiercely attacked in the West and had disappeared almost completely by the sixth century. Meanwhile, though, Manichanism had also spread to the east, to Persia and beyond. Muslim caliphs from the eighth century on persecuted the Manicheans, and by the 10th century, the seat of the religion had shifted to Samarkand, in Central Asia. Meanwhile missionaries carried the religion to the Uighur kingdom of Central Asia, where it became the state religion until 840, and it was practiced in China until at least the 14th century. The religious texts attributed to Mani and originally written in Syriac, an ancient Middle Eastern language, and later translated into Greek, Coptic, and Latin, were lost in the Middle Ages, but have since been partly recovered in China and Egypt.

Manigiri

The Manigiri are a subgroup of the YORUBA. They live in Benin and Togo.

Manja

The Manja are descended from BAYA ancestors who broke away from the main group. The majority live in the Central African Republic.

Manjaco (Mandyako; Manjago)

The Manjaco live in Senegal, Guinea-Bissau, and Gambia.

Manjago See MANJACO.

Mannaens

The Mannaens were an ancient people of northwestern Iran, first mentioned in records of the Assyrian king Shalmaneser III, who ruled from 858 to 824 B.C.E. (see ASSYRIANS). They were surrounded by three powerful empires, those of the Assyrians, the URARTIANS, and the MEDES. Their name appears for the last time in historical record in the seventh century B.C.E., when the Scythians invaded the region and the Medes were coming to power. The Mannaens were subsumed into the empire of the Medes.

Mano See MA.

Manyica See MANHICA.

Mao

The Mao are NILOTES from Ethiopia. The majority of the Mao are seminomadic or nomadic pastoralists.

Marait See MARARI.

Marakwet

The Marakwet are one of the several related groups that make up the KALENJIN. The Kalenjin are a large ethnic group in western Kenya.

Marari (Marait; Mararit)

The Marari are closely related to the ABU SHAR-IB. The Marari speak a TAMA language and live on and around the border between Sudan and Chad, mostly in Chad.

Mararit See MARARI.

Marave See MARAVI.

Maravi (Marave)

The majority of the Maravi live in northern Mozambique, where they migrated to from the territory of the present-day Republic of the Congo several hundred years ago.

Maronites

The Maronites are a primarily religious group living in Lebanon, Syria, and Israel. A large Maronite diaspora also lives in the United States, Canada, and Australia. Accurate figures are not available, but it is probable that the Maronite diaspora of over 3 million individuals is about three times larger than the Maronite population currently living in their homeland in the Middle East.

The defining cultural characteristic of the Maronites is membership of the Maronite Church, and the people are often referred to as Maronite Christians. The Maronite Church is one of the Christian Eastern Catholic churches. It was founded in the fifth century by Saint Maron (d. ca. 423), a monk born in present-day Syria who lived in the Taurus Mountains of present-day southern Turkey. According to Maronite tradition, Saint Maron's followers migrated into the mountains of present-day Lebanon following his death. From that time the mountains of Lebanon have been the spiritual heartland of the Maronites and have also frequently served as a retreat or fortress in the face of invasion and persecution. From their earliest settlements in Lebanon, Maronite missionaries spread their version of Christianity to the coastal cities and into the Bekaa Valley.

Early in the seventh century ARABS conquered much of the Middle East but paid little attention to the mountain fastnesses of the Maronites. Surrounded by territory now ruled by the Muslim Arabs, the Maronites became isolated from the Christian centers of Rome and Constantinople, the capital of the Christian Byzantine Empire. In 687 the Maronites appointed their own patriarch (head of the church), which angered the emperor in Constantinople. Byzantine forces attacked the Maronites in 694 during an incursion into Arab-held territory but were defeated. The Maronites were, however, unable completely to withstand the growing power of the Arabs. They were forced to retreat deeper into the mountains and were subject to constant harassment from Arab raids. Despite their isolation, though, the Maronites were able to retain their unique culture and faith through the centuries. When the Christian Crusades began late in the 11th century, the Maronites swiftly allied themselves with the European invaders and participated in many of their campaigns. The Crusaders were finally defeated and driven out of the Middle East by the end of the 13th century, leaving the Maronites open to reprisals from the Muslim Mamluk armies. The second half of the 13th century also brought conflict with invading MONGOLS.

The Maronite homeland was part of the Ottoman Empire for more than four centuries, from the early 16th century until the dissolution of the empire in 1918 (see OTTOMANS). During this period the Maronites struggled to maintain their unity and frequently rebelled against Ottoman rule. At times the Maronites enjoyed a high degree of autonomy within the empire, but they were also subjected to punitive expeditions by their Ottoman overlords when their power became too great. The first half of the 19th century was a period of great hardship for the Maronites in Lebanon. With Ottoman support, the DRUZE conducted a series of assaults on Maronite settlements between 1840 and 1860, resulting in the deaths of many thousands. The Druze, a nominally Muslim people who lived in the same areas as the Maronites, had long been rivals of the Maronites. In 1860 French troops landed in Lebanon to protect the Christian Maronites, forcing the Ottoman Empire to conclude an agreement with France, Britain, Austria, and Prussia over the future security of the Maronites. This agreement effectively reduced the size of Lebanon to the area around Mount Lebanon and installed a non-Lebanese governor, appointed by the Ottomans, who was to be supported by an advisory council made up of representatives from each of the territory's religious groups. Although the agreement removed the immediate threat of extermination, the Maronites were resentful of the imposition of a non-Maronite governor. A Maronite nationalist uprising took place in 1866 under the popular leader Youssef Karam and achieved a series of victories against Ottoman forces. Although close to achieving his goal of a fully independent Maronite Lebanon, Karam was forced to abandon his uprising when the European powers made it clear that they would be unwilling to recognize or support such a state, since to do so would undermine the agreement they had made with the Ottomans in 1860.

Despite Youssef Karam's unsuccessful rebellion, Lebanon retained its autonomy within the Ottoman Empire until 1915. During World War I the Ottomans allied themselves with Germany and Austria against Britain, France, and their allies. In 1915 the Ottomans revoked Lebanon's autonomy and installed a harshly repressive regime intended to extinguish Lebanese nationalism once and for all. Thousands of Maronites were imprisoned or forcibly exiled, and public executions of leading figures from the Maronite, Druze, and other Lebanese communities were carried out. The Ottomans also precipitated a devastating famine by commandeering Lebanon's agricultural produce. Eyewitness accounts suggest that at least 120,000 Lebanese, many of them Maronites, starved to death from 1916 to 1918, reducing the population by about one third.

Following the defeat of the Ottoman Empire in World War I, Lebanon became part of the territory mandated to French administration by the League of Nations (the predecessor of the United Nations). Lebanon became independent in 1946, at which time Maronite Christians made up about 50 percent of the population and were the largest minority. Lebanon's constitution was intended to guarantee political representation for each of the nations ethno-religious groups, and the office of the president was reserved for a Maronite. In the decades after independence shifts in the demographics of Lebanon significantly reduced the Maronite majority, leading to resentment among other groups and a civil war that raged between 1975 and 1990 (*see also* LEBANESE: NATIONALITY). Christians make up about 40 percent of the present-day population of Lebanon, though only a fraction are Maronites.

Marsh Arabs

The term "Marsh Arabs" is used to refer to a number of Arab tribes and tribal confederations with a traditional homeland in the wetlands between and around the most southerly stretches of the Tigris and Euphrates Rivers in Iraq. The wetlands, or marshes, in which the Marsh Arabs live are created and sustained by the annual flood cycles of the Tigris and Euphrates. For much of the year most of this area is accessible only by boat. This geographical isolation has created a degree of cultural isolation among the Marsh Arabs. Although Marsh Arabs belong to numerous different tribes, they share common ways of life and customs as a result of their unique habitat. They also have a tradition of independence from the dominant culture of the surrounding area.

The origins of the Marsh Arabs are unclear. There is archaeological evidence of reed-built houses and villages similar to those built by the modern Marsh Arabs dating from the 21st century B.C.E., but the first recorded mention of the Marsh Arabs themselves dates from the ninth century C.E. Historians have speculated that the modern Marsh Arabs are the descendents of BEDOUIN Arabs who migrated into the area as part of the expansion of Muslim Caliphate in the seventh or eighth century and that these people adopted the lifestyles, including the architecture, of earlier marsh-living peoples. Until the end of the 20th century most Marsh Arabs continued to live in reed huts and to follow the traditional pattern of raising buffalo or cultivating small areas of rice, barley, millet, or wheat.

The Marsh Arabs' way of life was dramatically disrupted in 1991 when the then dictator of Iraq, Saddam Hussein, undertook a program to drain the marshes. Drainage and irrigation projects carried out by the Iraqi government had begun to affect the habitat in the 1970s, and by the mid-1980s there was a low-level but continuous insurgency in operation among the Marsh Arabs. The majority of the Marsh Arabs are Shiites and as such were regarded with indifference or open hostility by the nominally Sunni government. A general uprising of insurgent Shii groups in southern Iraq, including Marsh Arab elements, following Iraq's defeat in the First Gulf War (1990–91) was brutally suppressed by Hussein's forces. As a punishment Hussein ordered the marshes drained and the Marsh Arabs relocated. Dams and channels were built using forced labor that effectively transformed much of the marshes into an arid wasteland. Following Hussein's removal from power by U.S. and coalition forces in 2003, these barriers were dismantled and water flowed back into the former marshes. Although much of the area quickly returned to its former state, it is estimated that as few as 10,000 to 15,000 Marsh

MAURITANIANS: NATIONALITY

nation:
Mauritania; Islamic Republic of Mauritania

derivation of name:
From a Latin phrase meaning "land of the Moors"

government:
Republic

capital:
Nouakchott

language:
The country's official language is Arabic. Pulaar, Soninke, French, Hassaniya, and Wolof are also spoken.

religion:
More than 99 percent of the population is Muslim (principally Sunni).

earlier inhabitants:
Unknown

demographics:
Persons of mixed Arab and Berber ancestry (known as Moors) make up about 30 percent of the population. Persons of mixed Moor and black African ancestry make up about 40 percent. The remaining 30 percent consists of several black African ethnic groups including the Tukulor, Sarakole, Fulani, Wolof, and Bambara.

Arabs, out of an original population of 500,000, continue to inhabit the area.

Marya

The Marya are one of central Eritrea's main ethnic groups.

Masai *See* MAASAI.

Masalit (Kaana Masala)

The Masalit mostly live in Darfur Province in western Sudan, and a minority live farther west in Chad.

Masheba *See* CHEWA.

Massa (Banana; Walia)

The Massa live in northern Cameroon and southern Chad.

Matabele *See* NDEBELE.

Matakam

The Matakam live in northern Cameroon and northern Nigeria.

Matambwe *See* MAKONDE.

Matheniko

The Matheniko are a subgroup of the KARAMO-JONG. They live in northeastern Uganda.

Matumbi (Kimatumbi)

The Matumbi are a BANTU people who live on the Tanzanian–Mozambique border, mostly in Tanzania.

Mauritanians: nationality (people of Mauritania)

GEOGRAPHY

The Islamic Republic of Mauritania, situated in western North Africa, is a desert country sparse in both agricultural resources and population. It has an area of approximately 398,000 square miles and has borders with the western Sahara (claimed by Morocco) to the northwest, Mali to the south and east, Algeria to the northeast, and the Atlantic Ocean on the west coast. Nouakchott, the capital city, is located on the western coastal zone and is the most populated urban area. Other important towns include Nouadhibou, located on a 30-mile long peninsula in the northwestern corner, and Rosso and Bigue on the northern bank of the Senegal River that forms the western part of Mauritania's southern border. Most of Mauritania is dominated by the Sahel, an area of flat dry plains. As such, there are only a few isolated mountains, peaks, and plateaus and one or two oases and trading posts such as Atar and Tidjkida. The largely uninhabited northeast is a large region of seemingly endless sand dunes. Although the southern regions experience some rainfall, and even flash flooding during the rainy season from July to September, only an average of about 19 inches of rain falls per year. The dry, northern Saharan and Sahel region of Mauritania can go for years without any rainfall.

Despite harsh desert conditions, Mauritanians have survived for centuries as nomads, using camels to carry products across the Sahara Desert. There is some evidence from rock carvings of elephants and lions that Mauritania was not as dry centuries ago as it is today and may have had more in common with the Serengeti than the Sahara of today. The gradual drying and desertification of the country is still in progress. The desert continues to rapidly encroach on the very few agricultural areas that remain; less than half of 1 percent of the country is arable land. Most agricultural production is focused on the northern bank of Senegal River. Locust infestations often destroy those crops that survive the harsh conditions.

INCEPTION AS A NATION

In the 11th century C.E. a group of Muslim BERBERS known as the Almoravids established an empire in northwest Africa that included the territory of present-day Mauritania. Following the fall of the Almoravids in the 12th century, the area came under the power of the Mali Empire and then the Songhay Empire that succeeded it. Moroccan invaders took control in the 1590s.

European involvement in Mauritania began with the arrival of Portuguese explorers and traders along the coast in the 15th century. Attracted by the lucrative trade in slaves, gold, and gum Arabic, the British, French, and Dutch vied for control of the coast for the next three hundred years. In 1815 France gained control of Senegal as part of the peace settle-

Mauritanians: nationality time line

C.E.

eighth century The Sanhaja Berber tribes arrives in the region of Mauritania. They establish a confederation and a capital at Aoudaghost, allowing them to control the trans-Saharan trade.

10th–11th centuries Islam spreads into Mauritania along trade routes.

1039 Abd Allah bin Yasin, a Muslim religious reformer, arrives in Mauritania and converts the Berber tribes to a strict form of Maliki Islam. The Almoravid movement begins.

ca. 1062 The Almoravids conquer much of North Africa and build the new capital of Marrakech. They soon conquer southern Spain as well.

1076 The Almoravids conquer Koumbi Saleh from the Ghana Empire and extend their control over much of Senegal.

1133–49 The Almohads, Berber tribes from the Atlas Mountains who follow the Mahdi, or Islamic messiah, Ibn Tumart, defeat the Almoravid Empire.

13th century The Mali Empire conquers most of the territory of present-day Mauritania.

14th–15th centuries Several Arab tribes, originally from Yemen, spread into Mauritania and conquer important trading towns.

1674 Arabs conquer both Berber and black African tribes, securing their position as the rulers of Mauritania for centuries to come.

1840 A French ordinance establishes Senegal and Mauritania as a French possession.

1960 Mauritania becomes an independent nation.

1976 Mauritania annexes the southern third of western Sahara but withdraws after resistance from the western Saharan Polisario group.

1984 A coup brings Maaouiya Ould Sid Ahmed Taya to power.

1989 Race riots in Mauritania and Senegal force tens of thousands of black Mauritanians to migrate into Senegal.

1992 Taya is elected president.

1997 Taya wins a second presidential term; elections boycotted by opposition parties.

2005 President Taya is overthrown in a bloodless coup.

2007 Multiparty elections take place. Sidi Ould Cheikh Abdallahi wins the presidency. Parliament bans slavery.

2008 Attack on the French embassy in Nouakchott is blamed on Muslim extremists. President Abdallahi is overthrown in a military coup.

ment that ended the Napoleonic Wars in Europe and gradually extended its influence over the peoples to the north of the Senegal River in the territory that was to become Mauritania. French penetration of the arid regions was slow, and concerted efforts to subdue the nomads of the north militarily did not take place until the early 20th century. In 1920 Mauritania was established as a French colony, and Mauritania became one of the eight states that made up French West Africa.

In 1946, following World War II, the French government reorganized all its foreign colonies under a new organization known as the French Union. Under the French Union all peoples living within the former French colonies were granted French citizenship, and a greater degree of local administration was encouraged. In 1958 the French Union was replaced by the French Community, which gave a large degree of autonomy to the former colonies with the understanding that France would not oppose their eventual evolution toward full independence.

Mauritania achieved full independence from France in November 1960. The new state did not adapt very quickly to modern administrative patterns, and traditional, nomadic tribal institutions generally ruled on a local level. There was a struggle for power between black, Berber and Arab groups and parties as various tribes vied for power. In 1965, however, the Mauritanian People's Party (PPM) made up of black, Arab, and Berber members gained control as the single legal party. The PPM provided some stability and a semblance of unity to Mauritanian politics, but also quelled dissent. Mauritania became involved with the western Sahara conflict after the Moroccan Green March, or expansion, into the region in the 1970s. Morocco had often claimed authority over Mauritania as a whole, and Mauritania's leaders were keen to prevent any further expansion of Morocco in the region. Mauritania even annexed the southern third of the western Sahara in 1976 but soon relinquished its claims after suffering raids from the western Saharan nationalist Polisario front. Mauritania has generally been ruled by dictatorial regimes until the bloodless coup of 2005 and the multiparty parliamentary, senatorial, and presidential elections that followed.

CULTURAL IDENTITY

Despite rapid urbanization, recent attempts at modernizing the state bureaucracy, and limited democratic reform, the cultural identity of Mauritanians is still largely based on its long history of tribalism. Mauritania has been a crossroads for nomadic groups and traders for centuries. The harsh geography discouraged the development of permanent, centralized governments. Even so, Islam and trade often provided opportunities for unity between tribal groups. Archaeological evidence suggests that Berber and African tribes have both inhabited the region of Mauritania for millennia, having migrated north from the forested regions of the Niger River. Following a nomadic existence, these tribes generally maintained an independent way of life, but they would also form confederations to ensure the flow of trans-Saharan trade. The Sanhaja Berber confederation of tribes settled at Aoudaghost and other trading posts on the important Saharan route. The route started at Sijilmasa in eastern Morocco and made its way south to Koumbi Saleh, the capital of the Ghana Empire. It generally took about 50 days to complete the journey on camelback. Koumbi Saleh was a diverse, cosmopolitan center inhabited by Muslim and non-Muslim traders and ruled by a non-Muslim king. By the early 11th century, however, various Sanhaja tribes had fallen into internecine warfare over control of trading routes. In the mid-11th century, however, a period of religious fervor reunited the Sanhaja tribes. Yahya ibn Ibrahim, an important chief

of the Djodala, one of the Sanhaja Berber tribes, returned from the Muslim pilgrimage to Mecca with a Sanhaja theologian named Abd Allah bin Yasin. Around 1042 bin Yasin's inspired group of followers, the Almoravids, built a fortified religious center, or *ribat,* and conquered the surrounding tribes. By 1186 the Almoravids had crossed the straits of Gibraltar and conquered Muslim Spain. By the end of the 11th century the Almoravids, starting as a mere band of religiously inspired tribes in Mauritania, had spread Almoravid, Maliki Islam throughout West Africa and southern Spain. The rise of the Almoravids signaled the beginning of Islam as a central part of Mauritanian society. Although its role in North African history diminished after the conquest of the Almoravids, Mauritania never ceased to be a crossroads of trade.

The ancient pursuit of trans-Saharan trade is another common factor of Mauritanian identity. Even after the Europeans conquered coastal areas and the Senegal River, Mauritania was still used for the transport of goods between Morocco and sub-Saharan Africa. Despite the almost universal embrace of Islam and trade, Mauritanian society is currently divided into competing ethnic groups: blacks, the Arab Maures, and the Berbers. In 1674 the ARABS, who had migrated from the north, gradually gained ascendancy over both the Berbers, who turned to religious practices, and the blacks who were enslaved or pushed into regions south of the Senegal River. Arab control of Mauritanian society generally remains to this day, and despite the objections of Western governments and human rights groups, slavery is still routinely practiced in many areas. Although interior regions of Mauritania were generally isolated from European influence, even Mauritania could not avoid partial colonization by European powers.

The influence of Europe has had an important impact on the nature of Mauritanian government, language and administration. The history of European interest in Mauritania begins in the 18th century when various European traders recognized the north bank of the Senegal River as a source of gum Arabic, used in printing, from acacia trees. In 1815 France gained power over the coast of West Africa to the Senegal River. In 1904, however, Mauritania was recognized by the French government as a separate territory to be administered by a delegate general at the trading city of Saint Louis. Even as they systemized the administration of West Africa and Mauritania, the French relied on the cooperation of local chiefs. France's administrative structure remains to this day. Both French and Arabic is spoken by the Mauritanian elite. Recently, however, Mauritanians have been eager to reassert their Islamic identity as they seek economic assistance from wealthy Arab nations.

The three main cultural and ethnic groups in Mauritania—blacks, Berbers, and Arabs—all have different histories and identities. Even so, all three groups have been defined by a history of nomadism, trade, and conquest across the Saharan region. Even after the establishment of modern boundaries, borders are regularly violated and crossed by arms traders, smugglers, and legitimate salt and mineral traders who use the same ancient trading routes and often prefer the camel over expensive, motorized transport. The desert of Mauritania is forbidding, but ever since the rise of the Almoravids in the 11th century it has also proven to be an almost impenetrable refuge for independent groups and religious revolutionaries. Recently, Mauritanians have been exposed to modern expectations and cultural influences, especially as traditional nomadic groups settle in the cities. Also, despite its location on the periphery of the Muslim world, Mauritania has not been exempted from the rise of modern, political Islam and fundamentalism. As a result the local traditional values of Mauritanian society, especially the high status of women in matriarchal nomadic tribes, has come into direct conflict with strict interpretations of Islamic law.

Like most tribal peoples, Mauritanian culture is dominated by poetry and the oral arts; the blue-veiled TUAREG of northern Mauritania have become famous for their epic songs. Black and Berber groups also maintain their own cultural traditions through song and complex tribal ceremonies. Architecturally, Mauritanian towns are famous for their magnificently decorated red and white plaster houses and unique mosques. The nomadic tent is a treasure trove of tribal folk art. Traditional symbols printed on camel skin sheets are used to predict the future, intricately carved Quran boxes protect from evil spirits, and carpets woven with narrative, symbolic designs tell the stories of ancestors. The camel hair tents are also decorated with splashes of color and symbols to protect the tent dweller from the dangers of the desert.

FURTHER READING

Simonetta Calderini. *Mauritania* (Santa Barbara, Calif.: Clio Press, 1992).
Robert E. Handloff (ed.). *Mauritania, a Country Study* 2nd ed. (Washington, D.C.: Library of Congress, 1990).
Jesse Sage and Liora Kasten. *Enslaved: True Stories of Modern Day Slavery* (New York: Palgrave Macmillan, 2006).

Mauritians: nationality   (people of Mauritius)

GEOGRAPHY

The Republic of Mauritius is an island nation situated about 560 miles east of Madagascar and 1,250 miles east of mainland Africa in the Indian Ocean. The nation consists of the island of Mauritius, the two Agalega Islands (North Island and South Island), the Cargados Carajos Shoals (also known as the Saint Brandon Rocks), and Rodriguez Island. The Republic has a total area of about 784 square miles. The island of Mauritius at 720 square miles makes up more than 90 percent of the total area of the nation; Rodriguez Island has an area of 43 square miles; and the Agalega Islands have an area of 27 square miles. The Cargados Carajos Shoals consist of about 16 small islands that are part of an extended barely submerged coral reef. The Agalega Islands lie about 700 miles north of the island of Mauritius; Rodriguez is situated about 350 miles east of the island of Mauritius; and the Cargados Carajos Shoals lie about 185 miles northeast of the island of Mauritius.

Mauritius, Rodriguez, and the Cargados Carajos Shoals are part of the Mascarene Archipelago. The island of Mauritius has a narrow coastal plain that rises to a central plateau with an altitude of 900 to 1,900 feet and is ringed by coral reefs. The highest point on the island, Piton de la Petite Rivière Noire, has an altitude of 2,717 feet. Rodriguez has a similar geography, with a high point of 1,160 feet.

About 97 percent of the population of the Republic of Mauritius live on the island of Mauritius, which has one of the world's highest population densities. The second most densely populated island is Rodriguez. Both the Agalega Islands and the Cargados Carajos Shoals are inhabited but have permanent populations of just a few hundred. The nation's capital city, Port Louis, is on the island of Mauritius.

INCEPTION AS A NATION

There are records of Arab and South Asian sailors visiting the island of Mauritius in the 10th century, but there seem to have been no

MAURITIANS: NATIONALITY

nation:
Mauritius; Republic of Mauritius

derivation of name:
Named for Dutch noble Maurice of Nassau (Maurits van Nassau)

government:
Parliamentary democracy

capital:
Port Louis

language:
The country's official language, English, is the first language of only about 1 percent of the population. Creole is spoken by 81 percent of the population, Bhojpuri (an Indian language) by 12 percent, French by 4 percent, and a range of other Indian, Chinese, and African languages by the remaining 2 percent.

religion:
About 48 percent of the population are Hindu, 24 percent are Roman Catholic, 17 percent are Muslim, and the majority of the remainder belong to other Christian denominations.

earlier inhabitants:
Uninhabited

demographics:
Indo-Mauritians make up about 68 percent of the population, Creoles 27 percent, Sino-Mauritians 3 percent, and Franco Mauritians 2 percent.

Mauritians: nationality time line

C.E.

1507 Portuguese sailors visit Mauritius, which is then uninhabited.

1598 Dutch claim sovereignty over the island, naming it Mauritius.

1638–58 Dutch establish colony on Mauritius; eventually abandoned.

1664–1710 Second Dutch colony on Mauritius; also abandoned. The dodo, a bird unique to Mauritius, becomes extinct through overhunting.

1715 France claims sovereignty over Mauritius and renames it Ile de France.

1720s Port Louis founded.

1810 Britain takes control of Mauritius after defeating French forces.

1834 Slavery is abolished throughout the British Empire.

1835 Indentured labor system introduced; thousands of workers begin to arrive from India.

1910 Indentured labor system ended.

1926 First Indo-Mauritians elected to the government council.

1936 Mauritian Labor Party (MLP) founded by Maurice Cure.

1948 New constitution extends suffrage to most Indo-Mauritians and Creoles.

1957 Internal self-government granted to Mauritius.

1958 Suffrage extended to all Mauritians over 21.

1959 MLP led by Seewoosagur Ramgoolam wins first elections under universal adult suffrage.

1968 Mauritius becomes independent.

1968 Mauritian Militant Movement (MMM) founded as main opposition party.

1971–76 State of emergency declared following general strikes called by the MMM.

1982 Anerood Jugnauth elected prime minister.

1983 Jugnauth founds the Militant Socialist Movement.

1992 Mauritius becomes a republic. Cassam Uteem of the MMM becomes the first elected president.

1995 MPL leader Navin Ramgoolam becomes prime minister.

1999 Four days of rioting by Creoles after popular Creole musician dies in police custody.

2000 Anerood Jugnauth elected prime minister again.

2002 President Uteem refuses to sign a controversial antiterrorism bill and resigns. Karl Hoffman elected president.

2005 Navin Ramgoolam elected prime minister again.

2006 Chagos islanders make their first visit to the islands since eviction by the British government 40 years before.

2007 British courts rule that Chagos Islanders should be allowed to return to live on the islands.

inhabitants. When Portuguese explorers visited the island in 1507 they were uninhabited, and they were still uninhabited in 1638 when the Dutch established their first settlement. The Dutch colony was abandoned in about 1710 and France, which had already claimed and settled the nearby island of Réunion, extended its control over the islands in 1715. Inhabitation of the islands has been continuous since that time. Port Louis was established as a base for attacking British interests in India, and French settlers began to establish a series of plantations using African slaves for labor. Britain seized control Mauritius in 1810 during the Napoleonic Wars, and the territory remained a British possession until independence in 1968.

Britain's chief aim in holding Mauritius was to deny its use as a base for the French navy, so there was little investment in the island and little British settlement. Consequently, the French landowning community that continued to live on the islands remained the dominant cultural and political force. Mauritius became a major sugar producer in the 19th century, and it was the French community that owned the sugar plantations and the refineries. After slavery was abolished across the British Empire, many former African slaves stopped working on the plantations and either left the islands or moved into other occupations. To replace the lost workforce, a system of indentured labor was introduced that brought almost half a million Indians to work on the islands' plantations from 1835 to 1910, when the system ended. Africans, Malagasy, and Chinese also migrated to the islands as indentured workers, but in much smaller numbers.

A Government Council was introduced to Mauritius in 1831, and a new constitution introduced in 1886 provided for a council of 27 members, 10 of whom were elected. Voting rights were restricted to land owners, thereby excluding the great majority of the nonwhite population from political representation. Property qualifications were removed for suffrage in 1947, and the vote was also extended to women under the constitution adopted in that year. From 1948 Mauritians of Indian decent, who make up more than 65 percent of the population, have dominated parliament. Internal self-government was introduced to Mauritius in 1957, and full independence followed in March 1968.

In 1965, immediately prior to independence, the British government detached the Chagos Islands, which had been a dependency of Mauritius since 1814, and formed a separate entity known as the British Indian Ocean Territories consisting of these islands alone. In 1966 the British government purchased all the privately owned land on the islands and began forcibly evicting the inhabitants in order to allow the construction of a large military base on the largest island, Diego Garcia, that was to be leased to the United States. Construction of the military facilities began in 1971, and since that time the original inhabitants of the islands, known as Chagossians, have been campaigning for the right to return to their homes. Mauritius currently claims sovereignty over the Chagos Islands, although there is little likelihood of their claim being recognized while it remains a strategically important British and U.S. military base.

CULTURAL IDENTITY

Mauritius is regarded as one of the most politically stable and economically successful of all postcolonial African nations. Historically, the islands' chief export was sugar, and this has remained one of the nation's most important industries. Since a severe drought in 1999 that severely damaged the sugarcane crop, however, the Mauritian government has pursued a vigorous policy of economic diversification that has attracted considerable foreign investment. Tourism and banking have become major growth industries, adding substantially to the nation's underlying economic strength. Mauritians have enjoyed steadily improving average life expectancy and public infrastructure since independence.

Mauritian society consists of four groups with distinctive ethnohistorical roots. Indo-Mauritians, the largest group, are largely the descendents of indentured workers who came to the islands in large numbers between 1935 and 1910. The Creoles are the descendants of either African slaves who were freed in the 1930s and remained on the islands or indentured African and Malagasy workers who arrived after 1935 or have a mixed heritage. Franco-Mauritians, who make up just 2 percent of the population, are the descendents of the original French settlers who came to the islands in the 18th century or later. Sino-Mauritians, who make up about 3 percent of the population, are the descendants of Chinese indentured workers or Chinese people who have migrated to Mauritius more recently to work in the country's growing textile industry. Although Indo-Mauritians dominate the political arena, the very small Franco-Mauritian community retains a level of influence disproportionate to its size thanks to its hereditary ownership of land. The Creoles are the most economically disadvantaged group.

Despite the diversity of very different ethnic groups that make up Mauritian society, interethnic conflict has been rare, although not unknown. In 1964 and 1968, as Mauritius was making the transition to independence, there was considerable violence between Muslims and Creoles and between Hindus and Creoles over the political future of the country, and violence occurred again in 1999 following the establishment of an unpopular government coalition. Unlike other nations with a broad ethnic mix, Mauritius has followed a policy of preserving and celebrating the different cultures that they represent rather than attempting to foster a sense of a unified identity. In one sense there is no single Mauritian national identity, since the various groups that make up the population have retained many of the traditions, religious beliefs, and customs from the homelands of their ancestors. In another sense the tradition of retaining distinctive customs while tolerating the distinctive customs of other groups is a defining feature of Mauritian national identity. Marriages between members of different ethnic groups are rare but becoming more common as the country's expanding and diversifying economy begins to break down traditional ways of life.

FURTHER READING

Richard B. Allen. *Slaves, Freedmen, and Indentured Laborers in Colonial Mauritius* (Cambridge, U.K.: Cambridge University Press, 1999).

Muniśvaralāla Cintamani. *Story of Independence of Mauritius* (New Delhi: Star Publications, 2003).

Saroja Sundararajan. *From Bondage to Deliverance: Indentured Labour in Mauritius and British Guiana* (New Delhi: Allied Publishers, 2006).

Stephen Taylor. *Storm and Conquest: The Clash of Empires in the Eastern Seas, 1809* (New York: Norton, 2008).

Megan Vaughan. *Creating the Creole Island: Slavery in Eighteenth-Century Mauritius* (Durham, N.C.: Duke University Press, 2005).

David Vine. *Island of Shame: The Secret History of the U.S. Military Base on Diego Garcia* (Princeton, N.J.: Princeton University Press, 2008).

Mavia (Chimaviha; Mabiha; Mawia)

The Mavia are a subgroup of the MAKONDE. They live in northern Mozambique and southern Tanzania, mostly in Mozambique.

Mawia *See* MAVIA.

Mayombe (Maiombe)

The Mayombe are a subgroup of the KONGO. They live in Cabinda, the northern extension of Angola, and in the Democratic Republic of the Congo.

Mazandarani (Tabari)

The Mazandarani are a people of the Iranian province of Mazandaran, south of the Caspian Sea and north of the capital city of Tehran, bounded by Golestan on the east and Gilan on the west. The Caspian Sea forms the northern boundary, while the Elburz Mountains, running parallel to the Caspian coast, form a barrier to the south. Aside from the coastal plain, the region is very mountainous and watered by numerous rivers. The Mazandarani language is a Northwest Iranian language, related to Kurdish and Balochi. Most Mazandarani also speak Persian, the official language of Iran. Census figures of 2006 put the population of the province at nearly 3 million. The total population of Iran is about 70.5 million.

In ancient Avestan and Pahlavi texts, the Mazandaranis are described as foreign and distinct from the PERSIANS, and they are alleged to descend from different ancestors from the Iranians (*see* IRANIANS: NATIONALITY) and the ARABS. The Arabs, who ruled the area from 644 C.E., knew the region as Tabaristan ("the land of the Tabaris"), but the name Mazandaran came into use again under the rule of the SELJUKS (1037–1300). Important figures who came from this region include the Arabic historian al-Tabari (d. 923 C.E.), whose name indicates that he came from Tabaristan. Al-Tabari is one of the towering figures of Islam, known mainly for his comprehensive *History of Prophets and Kings,* which begins with creation and the biblical patriarchs, then continues on to the life of Muhammad, through the rule of the Muslim caliphs and dynasties, up to al-Tabari's own era. Al-Tabari's other major work is his commentary on the Quran, still regarded as one of the essential works in Muslim religious studies. In modern times, the region was the homeland of Reza Shah Pahlavi, who ruled Iran from 1925 until 1941, when the occupying armies of the British and the Soviet Union forced him to abdicate in favor of his son, Muhammad Reza Shah, who ruled Iran to 1979, when he was forced into exile and the monarchy was ended by the Islamic Revolution.

Mbai *See* MBAY.

Mbaka (Bwaka; Ngbaka)

The Mbaka live in the Central African Republic and the Democratic Republic of the Congo. Jean-Bedel Bokassa, ruler of the Central African Republic between 1966 and 1976, was a Mbaka.

Mbaka-Mandija

The Mbaka-Mandija have relatively recently emerged as a separate ethnic group from the intermingling of Baya and Mbaka people. They live in the Central African Republic.

Mbala

The Mbala are a Bantu people who live in the south of the Democratic Republic of the Congo. The majority live in and around Kikwit on the Kwilu River. The Mbala language is related to that of the Kongo.

Mbay (Mbai)

The Mbay, a subgroup of the Sara, are probably of Nilotic origin (*see* Nilotes). They live largely in southern Chad.

Mbeere

The Mbeere live in south-central Kenya in the plains below the town of Embu on the slopes of Mount Kenya, roughly 100 miles northeast of the capital, Nairobi.

It is not known when the Mbeere settled in the area that is their present-day homeland, but they were certainly well established in this region by the mid-19th century. The Mbeere are a Bantu people—their language, which is called Kimbeere, belongs to the Bantu subgroup of the Benue-Congo group. The Mbeere are sometimes classified as a subgroup of the Kikuyu, who are also a Bantu-speaking people. Also like the Kikuyu, the Mbeere believe in a high-god called Ngai, who is said to live at the top of nearby Mount Kenya. In the 20th century, however, many Kikuyu have converted to Christianity.

Mbenga   *See* Mbuti, Twa, and Mbenga.

Mbila   *See* Safwa.

Mbochi   (Boubangui; Mboshi)

The Mbochi live in the central Republic of the Congo, the west of the Democratic Republic of the Congo, and eastern Gabon.

Mbole

The Mbole are a subgroup of the Mongo of Central Africa. The Mbole live in the central Democratic Republic of the Congo west of the Lokmani River.

Mboshi   *See* Mbochi.

Mbugwe

The Mbugwe live in central Tanzania to the east and south of Lake Manyara. They are a Bantu people.

Mbulu   *See* Iraqw.

Mbun

The Mbun are a historically important Bantu people of Central Africa. They once dominated the Adamawa highlands region of present-day Cameroon. They now live in southern Chad, northern Cameroon, and the west of the Central African Republic.

Mbundu

The Mbundu account for about one quarter of Angola's total population. They inhabit north-central Angola, including the capital, Luanda. The Mbundu language, Kimbundu, is a Bantu language.

Toward the end of the 15th century, the Mbundu founded the Ndongo Kingdom. The ruler of Ndongo was known as the *ngola*. In the 17th century, the Ndongo Kingdom was ruled by Nzinga Mbandi, or Anna Nzinga (1623–63). This famous African queen was a leader of anti-colonial resistance. In the mid-20th century, the Mbundu were central in the battle to expel the Portuguese. The leading nationalist movement, the Popular Movement for the Liberation of Angola (MPLA), drew much of its support from the Mbundu. When independence was achieved in 1975, however, the country was plunged into civil war that continued until 2002.

Mbunga

The Mbunga are a Bantu people who live mostly in Tanzania.

Mbute   *See* Vute.

Mbuti, Twa, and Mbenga

The Mbuti, Twa, and Mbenga are the three major groupings of the tropical forest-forager peoples (forest-dwelling people who live mainly by hunting and gathering) of Central Africa. These people are scattered across nine countries from the Atlantic coast in the west to Uganda in the east.

The Mbuti live in the Ituri Forest of the northeast of the Democratic Republic of the

MBUTI, TWA, AND MBENGA

location:
Central Africa

time period:
3,000 B.C.E. to present

ancestry:
Unknown

language:
Niger-Congo and Nilo-Saharan

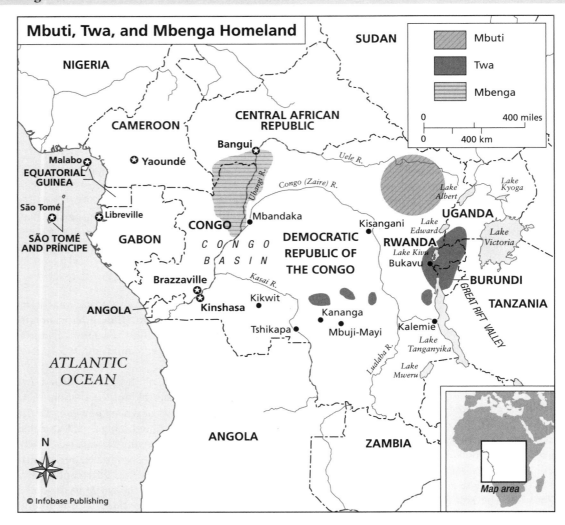

Mbuti, Twa, and Mbenga Homeland

© Infobase Publishing

Congo. About 100,000 Twa live in the area around Lake Tumba in the west of the Democratic Republic of the Congo, and there are a further 30,000 in the high forests along the borders of the Democratic Republic of the Congo, Uganda, Rwanda, and Burundi.

The Mbenga peoples—the AKA, BAKA, BONGO, and KOLA—number about 45,000. About 20,000 Aka live in the northern Republic of the Congo and the south of the Central African Republic. Some 20,000 Baka live in southeast Cameroon, the northwest Republic of the Congo, and northern Gabon. There are about 2,000 Bongo in the western Republic of the Congo and southern Gabon. The Kola number around 3,000 and live in southwest Cameroon.

ORIGINS

The origins of tropical forest-foragers—sometimes derogatorily referred to as PYGMIES because of their short stature—are obscure, but they have been living in the dense tropical rainforests, forests, marshes, and sometimes the savannas (grasslands with scattered trees and shrubs) of Central Africa for thousands of years. They were probably the region's first inhabitants and were known to the ancient Egyptians nearly 5,000 years ago.

LANGUAGE

There is no common tropical forest-forager language, as most groups speak the language of their nearest neighbors. The Mbuti and Twa peoples are BANTU speakers, and the languages of the Mbenga peoples are Bantu or Ubanguian. Two other Central African forest peoples, the Asua and Efe, speak a Sudanic language.

HISTORY

Until comparatively recently, the outside world—apart from their closest neighbors—knew very little about the forest-forager peoples. About 2,000 years ago Sudanic and

Bantu-speaking peoples from the north, east, and southeast began to settle and farm on the fringes of the rainforests. These settlers cleared large areas of forest for their farmland but found the forest itself hostile and threatening. In contrast, the forest dwellers felt safe in the forest and were threatened by its destruction.

The settlers and the forest people developed a relationship that was generally of benefit to both groups. The individual groups of forest people allied themselves with neighboring settlers, adopted their languages, and supplied them with forest products in exchange for corn, bananas, rice, metal, and other village products. By providing the villagers with the forest products that they needed, the forest-dwellers ensured that the villagers did not need to enter the forest themselves, thus preserving their environment. This mutual arrangement still survives, but in many parts of Central Africa has been under increasing threat.

This threat began with the colonization of Central Africa by European powers, especially France and Belgium. In the late 19th and early 20th centuries, the colonial governments began forcing villagers to grow crops such as rubber for export. In turn, the hard-pressed villagers needed their forest neighbors' labor to produce food crops. At the same time, large areas of the forest were taken over by trading companies, and the forest people were made to supply them with valuable products such as ivory and antelope skins. As a result, many of the forest people became dependent on villagers.

For a while, this suited the colonial governments, but policies changed in the 1930s, and attempts were made to govern the forest peoples directly and "free" them from the domination of the villagers—in reality, an attempt to make them dependent on the state instead. In the 20th century, Mbuti, Twa, and Mbenga groups were all affected by deforestation, government policies, and regional conflicts. In the early 1990s, the Twa of Rwanda were caught up in the violence between the principal HUTU AND TUTSI ethnic groups (*see* RWANDANS: NATIONALITY). More than 3,000 were killed in the genocide of 1994. The Mbuti of the Democratic Republic of the Congo were victims in the Second Congo War (1997–2003). Allegations have been made to the United Nations that thousands of Mbuti were murdered by combatants during the war.

CULTURE

Specialists at extracting resources from the forest, the ways of life of the Mbuti and other

Mbuti, Twa, and Mbenga time line

B.C.E.

ca. 3000 Ancient Egyptians in contact with rainforest peoples

ca. 200s Bantu-speakers begin to arrive.

C.E.

500s First recorded sightings of rainforest peoples

1884 German colony of Kamerun established.

1885 Belgian king's Congo Free State is established.

1908 Belgian government takes over Free State as Belgian Congo.

1916 Kamerun occupied by Britain and France.

1960 Belgian Congo and French Congo independent, both as Republic of Congo. Gabon independent. French Cameroun independent as Cameroon.

1961 British Cameroon independent; south as part of Cameroon

1994 Twa in Rwanda caught up in genocide between Hutu and Tutsi ethnic groups.

1997–2003 Second Congo War; thousands of Mbuti are massacred by combatants.

forest peoples is usually a seminomadic existence, based on hunting game and gathering forest products such as fruit, nuts, and wild honey. Communities live in forest camps for several months a year. To set up a camp, a group clears a patch of undergrowth and builds small, conical huts made of bent branches covered in leaves and furnished with benches and beds made of sticks. When the camp has been built, the group spends part of each day gathering food and hunting game, such as antelope and monkeys, with bows and arrows, spears, or nets. The rest of their time is spent on activities such as making and repairing weapons, weaving baskets, making cloth out of beaten tree bark, and on communal entertainment such as storytelling, singing, and dancing. When food becomes scarce in the area, the group moves on to another site.

In the present day, none of the forest-forager communities live in isolation. Forest products are traded with settled farming communities for food products such as cassava and corn or for goods such as iron tools, tobacco, salt, and clothes. Time has to be spent near a village so that these exchanges can be carried out. Many also provide labor for the villagers by, for instance, working in gardens. To outsiders it has often appeared that the forest-foragers are the servants of the villagers, but their ability to live in the forest keeps them independent.

Since the colonial era, vast areas of rainforest have been cleared for timber or to make way for cattle ranching or plantations of tea, coffee, rubber, cotton, and other cash crops. This large-scale destruction of the Twa and Mbenga lands has led to huge changes in their lifestyles—the Mbuti lands in the Ituri Forest have largely been spared so far because they lack the "high-grade" timbers in demand in Europe. As a result of these changes, many people can no longer follow their hunting-gathering way of life and have become an impoverished rural labor force. Since the Gishwati Forest was virtually all cut down for tea plantations and pasture in the 1980s, for example, the Impunyu Twa of Rwanda have largely abandoned hunting and gathering and are now mostly employed as domestic servants or landless laborers, or have to beg to survive.

Even forest conservation measures, such as the establishment of national parks, have caused problems for tropical forest-foragers, for most were created without consultation of the indigenous peoples of the forest. Conservation laws introduced to Rwanda in 1973 have made hunting and gathering virtually illegal. Most national parks restrict or prohibit the access of people to forests, forcing them to live on the fringes of the settled community. One exception is the Okapi National Park in the Democratic Republic of the Congo, where many Mbuti who were originally excluded are now employed as trackers.

Many groups now follow a settled lifestyle. In an often misguided attempt to integrate them into national life, forest dwellers have been encouraged to abandon the forest and farm since the colonial era. Some communities have therefore been sedentary farmers for generations, and most now incorporate at least some form of cultivation into their lifestyle. The Bongo of the southwest Republic of the Congo, for example, raise chickens for local markets and supply firewood, no longer relying on hunting and gathering. Recent research suggests that groups that continue their hunting and gathering way of life actually tend to be better nourished than other African peoples. Economic and political pressures mean that many rely on agricultural produce for most of their food though.

Government and Society

While living in the forest, the Mbuti, Twa, and Mbenga peoples live in bands of between seven to 30 households. These communities are renowned for their egalitarianism, for their social

A Mende woman with an elaborate hairstyle

organization is based on cooperation, equality, and sharing. Decisions affecting the group are made collectively, and food that is collected is distributed equally throughout the group. Conflicts and disputes are resolved using humor and ritual rather than confrontation. If any members of the group are unhappy with decisions or wish to leave, then they can set up their own community. As a result, groups are fluid and people move freely between one group and another—to visit relatives or to stay for good.

Often specific bands of forest foragers have historical ties with a certain group of villagers. The commercial exploitation of forests has not only affected people's way of life, however, but also their social structures. These reciprocal relationships between foragers and villagers, now forced to compete for land and revenue from the destruction of forests, have broken down in many cases and resulted in outright exploitation or discrimination to the disadvantage of the more vulnerable forest-foragers.

By taking care of tax returns and other official matters on their behalf, villagers have often established themselves as intermediaries with officialdom for the forest-dwellers. This can work against the interests of the people, as they are left unable to easily get hold of official documents needed to prove their citizenship and exercise their political rights. One of the greatest threats to the independence of these people is that none of the countries in which they live recognize that they have any legal rights to the land they inhabit. The Mbuti, Twa, and Mbenga peoples are therefore often politically marginalized and discriminated against. To counteract this, some Twa people have set up political and cultural organizations.

Responsibilities are decided according to age and gender. Each age group—children, young people, adults, and the elderly—has its own duties and responsibilities. Hunting is basically a male activity, but women and children help by driving the game toward the hunters; women also do most of the food gathering.

Religion

Religions vary between the various groups, but most involve a recognition of the central role that the forest plays in the communities' survival. Many forest people believe in a spirit world inhabited by the souls of the dead and presided over by the spirit of the forest itself. To them, the forest is a living being that is to be loved and respected, and most of their rituals are concerned with honoring it and the food it provides. All groups have healers and their own hunting rituals as well as ceremonies concerning the collection of honey. There are cultural and religious prohibitions against overhunting.

Medes

The Medes were an ancient Iranian people who established the earliest known Iranian Empire. Their traditional homeland was in the northwest of present-day Iran, an area they are believed to have migrated to from Central Asia in the second millennium B.C.E. Between the 10th and eighth centuries B.C.E. the Medes were subjects of the Assyrian Empire (see ASSYRIANS). At the beginning of the seventh century B.C.E., however, the Medes and the CHALDEANS threw off Assyrian domination and Media emerged as an independent power.

Little is known about the emergence and growth of the Median Empire, since there are no known surviving historical records from Media itself. Historians believe that the Medes extended their control over large areas of present-day Iran and Iraq and into the Anatolian Peninsula.

The empire of the Medes was the immediate predecessor of the first Persian Empire, also known as the Achaemenid Empire (see ACHAEMENIDS). The PERSIANS were a closely related subject people under Median rule. In 553 B.C.E. Cyrus the Great rebelled against his grandfather, the Median king Astyages, and won a

decisive victory in 550 B.C.E. that marked the establishment of a new Persian dynasty. Although defeated by the Persians, the Medes remained a prominent people in the empire, so much so that the early Achaemenid Empire is sometimes referred to as the Median and Persian Empire. Median customs, dress, and traditions were inherited by their Persian successors and came to form part of the foundation of Persian imperial culture. The Median capital, Ecbatana, near the present-day Iranian city of Hamadan become the summer residence of Persian rulers, and Medians were widely employed as officials, provincial governors, and generals.

Mbwera *See* SHIRAZI.

Meidob (Tiddi)

The Meidob live in the Meidob Hills in Sudan's western Darfur Province. They claim to descend from Nubian ancestors (*see* NUBIANS).

Mende

Most Mende live in central and southeast Sierra Leone, where they are that nation's largest single ethnic group. A few also live in Liberia.

<table>
<tr><td colspan="2">**MENDE**</td></tr>
<tr><td>**location:**
Sierra Leone and Liberia</td></tr>
<tr><td>**time period:**
15th century C.E. to present</td></tr>
<tr><td>**ancestry:**
Mandé</td></tr>
<tr><td>**language:**
Mandé (Niger-Congo)</td></tr>
</table>

ORIGINS

During the 13th and 14th centuries, the ancestors of the Mende lived around the upper stretches of the Niger and Senegal Rivers in what is now Guinea. These lands formed part of the medieval Empire of Mali. Mali was declining in the 15th century when the Mende probably moved slowly south as part of a wave of Mandé-speaking migrants that spread across West Africa.

LANGUAGE

The Mende language, also called Mende, belongs to the Mandé language group.

HISTORY

According to Mende oral history, in the beginning of the 16th century a group of MANDING (another Mandé language) speakers called the Mani were exiled from the Empire of Mali. Under their queen, Mansarico, they traveled southwest, finally settling in the Cape Mount area of modern Liberia around 1540. From there, the Mani conquered much of present-day Sierra Leone, establishing many subkingdoms. The resulting peoples of mixed Mani and local

The traditional script used to write the Mende language. The Mende use the Roman script today.

descent formed new ethnic groups, the largest of which was the Mende.

In the early 18th century, the Mende began migrating west of the Sewa River. They gained control of the southern half of modern Sierra Leone by the early 19th century. By 1896, however, they were conquered by the British. The Mende people were among the most active in the fight for independence from colonial rule. Sierra Leone became independent in 1961, with Milton Margai, a Mende, as head of state.

In the 1990s, both Sierra Leone and Liberia were hit by civil wars. In 1991, rebels launched an attack on Sierra Leone, and the country was ripped apart by fighting between government and rebel troops. The aims of the rebels were to expel foreigners from the country and take control of the rich diamond-mining regions. The people most affected by the conflict were ordinary civilians. Many Mende suffered through loss of employment and land, and many were victims of brutality meted out by both the government and rebel troops. The fighting was ended by a cease-fire in 2002. Liberia too has suffered from a prolonged period of recurring fighting among various rebel groups between 1989 and 2003.

CULTURE

The majority of the Mende people live in rural areas and make their living from the land. Rice, cassava, and yams are important food crops. The Mende also produce crops to sell, especially coffee, cocoa, ginger, kola nuts, groundnuts (peanuts), and cassava. Most rice is grown on upland farms by a system called shifting cultivation. This involves clearing patches of forests, growing crops on the cleared land for a few years, and then moving on to let the soil recover fertility. An increasing population and the growing levels of urbanization, however, have pushed farmers into using more intensive methods of cultivation. Since 1923 they have been encouraged to reclaim and farm swamplands. Diamonds have been Sierra Leone's most important export since the 1930s. Originally, diamond mining was monopolized by a government-run company. Widespread diamond smuggling and illicit mining in the 1950s forced the government to allow the licensing of independent diggers. Today, many Mende men work as diamond diggers, either independently or as part of a gang employed by a company.

Government and Society

The basic economic and social unit in Mende society is the *mawe*. Simply put, this is a farming household. It comprises one or more older men and their wives, their children, wives and husbands of these children, and any grandchildren. Although the senior male is head of the household, the functioning of the *mawe* is controlled by the women. The senior wife organizes the farmwork, which is done by both men and women. She also has her own plot of land on which she can grow cash crops. Senior wives are therefore largely responsible for the wealth and prosperity of a *mawe*.

Most Mende belong to one or more *hale* (secret societies). These act as unifying and controlling forces in Mende society. *Hale* lay down various rules, sanction acceptable forms of behavior, prohibit unacceptable behavior, and

Mende time line

C.E.

1235–ca. 1500 Empire of Mali: Mende ancestors part of empire

1400s Mende begin moving southwest into present-day Sierra Leone and Liberia, conquering local peoples.

ca. 1500 Mani people exiled from Mali.

ca. 1540 Mende ancestors settled in Cape Mount area (Liberia).

1800s Christianity spreads in Sierra Leone.

1808 British rule established in Freetown (Sierra Leone).

1847 Liberia established by freed American slaves.

1896 A British protectorate declared over Sierra Leone.

1898 Mende revolt sparked by the "hut tax"; revolt suppressed.

1961 Sierra Leone becomes independent.

1991–2002 Sierra Leone Civil War; Mende elements (known as the Kamajors) dominate the Civil Defence Forces (CDF) the leading paramilitary organization supporting the government of President Kabbah.

2007 Two former leaders of the CDF are convicted of war crimes committed during the Sierra Leone Civil War.

See also SIERRA LEONEANS: NATIONALITY

generally provide cultural and social unity to the Mende. They are both religious and political organizations. The officials serve as contacts with spirits who affect human affairs, while, in the past, chiefs depended for their authority on support from the men's *hale*, Poro. Historically, these societies were very important as the Mende were rarely under the rule of any particular nation or state.

The most important *hale* are the men's society Poro, and the women's society, Sande. At puberty, almost all boys and girls join one or the other. Initiation into Poro and Sande takes place in secret. Initiates are taken to a camp in the forest where they live in seclusion for weeks. Sande and Poro mostly teach Mende ideals of manhood and womanhood, though Poro also settles disputes and regulates trading. Other secret societies include the Humui, Njayei, and Kpa. The Humui regulates sexual behavior; the Njayei uses herbs and other substances to cure madness, which is attributed to breaching this society's taboos; and Kpa apprentices learn to use herbs to treat minor ailments.

Recently, the activities of secret societies have been drastically affected by foreign ideas and by changes in Sierra Leonean society. Many of the rites are no longer performed in larger urban areas. In such areas, it would be impossible to ensure that everyone in the vicinity followed the necessary prohibitions on behavior while the events took place; people no longer observe taboos as they once did. In cities, initiation into Poro now involves simply paying the society's membership fees. Sande no longer circumcises girls and has incorporated prenatal and postnatal education, as well as medical developments, into its initiates' lessons. Newly initiated girls return smartly dressed in modern adult clothes.

Religion

The majority of the Mende profess either Christianity or Islam. The Mende religion is still widely followed, even by converts to these world religions. The Mende religion involves belief in a supreme god, Ngewo, who created everything; belief in an afterlife; various nature spirits associated with such things as forests and rivers; spirits linked to particular *hale*; and the reverence of ancestor spirits.

Masked members of the Poro and Sande societies represent spirits at ceremonies. These are held to mark events such as the coming out of a group of initiates or, in the past, to make crops grow. Dancing and singing play an important part of Sande initiations, at the climax of which a woman disguised as a spirit whips away witches and unfriendly spirits. Today, these dances are performed to entertain.

See also SIERRA LEONEANS: NATIONLITY; LIBERIANS: NATIONALITY.

FURTHER READING

Arthur Abraham. *An Introduction to the Precolonial History of the Mende of Sierra Leone* (Lewiston, N.Y.: Edwin Mellen Press, 2003).

Mariane C. Ferme. *The Underneath of Things: Violence, History, and the Everyday in Sierra Leone* (Berkeley: University of California Press, 2001).

Ruth B. Phillips. *Representing Woman: Sande Masquerades of the Mende of Sierra Leone* (Los Angeles: UCLA Fowler Museum of Cultural History, 1995).

Merina

The Merina are one of Madagascar's most influential ethnic groups. They are the largest ethnic group on the island, where they are concentrated in the center. They have long dominated the country's politics and founded the Merina kingdom in the 15th century (*see also* MADAGASCAN PEOPLES).

Meru

The Meru live in northern Tanzania and across the border in southern Kenya. They are a BANTU people.

Merule   *See* MURLE.

Messiriya

The Messiriya are one of the main BAGGARA subgroups. The Baggara are a Sudanese people of BEDOUIN and black African descent.

Metoko

The Metoko are a subgroup of the MONGO of Central Africa. The Metoko live in the central Democratic Republic of the Congo west of the Lokmani River.

Mfengu   (Fingo)

The Mfengu are a XHOSA-speaking people. They live in the Transkei and Ciskei regions on the eastern seaboard of South Africa.

Miango   *See* IRIGWE.

Mihavane *See* LOMWE.

Mijikenda

The Mijikenda inhabit the coast of Kenya; historically they were concentrated between the towns of Kilifi and Vanga. The Mijikenda are made up of nine closely related groups: the CHONYI, the DIGO, the DURUMA, the GIRIAMA, the JIBANA, the KAMBE, the KAUMA, the RABAI, and the RIBE. The nine Mijikenda groups speak different dialects of the same Mijikenda language. The Giriama are the largest group, followed by the Duruma.

The Mijikenda are a BANTU people who probably migrated into East Africa from the Katanga region in the modern-day Democratic Republic of the Congo of Central Africa sometime early in the first millennium C.E. The Mijikenda are also known as the Nyika—a name for the dry, waterless regions they had to cross during their migration to reach the coast. Early 17th-century oral history relates how several Mijikenda groups, including many Giriama, migrated south from the northern Kenyan coast around Lamu as a result of pressure from the SOMALIS and OROMO. The Giriama built a fortress on top of a hill near Kilifi, roughly 100 miles south.

Mikhifore

The Mikhifore are related to the Malinke and speak a MANDING language. They live in Sierra Leone, Liberia, and Guinea.

Mileri

The Mileri are a TAMA-speaking people of Sudan and Chad, though the majority of the Mileri live in Sudan.

Mima

The Mima live in southern and western Sudan, largely in urban areas. They are closely related to the MIMI of Chad.

Mimi

The Mimi live in eastern Chad. They are closely related to the MIMA of Sudan.

Mina (Popo)

The Mina are a small but socially important ethnic group in both Togo and Benin. The Mina are concentrated in the south of these two countries. They are part of the EWE cluster of peoples.

Minianka

The Minianka are a northerly subgroup of the SENUFO. They have only recently been absorbed into that group. They live largely in the north of Ivory Coast and the south of Mali and Burkina Faso.

Mirifab

The Mirifab have both Arab and Nubian ancestors (*see* ARABS; NUBIANS). The majority of the Mirifab live in north-central Sudan.

Mobeur

The Mobeur are partly descended from the KANEMBU. They live in eastern Niger and northeastern Nigeria.

Mole-Dagbane (Gur; Voltaic)

The Mole-Dagbane peoples of West Africa are united by related languages. There are more than 9 million Mole-Dagbane people, including the MOSSI, MAMPRUSI, and GRUSI.

Mom *See* BAMUM.

Mongo (Lomongo)

The Mongo people inhabit the Congo River Basin in the central Democratic Republic of the Congo. They include a number of smaller groups such as the MBOLE, NTOMBA, METOKO, LENGOLA, and the TETELA.

ORIGINS

Bantu speakers began to settle in the Congo Basin during the first centuries of the Common Era and gradually displaced and absorbed the local tropical forest-foragers. These settlers and the indigenous peoples are ancestors of the present-day Mongo population.

LANGUAGE

The Mongo language is also called Mongo.

HISTORY

Initially the Mongos' ancestors engaged in fishing, hunting, and yam farming, but by 1000 bananas had become the staple crop. Over the years, new areas of forest were cleared for set-

MONGO

location:
Congo River Basin

time period:
First century C.E. to present

ancestry:
Bantu

language:
Bantu (Niger-Congo)

assumed greater importance and was integrated with trapping, hunting, gathering, and fishing. The balance of these activities depended on local environmental conditions.

In the mid-19th century, the increased European demand for ivory stimulated Mongo traders to buy ivory from specialized elephant hunters, in particular from Twa hunters (*see* MBUTI, TWA, AND MBENGA). The Mongo traded crops such as cassava, tobacco, and corn; crafts such as raffia (palm fiber) production, pottery, and basketry; and specialized products such as knives, iron, salt, and dugout canoes with neighboring peoples and European traders. In exchange, they received other regionally produced crafts, pieces of copper or brass, and European-manufactured goods. The village elders, and the village chief himself, exercised strong control over local trade, and together with the traders themselves, they were able to amass power and fortune as a result.

Following Belgian king Leopold II's establishment of the Congo Free State in 1885, the Mongo peoples endured a period of harsh exploitation under the new regime. Leopold's rule was characterized by abuse, brutality, and the committing of atrocities in order to protect and maintain the lucrative rubber trade. Some communities waged war against the white rubber agents or opted for migration. The leaders of rebellious communities were punished or humiliated if caught. International outcry led to the Belgian government taking over in 1908, which resulted in a less oppressive, if nonetheless strongly colonial, period of government until independence in 1960.

Mobutu Sese Seko came to power after a military coup in 1965 and was elected president in 1970. During the 1970s, he promulgated a strong national identity; European place names were Africanized and the country was renamed Zaire. During the 1980s, Mobutu came under growing international criticism at human rights abuses in Zaire, then a one-party state. Mounting tensions led to Mobutu calling a National Conference in 1991 to draft a multiparty constitution. Mobutu refused, however, to grant sovereignty to the National Conference. Civil war broke out in the east in 1996, and in 1997 Mobutu was overthrown by a rebel force led by Laurent Kabila. Kabila promptly renamed the country the Democratic Republic of Congo.

CULTURE

In the face of political uncertainty and social unrest, many Mongo communities continue

An Ndengese sculpture. The Ndengese are a Mongo clan.

tlement and agriculture, populations increased, and surplus labor was freed to engage in specialized arts and crafts activities. By the 19th century, many villages engaged in craft production such as pottery making, ironworking, and the construction of dugout canoes. Agriculture

Mongo time line

C.E.

200s Bantu-speaking people begin to settle in the Congo Basin.

1500s Portuguese begin settling on the Angolan coast and start trading with the Mongo peoples via intermediaries such as the Ovimbundu.

1885 Belgian king's Congo Free State is officially established.

1908 Belgian government takes over Free State as Belgian Congo.

1960 Belgian Congo gains independence as Congo.

1971 Congo renamed Zaire.

1997 Zaire renamed the Democratic Republic of the Congo.

1998–2003 Second Congo War; millions of Mongo are killed or displaced in the fighting.

See also CONGOLESE (DEMOCRATIC REPUBLIC OF THE CONGO): NATIONALITY

to engage in a part hunter-gatherer, part agricultural way of life. A wide range of produce is gathered from the rainforest: fruits, vegetables, palm kernels (seeds), mushrooms, snails, and edible insects, as well as roots and vegetation used for beverages, spices, and medicines. Shifting cultivation—in which newly cleared areas of vegetation are cultivated for three to five years before being left to revert to natural vegetation—is still commonly practiced. Cassava and bananas, for example, are often grown in this manner. Oil palms are harvested in partially cleared terrain and provide a range of products: fruits for oils in cooking and cosmetic products; fronds for housing and craft production; and sap, which is fermented to make wine.

Corn, groundnuts (peanuts), and beans were introduced as cash crops by Portuguese colonists in the late 16th century. The Mongo people were responsive to trading opportunities and adapted their subsistence activities accordingly. Present-day cash crops include coffee, palm products, rubber, cotton, sugar, tea, and cocoa, many of which are grown on large plantations.

Much of the farming and gathering is done by women, who also engage in seasonal fishing. The more prestigious activities of hunting larger forest animals and trapping smaller ones are generally carried out by men. As agriculture has become an increasingly important subsistence activity in the 20th century, the relative workload of women has increased.

Government and Society

Despite aggressive colonization and the subsequent creation of a national identity, many distinctive aspects of Mongo culture have survived in the wider Zairean community. Mongo society is centered on the household. Each household has 20 to 40 members and is led by a senior male elder, commonly referred to as *tata* (father).

Several households in the same area generally form a village of 100 to 400 people led by a village chief, the *bokulaka,* and a council comprising the compound elders. In the past, high status was conferred by birthright or in response to good leadership skills and recognition of the individual's and family's economic power and influence. At times of instability—when communities were threatened by war, for example—villages would form coalitions, with decisions at the district level being made by a loose collection of village chiefs, prominent male elders, and religious practitioners.

Women in Mongo society were given much less power and authority than men. Women did not play a part in decision making at the community level, and within the household, they had to defer to men. In general, they received harsher penalties than men if found guilty of certain crimes such as adultery.

Religion

Although many Mongo have converted to Christianity, a significant number of Mongo beliefs and practices have survived. Belief in witchcraft is strong, and the veneration of ancestors, which played a central role in the Mongo religion, is still widely practiced.

The Mongo oral tradition is very rich, with poems and songs that celebrate community life and provide guidance on how to live in harmony with community members. Folk tales, which were usually centered on a piece of wisdom, were an essential part of a child's education as were proverbs. These proverbs dealt with all aspects of life, especially promoting the importance of the family, respect for authority, and the mutual obligations of members of a community. Hunting and trapping feature strongly in many local proverbs and fables, and in rituals and ceremonies, indicating the high esteem and importance of these activities.

See also CONGOLESE (DEMOCRATIC REPUBLIC OF THE CONGO): NATIONALITY.

FURTHER READING

Richard Bjornson. *The African Quest for Freedom and Identity: Cameroonian Writing and the National Experience* (Bloomington: Indiana University Press, 1991).

Samuel Henry Nelson. *Colonialism in the Congo Basin, 1880–1940* (Athens: Ohio University Center for International Studies, 1994).

Mongols

The Mongols can be broadly defined in two ways—as a wide range of ethnic groups originating in the geographic area later named Mongolia, and found today in the modern nations of Mongolia, Russia, and China, or as those peoples across the Middle and Far East who speak any of the remarkably homogenous dialects of the Mongolian language (a subset of the Turkic language group). There is considerable overlap between these definitions.

The term *Mongol* is first seen in the records of the eighth century C.E. Tang dynasty of China, in reference to peoples inhabiting a region around the Onon River. These groups were descendants of seminomadic peoples (including the originators of the Huns) who warred among themselves and with neighboring states over territory, particularly with China.

It was only in the 13th century that the emergence of a single feudal state and the rise to power of the warlord Temujin, later titled Chinggis Khan ("great chieftain"), allowed the development of a united political and military identity that would form the core of the largest contiguous land empire in world history, reaching as far west as Syria. This period had a profound impact on the cultural and ethnographic development of the Middle Eastern lands, and therefore acts as a natural focus for historical research into Mongolian influence in Europe. In fact, only a small proportion of the empire was ethnically Mongolian like its Khan leaders, yet many of the indigenous peoples of the Middle East already owed some of their ethnic heritage to those TURKIC PEOPLES that eventually formed the Mongols.

ORIGINS

The earliest known period of Mongolian history is dominated by two nomadic ethnic groups, the Xiongnu and the Yuezhi. Despite warfare between these and other communities of the fifth century B.C.E., there was a great deal of ethnic and cultural fluidity, so it is misleading to exclusively identify any particular group with the development of the Mongol people. Invasions, migrations (willing or forced), geographically fluctuating regional control, and strong trading networks extending west and east further complicate this picture.

Kublai Khan (1215–94), ruler of the Mongols and emperor of China, in a portrait painted shortly after his death

Each of these primary nomadic groups migrated westward. The Yuezhi (driven out by the Xiongnu) went on to form the Kushan Empire (*see* KUSHANS) in the first to third centuries C.E., encompassing the territory of the modern nations of Iran, India, and Afghanistan. Descendents of westward-migrating Xiongnu became the Hun Empire, occupying the steppes of Central Asia from the third century C.E. and, under the leadership of warlord Attila, expanding westward to threaten the Roman Empire.

These early migrations, among many others, formed the basis for the modern definition of Turkic cultures—a broad ethnic category of historical and modern peoples associated by cultural and linguistic similarities. Many of the cultures of central Asia and the Middle East therefore shared the same genetic heritage as the Mongols, who applied a more direct influence on their development during the time of the Mongol Empire.

LANGUAGE

Language has been a major unifying force throughout Mongolian history. The modern Mongolian languages and their many dialects evolved from the many Turkic languages spoken up to around the 12th century. It has been proposed that these languages are so distinct and internally consistent that they deserve to be classified as Mongolic, alongside Turkic, under the supra-category of Altaic.

MONGOLS

location:
From northern China across Central Asia as far as Palestine

time period:
Fifth century B.C.E. to 14th century C.E.

ancestry:
Altaic; Mongolic

language:
Mongolic

Mongols: time line

B.C.E.

fifth century War between Xiongnu and Yuezhi

third century Xiongnu descendents form the Hun Empire in Central Asia.

C.E.

first–mid-10th centuries Rise of number of shortlived semi-nomadic Mongolian empires; war with Chinese Tang dynasty; consolidation of ethnically Mongolian but politically distinct, disunited peoples

1162 Temujin born on the banks of the Onon River.

1206 Temujin appointed Chinggis Khan of all Mongolian clans.

1227 Death of Chinggis Khan: empire divided between three Khan heirs.

1235 Major Mongol advance into Eastern Europe

1258 The Battle of Baghdad

1260 The Battle of Ain Jalut: first major Mongol defeat at hands of Mamluks

1260–94 Rule of final Great Khan, Kublai Khan; time of conflict between regional Khans

1299 Damascus sacked by Mongols, and Syria taken by Ghazan Khan; subsequently retaken by Mamluks.

14th century Mongol Empire fragments and shrinks because of internal power struggles and subsequent military disunity; encroachment of empire of warlord Timur.

15th century on Reversion to localized nomadic traditions for remainder of medieval period and until early 20th century

The first unified Mongolian script was adapted from that of the Uyghers, a Turkic people, during the time of the Mongol Empire. This language, now referred to as Classical Mongolian, is used in Mongolia today (in the form of the official language Khalkha, spoken by almost four-fifths of Mongolian peoples) with relatively few modifications from its original form. The Classical Mongolian language was one of the tools most successfully employed to provide the Mongol Empire with a strong sense of unity.

HISTORY

The traditional social structure of the Mongolians was nomadic: seasonal relocation of population centers in search of pasture for livestock. This lifestyle does not encourage the accumulation of material resources, so the early Mongolian nomadic economy was supported by trade and warfare (via plunder). Prior to the 13th century, the different Mongolian peoples warred with outside neighbors and among themselves, without the development of any large, long-lived power structures.

The ascendancy of the warlord Temujin to the title of Chinggis Khan in 1206 marked the first Mongolia-wide political unification of the major disparate ethnic and linguistic groups in the region. By the time of Temujin's death in 1227, the Mongol Empire had successfully invaded westward as far as the western edge of modern Kazakhstan. Thirty years later, under the rule of Temujin's grandson Hulegu, attempts we made to subsume the predominantly Muslim lands of the Middle East into the Mongol Empire.

In accordance with the strict Khanate system of military law, all communities encountered during expansion of the empire were encouraged to submit without struggle, to be rewarded with the benefits of a place in the feudal hierarchy. Total destruction was threatened to those who resisted. The Battle of Baghdad (1258) served as an example of the kind of punishment that awaited defiance. After a 13-day siege, this Islamic state capital was overrun by the Mongols, its population massacred, and its urban framework destroyed, including much or all of its precious irrigation network.

The westward expansion of the Mongol Empire was first checked in 1260 at the Battle of Ain Jalut by a military force of Egyptian Mamluks mustered by their ruler, Saif ad-Din Qutuz. The threat of Mongol attacks led Egypt to rely on its military more and more, and to organize its economy and government around it. Egypt, the only Middle Eastern state to deter invasion by the Mongol Empire, nurtured a pragmatic alliance with the Islam-converted Berke Khan of the Kipchak Khanate, covering what is modern-day Russia. With Berke Khan's support, Hulegu's further incursions toward Egypt were undermined and repelled.

Other Middle Eastern states were conquered and subsumed upon capitulation, or brutally suppressed when they offered resistance. Although the Mamluk victory in 1260 pushed the Mongols out of freshly conquered Syria, in 1299 the Mongol Khan of Persia, Ghazan, attacked the Syrian capital of Damascus with a force of at least 80,000 Mongols and Mongolian allies. At the Battle of Wadi al-Khazander, Ghazan's forces defeated the defending Mamluk force. Despite the inhabitants of Damascus initially accepting the invading force, resistance grew until the city governor actively defied Mongol rule. At this point Damascus was put to siege, overwhelmed, and largely destroyed. A small Mongol force ruled over Syria for the following three months until Ghazan's forces were driven

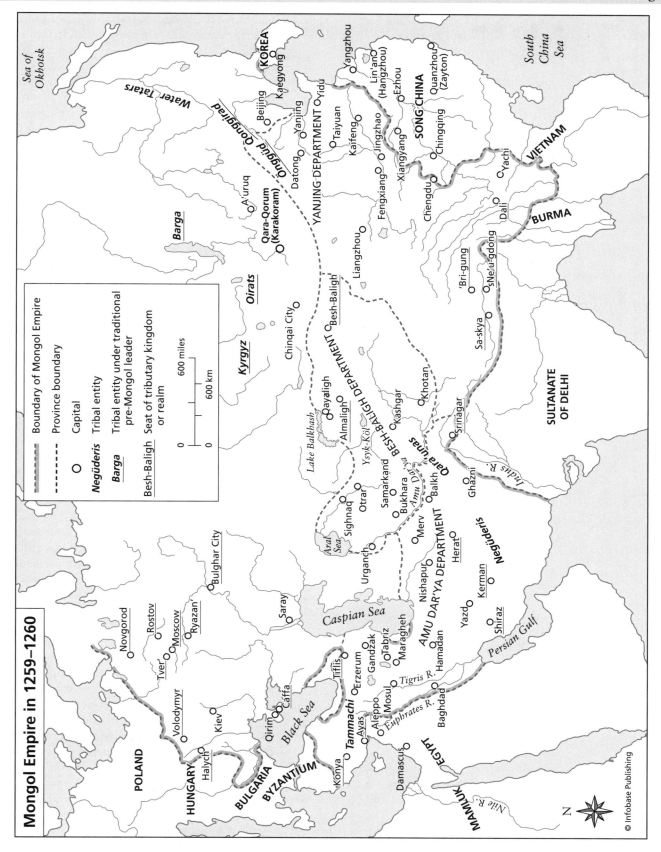

Mongol Empire in 1259–1260

Legend:
- ▬▬ Boundary of Mongol Empire
- - - - Province boundary
- ○ Capital
- *Negüderis* Tribal entity
- *Barga* Tribal entity under traditional pre-Mongol leader
- Besh-Baligh Seat of tributary kingdom or realm

600 miles
600 km

© Infobase Publishing

Sea of Okhotsk

KOREA
Kaegyong
Beijing
Yanjing
Datong
A'uruq
Qara-Qorum (Karakoram)
Barga
Oirats
Kyrgyz
Chinqai City
Chinqai Department
Besh-Baligh
Liangzhou
YANJING DEPARTMENT
Yidu
Taiyuan
Kaifeng
Jingzhao
Yangzhou
Lin'an (Hangzhou)
Ezhou
SONG CHINA
Quanzhou (Zayton)
South China Sea
Xiangyang
Chingqing
Fengxiang
Chengdu
Dali
Yachi
VIETNAM
BURMA
'Bri-gung
Ne'u-gdong
Sa-skya
Srinagar
SULTANATE OF DELHI
Khotan
Kashgar
BESH-BALIGH DEPARTMENT
Ysyk-Köl
Almaligh
Qayaligh
Lake Balkhash
Qara Unas
Ghazni
Indus R.
Water Tatars
Önggüd Qonggirad

Sighnaq
Otrar
Samarkand
Bukhara
Amu Dar'ya
Balkh
Merv
Nishapur
Herat
AMU DAR'YA DEPARTMENT
Kerman
Negüderis
Yazd
Shiraz
Persian Gulf

Aral Sea
Urganch
Saray
Caspian Sea
Hamadan
Maragheh
Tabriz
Gandzak
Baghdad
Tigris R.
Mosul
Aleppo
Euphrates R.
MAMLUK EGYPT
Nile R.
Damascus

Novgorod
Rostov
Tver'
Moscow
Ryazan'
Bulghar City
Volodymyr
Kiev
Halych
POLAND
HUNGARY
BULGARIA
Qirim
Caffa
Black Sea
BYZANTIUM
Konya
Tammachi
Ayas
Tiflis
Erzerum

N

out by a substantial Mamluk force. Despite a number of Mongol assaults, Syria would never again fall to the now waning empire.

The disintegration of the Mongol Empire is directly related to the internal power struggles among the successors to Chinggis Khan, who had created the position of Great Khan to oversee the four regional Khanates of the Empire. The final Great Khan was Kublai Khan, who ruled from 1260 to 1294, but even in this period conflict arose, such as that between Berke Khan and Hulegu (see above). Increasingly, domestic politics undermined the united leadership necessary for concerted expansion of the empire—for example, the need for successors to return to Mongolia for elections—and provincial divisions grew and grew until the Mongol Empire fragmented into four distinct dominions.

CULTURE

The cultural template of the empire was largely fluid and inclusive. This approach allowed the Mongolian political structure to govern without resorting to a large administrative framework to "Mongolize" the empire (define and enforce an existing rigid Mongol culture). The most uniform and unchanging aspect of the Mongolian culture was its military foundation.

Historian Samuel Huntingdon argues that the relatively uncomplicated political framework of the empire arose because of a lack of ecological pressure on the Mongols to change their pastoral, militaristic organization. Trade and warfare supplied the goods to fuel domestic demand without the need for widespread agricultural sedentism (although archaeological evidence suggests a number of Khans used fixed headquarters surrounded by cultivated land). The enormous mobility of the Mongol forces gave them the great tactical advantage of being able to move much more rapidly than their enemies.

Little occupational specialization existed in the empire: boys were initiated into a life in the military at the age of 15 and remained politicized warriors until death. The military emphasis was on the individual in ultimate power, not his role or traditional clan-based associations. This practice was designed to neutralize traditional power structures and better secure non-Mongol allied support. The most important piece of military equipment was the small Mongolian horse that soldiers were trained to use from childhood. These animals had great reserves of endurance and enabled rapid army movement and a signaling system with a range of 200 miles a day (using remounts). In battle, Mongolian heavy cavalry was supported by mounted archers using long-ranged composite bows, the former often employing a feigned retreat tactic to lure the enemy into archery range. Chinese technology, including gunpowder, catapults, and battering rams, was used during sieges.

The most distinctive item of Mongol clothing was the kaftan, a type of sleeved cloak fastened at the front, with great variety of design according to wealth and status and the seasonal climate. Since Mongolian tradition taught that washing clothes would pollute the land and anger the pagan gods, kaftans were not cleaned and were worn until they disintegrated.

The Mongolian nomadic lifestyle hindered the development of permanent architecture, and even today the *ger,* a large collapsible wooden frame covered in felt, is still widely used. The popular although inaccurate name for this dwelling is *yurt,* which comes from a Turkic word meaning "camping ground." The wooden *ger* frame represented an important piece of Mongol material wealth, to be handed down through generations.

The process of cultural inclusion was never more obvious when it came to religion. Mongolian paganism and shamanism followed the empire as it spread, and policy divination from readings of nature and scapulomancy was common (partly because it was a foolproof method of achieving political consensus). Alongside these practices, without apparent contradiction, was complete freedom of worship. Members of the empire could practice Buddhism, Islam, or Christianity, as explicitly stated in the Great Yasa, the Imperial code of laws originating in the maxims of Chinggis Khan. At the same time, the laws of the empire were strictly enforced: For example, unauthorized raiding was banned, and theft of animals was punishable by death. A police force was even used to ensure the main highways remained safe.

This policy of carefully managed openness to outside influence was designed to transcend traditional religious and cultural barriers and tie members of the empire directly to the Mongol political hierarchy. However, it can also be seen as a very practical response to the problem of managing a large group of diverse peoples: Without a specialized administrative class, the Mongols could not supply experienced administrators to manage the sedentary governments they absorbed into the fringes of the Empire.

These posts were therefore filled with "Mongolized" natives.

The influence of the Mongols on middle and western Asia can be seen in the centuries before the time of the Mongol Empire, but for the cultures of the Middle East, the Mongol invasions of the 13th and 14th centuries represented both a violent interruption and an influx of cultural influences and opportunities.

The Mongol confederation was neither an ethnologically or linguistically homogenous group, and relied on constant movement to survive since it was founded on a politically unstable nomadic system of government. The reliance on "personal rule" and the lack of a bureaucratic class meant that Mongol rule abroad would be temporary, however much upheaval accompanied its inception. In many countries, it would not take long for existing power structures to reassert themselves; for example, the Mamluks again took control of Syria after 1300 and held it for another century.

The legacy of the Mongol Empire is often thought of as destruction. In fact the spread of culture and ideas across the empire can be viewed as a positive proto-globalization episode. In the aftermath of the empire's fragmentation, the Mongols themselves receded eastward to eventually stabilize to the north and south of the modern nation of Mongolia. Today, some 2.7 million people in the region can be classed as ethnically Mongolian, with a further 6.3 million who speak Mongolian dialects abroad.

FURTHER READING

Christopher P. Atwood. *Encyclopedia of Mongolia and the Mongol Empire* (New York: Facts On File, 2004).

Thomas T. Allsen. *Culture and Conquest in Mongol Eurasia* (Cambridge: Cambridge University Press, 2001).

Ronald Findlay and Mats Lundahl. "The First Globalization Episode: The Creation of the Mongol Empire or the Economics of Chinggis Khan." In Göran Therborn and Habibul Haque Khondkar, eds. *Asia and Europe in Globalization: Continents, Regions, and Nations* (Leiden, Netherlands: E. J. Brill, 2006).

Robert L. Worden and Andrea Matles Savada, eds. *Mongolia: A Country Study* (Washington, D.C.: Federal Research Division of the Library of Congress, 1989).

Moors

The term *Moor* has been applied to many different peoples over the centuries. For years it was used to describe the people of Morocco and also the Muslims from North Africa who conquered large parts of Spain in the Middle Ages. Today, it generally refers to the people who make up 70 percent of the population of Mauritania. It also applies to a few of the people of Western Sahara, which has been occupied by Morocco—and, for a while, Mauritania—since 1975.

There are two main Moor groups: the BIDANIS, or "White Moors," who are of Berber-Arab origin (*see* BERBERS; ARABS); and the SUDANIS, or "Black Moors," who are largely of black African origin and are related to the FULANI, SONINKE, TUKOLOR, WOLOF, and other peoples.

ORIGINS

The original ancestors of today's Moors are said to have moved into what is now Mauritania in the 11th century with the spread of the Berber Almoravids led by Abu Bakr. Others followed in subsequent centuries.

MOORS

location:
Mauritania and Western Sahara

time period:
11th century C.E. to present

ancestry:
Berber, Arab, and black African

language:
Semitic (Afro-Asiatic)

Moors time line

C.E.

ca. 1070 Moors arrive in West Africa with invading Almoravids.

ca. 1400s Trade with Europeans begins.

1644–74 Cherr Baba War; Hassani and Zawiya Moors emerge.

1700s–1800s Moors involved in flourishing gum arabic trade.

1903 Mauritania becomes a French colony.

1959 Moktar Ould Daddah elected prime minister of Mauritania.

1960 Mauritanian independence

1960s Discovery of iron ore and copper deposits in Mauritania

1960s–80s Recurring droughts cause famine in Sahelian countries.

1966 Arabization campaign; violence erupts between Moors and other peoples.

1976 Mauritania and Morocco invade Western Sahara.

1979 Mauritania renounces claim to Western Sahara. Morocco occupies territory abandoned by Mauritania and many Moor refugees are displaced to refugee camps in Algeria.

1979–91 Western Saharan rebels Polisario fight for independence from Morocco. Fighting ends with a United Nations sponsored ceasefire.

1996 United Nations staff intended to oversee a referendum on independence for Western Sahara are withdrawn.

1997–2004 A series of United Nations sponsored negotiations fail to resolve the question of independence from Morocco.

2008 Polisario and Morocco hold talks in New York without reaching agreement.

LANGUAGE

The language of almost all the Moors is Arabic. French is also widely spoken in Mauritania—a relic of colonial days. A few Moors speak Berber languages.

HISTORY

The Moors fall into several subgroups. Two of the largest are the Hassani and Zawiya, both Bidani. The Hassani descend from a group of Arab people who settled in Mauritania from the 15th century onward. Moorish history holds that the division into Hassani and Zawiya occurred as a result of the Cherr Baba War between the Berbers and the Arabs in 1644–74.

There have long been rivalries between the majority Moor population and the minority black African population of Mauritania. Since the 1980s, this animosity has often turned into open conflict; there have been many instances of violence. The government troops' support of the Moors in these conflicts has led to the death of hundreds of black African Mauritanians.

CULTURE

About 60 percent of Moors live in rural areas, and the rest in towns. Industrialization and urbanization are attracting many people away from their nomadic ways of life, in which they travel over a large area with their herds of animals in search of water and pasture. Many people now work in the copper and iron mines concentrated in the northwest. Young Moors from all ranks study at the University of Nouakchott, Mauritania's capital, or at other universities in Africa or abroad.

Most of Mauritania is desert, unsuitable for agriculture. For this reason, many Moors are nomads. Cattle are the mainstay of the nomads, but they also keep flocks of sheep and goats, as well as camels, donkeys, and horses. Most of the cattle are in the southern part of the country, where the Sahara Desert gives way to the semidesert region of the Sahel. During the wet season, the cattle herders roam the Sahel, moving to pastures along the banks of the Senegal River during the dry season. Camels, goats, and sheep are herded in the desert.

Settled farmers live in the southern region, where they grow corn, dates, melons, millet, pulses, rice, sorghum, and vegetables and raise chickens. Many farmers also live in the scattered oases (fertile pockets in the desert), where there is enough water for agriculture. Men do most of the herding and heavy agricultural work. Women make goods from leather and weave cloth, including the fabric of tents. Among the nomads, it is the women who set up the tents and take them down again.

During the 1960s and 1980s, droughts struck Mauritania; the country was devastated and the nomadic Moors, in particular, were badly affected. Growing crops on the flood plains of the Senegal River was impossible because it failed to flood, over a million cattle were lost, and death rates for vulnerable people rose. Refugees flocked to urban areas in search of emergency food supplies, putting great strain on the resources of these areas.

Over the years, patches of the fragile Sahelian lands have been turning into desert, threatening the farming and grazing lands of the Moors. This process of desertification has been worsened by drought and also threatens the ability of rural people to make a living from the land. Drought and desertification have caused not only great immediate distress but also disrupted the nomadic pattern so severely that many will probably not return to that lifestyle. For example, in 1963, 83 percent of the population was nomadic, but by 1980 this figure was only 25 percent. Drought and desertification have also caused the remaining nomadic Moors to alter their habits. For instance, they may stay in one place for longer if they know there is a water supply available. This has put many cattle herders into conflict with the settled farming populations. In fact, in recent decades there have been many instances of violent conflict between the Moor and non-Moor populations.

Government and Society

There are many clans within the subgroups, and a strong class structure exists. The highest class is that of the nobles. Some subgroups serve the nobles, and slavery was not abolished in Mauritania until 1980. Below the nobles come smiths, wandering entertainers, and the *imraguen,* or fishermen, on the coast. Each subgroup has its own code of laws and has civilian and religious leaders who inherit their positions from their fathers. Some Moors are *marabouts,* or holy men. A few families are considered particularly holy because they are claim descent from of the prophet Muhammad. In the past, the Bidanis were considered superior to the Sudanis, though a Sudani of noble birth could outrank an ordinary Bidani—the division was based on class, not color. People tend to marry within their clans. One man may have several wives, but men generally marry a new wife only after divorcing the previous one, rarely keeping more than one or two wives at a time.

Religion

The vast majority of Moors are Muslim.
See also MAURITANIANS: NATIONALITY

Moroccans: nationality (people of Morocco)

GEOGRAPHY

The Kingdom of Morocco, excluding the disputed western Sahara territory claimed by Morocco, has an area of approximately 178,600 square miles. It is bordered by the Atlantic Ocean on the west and the Mediterranean Sea to the north. Algeria is located on a disputed eastern border, and Western Sahara and Mauritania are to the south. Only a few miles of ocean separate Spain from Morocco at the straits of Gibraltar. Although Morocco is an African country, its history and geography make it an important crossroads between Europe and the Muslim world.

Geographically speaking, Morocco is most famous for the Atlas Mountains that form the spine of the country. The Rif, a smaller mountain range, is also located in the north. These mountains have had an important influence on Moroccan history and identity, especially among the Berber tribes who have inhabited them in relative isolation for millennia (*see* BERBERS). Although Morocco is popularly depicted as hot, dry, and mountainous, extensive green, fertile plains along the Atlantic coast are inhabited by both ARABS and Berbers, and the west side of the Atlas received adequate rainfall for agriculture. Many parts of Morocco are, in fact, far more fertile than southern Spain. Only the eastern and southern sides of the Atlas Mountains could be properly described as desert. Even here, fertile wadis, or seasonal rivers fed by mountain snow, flow into vast palmeries harvested mainly for dates. Only a few parts of Morocco are covered by sand dunes, or ergs, blown in by the sandstorms that occasionally hit the country from the Sahara Desert to the east. The summers and winters are fairly mild on the coastal plains, especially around the main cities of Casablanca and Rabat, but inland areas such as Marrakech or Ourzazate can experience extremely hot summers and cold winters.

The main rivers in Morocco are the Bou Regreg that passes though Rabat, the Oum al-Rabia south of Casablanca, the Wadi Tansift on the Haouz plain near Marrakech, and the Sous River that forms the relatively fertile Sous valley south of the Atlas and north of the Anti-Atlas. Transport, especially in the nearly inaccessible but fertile valleys of the mountain regions, has traditionally been performed on pack animals led through treacherous mountain passes. This lack of easy access to the Atlas Mountains has had a profound impact on Moroccan history and society; it made the traditional Berber residents of those valleys largely isolated, rebellious and independent from central control.

INCEPTION AS A NATION

Although Berber tribes inhabited the region of Morocco before recorded history and the PHOENICIANS built settlements such as Lixus on the Atlantic Coast in the 12th century B.C.E., some of the first notions of a "Moorish," or Moroccan, kingdom began with the founding of the independent Roman kingdom of Mauretania Tigitania under Juba II in the first century C.E. (*see* MOOR). Although Mauretania Tigitania soon lost its independence and was integrated into the imperial Roman state, recent archaeological evidence suggests the capital Volubilis survived as a living city until after the Arab invasion in the early eighth century C.E. Although Uqba bin Nafia is often credited with the Arab invasion of Morocco after 685 C.E., it was not until a century later that Musa bin Nusayr took Tangier in the North as a base of operations for the conquest of Spain and began to rigorously convert the Berbers.

The founding of Fez, located near Volubilis, by Idris I, signaled the beginning of an orthodox, Islamic dynasty in Morocco. The Idrissids created a system of government dominated by an Arab ruling class. Islam spread quickly throughout Morocco and was adopted by the Berber tribes, but not always the same form of Islam preached by the Arabs. Some Berbers, especially the Berghwata on the Atlantic coast, adapted the tenants of Islam to Berber culture and language, even creating a Berber Quran. Also, in defiance of the Sunni Idrissids, several of the Berber tribes surrounding Fez supported Kharijite Islam, a egalitarian form of Islam well adapted to tribal societies that does not recognize descent from the prophet Muhammad, and hence Arab ancestry, as a precondition of leadership. There were a few power centers such as Fez in the early centuries of Islam, but Morocco could not be properly considered a state or even a unified territory. Even the Idrissid Kingdom dissolved.

MOROCCANS: NATIONALITY

nation:
Morocco; Kingdom of Morocco

derivation of name:
From Marruecos, the Spanish name for the city of Marrakesh.

government:
Constitutional monarchy

capital:
Rabat

language:
The country's official language is Arabic. Various Berber dialects are spoken in isolated areas.

religion:
More than 98 percent of the population are Muslim (principally Sunni). Christians and Jews make up the remainder.

earlier inhabitants:
Unknown

demographics:
99 percent of the population are of mixed Arab and Berber ancestry. Non-Moroccans make up the remainder.

By the 10th century, the Fatimids to the east and the Umayyads in Muslim Spain both vied for control of the extreme Maghreb—the region that is now known in English as Morocco. Berbers, protected in their mountain valleys, lived a completely independent existence outside of any semblance of government control. The first unified and functioning systems of power over the area now known as Morocco began only with the rise of three great Berber tribal dynasties: the Almoravids, the Almohads, and the Marinids.

The first of these dynasties, the Almoravids of the Sahara Desert and the Almohads of the High Atlas Mountains, were essentially founded on the integration of the ideals of Islam with the toughness and spirit of Berber tribalism. Remarkably, tribes that had lived for centuries in the desert or the mountains independent of central control suddenly gave up many of their former loyalties and united under the banner of Islam. The Almoravids, led most famously by Yusuf bin Tashfin, who established the city of Marrakech around 1062, created a unified system of Maliki Islamic law adapted to Saharan, Berber traditions such as the male mouth veil. The Almohads led by Ibn Tumart, who claimed to be the Muslim messiah (or *mahdi*), and who promised a new era of Islam originating from the mountain Berber tribes of Morocco, replaced the Almoravids. In 1147 the successor to the *mahdi*, Caliph Abd al Mumin, conquered Marrakech from the Saharan Almoravids and spread the borders of the Almohad Empire into Spain and Tunisia. Although the Marinids, who conquered the last of the Almohads by 1269, were not inspired by a strong religious vision, they were able to control large parts of what is now known as Morocco. They were not, however, able to control the same vast territories conquered by the Almoravids and Almohads. Still, their capital, Fez, became a brilliant cultural center that attracted Andalusian scholars and artisans who fled Spain during the Christian conquests.

While the rise and fall of the Almoravid, Almohad, and Marinid dynasties was dramatic, a far more gradual demographic and cultural change was altering the nature of Moroccan society in this period—the migration of large numbers of Arab tribes and Arabic speakers into Morocco. Whereas Arabs and Arabic had previously had an only superficial impact on the predominant Berber culture, language and traditions of Morocco, the migrations of BEDOUIN Arab tribes, including the BANI HILAL, to

The gravestone of a king of the Marinid dynasty of Morocco, Sultan Abu Yaqub Yusuf, who reigned from 1286 to 1307.

Morocco, the recruiting of Arab armies by Berber chiefs, and the intermarriage of Berbers and Arabs, especially on the coastal plains, would change Morocco into a much more integrated Arab and Berber society. Indeed, throughout the political upheavals and the conquest of coastal cities by Europeans that characterized the 16th to the 18th centuries in Morocco, Arab descent, especially descent that could be linked to Fatima, the daughter of the prophet, was held in highest esteem.

The sharifs, or those who claimed descent from the prophet, became the rulers of groups of Berber and Arab tribes and sometimes founded dynasties, the most famous being the Saadian dynasty. The great Saadian ruler, Sharif Ahmad al-Mansur (1578–1610), successfully destroyed the Askia Empire of Gao and conquered Tombouctou, making the Saadians masters of the trans-Saharan gold and salt trade. Sudden wealth and plunder from sub-Saharan Africa flooded into Morocco and led to the foundation of spectacular monuments in Marrakech. The conquest also increased contacts between North Africa and sub-Saharan Africa. The *makhzen,* or the government bureaucracy, was created to counterbalance the

A colonnade in the Kutubiya Mosque in Marrakech, Morocco. Built in the mid-12th century the colonnade features a series of horseshoe arches.

need to rely on Berber tribes for support. The establishment of the *makhzen* began the long and gradual but eventually very effective erosion of tribal power in favor of central power in Morocco. Soon, however, even the relatively well-organized Saadian Empire fell to infighting between rival tribes.

The Sharifian successors of the Saadians, the ALAWIS, however, were much more successful. Indeed, the Alawis, ancestors of the present king of Morocco, established one of the longest-lived dynasties in world history. One important reason for the long-term success of the Alawis, sharifs who originated in the Tafilalt region east of the Atlas near Erfoud, was the vigorous reign of Moulay Ismail (1672–1727). Moulay Ismail reestablished the bureaucracy, the Makhzen, pacified the tribes with a series of garrisoned *kasbahs* (or forts) along mountain passes, recaptured coastal cities from the Europeans, commanded a magnificent court at Meknes, and formed a corps of loyal slaves for his personal protection. The death of Moulay Ismail led to the gradual decline of his empire under a series of less competent rulers. There were several attempts by his successors to re-

assert centralized control, but none could deal decisively with the rise of European colonialism, despite many successful attempts to play one European power against the other. By 1912, however, the sultan was compelled to recognize a French protectorate over much of Morocco even as he maintained some superficial elements of sovereignty. The Spanish claimed their sphere of influence in the north, and Tangier remained an international zone.

The age of the European protectorates, which introduced European languages, systems, institutions, and ideas of modernity to Morocco's traditional society, would have a profound impact on Moroccan society. By the end of World War II, however, Sultan Muhammad V and a group of Moroccan nationalists began to assert themselves, often using the very rhetoric of modernization, self-determination, and nationalism they were exposed to from France. In 1953 the French sent the sultan, who had become the symbol of Moroccan resistance, into exile in Madagascar, but public disturbances quickly compelled the French to recall him. Sultan Muhammad V established the modern, independent state of Morocco in 1955. The Spanish gave up their possessions in the north in 1956 but retained Ceuta, Mellila, and a few Mediterranean islands whose sovereignty is still disputed. Hassan II, the successor to Muhammad V, continued the series of reforms and modernizations initiated by his father, even as he was frequently threatened by assassination and palace revolts. He maintained a close relationship with the United States and Europe, even as he alienated international opinion with his Green March, or migration, of Moroccans south into western Sahara, which established Moroccan claims over the territory even as Saharans, represented by the radical Polsario front, resisted Moroccan incursions. The United Nations is still monitoring the western Sahara, which is considered disputed territory. Its few settlements, situated around important mining operations, are administered largely by Morocco.

Hassan II and his ministers had a reputation for ruthlessness and the suppression of dissent. The death of Hassan II and his succession by the current king, Muhammad VI, has led to an opening of Moroccan society and the establishment of important democratic reforms in the parliament. Even so King Muhammad VI still retains supreme power and is considered the highest authority in matters both religious and political. Family law and the status of women,

Moroccans: nationality time line

B.C.E.

12th century Phoenicians build trading settlements on the Moroccan coast.

fifth century The Carthaginian explorer Hanno establishes seven colonies on the Moroccan coast, including Tangier and Sale.

C.E.

42 The Kingdom of Mauretania Tigitania with its capital at Volubilis in Morocco is annexed as a province of Rome.

fifth century Roman rule collapses after the invasion of Germanic tribes, the Vandals, who sailed from Spain to North Africa in 429.

sixth century Byzantines occupy the ports of Tangier and Ceuta.

seventh century Musa bin Nusayr begins the systematic conversion of Berbers and recruits them into the army that invades southern Spain.

684 The Muslim conqueror Uqba bin Nafia founds Qayrawan in Tunisia and raids into Morocco as far as Massa on the Atlantic coast.

eighth century The Idrissid dynasty founds the trading city of Fez as its capital and attempts to control most the north of Morocco.

10th century The Idrissid dynasty rapidly declines as the Umayyads in Spain and the Fatimids in Tunisia attempt to control Fez.

ca. 1062 Yusuf bin Tashfin, leader of the Almoravids, a group of Berber tribes from the Sahara Desert, founds Marrakech and conquers much of North Africa and Andalusia.

1147 Abd al Mumin, leader of the Almohads, conquers Marrakech from the Almoravids and rules over all of North Africa to Libya as well as much of Andalusia.

13th century Collapse of the Almohad Empire

1269 The Marinids, led by Aby Yahya, conquer Marrakech from the Almohads.

1471 The Portuguese conquer Tangier and found fortified trading ports on the Atlantic coast.

once exclusively decided by sharia, or Muslim law, that dated back to the seventh and eighth centuries, were reformed to give women a more equal standing. The king also made efforts to manage the recent growth of Berber identity and nationalism in the country by mandating the teaching of Berber in Moroccan schools. Economically, Morocco is moving forward rapidly, having formed free trade agreements with both Europe and America.

CULTURAL IDENTITY

Moroccan culture is defined by both extreme isolation and expansive integration. While most of the Middle East and North Africa were under the sway of the Ottoman Empire for centuries, Morocco remained outside of Ottoman Turkish control, allowing it to maintain a peculiar cultural, political, and religious identity that, in many ways, resembles that of the pre-Ottoman age. Moroccan cuisine, metallurgy, and crafts have more in common with the cuisine and art of Damascus and Baghdad in the ninth century than with Cairo or Beirut today.

Unlike other Muslims countries such as Saudi Arabia, where there is a very difficult balance between the authority of clerics and the authority of the monarch, Moroccans believe their king, a successor of the prophet Muhammad, to be endowed with special *baraka,* or spiritual blessing, and believe that he, not Muslim clerics in Cairo or Mecca, is "the prince of believers" and the ultimate arbiter in all religious matters. While fundamentalist ideas have gained a foothold in recent years, often in opposition to the corruption the monarchy's bureaucracy (known as the *makzen*), Morocco has traditionally been a center for Sufism, or mystical Islam. Great Sufi leaders and descendants of the prophet Muhammad can become living saints who, it is believed, provide *baraka* or even intervene for the faithful. These saints were essential for the stability of Moroccan

1550–78	The Saadians capture Fez, overthrow the Marinids, and arrest the advance of the Portuguese at Qasr al Kabir.
1610	Death of the Saadian ruler Ahmad al Mansur
1664–72	After the disintegration of the Saadian Empire, the Alawis from the Tafilalt east of the Atlas conquer much of Morocco.
18th–19th centuries	Morocco is nominally ruled by the Alawis.
1844	Franco-Moroccan war begins after Moroccans back rebellions over the French colonization of Algeria.
1894	The Alawite sultan Moulay Hasan dies after having failed in his attempts to regain control over much of Morocco.
1912	The Alawite sultan recognizes a French protectorate over much of Morocco. Spain gains control of the north, and Tangier becomes an international zone.
1953	The French exile Sultan Muhammad V to Madagascar for his support of Moroccan nationalism.
1955	Muhammad V returns as king of an independent Morocco after severe protests against the French.
1961	Hassan II becomes king of Morocco.
1970s	Hassan II instigates the Green March and claims to annex western Sahara.
1997	A bicameral legislature with limited powers is established in Rabat.
1999	Muhammad VI ascends to the throne.
2003	Casablanca is hit by terrorist attacks attributed to local al-Qaeda elements.
2006	A free trade agreement between Morocco and the United States is implemented.
2007	A series of suicide bomb attacks take place in Casablanca.
2008	Moroccans suspected of involvement in the 2003 bombings are arrested in Spain. The suspected leader of al-Qaeda in Morocco is put on trail for murder.

tribal society because they provided neutral arbitration in tribal disputes.

Despite these religious peculiarities, Moroccan's see themselves as firmly within the wider Sunni, or orthodox, Muslim community. Likewise, the geography of Morocco has led to opportunities both for isolation and integration with surrounding areas. Even as a Moroccan mountain village or desert tribe can seem isolated from the rest of world, the cities of Morocco are bustling centers of integration and multiculturalism. Moroccans have extensive ethnic, historical, and artistic ties with sub-Saharan Africa established through the gold and salt trade across the vast, Saharan desert sea. There are also ties with Europe. Many Andalusians fled to Morocco after the Christian conquest, and the influence of the French and Spanish protectorates is manifested in the building of European cities next to the traditional Muslim city. Finally, there are extensive ties between Morocco and the Middle East through the yearly pilgrimage to Mecca and the Arab identity of a large number of Moroccans.

FURTHER READING

Paul Bowles. *Morocco* (New York: H. N. Abrams, 1993).

A. M. Findlay. *Morocco* (Oxford, England: Clio Press, 1995).

Dorothy Kavanaugh. *Morocco* (Philadelphia: Mason Crest Publishers, 2008).

Raphael Chijioke Njoku. *Culture and Customs of Morocco.* Culture and customs of Africa (Westport, Conn.: Greenwood Press, 2006).

C. R. Pennell. *Morocco Since 1830: A History* (New York: New York University Press, 1999).

Mossi

Mossi as a term refers to a number of different ethnic groups who have similar cultures and lifestyles but maintain some distinct ethnic identity. The YARSE, for instance, are one group

MOSSI

location:
Burkina Faso

time period:
15th century C.E. to present

ancestry:
Bantu

language:
Bantu (Niger-Congo)

Mossi time line

C.E.

late 1400s White Volta area invaded by horsemen from Ghana; Mossi society founded. Ouagadougou Kingdom founded by Naba Oubri.

mid-1500s Ouahigouya (or Yatenga) kingdom founded by Naba Yadega.

1591 Mossi defeated by Moroccan invaders.

1744–45 Asante Empire occupies Dagomba, a Mossi kingdom.

1897 France takes control of Ouagadougou.

1919 Upper Volta declared a separate colonial territory under France.

1960 Upper Volta becomes independent.

1984 Upper Volta renamed Burkina Faso.

See also BURKINABE: NATIONALITY

within Mossi society. Together, the groups that make up Mossi society represent half the population of Burkina Faso.

Most of the Mossi live in Burkina Faso, but some have emigrated to live and work in cities or on plantations in Ghana, Ivory Coast, and France.

ORIGINS

Mossi oral history states that Mossi society originated in the 15th century when a cavalry group from northern Ghana rode north in search of land. The invaders conquered the various farming peoples who inhabited the valley of the White Volta River and settled among them. Some of the peoples in the area fled to locations where the invaders' horses could not follow, such as to Mali's isolated Bandiagara Cliffs, where the DOGON people sought refuge. Other peoples, however, remained behind in the newly created kingdoms, which included OUAGADOUGOU, YATENGA (or Ouahigouya), Dagomba, and Namumba and became part of a new society known as the Mossi.

LANGUAGE

The Mossi language, called Moré (or Moore or Molé), is one of the Niger-Congo family of languages.

HISTORY

The Mossi conquerors became the ruling class and were known as the *nakomsé* (meaning "the right and power to rule"). The defeated farmers became the commoners and were called *nyonyosé* (meaning "the ancient ones" or "children of the earth," references to their origins as the original inhabitants of Mossi territory). The *nakomsé* generally respected the *nyonyosé*, maintaining preexisting clans and assimilating many of their traditions into the new society. This reduced the likelihood of revolt and explains the cultural variations that are still found in Mossi society. Today, there continues to be a distinction between *nakomsé* and *nyonyosé* in terms of power relationships, but these have been lessened by intermarriage.

In 1897 France gained control of Mossi territory: Mossi myth explains that they were conquered not because they were weaker than the French but because the ruler of Ouagadougou had ignored the warnings of the gods. French direct influence over the Mossi remained limited, however, because the conquerors did not consider the area to be economically important. France's administrative hold over the Mossi remained weak, and it was subject to frequent revolts over such issues as the imposition of taxes, forced labor, and military conscription. When Burkina Faso (then known as Upper Volta) gained its independence from France in 1960, its first president, Maurice Yameogo, was a Mossi.

CULTURE

In the 17th and 18th centuries, large towns and markets developed through which goods such as salt and dried fish were imported and cotton cloth, livestock, and surplus grain exported. This led to specializations within Mossi society and the creation of specialized occupational groups such as blacksmiths and weavers. These were once associated with separate ethnic groups; the Yarse, for example, were largely weavers and traders. But these distinctions were flexible, so that a person could change from one group to another.

Since the integration of weavers of MANDÉ origin into Mossi society in about 1600, the Mossi have been renowned for their cotton and silk weaving. Some Mossi groups tell a creation myth that recalls how the founding ancestor was a weaver who descended to earth on the threads from his loom. Weaving is done by men during the dry season, but it is the women who dye the woven strips in pits filled with indigo dye. The resulting blue-and-white strips are combined to form a larger cloth. Despite competition from industrial textile mills, this traditional cloth is still highly sought after and is passed down through the generations in families.

Most Mossi, however, live in rural areas and are subsistence farmers, producing cereals,

A Mossi woman with an elaborately decorative hairstyle.

yams, and legumes and providing for themselves off the land. Poor soil and an increasing population, however, have made it more difficult to grow enough crops. For this reason, over the years Mossi farmers have shifted their farms, leading to a continuous shifting of the population. This has further contributed to the diversity of Mossi society.

The Mossi are well known for their masks used in celebrations. In the past, only the *nyonyosé* used masks, typically painted intense shades of red, white, black, and sometimes brown. Masks are owned by individual families or clans and are passed down through generations. The masks can be used to invoke protection and serve as a direct means of communication with the owners' ancestors and celebrate individual and group identity. In some regions, women and children are prohibited from viewing mask appearances, while in others men and women, old and young, participate in performances. Mossi masks, which are usually tall, are often carved from the soft, fine-grained, and very lightweight wood of the ceiba tree. Ceiba wood is very susceptible to insect damage, however, and every year, after the harvest but before the dry season, all the masks in a village are soaked in a river or a swamp to kill any insects and to remove the paint applied to the masks the previous year.

Government and Society

Mossi society is based on extended families, each of which typically consists of the head of the family, his wife, their children and grandchildren, and other close relatives. These extended families are grouped together into clans. The members of a clan have the same surname and claim descent from a common ancestor, and each clan is symbolically represented by an animal.

Religion

Muslim traders from the north helped to introduce Islam to West Africa in the early years of the second millennium. Since this date, most have converted to Islam; nevertheless many Mossi people have remained faithful to the Mossi religion, which is based on the devotion to ancestors and spirits.

See also BURKINABE: NATIONALITY

FURTHER READING

Elliott P. Skinner. *The Mossi of Burkina Faso: Chiefs, Politicians, and Soldiers* (Prospect Heights, Ill.: Waveland Press, 1989).

Elliott P. Skinner. *The Mossi of the Upper Volta: The Political Development of a Sudanese People* (Stanford, Calif.: Univ. Pr, 1964).

Mouroum

The Mouroum are a subgroup of the SARA and live in Chad.

Mozambicans: nationality (people of Mozambique)

GEOGRAPHY

Mozambique is a nation on the eastern coast of southern Africa. It has an area of about 309,000 square miles and is bordered by six other nations. Tanzania lies to the north; Malawi, Zambia, and Zimbabwe to the west; and South Africa and Swaziland to the south. Mozambique's Indian Ocean coastline extends for about 1,500 miles. The strait that lies between Mozambique and the island of Madagascar, known as the Mozambique Channel, ranges from 250 to 600 miles wide.

Almost half of Mozambique consists of coastal lowlands rising gently toward a western plateau with an elevation of about 600 to 2,000 feet. Further west, toward Mozambique's borders, are a higher plateau and a spine of mountains. The highest mountains lie along the

---

MOZAMBICANS: NATIONALITY

nation:
Mozambique; Republic of Mozambique; formerly the People's Republic of Mozambique

derivation of name:
Named for the Island of Mozambique a former Arab trading center and port off the coast of northern Mozambique

government:
Republic

capital:
Maputo

language:
Portuguese is the country's official language, although it is spoken by less than 10 percent of the population as a first language. Indigenous languages include Emakhuwa, Xichangana, Elomwe, Cisena, Echuwabo, and dozens of others.

religion:
Roman Catholic (25 percent); Muslims (15 percent); other Christian denominations (15 percent); indigenous belief systems or no religion (45 percent).

earlier inhabitants:
Khoisan; San

demographics:
Indigenous ethnic groups make up more than 99 percent of the population. There are 10 ethnic (linguistic) clusters. The largest are the Makua-Lomwe group (37 percent), the Tsonga (23 percent), the Shona (9 percent), the Yao (or Ajawa), the Makonde, the Nguni, the Chopi, and the Maravi.

Mozambicans: time line

C.E.

third–fifth centuries Bantu-speaking people migrate into Mozambique.

eighth century Arabs establish trading posts along the coast of Mozambique.

1498 First Portuguese explorers arrive in Mozambique. Portuguese trading posts are established.

16th–17th centuries Portuguese extend their control inland but are met with fierce resistance. Portuguese plantations established.

18th–19th century Mozambique becomes a major source of slaves following the British campaign against slave trading on Africa's west coast.

1878 Portugal begins the establishment of trading companies chartered to exploit Mozambique's resources. Indigenous peoples are forced to labor on plantations and in mines.

1902 The city of Lourenco Marques (later renamed Maputo) becomes the capital of the colony.

1932 Portuguese trading companies are closed down and the Portuguese government takes direct control of Mozambique.

1950s–60s Thousands of new Portuguese settlers are attracted to Mozambique by its strong economic growth. The exploitation of indigenous peoples continues.

1962 Exiled independence activists found the Mozambique Liberation Front (FRELIMO) in Tanzania.

1964 FRELIMO begins military operations against the Portuguese authorities in Mozambique.

1974 The government of Portugal is deposed and peace negotiations with FRELIMO begin. The majority of Portuguese settlers leave Mozambique.

1975 The People's Republic of Mozambique gains independence. Samora Machel is the country's first president.

1976 Lourenco Marques is renamed Maputo.

1976 The Mozambique National Resistance (RENAMO) is established with Rhodesian backing to conduct operations against the Mozambican government.

1980 South Africa continues to support RENAMO after the collapse of the Rhodesian government.

1986 Machel is killed in an air crash. Joachim Chissano replaces him as president and leader of FRELIMO.

1990 A new constitution allows for the formation of opposition parties for the first time.

1992 RENAMO signs a peace deal with the government.

1994 Chissano is reelected president in the country's first open elections. RENAMO forms the main opposition.

1999 Chissano is reelected for a second term.

2000–01 Serious floods displace hundreds of thousands of Mozambicans.

2005 Armando Guebuza of FRELIMO elected president. FRELIMO has been in power for 30 years.

2006 World Bank cancels most of Mozambique's crippling debt.

2008 Thousands of Mozambicans working in South Africa return home to escape ethnic violence.

border with Zimbabwe and include Mozambique's highest point, the peak of Mount Binga, at about 7,990 feet. Numerous rivers flow from the western highlands through Mozambique to the Indian Ocean. The largest and most economically important of these are the Zambezi and Limpopo. Thick forest predominates in the wetter regions of the country, while much of the uplands have poor soil and are covered by dry savanna. The southwest is the driest and least agriculturally productive area.

About 40 percent of Mozambique's population lives in its urban centers. Of these the capital, Maputo, is the largest and is located on the

A Mozambican woman using a bark extract on her skin to protect her from the sun

coast in the extreme south. All of Mozambique's major cities are located on the coast. Beira, Mozambique's second city, is a few hundred miles north of Maputo. Both Maputo and Beira are major ports and industrial centers.

INCEPTION AS A NATION

The earliest known inhabitants of the area now encompassed by the borders of Mozambique were the ancestors of the modern SAN and KHOIKHOI peoples. These groups were largely displaced or assimilated by an influx of BANTU peoples that occurred between the third and eighth centuries C.E. The eighth century also brought the first Arab traders and settlers to the coast of southeast Africa. These Arab trading settlements had developed into major commercial centers by the 14th century. They conducted trade with the indigenous peoples of the interior, and the raw materials they obtained were fed into the great network of trade routes that extended around the Indian Ocean from the coast of southern Africa to the southern tip of India. The trade in slaves was a part of this system.

The Portuguese expedition led by the explorer Vasco da Gama brought the first Europeans to Mozambique in 1498. Portuguese trading posts soon sprang up along the coast, and there was considerable rivalry between the long-established ARABS and the newly arrived Europeans for control of trade. The Portuguese also introduced the first systematic and large-scale exportation of slaves from Mozambique. At the time of the arrival of the Portuguese, the Zambezi basin was under the control of the Maravi Kingdom of the Mwene Matapa people. Throughout the 16th century the Portuguese slowly extended their control inland in the face of strong opposition from the indigenous kingdoms. The Mwene Matapa accepted Portuguese rule only in 1629. The difficulty of subduing this opposition meant that Portuguese control was effectively limited to the coastal strip and the lower reaches of the valley of the Zambezi River until well into the 19th century. Portuguese control in practice usually meant control administered by Portuguese or mixed African-Portuguese estate owners, who quarreled among themselves to extend their petty fiefdoms and ruled through private armies.

By the end of the 19th century Portuguese control of much of Mozambique had been firmly established and agreements with other European colonial powers had fixed the borders of what was to become the modern nation of Mozambique. At the beginning of the 20th century Mozambique was administered by a series of private companies chartered by the Portuguese government. Although slavery had been outlawed by Portugal in the 1840s, the plantations and gold mines of Portuguese Mozambique were effectively run on a forced labor system.

Opposition to Portuguese rule had resulted in sporadic revolts throughout the early decades of the 20th century, particularly in 1917 following the mass conscription of Mozambicans to fight in World War I, but it gained strength in the 1950s. The late 1950s and early 1960s saw the advent of the Pan-African movement, which focused the frustrations of African people all across the continent over their status as colonial subjects. In 1962 several small liberation movements that had developed in Mozambique united to form the Mozambique Liberation Front (FRELIMO). Military operations by FRELIMO against Portuguese targets in Mozambique began in 1964. Vicious fighting continued for 10 years as FRELIMO slowly but steadily extended its control over rural parts of the country and the Portuguese government committed more and more troops and resources to halt their advance. In 1974 a revolution in Portugal deposed the dictatorial government that had ruled the country since 1928 and peace negotiations with FRELIMO followed soon after. Within a year Mozambique achieved independence (June 1975) as the People's Republic of Mozambique. Samora Machel, the leader of FRELIMO since 1970, became the new nation's first president.

CULTURAL IDENTITY

Within days of independence, Mozambique became embroiled in a conflict that was to result in many more years of bloody fighting and hardship for the Mozambican people. The new government of Mozambique quickly proclaimed its support for the independence movement in neighboring Rhodesia (now Zimbabwe). Rhodesian rebel groups quickly established themselves inside Mozambique and used the border region as a base from which to launch attacks into Rhodesia. The Rhodesian government retaliated with cross-border strikes that forced many from their homes and caused economic chaos. Fighting along the Mozambican-Rhodesian border ended in 1980 when the Rhodesian government fell and the country became Zimbabwe, but from 1976 an anti-Mozambican government group known as the Mozambique National Resistance (RENAMO) was conducting devastating guerrilla operations inside Mozambique. RENAMO was heavily funded by the Rhodesian government before 1980 and by the South African government after 1980. It claimed to represent the interests of Portuguese and other European settlers in Mozambique, but in reality it was little more than an illegal army operated by the Rhodesians and South Africans as part of their campaigns against the newly independent nonwhite-ruled nations of southern Africa.

RENAMO focused its operation on the disruption of infrastructure such as railways and bridges, causing great damage to the Mozambican economy. Coupled with corruption within the state itself, a series of devastating floods and droughts throughout the 1970s and 1980s and ill-advised Marxist policies, the overall effect was to cripple Mozambique's economy, leading to mass migrations out of the country and the deaths of hundreds of thousands of people. The first 20 years of Mozambiques's existence as an independent nation was a catalog of war, economic hardship, and natural disasters.

A peace deal that ended the civil war in 1992 was followed by years of negotiations and United Nations intervention to establish a multiparty system and to disband the many armed groups that the decades of conflict had spawned. FRELIMO retained power in the country's first open elections in 1994, and stability gradually returned to the country. From the mid-1990s millions of displaced Mozambicans began to return home, and the country's economy slowly but steadily improved. Floods and droughts have continued to hamper development, however, and Mozambicans remain among the poorest people on earth.

Mozambique has traditionally been culturally and linguistically along the Zambezi River. The area to the south of the Zambezi was much more strongly influenced by Portuguese culture, while the area to the north was always more remote and retained a greater degree of its indigenous culture. The north was the stronghold of FRELIMO during the struggle for independence, largely because of its remoteness from the urban center of Maputo in the far south and the other coastal cities. A larger proportion of the northern population retains their traditional seminomadic lifestyle, while the population of the south and the coastal strip tend to be more settled and urban.

There are about 10 major ethnic groupings in Mozambique. The largest north of the Zambezi is the MAKUE-LOMWE group of peoples, who make up about 40 percent of the country's population. To the south of the Zambezi the largest ethnic group is the TSONGA, who account for almost 25 percent. Other significant groups include the Ajawa, the MAKONDE, the NGUNI, the MARAVI, the Chopi, and the SHONA. There is little history of interethnic conflict in Mozambique. The long war for independence against Portugal proved to be a uniting factor in Mozambican history, and the civil war that followed was not primarily ethnic in origin.

Forced displacement both within Mozambique and across its borders was a fact of life for millions of Mozambicans from the mid-1970s to the mid-1990s. In 1992 an estimated 1.5 million displaced Mozambicans were in neighboring countries and a further 4 to 5 million within the country. Following the end of the civil war, the United Nations conducted the largest repatriation project ever been undertaken in Africa, bringing the great majority of displaced Mozambicans back to Mozambique.

FURTHER READING

James Ciment. *Angola and Mozambique: Postcolonial Wars in Southern Africa* (New York: Facts On File, 1997).

Alice Dinerman. *Revolution, Counter-Revolution and Revisionism in Post-Colonial Africa: The Case of Mozambique, 1975-1994.* Routledge studies in modern history, 3 (London: Routledge, 2006).

George O. Ndege. *Culture and Customs of Mozambique.* Culture and customs of Africa (Westport, Conn.: Greenwood Press, 2007).

Jessica Schafer. *Soldiers at Peace: Veterans and Society After the Civil War in Mozambique* (New York: Palgrave Macmillan, 2007).

Jason Sumich. *Strong Party, Weak State?: Frelimo and State Survival Through the Mozambican Civil War : an Analytical Narrative on State-Making* (London: Crisis States Research Centre, 2007).

Rachel Waterhouse. *Mozambique: Rising from the Ashes* (Oxford: Oxfam, 1996).

Harry G. West. *Ethnographic Sorcery* (Chicago: University of Chicago Press, 2007).

Mpondo

The Mpondo are a large ethnic group in South Africa living primarily in the Transkei region, which lies between the Drakensberg Mountains and the Indian Ocean coast in southeastern South Africa. They are spread along the north-eastern coastal region of Transkei, roughly from Port St. Johns to the border with the Kwa-Zulu-Natal Province to the north.

The Mpondo are XHOSA-speaking people, and they share a common origin with the THEMBU and Xhosa proper. Like other NGUNI BANTU people, the Mpondo ancestors were established in South Africa by at least the 16th century. By the 18th century, the Mpondo were living in large clan-based chieftaincies east of the Kei River. The present-day Mpondo are still divided into clans.

Mpongwe

The Mpongwe are a small ethnic group in Gabon. They have been highly influential in that country, however, dominating the teaching and business professions.

Mumuye

The Mumuye are a BANTU people of Nigeria. They live in and around the Jos Plateau in north-central Nigeria.

Muntafiq

The Muntafiq are an Arab tribe, part of the Banu Uqayl, which in turn are part of the larger group of tribes, the Banu Emir bin Sasaa. Not much is known of the early history of the Muntafiq, although they are said to have lived in the southwest of Yamama, in central Arabia. In the early days of Islam, members of the tribe were sent to the prophet Muhammad as representatives of the Banu Uqayl. During the era of the Muslim conquests (roughly the mid-seventh to mid-eighth centuries), the tribe established itself in the marsh area of southern Iraq between the important cities of Kufa and Basra. From the 17th to the 19th century they were one of the dominant tribes in the region between Baghdad and Basra. For a while the tribe held the city of Basra, until it was retaken by the OTTOMANS in 1705. The tribe prevented incursions of the Wahhabis, the religious reformers from the Arabian heartland, into the more northerly territory they held. The ruling family were the Saadun, who traced their roots to the family of the prophet Muhammad. They had migrated to Mesopotamia from the Hijaz, the western coastal region of the Arabia, in probably the 15th century. While the Saadun were Sunni Muslims, most of the tribesmen were Shia.

While the tribe was originally nomadic, by the 19th century its members increasingly became sedentary farmers. The tribe also functioned as protectors of the caravan routes between Baghdad and Basra and supplied horses to the British in India. In the 1870s and after, the Saadun family's power began to erode for reasons related to Ottoman land reform, and by the beginning of the 20th century, the family had lost much of its status. Nevertheless, the city of Nasiriyya on the Euphrates River in southern Iraq, near the ruins of the ancient city of Ur, was founded about 1870 by a Muntafiq shaykh Nasir Saadun Pasha. Muntafiq territory was notoriously lawless during and after World War I. The prime minister of Iraq in 2008, Nuri al-Maliki, is reportedly a member of the Muntafiq tribe. He is a Shii Muslim and was a leader in the resistance to the rule of Saddam Hussein, who was overthrown in 2003.

Murle (Ajibba; Beri; Merule)

The Murle live primarily in Sudan. Originally from Ethiopia, the Murle only number a few thousand in that country today.

Mutayr (Mutair; Mutayyir)

The Mutayr are a major Arab tribe centered in north-central Saudi Arabia, extending east to Kuwait (*see* ARABS). The tribe's members are traditionally nomadic (BEDOUIN) camel herders. Considered one of the "noble" tribes, their ancestral land is the area between the holy cities of Medina and Mecca. They speak a dialect of Arabic. During the 18th century, they fought a long series of wars with the Anaza over pasturage in the central region of the Arabian Peninsula, the Najd, and succeeded in forcing the Anaza northward. In the 19th century, they resisted the growing power of the SAUD (Al Suud) and sometimes allied themselves with the RASHID against Ibn Saud, even though the Rashid are a tribe of SHAMMAR, traditional enemies of the Mutayr. By the 1920s, though, the Mutayr had joined the Ikhwan ("Brothers") movement of Arab tribesmen who took up the cause of resurgent Wahhabism, the reformist Muslim ideology championed by Ibn Saud, first preached by Muhammad ibn Abd al-Wahhab in the mid-18th century. In the name of the Ikhwan and Ibn Saud, the Mutayr led attacks into the western region called the Hijaz, where the holy cities of Medina and Mecca are located, and also into Shammar territory in the central area of the peninsula, and east to Kuwait. The Ikhwan movement was largely responsible for bringing most of the Arabian Peninsula under the control of Ibn Saud and led ultimately to the establishment of the Kingdom of Saudi Arabia (*see* SAUDI ARABIANS: NATIONALITY).

The Mutayr also played a prominent role in an unsuccessful Ikhwan rebellion against Ibn Saud that began in 1927 and was not finally quelled until 1930. During this revolt, the Ikhwan repeatedly defied Ibn Saud's authority, violently spreading their own brand of Wahhabism, which was even more radical and zealous than Ibn Saud's. The revolt ended with the Mutayr leader and other leaders involved in the rebellion imprisoned or dead and power consolidated under Ibn Saud. After the establishment of the Saudi state in 1932, members of the Ikhwan came to dominate the Saudi National Guard and some joined the Mutawain, the feared religious police.

Mwela *See* MWERE.

Mwenga *See* LEGA.

Mwera *See* MWERE.

Mwere (Chimwere; Mwela; Mwera)

The Mwere are a people of southeastern Tanzania. They are sometimes considered to be a subgroup of the YAO.

Mysians

The Mysians were an ancient people mentioned in the Greek epics the *Iliad* and the *Odyssey* as allies of the Trojans. The area known as ancient Mysia is in northwest Anatolia (modern-day Turkey), bounded by the Sea of Marmara in the north and the Aegean to the west, and includes the ancient cities of Troy and Pergamum and the territory of Aeolis. There is no historic evidence that Mysia was ever an independent polity. It was ruled by Lydia, which reached the height of its power from 700 to 550 B.C.E., then by Persia. and was taken by the king of Pergamum in about 190 B.C.E. (*see* LYDIANS: PERSIANS). It was incorporated into the Roman province of Asia in 129 B.C.E., which is the last the Mysians appear in the historical record (*see* ROMANS).

Nabataeans (al-Anbat)

The Nabataeans were a nomadic Arab people who migrated in the sixth century B.C.E. from the northern area of modern-day Jordan to the region south of the Dead Sea that was to become the heartland of their sedentary civilization. By the second century B.C.E., from their capital city of Petra, in present-day Jordan, they ruled an area that included most of what is today southern Jordan, southern Israel, and the northwest corner of Saudi Arabia. They spoke Arabic and wrote inscriptions, some of which have survived because they were carved on rock, in an Aramaic script that was deciphered in the mid-19th century. Their gods were most likely celestial gods who were also worshiped in other Arabian cultures. While agricultural towns and villages dotted their realm, their major business was trade, especially conveying products such as frankincense and myrrh from the southern Arabian Peninsula to Egypt and the areas along the eastern Mediterranean coast. The Greek geographer Strabo (d. after 21 C.E.) described Petra as a magnificent, cosmopolitan city inhabited by people who prided themselves in their wealth and the niceties of their highly developed urban lifestyle. In 106 C.E. Nabataean lands were subsumed in the Roman province of Arabia, under Trajan. While a major earthquake devastated the area in 363, recent archaeological evidence suggests that the city continued to thrive into the sixth century. The monumental ruins of Petra, with the iconic "Treasury" and other structures carved into the rose-colored rock, are a major tourist attraction today.

Nagot (Edo Nago)

The Nagot are a YORUBA people who live in southern Nigeria.

Nama

The Nama are a KHOISAN people originally of Namibia and more recently Botswana. Many fled to Botswana from Namibia in the early 1900s to escape an anti-German rebellion.

Namchi

The Namchi are closely related to the BAYA and MBUN people of Central Africa. They live in the west of the Central African Republic and the east of Cameroon.

Namibians: nationality (people of Namibia)

GEOGRAPHY

Namibia is a nation on the southwest coast of Africa. It has an area of about 319,000 square miles and is bordered by four other countries. South Africa meets Namibia's southern border, and Botswana is on its eastern border. A long thin finger of Namibian territory known as the Caprivi Strip extends from the northeast corner of the main body of Namibia's land area into

(continues)

earlier inhabitants:
Khoisan; San

demographics:
Black Africans make up about 88 percent of the population, white Africans about 6 percent, and people of mixed ancestry about 6 percent. The Ovambo people make up about 50 percent of the population, and the Kavango another 9 percent. Other ethnic groups include the Herero (7 percent), Damara (7 percent), Nama (5 percent), Caprivian (4 percent), Baster (2 percent), and Tswana (0.5 percent).

———◆———

the heart of the continent. The Caprivi Strip is bordered by Botswana to the south and Zambia and Angola to the north. The point at which the Caprivi Strip ends in the east is adjacent to the extreme western corner of Zimbabwe, but the two countries do not technically share a border. Angola dominates the bulk of Namibia's northern border. Namibia's coastline extends for approximately 980 miles along the South Atlantic Ocean. From 1977 to 1994 a 433-square-mile coastal enclave known as Walvis Bay was administered by South Africa, but today this territory is within the boundaries of Namibia.

An arid plateau extending from the north to the south dominates the center of. The coastal fringe includes a very arid area known as the Namib Desert, and a portion of the Kalahari Desert intrudes into the eastern part of the country. The central plateau rises from the coastal desert area to form a steep escarpment up to 2,000 feet high. Although the landscape of the plateau is very arid, it receives enough rainfall to support sparse savanna, unlike the coastal strip, which is almost completely devoid of plant life. Namibia's only permanent flowing watercourses lie along its borders. The Kunene, Okavanga, and Zambezi Rivers form parts of its northern borders with Angola and Zambia; and the Orange River marks its border with South Africa in the south. The majority of Namibia's small population lives on the central plateau and the country's capital, Windhoek, is also located there. Walvis Bay, Namibia's second largest city and its primary port, is located on the coast. Taken as a whole Namibia is the word's second most sparsely populated nation; only Mongolia has fewer people on average per square mile of territory.

INCEPTION AS A NATION

The huge and sparsely populated area encompassed by the borders of the modern nation of Namibia has never been the homeland of a single ethnically or linguistically related people. The earliest known inhabitants were SAN and KHOISAN peoples, and rock paintings discovered in the northeast of the country indicate human habitation stretching back several thousand years. BANTU-speaking peoples are believed to have migrated into the area from the 15th century C.E. and by the 19th century made up the majority of its inhabitants.

Colonial interest in Namibia was limited because of the extreme aridity of its interior and the absence of readily obtainable resources. The exception to this rule was Walvis Bay, a natural deepwater harbor that was first visited by Portuguese explorers in the 1480s and became a regular hunting ground for European whalers in the centuries that followed. Like Cape Town in South Africa, Walvis Bay also became an important resupply point on the sea route from Europe to India. The Dutch were the first Europeans to assert colonial control over a portion of Namibia when the Dutch East India Company added Walvis Bay to the Cape Colony in 1793. Control of the Cape Colony, including the enclave of Walvis Bay, passed to the British in 1797 and remained in British hands until 1910, when the Cape Colony joined the Union of South Africa (the predecessor of the modern nation of South Africa).

Neither the Dutch nor the British made any effort to extend their control inland from Walvis Bay, but in the 1880s Germany launched a series of military expeditions to occupy the interior of Namibia and forestall a rumored British intention to declare the entire region a protectorate. German forces quickly conquered much of the territory of modern Namibia, and in 1884 the German colony of South West Africa was declared. Revolts against German rule by indigenous peoples were frequent and on several occasions necessitated the deployment of large expeditionary forces from Germany to defeat them. From 1892 to 1905 a series of uprisings by the HERERO and NAMA peoples were brutally suppressed by German troops, resulting in the death of up to 80 percent of the Herero population.

During World War I South African troops invaded South West Africa and made significant gains. Following Germany's defeat in Europe in 1919, South West Africa was mandated to South Africa by the League of Nations (the predecessor of the United Nations). Following the end of World War II in 1945, South Africa was refused permission to annex South West Africa and incorporate it as a province by the United Nations. Despite this ruling, South Africa increasingly treated South West Africa as if it were an integral part of the nation in the decades that followed; in the 1960s and 1970s South Africa extended its apartheid policies to South West Africa, set up administrative "ethnic homelands," and encouraged the settlement of white South Africans. In 1958 an independence movement known as the Ovamboland People's Congress was formed in South West Africa, and in 1960 this movement became known as the South West Africa People's Organization (SWAPO). International opposition

Namibians: nationality time line

C.E.

1884 Germany establishes the colony of South West Africa.

1886–90 Agreements between Germany, Britain, and Portugal over the territory of South West Africa result in the present-day borders of Namibia.

1892–1905 Uprisings by Herero and Nama peoples are suppressed by Germany resulting in great loss of life.

1915 South Africa invades South West Africa.

1920 South Africa is mandated by the League of Nations to administer South West Africa.

1958 Ovamboland People's Congress established with the aim of achieving independence for South West Africa.

1960 Ovamboland People's Congress renamed South West Africa People's Organization (SWAPO).

1966 SWAPO begins military operations against South African occupation.

1968 South West Africa renamed Namibia by United Nations.

1972 SWAPO recognized as the rightful political representatives of Namibia by the United Nations.

1988 South Africa agrees to Namibian independence.

1989 SWAPO wins elections to form a transitional government in Namibia.

1990 Namibia achieves independence. SWAPO leader Sam Nujoma is the nation's first president.

1994 Wavis Bay enclave incorporated into Namibia. Nujoma wins a second term as president.

1998–99 Separatist groups in the Caprivi Strip allege persecution by the Namibian government.

1999 Nujoma wins a third term as president.

2003 Black farm workers threaten to occupy white-owned farms.

2004 Germany issues an official apology for the massacre of Herero people during the uprisings of 1892–1905.

2005 Leading SWAPO politician Hifikepunye Pohamba replaces Nujoma as president.

2007 A group convicted of organizing rebellion in the Caprivi Strip are imprisoned.

to South Africa's continued de facto rule over South West Africa grew in the late 1950s and early 1960s, and in 1961 the United Nations called for independence for the territory and an end South African occupation.

SWAPO launched military operations against South African occupation in 1966, and in 1968 the United Nations officially recognized the name of the territory as Namibia and declared its occupation by South Africa to be illegal. Despite United Nations support, SWAPO's war against South Africa was to continue for 25 years. Many of SWAPO's military camps were across the border in Angola and Zambia, so South African forces frequently launched punitive strikes into these countries. South African rule in Namibia came to an end as the result of an agreement with Angola that guaranteed the withdrawal of Cuban troops from Angola and the repatriation of SWAPO fighters to Namibia.

United Nations–sponsored elections took place in 1989, and Namibia became formally independent in March 1990. Representatives of SWAPO formed the largest party in the new national assembly, and SWAPO leader Sam Nujomo was sworn in as the nation's first president.

South Africa retained control of an enclave around Walvis Bay until 1994, when it was formally incorporated into Namibia following three years of negotiations between the South African and Namibian governments.

CULTURAL IDENTITY

Namibia is an ethnically diverse nation, but a single ethnic group, the Ovambo people, makes up about 50 percent of the population. The rejection of ethnic segregation was one of the guiding principles of SWAPO, a response to the rigid racial stratification and "ethnic homeland" system that was imposed under South

African rule. The nation's constitution, laws, and administrative divisions were drawn up specifically to eliminate these divisions. About 8 percent of the population is of primarily European descent and another 7 to 8 percent are of mixed European-African descent. A deliberate policy of national reconciliation following Namibian independence was largely successful at integrating this significant non-African minority into the new political reality. Despite these efforts, some ethnic tensions have surfaced in the country as smaller ethnic groups have made land claims in areas they regard as their traditional homelands. The overwhelming dominance of SWAPO and its predominantly Ovambo supporter base has also given rise to a leading opposition party made up primarily of the representatives of smaller ethnic groups.

Under South African rule whites and people of mixed ancestry were concentrated in the urban centers, particularly in the center and south of the country, while indigenous peoples who made up the great majority of the population were dispersed across rural and remote areas or housed in substandard accommodation on the outskirts of cities. This pattern has largely persisted in the short time since independence. Gradual economic change, however, is creating an influx to the cities of the rural poor, which is putting a great strain on services and feeding an increase in unemployment. The economic elite of the nation has remained almost intact, with the great majority of large businesses still under the control of the ancestors of white European and South African settlers. In the political and administrative arena, however, formerly oppressed groups are rapidly gaining parity if not dominance.

An overwhelming majority of Namibians remain extremely poor and support themselves by subsistence agriculture. Namibia has one of the most unequal income distributions in Africa, a consequence from the years of South African rule. Although the export of raw materials such as diamonds, uranium, copper, and other minerals accounts for a large proportion of Namibia's foreign earnings, about 80 percent of the nation's economic activity is accounted for by agriculture, and the majority of this is conducted at a very low level of technological development.

FURTHER READING

Gary F. Baines and Peter C. J. Vale. *Beyond the Border War: New Perspectives on Southern Africa's Late-Cold War Conflicts* (South Africa: Unisa Press, 2008).

Lionel Cliffe et al. *The Transition to Independence in Namibia* (Boulder: Lynne Rienner, 1994).

Laurent C. W. Kaela. *The Question of Namibia* (Houndmills, U.K.: Macmillan Press, 1996).

Colin Leys. *Namibia's Liberation Struggle: The Two-Edged Sword* (London: J. Curry, 1995).

David Robbins. *On the Bridge of Goodbye: The Story of South Africa's Discarded San Soldiers* (Johannesburg: Jonathan Ball, 2007).

Donald L. Sparks. *Namibia: The Nation After Independence* (Boulder, Colo.: Westview Press, 1992).

Elizabeth Marshall Thomas. *The Old Way: A Story of the First People* (New York: Farrar, Straus and Giroux, 2006).

Namnam

The Namnam are a MOLE-DAGBANE people. The majority of the Namnam live in eastern Ghana.

Namwanga

The Namwanga live in the far northeast of Zambia. Many of the Namwanga are Jehovah's Witnesses.

Nandi

The Nandi are one of the largest of the several related groups that make up the KALENJIN. The Nandi people live in western Kenya. The ancestors of the Kalenjin were highland NILOTES, who began dispersing from their original cradleland at the northernmost tip of Lake Turkana in present-day Ethiopia to East Africa during the first millennium B.C.E. The separate Kalenjin groups such as the Nandi emerged as the highland Nilotes spread out over the region and mixed with people already living there. The Nandi did not emerge as a distinct ethnic group until sometime after 1000 C.E., separating from the KIPSIGIS as late as about 1600 to 1800. While both Nandi and Kipsigis are very similar Kalenjin languages, they are distinguishable by small differences in sounds and terms used, comparable to the difference between American and British English.

Nanerge

The Nanerge are part of the SENUFO group of people. Closely related to the MINIANKA, they are concentrated around the border between Mali and southwestern Burkina Faso.

Nankansi *See* GRUSI.

Nar

The Nar are a subgroup of the SARA. The majority live in southern Chad.

Nbule *See* BAFOU.

Ndau (Buzi; Vandau)

The Ndau are a subgroup of the SHONA. They live in southeastern Zimbabwe and Mozambique.

Ndebele (Matabele)

The Ndebele live in the Transvaal province of South Africa and in Zimbabwe. They are commonly divided into two separate groups: the Northern Ndebele and the Southern Ndebele. The Southern Ndebele are subdivided into two main branches: the NDZUNDZA and the MANALA, which take their names from early leaders. The Northern Ndebele have been absorbed into the SOTHO population and are no longer considered a distinct ethnic group.

The Ndebele of southern Zimbabwe are also known as the Matabele, and the area in which they live is called Matabeleland. The Ndebele and Matabele both refer to themselves as AmaNdebele. The histories and cultures of the Ndebele and the Matabele are closely connected and the two groups are treated as branches of the same Ndebele people. (*See also* ZIMBABWEANS: NATIONALITY.)

ORIGINS

The Ndebele story begins with the NGUNI, a BANTU-speaking people who arrived in southern Africa at the beginning of the second century. The Ndebele of today are one of many ethnic groups descended from the original Nguni settlers. ("Ndebele" is the Sotho name for "Nguni.") History suggests that they probably split off some time in the late 1500s under a chief named Musi. Early on, the Ndebele split into two groups—Northern and Southern—most of whom migrated from present-day KwaZulu-Natal northward to modern Transvaal, where the Northern Ndebele gradually became absorbed by their Sotho neighbors. In the 1700s, the Southern Ndebele fragmented into different groups. Two branches survived this fragmentation into the present day: a smaller group, led by Manala, and a larger group, led by Ndzundza.

An Ndebele woman wearing beaded hoops. Hoops of this kind are traditionally worn by married women only.

NDEBELE

location:
South Africa and Zimbabwe

time period:
Second century C.E. to present

ancestry:
Bantu

language:
Bantu (Niger-Congo)

LANGUAGE

The language of the Ndebele of South Africa and Zimbabwe is called Ndebele (or isiNdebele).

HISTORY

The Ndzundza Ndebele reached a height of prosperity in the mid-19th century under the rule of King Mabhogo, but they were finally conquered by the Boers' South African Republic (Transvaal) in 1883. All the Ndzundza lands were confiscated and the people forced to work for the BOERS (Afrikaner farmers) virtually as slaves (*see* AFRIKANERS). After the Union of South Africa was created in 1910, the Ndebele came under white-minority rule.

The Ndebele of present-day Zimbabwe (also known as the Matabele) are also descended from early Nguni settlers, but they did not emerge as an independent people until the 19th century. In the early 1800s, South Africa was dominated by the ZULU led by Shaka. His lieutenant was Mzilikazi of the Khumalo people—a Ndebele group that had not migrated to the Transvaal but remained in present-day KwaZulu-Natal. In 1823 Mzilikazi rebelled against Shaka during the violent Mfecane era and led the Khumalo northward to

Ndebele time line

C.E.

200s Bantu-speaking peoples begin to arrive in southern Africa.

1500s Ndebele groups emerge.

1700s Southern Ndebele fragment.

1819–39 Mfecane period of mass migrations and wars

1820s Mzilikazi founds Ndebele state.

1836–48 Great Trek brings Boers into conflict with people inland.

1837 Mzilikazi and followers migrate north.

ca. 1840 Mabhogo's reign over Ndzundza Ndebele begins.

1883 Ndebele conquered by Boers.

1890 British South Africa Company colonizes Southern Rhodesia.

1896 Shona and Matabele at war with British colonizers.

1910 White-minority-ruled Union of South Africa created.

1923 British government takes control of Southern Rhodesia; white immigration encouraged.

1948 Apartheid begins in South Africa.

1965 White-minority rule established in Southern Rhodesia as Rhodesia.

1967–75 Period of guerrilla warfare against white Rhodesians.

1980 Rhodesia independent as Zimbabwe

1980–88 Conflict between Shona-dominated government of Zimbabwe and Ndebele elements. Thousands of Ndebele are killed. Conflict ends in a power-sharing agreement.

2002 Zimabwean president Robert Mugabe posts Shona-dominated police in Ndebele regions to monitor preidential elections, provoking unrest.

See also ZIMBABWEANS: NATIONALITY

safety. Mzilikazi settled north of the Vaal River and established a powerful Ndebele kingdom near present-day Pretoria. This kingdom was attacked repeatedly by Zulu, GRIQUA, and Kora people and finally by Boers on the Great Trek. In 1837 Mzilikazi led his people across the Limpopo River to a new settlement that he called Bulawayo (meaning "Great Place"), in present-day Zimbabwe, which is where they came to be known as the Matabele.

The Ndebele of Zimbabwe came into conflict with the British in the late 1800s when the British South Africa Company, headed by the imperialist Cecil Rhodes, occupied most of the region. In 1890, the Ndebele found themselves the second-largest ethnic group in a British-dominated territory called Southern Rhodesia, named for Rhodes.

In 1973, under apartheid (the racist doctrine of "separate development"), the Ndebele of South Africa were given a homeland called KwaNdebele, which was in territory that had not previously formed part of their traditional range. Great conflict arose in the 1980s between the government-appointed regime of the homeland and the supporters of the Ndebele monarch: 160 died, 300 were detained, and hundreds simply disappeared. The homelands were abolished in 1994 following the ending of apartheid legislation in 1991.

Meanwhile, the Ndebele of Zimbabwe experienced years of oppression at the hands of the white-minority governments of Southern Rhodesia and Rhodesia. After a prolonged guerrilla war, majority rule was introduced with the birth of the independent state of Zimbabwe in 1980. Even after independence, the Matabele suffered the effects of a power struggle between the leaders of two former rebel groups: Robert Mugabe—the new prime minister—and Joshua Nkomo, whose opposition party drew most of its support from Matabeleland. Government reprisals against dissidents in Matabeleland were harsh and culminated in brutal massacres in the 1980s.

CULTURE

The ways of life of the Ndebele in South Africa and Zimbabwe are still greatly affected by the legacy of white-minority rule. In South Africa and Rhodesia, the best farming land was allocated to whites, and despite land-redistribution plans in independent Zimbabwe and the end of apartheid in South Africa, the situation has not improved greatly. Most Matabele households rely on food-crop farming augmented by the sale of cash crops and surplus produce, casual employment, money sent by family members working as migrant laborers, and wages from working as farm laborers. Today, the majority of Ndebele work for wages in a variety of jobs including farm labor, but some with access to land still farm. Even today, some Ndebele farm laborers work under the same conditions as they did in the 1880s for the Boers and still do not receive any wages. The main food crops grown are corn, wheat, millet, and sorghum as well as, in South Africa, pumpkins, beans, and potatoes. In Zimbabwe, the main cash crops are cotton, tobacco, and sugar.

Government and Society

Families are based on men as heads of households, and in the countryside three generations often share the same home or live close together.

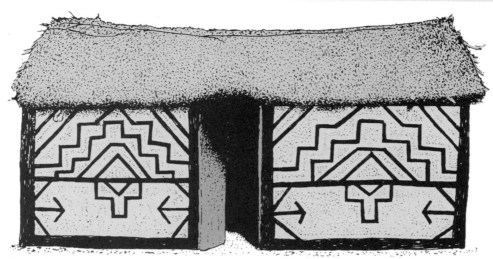

An Ndebele house decorated with geometric designs. Ndebele women are renowned for their decorative skills.

Because so many Ndebele women, as well as men, go to distant parts to work, grandparents frequently bring up the children. Inheritance of property generally passes to the youngest son. A man may still have more than one wife, though having only one wife is the general rule in South Africa. A woman, however, can have only one husband.

Historically, the Ndebele and Matabele were ruled by kings and paramount chiefs, and vestiges of this system remain today. Chiefs retain some authority, but they have to work within the modern systems of government in both countries. Justice was administered by a group's local court, and some disputes are still settled in this way.

Religion

The majority of Ndebele are Christians; most have converted since the emergence of the many independent African-run Christian churches. Certain features of the Ndebele religion are still widely followed. The most important of these is belief in amaNdlozi, the revered ancestors of the family, who are also believed to be spirit guardians. The Ndebele also maintain their beliefs in healing through spiritual forces. This is carried out by *sangomas* (diviners), who may be men or women, and *nyangas* (essentially herbalists), who are always men.

See also SOUTH AFRICANS: NATIONALITY; ZIMBABWEANS: NATIONALITY.

FURTHER READING

Sue Derwent. *The Ndebele: Africa in Colour* (Cape Town, South Africa: Struik Publishers, 1998).

Micere Githae Mugo. *African Orature and Human Rights in Gikuyu, Shona, and Ndebele Zamani Cultures* (Harare, Zimbabwe: SAPES Books, 2004).
Pathisa Nyathi. *Traditional Ceremonies of Amandebele* (Gweru, Zimbabwe: Mambo Press, 2001).

Ndembu

The Ndembu are one of the many groups that make up the LUNDA people. The precolonial Lunda Empire brought together a variety of Central African peoples, who, like the Ndembu, are often just referred to as the Lunda. While living in the northwest of modern-day Zambia, the Ndembu inhabit the southern regions of the historic Lunda Empire, which was in what is now the southern Democratic Republic of the Congo. For this reason the Ndembu are also known as the Southern Lunda.

The Ndembu separated from the Northern Lunda in the 18th century, leaving the lands of the Lunda Empire and migrating south. During the 19th century the Ndembu were regularly raided, and many were enslaved by CHOKWE and OVIMBUNDU slave traders. A small Ndembu community was established in Angola in the early 20th century when some crossed the border to escape taxation by the colonial British.

Ndundza

The Ndundza are one of the main NDEBELE groups. The Ndebele live in South Africa.

Ndwandwe

The Ndwandwe are a NGUNI people of South Africa and Swaziland. They once controlled a powerful kingdom in southern Africa under their leader Zwide in the early 19th century.

Nestorians

Nestorians are Christians more accurately known as East Syrian Christians, or members of the Church of the East or the Assyrian Church of the East. The name Assyrian was adopted in the 19th century, following Western archaeologists working in Nineveh, in modern-day Iraq, who suggested that this Christian community descended from the ancient ASSYRIANS. The language used in their religious rituals is Syriac, an ancient Semitic language related to Aramaic, the language of Jesus. The term *Nestorian* derives from the name Nestorius, bishop of Constantinople, whose teachings were condemned by the Council of Ephesus in 431. It is uncertain exactly what Nestorius's teachings were, as they survive only in fragments, but he was charged with heresy for teaching that Christ had a dual nature, as a man and as the divine Son of God. According to some scholars, politics more than religion caused the condemnation of Nestorius and the subsequent break with the Byzantine Church. Persecuted by the Persian Sassanians, the Nestorians welcomed the Arab conquerors in the seventh century, and under Muslim rule, they were protected as "people of the book" (*see* SASSANIANS).

Nestorians were ambitious missionaries and traders, and as early as 635 they had reached Central Asia and China, although by about 1200 the religion had vanished from China. Nestorian missionaries also established themselves in India, especially along the Malabar Coast, where East Syrian Christian communities still survive. While under some Muslim rulers, Nestorians, along with other Christians, suffered various sorts of religious persecution, ninth- and 10th-century Abbasid rulers accorded them positions of prestige. During that period many illustrious physicians, scientists, philosophers, and government officials came from this community, and the famous translations of Western classical works, such as those of Aristotle and Hippocrates, were overseen by Nestorians. In the 14th century, the Mongol conqueror Timur (Tamurlane) destroyed the Nestorian church east of Iraq, except in India.

Ngama

The Ngama are a subgroup of the SARA. They live in southern Chad.

Ngambay

The Ngambay are a subgroup of the SARA. They live in southern Chad.

Ngan *See* BENG.

Ngbaka *See* MBAKA.

Ngichoro

The Ngichoro are one of the two main subgroups of the TURKANA. The Turkana live in northwest Kenya.

Ngimonia

The Ngimonia are one of the two main subgroups of the TURKANA. The Turkana live in northwest Kenya.

Ngizm

The Ngizm are a subgroup of the KANURI. They live in northeastern Nigeria.

Ngonde

The Ngonde live in Malawi and are closely related to the NYAKYUSA of southwestern Tanzania. The Ngonde inhabit the lands at the northern end of Malawi, just across the border and the Songwe River from the Nyakyusa. The Ngonde and the Nyakyusa languages are closely related BANTU languages.

The Ngonde's home on the shores of Lake Malawi was an important crossroads of historical trade networks, allowing the Ngonde to profit from the lucrative ivory trade but exposing them to the raids of slave traders. A powerful Ngonde kingdom (or chiefdom) arose in the 19th century, stimulated by the trade in ivory and slaves. This coincided with one of the most violent periods in Ngonde history—a SWAHILI slaver set up business in Ngonde country, initially with Ngonde consent, but Ngonde villages were attacked by the Swahilis and many people captured or killed.

Ngoni

Many East Africans who descended from NGUNI refugees and fled from the violence of the Mfecane in the mid-1800s are known collectively as Ngoni peoples. The Mfecane (the Nguni word for "crushing") is used to refer to the period (1819–39) of mass migrations and wars in the southeastern half of southern Africa. The Mfecane was triggered by the rise of the ZULU kingdom under Shaka. In Mozambique, the Ngoni refugees adopted Zulu battle tactics and raided the local TSONGA and Portuguese trading settlements on the coast, dominating the region by the 1830s. Led by Shaka's former general, Soshangane, the Ngoni established a military empire called Gaza. Gaza was a major obstacle to the Europeans trying to colonize Mozambique in the 1890s. Ngoni states were also established in Central Africa by Ngoni refugees. These were eventually absorbed into local groups, forming centralized chieftaincies.

Ngqika

The Ngqika are one of the main XHOSA groups. The Xhosa are a large group of peoples united by a common language in South Africa.

Nguin *See* BENG.

Ngulu *See* LOMWE.

Nguni

There are two major black African cultural and linguistic groupings in southern Africa: the Nguni and the SOTHO-TSWANA. Both, along with other BANTU speakers, share a common origin centuries ago in eastern Nigeria. The Nguni arrived in southern Africa in the early third century C.E., and it is possibly from the TSONGA of Mozambique that the earliest Nguni trace their origins. In southern Africa, the Nguni are concentrated in the southeast of the region, mostly between the Drakensberg Mountains and the sea. The larger Nguni groups in this area include the ZULU, SWAZI, and the XHOSA. Other groups, such as the NDEBELE, live in regions farther north, where they were displaced during the Mfecane period. The Mfecane (the Nguni word for "crushing") is used to refer to the period (1819–39) of mass migrations and wars in the southeastern half of southern Africa. The Mfecane was triggered by the rise of the Zulu kingdom under Shaka.Many East Africans descended from Nguni refugees who fled from the violence of the Mfecane in the mid-1800s are known as NGONI peoples.

Nguru

The Nguru are part of the ZARAMO, a BANTU people of East Africa. The Nguru live mostly in the mountainous highlands of coastal Tanzania.

Nigerians: nationality (people of Nigeria)

GEOGRAPHY

The Federal Republic of Nigeria is the most populous African nation, it is situated on the west coast of the continent with a coastline on the Gulf of Guinea and has an area of about 357,000 square miles. Nigeria has borders with four other nations. Benin lies to the west, Niger to the north, Chad to the northeast, and Cameroon to the east and south. Nigeria's border with Chad in the extreme northeast corner of the country bisects Lake Chad.

Nigeria's coastal plain is dominated by a belt of mangrove forest and intersected by the many branches of the delta of the Niger River's as well as numerous other rivers and streams flowing into the sea. Inland from the mangrove forests is a wide belt of gently hilly terrain covered by tropical rain forest that rises gradually to a central plateau with an average elevation of about 2,000 feet. The north of the country is generally drier and is typically characterized

A full-size terra-cotta head produced by an artist of the Nok culture that inhabited northern Nigerian between ca. 500 B.C.E. and 200 C.E.

NIGERIANS: NATIONALITY

nation:
Nigeria; Federal Republic of Nigeria

derivation of name:
From the Niger River

government:
Federal republic

capital:
Abuja

language:
English is the country's official language. Hausa, Yoruba, Igbo, and Fulani are the most widely-spoken indigenous languages.

religion:
About 50 percent of the population are Muslim, 40 percent are Christian, and the remaining 10 percent follow traditional indigenous faiths.

earlier inhabitants:
Nok

demographics:
Nigeria has more than 250 ethnic groups. Of these the largest are the Hausa and Fulani making up about 29 percent of the population, Yoruba (21 percent), Igbo (18 percent), Ijaw (10 percent), Kanuri (4 percent), Ibibio (3.5 percent), and Tiv (2.5 percent).

Nigerians: nationality time line

C.E.

1804 Usman dan Fodio begins a jihad (Islamic holy war) against the Hausa, creating the Sokoto caliphate.

1861 Britain annexes Lagos.

1886 The Royal Africa Company establishes a protectorate over much of western Nigeria.

1892 Benin agrees to become a British protectorate.

1893 The Yoruba agree to accept a British protectorate.

1900 The British government assumes jurisdiction over Royal Africa Company territory.

1902 Britain conquers the Ibo.

1903 Britain completes the conquest of the Sokoto caliphate.

1914 Britain conquers Abeokuta, the last independent state in Nigeria.

1914 Britain forms the colony and protectorate of Nigeria.

1918 Abeokuta rebels against British rule.

1929 Ibo and Ibibio women protest against British rule.

1946 A new constitution gives Nigerians a role in government.

1954 Federal government model established.

1960 Nigeria becomes independent of Britain.

1963 Nigeria declares itself a republic.

1966 Military takes over the Nigerian government: Yakubu Gowon becomes leader of Nigeria.

1967 Eastern Region under Ojukwu declares independence as Biafra: civil war breaks out.

1970 Biafra surrenders ending the civil war.

1975 Gowon is replaced by Murtala Muhammad in a bloodless coup.

1976 Muhammad is killed in a failed coup attempt: Olesegun Obasanjo succeeds as leader.

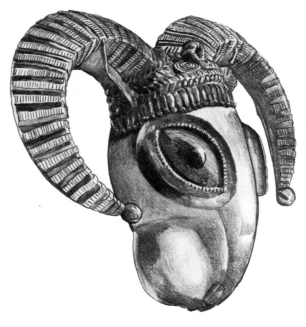

A 15th-century sculpture created by the Owo people of Nigeria

by savannah while the south is wetter and more densely forested.

Nigeria's major waterway is the Niger River, the third largest river in Africa. It enters the country in the northwest across the border with Niger and flows in a generally southerly direction towards the Gulf of Guinea. The Benue River, the Niger River's major tributary, enters Nigeria in the east and flows generally west towards its confluence with the Niger near the town of Lokoja close to the geographical center of the country.

Approximately 50 percent of the population of Nigeria lives in urban areas and Lagos, the country's largest city, is one of the most densely populated urban areas in Africa as well as one of the largest and most rapidly expanding cities on the continent. Lagos, situated on the coast close to the western border with Benin, was Nigeria's capital city until 1991 when the seat of government was moved to the much

1978	Obasanjo approves a democratic presidential constitution to come into effect in 1979.
1979	Alhaji Shehu Shagari's National Party of Nigeria wins federal elections. Shagari takes office as president.
1983	Shagari's government is overthrown by a coup: Muhammad Buhari becomes president.
1985	Buhari overthrown by Ibrahim Babangida.
1988	Elections for local and national government prepare for return of civilian government.
1991	Seat of government is transferred from Lagos to Abuja.
1993	Interim government takes office under Babangida. Social Democratic Party of Moshood Abiola wins federal elections but Babangida annuls the result and picks a non-elected civilian government. Government overthrown by military coup of Gen. Sanni Abacha.
1994	Abiola declares himself president and is arrested for treason.
1995	Author Ken Saro-Wiwa and other members of the Movement for the Survival of the Ogoni People executed.
1998	Death of Abacha: he is succeeded by Abdulsalam Abubakar.
1998	Riots follow the sudden death of Moshood Abiola
1999	Former military dictator Olesegun Obasanjo is elected president.
2000	Muslim-Christian clashes occur in the north.
2003	Obasanjo elected to a second presidential term.
2004	Muslim and Christian militias engage in fighting in the central Plateau State. Criminal gangs clash in the important oil-producing city of Port Harcourt.
2006	The Sultan of Sokoto, spiritual leader of Nigeria's Muslims, is killed in a plane crash. Militants in the Niger Delta attack oil facilities and kidnap foreign oil workers.
2007	Umaru Yar'Adua wins presidential elections.
2008	Nigerian oil production falls as a result of attacks on oil facilities by militants. More than 200 people are killed in violence between Muslims and Christians in central Nigeria.

smaller and newly constructed city of Abuja in the geographical center of the country. Other large cities include Kano, in the north of the country; Ibadan, just north of Lagos; and Kaduna, in the north central region, all of which are significantly larger and more populous than the capital.

INCEPTION AS A NATION

The Nok culture emerged in what is now Nigeria around 2,500 years ago. Nok is the earliest known civilization of West Africa. In the 20th century several fine terra-cotta figurines were unearthed near the village of Nok, after which the ancient culture has been named. "Nok" figurines have since been found over a much wider area. Little is known of the culture, but it was in existence from about 500 B.C.E. to 200 C.E. Initially a Stone Age culture, the people of Nok made the transition to an Iron Age culture; iron-smelting furnaces dating from 300

B.C.E. have been found in Nigeria. Some historians once thought that the Nok culture represented the earliest beginnings of iron-working. This is now known to be untrue, but Nok culture does represent the earliest know evidence of a developed sculptural tradition in Africa south of the Sahara. Other early cultures centered within the territory of modern Nigeria include the Ife culture, which emerged around 1000 C.E., and the Kingdom of Benin, whose greatest period was between the mid-15th and mid-17th centuries.

The early development of northern Nigeria was influenced by the empires that dominated the West African savanna belt. Northern Nigeria bordered the Kingdom of Kanem but, in the 14th century, Bornu in northeastern Nigeria became Kanem's political center. After the collapse of Songhay in 1591, Kanem-Bornu became powerful, but it too began to decline in the late 17th century. From the 14th century,

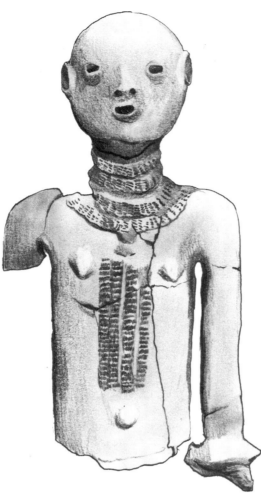

A fourth-century terra-cotta human figure from northern Nigeria.

wealthy Hausa city states developed in northern Nigeria, but, in 1804, these were conquered by the Fulani Muslim cleric, Usman dan Fodio, who founded the Sokoto Caliphate.

The Portuguese were the first Europeans to reach the Nigerian coast, which soon became important in the slave trade. Britain banned slavery in 1807 and, in 1851, the British seized the port of Lagos, using it as a base for curbing the slave trade. Lagos became a British colony in 1861 and, in the 1880s and 1890s, Britain extended its influence in southern Nigeria through a series of treaties with local rulers. In 1903, Britain conquered the Sokoto Caliphate in the north and, in 1914, most of the present-day territory of Nigeria was united as a single British colony.

From the 1920s, Nigerians began to demand more representation in government. However, differences between the country's rival ethnic groups caused disunity. The constitution of 1954 created a federal system of government that devolved significant powers to the three principal regions; North, East, and West. These divisions, roughly corresponding to the tripartite geographical division of the country created by the course of the Niger and Benue Rivers, essentially recognized the major ethnic groupings in the territory; the Hausa in the north, the Yoruba in the west, and the Igbo in the east. They also reflected the principal colonial territories that had existed before the unification of 1914. In 1957 the East and West regions became self-governing with the North region achieving the same status in 1959. In October 1960 all three regions became fully independent from Britain but continued to operate under a singe federal government structure. Three years later, in 1963, proclaimed itself a federal republic with Nnamdi Azikiwe as its first president. As part of the transition to a republic a fourth region, the Midwest, was formed.

CUTLURAL IDENTITY

Nigeria is a nation that encompasses a highly diverse set of ethnic and religious identities. The three major ethno-linguistic groups are the Yoruba, who predominate in the Ogun, Ondo, Oyo, and Osun states of the west; the Igbo, who predominate in the Anambra, Imo, Abia, and Enugu states of the east; and the Hausa and Fulani who make up the largest single groups in the Sokoto, Kaduna, Jigawa, Katsina, and Kano states of the north. Other significant groups include the Kanuri, the Edo (or Bini), the Ibibio, the Ijaw, the Tiv, and the Nupe.

The Edo people of southern Nigeria are descendants of the Bini, who established the historic Kingdom of Benin—famed worldwide for its beautiful bronze sculptures. The capital of the kingdom was Benin City, which was founded by the Edo sometime before 1300 C.E. The Kingdom of Benin reached its height between the 14th and 17th centuries, amassing wealth from the trade in ivory, pepper, palm oil, and slaves. The kingdom was ruled by an oba, and the Benin division of the modern Edo province still boasts a ceremonial oba. The Edo retain a strong tradition of metalworking and many still practice the art of lost-wax metal casting that was used to produce the famous Benin bronzes.

The decades after Nigerian independence were fraught with interethnic violence and political instability. In 1966 the elected government was overthrown by a military coup and Nigeria's first prime minister, Sir Abubakar

Tafawa Balewa, was killed. Balewa was a northerner, while the new military head of state, Johnson Aguiyi-Ironsi, was an Igbo. He abolished the federal system of government and appointed many Igbos to high office. This led to rioting in the north. In July 1966, Aguiyi-Ironsi was killed and Yakubu Gowon, took power, but Odumegwu Ojukwu, military governor of the Eastern Region, opposed his appointment. In 1967, in an attempt to give power to more ethnic groups, Gowon replaced the four regions with 12 states, but Ojukwu refused to accept the division of the Eastern Region. In May 1967, he proclaimed the Eastern Region an independent republic called Biafra. Civil war followed until Biafra, suffering from a famine created by a food blockade, surrendered in January 1970. Between 500 thousands and 2 million people are estimated to have died in the conflict, most as a result of starvation.

From the early 1970s, oil exports boosted the economy, but political problems continued. Gowon was overthrown in 1975. His successor, Murtala Ramat Muhammed, was also killed in 1976 and was succeeded by Olusegun Obasanjo, who increased the number of states in Nigeria to 19. Obasanjo also ended military rule in 1979. The elected President Shehu Shagari began the building of a new federal capital at Abuja in central Nigeria to replace Lagos. Shagari was overthrown in 1983 and Muhammadu Buhari set up another military regime. He was replaced in 1985 by Ibrahim Babangida, who promised a return to civilian rule. However, after presidential elections in 1993 were annulled, General Sanni Abacha took power and delayed the return to democracy.

When Abacha died in 1998, he was replaced by General Abdulsalam Abubakar, who restored civilian rule. In elections in 1999, Olusegun Obansanjo, the former army leader, was elected president, while his People's Democratic Party won a majority in parliament. By 1999, the Republic of Nigeria was divided into 36 states, plus the capital Abuja. However, Obasanjo faced many problems in maintaining national unity. In 2000, Christian-Muslim clashes occurred when some northern states adopted sharia (Islamic law), while Hausa-Yoruba conflict broke out in the southwest. The following year hundreds were killed in interethnic fighting in Benue state, many by federal troops sent into the region to quell the conflict. In 2002 fighting in Lagos between Muslim Hausas and Christian Yorubas resulted in more than 100 dead and thousands displaced from

A Nigerian man from the predominantly Muslim north of the country.

their homes while riots in the predominantly Muslim northern city of Kaduna over the planned Miss World beauty pageant resulted in 200 more deaths. Further violent disturbances along ethnic lines have continued to take place throughout the first decade of the 21st century.

In addition to the violence created by ethnic and religious divisions Nigeria has been subject to increasing lawlessness and corruption centered on its oil industry. Nigeria is one of the world's largest oil producers but the people who live in the oil rich regions of the country, principally the area of the Niger Delta, receive little of this income. The OGONI people have been at the forefront of resistance to the activities of oil companies. Since 2006 an organization known as the Movement for the Emancipation of the Niger Delta (MEND) has conducted a series of violent attacks against oil companies severely disrupting production at times. Criminal gangs involved in a substantial black-market trade in oil and the numerous politically motivated insurgents fighting to secure greater control of their regional resources have combined to make this one of the most dangerous parts of the country.

The presidential elections of 2003, which resulted in a second presidential term for Olusegun Obasanjo, marked the first transition from one democratically elected civilian administration to another in Nigeria's post-independence history. Despite allegations of electoral irregularities made by international observers this marks an important step in Nigeria's transition towards stable democratic governance. Increasing oil prices have enabled Nigeria to pay the majority of its foreign debts and have given Nigeria one of the world's fastest growing economies. Endemic corruption, inter-ethnic violence, and the very limited benefits derived from oil wealth by the majority of the population remain major challenges.

FURTHER READING

Alamieyeseigha, D. S. P., Steve S. Azaiki, and Augustine A. Ikein. *Oil, Democracy, and the Promise of True Federalism in Nigeria* (Lanham, Md.; Plymouth: University Press of America, 2008).

Falola, Toyin. *Culture and Customs of Nigeria* (Westport, Conn.: Greenwood Press, 2001).

Ikein, Augustine. *The Impact of Oil on a Developing Country: The Case of Nigeria* (New York: Praeger, 1990).

Kashi, Ed, and Michael Watts. *Curse of the Black Gold: 50 Years of Oil in the Niger Delta* (Brooklyn, N.Y.: PowerHouse Books, 2008).

Smith, Daniel Jordan. *A Culture of Corruption: Everyday Deception and Popular Discontent in Nigeria* (Princeton: Princeton University Press, 2007).

Umoren, Joseph A. *Democracy and Ethnic Diversity in Nigeria* (Lanham, Md.: University Press of America, 1996).

Uwazie, Ernest E. et al, eds. *Inter-Ethnic and Religious Conflict Resolution in Nigeria* (Lanham, Md.: Lexington Books, 1999).

Nigeriens: nationality (people of Niger)

GEOGRAPHY

Niger is a landlocked country in North Africa. It has an area of about 490,000 square miles and is bordered by seven other nations. Algeria and Libya meet Niger's northern borders; Chad lies to the east, Nigeria to the south; Benin and Burkina Faso meet the southwest corner of the country; and Mali lies to the west.

About 80 percent of the area encompassed by the borders of Niger lies within the extremely arid and almost lifeless Sahara Desert. Most of this area is flat and dominated by rolling sand dunes. A range of highlands stretch along the northern border with Algeria and Libya at an average altitude of about 2,000 feet, including Niger's highest point, the 6,380-foot-high peak of Mount Gréboun. It is only the southern 20 percent of the country, and particularly the southwest corner, that can support agriculture. The extreme southeast of the country is on the fringes of the much wetter tropical-forest region of the Niger River basin. The Niger River is the only major year-round watercourse in the country; it flows from northwest to southeast through the southwest corner of the country. Niger's capital city, Niamey, is situated on the banks of the Niger River. The southeast corner of Niger includes part of the marshy fringes of Lake Chad. The lake has shrunk to such an extent over the past century, however, that the open waters of the lake itself no longer lie within Niger's borders.

The arid north of the country is very sparsely populated; the bulk of the population is concentrated in the southwest and along a narrow southern band that borders Nigeria. Zinder, the country's second largest city, and Maradi, its third largest, are both situated close to the Nigerian border in the south. Both lie on ancient trade routes across the Sahara Desert that connected the ancient kingdoms of the interior of central Africa to the Mediterranean coast.

INCEPTION AS A NATION

The evidence of ancient rock paintings discovered in the mountains of northern Niger indicate that 10,000 years ago the Sahara Desert was far smaller than it is today and that northern Niger was covered by fertile grasslands that supported a range of plant and animal life as well as human pastoralists. The rapid expansion of the Sahara Desert is believed to have begun around 2000 B.C.E. and continues to the present day. As the desert expanded, human settlements were forced to withdraw to oases or to move south. Over hundreds of years trade routes developed across the desert along which nomadic traders carried high-value raw materials such as salt and spices from the empires of West Africa to Egypt, Ethiopia, and Morocco. Many of these routes passed through the territory of modern Niger.

In the 1300s C.E. the Mali Empire, which extended from the Atlantic coast of the modern nation of Mali along the upper reaches of the Niger River and deep into modern Niger at its greatest extent, quickly grew as a regional

---

NIGERIENS: NATIONALITY

nation:
Niger; Republic of Niger

derivation of name:
From the Niger River

government:
Republic

capital:
Niamey

language:
The country's official language is French. Hausa and Djerma, the languages of the two largest ethnic groups, are widely spoken.

religion:
About 90 percent of the population are Muslim, about 5 percent are Christian, and the remaining 5 percent follow indigenous belief systems.

earlier inhabitants:
Unknown

demographics:
The Hausa people make up about 56 percent of the population and the Djerma another 22 percent. Other significant groups include the Peul (8.5 percent), the Tuareg (8 percent), and the Kanuri (4.3 percent).

Nigeriens: time line

C.E.

1904	France occupies Niger.
1922	Niger becomes a French colony.
1958	Niger becomes an autonomous republic within the French Community.
1960	Niger becomes an independent nation with Diori Haman as president.
1968–73	Severe drought in Niger
1974	Haman deposed in a military coup led by Seyni Kountche.
1987	Kountche dies and Ali Seybou becomes president.
1989	A new constitution marks a return to civilian government. Seybou wins presidential elections.
1990	Political opposition parties legalized. Tuareg rebellions in the north begin.
1993	Niger's first multiparty elections take place. Mahamane Ousmane is elected president and his Alliance of the Forces of Change party wins a majority in parliament.
1996	A military coup deposes Ousmane. Elections under a new constitution bring coup leader Ibrahim Mainassara to power.
1999	Mainassara assassinated in a coup led by Daouda Malam Wanké; Mamadou Tandja is elected president the same year.
2004	Tandja wins a second presidential term.
2005–06	Drought and crop failures threaten millions with starvation.
2007	Antigovernment Tuareg insurgents in the north escalate attacks.

power in West Africa. From the early 1400s the slow decline of the Mali Empire allowed the emergence of the even larger SONGHAY Empire, which came to control much of the Niger River and most of modern Niger by about 1500. During the same period the HAUSA people founded a series of states in the south of the present-day Niger, while the north was controlled by Arabized BERBERS and TUAREG. The early 19th century brought a series of invasions and attacks by the FULANI, who sought to bring their own brand of Islam to the region.

The early 19th century also brought the first Europeans to Niger; these were explorers seeking the mouth of the Niger River. The Niger River fascinated European explorers because its source is close to the Atlantic coast in Guinea but it flows inland rather than toward the sea. At the time, when the geography of the interior of Africa was largely unknown to Europeans, many explorers believed that it might empty into a vast inland sea in the center of the continent. The Fulani, Tuareg, Hausa, and Bornu (successor to the Songhay Empire) states fought frequent wars for control of the region's trade routes throughout the 19th century. From the late 19th century the French, who already had colonial interests in regions to the west of Ni-

ger, began to extend their influence eastward. French military expeditions met with fierce resistance from the well-armed and experienced forces of the Fulani, Tuareg, Hausa, and Bornu, but their more advanced weaponry allowed them to gradually establish a foothold in the south of present-day Niger, particularly around Lake Chad.

The colonial territory of French West Africa, originally formed in 1895 by the union of the French colonial territories of Senegal, French Sudan, French Guinea, and Ivory Coast, was extended to include Niger and Mauritania as "Military Territories" in 1904. Opposition to French rule in Niger was never completely suppressed, and there were frequent uprisings, notably during World War I when Tuareg warriors attacked the town of Zinder. Niger was finally designated a French colony only in 1922.

In 1946, following World War II, the French government reorganized all its foreign colonies under a new organization known as the French Union. Under the French Union all peoples living within the former French colonies were granted French citizenship, and a greater degree of local administration was encouraged. In 1958 the French Union was replaced by the French Community, which gave a large degree

Salt pits near the oasis town of Bilma in Niger. Salt is dug from the pits, dried in the sun, and sold to traders who carry it hundreds of miles across the Sahara.

of autonomy to the former colonies with the understanding that France would not oppose their eventual evolution toward full independence. As with most of the other members of the French Community, Niger declared its independence in 1960. Following Niger's declaration in August 1960, Hamani Diori was sworn in as the nation's first president.

CULTURAL IDENTITY

Niger's first president, Hamani Diori, had been closely involved in the negotiations with France that led to Niger's independence and remained on good terms with the French government after 1960. Niger received economic and technological assistance from France in the 1960s, allowing Diori to remain relatively popular. The early 1970s, however, brought devastating droughts to Niger and other Sahelian nations, resulting in great suffering for the majority of the population and a rapid decline in the government's popularity; corruption and poor organization were responsible for worsening the situation. In 1974 this growing opposition reached a crisis point when a violent military

coup led by Seyni Kountché overthrew Diori's government. The new government did not hold general elections.

Following Kountché's death in 1989, another military officer, Ali Seybou, was appointed president. Seybou's attempt to formalize one-party rule, something that had been a political reality since 1974, met with strong opposition, particularly among the nascent labor movement in the country. A national strike forced the government to concede the desirability of a multiparty system, so a new constitution was drawn up and brought into force in 1992. Mahamane Ousmane, the representative of a coalition of opposition groups known as the Alliance of the Forces of Change, won the presidency in the country's first open and democratic elections, although the election was delayed until 1993 because of a violent separatist insurgency that flared up among the Tuareg peoples in the north. Continued violence in the north, which was partly motivated by the perceived predominance of ministers from the Djerma-Songhay ethnic group in the new government, continued into 1995. Political chaos and infighting led to a second coup in 1996 in which Ibrahim Baré

Mainassara seized power. Mainassara quickly declared himself the winner of a presidential election that international observers widely condemned as fraudulent. Three years later he was assassinated in another coup led by Daouda Malam Wanké to power. Wanké returned the country to democratic rule and a new round of open presidential elections in 1999.

Niger spans a cultural divide that has existed for centuries. The north of the country is within the cultural sphere of North Africa and is inhabited by largely nomadic Arabic speaking Berber peoples, such as the Tuareg. The southern fringe of the nation is far more populous and inhabited by sedentary farmers. The culture of the south is more typical of West African nations than of North Africa. The Hausa are the country's largest ethnic group, making up more then 50 percent of the population, and are concentrated in the southwest. The second largest ethnic group, the Djerma-Songhay, live in southcentral and southeast Niger. Despite this divide and the occasional tensions it has produced, the entire country has been strongly influenced by Muslim culture and there is no religious fault line. About 80 percent of the population are Muslim.

Tensions between the north and south that initially caused conflict in the mid-1990s have recently reemerged. The peoples of the north cite underdevelopment in their region and a lack of political influence as their chief grievances. In 2007 a new rebel group called the Niger Movement for Justice instigated a campaign of violence and kidnapping against government troops. Drawing support primarily from the Tuaregs of northern Niger, the activities of the Niger Movement for Justice have also spread to neighboring Mali, a nation that also has a significant population of impoverished Tuareg.

Poverty and underdevelopment remain serious problems for Nigerians more than 45 years after independence. Niger's most valuable export is uranium, but large and unpredictable price fluctuations have meant that a long-term program of development has not been possible. The slow but relentless expansion of the Sahara Desert southward is also threatening agricultural production. Droughts are frequent and starvation a regular occurrence among the nation's poorest people. Niger has the highest child mortality rate in the world and, thanks to an almost complete lack of primary education, one of the world's highest rates of illiteracy. The United Nations rates Niger as the world's poorest nation.

The practice of slave ownership continues to be a major social issue in Niger. Although the colonial French authorities banned slave trading early in the 20th century, the ownership of slaves was not officially outlawed until 2003. Despite this recent law it is estimated that as many as 8 percent of Nigerians are effectively enslaved. Slaves are required to work for their "owners" in exchange for food and clothing. They are born into slavery as the children of men and women who are themselves slaves and whose ancestors may have been slaves for hundreds of years. The concept of slavery is deeply ingrained in Nigerian culture, so the law banning the practice has had very little impact on the reality of slavery. In many cases owners of the slaves are themselves illiterate and unaware of the law, and there is little money the government can use to enforce the law.

FURTHER READING

Samuel Decalo. *Historical Dictionary of Niger*, 3rd ed. (Lanham, Md.: Scarecrow Press, 1996).
F. A. Fugelstad. *History of Niger, 1850–1960* (London: Oxford University Press, 1984).
William F. S. Miles. *Hausaland Divided: Colonialism and Independence in Nigeria and Niger* (Ithaca, N.Y.: Cornell University Press, 1994).
Richard L. Roberts. *Warriors, Merchants, and Slaves: The State and the Economy in the Middle Niger Valley, 1700–1914* (Stanford, Calif.: Stanford University Press, 1987).
Marion Van Offelen and Carol Beckwith. *Nomads of Niger* (New York: Harry Abrams, 1983).

Nikki

The Nikki are part of the BARIBA and live in Benin.

Nilamba   *See* IRAMBA.

Nilotes

The majority of the modern-day population of East Africa is descended from three main African groups: CUSHITES, BANTU, and Nilotes. In turn, the Nilotes are divided into three main groups: Highland, Plains, and River-Lake. All three groups share a common homeland in the southwestern borders of the Ethiopian highlands in the Nile River region of southern Sudan. Their migration, which was gradual and occurred over several centuries, was perhaps triggered by overpopulation, the need to find more land to graze cattle on, or pressure from other ethnic groups.

NUBA

location:
Kenya and Tanzania

time period:
17th century C.E. to present

ancestry:
Nilotic

language:
Nilo-Saharan

From 1000 B.C.E. to 1500 C.E. the Highland and Plains Nilotes migrated into the highlands and plains of Kenya and Tanzania. The River-Lake Nilotes, however, followed the Nile Valley and settled in the lakes region of northern Uganda. The Plains Nilotes emerged as a new and powerful force in East Africa during the second millennium. The Maasai, Turkana, Karamojong, and Iteso people are Plains Nilotes. The Kipsigis, Nandi, and other Kalenjin peoples are Highland Nilotes. Lwo-speaking peoples such as the Alur and the Anuak are descended from River-Lake Nilotes.

Nilotic   *See* Nilotes.

Nladja-Wron   *See* Alladian.

Nogais   (Nogays, Noghays)

The Nogais are a Turkic people (*see* Turkic Peoples) of the Caucasus region of Central Asia who today live in North Dagestan, in the Russian province of Stavropol, and in Chechnya. The total population living in the Caucasus is estimated at 70,000. A population of similar numbers lives in Turkey, mainly the central area of Ankara, their ancestors having immigrated there in the mid-1860s because of pressure from Russian settlers in the north Caucasus. During that time, many Nogais also immigrated to Romania. The Nogais, who are Sunni Muslims, speak various closely related dialects of Nogai, a Turkic language written with the Cyrillic, or Russian, alphabet. The Nogais were traditionally nomadic cattle breeders and farmers. In the 14th century C.E. they separated from the Golden Horde, the Mongol state founded in the mid-13th century, which included most of what is today Russia. The Nogais take their name from Nogai Khan, who was a great-grandson of Chinggis Khan and ruler of the Golden Horde. He was killed in battle in 1299. Their traditional pasture areas were in the area of the Volga River, but Kuban Cossacks pushed them into the Caucasus region by. Land rights continue to be an unresolved issue in the Caucasus, as some of the Nogai pasturelands fall along the border of the Russian Republic of Kalmykia and Dagestan.

Nono

The Nono are closely related to the Manding people and live primarily in Mali.

North Mugirango

The North Mugirango are one of the main subdivisions of the Gusii. The Gusii are a large ethnic group of western Kenya.

Nsenga

The Nsenga are closely related to the Bemba and live in eastern Zambia and across the border in Mozambique.

Ntomba

The Ntomba are a subgroup of the Mongo of Central Africa. The Ntomba live in the central Democratic Republic of the Congo along the Maringa River.

Ntumu

The Ntumu are a Fang subgroup living in Equatorial Guinea, Cameroon, and Gabon.

Nuba

The Nuba live in the Nuba Hills of Kordofan province, southern Sudan. This region lies west of the White Nile River and south of Khartoum, the Sudanese capital. The Nuba fall into more than 60 groups and many more subgroups. (The Nuba should not be confused with the Nubians, who originate from the region now covered by Lake Nasser.)

ORIGINS

Although very little is known about Nuba history until the Arab invasion of North Africa in the seventh century, it seems they have lived in their present location for centuries. Three hundred years before the Arab invasion, references had already been made to the presence of people called the "Black Noba," who were probably ancestors of the modern Nuba. Some Nuba groups claim to have always lived in the Nuba Hills. Since the 18th century, others have moved up into the hills in retreat from Baggara raids or, in the late 19th century, Mahdist troops.

LANGUAGE

The Nuba speak over 50 different languages of the Koalib, Tegali, Talodi, Tumtum, and Katla groups of the Niger-Kordofanian family.

HISTORY

During the lengthy Sudanese civil war between the Islamic north and the mainly non-Muslim south, the Nuba were drawn into conflicts with their Islamic neighbors, the Baggara. The government armed the Baggara, which resulted in thousands of Nuba being killed. Many thousands more were deported from the hills to government-run "peace villages," where they are under pressure to convert to Islam or to join the government troops fighting the southern rebels. There were also reports of rebel groups forcibly conscripting civilians. Since 2002 a ceasefire has been generally observed by both sides.

CULTURE

Most Nuba are farmers and live in permanent settlements. They cultivate the land with hoes, and terrace and irrigate their fields. Common crops are millet, sorghum, and corn. Other crops include cotton, gourds, melons, okra, onions, cucumbers, peppers, and sesame. The Nuba also keep cattle and goats, which provide milk, and chickens, donkeys, horses, and sheep. Except in the few Muslim subgroups, many Nuba also raise pigs. Normally, men work on the land and milk the cattle and goats, while women look after the chickens and pigs and gather wild foods such as nuts. Women also work in the fields to help with harvesting. In the 1970s, oil companies began drilling in the oil-rich south of Sudan, employing many Nuba men. Since the outbreak of the civil war, however, exploitation has largely ceased and job opportunities in the industry have dried up.

The traditional Nuba home is a cylindrical mud structure with a cone-shaped thatched roof. Entrances are generally keyhole shaped. Home to a family may consist of five of these grouped around a courtyard. In towns scattered around the Nuba Hills, where many of the administrative centers are, the Nuba work and live in flat-roofed buildings of brick or stone.

The Nuba are famous for their elaborate forms of personal art, which involve scarring and painting their bodies. The patterns used to decorate the skin are rich in symbolism. Both men and women have this decorative scarring, but for women it denotes important milestones, and the scarring process continues for many years. The skin is cut in patterns and then rubbed with ash, saliva, or sesame oil. The first scarring is done in childhood or at the start of puberty, and the final scarring takes place after a woman has weaned her first child. The scars fade with age and become less prominent. As the Nuba are otherwise occupied by the current civil war, however, many personal art forms are in danger of falling into disuse.

A popular social activity among the Nuba is wrestling. Boys begin their training at the age of 13 or 14. From that time onward, a boy ideally spends at least half his time at a camp where he learns and practices wrestling. As he progresses, he passes through four grades. Each grade has a belt or sash. White is the lowest grade; the belts of higher grades are made of colored cloth or goatskin, with a cow's tail as a badge of rank. The most accomplished wrestlers adorn their belts with brass bells. A wrestler paints his body with patterns in yellow or white. He also shaves his head and smears it with ashes mixed with milk. Nowadays, however, few can spare time for wrestling in the midst of a civil war.

Government and Society

Nuba society has been drastically affected by the decade-long civil war. Many Nuba have been killed during the conflict, and a large proportion of Nuba men and boys have been forcibly conscripted into either the rebel armies or government forces. With many Nuba living in the so-called peace villages or in refugee camps in neighboring countries such as the Democratic Republic of the Congo and the Central African Republic, Nuba social structures, which differ

Nuba time line

C.E.

300s	"Black Noba," probable ancestors of present-day Nuba, recorded in southern Sudan.
640	Arabs begin conquest of North Africa; Islam introduced.
1700s	Arab slave raids against the Nuba. Baggara raids begin; more Nuba retreat into hills.
1821	Trade routes opened from north to south Sudan; as a result, southern population is reduced by disease and slave trading.
1882	Anglo-Egyptian forces conquer Sudan; Mahdi begins campaigns; more Nuba retreat into hills.
1898	Anglo-Egyptian force conquers Mahdist State.
1955	First civil war between south and north Sudan begins.
1956	Sudanese independence
1983–96	Many Nuba join Sudanese People's Liberation Army (SPLA), a southern-based rebel group.
1990s	Famine hits Nuba Hills. Reports of "ethnic cleansing" of the Nuba by Baggara militias
1992	Relocation camps for Nuba, so-called peace villages, set up by government.
2002	The SPLA and the Sudanese government agree a ceasefire.

See also SUDANESE: NATIONALITY

NUER

location:
Sudan

time period:
1000 C.E. to present

ancestry:
Nilotic

language:
Nilo-Saharan

from group to group but are generally based around clans, are gradually being dismantled.

Religion

The majority of the Nuba follow the Nuba religion, which differs in nature from group to group. A minority of Nuba are Christians, however, and an even smaller proportion are Muslims.

FURTHER READING

Ludewig, Alexandra. *Leni Riefenstahl's Encounter with the Nuba: In Search of the Sublime* (London: Interventions, 2006).

Rahhal, Suleiman Musa. *The Right to Be Nuba: The Story of a Sudanese People's Struggle for Survival* (Lawrenceville, N.J.: Red Sea Press, 2001).

Rodger, George. *Village of the Nubas* (London: Phaidon, 1999).

Sesana, Renato Kizito, and Silvano Borruso. *I Am a Nuba* (Nairobi, Kenya: Paulines Publications Africa, 2006).

Steidle, Brian, and Gretchen Steidle Wallace. *The Devil Came on Horseback: Bearing Witness to the Genocide in Darfur* (New York: PublicAffairs, 2007).

Nubians

Nearly 3,000 years ago in what is now southern Egypt and northern Sudan, the Kingdom of Nubia became independent from ancient Egypt, which lay downriver along the Nile. For a while, the Nubians even controlled ancient Egypt (*see* EGYPTIANS). Until recently, descendants of the historical Nubians still lived in this region. The 1960s saw the building of the Aswan High Dam on the Nile River, forcing more than 100,000 Nubians to relocate to elsewhere in Egypt and Sudan after much of Nubia was flooded. The region is now covered by Lake Nasser. UNESCO launched a campaign to save the historical treasures of Nubia, which include temples (Abu Simbel, for example), statues, fine pottery, and tombs full of gold and silver jewelry, bronze work, and other treasures. While greatly influenced by its powerful northern neighbor, Nubian culture was distinctly African in its origin and expression. (*See also* SUDANESE: NATIONALITY.)

A bronze statue of a Nubian king from the eighth century B.C.E.

A Nubian bowl featuring dramatic geometric patterning

Nuer

The Nuer are a Nilotic people who live in southern Sudan. The Nuer are closely related to the DINKA, another Nilotic group (*see* NILOTES).

ORIGINS

Along with other Nilotic peoples, the Nuer originated in a region to the southwest of their present location. Over the years, they migrated to their present homeland. This gradual process of migration was forced to halt when the British and Egyptians conquered Sudan in 1898.

LANGUAGE

The Nuer language is also called Nuer and belongs to the Nilotic language group.

HISTORY

After Sudan achieved independence in 1956, an ongoing civil war tore the country apart; many Nuer temporarily fled to neighboring countries, and their herds were drastically reduced. This civil war ended in 1972 after the south, an area populated by many different ethnic groups, was given regional autonomy.

In 1983 the Sudanese government adopted sharia (Islamic holy) law, triggering another civil war between the Muslim north and the largely non-Muslim south. Conflict between the north and south continued throughout the 1990s despite numerous peace talks. The Sudan People's Liberation Movement (SPLM) and its military arm, the Sudan People's Liberation Army (SPLA), waged a continuous guerrilla war against government forces until a ceasefire was finally agreed in 2002 and a final end to hostilities in 2005.

CULTURE

The vast majority of Nuer are seminomadic pastoralists who rear cattle, an activity they combine with growing crops. The Nuer live in a region that is largely savanna (grasslands with scattered tree and shrubs), but some of their land is in the Sudd—a seasonally swampy region. During the rainy season, from May to December, the pastures around the rivers flood and become uninhabitable swamps, so the Nuer move to settlements on higher ground. During this season, the women cultivate crops such as peanuts, millet, and corn, while the men graze their herds nearby. As the swamps dry out during the dry season, from January to May, the Nuer men and their herds follow the receding rivers to new pastures.

In the 1970s, drilling for oil by the U.S. company Chevron brought trucks and bulldozers to Nuer territory. Many Nuer took work on oil rigs. Production was stopped indefinitely in 1986, however, after several Chevron employ-

---

Nuer time line

C.E.

ca. 1000 Nilotic peoples settled in region to the far southwest of Bahr al Ghazal River.

ca. 1700s Nuer people begin to migrate eastward.

1821 Trade routes opened from north to south Sudan, leading to a reduced southern population through disease and slave trading.

1840s–50s Arab slave trade develops in Nuer territory; Nuer are targeted by slave raiders.

ca. 1850 Active period of eastward Nuer migrations begins.

1898 Britain and Egypt colonize Sudan. Boundaries between Nuer and Dinka fixed.

1955–72 First Sudanese civil war between north and south

1956 Sudanese independence

1972 End of first Sudanese civil war; south granted regional autonomy.

1983–2002 Second Sudanese civil war; the south is devastated by government forces and fighting ends with a ceasefire.

See also SUDANESE: NATIONALITY

---

ees were kidnapped and murdered by rebels. Although the lifestyle of many Nuer was altered from seminomadic pastoralism to wage labor, the work brought in much-needed cash for families and villages.

Cattle are central to the Nuer way of life and are rarely killed for their meat alone. Cows are important as they provide milk; the Nuer milk-based diet is supplemented by some fishing and hunting. Cattle are important in many other ways. The prestige of the head of the household is determined by the size of the herd owned by the family. Cattle are sometimes sacrificed in religious rituals, and they are presented by the groom to his bride's family upon marriage. Young men often take a name based on the color of their favorite bull.

Because of their major role in Nuer culture, cattle are often the source of conflict; a cow owned by one man might eat the crops of another, for instance. They are also often the means of resolving conflicts, however, and not just those caused by cattle. Serious disputes are referred to the *kuuarmuon* (the chief and local magistrate), who determines the appropriate compensation, which is often takes the form of a payment of cattle.

Government and Society

The Nuer are organized into many clans. Territory and other resources are divided by clans.

Members of a particular clan do not marry one another. Upon marriage, the Nuer, like many African people, practice a system called bride-wealth, which involves a gift—usually cattle—given by the bridegroom to the bride's family. An ideal arrangement might be a gift of 40 cows to be given to the father of the bride-to-be; these would then be distributed to the bride's relatives. Few can afford this amount while they are at war, however. Bride-wealth does not represent payment for the woman but compensation for her family's loss of a working member. It is also considered a token of respect. Marriages are considered legal only after the bride-wealth has been received in full.

Children are important in that they link the families of their mother and father. This is believed to reduce potential conflicts between families because they share an interest in the child's well-being. In Nuer eyes a marriage is not finalized until the woman has given birth to at least two children. This, combined with the fact that it may take many years to complete the bride-wealth, makes Nuer marriages a lengthy process.

Nuer couples can divorce, but bride-wealth complicates this if there are children. With no children, the bride's family returns all the bride-wealth, and the couple is free to divorce and remarry. If the couple has had only one child, the husband can ask for the bride-wealth to be returned, but some will be retained by the bride's family in exchange for the one child, who remains part of the husband's family. If more children are born, the bride's family will be justified in retaining more or all of the bride-wealth, making divorce an expensive option for the husband.

Religion

Although some Nuer have converted to Christianity, the vast majority follow the Nuer religion, which is centered around a creator god called Kowth. The Nuer pray to Kowth for health and good fortune and offer sacrifices of cattle. There is no organized hierarchy of religious officials, though some people act as diviners and healers. According to Nuer religion, the first Nuer, Djagay, came out of a hole in the ground.

See also SUDANESE: NATIONALITY

FURTHER READING

Stephanie Beswick. *Sudan's Blood Memory: The Legacy of War, Ethnicity, and Slavery in Early South Sudan* (Rochester, N.Y.: University of Rochester Press, 2004).

———. *The Nuer, a Description of the Modes of Livelihood and Political Institutions of a Nilotic People* (Oxford, U.K.: Clarendon Press, 1940).

Sharon Elaine Hutchinson. *Nuer Dilemmas: Coping with Money, War, and the State* (Berkeley: University of California Press, 1996).

E. E. Evans-Pritchard. *Nuer Religion* (Oxford, U.K.: Clarendon Press, 1956).

Douglas Hamilton Johnson. *Nuer Prophets: A History of Prophecy from the Upper Nile in the Nineteenth and Twentieth Centuries.* Oxford Studies in Social and Cultural Anthropology (Oxford, U.K.: Clarendon Press, 1997).

Douglas Hamilton Johnson. *The Root Causes of Sudan's Civil Wars* (London: International African Institute, 2004).

Nupe

The Nupe people live in west-central Nigeria. Their language is related to that of the YORUBA and the IGBO.

Nuristanis

Nuristanis (Nuri, Kaffir, or Kafir, the latter two names from the Arabic for "infidel" or "unbeliever") are an Afghani people. Their homeland is Nuristan, which is in the remote Hindu Kush mountain area northeast of Kabul, Afghanistan, largely centered in the northern areas of Nangarhar province and the adjoining Chitral area of Pakistan. Nuristanis are estimated to number about 65,000 in Afghanistan and about 3,000 in Pakistan. They speak Nuristani, an Indo-European language of the Indo-Aryan subgroup, which also includes Hindi and Urdu. Historically the Nuristanis were designated *kaffir* (or *kafir*)—"unbelievers"— and their territory Kafiristan, "the land of the infidels," because they continued to practice their polytheistic religion long after Islam had become dominant in the region. The remoteness of their territory, some of which is accessible only by footpath, allowed them to maintain their distinctive culture and religion. However, at the end of the 19th century, Abd al-Rahman Khan, the Afghani prince under whose leadership the boundaries of modern Afghanistan were largely defined, extended his sovereignty to Kafiristan and forced the inhabitants to convert to Sunni Islam. Their territory was then renamed Nuristan, "land of light." While most Nuristanis are dark haired and brown eyed, there are also a number of blue-eyed blondes in the population, seemingly providing support for the popular claim that the group descends from the army of Alexander the Great, which passed through the region in the fourth century B.C.E. on the way to India.

Nyakyusa

The Nyakyusa are closely related to the NGONDE of northeastern Malawi and inhabit the lands at the northern end of Lake Malawi in the southwest of Tanzania, just across the border and the Songwe River from the Ngonde. The Nyakyusa and the Ngonde languages are closely related BANTU languages. The Ngonde-Nyakyusa peoples originally came from Bukinga (meaning the land of the Kinga people) in the Livingstone Mountains, which run along the northeastern edge of Lake Malawi in present-day Tanzania. The Nyakyusa chiefs claimed descent from the Kinga, while the "commoners" were supposed to have descended from local people conquered by the Kinga leaders.

The Nyakyusa and Ngonde were famous for their age-system of social organization, which the Nyakyusa have not practiced, however, since the 1950s. Different generations lived in separate "age villages." Every 30 or 35 years there was a ceremony in which fathers handed over power, land, and goods to their son's generation and became priests. The last such ceremony held by the Ngonde was in 1913.

Nyamwezi

The Nyamwezi live in west-central Tanzania, where they are one of about 120 ethnic groups. Their name, originally Wanyamwezi (meaning "People of the Moon"), was given because they came from the west, where the new moon is first seen. Their homeland is known as Unyamwezi.

ORIGINS

Oral history holds that the region of Unyamwezi was uninhabited until the 17th century. Then, chiefly families began to arrive from various directions. The earliest records are from the late 1600s and concern the Galagansa, a western group.

LANGUAGE

The Nyamwezi speak a language called Nyamezi (or Kinyamwezi). In addition, many Nyamwezi speak Swahili (or Kiswahili), English, or both.

HISTORY

The Nyamwezi formed a number of semi-independent, self-governing units called *ntemi* (chiefdoms). A few powerful *ntemi* such as the Ha, Zinza, and NGONI dominated the others. By about 1800 traders from these groups were visiting the east coast—whose inhabitants gave them the name Wanyamwezi. The Nyamwezi gained a considerable reputation as pioneers of long-distance trade in East and Central Africa by organizing trading caravans. The principal trade was in iron—made and worked by the northern Nyamwezi—and salt. Later, copper and ivory became the main commodities. There was also some slave trading. During the 1800s the Nyamwezi bought guns, and some groups established standing armies. There were several wars among the chiefdoms and armed conflict with the Arab traders from the coast (*see* ARABS).

In the 19th century, a *ntemi* chief named Mirambo managed to establish his dominance over several chiefdoms. Mirambo's short-lived empire came into conflict with Arab traders but broke up soon after his death in 1884. During the 1890s German colonists took control of mainland Tanzania, which they ruled as German East Africa. Britain took over after World War I. In 1951 the British evicted 3,000 Africans from their land to make way for white farmers.

Tanganyika became independent in 1961 and, on union with the island of Zanzibar in 1964, became Tanzania. In 1965 the two parts of Tanzania were allowed only one political party each, and two years later the country adopted a policy of socialism and self-reliance set out under the Arusha Declaration. Attempts to reorganize Tanzanian society along socialist lines

Nyamwezi time line

C.E.

1600s Nyamwezi settle in present-day area of west-central Tanzania.

1800s Nyamwezi develop trade links with east coast.

1860–70 Mirambo controls Ugowa and begins empire building.

1871–75 Mirambo frequently at war with Arabs from the coast.

1884 Death of Mirambo; empire begins to disintegrate.

1885 German Protectorate includes Unyamwezi.

1898 First "hut-tax" collected by Germans.

1920 Britain administers Germany's East African colonies.

1951 3,000 Africans evicted to make way for white farmers.

1961 Tanganyika wins independence.

1964 Tanganyika and Zanzibar unite to form Tanzania.

See also TANZANIANS: NATIONALITY

A traditional Nyamwezi house

Although most people are dependent on agriculture, trading is still important. During the colonial era, Nyamwezi trading caravans to the coast ceased. Instead, the Nyamwezi were often engaged as porters. Many also came to be employed as migrant laborers, and this is still true today. For many years, the independent Tanzanian government discouraged private trade as part of its socialist stance. More recently, private businesses have been encouraged, and many Nyamwezi are now involved in trade again. The basic food is bugalli, a form of porridge made from grains and eaten with meat and vegetables. The Nyamwezi make beer from corn or sorghum, and also drink coffee and tea.

Government and Society

Nyamwezi society is very open and well adapted to absorbing newcomers, including those from other ethnic groups. People who are not Nyamwezi but live among them are encouraged to follow their own ways of life and not to conform necessarily to Nyamwezi traditions. This cosmopolitan outlook on life could, in part, be thanks to their long history of trade and traveling for commercial reasons. As a result, many people regard themselves as Nyamwezi even though their ancestors had no connection with any of the original groups. The political functions of the chiefs have now been abolished, but they still retain their social status.

Religion

A few Nyamwezi have converted to Christianity or Islam but neither of these religions have flourished among the Nyamwezi. Many still follow the Nyamwezi religion. Generally, the Nyamwezi believe in a supreme god, variously referred to as Likube (High God), Limatunda (the Creator), Limi (the Sun), or Liwelelo (the Universe). This god is rarely worshipped directly. Ancestor reverence is the main component of the religion that is practiced daily. The ancestors of each family are thought to affect the lives of their descendants. Chiefs' ancestors, however, have a more widespread influence over all the inhabitants of their former domains. People make offerings, mostly of grain but occasionally of sheep or goats, to show respect to their ancestors, having first invoked the help of Likube.

There are also spirits who are believed to influence the lives of people, and specific societies or cults are devoted to them. The Baswezi society, for example, recruits people who have

had limited success but great impact on all Tanzanians, including the Nyamwezi. Agriculture, in particular, was widely affected by villagization policies—the creation of new rural villages (*ujamma*), collectives, and large farming cooperatives. Although the planned improvements in agricultural production were never realized, social benefits in the area of health and education were achieved. After the retirement in 1985 of President Julius Nyerere—who oversaw the socialist era—the worsening economic crisis led to the abandonment of socialism. (*See also* Tanzanians: nationality.)

CULTURE

Many Nyamwezi live and work outside their homeland, where they are engaged in various professions. Nevertheless, for the majority, growing crops and raising animals is their livelihood. The territory of the Nyamwezi is undulating country, some of it forested or dry grassland, which is unsuitable for agriculture or grazing. There is a dry season lasting from May to October and a wet season from November to April. Farming is mostly confined to the wet season. The Nyamwezi still cultivate some of their land with hand hoes, but plows drawn by oxen or tractors are becoming more common. Cereal crops include corn, millet, sorghum, and rice. Other food crops include beans, cassava, mushrooms, onions, groundnuts (peanuts), spinach, and tomatoes. Fruit crops include bananas and oranges. The major cash crops are cotton, sunflowers, rice, and tobacco. The Nyamwezi raise large numbers of cattle and also keep, goats, sheep, and chickens.

been attacked or possessed by the Swezi spirit. Many people believe in *bulogi* (witchcraft) and attribute misfortunes or illness to its practice. Religious practitioners or diviners called *mfumu* are often consulted during trouble or illness; they interpret the belief system for their clients and use several methods to divine the forces active in a person's life and arrive at remedies. Most *mfumu* act as medical consultants, using herbal medicines. The Nyamwezi are equally happy to make use of modern hospitals and medical facilities.

FURTHER READING

Abrahams, Raphael Garvin. *The Nyamwezi Today: A Tanzanian People in the 1970s* (Cambridge, U.K.: Cambridge University Press, 1981).

Brandström, Per. Boundless Universe: The Culture of Expansion Among the Sukuma-Nyamwezi of Tanzania (Uppsala, Sweden: Department of Cultural Anthropology, Uppsala University, 1990).

——.Who Is a Sukuma and Who Is a Nyamwezi: Ethnic Identity in West-Central Tanzania (Uppsala, Sweden : African Studies Programme, Department of Cultural Anthropology, University of Uppsala, 1986).

Nyankore

The Nyankore are a BANTU people of East Africa living primarily in southwestern Uganda. They were the founders of Uganda's historic Ankole Kingdom, which was abolished in 1966 along with the NYORO, TORO, and GANDA kingdoms.

Nyaribari

The Nyaribari are one of the main subdivisions of the GUSII. The Gusii are a large ethnic group of western Kenya.

Nyika *See* MIJIKENDA.

Nyoro (Banyoro)

The Nyoro people live in the lakes region of northwestern Uganda. The main area they inhabit is bounded on its western side by Lake Albert, on the north and northeast by the Victoria Nile River, and by the Muzizi River in the southeast. The southern borders are less clearly defined.

ORIGINS

Nyoro history is centered around that of the medieval empire of Bunyoro-Kitara and later the Bunyoro Kingdom. Oral history attributes

---

Nyoro time line

C.E.

1000s–1300s Bantu speakers migrate to lakes region of present-day northwest Uganda.

ca. 1350–ca. 1500 Bachwezi dynasty rules over Bunyoro-Kitara Empire.

ca. 1500 Babito rule begins in Bunyoro.

ca. 1550 Bunyoro Kingdom at greatest extent

ca. 1830 Babito prince founds independent Toro Kingdom.

1859–70 Bunyoro-Toro civil war

1870–98 Reign of Omukama (King) Kabalega

1872 Battle of Baligota Isansa; British forces defeated.

1896 Bunyoro and Toro made British protectorates.

1900 Uganda Protectorate established; Bunyoro and Toro Kingdoms included under the Protectorate.

1962 Uganda wins independence.

1993 Buganda and Toro Kingdoms restored.

See also UGANDANS: NATIONALITY

---

the founding of the first Bunyoro-Kitara Empire to the mythical Abatembuzi (or Tembuzi) people. They were succeeded by the Bachwezi (or Chwezi) dynasty (ca. 1350–ca. 1500), about whom little is known with certainty except that they were a immigrant, cattle-herding people. The Bachwezi established a centralized monarchy over the local Bantu peoples. They had a hierarchy of officials and also maintained an army. After the death of the last Bachwezi *bakama* (king), Wamara, the Bunyoro-Kitara Empire broke up into several separate states, one of which was Bunyoro.

LANGUAGE

The Nyoro speak a language also called Nyoro, which belongs to the wider Bantu group of languages.

HISTORY

The Babito dynasty took control of Bunyoro around the start of the 16th century. The Babito were originally Lwo-speaking River-Lake NILOTES—peoples who migrated from the Nile River in present-day southern Sudan to the lakes region of modern Uganda. Under their first *omukama* (ruler), Mpuga Rukidi, the Babito took over the country from the Bachwezi but kept many of the previous dynasty's rituals and customs. Raids against neighboring peoples expanded Bunyoro. By 1870 it extended to the

---

NYORO

location:
Uganda

time period:
17th century C.E. to present

ancestry:
Bantu

language:
Bantu (Niger-Congo)

north and east of the Nile and to the west of Lake Victoria.

Bunyoro was governed as a loose federation of *saza* (provinces), each under a chief appointed by the *omukama*. These *saza* were semi-independent, and some on the edges of Bunyoro territory broke away to form independent states. During the long reign of Omukama Kyebambe Nyamutukura III (1786–1835), for instance, four of his sons turned against him. One of them, Kaboyo Omuhanwa, took the *saza* of Toro and established his own kingdom. Toro then became one of the border regions in dispute between the various Nyoro factions.

Omukama Kabalega (r. 1870–98) tried to unite Bunyoro once again and regain the ascendancy it had lost on the rise of Buganda, a kingdom to the southeast. Kabalega created the Abarusura, a standing army of 20,000 men in 10 divisions, each with its own commander. One division, under Kabalega's greatest general, Rwabudongo, went to the capital Masindi to maintain law and order. Omukama Kabalega defeated the British in 1872 at the battle of Baligota Isansa, when the British tried to set up an Egyptian protectorate in the northern part of Bunyoro. Kabalega later led a guerrilla war against the British for seven years until they deported him to the Seychelles in 1897. Toro and Bunyoro had already been made British protectorates in 1896. In 1900 they became part of the British Uganda Protectorate.

In 1962 Uganda gained its independence. In 1967 President Milton Obote abolished all of Uganda's kingdoms, including Bunyoro. From 1971 to 1979 Uganda was ruled by the dictatorial Colonel Idi Amin Dada. After he was ousted in 1979 by joint Tanzanian and Ugandan forces, the country was torn apart by civil war. After the end of this war in 1986, Uganda came under military rule until 1994. In 1993 Uganda's monarchies were restored but with ceremonial and cultural roles only. Solomon Gafabusa Iguru was crowned as Omukama of Bunyoro in 1994.

CULTURE

Most Nyoro are farmers, living in scattered settlements rather than villages. The most common cash crops are coffee, cotton, and tobacco. Bananas, usually beer-making varieties from which *mwenge* is brewed, are also used. The staple food is finger millet, although vegetables such as sweet potatoes, cassava, peas, and beans are also grown. Corn cultivation is rapidly expanding both as a food and a cash crop. In pre-colonial times, the Nyoro were cattle farmers, but the herds were ravaged by the wars and rinderpest (a cattle disease) epidemics of the 19th century. Now the tsetse fly—which carries both cattle and human diseases—prevents large herds from being kept in modern Uganda. Instead, most farmers keep a few goats or sheep and chickens.

Before Amin's era, Uganda had one of the richest economies in tropical Africa. Political insecurity, the expulsion of Ugandan Asians (who owned many businesses), hasty nationalization, and the civil war devastated Ugandan industries. This has affected the Nyoro as much as any other people in Uganda, despite improvements since the late 1980s, though locally based industries such as salt making and blacksmithing have survived. The Nyoro have made salt since the time of the Bunyoro Kingdom. Iron ore is plentiful, and the Nyoro have long been skilled blacksmiths. In 1990 Uganda and the Democratic Republic of the Congo agreed jointly to exploit petroleum reserves found beneath Lake Albert, and subsequent development of this resource has brought social changes to the Nyoro.

Government and Society

In the past, Nyoro people were divided into three main subgroups based on ethnic origin: the Babito (who took over Buganda from the Bachwezi), who always produced the hereditary *omukama*; the aristocratic, cattle-owning Bahima pastoralists (livestock raisers); and the Bairu cultivators, the largest group. While the Bairu are indigenous to the region, the Babito and the Bahima originally arrived as invaders. Intermarriage and mixing over the years, however, has blurred any ethnic basis for distinction between the three groups. Today, the divisions are more a matter of class than ethnicity or occupation, if they are considered at all. The Babito were originally Lwo-speaking peoples, while the Bairu spoke a Bantu language. All Nyoro now speak the same language.

Religion

The Nyoro are predominantly Christian, though a few are Muslims. Many Nyoro still follow the Nyoro religion, inherited from the Bachwezi Empire in which the rulers were viewed as hero-gods. Even after the Bachwezi dynasty ended, senior mediums of the Bachwezi gods passed on advice to the *omukama* on how to maintain his personal fertility, achieve success in warfare, and promote the fruitfulness of the land. As well as being thought of as the ancient rulers of the kingdom, the Bachwezi gods are each associated with a place, event, element, or idea. Examples include, Mugizi, the god of Lake Albert; Nduala, the god of pestilence; Muhingo, the god of war; and Kaikara the harvest goddess.

See also UGANDANS: NATIONALITY

FURTHER READING

David Kihumuro Apuuli. *A Thousand Years of Bunyoro-Kitara Kingdom: The People and the Rulers* (Kampala, Uganda: Fountain Publishers, 1994).

J. W. Nyakatura. *Anatomy of an African Kingdom: A History of Bunyoro-Kitara* (Garden City, N.Y.: Anchor Press, 1973).

John O'Donohue. *Gods and Ghosts: Traditional Religion in Buganda and Bunyoro* (Wandegeya, Kampala, Uganda: Journal of African Religion and Philosophy, 1997).

Nzima

The Nzima are an AKAN people. They live mostly in southern and central Ghana and across the border in Ivory Coast. The Nzima language (also known as Appolo) is a Bantu (Niger-Congo) language. The Nzima are principally settled farmers and are known for their traditional satirical *avudewene* songs, which are performed at annual religious festivals across Nzima territories.

Odjukru *See* ADJUKRU.

Oghuz

The Oghuz are one of the principal branches of the TURKIC PEOPLES and were the group whose migrations from Central Asia most affected the Middle East. The term "Oghuz" cannot be taken as a simple ethnic designation, since it refers more generally to those Turkic peoples who, following the collapse of the Göktürk Empire, migrated west beginning in the eighth century. The same group is also sometimes referred to as the "Western Turks." The Oghuz originated in the region known as Turan (a Persian-language term referring to the Ural-Altay area or to Central Asia in general). According to Arab sources, the Oghuz were present in Transoxiana, the area comprising modern-day Uzbekistan, Tajikistan, and parts of Kazakhstan, from the late eighth century. From this region the Oghuz later migrated into Anatolia and founded the Seljuk Empire (1037–1194) and the Ottoman Empire (1299–1922) (*see also* SELJUKS; OTTOMANS).

Oghuz Turkic is one of the principal subdivisions of the Turkic language family and is also referred to as Southwestern Turkic.

Ogoni (Kana; Khana)

The Ogoni live in the Ogoni region of southeastern Nigeria. They have come to world attention through their conflict with oil companies and

An Ogoni mask in the form of a bush pig

the Nigerian government over the use of their land to explore for oil. Ogoni activist Ken Saro-Wiwa, along with eight others, was executed by the Nigerian military government in 1995. International outcry led to Nigeria's suspension from the Commonwealth of Nations (a voluntary association of former British colonies). Commonwealth membership was restored in 1999 following the restoration of civilian government. Sporadic violence between Ogoni groups opposed to the policies of oil companies and government troops have continued since Ken Saro-Wiwa's death.

Okak

The Okak are a subgroup of the Fang of Central Africa. They live in Equatorial Guinea, Cameroon, and Gabon.

Okiek

The majority of the Okiek people inhabit the highlands of west-central Kenya, though smaller groups live across the border in Tanzania. They are sometimes also called the Athi or Dorobo, but these are confusing terms originally used by the Maasai to refer to many different non-Maasai groups. There are more than 20 different Okiek groups, including the Akie of northeastern Tanzania, the Digiri and Omotik of the savanna regions of west-central Kenya, and the Kaplelach and Kipchornwonek, who live on the southern slopes of the Mau Escarpment in western Kenya.

The ancestors of the Okiek were the Kalenjin, highland Nilotes who began dispersing from their original cradleland at the northernmost tip of Lake Turkana in present-day Ethiopia to East Africa during the first millennium B.C.E. The separate Kalenjin groups such as the Okiek emerged as the highland Nilotes spread out over the region and mixed with people already living there. Although Nilotic peoples are historically associated with cattle herding, the Okieks have historically been hunters and gatherers in forest regions. As a result, the Okiek, who are in a minority, have been considered inferior by their cattle-herding neighbors. Modern-day Okiek people farm, keep livestock, gather honey, and work in towns; hunting and gathering are now supplementary activities.

Omanis: nationality (people of Oman)

GEOGRAPHY

Oman is a nation situated at the southern end of the Arabian Peninsula. It has an area of approximately 115,000 square miles and is bordered by three other countries. Yemen lies to the southwest, Saudi Arabia to the west, and the United Arab Emirates (UAE) to the northwest. Oman's border with the UAE is complex because two enclaves of Omani territory are separated from the main body of Oman by UAE territory. The Omani enclave of Madha is completely surrounded by UAE territory and itself contains the smaller completely enclosed UAE enclave of Nahwa. The Omani enclave of Musandam occupies the tip of the Musandam Peninsula and borders the extreme northeast corner of the UAE. Oman's 1,300-mile coast extends along the Gulf of Oman in the north and along the Arabian Sea in the southeast. The coast of the Omani enclave of Musandam fronts the Strait of Hormuz at the entrance to the Persian Gulf. Omani territory includes a group of small islands known as the Khuriya Muriya Islands and the larger island of Masirah, both close to the Arabian Sea coast of the Omani mainland. At its closest point the territory of Iran lies just 21 miles away from the territory of Oman across the Strait of Hormuz, one of the busiest and most economically important sea channels in the world. The precise border between Oman and the UAE remains in some dispute.

There are three distinct geographical regions in Oman. A narrow, relatively fertile, coastal plain extends along the northeast coast. This is the most densely populated part of the country, and most of the urban centers, including the capital city Muscat, are situated here. The southern end of this coastal strip narrows to almost nothing and gives way to a very rugged rocky coast lined by cliffs. Inland from the northern coastal plain the Hajar Mountains mark the division between the lowland coast and the desert plateau of the interior. South and east of the mountains the bulk of the country's interior is extremely arid and very sparsely populated. The extreme southern part of the country, a region known as Dhofar, is also geographically distinct. This highland region receives substantial rainfall from the annual southwest monsoon and consequently is much more fertile and has constantly flowing watercourses. Dhofar is Oman's second-most densely populated region.

INCEPTION AS A NATION

The territory of modern Oman has been home to distinctive and influential civilizations since the beginning of recorded history. The Aad people are believed to have been established in part of eastern Yemen and western Oman from about 3000 B.C.E. A city known as Iram is mentioned in numerous ancient sources as a wealthy trading power in the region and as the source of the valuable fragrant resin known as frankincense. Over time Iram became an established part of Arabic folklore as a fabulously wealthy

---

OMANIS: NATIONALITY

nation:
Oman; Sultanate of Oman

derivation of name:
From the ancient historical name Uman

government:
Monarchy

capital:
Muscat

language:
Arabic is the country's official language, but English is taught to all school students. Minority groups speak Balochi, Urdu, and other Indian dialects.

religion:
The overwhelming majority of the population is Muslim. Up to 75 percent of the population belong to the Ibadi denomination of the Muslin faith, and most of the remainder is Sunni Muslim. There are small groups of Hindus and Christians.

earlier inhabitants:
Semites

demographics:
About 80 percent of the population identify as Omani, although these include significant minorities with Iranian, South Asian, or East African heritage. About 20 percent of the population is made up of resident non-nationals.

lost city. In the 1980s a group of archaeologists and explorers using data from space-based observation platforms discovered the ruins of an ancient city in the Dhofar region of Oman that are believed to be the remnants of the city of Iram. The city was probably abandoned before the first century B.C.E. There are numerous archaeologically important sites in the north of Oman, particularly along the coast, where evidence of Neolithic agriculture has been found as well as artifacts that demonstrate trade links with ancient Mesopotamian civilizations such as Babylon and Sumer.

From the fourth to the seventh century C.E. the southern part of the Arabian Peninsula came under the control of the Iranian Sassanid Empire (*see* SASSANIANS). The seventh century saw the emergence of Islam and the rapid spread of Muslim power across the entire Arabian Peninsula, including Oman. Until the 16th century Oman was a largely self-governing region under a series of hereditary Muslim imams and the wider authority of successive Muslim empires. Throughout this period the Omanis were a prosperous people heavily involved in maritime trade around the Indian Ocean and the Persian Gulf. At the beginning of the 16th century the Portuguese captured Muscat and other Omani coastal towns and established forts to protect their maritime trade routes. By 1650 the Portuguese had been driven out by the Omanis and an Omani trade empire encompassing Mombasa and Zanzibar on the east coast of Africa and parts of India began to emerge. The Omanis established trade links with several European nations and were involved in the East African slave trade.

Apart from a brief period from 1737 to 1749 when Iran invaded and occupied Oman, the country has been an independent self-governing nation for centuries. During the 19th century Oman lost its overseas colonies in Africa and India to the British and concluded a series of maritime and nonaggression pacts with Britain but never became a protectorate. Territories on the southern coast of the Persian Gulf, which had historically been included in the geographical term "Oman," did become British protectorates during the 19th century and were sometimes referred to as Trucial Oman or the Trucial Sates. These became independent as the United Arab Emirates in 1971.

Since 1749 Oman has been ruled by the Al Bu Said dynasty. On two occasions during the 20th century separatist movements threatened to divide the nation, but neither succeeded.

From 1913 powerful imams (religious leaders) began agitating for a separate state in the interior of Oman, and for a time the power of the Al Bu Said sultan was effectively limited to the northern coast. A British-brokered peace deal restored the sultan to effective control of the entire country in 1920. From 1965 to 1975 rebels in the culturally distinct Dhofar region in the south fought to secede from Al Bu Said rule. This rebellion was also defeated and the country remained unified.

Sultan Said bin Taimur, who ruled Oman from 1959 until 1970, imposed a strictly traditionalist and isolationist regime on the country. These were years of great economic hardship and repressive fundamentalist religious rule for the Omanis. The removal of Sultan Said bin Taimur by his son Qaboos in a bloodless coup in 1970 marked the beginning of a new era in Omani history and coincided with the start of the rapid growth of the Omani economy fueled by the export of oil. The last decades of the 20th century saw Oman emerge as a modern and increasingly democratic nation fully integrated into the global economy.

CULTURAL IDENTITY

Modern Omani culture has its roots in strong seafaring and mercantile traditions, the beliefs and traditions of Islam, and the wider Arabic culture of the Arabian Peninsula. African and Portuguese elements have also contributed. Oman is the only country in which the Ibadi denomination of Islam predominates; it is the faith of 50 to 70 percent of the population. Ibadis are also found in Algeria and Libya, but in far fewer numbers. The Ibadi denomination is believed to have emerged very early in the history of Islam, probably within a few decades of the death of the prophet Muhammad in 632 C.E. The Ibadi movement may have developed from the Kharijite sect of southern Iraq, although the Ibadis of Oman repudiate the association. Ibadism differs from the larger Sunni and Shii schools of Islam on several theological points, but many of its core beliefs are identical to those held by the wider Muslim community. In modern times the Ibadi have abandoned some of their isolationist tendencies, such as their reluctance to associate with non-Ibadi Muslims, but remain one of the more traditionalist sections of the Muslim world.

Oman has a diverse ethnic mix. Its close proximity to Iran and centuries of trade with East Africa and South Asia have brought many traders and settlers to Oman. As well as the

The Riyam Dome in the city of Muscat, Oman

Arab majority there is a significant minority of BALOCHS whose ancestors originated in southern Iran, as well as large communities of Indians, Pakistanis, Bangladeshis, and Sri Lankans. East Africans have also been a part of Omani society for centuries. The Dhofar region of southern Oman is separated from the populous north of the country by the inhospitable dessert known as the Empty Quarter and has always been culturally distinct. The indigenous peoples of the region speak several southern Semitic languages (known as the modern South Arabian languages), which are descended from the ancient Semitic languages spoken in the southern Arabian Peninsula before the spread of Arabic. The largest of these groups are the Mahra people, who speak the Mehri language, and the Qara people. Both of these groups have historically had closer cultural ties with Yemen than with Oman. Historically the Omani sultans' rule of Dhofar has been exploitative. During the first half of the 20th century, economic exploitation of the region by the Omani ruling family was particularly onerous and led to a bloody rebellion that lasted from 1965 to 1975. The rebellion was finally defeated with support from British troops, but it was a catalyst for the reforms in the country from 1970 onward.

Under the rule of Sultan Said bin Taimur, who came to power in 1938, Oman was almost totally economically and culturally isolated from the rest of the world. The sultan's rule was absolute and society was organized along essentially feudal lines. Running water and electricity were unknown across most of the country, building methods that had not changed in centuries continued to be used, there were very few paved roads or motor vehicles, and the bulk of the population lived by subsistence farming or fishing. The Dhofar rebellion, which began in 1962, highlighted dissatisfaction with the sultan's rule and increased the pressure for change. In 1970 Sultan Qaboos Bin Said deposed his father and quickly set about modernizing the country. Oman's growing revenue from the export of oil allowed Qaboos to invest heavily in infrastructure such as roads, electricity, and water distribution, and to rapidly develop an extensive public welfare program including the building of schools and hospitals. Sultan Qaboos remains absolute monarch of the state and rules by decree, although significant steps toward democracy have been taken. In 1997 women were permitted to stand for election to the national consultative committee (a body with limited advisory powers to the sultan) and in 2002 voting rights were extended to all citizens over the age of 21.

Omani society, like other societies in the Persian Gulf region, is strongly delineated by

Omanis: nationality time line

B.C.E.

sixth–fourth centuries The Achaemenids have either direct control or strong influence over the coast of Oman.

C.E.

first century Ptolemy I maps the Arabian Peninsula, including references to Dhofar and the market-place of the Omani.

third–seventh centuries The Iranian Parthian and Sassanid dynasties control Oman as part of their empires.

seventh century Islam is established in Oman. Iranian power is destroyed.

1507 The Portuguese capture Muscat and establish forts along the northern coast of Oman.

1650 The Portuguese are driven out of Oman by the Omanis.

1749 The Al Bu Said dynasty comes to power in Oman.

17th and 18th centuries Oman establishes a maritime empire than encompasses Zanzibar and Mombasa in East Africa as well as parts of India.

19th century Oman's foreign colonies are seized by the British.

1913 Control of the country is divided between Ibadite imams, who rule the interior, and the sultan, who rules the coastal area.

1959 Sultan Said bin Taimur regains control of the interior after decades of intermittent conflict with Ibadite imams.

1965–75 Rebellion in the southern Dhofar region

1970 Sultan Said bin Taimur overthrown by his son, who becomes Sultan Qaboos bin Said. Sultan Qaboos bin Said begins a liberalization and modernization program.

1997 Two women are elected to the Consultative Council for the first time in Omani history.

2002 Voting rights are extended to all Omanis over age 21.

2003 First elections to the Consultative Council under the new extended franchise

2004 Oman's first female minister appointed.

2007 Cyclone Gonu kills more than 50 Omanis and disrupts oil production.

---

clan or tribe. The Al Bu Said clan, which has ruled Oman since the mid-18th century, forms the elite of Omani society, and its members have held many of the most important positions in government and industry for centuries. Long-established and wealthy merchant families make up the second tier of Omani society, some of which are of Iranian or South Asian ancestry. These families became firmly entrenched as the nation's economic elite during the reign of Sultan Said bin Taimur and continue to benefit from their close association with the ruling family today. Although not directly involved in oil refining and export, they tend to have a monopoly on the supply of raw materials for government projects and to foreign companies established in Oman. A small but growing professional middle class has emerged as a result of the establishment of universal education but has had little success penetrating into positions of political power. The traditional power of tribal rulers, or shaykhs, who once enforced the sultan's authority at a local level has diminished considerably with the establishment of a centrally administered welfare state.

Male and female roles remain highly traditional. The public realm is regarded as primarily male, while females are expected to remain at home. Traditional male and female dress also continues to be common, especially outside of the main urban centers. Males commonly wear an ankle-length overgarment known as a *dishdasha*, which often indicates their tribal affiliation through color or the style of collar. Until recently all men wore a traditional Omani curved dagger, known as a *khanjar*, in their belts but this is now largely reserved for formal occasions. Women's attire is often highly colored and accompanied by elaborate jewelry, but in public a full-length black gown that covers the entire body is often worn. Face veils are common but not universal.

At the beginning of the 21st century Omanis were considerably wealthier and better educated than they had been 50 years before. The revenue from oil that has allowed much of this transformation is likely to diminish significantly in the coming decades, and Oman faces the challenge of building new industries to sustain its development. The tension between the established aristocratic class and a growing educated middle class is likely to increase as this transition is made, and even more so if the transition fails to be made.

FURTHER READING

Dionisius A. Agius. *Seafaring in the Arabian Gulf and Oman: The People of the Dhow* (London: Kegan Paul, 2005).

P. S. Allfree. *Warlords of Oman* (London: J. A. Allen, 2008).

John Burrowes. *Sultan Qaboos: The Remarkable Story of a King and His Country* (London: Motivate, 2008).

Christine Drake. *The Sultanate of Oman* (Seattle, Wash.: Market House Book Co, 2004).

Donald Hawley. *Oman* (London: Stacey International, 2005).

Oman, Ministry of National Heritage and Culture. *Oman: A Seafaring Nation* (Sultanate of Oman: Author, 2005).

Francis Owtram. *A Modern History of Oman: Formation of the State Since 1920.* Library of Modern Middle East Studies, 30 (London: I.B. Tauris, 2004).

John Peterson. *Oman at War: The Sultanate's Struggle for Supremacy* (London: Saqi, 2007).

Uzi Rabi. *The Emergence of States in a Tribal Society: Oman Under Sa'id Bin Taymur, 1932–1970* (Brighton, U.K.: Sussex Academic Press, 2006).

Omotic

Omotic peoples account for well over 1.5 million people divided into 80 different ethnic groups. Their territories range from the lakes region of East Africa to southern Ethiopia. There are more than 25 Omotic languages.

Omotik

The Omotik are a subgroup of the OKIEK of west-central Kenya. The Okiek are, in turn, part of the KALENJIN.

Oquies *See* AKWAMU.

Oring

The Oring live in Cross Rivers State, southeastern Nigeria, and farther east into western Cameroon. They speak a BANTU language.

Oromo

The Oromo are a large ethnic group living in Ethiopia. Other African peoples call them Galla, a name the Oromo themselves dislike. Their territory, Oromia, covers southeastern Ethiopia and part of northern Kenya. It is almost as large as Texas in the United States and was once an independent country.

The Oromo probably make up roughly half of the population of Ethiopia. There are nine main subgroups. They are the ARUSI, BARARETTA, BORANA, ITU, MACHA, RANDILI, TULAMA, WALEGA, and WOLLO. Altogether, there are about 200 different subgroups.

ORIGINS

The Oromo are a Cushitic people. The CUSHITES originated in the Ethiopian highlands and were the first food producers in East Africa. Historians think that the ancestors of the Oromo lived in Ethiopia at least 5,000 years ago. From the highlands of Ethiopia the Cushites gradually expanded to occupy most of northeast Africa, slowly migrating south and east to their present homeland.

LANGUAGE

The Oromo language, also called Oromo, belongs to the Cushitic language group.

HISTORY

The Oromo began expanding northward in the 1500s, and by 1563 they controlled about one third of Ethiopia. Sometime after 1600 they began raiding southward, and by 1699 they had reached Malindi, Kenya. In 1788 one of their chiefs, Ali, founded the Kingdom of Begemder in central and northwest Ethiopia. Other Oromo chiefs founded kingdoms in the early 1800s. Oromo chiefs served as ministers in the Ethiopian government, which they dominated.

In 1853 Kassa, a former bandit, overthrew Ras Ali of Begemder and married the successor to the Begemder throne. In 1855 he made himself emperor of Ethiopia, with the title of Tewodros (or Theodore) II. Later, he was overthrown by a British expeditionary force. In 1880 Menelik II, the AMHARA ruler of the Ethiopian province of Shoa, began to overrun Oromia. He became

OROMO

location:
Ethiopia and Kenya

time period:
16th century C.E. to present

ancestry:
Cushitic

language:
Cushitic (Afro-Asiatic)

An Oromo woman filling a container made from goat skin

emperor of Ethiopia in 1889 and by 1900 had completely conquered Oromia. Menelik made the Oromo into slaves, and he and Queen Taitu personally owned 70,000 of them. The unfortunate Oromo fared little better under the last Ethiopian emperor, Haile Selassie I (r. 1930–74), or under the Italians, who occupied the country from 1935 to 1941. Thousands of Oromo died in the civil war that racked Ethiopia from the 1960s to 1991. In this war, the Oromo and other ethnic groups strove to win independence. By 1993 only the Eritreans had attained it. Since 1995 the Oromo have frequently been victimized with Oromia virtually under army occupation, and many Oromo have become victims of summary rape, torture, or execution at the hands of government troops.

Numerous Oromo groups have continued to agitate for independence through political and military means. The Oromo Liberation Front (OLF), established in 1973, is a lead-ing militant nationalist organization that has undertaken numerous violent attacks against Ethiopian government targets and has been increasingly active since 2005. The Islamic Front for the Liberation of Oromia (IFLO) was an Islamic group that opposed the government of Mengistu Haile Mariam and briefly took part in the coalition government that was established following his removal from power. Since 2005 the IFLO has renounced its strictly Islamic stance and renamed itself the Front for Independent Democratic Oromia. The Oromo Peoples' Democratic Organization (OPDO), founded in 1989 in opposition to the OLF has become a significant force in Ethiopian politics as part of the Ethiopians Peoples' Revolutionary Democratic Front (EPRDF) alliance, which won more than half the seats in national legislative elections in 2005. The OPDO also gained more than 70 percent of the seats in regional assembly elections for Oromia in the same year.

CULTURE

The Oromo were originally a cattle-herding people, moving from place to place. Many, particularly in the lowlands of the south, are still pastoralists. They keep cattle, sheep, and goats, with donkeys as beasts of burden. Some groups have horses and camels, and one small group keeps pigs. They do no hunting or fishing, and milk, meat, and butter are the main items of their diet. In the highlands they are sedentary farmers, growing cereals and coffee as well as keeping animals, including chickens and goats. Work is divided between the sexes: Men tend to do all the herding, while women do the milking and look after the plants. The Oromo cultivate the soil with plows drawn by pairs of oxen.

Clothing varies from one subgroup to another. In isolated areas traditional dress predominates. This includes, for men, a *waya*, a togalike garment, or a short kilt, and, for women, leather skirts, often with a cotton top. Men generally wear their hair short, while women have many elaborate hairstyles.

Government and Society

In their days of independence, the Oromo were governed under a democratic system called the *gadaa*, a system that has been in existence for more than five centuries. The leaders were elected by adult males who had attained certain grades in the *gadaa* system. There were 11 of these grades, the first three being for boys. The sixth grade, also called *gadaa*, was that of the ruling class. Its members held office for only eight years. After that they became advisers for three grades, totaling 24 years. At the final grade they were retired. The system provided training so that when men entered the *gadaa* grade they were fully equipped to run their local government. Under the republican government of Ethiopia, the system has declined and many of its attributes are banned, though in principle it still exists.

The Oromo have a rich culture, which is slowly being eroded by their position in Ethiopia. They had their own calendar, based on a lunar month of 29 days. The Oromian year is 354 days long, so their calendar is out of step with the sun. Each day of the month has its own name, but as there are only 27 names; each month begins on a different day. In many parts of Oromia, the Oromo calendar has given way to the Muslim calendar.

Oromo blacksmiths make tools, spears, and other objects from iron. Goldsmiths make ornamental work such as bracelets from gold, which is panned in Oromia, and from silver. The silver is imported, mainly in the form of Maria Theresa dollars. These old Austrian coins were used as currency in East Africa for many years and were still being minted in the 20th century—always dated 1780. Oromo woodworkers fashion tools and plows, spears and bows, and simple tables. They make small barrels that are hung in trees as beehives. Some honey barrels are made of reeds. Weavers make plain cloth on simple looms.

Religion

Most Oromo follow either Islam or Christianity, and some still practice the Oromo religion,

Oromo time line	
C.E.	
1500s	"Great Migration" into highlands of Ethiopia
1600s–1700s	Oromo begin to expand southward and settle.
1788	Begemder Kingdom founded.
1825–50	Sudanese slave trade flourishing in Oromia.
1850s–90s	Oromo monarchies in southwest Ethiopia
1853	Begemder king overthrown.
1889–96	Oromo influence in decline in East Africa
1935–41	Ethiopia invaded and occupied by Italy.
1961	Ethiopian civil war begins.
1974	Military coup overthrows Haile Selassie I; Ethiopia declared a socialist state.
1975	Oromo Liberation Front (OLF) formed; active near Kenyan and Sudanese borders.
1977	Mengistu Haile Mariam takes power in Ethiopia.
1980s	Severe droughts cause famine throughout decade. OLF support increases.
1991	Mengistu loses power; OLF part of new government; end of civil war, and Eritrean liberation from Ethiopia follows.
1992	OLF leaves government after dispute; renews rebellion; 20,000 Oromo detained.
1994	Ethiopia organized into nine states based on ethnicity; Oromo state formed.
1995	Small OLF bands still active. Dr. Negasso Gidado elected Ethiopian president; 280 Oromo rebels on trial
2005	Oromo Peoples' Democratic Organization (OPDO) wins 70 percent of seats in regional assembly elections for Oromia and forms part of ruling national coalition.
2008	Oromo journalists claim 400 Oromos have been massacred in the Benishangul-Gumuz region of northwest Ethiopia.

See also ETHIOPIANS: NATIONALITY

The tomb of an Oromo holy man known as Shaykh Husayn. The Oromo traditionally make pilgrimages to tombs and shrines of this kind.

which features one supreme god, Waqaayo, plus a great many *ayanas,* or saints. Religious leaders are known as *quallus,* and their office is hereditary. There are also female religious leaders, *qalittis.* Some Muslim and Christian Oromo follow the Oromo religion at the same time. Islamicization was made easier by the Oromo's eagerness to resist the domination of the Amhara, who are predominantly Christian.

The Oromo believe in life after death. They used to hold a special prayer ceremony before the annual harvest, but the republican government of Ethiopia has made the ceremony illegal. The Oromo religion and its practices have survived mainly in southern Ethiopia. These practices include ceremonies to honor or celebrate birth, circumcision, marriage, and death.

See also ETHIOPIANS: NATIONALITY.

FURTHER READING

Mekuria Bulcha. *The Making of the Oromo Diaspora: A Historical Sociology of Forced Migration* (Minneapolis, Minn.: Kirk House Publishers, 2002).

Belletech Deressa. *Oromtitti: The Forgotten Women in Ethiopian History* (Raleigh, N.C.: Ivy House Publishing Group, 2003).

Asafa Jalata. *Oromia and Ethiopia: State Formation and Ethnonational Conflict, 1868–2004* (Trenton, N.J.: Red Sea Press, 2005).

Asmarom Legesse. *Oromo Democracy: An Indigenous African Political System* (Lawrenceville, N.J.: Red Sea Press, 2000).

Richard Pankhurst. *The Ethiopians: A History* (Oxford, U.K.: Blackwell, 2001).

Mengasha Rikitu. *The Oromo of the Horn: Cultural History: Past and Present* (London: Biiftuu Diiramaa Association, 2001).

Oron

Oron is the name of an IBIBIO language and the people who speak it. The Oron live in southeastern Nigeria.

Ossetians (Ossetes)

The Ossetians are a people of the North Caucasus who speak Ossete, an Indo-European language of the Northeast Iranian branch. The two main dialects are called Iron, or Eastern, and Digor, or Western. The Ossetians live mostly in Russia, where they number about 500,000 in a total population of 142.8 million. A small number of Ossetians live in modern-day Georgia, where they make up less than 1 percent of the population of 4.3 million and have agitated for independence since 1989, with sporadic violent flare-ups. The Ossetians are descendants of the Alans, whose ancestry can be traced back to the ancient Scythian and Sarmatian tribes who inhabited the steppes north of the Black Sea. In about the fourth century C.E., displaced by the Huns, the Alans moved southward into the Caucasus. There they developed ties with the Byzantine Empire and by the 10th century had converted to Christianity. In the 13th century the MONGOLS invaded, and the Alans scattered, some migrating to modern-day Hungary and farther west into Europe, others to China. Those who stayed in the Caucasus moved deeper into the mountains and abandoned their nomadism in favor of the agriculture and herding. They intermarried with the locals and by the 16th century had reemerged as an ethnically distinct group, the Ossetians. The majority are Orthodox Christians with Sunni Muslims making up about 20 to 30 percent of the population. Those who became Muslims converted between the 16th and 19th centuries, influenced by neighboring KABARDS, who had converted to Islam by the end of the 17th century and with whom Christian Ossetians have had a relationship largely defined by conflict. As with other groups of the North Caucasus, both Christian and Muslim practice among the Ossetians still shows strong undercurrents of the pagan beliefs of their ancestors. In 1944 the Digor, along with other Muslim minorities of the North Caucasus, were caught up in Stalinist purges and deported to Central Asia. In the late 1950s survivors were allowed to return to their homelands, although some remained in Central Asia.

Otman

The Otman are an AMARAR subgroup. The Amarar are, in turn, a subgroup of the BEJA. They are a Cushitic people, and the majority live in a large area bordered on the east by the Sudanese Red Sea coast (see CUSHITES).

Ottomans

The Ottomans were a TURKIC PEOPLE who founded one of the largest and most powerful empires in world history. At its height in the 16th and 17th centuries the Ottoman Empire encompassed territory spanning three continents: from southeastern Europe through the Middle East into North Africa and stretching from the Atlantic coast of modern-day Morocco in the West to the Caspian Sea and the Persian Gulf in the East; and from modern-day Austria and the Ukraine in the north to Sudan, Somalia and Yemen in the south. For 600 years the empire was the mediator of interactions between East and West. The Ottoman Empire came to end with the declaration of the Republic of Turkey in 1923.

The term *Ottoman* refers to Osman I (r. 1299–1324), the founder of the Ottoman dynasty who declared his independence from the Seljuk Turks in 1299 and himself conquered nearby tribes. His son Orhan (r. 1324–62) renamed the tribe after his father. The village of Sogut—located in what is now the Bilecik province of Turkey—where Osman was born remained the capital until replaced by Bursa, captured from the Byzantines in 1326. It was Orhan's son Murad I (r. 1362–89) who named the dynasty and who assumed the title sultan.

ORIGINS

The Ottoman dynasty emerged as an independent power in western Anatolia (modern Turkey) in the last decades of the 13th century. From the 11th to the 13th century Anatolia had been ruled by the SELJUKS. During the 13th century, however, Seljuk power faded and a number of small independent kingdoms emerged in the region. One of these independent states was the foundation of the Ottoman Empire.

Osman I's father, Ertugral, was descended from the Sogut tribe of western Anatolia. The Sogut were a subbranch of the Kayi (or Kai) subtribe of the Seljuks, whose origins lay among the Central Asian Turkic peoples whose westward invasions began in the 10th century. They reached Anatolia in the 12th and 13th centuries. Both the Seljuks and the Ottomans were descendants of the larger Central Asian OGHUZ (Turkic) Turks of the Ural-Altay region whose migrations westward had begun in the ninth century. Tradition has it that on his own westward journey Ertugral came across two warring armies, sided with the apparently losing side, turned the tide, and was rewarded by the victor—a Seljuk warlord—with the territory of Sogut.

The House of Osman ruled the Ottoman Empire until 1923, although the family's distinctly Turkish ethnicity was lost early in its history as the sultans intermarried with non-Turks to solidify political and military conquests or alliances and treaties.

As Osman expanded his territory he came into conflict with the Byzantine Empire to the west. Following Osman's death the empire expanded into the Balkans and the eastern Mediterranean. The expansion was briefly checked by Tamurlane's 1402 invasion of Anatolia and the subsequent decade of civil strife. The 1453 capture of the Byzantine capital of Constantinople by Mehmed II, "the Conqueror" (r. 1444–46 and 1451–81), signaled the resumption of Ottoman territorial ambitions. Though Mehmed's Italian campaign stalled at his death, Selim I

OTTOMANS

location:
Anatolia

time period:
13th century to 1922

ancestry:
Turkic

language:
Turkic

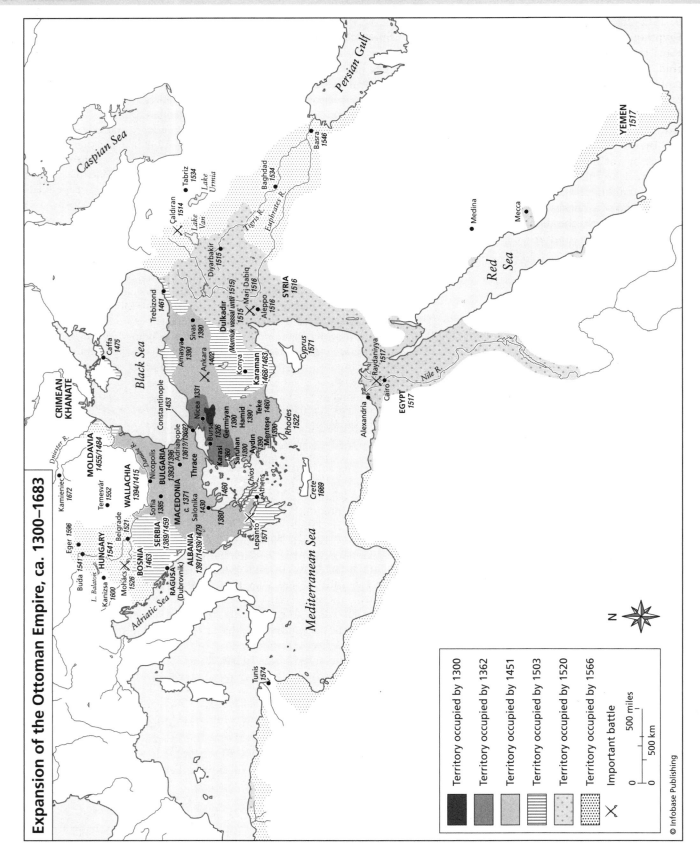

Expansion of the Ottoman Empire, ca. 1300–1683

Caspian Sea

Persian Gulf

YEMEN
1517

Tabriz
1534

Baghdad
1534

Lake
Urmia

Basra
1546

Çaldiran
1514

Lake
Van

Medina

Mecca

Red
Sea

Diyarbakir
1515

Trebizond
1461

Black Sea

Caffa
1475

CRIMEAN
KHANATE

Marj Dabiq
1516

Dulkadir
(Mamluk vassal until 1515)

Aleppo
1516

SYRIA
1516

Cyprus
1571

Sivas
1390

Amasya
1390

Ankara
1402

Nicea 1331

Konya

Karaman
1468/1483

Raydaniyya
1517

Cairo
1517

EGYPT
1517

Nile R.

Alexandria

Tigris R.

Euphrates R.

Dniester R.

MOLDAVIA
1455/1484

WALLACHIA
1394/1415

Danube

Constantinople
1453

Adrianople
1361/1369?

Bursa
1326

Germiyan
1390

Hamid
1390

Teke
1460

Mentese
1390

Aydin
1390

Saruhan
1390

Karasi
1460

Thrace

Rhodes
1522

Kamieniec
1672

Nicopolis
1393/1396

BULGARIA
1393/1396

Sofia
1385

MACEDONIA
c. 1371

Salonika
1430

Chios

Athens

Crete
1669

Temesvár
1552

SERBIA
1389/1459

Belgrade
1521

ALBANIA
1391/1439/1479

Eger
1596

Buda 1541

HUNGARY
1541

BOSNIA
1463

RAGUSA
(Dubrovnik)

L. Balaton

Kanizsa
1600

Mohács
1526

Lepanto
1571

Tunis
1574

Adriatic Sea

Mediterranean Sea

N

Territory occupied by 1300
Territory occupied by 1362
Territory occupied by 1451
Territory occupied by 1503
Territory occupied by 1520
Territory occupied by 1566
Important battle

500 miles

500 km

© Infobase Publishing

(r. 1512–20) resumed that expansion to take Egypt and to push toward the Red Sea. Suleyman "the Magnificent" (r. 1520–66) took Belgrade in 1521, besieged Vienna in 1529, and captured Baghdad from Iran in 1535. The diversity of the empire's peoples was further enhanced by the arrival of large numbers of Spanish Jews and ARABS in 1492.

The ethnic, religious, cultural and linguistic diversity of all these peoples broke down the Ottomans' original, overtly tribal outlook in favor of a more cosmopolitan discourse. This diversity also encouraged a system of administration sufficiently complex to accommodate a large degree of religious and cultural diversity and independence and to allow local political and administrative autonomy.

LANGUAGE

Ottoman Turkish evolved commensurate with the development of the empire itself. Old Ottoman Turkish, related to Anatolian Turkish and closely akin to the Seljuk variant of Turkish, was the language used until the 16th century. In practice, this language contained many borrowings from Persian and Arabic. Persian in fact had been the language of the Seljuk court. It has been argued that only via Persian did this Turkish came into contact with and borrow heavily from Arabic; Persian itself contained much Arabic by the time Turkish tribes arrived in Iran from Central Asia several centuries after the seventh-century Arab conquest of Iran.

Middle Ottoman was that language used in poetry and administration from the 16th century until the mid-19th century reforms known as the Tanzimat ("Reorganization"). Among the educated classes, knowledge of both Persian and Arabic was required—to such an extent that it has been argued that Persian, in fact, was the court language, if unofficially, in this period. As such, Middle Ottoman was unintelligible to the middle and lower classes.

New Ottoman is usually dated from the mid-19th century. There were several efforts in the 19th century to purge the language of its Persian and Arabic elements (see "Literature" below). Until 1928 Ottoman Turkish was written in a form of Arabic script that was also heavily influenced by Persian.

In 1928, following World War I, the dissolution of the Ottoman Empire, and the establishment of the Republic of Turkey, language reforms instituted by Kamal Ataturk also attempted to purge Persian and Arabic loanwords in favor of Turkish alternatives. As part of these

Suleyman I: The Lawgiver

Known in the West as Suleyman the Magnificent and in the Middle East and Asia as Suleyman the Lawgiver, Suleyman I was the 10th sultan (ruler) of the Ottoman Empire. His 46-year reign coincided with the peak of Ottoman power and cultural achievement and established the template for Ottoman government for centuries after his death.

Suleyman was born in 1494 in Trabzon, a coastal city in present-day northeast Turkey, the son of Selim I (r. 1512–20). His father, Selim I, had greatly increased the size and wealth of the Ottoman territories during his relatively short reign, most notable bringing Syria, Palestine, and Egypt under Ottoman suzerainty. As a young man Suleyman was appointed governor to a series of Ottoman territories before succeeding his father as sultan at the age of 26.

Suleyman I pursued the aggressive expansionist policy of his father. The year following his ascension to the throne Suleyman captured Belgrade (the capital of modern Serbia) and then turned his attention in 1522 to the island of Rhodes, which was then ruled by the Christian Knights Hospitaller, capturing it after a six-month siege. In 1526 Suleyman led an army that defeated the forces of the king of Hungary at the Battle of Mohács, effectively establishing the Ottomans as the most powerful force in southeast Europe. In 1529 Suleyman's forces besieged Vienna (the capital of modern Austria). Although the city was not captured, the siege demonstrated the Ottomans' ability to strike into the heart of Europe and reaffirmed their control of Hungary and the Balkans.

During Suleyman's reign the Ottomans also made territorial gains in the Middle East and Africa. Baghdad fell to Ottoman forces in 1535 during a campaign against the Persian Empire of the Safavid dynasty. Further campaigns brought lower Mesopotamia, the mouths of the Euphrates and the Tigris Rivers, and parts of the Persian Gulf coast under Suleyman's control. Large areas of North Africa west of Egypt also fell to Suleyman. At his death the Ottoman Empire was approximately twice the size it had been when he became sultan.

In addition to the military conquests achieved under Suleyman I's reign, the Ottoman Empire reached new peaks of cultural achievement. In much of the area formerly ruled by the Ottomans, Suleyman is remembered as the Lawgiver. During his reign he systematically collected and rationalized the legal judgments that had been handed down by his nine predecessors and formed them into a single body of imperial law known as the kanuni Osmani, or Ottoman laws. These were to form the core of imperial Ottoman legal practice for the next three centuries. Suleyman's reforms included reducing the tax burden on Christians living in the empire and the renunciation of anti-Jewish activities.

Education and patronage of the arts were also very important to Suleyman. Artists and craftsmen from all over the empire were attracted to Suleyman's court by his reputation for generous patronage. The period of Suleyman's rule has been called the golden age of Ottoman culture. Suleyman himself was a gifted poet, and some of his verses are still remembered as Turkish proverbs today. Lasting and visible monuments to this period of creativity include the Suleymaniye Mosque in Istanbul and the Selimiye Mosque in Edirne as well as hundreds of other monuments and buildings constructed by Mimar Sinan, the sultan's chief architect. At the time of Suleyman's death in 1566 the Ottoman Empire was the preeminent military and cultural state in the world.

reforms a modified Latin script replaced the Arabic script. In practice, however, modern

Ottomans time line

C.E.

1299 Osman I, founder of the Ottoman dynasty, declares independence from Seljuks.

1324 Death of Osman I; succession of his son Orhan I.

1326 Bursa surrenders to Ottoman forces; becomes Ottoman capital.

1354 Ottomans capture Gallipoli.

1385 Ottomans capture Sofia.

1389 First Battle of Kosovo; Serbs forces defeated but Ottomans retreat.

1394 Ottoman forces cross the Danube River.

1402 Tamurlane's invasion of Anatolia briefly checks Ottoman expansion.

1444–81 Reign of Mehmed II the Conqueror, interrupted 1446–51.

1423–30 Wars with Venice

1448 Second Battle of Kosovo; Ottomans victorious.

1453 Ottomans capture Constantinople.

1462 Armenian patriarch of Bursa becomes head of Armenian millet.

1463 Decree of sultan to Christians in Bosnia and Herzogovina.

1480 Ottoman forces invade Italy.

1492 Jews expelled from Spain are welcomed into the Ottoman Empire by Bayezid II.

1499–1503 Wars with Venice

1512–20 Reign of Selim I

1514 Ottomans defeat Safavid (Iranian) army at Chaldiran.

1517 Ottomans occupy Egypt.

1520–66 Reign of Suleyman "the Magnificent"

1521 Ottomans capture Belgrade.

1529 Ottomans lay siege to Vienna.

1535 Ottomans capture Baghdad from Safavids.

1543 Ottomans capture Nice.

1556 Death of poet Fuzuli

1557 Completion of Suleymaniye mosque in Istanbul by Sinan.

1571 Defeat of Ottoman navy at Battle of Lepanto.

1574 Completion of Selimiye mosque in Edirne by Sinan.

1622 Janissary revolt

Turkish as spoken in Turkey still retains much Persian and Arabic.

HISTORY

The Rise of the Ottomans (1299–1453)

The rise of the empire may be dated from the reign of Osman I. In 1299 Osman declared his independence from his Seljuk overlords, who had given his father, Ertugrul, the territory in which he founded the town of Sogut. Osman's forces harried the wealthy territories of the adjacent, increasingly weak Byzantine Empire. His victories against the Byzantines attracted more warrior immigrants and forced Byzantine forces to withdraw westward. Osman conquered Ephesus, then areas around the Black Sea, and, finally, the Byzantine stronghold of Bursa in 1326.

Osman was succeeded by Orhan, who took western Anatolia and married a Byzantine

1703–30 Reign of Ahmed III

1712 Ottoman defeat of Russian forces

1718–30 Tulip Period

1730 Death of poet Nedim

1774 Treaty ending Russo-Turkish War. Russians given right to intervene on behalf of Orthodox Christians.

1821–29 Greek War of Independence against Ottomans

1827 Battle of Navarino; Western forces defeat Ottoman navy.

1826 Janissary corps abolished.

1830 Algeria invaded by the French.

1832 Treaty of Constantinople grants Greece independence from Ottomans.

1838 British-Ottoman commercial treaty

1839–76 Tanzimat (or "reform") period

1848 Completion of Muhammad Ali mosque in Cairo

1853–56 Crimean War

1853 Completion of Dolmabahce palace in Istanbul

1856, 1859 Laws guaranteeing equality of all under the law, and Ottoman citizenship

1863 Promulgation of Armenian Constitution

1876 Proclamation of constitution

1877–78 Russo-Turkish War

1881 Tunisia comes under French control

1882 Egypt comes under British control.

1906 Establishment of Committee of Union and Progress

1908 Constitution restored.

1912–13 First Balkan War; loss of remaining Ottoman territory in Europe

1912 Parliament closed.

1913 Coup and "Rule of the Three Pashas"

1914 Start of World War I; Ottomans ally with Central Powers.

1915 Onset of Armenian massacres

1916–18 "Arab Revolt" against Ottomans; end of World War I. Partitioning of Ottoman territories under British and French mandates

1923 Proclamation of Turkish Republic

princess whose father he aided in the overthrow of the Byzantine emperor. The 1354 capture of Gallipoli gave the Ottomans a foothold on the European mainland. Orhan's son Murad I brought most of the Balkans under Ottoman control, took the title of sultan, and systematized the Janissary corps—a military force composed of the children of conquered peoples—that his father had initiated. In 1389, four years after Sofia had fallen to the Ottomans, Murad was assassinated during the First Battle of Kosovo with Serbian forces. His son Bayezid (d. 1403), born of a woman of Greek descent, took over in the middle of the battle. A year later the Serbs declared themselves to be Ottoman vassals, and Murad married a Serbian princess. In 1394 Bayezid crossed the Danube and, in the same year, commenced the siege of Constantinople. A crusade called to lift the siege was defeated, but Bayezid himself abandoned the siege to face the invading Tamurlane at Ankara in 1402. He was seized and imprisoned during the battle. At his death his sons fought among themselves. One son, Mehmed I (d. 1421), emerged as sultan to reunite the empire. The reign of his son Murad II (d. 1451) was marked by wars in the Balkans and Anatolia and civil strife. Murad expanded into the Balkans, and in the 1448 Second Battle of Kosovo defeated a coalition of western forces. Murad was succeeded by Mehmed II "the Conqueror" (d. 1481), his son by a Serbian woman. In 1453 Mehmed II captured Constantinople, ending the Byzantine Empire, and named it his capital (the name of "Istanbul" in fact predated the capture). His 1456 siege of Belgrade failed, but Mehmed did seize areas in the Peloponnesus and captured Trebizond in the early 1460s. Already linked by blood to the Byzantine royal family, Mehmed then declared the Ottoman Empire to be the successor to the Roman Empire and took the title Caesar (or Kaysar), He invaded Italy in 1480.

The Empire at Its Height (1453–1699)

The seizure of Constantinople in 1453 marked the Ottoman Empire's emergence as the preeminent force in the eastern Mediterranean, southeast Europe, and western Asia. Mehmed's grandson Selim I (r. 1512–20) defeated Iran's Safavids in 1514 and then turned south to take Syria, Egypt and the Red Sea region. Selim's son Suleyman "the Magnificent" (r. 1520–66) took Belgrade in 1521, failed to take Vienna in 1529, brought Transylvania and Moldavia under Ottoman tutelage, and seized Baghdad from the Safavids in 1535. With the Ottoman navy in control of the Mediterranean, Suleyman solidified the empire's control of territory from Egypt into North Africa; he captured Nice in 1543.

The century following Suleyman's death witnessed defeats at the hands of the Europeans and Safavid Iran. The Europeans' defeat of the Ottoman navy at Lepanto in 1571 checked the empire's control of the seas, and defeat at the Battle of Vienna in 1683 marked the end of Ottoman overland expansion into Europe. The internal Jelali revolts, which spanned the later 16th and early 17th centuries, and Janissary revolts in 1622 limited the center's response to these external challenges, though under Murad IV (r. 1612–40) some lost territory was retaken.

The Sultanate of the Women and the Tulip Era

From the mid-16th century onward, however, the empire was also transforming itself from a state geared for war and expansion to one equipped to administer the territories it had so rapidly acquired. The bureaucratization of the empire in turn enhanced the standing and authority of the palace itself and, especially, the sultan as the center of Ottoman government. This transformation also enhanced the power of those with influence at the palace, including the woman of the imperial family and their retainers. The term "Sultanate of the Women" is used to refer to the period from the mid-16th to the late 17th century in which the mothers of young sultans acquired and exercised power on behalf on their sons.

The 18th century witnessed the beginnings an administrative decentralization of those portions of empire located furthest from the capital. In return for continued recognition of the center's authority, Egypt and parts of North Africa in particular acquired much autonomy. This period also saw a change in attitude toward Europe. During the long reign of Ahmed III (r. 1703–30), friendly relations with France were cultivated and, following the Ottoman defeat of Russian forces in 1712, the Russians made peace with the sultan. The name given the period, the "Tulip Era" (1718–30), derived immediately from the elites' preoccupation with the flower; more importantly, the term reflects the shift in the center's interests to peacetime pursuits. Selim III (r. 1789–1808), for example, was fond of music, poetry and calligraphy. Responding both to Austrian and Russian pressures and to Napoleon's brief invasion of Egypt in 1798, Selim reorganized the Ottoman military and administrative system along Western lines.

The Period of Reform (1828–1908)

The latter changes provoked domestic opposition among the most affected elements, chiefly the Janissary corps and certain clerical elements. Supported by key clerics, the Janissaries murdered Selim in 1807. The Janissary rebels were defeated in 1826 by Mahmud II (r. 1808–39). His reign witnessed Greece's winning of independence from the empire in the aftermath of the 1827 western victory over the Ottoman navy and France's 1830 invasion of Algeria. Mahmud nevertheless dismantled the Janissary corps and established a new military force, including a reformed navy, laying the groundwork for later changes. The reforms of the Tanzimat period (1839–76) included establishment of a conscripted army, banking changes, and the rise of a factory system of production.

In 1876 a constitution was proclaimed, backed by a group of reformers called the Young Ottomans, as part of a series of reforms these Western-educated elements believed would save the empire from decline. A military coup the same year deposed the ruling sultan and Abdulhamid II (r. 1876–1909) became a constitutional ruler but suspended the parliament. In the aftermath of the Russo-Turkish War of 1877–78 and the loss of Cyprus, the empire sought new alliances with the British and French to counter Russian power.

In 1908 the Young Turk revolution resulted in the repromulgation of the 1876 constitution and the reconvening of the parliament. The Young Turks were the ideological descendants of the Young Ottomans. Drawn from a range of the empire's different ethnic groups, the Young Turks advocated a more secular society and limits on the sultan's power but also an increase in the power of the state, to safeguard the empire. In the face of rising nationalist sentiments among the empire's various divergent members and the losses of Bosnia and Herzegovina to Austria-Hungary, Libya to the Italians, and the Balkans in the Balkan Wars (1912–13), the Young Turks were, in fact, committed to the empire. The loss of this territory engendered the 1913 coup and the "Rule of the Three Pashas," key ministers in the government during World War I who organized the Ottoman-German alliance. It was during World War I that the empire's Armenian population was charged with supporting Russian interests and experienced what has been called the first real genocide of the 20th century, though successive Turkish governments have rejected claims that the deaths that did occur were the result of official, systematic government policy (*see* ARMENIANS).

The Empire in World War I and Its Dissolution

The combination of the British-assisted "Arab revolt" (1916–18) and World War I led to the empire's defeat. Immediately after the war the empire was partitioned. Britain gained a mandate over Iraq, Palestine, and Transjordan, and the French gained control over Syria and Lebanon. Turkish nationalist elements meeting in Ankara in 1920 rejected both the partitioning and the Ottoman government in Istanbul. Two years later, these forces reclaimed Istanbul and abolished the Ottoman sultanate, with which the Ottoman Empire officially ended. The Republic of Turkey was declared the next year.

CULTURE
Economy

At its height the economic activity of the empire comprised agriculture, trade and merchant activity, and small and medium production.

In its early period cities were the focus of trade and merchant activity, and adjacent rural areas supplied urban areas with food and raw materials. The taxes and levies imposed on the goods passing between Europe and points further east that passed through the empire were an additional source of wealth.

As the empire expanded, the Ottoman sultans strove to develop key cities as important commercial and industrial centers. Bursa, the capital until the capture of Constantinople, imported silk from Iran, and its artisans created silk products for the imperial court. Edirne (Adrianople), located on the European mainland, was another commercial and light manufacturing center. After capturing Constantinople in 1453, Mehmed II rebuilt the city as an economic center. He built the city's grand bazaar, waterways, the great Fatih mosque complex, and the Topkapi Palace. In 1492 his son and successor Bayezid II (r. 1481–1512) welcomed ARABS and JEWS fleeing the Spanish Inquisition. The Jewish refugees introduced the first Gutenberg printing press and contributed much to the economic growth of both Istanbul and the empire. Orthodox GREEKS also played a key role in the life of the empire in this period.

Beginning in the late 1500s and especially in the 1600s, the Dutch and English maritime trading companies established a presence in the empire, Safavid Iran, the Persian Gulf, and the Indian subcontinent. Within a century the rise of the European trading systems challenged the empire's preeminence as the crossroads for the West–East overland trade, and the volume of some luxury items moving across the empire began to suffer. The influx of gold and silver that had been coming to Europe from the New World encouraged widespread price inflation and currency devaluation.

The 1838 British–Ottoman commercial agreement facilitated direct connections between British merchants and various Ottoman millets, thus bypassing the Istanbul-controlled internal trading system. The treaty reflected the onset of the Industrial Revolution in Europe and England. The consequent appearance of cheap European manufactured products in the empire began to damage traditional industries and trade.

Following the Crimean War (1853–56)—the origins of which lay in Russian efforts to counter rising French influence among Ottoman Christians, and subsequent British, French, Austrian, and Prussian assistance to the sultan—merchants and traders from the empire's European allies appeared throughout the empire in strength. These sought to reshape the economy even more favorably to their interests. The 1873 crash of the Vienna stock market severely affected the empire. The Ottoman government (known as the Porte) was forced to default on the European loans it had taken out to underwrite reforms. The ruling sultan, Abd al-Aziz (r. 1861–76), was eventually deposed as a result and a Council for the Administration of the Ottoman Public Debt was established. The OPDA encouraged further European investment in the empire, financing railroads and other industrial-scale activities. From 1890 to World War I, the empire's economic activity increased substantially, but based only on these large foreign investments. The latter included German investment in railroads.

Government and Society

The expansion of the empire encouraged greater bureaucratization. The sultan stood at the apex of the Ottoman government, but civil officials increasingly carried out judicial, financial, and other administrative duties, and military officials undertook other executive functions.

The sultan had a coterie of advisors and ministers. These included the various viziers of the divan (council). The Grand Vizier led the debates of the divan and reported its findings to the sultan; the membership of the Ottoman divan rose from three in the 14th century to eleven 300 years later. The name Sublime Porte, by which the Ottoman political center was later known, referred to the sultan's open court over which the Grand Vizier presided.

The Ottoman family's intermarriage with non-Turks led to growth in the household itself. The sultan's harem gradually developed its own internal administration. The mother of the sitting sultan presided over the harem. Beneath her in authority was the mother of the sultan's firstborn son, then his other wives and then his concubines. During the 16th and 17th centuries, during the Sultanate of the Women, the harem exercised considerable influence.

The palace also developed its own school system for the training of Muslim and non-Muslim government functionaries. Some thousands of the latter, in a process called the *devshirme* ("collecting"), were forcibly recruited from among Christian communities conquered by the Ottomans. The system had its origins among earlier Muslim states but made its appearance among the Ottomans under Murad I (r. 1359–89), himself the son of a Byzantine princess. The best and brightest of these youth were sent to the palace school system to become civil administrators. The remainder were consigned to the Janissary corps. Although these youth were formally required to convert to Islam, the practice of allowing non-Muslims into service further diluted the control of the empire by the original Turkish elites. The *devshirme* system was in decline by the 16th century and was abolished in the 17th, especially under pressure from Turkish elites who wanted their sons to be selected for training and service at court in preference to foreigners; this service thereafter became voluntary. The Janissary corps was abolished in 1826 following a series of revolts against efforts to curb their independence.

Initially the empire was administered through preexisting territories called *beyliks* whose leaders (*beys*) acknowledged Ottoman authority. In the 14th century a system of *sanjaks* was established. With the further expansion of the empire, the *sanjak* system became a secondary tier of administration subsumed under larger *beylerbeyliks,* presided over by a governor-general (*beylerbey*). These divisions also became known as *eyalets* or *vilayets* (provinces), and the number of these expanded greatly with later territorial acquisitions. These were subdivided into *sanjaks* and further into *timars* (fiefs). The latter was a form of land tenure granted a local administrator in return for services, usually military.

Outside the *vilayet* system were vassal and tribute-paying territories. Some of these served as buffer states between the empire and the Western powers, while others were small areas (for example, Mount Lebanon) deemed not worth the military effort to conquer.

The Tanzimat reforms were implemented to strengthen the empire against European influence. Many of these changes, such as the introduction of paper banknotes, the reorganization of the financial and military sectors and the civil and criminal codes, as well as the establishment of universities and a stock exchange in Istanbul, were in fact based on European models. The period also witnessed the abolition of the poll tax on non-Muslims, the lifting of barriers to non-Muslims' joining the military, and 1856 and 1869 laws that

Hagia Sophia in Istanbul. Built by the Byzantine rulers of Constantinople (the former name for Istanbul) between 532 and 537 the building was converted into a mosque and expanded after the Ottoman conquest of the city in 1453.

guaranteed equality under the law to those of all faiths and the creation of a common Ottoman citizenship. In 1863 the government approved an Armenian national constitution. The 1876 national constitution limited the powers of the sultan. Although the constitution and the parliament were suspended, the Young Turks reestablished both, and their Committee of Union and Progress dominated the political scene until 1918. The palace closed the parliament in 1912, but in 1913 the CUP seized power in the Bab-I Ali coup and set up its own government. The CUP was linked to the state's anti-Armenian actions during the early years of World War I. In 1918 many CUP members were put on trial by the sultan. The remainder were eliminated in 1926 in the aftermath of the empire's 1923 abolition.

Military Practices

Initially the Ottoman military consisted of large numbers of mercenary and *ghazi* warriors (fighters for the faith of Islam), the bulk of whom had settled in Anatolia after fleeing the Mongol invasions. These troops fought for the defense and expansion of Islam in return for booty. Orhan organized a standing army paid by salary and composed mainly of foreign mercenaries. These became so powerful that Murad I formed his own personal military force, including the Janissary corps, to counter the growing political ambitions and influence

of the standing army. The members of modern Europe's first standing army were paid salaries, had their own uniforms and distinctive music, lived in barracks, and considered the corps their own family.

In 1389 local conscription was introduced, and in times of danger local authorities had to provide fully equipped recruits for service. This force, called the Azabs, were also used as support troops for the main military forces.

The Ottomans also had a cavalry force, the best-known element of which was the Sipahi corps, also founded during the reign of Murad I. Initially also recruited via the *devshirme* system, by the reign of Mehmed II these were mainly ethnic Turks.

The Ottoman navy dated from the early 14th century. The force assisted the empire's expansion into the Balkans and the Black Sea, the wars with Venice (1423–30 and 1499–1503), invasions of Albania (in 1448, 1450, and again in 1497), the 1453 capture of Constantinople, and the expansion into Syria, Egypt, and North Africa. In the mid-1500s the fleet defeated European fleets in the Mediterranean Sea, and Persian Gulf–based forces challenged Portuguese interests. The navy suffered a minor setback at the hands of a Western alliance at the 1571 Battle of Lepanto, which was its first defeat. A year later, with new ships, the navy resumed its expansion. In the early 17th century the Ottomans were even able to raid coastal areas of Britain.

Naval defeats in the next century spurred the Porte's recommitment to the navy. By the late 1800s the Ottoman navy was the world's third largest. The economic misfortunes suffered by the empire in this period, however, meant that this force could not be maintained. German support for the Ottoman navy was a factor in the empire's alliance with Germany, but the Western allies disbanded the Ottoman navy after World War I.

Architecture

Early Ottoman architecture was heavily influenced by the Seljuk style, particularly a preoccupation with the single dome. Interaction with the Byzantine Empire exposed the Ottomans to an imperial architectural tradition, and the Ottomans sought a distinctive style that was nevertheless linked to the Byzantine tradition. This combination was visible in Istanbul's Hagia Sophia, the patriarchal basilica of the Eastern Orthodox Church that Mehmed II refashioned into a mosque following his conquest of the city in 1453. The new structure remained the city's central mosque for the next five centuries and was the model for many later Ottoman mosques. Sinan, a Christian by birth recruited into the *devshirme* system to become chief architect from 1538 to 1588, was responsible for more than 300 buildings, including Istanbul's famous Suleymaniye mosque. Under Sinan the empire achieved a unique style of expression that also built on the past. His masterpiece, the Selimiye mosque complex of Edirne, was completed in 1574. Subsequent mosques carried on this optimistic sense of identity.

In the 18th century Ottoman architects became enamored of the European baroque and rococo styles. During the Tulip period baroque styles were used in mosque architecture. The Armenian Balyan family, who dominated the center's architecture in the 18th and 19th centuries, successfully fused Ottoman-Turkish and Western architectural styles. The best example of their style, Istanbul's Dolmabahce Palace, completed in 1853, was the empire's first European-style palace.

The tastes and styles that dominated the capital to varying extents reached the empire's provinces, in Cairo's Muhammad Ali mosque, completed in 1848, for example, as well as in Damascus and Jerusalem.

Literature

The highly stylized Ottoman poetry known as divan poetry had its roots in Seljuk poetry.

Ottoman court-based poetry drew on both the Persian and, to a lesser extent, Arabic traditions of poetry. From the Persian came *gazel* poetry (based on couplets sharing a rhyme and refrain) and *mesnevi* (consisting of a indefinite number of couplets), and from the Arabic, most likely via Persian, came the *kaside* (derived from pre-Islamic Arabia, also couplets with a single meter, with every line rhyming). Persian poetical meters were adopted and many Persian and Arabic words were also incorporated. As its Persian counterpart, the Ottoman *mesnevi* possessed a literal—sometimes ostensibly romantic—and spiritual level of meaning. This genre of poetry was often heavily influenced by Sufi mystic thought.

The tradition takes its name from the term divan, referring to the collected works of a poet. The best-known divan poets included Fuzuli (d. 1556), who composed in Ottoman Turkish, Persian, and Arabic, and Nedim (d. 1730), of the Tulip period, who was well known for reinvigorating the genre with popular elements. The mainly oral tradition of folk poetry was based on the quatrain and was intimately associated with folk music. More than the divan poetry, this tradition was influenced by Sufi and Shii tradition. The Ottoman prose tradition in nonfiction comprised works of history, travelogs, and the writings of prominent Ottoman officials, biographies of important figures, and works in the "Mirrors for Princes" genre.

Works of fiction were composed using rhyming prose. Prose fiction appeared from the Tanzimat period, concomitant with reforms to the language itself that aimed to cultivate a spirit of national consciousness and to strengthen the empire by returning to the language's distinctly Turkish roots. European, and especially French, literary styles—the novel and short story and French poetical styles—appeared on the scene at the same time. The "New Literature" movement in the last decade of the 19th century witnessed an effort among prose writers and poets to promote Western, and especially French, notions of elite art. From the beginning of the 20th century and the appearance of the Young Turks, the idea of a pan-Turkish literature, shorn of Persian and Arabic influences, reappeared.

Persian tradition also influenced Ottoman miniature painting, both as separate works of art or for the illustration of manuscripts. The Ottomans also developed a distinctive form of calligraphy, the *divani* form of Arabic script, which was most popular during the reign of

Suleyman the Magnificent. Divani was used for all official decrees and correspondence.

The Ottomans were also known for their carpets and jewelry. Ottoman music, based in palaces and among Sufi orders, derived from Persian court music but achieved its own distinctive form by the 17th century. The expansion of the empire encouraged a diversified musical tradition, reflective of the musical traditions of the different peoples of the empire. The distinctive music developed in the Janissary corps influenced such European composers as Mozart and Beethoven.

Religion

The Ottomans were Sunni Muslims, like their Seljuk forbearers. At its height in the 16th century, however, the empire included peoples of many different faiths. Ethnic differences were not, however, officially recognized as the basis for organizational units. The millet system had its origins in the guarantees of religious freedom made to Jews and Christians as "people of the book" in the early years of Islam. In the Ottoman system, recognized confessional (religious) minorities were permitted virtually to rule themselves, with the heads of these reporting to the sultan.

Overall the empire was extremely tolerant of these differences. Thus, following his 1453 capture of Constantinople, Mehmed II, to keep the Byzantine church functioning, made the patriarch of the church chief administrator and overlord of the city's orthodox believers. In 1462 Mehmed brought the Armenian patriarch of Bursa to Constantinople and made him head of the Armenian millet. In 1463, following his conquest of Bosnia and Herzogovina, he issued a *firman* (decree) that guaranteed the rights of this region's Christians. Mehmed also established the institution of *hakham bashi,* or chief rabbi of the Jewish millet. Mehmed's successor, Bayezid II, his son from a Greek Orthodox noblewoman, welcomed those Jews (and Arabs) who, refusing to convert to Christianity, were expelled from Spain in 1492. He sent the Ottoman navy to rescue them and threatened with death any who treated the refugees harshly.

By the 19th century, several Christian and Armenian millets were in existence as well as the Jewish one. Non-Sunni Muslims were recognized as members of the Sunni millet.

The growing European presence in the empire allowed the Western powers to petition the Porte for, and receive guarantees of, the protection of their representatives, missionaries, and religious pilgrims visiting the Holy Lands. In a series of agreements called the "capitulations" signed with the Porte, these were to be subject to the laws of their own country, not those of the empire. The 1774 treaty ending the Russo-Turkish War gave the Russian tsar the right to intervene in Ottoman politics to protect members of the Eastern Orthodox Church. The French had made similar claims for Ottoman Catholics since the previous century, and an 1838 treaty between the British and the Porte reconfirmed these earlier capitulatory agreements. By these the empire lost even indirect authority over its millets. Each of the millets and many other ethnic groups in the empire also felt the stirrings of 19th-century European nationalism; these, for example, encouraged the Greeks' struggle for independence.

The Tanzimat reforms aimed partly to create a sense of Ottoman identity. The 1876 constitution established freedom of belief and equality of citizenship across the empire. The CUP, in its early years (1906–08), peopled by different ethnic groups, later turned against religious and ethnic minorities. The empire's Armenians were in particular scapegoated following the failure of an offensive against Russia in the early years of World War I.

FURTHER READING

Gábor Ágoston and Bruce Alan Masters. *Encyclopedia of the Ottoman Empire* (New York: Facts On File, 2009).

Walter G. Andrews et al., trans. *Ottoman Lyric Poetry: An Anthology* (Austin: University of Texas Press, 1997).

C. G. A. Clay. *Gold for the Sultan: Western Bankers and Ottoman Finance 1856–1881: A Contribution to Ottoman and to International Financial History* (London: I. B. Tauris, 2000).

Suraiya Faroqhi. *The Ottoman Empire and the World Around It* (London: I. B. Tauris, 2004).

W. Feldman. *Music of the Ottoman Court: Makam, Composition and the Early Ottoman Instrumental Repertoire* (Berlin: WB-Verlag fur Wissenschaft und Bildung, 1996).

G. Goodwin. *A History of Ottoman Architecture* (Baltimore, Md.: Johns Hopkins University Press, 1971; London: Thames & Hudson, 1987, 2003).

R. Hillenbrand and S. Auld, eds. *Ottoman Jerusalem: The Living City, 1517–1917* (London: Al-Tajir, 2000).

H. Inalcik and D. Quataert, eds. *An Economic and Social History of the Ottoman Empire, 1300–1914.* 2 vols. (Cambridge, U.K.: Cambridge University Press, 1994).

H. Lowry. *The Nature of the Early Ottoman State* (Albany: State University of New York Press, 2003).

L. Pierce. *The Imperial Harem: Women and Sovereignty in the Ottoman Empire* (New York and Oxford: Oxford University Press, 1993).

Donald Quataert. *The Ottoman Empire, 1700–1922*, 2nd ed. (Cambridge, U.K.: Cambridge University Press, 2005).

Ouagadougou (Wagadugu)

The Ouagadougou area a part of the Mossi. They live in and around the city of Ouagadougou in central Burkina-Faso.

Ouara *See* Wara-Wara.

Ouassoulounke (Wassalunka)

The Ouassoulounke are a Manding people. They live in the Wasulu region of southwestern Mali.

Ouatchi

The Ouatchi are an Ewe people living mostly in southern Togo but also in Benin.

Ovahimba

The Ovahimba are a subgroup of the Herero. The majority live in northeastern Namibia.

Ovambo

The Ovambo are concentrated on the high, flat, stoneless plains between the Kunene (Cunene) and Okavango (Cubango) Rivers in the far north of Namibia and the far south of Angola. The 150,000 Angolan Ovambo are one of that country's smaller ethnic groups, but the half million Namibian Ovambo constitute almost half of Namibia's population. Many Ovambo have migrated to live elsewhere in Namibia, where they work, either on a permanent or temporary basis, on farms, in mines, and as civil servants. Due to the policy of apartheid and South Africa's policy of "divide and rule," many people have come to reject being labeled "Ovambo," instead preferring to be identified simply as Namibians.

ORIGINS

It is believed that the Ovambo migrated to their present homeland from the northeast—in the area of present-day Zambia—sometime around the 15th or 16th centuries. The Ovambo have a close cultural and historical relationship with the Herero, who live farther south: Ovambo legend states that the two peoples are descended from brothers who parted when they reached the present home of the Ovambo, known as Ovamboland.

LANGUAGE

The Ovambo are a Bantu-speaking people whose main language is Ovambo, also called Ambo. There are linguistic differences between Ovambo subgroups, but their dialects are easily mutually intelligible.

HISTORY

In 1884 Namibia became a colony of Germany, but because of difficulties in controlling the smaller Herero and Nama population to the south, the Germans never took much interest in the areas of Ovambo territory under their jurisdiction. In 1915 Namibia (as South West Africa)—and with it much of Ovamboland—came under South African administration. The South Africans took more interest in Ovamboland, and in the 1920s and 1930s they crushed numerous Ovambo rebellions. The Portuguese had occupied the Angolan coast since the late 15th century, but until they ruthlessly asserted their claims to part of southern Angola in the early 20th century they took little interest in the isolated Ovamboland.

South Africa's policy of apartheid, introduced in 1948, was also forced on Namibia. In 1973, Ovamboland was declared "independent" by South Africa. This independence was rejected by the overwhelming majority of Ovambo and by the international community. An assembly of mainly South African–appointed chiefs was created. The chief minister, Filemon Elifas, was assassinated in 1975 for his brutal reign of fear, which was backed by the South African army and police. Absences from Ovamboland were allowed only with a work permit—and then without any accompanying family members. Frustration with this system and with the lack of opportunities in Ovamboland, resulting from overpopulation and overgrazing, led to the development of an Ovambo workers' movement.

In 1960 the South West Africa People's Organization (SWAPO) emerged from the opposition to South African rule. After more than 20 years of armed struggle, SWAPO led Namibia to independence in 1990. Although SWAPO has been accused by its opposition of being dominated by Ovambo, it upholds strong nontribal and nonracial principles. Ovambo,

OVAMBO

location:
Namibia and Angola

time period:
15th century C.E. to present

ancestry:
Bantu

language:
Bantu (Niger-Congo)

however, do make up almost half Namibia's population, and Ovamboland was in the front line of the guerrilla war, so it is not surprising that many of the organization's members and leaders are Ovambo.

CULTURE

The northern part of Ovamboland is open wooded grassland, but the south is more arid grassland. It is subject to two to three months a year of heavy rain that causes widespread flooding of the silt-covered plain, followed by nine or 10 months of drought. To adapt to these harsh conditions, the Ovambo have taken advantage of what resources are available. Cultivation is largely the preserve of women. The staple crop is millet, pounded into flour and eaten in the form of a dry porridge, while corn is produced for making beer. Beans, sweet potatoes, groundnuts (peanuts), melons, and pumpkins are also cultivated. Men tend the livestock: Cattle and goats are raised, but, due to flooding, local grazing conditions are not as favorable as they are to the south in Herero territory. Since the late 19th century, Ovambo men have traveled south to work in Namibia's mines or on the railroads, while many women have left Ovamboland to work as domestic servants.

Most Ovambo live in compounds (a linked group of houses) completely encircled by a fence. Husbands, wives, young men and women, and visitors all live in separate buildings. Encircling the compound is a cattle enclosure, which also includes safe storage areas for grain and other goods.

The western Ovambo groups have developed a reputation for their skills in copper and ironworking, making practical implements such as knives and hoes. As there are no iron or copper deposits in Ovamboland, it is assumed that the Ovambo knew the art of smelting iron before they settled in their present lands. Apart from metalworking, other major handicrafts include pottery and basketry.

Government and Society

A special feature of Ovambo society is its matrilineal succession. Children inherit from their mother or their maternal aunts and uncles. Only mothers are considered to be the immediate relations of their children, as suggested by the Ovambo proverb, "The family does not come from the penis"; the closest relative a father had was his own sister. A husband, wife, their children, and any elders make up the basic family unit, but the maternal uncle is regarded as the family leader, so he is accorded great respect.

Despite this matrilineal inheritance, official positions are the preserve of men. Social status depends on a man's ancestry, age, and number of cattle. Historically, the ruling elite had the means to survive extended periods of drought and build up grain stocks as well as distribute aid to the poor, thereby earning prestige.

Religion

The Finnish Missionary Society has had a continuous presence in Ovamboland since 1870, and its missionaries have established schools, clinics, and churches. The first baptisms took place in 1883. Most Ovambo are now members of the Lutheran Ovambokavango Church; a minority in Namibia are Anglicans, and in Angola a minority are Catholics.

See also NAMIBIANS: NATIONALITY; ANGOLANS: NATIONALITY

FURTHER READING

Maija Hiltunen. *Witchcraft and Sorcery in Ovambo* (Helsinki: Finnish Anthropological Society, 1986).

Ovambo time line

C.E.

ca. 1500s Ovambo arrive in Namibia.

1500s Portuguese establish colony in present-day Angola.

1884 Germany colonizes Namibia as South West Africa; Christianity introduced to the region.

1915 German South West Africa occupied by South Africa.

1920s–30s Numerous Ovambo rebellions quashed by South Africa.

1948 Form of apartheid introduced to South West Africa.

1950s–60s Main Angolan independence movements formed.

1960 South West Africa People's Organization (SWAPO) founded.

1966 Conflict between SWAPO and South African troops begins.

1969 South Africa's occupation of South West Africa declared illegal by United Nations.

1973 "Independent" Ovamboland homeland created in South West Africa.

1974 Portuguese revolution; Angola promised independence.

1975 Civil war breaks out in Angola. Autocratic Ovamboland ruler Filemon Elifas assassinated.

1989 Apartheid legislation repealed in South West Africa.

1990 Namibia independent; peace accord in Angola

See also ANGOLANS: NATIONALITY; NAMIBIANS: NATIONALITY

Lovisa T. Nampala, Vilho Shigwedha, and Jeremy Silvester. *Aawambo Kingdoms, History and Cultural Change: Perspectives from Northern Namibia.* Basel Namibia Studies Series, 8/9 (Basel, Switzerland: P. Schlettwein, 2006).

Frieda-Nela Williams. *Precolonial Communities of Southwestern Africa: A History of Owambo Kingdoms, 1600–1920* (Windhoek: National Archives of Namibia, 1991).

Ovimbundu (Umbundu)

The Ovimbundu form the largest ethnic group in Angola. They are concentrated around the Benguela highlands of central Angola.

OVIMBUNDU

location:
Angola

time period:
16th century C.E. to present

ancestry:
Bantu

language:
Bantu (Niger-Congo)

ORIGINS

The Ovimbundu emerged as a distinct group in the 16th and 17th centuries. They arose from the merging of two ethnic groups: the Jaga, a LUNDA people from northeast Angola who invaded central and western Angola and settled with the indigenous populations—the second group. The Ovimbundu were firmly established by the 1770s, with royal families providing both political and ritual leadership through the king and his counselors. Originally, they incorporated many of the warrior traditions of the Lunda, but these were diluted as the Ovimbundu became primarily a trading people.

LANGUAGE

The Ovimbundu language is called Umbundu.

HISTORY

The economic history of the Ovimbundu is largely a record of violent contact with, and then commercial exploitation by, Portuguese colonists beginning in about 1600. The slave trade remained an important element of the Ovimbundu economy until the early 20th century, during which time over 3 million slaves had been exported, mainly to Brazil.

The geographic location of the Ovimbundu kingdoms—between the coast and the peoples of the interior—promoted a rich trading economy in the 19th century, with the Ovimbundu acting as middlemen. By the mid-19th century, Ovimbundu trading caravans were journeying across the continent dealing in slaves, ivory, wax, and rubber. They were soon numbered among the greatest traders of Africa, with caravans sometimes comprising thousands of people. The height of the Ovimbundu economy was reached between about 1874 and 1900, when high-grade rubber became almost the

sole export from the coastal port of Benguela. Increased competition with rubber from West Africa, Asia, and South America led to a huge fall in the price paid for Angolan rubber, which was classified as third grade. Coupled with continuing injustices and exploitation by the Portuguese, this decline triggered the Bailundo War of 1902 and 1903.

The Portuguese occupation in subsequent years and the collapse of Ovimbundu caravan trading by 1911 resulted in widespread famine. In response to forced labor, heavy taxation, discrimination by the Portuguese, and repression of all political protest, the Angolan war of liberation began in 1961. Initially, it was fought by the Marxist-Leninist Movimento Popular Libertação de Angola (MPLA) and the Frente Nacional de Libertação de Angola (FNLA). The MPLA received backing from Cuba and the USSR. In 1967, when União Nacional para a Independência Total de Angola (UNITA) was formed, much of its support was drawn from the rural Ovimbundu.

Angola became independent in 1975, by which time the MPLA and UNITA were fighting each other in a civil war. UNITA received military assistance and arms from the United States and South Africa. By early 1976, the MPLA had taken control of most of Angola and formed the government, but it remained in conflict with the UNITA guerrilla movement led by Dr. Jonas Savimbi throughout the 1980s. Multiparty elections took place in 1992, which the MPLA leader José Eduardo dos Santos won. Savimbi refused to accept the election results, however, and there was a return to civil war, which continued until 2002 when UNITA agreed to a cease-fire.

CULTURE

The lifestyles of the Ovimbundu, and all other Angolans, have been drastically affected by the 25-year-long civil war. Combined with poor transport and marketing facilities, drought, shortages of raw materials, and the concentration of government spending on defense, the development of both agriculture and industry have been severely hampered. As a result, there are serious food shortages and malnutrition is widespread. The presence of an estimated 9 million land mines left over from the civil war not only endangers the lives of civilians but has left much fertile land uncultivated.

Although many Ovimbundu live and work in Angola's towns and cities, during the war there was a general population shift from cities to rural areas. Many urban Ovimbundu have fled to the rural communities of central Angola to avoid persecution. The civil war has created a large population of internally displaced people. In rural areas, the Ovimbundu have become concentrated in villages fortified against antigovernment rebels and government troops.

Most Ovimbundu make their living as farmers. Cassava is the staple food crop. Cash crops include corn, palm oil, palm kernels, cotton, coffee, bananas, and sisal (a fiber crop). Farming and cattle rearing are the mainstays of many communities—the Ovimbundu highland areas are relatively free of the tsetse fly (a disease-bearing fly), which prevents animal husbandry in much of Angola.

Government and Society

From the 17th until the 19th centuries, Ovimbundu society adapted itself to a cattle-rearing and crop-farming economy that was heavily involved in trade. During this time, a double-descent kinship system helped maintain social cohesion. In this system, each individual belonged to both a local patrilineal group and a more dispersed matrilineal grouping. Membership of the patrilineal group gave an individual claims to land and residence rights, while membership of the matrilineal group conferred the right to inherit movable property. Matrilineal kin also provided financial resources for trading enterprises and so underpinned the Ovimbundu economy. This dual system helped to separate village and chiefdom concerns from the inheritance of wealth gained from trade.

The economic and cultural domination of the Ovimbundu by the Portuguese, combined with the decline of the Ovimbundu trading economy, has eroded much of this system of social organization. In modern Ovimbundu society, the nuclear family of husband, wife, and children is now the basic social unit, and there is little distinction between matrilineal and patrilineal kin.

Religion

Over half of Ovimbundu people are Christian. Of these, over three quarters are Catholic. Ovimbundu religious beliefs are also still widely held. The Ovimbundu religion involves the belief that the chief and certain family members—especially his principal wife (*inakulu*)—are imbued with certain powers. Through

Ovimbundu time line
C.E.
ca. 1500s Portuguese begin settling on Angolan coast and start trading with the Ovimbundu peoples.
ca. 1580 The Jaga Lunda people settle in the highlands of Angola.
1902–03 Bailundo War fought against Portuguese colonization.
1911 "Year of the Great Hunger": The last Ovimbundu trading caravans do not return and many die from hunger.
1961 Start of Angolan War of Independence fought by the MPLA and the FNLA
1967 Jonas Savimbi forms UNITA, which recruits from Ovimbundu.
1975 Angola gains independence; civil war is being fought by Soviet- and Cuban-backed MPLA and U.S.- and South African–backed UNITA
1976 Government formed by MPLA.
1988 South African and Cuban forces begin to leave Angola.
1991 Peace agreement signed by UNITA rebels and government.
1992 First democratic elections are won by MPLA. UNITA refuses to accept election results and civil war breaks out again.
1994 Lusaka Protocol signed, but hostilities continue.
1995 Savimbi recognizes MPLA leader José Eduardo dos Santos as president and declares war to be at an end.
1999 UN peacekeeping mission withdraws as civil war resumes in Angola.
2002 Civil war ends as UNITA accepts a cease-fire agreement.

See also ANGOLANS: NATIONALITY

rituals and ceremonies, the chief and his family exercise power over the fertility of people, animals, and plants. Much of Ovimbundu art is associated with the cult of the sacred chief and royal family; the carvings on wooden statues, staffs, and musical instruments particularly reflect this.

See also ANGOLANS: NATIONALITY.

FURTHER READING

Linda M. Heywood. *Contested Power in Angola, 1840s to the Present* (Rochester, N.Y.: University of Rochester Press, 2000).

Merran McCulloch. *The Ovimbundu of Angola.* Ethnographic Survey of Africa: West Central Africa, pt. 2 (London: International African Institute, 1952).

Oyo

The Oyo are a major YORUBA subgroup. The majority live in Oyo State, western Nigeria.

Padhola (Adhola; Dhopadhola)

The Padhola live in the northeast of the Democratic Republic of the Congo and the west of Uganda. They are a Nilotic people sometimes argued to be part of the Luo cluster (*see* NILOTES).

Palestinians

PALESTINIANS

location:
Palestinian Territories and Israel

time period:
Seventh century C.E. to present

ancestry:
Semitic

language:
Arabic (Semitic; Afro-Asiatic)

The name *Palestinians* can be traced back to the Philistines, one of the SEA PEOPLES from the Aegean Sea, who arrived in the area identified today as Palestine in the 12th century B.C.E. They settled mainly on the coastal plain from what is now Gaza north to Mount Carmel, and their name appears frequently in the Hebrew Bible. The name for the land of the Philistines was taken into Assyrian as "Palastu," into Greek as "Palaistine," and into Latin as "Palaestina." The Arabic word is "Filastin."

The Palestinians of today are ARABS, both Christians and Muslims, who trace their heritage to the general area of the state of Israel and the Palestinian Territories, which include the West Bank (of the Jordan River), East Jerusalem, and the Gaza Strip.

ORIGINS

The Palestinian homeland coincides roughly with the territory the JEWS call Eretz Israel, "the land of Israel," and the fact that two peoples claim the same land has been the defining feature of modern Palestinian history and politics. An important point to keep in mind is that while the name *Palestine* has a long history, it was not always clearly defined politically, even though its inhabitants had a clear sense of their own connection to that particular land. The Arab population defined themselves in terms of family and tribal relationships and, through those connections, to specific villages or towns. While the Palestinians were not and are not differentiated from Arabs of neighboring countries in terms of language or ethnicity, their identity is rooted in a sense of place, a theme that runs throughout Palestinian literature, history, art, and scholarship.

The area has suffered from decades of political upheaval and violence, and while many Palestinians have remained in their homeland, many have fled or immigrated elsewhere. Worldwide, the population of Palestinians was estimated in 2006 to be 10.1 million. The Palestinians who live in the state of Israel are Israeli citizens and account for just over 20 percent of the population of that country, or about 1 million people (*see* ISRAELIS: NATIONALITY). Preliminary census figures for 2008 estimate the Palestinian population of the Palestinian Territories—that is, the West Bank, East Jerusalem, and the Gaza Strip—to be 3.8 million, indicating a 30 percent increase in the past decade and making this one of the fastest growing populations in the world. The Palestinian diaspora, which includes all those who have left their homeland, covers a wide range, from those living in poverty in refugee camps in southern Lebanon, Jordan, and Syria, to highly educated and successful professionals living in other Arab countries or in the West. As for those living in the diaspora, it is nearly impossible to estimate those numbers with accuracy because most countries do not provide population figures for this minority. It is thought that the diaspora population is at least 5.2 million. Of these, 2.7 million live in Jordan, Syria, and Lebanon and are registered as refugees with the United Nations Relief and Works Agency (UNRWA), established by a resolution of the United Nations in 1949 to provide humanitarian services to Palestinian refugees. As there has been no political solution to "the Palestinian refugee problem," in the words of UNRWA, the United Nations has repeatedly renewed the agency's mandate, most recently extending it to 2011. As of December 2007, the agency was providing education, health, relief, and social services to a total of more than 4.5 million Palestinians in the Middle East registered with the agency as refugees. (This figure includes the 2.7 million cited above, plus 750,000 in the West Bank and over 1 million in the Gaza Strip.) There are also sizable Palestinian communities in Europe, the United States, Latin America, and Australia. The large Latin American community dates from the Ottoman era (before 1918), when many Christian Palestinians emigrated, mainly from West Bank towns, including Ramallah and Bethlehem, establishing communities that continue to thrive in Chile, Brazil, El Salvador, Honduras, and Peru. Palestinians are such a part of the fabric of these societies that in the 2004 presidential election in Peru, both candidates were descendants of Palestinians who had emigrated there from Bethlehem in the early 20th century.

LANGUAGE

Palestinians are Arabic speaking, with some dialects so distinctive they can be traced to particular villages or towns. Many, especially those living or working in Israel, also speak Hebrew. English and French are also spoken among educated Palestinians.

HISTORY

Early History

The area defined as Palestine, homeland of today's Palestinians, was formally outlined under the British Mandate in Palestine, which went into effect in 1923, as part of the Western powers' division of the Ottoman Empire among themselves in the aftermath of World War I (*see* OTTOMANS). This does not mean, though, that Palestine did not exist before this. Many geographic names place Palestine in the center of Christian history and the life of Jesus—Jerusalem, Galilee, Jericho, and the Mount of Olives, to name a few. From the beginnings of Christianity, various Christian groups have laid claim (and disputed each other's claims) to sites such as the Holy Sepulchre in Jerusalem, where Jesus is said to have been buried. In the early years of Islam, in 636–38, Muslim armies spread north from their homeland in the Arabian Peninsula and conquered Palestine and neighboring Syria. Jerusalem is the third holiest city in Islam after Mecca and Medina, and it figures in some important events described in the Quran. It is from Jerusalem that the prophet Muhammad is believed to have ascended into heaven during his miraculous night journey. The site of his ascent is marked by the Dome of the Rock, the oldest surviving Islamic monument, built in 691–92, on a site abutting the Western Wall of the Jewish Temple, the holiest site in Judaism. In the early eighth century, under the Muslim caliph al-Walid ibn Abd al-Malik of the Umayyad dynasty, which had its capital in Damascus, the al-Aqsa Mosque was built, which together with the Dome of the Rock and a few other structures make up the 35-acre complex called the Haram al-Sharif, "Noble Sanctuary," the center of Muslim worship in Palestine.

Palestine, and Jerusalem in particular, was the prize sought during the Crusades, which were initiated in 1095, with the call of Pope Urban II to Christians to retake the "Holy Land" from the "infidels." In 1099 Jerusalem fell to the Crusaders, who established independent Latin kingdoms in Anatolia, Palestine, Syria, Jordan, and Lebanon. The renowned Muslim warrior Saladin (Salah al-Din) retook Jerusalem in 1187, although Europeans remained in control of some areas of Palestine. In 1291 the last of the Crusaders were defeated by the Mamluks, a Muslim dynasty centered in Egypt and Syria. The Mamluks maintained control until the early 16th century. In 1516 Palestine came under rule of the Ottomans, a dynasty founded by nomadic Turkmen in Anatolia, today Turkey, and it remained part of the Ottoman Empire until the empire was dismantled after World War I.

Zionism and World War I

In the 19th century Zionism, a movement advocating a return of Jews to Eretz Israel, found new resonance in Europe, and Jews, particularly those fleeing the pogroms of Russia in the

Palestinians time line

C.E.

636–68 Muslim armies conquer Palestine and neighboring Syria.

1099 Jerusalem falls to Crusaders, who establish Latin kingdoms in Palestine and other parts of the eastern Mediterranean.

1291 The last of the Crusaders are defeated by the Mamluks, who establish their rule over Palestine.

1516 Palestine comes under Ottoman rule.

1882 The First Aliya, or "ascent," of Jewish immigrants arrive, fleeing persecution in Russia and Central Europe. Immigration continues, with a Second and Third Aliya, ending in 1923.

1917 Under the terms of the Balfour Declaration, the British pledge to create a "national home" for Jews in Palestine.

1923 The British Mandate goes into effect in Palestine.

1936–39 Arab protests against British rule and Jewish immigration erupt into the Arab Uprising. In 1937 the Peel Commission recommends partition.

1947 A United Nations Special Committee again recommends partition.

1948 The independent state of Israel is declared on May 14; war breaks out, with Arab countries sending troops. The war ends in defeat for the Arabs, with an armistice in April 1949.

1950 The West Bank is officially annexed to the Hashemite Kingdom of Jordan.

1957 Yasir Arafat and others found the Palestine National Liberation Movement, or Fatah.

1964 The Palestine Liberation Organization (PLO) is founded by the Arab League.

1967 The Six-Day War ends with Israel capturing East Jerusalem and the West Bank from Jordan, and Sinai and the Gaza Strip from Egypt.

1973 The Yom Kippur (or Ramadan) War breaks out, as Syria and Egypt attack Israeli forces in the Golan Heights and the Sinai Desert but are forced to retreat.

1974 The United Nations accepts the Palestine Liberation Organization as representative of the Palestinian people and grants them permanent observer status. Chairman Yasir Arafat addresses the General Assembly.

1880s and 1890s, began emigrating to Palestine in growing numbers, joining an old, established Jewish community there. Their numbers were relatively small and included Jews not only from Russia and Europe, but also Jews from Yemen, North Africa, and Kurdistan. These immigrants were not necessarily united in religious motivation or ideology, although the ideas of the European Jewish thinker Theodor Herzl (d. 1904) were to have a profound effect on the end result, the founding of the state of Israel in 1948. Jewish immigration continued, known by the Hebrew word Aliya, meaning "going up" or "ascent." These waves are generally categorized as the First Aliya (1882 to 1903–34), the Second Aliya (1904–05 to 1914), and the Third Aliya (1918–19 to 1923). The Ottoman authorities and Palestinian notables showed some concern about the increasing numbers of these immigrants and attempted to control their purchase of land. The Ottoman government's wariness was based primarily on the fact that these immigrants were mostly Europeans, many of them from Russia, with whom the Ottomans had recently fought a war. Nevertheless the new immigrants were not always viewed negatively. While some Arab peasants were forced from their land when it was sold to Jewish settlers, others found work on lands acquired by Jews.

Another important current during the late 19th to early 20th centuries was European expansion of empire. Britain and France in particular staked their claims to various parts of North Africa and the Middle East, always with an aim of maintaining a balance of power among European interests. In 1914 World War I broke out, and soon much of the world was enflamed. Britain and other powers understood the strategic significance of Palestine. In an attempt to secure the support of European Zionists and Arab nationalists under Ottoman rule, Britain made conflicting promises that were to

1978 U.S. president Jimmy Carter, Egyptian president Anwar Sadat, and Israeli president Menachem Begin sign the Camp David Accords, in which Israel agrees to eventually grant the Palestinians "full autonomy" in the Occupied Territories.

1980 The Israeli parliament officially annexes East Jerusalem to Israel.

1982 The Israeli army invades Lebanon to destroy PLO bases there, with tens of thousands killed.

1987 The first Intifada, a popular and for the most part unarmed uprising, begins in Gaza and spreads to the West Bank.

1988 The PLO proclaims an independent Palestinian state in the West Bank and Gaza, and shortly after, Yasir Arafat declares the PLO's acceptance of Israel's right to exist and denunciation of terrorism.

1993 PLO chairman Arafat and Israeli prime minister Yitzhak Rabin sign the Oslo Accords, which are to lead to an independent Palestinian state.

1994 Rabin, Arafat, and Israeli foreign minister Shimon Peres are jointly awarded the Nobel Peace Prize.

1995 Yitzhak Rabin is assassinated by an Israeli student.

1996 Arafat is elected Palestinian Authority president. Shortly after, the PLO charter is amended, removing the call for the destruction of Israel.

2000 The Second Intifada begins.

2004 Palestinian Authority president Yasir Arafat dies.

2005 Mahmoud Abbas is elected president of the Palestinian Authority, but Hamas wins control of the PA. Western donor states cut off aid to the PA, declaring Hamas a terrorist organization.

2005 Israel evacuates Israeli settlements in Gaza and four on the West Bank.

2007 Battle of Gaza; Hamas and Fatah fight for control of the Gaza Strip. Fatah is defeated and the Gaza Strip comes under the de facto control of Hamas while the West Bank is controlled by Fatah.

2008 Peace talks stall as a new government is formed in Israel after Israeli prime minister Ehud Olmert, beset by charges of corruption, resigns.

have dire consequences for the Palestinians. In 1917 Britain made a pledge, known as the Balfour Declaration, after British foreign secretary Lord Balfour, to create a "national home" for Jews in Palestine. At the same time, seeking alliances with Arab leaders, Britain also promised independence to Arabs under Ottoman rule.

During World War I, the Ottoman Empire had joined with Germany and Austria-Hungary in an alliance known as the Central Powers. They were on the losing side, and in the peace talks held after the war, the victorious Allies divided up the Ottoman Empire largely along the national borders we see today in the Middle East. The League of Nations (the predecessor of the United Nations) awarded the British control of Palestine as a mandate, with the specific proviso that they were to honor the earlier Balfour Declaration made by the British, that is, to assist in establishing a Jewish homeland in Palestine.

In the period between World War I and World War II resistance to the aims of Zionism stiffened among some elements of the Palestinian leadership. Hajj Amin al-Husayni, a leading Palestinian cleric, was one of the most prominent opponents of Zionism in Palestine. During World War I al-Husayni had worked with the British recruiting Palestinians to fight in the Arab Revolt (1916–18) against Ottoman rule. Al-Husayni and many other Arab Palestinians believed that the British had promised independence and self-rule for Palestine once the Ottomans were defeated. Following the Balfour Declaration, however, al-Husayni became disillusioned with Britain's plans for post-war Palestine and began to organize resistance to the concept of a Jewish homeland in Palestine. At first al-Husayni's political efforts were directed towards the establishment of an independent Arab state, often referred to as Greater Syria, with its capital in Damascus and with Palestine

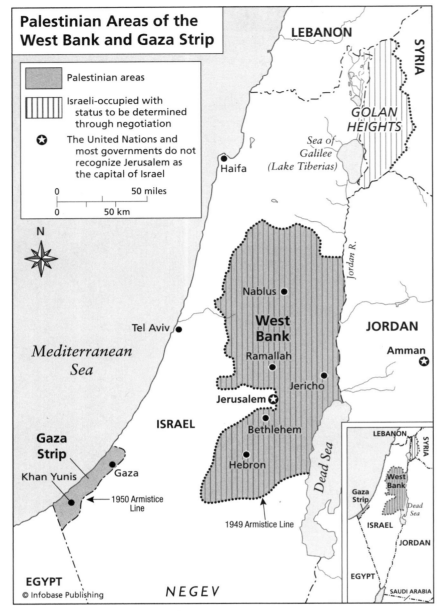

Palestinian Areas of the West Bank and Gaza Strip

Palestinian areas

Israeli-occupied with status to be determined through negotiation

The United Nations and most governments do not recognize Jerusalem as the capital of Israel

0   50 miles

0   50 km

N

LEBANON

SYRIA

GOLAN HEIGHTS

Sea of Galilee (Lake Tiberias)

Haifa

Jordan R.

Nablus

West Bank

Tel Aviv

JORDAN

Ramallah

Amman

Jericho

Jerusalem

ISRAEL

Bethlehem

Mediterranean Sea

Hebron

Gaza Strip

Khan Yunis

Gaza

1950 Armistice Line

Dead Sea

1949 Armistice Line

EGYPT

© Infobase Publishing

NEGEV

LEBANON

SYRIA

West Bank

Gaza Strip

Dead Sea

ISRAEL

JORDAN

EGYPT

SAUDI ARABIA

---

maintaining a balance between the Husayni clan, to which al-Husayni belonged, and the rival Nashashibi clan, members of which had also been elected or appointed to powerful positions in the British-run administration. The Husayni and Nashashibi families were among the most respected and wealthy of the established Palestinian Arab clans. Both families were at the center of nationalist and anti-Zionist movements in the first decades of the 20th century, but their political rivalry prevented them from forming a united movement that might have been more effective in achieving their aims. The British took advantage of this rivalry by ensuring that representatives from both clans held important positions, for example while Hajj Amin al-Husayni held the posts of grand mufti of Jerusalem (1921–48) and president of the Supreme Muslim Council (1922–37) Raghib al-Nashashibi, of the Nashashibi clan, held the post of mayor of Jerusalem (1920–34). It was not until 1936 that these rival clans achieved a degree of unity by forming the Arab Higher Committee. During this period al-Husayni controlled a secret organization known as al-Fedayeen ('the self-sacrificers'), which carried out anti-British and anti-Zionist activities, but he continued to engage in conventional political dialogue with the British as well.

The Arab Uprising

In the years that followed, there were numerous violent clashes in Palestine between Arabs and Jews, including a massacre of Jews in Hebron and Safed in 1929. Meanwhile, in Europe Adolf Hitler had come to power and Jewish immigrants began streaming into Israel. In 1936 Arabs staged a strike and boycott that was to evolve into armed resistance and a rebellion that lasted until 1939, known as the Arab Uprising. In response to the early unrest, the British commissioned an inquiry to address how the situation could be handled. In 1937 the Peel Commission issued a recommendation that the country be partitioned, giving the Jews a small area in northern and central Palestine, leaving the rest to the Arabs. Hostilities continued, however, and in 1939 the British convened another conference, this one issuing a White Paper declaring that the Mandate would end in 10 years with independence. Meanwhile Jewish immigration would be effectively limited to 15,000 per year until 1944. After that, Arab consent would be required for continued immigration, and restrictions were put the on sale of Arab land to Jews.

---

as one of its southern provinces. When Britain ceded control of Syria and Lebanon to France in 1920 the dream of a Greater Syria ended and al-Husayni turned his attention to the future of Palestine, and particularly Jerusalem, as a separate entity. In 1920 al-Husayni was convicted by the British authorities of inciting anti-Zionist riots in Jerusalem. In 1921, after having his conviction quashed, al-Husayni was elected grand mufti of Jerusalem, a post that was regarded as the preeminent clerical position among Jerusalem's Sunni Muslims. The following year he was elected president of the Supreme Muslim Council. Both of these positions were essentially in the gift of the British authorities who favored al-Husayni because of their policy of

Hajj Amin al-Husayni played a prominent role in the Arab Uprising. During the riots of 1929 he was widely accused of having instigated the violence, although evidence suggests that in fact he went to great lengths to calm the situation. By 1936, however, al-Husayni and other leaders had become convinced that open rebellion was the only way to stop what they saw as Britain's increasing support for Zionism. The formation of the Arab Higher Committee in 1936 was partly inspired by the general strike that started the uprising and one of the committee's first acts was to call on Palestinians to refuse to pay taxes. In 1937 the British moved to arrest the members of the committee but al-Husayni escaped to Lebanon and later to Iraq. Hajj Amin al-Husayni's nephew Abd al-Qadir al-Husayni also played a prominent role in the Arab Uprising and also fled to Iraq when it was finally suppressed. Abd al-Qadir al-Husayni was later to return to Palestine where he played a prominent part in the Civil War in Palestine (1947–48).

Britain and the rest of the world were soon engulfed in World War II. As German forces advanced across Europe, pressure mounted for the British to lift restrictions on Jewish immigration to Palestine. Zionist terrorist groups attacked British installations in Palestine, and the British were essentially fighting a war in Mandate Palestine, too. Hajj Amin al-Husayni made several attempts to form alliances with the Axis powers during the war and was active in producing propaganda for the Axis powers broadcast in the Arab world. Al-Husayni saw the Axis powers, particularly Nazi Germany, as potentially valuable allies in his aim to prevent the formation of a Jewish state in Palestine. There is no direct evidence that he was aware of or supported the policies that led to the Holocaust, but he was convicted as a war criminal after the war for his involvement in the organization and recruitment of Bosnian Muslims. He escaped after his conviction in 1946 and spent the rest of his life living in exile in Egypt and Lebanon.

The Establishment of Israel

As the war came to an end, and the full extent of Nazi crimes became apparent, calls for a re-thinking of Palestine were again raised. In 1947 the newly established United Nations sent a Special Committee to Palestine. This committee recommended partition, with the region including Jerusalem and Bethlehem to be administered by the United Nations.

The United Nations voted in favor of a plan to partition Palestine in November 1947 and the British withdrew from Palestine in May 1948. The conflict that took place during this period between Arabs and Jews living in Palestine is known as the Civil War in Palestine. Arab forces consisted principally of the Army of the Holy War (or Army of the Sacred Jihad), led by Abd al-Qadir al-Husayni, and the Arab Liberation Army, made up of recruits from several Arab countries and organized by the Syrian government. Jewish forces consisted primarily of the various elements of the Haganah (the Jewish paramilitary defense organization). British forces played little part in the conflict. Following the British withdrawal in 1948 and the almost simultaneous declaration of the state of Israel the fighting continued and several Arab nations became directly involved. This phase of the conflict is usually referred to as the First Arab-Israeli War or the 1948 Arab-Israeli War.

During the Civil War phase of the conflict Abd al-Qadir al-Husayni and his Army of the Holy War concentrated on attempting to isolate scattered Jewish settlements and Jerusalem by raiding Jewish convoys on the roads. These tactics were highly successful at first resulting in severe supply problems for Jewish populations and heavy losses for Jewish forces escorting convoys. Direct attacks on Jewish settlements were less successful, however, and Abd al-Qadir al-Husayni was killed in April 1948. As the conflict entered its second phase (the First Arab-Israeli War) Jewish forces began to turn the tide thanks to their greater cohesiveness and an influx of arms from foreign donors. The Haganah went on the offensive from April 1948 and rapidly defeated the poorly armed and disparate Arab elements opposing them. The death of Abd al-Qadir al-Husayni and the Jewish offensive had a profound effect on the morale of the civilian Arab population in Palestine; waves of Arab refugees intent on escaping the fighting rapidly depopulated large areas of Palestine.

Massacres were perpetrated on both sides. In April 1948 Zionist terrorists attacked the village of Deir Yassin, near Jerusalem, and massacred more than 100 men, women, and children, and this was to become, for Palestinians, the very icon of Zionist cruelty. In revenge, five days later Arabs attacked a Jewish convoy en route to a hospital, killing 78 people.

The question of precisely what occurred during the war has been the subject of much inquiry and debate, both sincere and politically

Edward Said: A Christian Wrapped in a Muslim Culture

Edward W. Said (1935–2003) was an enormously influential and widely respected Palestinian intellectual and voice for Palestinian independence. He once described himself as a "Christian wrapped in a Muslim culture," referring to the complexity of his cultural background. He was born into a Christian family in Jerusalem under the British Mandate and grew up in Jerusalem and Cairo. He traveled to the United States in 1951 to attend Mount Hermon School in Massachusetts. He graduated from Princeton University, then earned a Ph.D. in English literature from Harvard University in 1964. He spent most of his academic career at Columbia University in New York City, where he was eventually named University Professor, the most prestigious academic position at that institution. His early books include *Beginnings* (published in 1975), winner of Columbia's Lionel Trilling Award, which considered the notion of literary inspiration and was described by a reviewer as "an ingenious exploration of the meaning of modernism." The book that brought him widespread recognition (and, in some circles, notoriety) was *Orientalism*. Published in 1979, the book became the seminal text for "postcolonial studies," which takes as its starting point the notion that the way "the Orient," and particularly the Arab world, has been represented in Western scholarship is hopelessly tainted by implicit racism, imperialism, and cliché. The book was challenged and criticized, but nevertheless it started an entire new way of thinking about Western representations of the Eastern " Other."

Said was also politically involved. He became a member of the Palestine National Council in 1977 and helped draft the Palestinian constitution in 1988. His writings reflected his commitment to the Palestinian cause, among them *The Question of Palestine* (1979), *Blaming the Victims* (1988), and *The Politics of Dispossession* (1994).

Said was a deeply cultured man, described in the obituary published by the *New York Times* as a polymath. An accomplished pianist, he wrote about music for *The Nation* and collaborated with musicians including Daniel Barenboim and Yo-Yo Ma. The book he was working on when he died, in 2003 of leukemia, was *On Late Style: Music and Literature Against the Grain*, examining creative works produced late in an artist's life. His memoir *Out of Place* provides a detailed and often poignant depiction of, as Said phrased it, "an essentially lost or forgotten world."

motivated—did the Israelis undertake a deliberate policy of ethnic cleansing? Did Arab governments instruct the Palestinians to flee? Did they leave willingly, expecting to return, or were they driven out? As governments open more archives to inspection, historians continue to consider these questions. In any case, the end result of that war was that Israel came to control considerably more territory than was allocated by the partition; the Jewish population was soon bolstered by 350,000 new immigrants, most of them from Arab countries; 700,000 Arabs had become refugees; and something on the order of 450 Palestinian villages were destroyed. The events of 1948–49 are known to Palestinians as *al-nakba,* "the catastrophe." Since this time Palestinian refugees who fled during this period and their descendents have campaigned repeat-

edly for the so-called 'right of return.' Many Palestinians effected by the conflict believe they should be allowed to return to the homes and villages they abandoned, most of which are now within the state of Israel. The Israeli government has consistently refused to accept this principal suggesting instead that it can only be applied to locations within the Palestinian Territories or that financial compensation might be paid to those whose homes were within the borders of present-day Israel.

1948 to 1967: The Palestinian Fedayeen

Among the hundreds of thousands of Palestinian refugees that fled to neighboring countries such as Syria, Egypt, and Jordan between 1947 and 1948 paramilitary organizations soon began to emerge. Known collectively as the fedayeen these groups were primarily nationalist and socialist and drew their inspiration from other left-wing guerilla groups in Southeast Asia, Algeria, and South America. Their primary aims were the eradication of the state of Israel and the creation of an Arab Palestinian state in its place. Attempts by Palestinians to migrate into the newly established state of Israel were actively resisted by Israeli border guards. Fedayeen groups increasingly carried out covert crossings into Israel in the late 1940s. At first many of these operations were economically motivated with Palestinians attempting to return to their villages to harvest crops, recover abandoned possessions, or to continue interrupted trading. In the early 1950s these raids became more militaristic as fedayeen groups became more organized. Israel organized specialized military units to counter these incursions and began to carry out attacks on fedayeen bases in neighboring countries. In 1953 Israeli troops carried out a raid on the Palestinian village of Qibya in the Jordanian controlled West Bank in which dozens of Palestinians were killed and many buildings destroyed. Another notorious massacre of Palestinians by Israeli forces occurred in 1956 in the town of Kafr Kassem, a Palestinian community which lay just inside the borders of Israel. Many more Palestinians were killed in Israeli attacks on Palestinian communities in Jordan and Egypt and fedayeen attacks on Israelis resulted in hundreds of deaths between 1948 and 1956.

The Gaza Strip, a narrow strip of coastal territory bordering Egypt, became the focus of conflict between the fedayeen and the Israelis. The Gaza Strip was the sole territory of the

All-Palestine Government, an independent Palestinian state declared in October 1948 and was one of the principal destinations for Palestinian refugees. Egypt effectively controlled the Gaza Strip, although it made no claim to the territory, and following the Egyptian Revolution of 1952 and the rise to power of Gamal Abdel Nasser Egypt increasingly supported and armed the fedayeen groups based there. Israel's invasion of the Gaza Strip during the Suez War of 1956 was partly justified by Israel as an attempt to destroy the fedayeen. Israel occupied the Gaza Strip for four months until it was forced to withdraw under international pressure. The All-Palestine government continued to exercise nominal authority over the Gaza Strip until Egypt ceased to recognize it in 1959 and thereafter administered the territory via a military governor until the Six-Day War on 1967.

The Six-Day War and Its Aftermath

Relations between Arabs and Israelis remained hostile, with military buildups and threats and counterthreats exchanged, erupting in June 1967, when Israel made a preemptive strike against Egypt, destroying its air force within hours, quickly followed by strikes on Jordan, Syria, and Iraq. Israeli ground forces took Egypt's Sinai Peninsula (which reverted to Egypt following the 1979 peace treaty between Egypt and Israel). The war, known as the Six-Day War (also known as the 1967 Arab-Israeli War), ended quickly, with Israel in control of the West Bank and Arab Jerusalem (which had been under Jordanian rule since 1948), the Golan Heights (part of Syria), and the Gaza Strip (which had been administered by Egypt since 1948). Israel had tripled its territory, taking land that was populated by a million Palestinians, and more than 200,000 new refugees were created. Israel annexed East Jerusalem, razed and demolished houses, deported or jailed suspected terrorists, and destroyed some villages and towns. Jewish settlers began building permanent settlements in occupied lands. The United Nations Security Council met and passed Resolution 242, often cited in the coming decades. The resolution stresses "the inadmissibility of the acquisition of territory by war," a basic tenet of international law, and called for a just and lasting peace based on Israel's withdrawal from occupied territories and the right of every state in the region to "live in peace within secure and recognized boundaries free from threats or acts of force." The resolution also called for "a just settlement of the refugee problem." In the years

that followed, Israel held on to what became known as the Occupied Territories.

Meanwhile, the Palestine Liberation Organization (PLO) was founded in Cairo in 1964, with the stated goal of destroying Israel through armed struggle and restoring an "independent Palestinian state" between the Jordan River and the Mediterranean. Yasir Arafat was appointed its chairman in 1969.

The 1973 War to the Second Intifada

On October 6, 1973, Egypt and Syria made a surprise attack on Israel and retook the Sinai and the Golan Heights. Although the Arab countries were soon forced to retreat, this initial victory gave the Egyptians the standing to allow for peace negotiations, which took place in 1979 and led to Egypt's recognizing Israel, the first Arab country to do so. Under the terms of the treaty, Sinai was returned to Egypt. The 1973 Arab-Israeli War is also known as the Yom Kippur War or the Ramadan War.

Meanwhile, the PLO had based its fighters in Lebanon, establishing "a state within a state" (*See also* LEBANESE: NATIONALITY). In 1982 Israel invaded Lebanon to remove these fighters, who relocated to Tunis, on the coast of North Africa. In September of that year, Lebanese Phalangists, who were Christian allies of the Israelis, massacred 2,750 Palestinians—many of them women, children, and the elderly—living in the refugee camps of Sabra and Shatila, in southern Lebanon, which had been left undefended with the departure of the Palestinian military forces. In 1983, more than a year after their invasion, the Israelis withdrew from Lebanon, maintaining a "security zone" in southern Lebanon. In December 1987 the first Intifada began in the Palestinian Territories. *Intifada* is an Arabic word that literally means "shaking off," used here to describe a popular uprising that included general strikes, riots, and various forms of civil disobedience, to which the Israeli army responded with tear gas, plastic bullets, and live rounds, along with arrests, border closings, school and university closings, and other actions. It was during the first Intifada that Shaykh Ahmad Yassin founded Hamas, a name that means "zeal" in Arabic but is also an acronym for the Islamic Resistance Movement. Shaykh Yassin had been the head of the Gaza branch of the Muslim Brotherhood, an Islamist organization founded in Egypt in the 1928, and had spent time in an Israeli prison. Hamas not only offered an alternative political ideology; it also spent a great deal of its resources providing

Yasir Arafat: Icon of the Palestinian Movement

Yasir Arafat (1929–2004) was the iconic figure of the Palestinian nationalist movement, recognized throughout the world in his military fatigues and traditional checkered headdress, folded into an elongated diamond, a symbolic reference to the map of the longed-for Palestine. He was president of the Palestine Liberation Organization (PLO) Executive Committee from 1969 until his death. He was reportedly born in Cairo, Egypt, although there are also claims that he was born in Jerusalem or Gaza. In any case, his heritage was Palestinian: His family on his father's side were merchants from the Gaza Strip. His mother, who died when he was four, came from a prominent family of Jerusalem. After his mother's death, he was raised by various relatives in Jerusalem, Gaza, and Cairo. In 1949, the year after the war that resulted in the establishment of the state of Israel, he enrolled at Cairo University in Egypt, where he was elected president of the General Union of Palestinian Students. He graduated with a degree in engineering in 1957 and eventually settled in Kuwait. He continued his political activities and in 1959 founded the Palestinian National Liberation Movement, known by the acronym usually written in English as Fatah (meaning "victory" or "conquest"), which launched military operations against Israel. Fatah's stated goal was "Creating a democratic society in Palestine where Muslims, Christians, and Jews would live together in complete equality." Through his political activities in Egypt and in Kuwait, he forged alliances with men who were to become important figures in the PLO, which was founded in 1964.

Arafat has been described as "enigmatic," and his life was certainly a study in contradiction. While in the 1960s and 1970s he lent his authority to notorious acts of terrorism, including the massacre of Israeli athletes at the 1972 Olympics in Munich, he came to support a two-state solution to the Palestinian–Israeli conflict and was awarded the Nobel Peace Prize in 1994, jointly with Israeli prime minister Yitzhak Rabin and Israeli foreign minister Shimon Peres, in recognition of their efforts toward creating a viable peace. This agreement was the Oslo peace accords of 1993, promising mutual recognition, Palestinian self-rule in parts of Gaza and Jericho, and gradual transfer of authority from Israel to the Palestinians in other parts of the Occupied Territories. In 1994 Arafat was welcomed back to Gaza from Tunis, where he had lived in exile, and established the first Palestinian government. In 1996 he was confirmed as leader of the Palestinians, winning the presidential election with 88 percent of the vote. But support for him and his government was not universal. The Palestinian Authority clashed with the more radical Hamas, which continued to advocate military action against Israeli targets, including terrorism aimed at civilians. Some Palestinians felt that Arafat had betrayed their cause by agreeing to give up too much. Others chafed under his autocratic rule and accused him of corruption. Meanwhile, the Israeli government periodically sealed the borders of Gaza and the West Bank, preventing Palestinians from getting to their jobs in Israel and creating an economic disaster in the territories.

At times it seemed that a peace settlement the Palestinian people could accept was within reach. In 2000 American-brokered negotiations took place with Israeli prime minister Ehud Barak, but Arafat ultimately rejected the terms because they did not include implementation of a full right of return and because he considered Israeli security demands unacceptable. Shortly after this, the second Intifada broke out, and the Israeli government shelled the area surrounding Arafat's headquarters in Ramallah. Arafat holed up in his headquarters with a few aides, unable to leave, until nearly three years later, he was allowed to travel to Paris for medical treatment. He died in Paris a few days later.

social services—funding schools, orphanages, mosques, clinics, soup kitchens, and sports groups—to those who desperately needed it. Hamas was to become the primary opposition to Arafat's Fatah.

In 1988 Arafat unilaterally proclaimed a state of Palestine when Jordan renounced its territorial claim to the West Bank in favor of the PLO. Other conflicts in the Middle East and ill-conceived decisions on the part of Palestinian leadership added to Palestinian difficulties. In 1990, when Iraq invaded Kuwait, the PLO leadership took the side of Iraq. Kuwait then broke ties with the PLO, cut off the substantial financial aid it had been providing, and expelled 400,000 Palestinians who had been living and working in Kuwait. Many of them returned to the Territories or to Jordan—to economies already badly faltering and unable to absorb them.

Major powers, most notably the United States, continued to press for peace talks. In 1991 peace talks began in Madrid; in 1993, in Oslo, Norway, the PLO and Israel agreed to recognize one another, a major step. In 2000 meetings were held at Camp David between Israeli prime minister Ehud Barak and Arafat which were intended to produce a so-called final status settlement. The negotiations foundered over Palestinian demands for full implementation of the right of return, disagreements over territorial claims, and Israeli demands for control of Palestinian airspace and the right to deploy troops in Palestinian territory. A couple of months later, Arial Sharon, then leader of Israel's right-wing Likud Party, visited the Haram al-Sharif, the Muslim religious sanctuary in the heart of old Jerusalem. This visit was perceived as an insult and a threat, and against the background of the failed peace talks, the second Intifada broke out. The following February, Sharon was elected Israeli prime minister. Violence escalated, with assassinations, terrorist attacks, and military actions. Israeli troops shelled and surrounded the Palestinian government's West Bank headquarters in Ramallah, making it impossible for Arafat to leave. He remained a virtual prisoner there until he was allowed to fly to Paris for medical care shortly before his death in 2004. Earlier that year, Shaykh Yassin, the founder of Hamas, was assassinated by Israeli government forces, as was his co-founder and successor, Abd al-Aziz al-Rantissi, the following month. In January 2005 Hamas won the majority of seats in Palestinian elections, and in response, the United States, Israel, and several European countries cut off aid to the Palestinians. Ideological differences between Hamas and Fatah resulted in near civil war in Gaza and continuing factional fighting. Hamas allowed rocket attacks to be launched from Gaza into Israel, and Israel retaliated with air raids on Gaza. Abbas tried desperately to retain control and to convince outside powers to lift their embargo of aid to Palestinians, which remains in place as of 2009.

Continued rocket attacks on Israel launched from the Gaza Strip prompted Israel to block the supply of electricity, fuel, and many other commodities into the territory in 2007, causing great hardship to the population, and to seal its border completely in 2008. Israel conducted air and land attacks on targets in the Gaza Strip early in 2008 and launched another major offensive in December 2008 that continued until the end of January 2009.

CULTURE

Economy

The Palestinian economy before 1948 was largely based on agriculture, particularly the cultivation of olives, citrus and other fruits, wheat, barley, lentils, and vegetables. Approximately 250,000 acres were under cultivation. When the Palestinians fled their villages or were driven out by Israeli forces, many of their orchards were also destroyed, either intentionally or through neglect. The economy of the West Bank and Gaza is now heavily skewed toward the service industry, which accounts for 79 percent of the gross domestic product. Agriculture accounts for 8 percent and industry 13 percent. Unemployment is high (35 percent in 2006), and 80 percent of the population in the Gaza Strip lives below the poverty line, as does 46 percent of the population in the West Bank (2007 estimates). Frequent closure of crossing points into Israel, preventing the flow of goods and workers into Israel, along with economic sanctions, have had a devastating effect on the Palestinian economy.

Government and Society

A 1993 agreement between Israel and the PLO provided for Interim Self-Government Arrangements, a period of transitional Palestinian self-rule in the West Bank and Gaza. A Palestinian Authority (PA) was established and Israel relinquished to it certain responsibilities of government. However, with the outbreak of the second Intifada in 2000, Israel reoccupied most Palestinian-controlled areas. In April 2003 the so-called Quartet, made up of the United States, the European Union, the United Nations, and Russia, drew up a "roadmap" that outlined steps each side was to take, leading to a final, two-state solution—Israel and a democratic Palestine—by 2005. Many obstacles, including violence and accusations of noncompliance on both sides, prevented that from happening. PA president and long-time Palestinian leader Yasir Arafat died in 2004 and Mahmud Abbas, of the Arafat-founded Fatah Party, was elected president. The peace process seemed to be moving ahead, and in September 2005 Israel withdrew settlers and its armed forces from the Gaza Strip. However, in elections held in January 2006, Hamas, the Islamic Resistance Movement, which has the aim of creating an Islamic state in the West Bank and the Gaza Strip, won control of the Palestinian Legislative Council and shortly after, the PA. The international community and Israel refused to work with Hamas and crippling economic sanctions were put in place.

Dwellings and Architecture

Palestinians today live in every imaginable sort of dwelling—from modern apartment buildings, to elegant traditional homes, to village dwellings, to the overcrowded misery of the refugee camps—as one would expect of a diverse, widely scattered population. Perhaps the type of dwelling most evocative of Palestinian culture is the traditional village home, with its strong associations with homeland and what used to be.

Before 1948, more than one third of the Arab population of Palestine lived in urban centers but almost 90 percent of that population was uprooted and displaced. Scholars have often cited the collapse of Palestinian urban society as a factor with lingering negative consequences for Palestinians in Israel and the Palestinian Territories, as the urban dwellers were the better educated, the more affluent, and the "modernizers." Without them and the vibrant city life they had created, Palestinian society in Israel and the Territories has suffered immeasurably. The remaining two thirds of the pre-1948 population lived in agricultural villages.

Villages typically averaged about 700 inhabitants. A report to the British Mandatory government written in 1944 describes "the most notable feature of the typical Arab village" as "the concentration of the houses in a thick cluster on the high ground of the village lands." The houses were built close together, overlooking their orchards and fields, situated so that they encroached on the arable land as little as possible. Building materials were generally whatever was locally available: If the village was in a rocky area, the homes were built of stone. In coastal regions, homes were built of adobe. Some village residents—typically the more affluent—built their homes set apart from the rest of the village, and these were often built of "modern" materials—reinforced concrete. In the typical village home, a narrow passageway led from the street into the home's courtyard. Surrounding this central courtyard were rooms serving various purposes. The family lived in one of the rooms. Other rooms were for storage of grain or tools, a pen for sheep, a barn for dairy animals, and a space for chickens. The space for the family was often cramped and windowless, but people would spend most of their time outside, in the fields or in the village common spaces.

Home and everything that word connotes was and is the central element of Palestinian life. Traditionally, the completion of the building of a house was cause for celebration. When the roof was finished, family, friends, and neighbors, and particularly those who helped with the building, would be invited for a feast, with a sheep slaughtered on the threshold of the new home. The British authorities trying to put down the Arab Uprising of 1936–39 understood the significance of home and they used it as a powerful weapon. Under emergency regulations, the British commander was empowered to demolish a home if he suspected that shots had been fired from it or bombs thrown from it or that its inhabitants had participated in violence. Hundreds of homes were demolished under these regulations. This form of collective punishment was taken up by Jewish forces in the 1948 war and continues to be used by the Israeli government, despite protests from both Palestinians and Israelis and from international human rights groups. The Israeli Committee Against House Demolitions (ICAHD) estimates that 18,000 homes have been demolished in the Palestinian Territories, including East Jerusalem, since 1967, with 5,000 of those demolitions taking place since the start of the second Intifada in September 2000. The policy was halted in 2005, but in 2008, in the wake of a terrorist incident, Israeli prime minister Ehud Olmert and other government officials called for its reinstatement.

Clothing

While jeans and T-shirts and other Western clothing styles are a common sight in Palestinian cities and towns today, traditional Palestinian dress is still worn, particularly in villages and for celebrations. Traditional costume is so rich and varied, especially women's clothing, that it has been analyzed as a language in itself. A man's headgear, for instance, would immediately convey where he came from (town or village or nomadic tribe), his status, and his religion. A woman's dress would indicate her marital status, the social and economic status of her family, and the village or region she came from.

The basics of men's clothing—both for villagers and BEDOUIN—included a long shirtlike tunic *(thob)* that came at least to the knees. Various sorts of coats could be worn over that—a sheepskin coat with the wool worn towards the body, a cloth coat, or a sleeveless cloak *(aba* or *abaya)*. From the end of the 19th century, men began wearing a calf- or ankle-length coat, called a *qumbaz,* over the *thob,* and this item came to be an important gift given in ceremonies such as circumcision and marriage. For example, as part of the wedding ceremony, the bride would ride in procession on a horse or a camel from her family's home to her new home. Over her head would be draped a coat belonging to the groom, given by him to the bride's father and worn by the bride as a symbol that leaving her father's house, she was now under the protection of her husband. During the British Mandate, Western-style jackets often replaced the more traditional coats. Baggy pants worn under the *thob* were adopted by villagers and became common after about 1920. Belts and sashes of various types provided folds into which one could tuck or attach various items, including tools, a tobacco pouch, and possibly a dagger.

Both men's and women's traditional dress was modest and always included a head covering, a sign of modesty. Men wore a turban, or a *tarbush* (also called a fez—a cylindrical hat made of felt), or a Bedouin headdress made up of the headcloth *(kaffiya)* with a rope ring *(aqal)* to hold it in place. In the late 1930s, many village men began wearing the *kaffiya* and *aqal* exclusively as a declaration of Palestinian identity. At that time, the usual headcloth was white, but later the familiar black or red checked cloths became fashionable, especially after the 1967 war, as young men in particular adopted the headdress so strongly identified with Yasir Arafat.

Women's clothing worn at home, with family, was often a European-style dress (fustan), which became the fashion from about the late 19th century on, replacing the traditional long-sleeved shirt called a qamis. Ankle-length pants were worn under that, often with embroidered legs that would show under the shirt or dress. Outside the home, a woman would wear an outer dress (also called a thob) in some regions, or a sort of coat-dress in others, some with long pointed sleeves that had to be tied behind the neck to get them out of the way while the wearer worked. Dresses could also have straight, tight-fitting sleeves. In some areas, the dress was made of black cloth—usually cotton, but also taffeta or satin—while in other areas it was white. The dress could be decorated with appliqué (patches of material sewn on top of the dress) or inserts of luxurious fabric. The typical dress of many regions was decorated with embroidery, usually consisting of a rectangular chest panel, vertical panels on the skirt, and lines of embroidery across the sleeves. Dress styles and the motifs of the embroidery differ from village to village, as do the sashes or belts that are always worn with the outer dress.

In traditional Palestinian society embroidery was a highly valued skill, and as early as the age of six, girls would begin learning. Needlework was often an early evening social activity, after the day's work was done but the light was still sufficient for such close, detailed work. Women and girls would sit at their doorways and do their stitching, talking and helping the children who were still learning. Some villages were known for particularly fine work, and sometimes girls would be sent to these villages to learn their special style. In preparation for her eventual wedding, a young girl would be expected to embroider her bridal dress, which would be elaborately decorated, as well as various items for her new home—cushion covers and such. Part of the tradition was that the bride would make tobacco bags for the groom and his close male relatives, while the groom would often make the tassels for the bride's veil. Since women generally embroidered their own garments (although there were also professional dressmakers and embroiderers), they had some degree of control over the designs they used and the "language" associated with it.

Hand-embroidered garments and accessories are still produced today, sometimes as a cottage industry, often supported by relief and welfare organizations that provide microloans and assist with sales in the international market. These efforts not only provide much-needed jobs, they also ensure that these skills are not lost.

Transportation

The configuration of the Palestinian Territories present transportation difficulties in that the West Bank and Gaza, which, under current peace plans, are generally regarded as being the independent Palestinian state, are not contiguous. To get from one to the other, one must pass through Israel. The Israeli government, fearing attacks by Palestinian terrorists, has controlled access through Israeli territory by means of hundreds of checkpoints and border crossings, all of which can be closely monitored and even closed off. The difficulties this tight security has posed for Palestinian workers, businessmen, professionals, and others who need to travel—to jobs, for medical care, to visit relatives, for whatever reason—is one of the central issues that has to be worked out in any eventual peace agreement. Smooth, predictable travel across borders is essential if, for instance, Palestinian farmers are to transport their produce for sale in Israel, rather than risk watching it rot in the long lines at checkpoints. The far-reaching effects of stringent travel restrictions are illustrated by a 2008 incident in which seven Palestinian scholars from the Gaza Strip who had been awarded Fulbright scholarships to study in the United States were denied permission to travel and their scholarships were rescinded. Their fellowships were reinstated and permission granted to them to leave Gaza only after Secretary of State Condoleeza Rice directly intervened. Numerous other scholars have been denied permission to travel to accept study grants in other countries.

Movement within Palestinian territory has become even more complicated since 2002, when Israel began the erection of a wall in the West Bank, built in response to suicide bombings. The concrete barrier, which will extend 490 miles when completed, in places 26 feet high, veers into the occupied West Bank and has resulted in Palestinian farmers being unable to access their land, children being unable to get to their schools, and ambulances having to travel 60 miles around the barrier instead of to the hospital five minutes away but now inaccessible. According to a 2007 U.S. State Department report on religious freedom in Israel and the Palestinian Territories, construction of the barrier has involved confiscation of Palestinian property and displacement of Christian and

Muslim residents, and it has seriously restricted access of West Bank Muslims and Christians to holy sites in Jerusalem and the West Bank. Many Israelis see the wall as an essential security measure and point to the decline in suicide bombings as evidence of its effectiveness. Palestinians see it as a symbol of apartheid and a mechanism for Israel to annex more of their land. The Israeli Supreme Court has issued several rulings that parts of the wall must be moved because they create hardships for Palestinians. This is an issue that will no doubt be the subject of continuing debate.

Art

Before 1948 exhibitions of paintings or sculpture were practically unknown in Palestinian society, although handicrafts, calligraphy, and other forms of creative expression had long traditions. Ismail Shammout, often called the "father of Palestinian modern art," held an exhibition in Gaza in 1953, the first exhibition of Palestinian art in Palestine. Visual artists have often imbued their work with political meaning, sometimes evoking images of resistance and nationalism, in various media and styles including realistic, symbolic, and surrealistic. Palestinian paintings and sculpture are often figural and sometimes incorporate elements of calligraphy. Palestinian culture has produced many artists whose works have been exhibited around the world and are held in major collections in Europe, the United States, and the Middle East. Kamal Boullata is one of these artists to rise to prominence in the 1960s and after. Born in Jerusalem, trained at the Academy of Fine Arts in Rome, and now living and working in the south of France, Boullata is particularly known for his evocative use of calligraphy and geometric shapes. In addition to his paintings, he has also edited and illustrated books of Palestinian poetry and edited a collection of Palestinian children's art. Other prominent artists include Suleiman Mansour, whose metaphorical work *Camels of Hardship*, which depicts an old porter carrying Jerusalem on his back, was influential in establishing the New Vision movement after the outbreak of the first Intifada in 1987. Samira Badran is known for her apocalyptic images of the occupation. While Palestinian artists have begun to experiment with installation art, multimedia works, and photography, painting continues to be the preferred medium. In 2003 and 2005, major group shows were exhibited in the United States, traveling to a number of museums.

Literature

Palestinian novels and poetry are replete with imagery of the land—its smells, how it feels beneath the feet and in the hand, the olive trees, the figs, the orange trees—and the imagery of loss and longing. Poetry and the well-spoken word are highly valued in Arabic culture, and the words of many Palestinian poets are memorized and treasured. Among the best-known modern Palestinian poets are Mahmud Darwish (d. 2008), Jabra Ibrahim Jabra (also known for his novels and literary criticism), Rashid Hussein, Salma Khadra Jayyusi, and Fadwa Tuqan. Tuqan, who died in 2003 at the age of 86, was honored with prizes for her poetry, both at home and abroad, and was admired by Arab and Israeli feminists for also speaking out on women's issues. These lines reflect the simple, direct force of her poetry:

> I ask nothing more
> Than to die in my country
> To dissolve and merge with the grass,
> To give life to a flower
> That a child of my country will pick,
> All I ask
> Is to remain in the bosom of my country
> As soil,
> Grass,
> A flower.
>
> —Fadwa Tuqan

Among Palestinian novelists, Emile Habiby, an Israeli Arab, former member of parliament, and acclaimed journalist, is particularly known for his novel *The Secret Life of Saeed the Pessoptimist*, a satirical treatment of a comic hero, in the tradition of Voltaire and Swift, who becomes an hapless informer on the margins of both Israeli and Palestinian society. Ghassan Kanafani, an outspoken militant who was assassinated by a car bomb in 1972, is cited as among the first Palestinian writers to depict with empathy and sensitivity both Palestinian and Israeli sides, especially in his novella *Returning to Haifa*, included in the collection of his stories *Palestine's Children*. Young Palestinian writers are attaining wider recognition, and a range of Palestinian literature has been translated into English.

Religion

The majority of Palestinians are Sunni Muslims with a minority of Shia and a small community of Druze, most of them from the area of the

Sea of Galilee. Christian Arabs make up about 6 percent of the total, most of them Orthodox or Greek Catholic. Of Palestinians living in the Palestinian Territories, about 3 percent are Christian. As is evident from the discrepancy between the percentage of Christians in the diaspora and Christians remaining in the Territories, Christians generally have a higher rate of emigration than Muslims, both from the Palestinian Territories and from within Israel.

———◆———

The future of the Palestinians depends upon a final peace with Israel that will provide the security and resources needed for economic development, education, and optimism. Building infrastructure in areas long neglected, educating a population denied schooling because of violence and instability, and creating a viable economy will most require continuing and intense international investment and support.

FURTHER READING

Mourid Barghouti. *I Saw Ramallah,* trans. Ahdaf Soueif (New York: Anchor Books, 2003).

Meron Benvenisti. *Sacred Landscape: The Buried History of the Holy Land since 1948,* trans. Maxine Kaufman-Lacusta (Berkeley: University of California Press, 2000).

Rashid Khalidi. *Palestinian Identity: The Construction of Modern National Consciousness* (New York: Columbia University Press, 1997).

Gudrun Krämer. *A History of Palestine: From the Ottoman Conquest to the Founding of the State of Israel,* trans. Graham Harman and Gudrun Krämer (Princeton, N.J.: Princeton University Press, 2008).

Saree Makdisi. *Palestine Inside Out: An Everyday Occupation* (New York: Norton, 2008).

Philip Mattar. *Encyclopedia of the Palestinians, Revised Edition* (New York: Facts On File, 2005)

Benny Morris. *The Birth of the Palestinian Refugee Problem Revisited* (Cambridge, U.K.: Cambridge University Press, 2004)

Ibrahim Muhawi and Sharif Kanaana. *Speak, Bird, Speak Again: Palestinian Arab Folktales* (Berkeley: University of California Press, 1989).

Sari Nusseibeh. *Once Upon a Country: A Palestinian Life* (New York: Farrar, Straus and Giroux, 2007).

Danny Rubinstein. *The People of Nowhere: A Palestinian Vision of Home,* trans. Ina Friedman (New York: Random House, 1991).

Paphlogonians

The Paphlogonians, an ancient people of northwest Anatolia (modern-day Turkey), are mentioned in the Greek epics of Homer, the *Iliad* and the *Odyssey,* as allies of the TROJANS. Herodotus, whose work was known by 425 B.C.E. during the classical period of ancient Greece, mentions them in his *History* as having been conquered by the last Lydian king, Croesus (r. ca. 560–546 B.C.E.) and as fighting in the army of Xerxes, the king of Persia from 486 to 465 B.C.E. The Greek historian Xenophon also mentions their military strength. In 333 B.C.E. the Paphlogonians came under the rule of Alexander the Great. By the third century B.C.E., parts of Paphlogonia were ruled by native princes, while parts had come under the rule of the PONTIANS. By 6 B.C.E., the entire area was under Roman rule as part of the province of Galatia. The area was known for its timber production, and Mount Olgassys, included in Paphlogonian territory and one of the highest mountains in northern Anatolia, was said to be the home of the Greek gods.

Pare

The Pare are part of the larger grouping of SHAMBAA peoples, who inhabit the coastal lowlands of Tanzania. The Pare heartland includes the Pare Mountains in the northeastern corner of Tanzania.

The Shambaa are descended from both BANTU and Cushitic ancestors who migrated into East Africa hundreds of years ago (*see* CUSHITES). The first Bantu-speaking settlers reached the Pare region some time before the 16th century. From the 1700s on, there was a steady movement of Bantu speakers into the Pare region, where they intermingled with other groups and eventually organized themselves into lineage (family-based) groups. The northern Pare state of Gwena, ruled by the Wasuya lineage, was a stable and well-organized union that survived well into the 19th century. The leader, or *mangi mrwe,* ruled with the help of *chila* (councils), *wanjama* (ministers), and local chiefs (*wamangi*).

Parsis (Parsees)

Parsis are Zoroastrians who migrated from Persia to India beginning in about the 10th century C.E. to seek freedom to practice their religion unhindered. The name derives from the word for Persia, "Fars," and means literally "someone from Persia." The Parsis settled mostly in Gujarat, on the west coast of India, and the city of Mumbai (formerly Bombay) remains important as a center of the Parsi community. Beginning in about the 17th century, as Europeans began to take a more active interest in the Indian subcontinent and began settling in western India, the Parsis rose to prominence. They were well educated and soon established themselves as wealthy merchants and industrialists, particularly in the textile and steel industries, as well as in banking and insurance, and as physicians and lawyers. By the late 19th century, Parsis were also becoming important political leaders, among them Dadabhai Naoroji, known as "the Grand Old Man of India," who founded the Indian National Congress in 1885 and was the first Asian to be elected a member of the British Parliament (1892–95).

The Parsi community makes up a very small minority, estimated at perhaps only 100,000 worldwide, with a population of perhaps 70,000 in India, a country with a total population of more than 1 billion. Despite their small numbers, though, the Parsis have had a disproportionate—and remarkable—influence. They have founded some of the largest and most important businesses in India, including Tata Steel and Air India, the national airline. Since India's independence in 1947, Parsis have headed each branch of India's armed forces. Former president Indira Gandhi was married to a Parsi politician. Parsis are also known as generous philanthropists on an international scale. While small communities of Parsis have established themselves around the world since the 18th century, the latter part of the 20th century saw the diaspora grow. Many immigrated, often for educational purposes, to Europe, especially London, the United States, and Canada, with Zororastrian associations being established in New York, Toronto, Los Angeles, Chicago, and Vancouver. Of the Parsi communities in Muslim countries, the most influential is in Pakistan, where, while their numbers are small, they have held positions of prominence in government, the military, and business.

Parthians

Parthia occupied much of the territory of what is today northeastern Iran and was one of the great civilizations of the ancient world. It entered into the historical record during the third century B.C.E. and later grew into one of the most powerful empires of Asia, its territories spreading beyond Iran to include modern Iraq and Armenia plus regions within Georgia, Azerbaijan, Afghanistan, Turkmenistan, Tajikistan, Syria, Lebanon, Israel, Palestine, and Pakistan, although not all of the these territo-

ries were occupied conterminously. This empire existed for several centuries until Parthia was dissolved into the Sassanid Empire in the 220s C.E. (*see* SASSANIANS) The word *Parthia* was derived from the indigenous term "Parthava," which may in turn have been a local variant of the name Parsa, for Persian. Note, however, ancient Assyria also acknowledged a land named Partukka or Partakka in the region dating back to the seventh century B.C.E.

ORIGINS

The origins of Parthia itself are barely understood, as there is little historical material to provide information. It is first known as a satrapy of the Achaemenid Empire, the satrapy established when Media (of which Parthia may have been a part) was taken over during the conquests of Cyrus the Great (*see* ACHAEMENIDS). The conquest of Parthava probably occurred sometime between 546 and 539, and the word first appears in an inscription of around 520, when Darius I was on the Achaemenid throne.

LANGUAGE

Parthia had its own language known today as Parthian, and this was concentrated at first in the northwest territories of Iran. This language spread widely throughout the Parthian Empire and had an official status, and it is also closely related to Middle Persian. Note also, however, that Greek became an important additional language within Parthian territories as Greek influence was diffused by the conquests of Alexander the Great and the subsequent Hellenization of much of Asia (*see* GREEKS).

HISTORY

Parthia made a brief, unsuccessful attempt to shake off Persian rule in 521 B.C.E., but this was suppressed by the forces of the Parthian satrap, Hystaspes. Now that Parthia was subdued, its troops worked for the greater Persian good, with Parthian forces forming an important contingent of the Persian assault on Greece by Xerxes in 480 B.C.E. The Greek response came in 331 B.C.E., when the forces of Alexander cut through Asian territories. Parthia was defeated, although Alexander reconfirmed its existing satrap, Phrataphernes, as the local governor.

From the death of Alexander in 323 B.C.E., Parthia was ruled by a succession of satraps, not always with stability and frequently fighting off incursions from neighboring and distant countries. A critical juncture, however, came in 245

PARTHIANS

location:
Northeast Iran; their empire stretched across Iran, part of Iraq, and into Turkey

time period:
Third century B.C.E. to third century C.E.

ancestry:
Iranian

language:
Parthian (Indo-Iranian; Indo-European)

B.C.E. with the Parthian revolt against Seleucid rule. A new Persian kingdom was established, and amid political turmoil a Central Asian nomadic tribe called the Parni invaded (or simply migrated) and took over Parthia from 238 to 227 B.C.E., establishing a capital at Hecatompylos. The Parni subsequently become known as the Parthians, and their first king was Arsaces I. So began the reign of the Arsacid dynasty (238 B.C.E.–224 C.E.).

It was under Arsaces I and his successors that Parthia rose to become a power of imperial status. At first the Parthian rulers still paid tribute to the Seleucid rulers, but after 188 B.C.E. (or 187 B.C.E.), when Antiochus III died, there began a wave of Parthian expansionism under the Parthian king Mithridates I (171–138 B.C.E.). Bactria, Media, Babylonia and Elam were all conquered, with Mithridates taking over the Seleucid capital (Seleucia) and fighting off Seleucid attempts at reconquest. Under the subsequent rule of Mithridates II (123–88 B.C.E.), the boundaries of the growing empire were extended even further, reaching out to territories as far apart as Armenia and India.

Parthian power eventually came into direct conflict with another expansionist civilization—Rome. The turning point was 53 B.C.E., when Parthian territories were invaded from the west by Roman forces under Crassus. The ROMANS were aiming to capitalize on a period of general disorder throughout the Parthian Empire following the death of the Mithridates II, but Parthian military talents resulted in a massive defeat for the Romans at Carrhae—only 10,000 of 40,000 troops escaped. Rome was then distracted by domestic turbulence (the struggle for power between Pompey and Caesar), and in 41/40 B.C.E. the Parthians themselves attacked westward, the army led, ironically, by a Roman who had switched allegiance, Quintus Labienus, and the Parthian Pacorus, son of King Orodes (ca. 57–38 B.C.E.). The attack resulted in further large Parthian gains in Asia Minor, Syria, and Palestine. Labienus and Pacorus were both killed in a Roman counterattack, and Orodes was then murdered by his now eldest son, Phraates IV (ca. 38–2 B.C.E.), who took over the kingdom and defeated a further assault by Roman troops under Mark Antony.

These early wars set the scene for the subsequent centuries of conflict, as Rome and Parthia frequently clashed within the Middle Eastern and Central Asian territories, although after the defeat of Antony there was a period of some 20 years where peace reigned between

---

Parthians: time line

B.C.E.

546 Partharva becomes part of the Achaemenid Empire.

331 Parthia is defeated by forces of Alexander the Great and becomes part of his empire.

247 Parthian revolt against Seleucid rule

238–227 Parni tribe invade or migrate into Parthia. The Arsacid dynasty is established.

171–138 Mithridates I launches a major period of imperial expansion.

53 Parthian territories are invaded from the west by Roman forces under the Roman general Marcus Crassus, but the Romans are defeated at the battle of Carrhae.

ca. 40 The Parthians launch a major assault against the eastern territories of the Roman Empire and make further territorial gains in the Middle East.

C.E.

60 The Armenian settlement between Rome and Parthia brings a temporary truce between the two empires.

116, 161, 195, and 217 Major Roman campaigns against Parthia

224 The last Parthian ruler, Artabanus V, is overthrown by Ardashir from Fars, beginning the Sassanid dynasty.

---

the two empires, though not within the Parthian Empire itself, which descended into civil war following a rebellion against Phraates IV. However, disputes over Armenia around 65 C.E. brought Rome and Parthia back into direct conflict. Parthia lost out here, and Armenia went into the Roman fold, although the peace settlement allowed a Parthian ruler to sit on the Armenian throne, but under Roman authority.

The Armenian settlement was far from a long-term solution to Parthian–Roman tensions. Furthermore, the conquests of empire had allowed many nobles within the Parthian Empire to grow independently powerful, and Parthian central control became more challenged and fragile.

CULTURE

Economy

Once Parthia had expanded into an empire, it possessed an extremely vibrant economy. The economy was primarily agricultural, but the empire also forged international trade in goods such as silks and spices. Most importantly, Parthia dominated the Silk Road from China through to the Mediterranean, and thus was able to derive an income not only from the goods traded but also from the tolls imposed on traders passing through the territories.

The empire also yielded income through the payment of tribute to the king from the subject territories, a contribution that was central to the Parthian creation of some of its most impressive cities, such as Ecbatana, Rhagae, and Susa. Note that Parthia had a fully fledged system of coinage, with coins first being minted under the reign of Arsaces I. Subject territories were allowed to mint their own coins, an enlightened imperial policy.

Government and Society

As was seen above in the case of coinage, the Parthians allowed their subjects to maintain their own identities and social systems—such was seen as a way to promote longevity of rule by reducing the likelihood of rebellion. The Parthian king still retained a clear sense that he was overall ruler of the lands, and so took the title "King of Kings." Such centralization, however, was more about overall political muscle, and apart from the fact that the Parthian empire was fairly decentralized in structure. This was both a strength and a weakness: a strength in that the empire was fairly resilient to conquest (centers of power could be easily shifted), a weakness in that it allowed challengers to emerge. The king was not an untouchable authority. A powerful noble class had wide-reaching influence over government, both directly (in the cases of some particularly powerful families) through voting rights in legislative bodies and by the fact that every noble could wield his own army. The nobility also flexed clear authority over the lower orders of society. Horse ownership and riding, for example, were reserved purely for the Parthian aristocracy, clearly indicating their power by alluding to the importance of the horse for formerly nomadic peoples.

Military Practices

Parthia was known for its military prowess on horseback, combined with exceptional talents in archery. The early Parthians would attack their foes by riding around them at speed, their horses being partially protected from missiles by a thick layer of mail armor (formed by interlinked hoops of metal). By the time of the engagements between Parthians and Romans in the first century B.C.E., the Parthian cavalry had developed a high degree of sophistication, and through the efforts of the Parthian general Surena it had divided into two types. The light cavalry lacked any armor but consequently was very fast—ideal for raid-then-retreat archery attacks against enemy flanks. The heavy cavalry, by contrast, was extremely well protected with mail, and the riders wielded swords and lances to smash open enemy ranks with thunderous frontal assaults. It was such cavalry that inflicted the crushing losses on Crassus at the battle of Carrhae. One other interesting tactic was the so-called "Parthian shot" (or "Parthian shaft"). Here the light cavalry forces would feign retreat, and as they were being pursued the riders would literally turn around and sit backwards on the horse, firing arrows directly into the advancing enemy to deplete their ranks.

Dwellings and Architecture

Most Parthian buildings were constructed from bricks baked in a kiln or hardened in the sun before being used. Parthian engineers used the bricks with great versatility and could raise buildings in the unlikeliest of settings. The mountainous setting for Zahak Castle near Khorassanak, for example, is at 5,905 feet, and much of the building still stands today. It is made from bricks held together with mortar. A classic feature of Parthian architecture was an open-fronted hall known as an *iwan,* capped with a vaulted dome. In the palace at Ashur, the open fronts of four *iwan* are used to frame a central square, and this layout was to have an influence on the design of much later Islamic architecture. Decorative forms applied to buildings included glazing, stucco reliefs, frescos, and geometrical plaster moldings.

Art

The most basic form of Parthian art is fairly crude reliefs cut directly into rock, these forming features that surrounded both domestic and civic buildings. Typical scenes included horses, hunts, and battles. More sophisticated freestanding statuary was produced, however, carved from either stone or molded in bronze. The level of expression in these statues varies considerably and ranges from stiff, formulaic figures representing noble leaders through to flowing, naturalistic figures of women reclining or riders on horseback. Of course, the style of the art changed dramatically according to foreign influences, including influences from invaders (such as the Greeks and Romans) or from conquered territories.

Parthians expressed themselves in many other forms of decorative arts. Frescos were painted in vivid colors and with intense naturalism, while jewelry included some exceptionally fine pieces of lacework gold and silver, inlaid with turquoise and other richly colored stones. Parthian artists were also well known for their exquisite rhyton drinking horns made from carved ivory or heavily decorated silver and featuring realistic animal moldings, carvings, and images of divinities. Some historians who that the earliest techniques of weaving carpets originated in Parthia.

Religion

The Parthians practiced two of the world's most influential early structured religions—Mithraism and Zoroastrianism. The worship of the divinity Mithra actually predates Parthia's known existence, being frequently associated (although not identified) with the sun, and was a widely influential faith across Eurasia. In turn, Mithra became the pivotal deity in Zoroastrianism, Ahura Mazda, with an important role in overseeing truth, friendship, and love in interpersonal relationships. There is some evidence that the original scriptures of Zoroastrianism were actually laid down in Parthia.

———◆———

As the centuries progressed, the Parthians steadily lost territory to the Romans, who conducted major campaigns in 116, 161, 195, and 217. Parthia itself, however, managed to resist takeover until 224. In the end, it was internal threats that undid the last Parthian ruler, Artabanus V. Ardashir, a Parthian vassal in Persis, rose up against Artabanus and defeated him in battle, thus establishing the Sassanid dynasty and ending the age of Parthia, whose history was then absorbed into that of Persia.

FURTHER READING

Vesta Sarkhosh Curtis and Sarah Stewart. *The Age of the Parthians.* Idea of Iran, vol. 2 (London: I.B. Tauris, 2007).

Pashtuns

The Pashtuns are the largest ethnic group in Afghanistan and form a large minority in Pakistan. Pashtuns also live in eastern Iran, and there is an immigrant community in the United Arab Emirates.

Pazande See AZANDE.

Pedi

The Pedi are a SOTHO people who emerged as a distinct ethnic subgroup under the influence of the Bapedi Empire. Today the Pedi inhabit a region called Sekhukhuneland that is centered around the Olifants River in the northeastern tip of South Africa.

The Pedi are a BANTU people whose ancestors had settled their present lands by about 1000. By about 1400 the main Sotho clans had emerged, including the Pedi. During the 17th century the Pedi clan became dominant among the Northern Sotho and established the Bapedi Empire. Bapedi lasted for over 200 years and expanded the Pedi clan into a wider political and then ethnic grouping made of people who joined or were conquered by the Bapedi Empire. In the 19th century, Bapedi became a popular destination for Africans seeking to escape the harsh labor laws of the newly formed white-ruled South African Republic. In the 1860s open war broke out between the BOERS and the Pedi, led by their king, Sekhukhuni. The Boers were defeated, but three years later the British defeated the Pedi with the help of the SWAZI.

Pende

The Pende inhabit a region in the Democratic Republic of the Congo between the Kasai and Lutshima Rivers in the southwest of the country. The Pende are divided into two main subgroups: the eastern Pende (or Pende-Kasai) and the western Pende. The two groups differ linguistically, culturally, and economically from each other. For example, the eastern Pende are not as economically developed as the western Pende. The two groups are separated physically by the Loange River, and there are a great many more western than eastern Pende. The Pende probably originated from northern Angola, but fled to their present region to escape slave raids by the CHOKWE. The Pende religion involves a belief in Nzambi, who created the universe but is not often directly worshipped. The reverence shown to ancestors is a more immediate aspect of the Pende religion.

Persians

Persia has its origins in the Old Persian term *Parsa*, meaning "above reproach." In Greek mouths the word was reshaped in the sixth century B.C.E. into "Persis" then, through later Latinization, into "Persia." Persia was used alongside "Iran"—the indigenous term from the seventh century C.E., meaning "Land of the Aryans"—until 1935, when the then shah of Iran, Reza Pahlavi, insisted that "Iran" replace "Persia" as the preferred term in international

PERSIANS

location:
Iranian plateau

time period:
2700 B.C.E. to present

ancestry:
Iranian and Turkic peoples

language:
Iranian; Indo European

———◆———

usage. Despite some resistance from certain Western countries, particularly those with old colonial interests in the region, Iran became the accepted norm. The main geographical location of the Persian people is the Iranian plateau region, which has aquatic borders on the Caspian Sea, the Persian Gulf, and the Gulf of Oman, and modern land borders (clockwise from the west) with Iraq, Turkey, Armenia, Azerbaijan, Turkmenistan, Afghanistan, and Pakistan.

ORIGINS

Human activity within the Iranian plateau is ancient, with stoneworking, hunter-gatherer cultures dating back to 100,000 B.C.E. Agricultural communities, however, settled the territory between the 10th and seventh millennia B.C.E., leaving archaeological evidence of an advanced culture that included wine production and the use of horse-drawn cart transport. During the third and second millennia B.C.E. numerous tribes migrated into and out of the territory, with resulting tensions and struggles for power. One of the most important cultures to emerge during this period was that of the ELAMITES, concentrated in Khuzestan (a southwestern province of Iran), whose first king dates to around 2700 B.C.E. The Elamites established powerful dynasties and grand cities, including Susa. They traded with Assyria, Babylon, and Egypt, with whom they also warred, defeating Assyria and Babylon during the 13th and 12th centuries B.C.E. Elamite power declined over the next six centuries, but during this time other forces established themselves. Aryan tribes had moved into Iran from Central Asia during the second millennium. By the ninth century B.C.E. these tribes had differentiated into distinct groups, of whom the most important were the MEDES and the PERSIANS.

LANGUAGE

The overarching language of the Persians is Farsi, which is spoken not only in Iran but also in much of Tajikistan, Afghanistan, and Uzbekistan, with enclaves in Central Asia and China. Traditionally, Persian is separated into three historical strains: Old Persian (ca. 600–300 B.C.E.), Middle Persian (ca. 300 B.C.E.–800 C.E.), and Modern Persian (ca. 800 C.E.–present).

HISTORY

The Medians and the Achaemenids

The Median kingdom was founded, according to tradition, in the eighth century B.C.E. by one Deioces, who established a capital at Ecbatana (modern Hamadan) and laid the foundations for one of the most powerful empires of the ancient Middle East. Having defeated the encroaching ASSYRIANS in 612 B.C.E. (with the fall of Nineveh), the Medes carved out a kingdom extending from the Black Sea to Afghanistan, which was held together as much by mutual alliances as by conquest. The Persians, then a relatively minor people located in Fars in the southwest of Iran, were one of the groups under Median rule. It was under Cyrus II (ca. 585–530 B.C.E.) that the Persians ceased to be vassals and became rulers. In 553 Cyrus led his armies in a rebellion against Astyages (585–550 B.C.E.), who was his father-in-law and the Median king. With the help of the BABYLONIANS, the Persians captured Ecbatana and later removed Astyages from the throne.

Cyrus (also known as Cyrus the Great), the first king of what is known as the Achaemenid dynasty now presided over the Median Empire, and four years later took the title king of Persia, thereby stamping his ethnic identity on the conquered territory (see ACHAEMENIDS). Cyrus immediately embarked on a program of imperial expansion. His first objective was Lydia, a kingdom in western Anatolia (modern Turkey). Sardis, the capital of the LYDIANS, was put under siege and most of the Greek cities in Anatolia surrendered to the Persians. Lydia's king Croesus was captured in 546 B.C.E. In 540 B.C.E., Cyrus turned his attention to Babylon, previously his ally. The Babylonian king, Nabonidus, was not a popular ruler, a fact that helped Cyrus to a swift victory. Babylon fell in 539 B.C.E., giving Cyrus effective control of the entire Middle East. Cambyses II, Cyrus's son, inherited the throne in 530 B.C.E. The new king showed the same thirst for power as his father. In 525 B.C.E. he began a successful campaign to take Egypt. He was not to enjoy his victory for long, though; in 522 B.C.E. he died, possibly from an accidental sword wound, and was succeeded by one of his generals, Darius I (ca. 549–486 B.C.E.)

Darius's entire reign was characterized by rebellion, a virtually inevitable situation given the size of the Achaemenid Empire and the diversity of its subjugated peoples. The provinces under his control also had to pay high annual tributes in gold and silver, a practice that nearly bankrupted some states. Probably the most threatening rebellion came from within the Greek territories; many of the Ionian states rose up against Persian rule in 502 B.C.E. Persia suppressed these rebellions one by one, and then determined to invade the Greek mainland itself. At first victory seemed assured, with Macedon, Thace, Eretria, and various islands falling to Darius. However, in 490 B.C.E. the Persian army was soundly defeated at Marathon by a numerically inferior Greek army, a defeat that put a humiliating end to Darius's ambitions (*see* GREEKS).

Xerxes (r. 486–465 B.C.E.), the next Achaemenid ruler, continued the fight against Greece. The battle between Greece and Persia in the fifth century B.C.E. is one of the epic conflicts of ancient history. It took place in the context of Xerxes' successful suppression of revolts in Babylonia and Egypt. In 480 B.C.E. Xerxes launched a massive invasion of the Greek mainland. His progress was even greater than that achieved by Darius. He advanced his army through Attica and sacked and burned Athens. Shortly thereafter, however, he suffered a crushing naval defeat at Salamis (480 B.C.E.), where he lost 200 ships to the Greeks. Another major defeat came at Plataea in 479 B.C.E. The resultant Persian retreat finalized the destruction of the Greek expedition, and Persia lost most of its Greek territories.

Greeks and Parthians

Persian enjoyed relative peace with Greece for over 50 years, and from 393 B.C.E. even began to give Athens—previously its prime enemy—military and financial assistance in its war against Sparta. In 387 B.C.E. Persia headed negotiations to bring what is known as the Peloponnesian War to an end, although its principal motive was to gain reassurances that a newly powerful Athens would not try to take Persia's remaining possessions in Asia Minor.

The fourth century B.C.E. brought a truly seismic event in Persian history. The context for the century was a steady decline in Persian power, as more of the provinces of the Achaemenid Empire successfully broke away. In addition to these loses came the conquests of the Macedonian king Alexander the Great (356–323 B.C.E.) (*see* MACEDONIANS). Having effectively united Greece under his authority, Alexander turned his imperial ambitions east in 336 B.C.E. At the head of a large professional army, Alexander ousted Persia, now led by Darius III (336–338 B.C.E.), from its possessions in Asia Minor, achieving his first important victory at the Granicus River in 334 B.C.E., then capturing the Persian treasury at Sardis. Persia suffered further routs at the battles of Issus (331 B.C.E.)

and Gaugamela (329 B.C.E.), and steadily all of Persia's western provinces fell to Alexander's advance, despite Darius offering the Macedonian all the land west of the Euphrates River in return for peace.

The Greek onslaught was irrisistable. Babylon and Susa both fell in 331 B.C.E., and with them most of Persia's imperial wealth fell into the hands of Alexander's forces. Alexander next took Persepolis and its treasury. By this point only the city of Ecbatana remained as the last possible outpost of Persian resistance; Darius had ensconced himself there with a bodyguard force but was murdered by his own troops and Alexander's forces entered Ecbatana unopposed in 330 B.C.E.

Alexander's conquest of Persia marked the beginning of what is known as the Hellenistic Age, which was characterized by the spread of Greek culture across much of the known world. For the Persians conquest did not bring total subjugation. Alexander promoted interaction between GREEKS and Persians and left many of the Persian satrapies (provinces) in place, as well as encouraging Persian and Greek intermarriage at court level. Alexander died in 323 B.C.E., and the loss of his central authority caused the empire to fracture into numerous power blocs. Persia, along with Mesopotamia, Syria, and Bactria, came under the rule of the Seleucid dynasty from 312 B.C.E., the first ruler being Seleucus I (ca. 358–281 B.C.E.), a former Macedonian commander. The Seleucids had an especially troubled reign as they tried to rule over their fractious states. Furthermore, there were major new threats. Chief among these were the PARTHIANS, an aggressive tribe from the northeast of Iran. In 250 B.C.E., both Parthia and Bactria broke away from Seleucid rule, and although the Seleucids contained the Parthians, they could not defeat them. The Romans were also becoming interested in Persia, primarily because it wanted to quash Persian ambitions in Greece. The Seleucids were eventually military defeated by Rome and Parthia. The Parthian king Mithridates I (171–138 B.C.E.) took Persia itself in 139 B.C.E. and captured the last Seleucid monarch, Demetrius II Nicator.

The Parthian takeover inaugurated a new era for Persia. The Parthians eventually consolidated an empire that stretched from the Euphrates River to Afghanistan. Hellenistic influences were weakened under the Parthians, allowing older Persian customs and art to reassert themselves in the cultural life of the Iranian plateau.

Persians time line

B.C.E.

10th–seventh millennia Agricultural communities settle on the Iranian plateau.

ca. 2700 First recorded Elamite king.

eighth century Median kingdom is founded.

612 The Medes inflict a major defeat upon the Assyrians at Nineveh.

553 The Persians under Cyrus defeat the Medes in battle and capture Ecbatana.

550–539 Asia Minor and Babylon are added to the Persian Achaemenid Empire.

522 Darius I takes the throne of the Achaemenid Empire after the death of Cambyses II.

449 The long-running wars between the Greeks and the Persians are brought to a temporary end by the Peace of Callias.

336–330 Alexander the Great conquers all of the Persian territories, ushering in the Hellenistic Age.

312 The Seleucid dynasty is founded under Seleucus I.

139 The Parthians capture Seleucid monarch Demetrius II Nicator and conquer Media and Fars.

C.E.

222 The Sassanian dynasty begins when the vassal king Ardashir revolts and captures the Persian capital Ctesiphon.

642 The Sassanian dynasty comes to a decisive end with the Arab victory over Persia at Nehavand.

661 The Umayyad Caliphate is established.

750 The Umayyad Caliphate is overthrown by the revolt of Hashimiyya; Abbasid dynasty begins.

999–1010 Turkish forces take power from the Samanid dynasty and establish Mahmud, the ruler of the Ghaznavids, as ruler.

1051 The rule of the Ghaznavids and the Buyids is overthrown by the invasion of the Seljuk Turks, who establish Toghril I as king.

13th–14th centuries Persia is steadily conquered by the Mongols.

1387 The Mongol leader Timur establishes the Timurid dynasty over Persia.

1501 The beginning of the Safavid dynasty, the first ruler being Shah Ismail.

1722–36 The Safavid dynasty collapses under a series of invasions from Afghan, Russian, and Turkish forces.

1796 The Qajar dynasty begins after Agha Mohammed Khan Qajar takes power from the hands of the short-lived rule of Mohammed Karim Khan Zand.

1907 An Anglo-Russian Convention gives Russia power over the north of Persia, while Britain controls over the south.

1925 Despite British attempts to control Persia, Reza Khan takes over the Persian leadership, beginning the Pahlavi dynasty.

1941 Allied forces occupy Persia to protect their wartime oil supplies.

1943 The Tehran conference guarantees Iran's postwar boundaries and independence.

1979 Exile of the Mohammad Reza Pahlavi, the last shah of Iran, marks the end of millennia of rule by monarchy.

The Parthians and the ROMANS warred frequently, often in disputes over the Armenian homeland. These conflicts included some moments of Parthian military brilliance, such as at the Battle of Carrhae in 53 B.C.E., when the Parthian army destroyed that of the Roman commander Marcus Licinius Crassus, killing over 20,000 Roman troops, but many more

Parthian defeats. Parthia was vulnerable. It was split between seven ruling tribes, so there was always the potential for political fractures, and wars with Rome were costing a great deal of money and manpower. Under the rule of Artabanus V, rebellion finally came in earnest. In 224 C.E. Ardashir, a Persian vassal king (ruler of Fars and Kerman), began a revolt aimed at taking over the Persian state. In 222 C.E. Ardashir captured Ctesiphon, which was then the capital of Persia. Ardashir I became the first ruler of the Sassanian dynasty.

The Sassanian Empire

Ardashir I (r. 224–41) brought centralization to Persia once more, uniting the country under one ruler and avoiding the federal political structure of the Parthians. The Sassanian dynasty (the area ruled by the Sassanid dynasty) regarded itself as building on the legacy of the Achaemenid rulers Darius and Cyrus and continued those two kings' policy of imperial expansion (*see* SASSANIANS). Ardashir also invested his own brand of religious fervor, establishing the cult of Ahura Mazda as the official state religion. Other religions faced persecution, especially Christianity, since the Christians were seen as sympathetic to the Byzantines, who were then the Persians' chief opponents.

Under Ardashir and successive rulers, the Sassanian Empire grew steadily. High points of expansion came in 256, when Shapur (Ardashir's son) captured Antioch from the Romans (it was subsequently lost), and in 260, when a large Roman army was defeated at Edessa and the Roman emperor Valerian was captured.

The Sassanian Empire survived from 226 to 651. The beginning of its end can be traced to 590. In that year the Shah Hormizd IV (r. 579–590) was murdered and his son Khosrau II was forced to flee. In an unlikely alliance, Khosrau turned to the Romans for help, and the Byzantine emperor Maurice complied, gaining some Armenian and Mesopotamian territories in return and putting Khosrau on the throne in 591.

The deal between the Byzantines and the Persians was broken in 602, when Maurice was murdered by rebellious Byzantine troops. Khosrau subsequently decided to move against the Byzantine Empire. His advance was dramatic and ruthless. Syria fell between 611 and 613, bringing Antioch once again into Persian hands, and in 614 the Persian army advanced into Palestine. The advancing Persians killed thousands of Christians and destroyed hundreds of churches. On reaching Jerusalem in April 614, the Persians placed the city under siege for a month. When it finally fell, 60,000 Christians were murdered and over 30,000 put into slavery as punishment for their resistance. The Persians also looted the True Cross relic, an incendiary act to all Christian nations.

As the Christian world slowly began to mobilize, Khosrau continued his advance. In 626, the Persians laid siege to the city of Constantinople itself (Byzantium had been renamed Constantinople in 324). By this time, however, Constantinople was under the leadership of a new and highly competent leader, Emperor Heraclius. Khosrau rejected peace terms offered by Heraclius, but his confidence was misplaced. Heraclius had rebuilt his army and navy into a disciplined fighting force. The siege army was defeated and Heraclius went on the offensive from 622. Over the next two years Byzantine forces surged through Asia Minor, Armenia, and Azerbaijan to threaten Persia itself. In 627 the Byzantines defeated the Persians in a major battle at Nineveh in Mesopotamia, then pushed into Persia to take the capital Ctesiphon, obliterating Khosrau's palace. The True Cross was returned to Constantinople, and the Sassanian Empire was left tottering.

Arab Invasion and the Abbasid Caliphates

During the seventh century, a force arose in the Middle East that would change the political and religious future of the world. This force, both warlike and spiritual in nature, was that of the Muslim ARABS, who upon the death of the prophet Muhammad in 632 began a military drive out from what is today Saudi Arabia. Arab assaults on Persia began around 635 under the leadership of Abu Bakr, who had already taken Syria and Palestine. Persia was militarily weak at this time, having suffered recent defeats at the hands of the Byzantines. In 637 the Arab force pushed aside Persian resistance to take Ctesiphon, sending the five-year-old emperor, Yazdegerd III, fleeing with his family. He was assassinated in 651, but by this time the Sassanian dynasty had already come to an end with the Arabs' decisive victory at the Battle of Nehavand in 642. It was the beginning of Persia's subjugation under the Muslim caliphate (rule by an Islamic head of state, known as a caliph), which would last for the next century. In 661 the Umayyad dynasty became rulers of the Caliphate.

The Arab takeover of Persia was to have a profound impact upon the country, bringing an

Islamic monotheism that became the dominant faith of the Persian peoples during the centuries that followed. In the 740s there was a further transformation. Fault lines were widening in Arab unity, and in 747 the Hashimiyya movement, headed by Abu Muslim, began a revolt against the Umayyads. The rebels had a mix of religious and political grievances to air. In Persia, taxation was a major source of discontent, particularly what was seen as the unfair imposition of land and head taxes on those who had converted to Islam in the conquered territories. By 750 the Umayyads had been overthrown, and Persia came under the rule of the Abbasid dynasty, which would last from 750 to 821.

The time of the Abbasid caliphates was a culturally fascinating one for Persia, and for the Arabs who came into contact with the country. It saw intense intellectualism develop as Persian and Arabian cultures mixed and competed, with literary and philosophical output being especially strong. Persian artists and thinkers were salient in the Abbasid court in Baghdad, and many Arabs felt that their peoples were having their spiritual simplicity corrupted by Persian sophistication.

Persia soon became a source of trouble for the Abbasids. Rebellions began during the ninth century as Abbasid control of territories beyond its power base in Baghdad weakened. While Syria and Palestine saw their own uprisings, various groups within Persia steadily brought much of the country back under their control. Some groups—such as the Tahirids, Saminids, and Ghaznavids—took de facto control of their territories simply by running their provinces as their own. In eastern Persia, the Saffarid dynasty was more aggressive and built a small empire. The Saffarids even marched on Baghdad in 876, although that mission was defeated. Saffarid power was eventually replaced by that of another Persian dynasty, the Samanids, who built a capital in Bukhara. The Samanids, as other Iranian dynasties had done before them, revived many elements of Persian culture that had been smothered under Arab rule, especially indigenous festivals and the literary retelling of specifically Persian histories. Another dynasty that reignited Persian identity was that of the Buyids in the north of Persia, who in 945 entered Baghdad and took effective control of the caliphate (although they allowed the caliph to remain as a nominal post). The Buyids expanded their control over many provinces of Iran, including Fars, Jibal, Ravy, and Kerman.

The weakness of Samanid power lay in their Turkish slave guards, who grew in strength to form two threatening families—the Simjurids and Ghaznavids. The latter in particular rose, by the end of the 10th century, to threaten Samanid rule, making allegiances with other families inside Persia and attracting Turkish invaders from without. In 999 Turkish forces took over Bukhara, and by 1010 the effective leadership of Samanid territory had passed to Ghazni's ruler, Mahmud.

Mahmud was an ambitious man, and like many Persian leaders soon acquired imperial ambitions. He pushed out his territories west to Isfahan, one of Persia's most important cities, and east to northern India, but during the 12th century his empire, and Persia in general, succumbed to an outside force—the Seljuks.

Seljuks and Mongols

The Seljuk Turks, named after their ancestral chieftain, were a strong presence on Persia's northern borders by the end of the 10th century C.E., having migrated there from the Central Asia steppes. The Seljuks had territorial ambitions in Persia, particularly on those territories held by the Ghaznavids. With the death of Mahmud in 1030, and the ascendancy of his son Masud to the throne, the Seljuks identified a critical juncture in which to act. Under their sultan Toghril I, the Seljuks invaded Persia and overcame the Ghazavids, taking Isfahan in 1051. With the Ghazni suppressed Toghril's next target was the Buyids, and he marched on Baghdad, which also fell in 1051.

The Seljuks, like the Buyids, retained the caliphate but promoted their orthodox Sunni credentials by presenting themselves as the protectors of the caliph's spiritual authority. However, Toghril received the title King of East and West as a blunt recognition of his overarching political control. The Seljuks established an empire that was to last for the next 100 years, but their hegemony over Persia came to an end in the mid-13th century. Internally, Seljuk unity had started to dissolve during the 12th century through familiar causes—rival provincial governors establishing their own power bases in various regions of the country. But the final destruction of the Seljuks began in 1219 when the Mongols under Chinggis Khan began their expansion across Central Asia and into the Middle East. In 1256, Khan's grandson, Hulegu (1217–65) took most of Persia, with the remainder being absorbed by the conquests of Timur in the late 14th century.

Many Mongol leaders had a distinct antipathy toward Persian culture, and the invasions resulted in major cultural and agricultural destruction across Persia and a major drop in population levels (particularly among males, who were killed in their thousands). Some later rulers were more enlightened. Ghazan Khan (1295–1304), for example, vigorously encouraged Persian commerce by lowering taxes and improving agriculture and trade routes. Yet under Timur (1336–1405), who established the Timurid dynasty over Persia from 1387, Persia lived under a state of virtual persecution, with any rebellion put down through massacres on a tremendous scale. Ironically, the period of Timur's rule also saw the promotion of intellectual activities at his courts.

Safavids

The dynasty that would replace the Mongols in Persia first became established in northwestern Iran, although its origins lie more in Azerbaijan. The Safavids were a Shii order founded by Safi al-Din in 1301, and by the 16th century they had grown both powerful and radical. Under Shah Ismail (1487–1524), they began a campaign to take Persia and much of Central Asia for themselves. By 1501 they had succeeded in ousting the vestiges of Mongol power and establishing control over Mesopotamia and Persia.

The critical historical importance of the Safavids to the whole subsequent history of Iran is that Shii Islam went from being a minority religion in the country to being the majority, and official, religion. The process was slow and steady, but by the middle of the 17th century the transformation was effectively complete. Persia also became more defined as a state in its own right. Its international trade grew, with the consequence that Persia's arts and literature were influenced by foreign traders passing through though its cities and along its trade routes. It still, however, had to contend with a familiar range of threats from outside its borders, and Ismail's forces suffered a heavy defeat against the rising power of the Ottoman Turks in 1514 at Caldiran (*see* OTTOMANS).

The Ottoman Turks were no less of a problem for one of the greatest Safavid rulers, Abbas I (1587–1629). Abbas reformed the Persian army substantially, making it a much more professional force, and made a peace treaty with the Ottomans in which the borders of Iran were agreed. In 1598 Abbas also moved the Persian capital to Isfahan (from Kazvin) and helped develop it into one of the most spectacular and civilized cities in the world. Trade was broadened with foreign nations as Persia opening itself to commercial activity with the powerful English East India and Dutch East India companies. The governmental system was also reformed.

The year 1722, however, was the beginning of the end of the Safavid dynasty. The passage of time had already weakened its power somewhat, and so it was vulnerable to a raid by Afghan tribesmen, who invaded the country and captured Isfahan. At the same time Russian and Turkish troops also invaded. Apart from a brief period of Safavid restoration, by 1736 the dynasty had ended.

Qajar Dynasty and European Intervention

The ruler who took the Persian throne after the downfall of the Safavids was Nadir Shah (r. 1736–47). During the 11 years he was in power, Nadir drove the Russians, Turks, and Afghans out of Persia and then began campaigning beyond Persia's borders. Nadir achieved numerous victories in Central Asia and even, in 1739, attacked Mughal India, looting Delhi. Although the new empire brought enhanced wealth to Persia, from 1741 Nadir became increasingly paranoid and ruthless, and hence created many internal enemies. He was murdered in 1747, and Persia fractured into competing territories once again.

Central to the immediate post-Nadir history of Persia was the conflict between two factions, the Zand and the Qajar. From 1750 to 1779, the Zand were the more powerful, ruling over central and southern Iran under the leadership of Mohammed Karim Khan Zand. Karim Khan's rule was a relatively peaceful period in Persian history, with good commercial activity and levels of prosperity. However, following his death in 1779, buried enmities came to the surface, especially in the hands of Agha Mohammed Khan Qajar, a former prisoner of the Zand and a leader of the rebellious Qajar tribe (*see* QAJARS). Agha Mohammed began war against the weakened Zand, killing their leader in 1794 and taking control of most of Persia two years later, whereupon he took the title shah.

Iran's fortunes were reversed under the Qajar dynasty. Wealth plummeted through misuse and poor trade deals, and productivity fell. Iran became a battleground over which Britain and Russia contested their imperial ambitions. Britain was expanding its empire north from India, while Russia was growing in Central Asia. Russia aimed to gain access to the

Persian Gulf and Indian Ocean, while Britain wanted to check that ambition and protect its interests in northern India and Afghanistan. Iran quickly lost its Central Asian territories in a series of disadvantageous treaties and, worse still, tried to solve its financial problems by trading its assets to foreign powers. The Qajar rulers led ineffectively, and by the early 20th century foreign powers were effectively carving up Iran. One positive event in this period was the Constitutional Revolution of 1906, which imposed a constitution upon the country's monarchical structure.

In 1907 an Anglo-Russian Convention settled the imperial dispute by giving the signatories effective economic control over Iran, Russia taking the north of the country and Britain the south. Iran became particularly important to both parties when oil was discovered shortly thereafter.

The Birth of Modern Iran

World War I saw Iran become a battleground once again as Britain and Russia attempted to protect their oil interests from the Axis powers (which included the Ottoman Turks). Several German plots aimed at inspiring revolts were foiled, but in 1916 northern Persia saw direct fighting between the Russians and the Turks. Following the Russian Revolution of 1917, which seemed to leave the Turks with open access to Persia, a small British force held Persia until the armistice of 1918.

The end of the war left Britain with effective governance over Persia. Its attempt to establish Persia as a protectorate, however, was prevented by an Iranian soldier, Reza Khan, who organized a coup in 1921 and quickly rose in prominence under the shah. In 1925 he overthrew Ahmed Shah and took the throne of Iran for himself.

Reza Kahn established what was known as the Pahlavi dynasty, which ruled from 1925 until 1979. His impact on the country was powerful. He began to reverse Iran's economic decline, modernize its politics (with increased secularization), and instigated important reforms in education and law. During World War II the British once again occupied the country to secure its oil reserved, and Reza, who had sympathies with Germany, was forced to abdicate in favor of his son Mohammad Reza Pahlavi, who ruled for the next 38 years.

Although the Tehran Conference of 1943 guaranteed Iran's postwar boundaries and independence, the end of hostilities in 1945 brought tensions as Russia continued to occupy Iranian territories (principally Azerbaijan) until it secured promises of oil concessions in 1946. The postwar period was one of political instability in Iran. Parliamentary-style elections were held, but there was a high turnover of prime ministers (six by 1951 alone). In 1951 Iranian oil was nationalized, although this did not stop Iranian dependence on Western oil distribution channels.

The 1960s saw something of mixed fortunes in the Iranian domestic situation. A series of land reforms distributed Iranian land more equitably throughout the population, with the proportion of owner-occupied farmland rising from 26 percent to 78 percent by 1972. Education became more secular in outlook, and there were improvements in literacy. However, new tensions were emerging. The fundamentalist religious voice of the Ayatollah Ruhollah Khomeini criticized the government and its secular reforms, and even though he was exiled in 1964 (to Iraq, then France) his opinions still stirred a large percentage of the populace. Government-backed violence increased, with heavy-handed detentions in which torture and killing were commonplace, particularly after the assassination of Premier Hassan Ali Mansur in 1965. The economy also started to suffer as the government attempted to cope with surging population increases.

By the late 1970s public demonstrations against the shah were expanding in both size and fervor. Suspecting an imminent coup the shah fled Iran on January 16, 1979. This event marked the end of royal rule in Iran, a period of more than 4,500 years from the earliest Elamite kings. Although the transformation of Iran into a modern state had arguably begun in the 16th century under the Safavids, the events of 1979 mark a clear division between the ancient land of the Persians and the modern Iranian state.

CULTURE

The cultural history of the Persians is long and labyrinthine. In this account there is scope to only touch upon some of the major themes and issues from that history, and bring out salient examples of how the Persian world expressed itself and was administered.

Economy

The economic history of the Persians has been rooted in the need to find, or the disregard for, equitable solutions to taxation and wealth dis-

Detail of a fifth-century B.C.E. relief from the Persian citadel in Persepolis

tribution across a wide range or ethnic groups and needs. The financial foundation of much of the population has historically rested on basic village agriculture, and agriculture has remained important to the Iranian economy to this day. A 1991 census found that almost a quarter of the population was engaged in agricultural work, with major export industries in products such as dates and pistachio nuts.

Historically, however, the major economic equation that had to be negotiated was the relationship between a centralized ruler and his subject governors. If taxes were too high, there was a risk of promoting revolt; too low, and the military and civil needs of the government might not be met. Under Darius (who, it should be noted, introduced one of the world's first systems of coinage), for example, satraps and the rulers of vassal states each had to pay fixed annual amounts of gold and silver to the government coffers, but in agriculture the tax contributions were based on a percentage of the annual yield. An example of a less successful taxation system comes from the Arab rulers of the seventh century. After they had replaced the Sassanians, they appointed tax agents who thrived on extortion, something that bred animosity among Arab and Persian alike. A poll tax (known as the *jizyah*) on non-Muslims was frequently extended to Persians who had converted to Islam. Added to this was a lack of investment in agriculture that made agricultural taxes increasingly difficult to meet.

War has played a major role in Persian economic history and the financial effects of conflict have often been a primary cause for the downfall of empires. Wars were extremely expensive to fund and the loss of treasuries to invaders could prove devastating—as the Persians found during the conquests of Alexander the Great.

The modern economic history of Iran has been defined by oil and natural gas, the revenues from which today form nearly 50 percent of total government income. International trade in this, and other commodities, has been complicated by global politics. Since the Islamic revolution of 1979, Iran has been largely dependent on trade with Middle Eastern nations and those of the former Soviet Union.

Government and Society

The diverse ethnic and tribal identities of Persia have made it a complex entity to govern. One

A relief of King Darius I discovered on the wall of his palace at Persepolis

of the earliest systems of government, that of the Elamites, involved a ruling monarch served by vassal princes. Under the rule of Cyrus the Great in the sixth century B.C.E., the system of satrapies was in place. In this case an appointed satrap (governor) ruled over his own satrapy (province). Even though satraps were subordinate to the imperial ruler, they exercised almost total power within their own territories. Satraps had their own royal courts, controlled provincial military units, acted as final arbiter in disputes of law, and held sway over the province's finances. The system was generally a successful one, so much so that Alexander left it in place when he conquered Persia in the fourth century B.C.E. However, the danger in the satrapies was always that a governor might use his local power base to rebel against the king. As history shows, Persia has frequently endured upheavals in imperial and federal order as ambitious satraps have sought to gain more power.

A major influence over Persian government and society were the effects of takeovers by foreign powers. In some cases invaders were sensitive to local systems of government, as was the case with Alexander the Great, and indeed encouraged the exchange of political ideas and systems. Some were less than sensitive—the Mongol and early Arab leaders were known for imposing authority rather than inspiring it. Furthermore, the degree to which Persia could be called a centralized state varied considerably. In the first century C.E. the Parthians, for example, struggled to maintain control over an empire composed of 18 different kingdoms, with the nobility of each kingdom having its own tribal, financial, imperial, or nationalistic agendas. By contrast, the succeeding Sassanid Empire was far more centralized, with the king clearly governing via an aristocratic court. The centralization was aided by a new system of social classification in which people were ordered into one of four categories: soldiers, priests, secretaries, and commoners. By basing this system on birth, but making some allowance for progression by merit, the Sassanids engineered a social system in which all power rested squarely within the royal court, the umbrella under which all the other social classes sheltered.

Military Practices

The numerous empires won by various Persian dynasties through the ages is simple testimony to the professional and spirited military heritage of the Iranian peoples. The precise form taken by these armed forces, however, varied considerably over time.

During the period of the Greco-Persian wars in the fifth centuries B.C.E., the Persia army was a mixed body of light dagger- and spear-armed infantry, slingers, archers, and cavalry. Archers and infantry worked closely together. Archers shot into the mass of the enemy ranks, protected by a shield man standing in front (or, later, a freestanding wicker shield) while the infantry made stabbing and slashing attacks when the moment to advance was right. Persian archers used composite bows, which had a lethal range of several hundred yards in competent hands. The cavalry consisted of warriors on horseback or riding in horse-drawn chariots. In combat the cavalry made rapid maneuvers around the enemy ranks, firing arrows and launching javelins to break the enemy lines. Heavy cavalry armed with spears and swords could also be used to come into close contact with the enemy.

One of the most famous bodies of Persian soldiers was the "Ten Thousand Immortals."

These soldiers acted as both a royal guard and an elite body of standing infantry, and were so named because their numbers were never allowed to fall below 10,000 strong. In general, however, the Persian army was an amalgam of diverse forces, including bodies of infantry from numerous tribes and nations and large numbers of mercenaries. This social and ethnic diversity meant that Persian forces contained a broad mix of fighting styles and equipment that were not always easy to control. The Immortals plus several other key units of indigenous infantry typically occupied the center ranks while the possibly more unreliable troops from other tribes were arrayed in less vital positions.

Persia's military might was eventually overcome by the strength, speed, and discipline of the Greek hoplites (citizen-soldiers), plus the talents of the Greek navy, which outmaneuvered the Persian triremes at battles such as Salamis. In a syncretic style typical of the Persians, Greek hoplites were later incorporated into their own ranks. The Persians also learned from the Arab armies, who showed them the value of such practices as raiding and maneuver based on fleeting attacks and false retreats.

Dwellings and Architecture

Domestic dwellings in Persia, until the advent of modern building materials in the late 20th century, were constructed of stone or mud-brick. They were typically one- or two-story dwellings with thick walls to retain heat in winter, and to keep it out in the summer. In traditional houses, the front door opened into a small space called the *hashti,* which in turn gave access to a hallway known as the *dalan-e-vorudi.* From this hallway most of the other rooms of the house could be accessed. There was often also a central courtyard featuring water and plants. Decorative features were rendered in stucco.

Traditional Persian houses and larger buildings in hot arid areas often featured a cooling system that used an underground water reserve (*qanat*) and a wind tower (*badgir*). Even in the height of summer the water reserve remained cool, sometimes close to freezing, in the rock several feet below the surface. These water reserves were often part of underground irrigation systems. Cool air in the water chamber was drawn up into the building via a conduit through the action of the wind tower. Protruding several feet into the air above the dwelling, the wind tower had apertures that could be closed or opened. By opening the aperture facing away from the direction of the wind warm, air would be drawn up the wind tower from the interior of the house and cool air from the water chamber below would be drawn into the house to replace it. In the most sophisticated examples the interior of buildings could be kept cool enough to refrigerate meat and other perishables. In less sophisticate examples a *badgir* was used to provide ventilation only.

Iran is also been known for its impressive civic architecture. The styles of this architecture have shifted over the centuries, changing as the influences of different cultures have passed through the country. During the time of Cyrus, Darius, and Xerxes, for example, the great palaces illustrated Assyrian, Greek, and Egyptian mannerisms. The palace at Pasargadae, for example, had winged bulls at the gateways, imitating the Assyrian style. Similarly, columns from the palace at Persepolis feature Egyptian-style capitals with animal and palm motifs, but also show a Greek influence in the double Ionic decoration on the capitals. In overall layout, these great palaces were majestic and labyrinthine, with numerous colonnaded passageways, majestic hypostyle halls, and sumptuous gardens and courtyards.

A great shift in Persian architecture occurred during the transformation in the country's culture under Islam. Architectural principles were standardized under the Islam system of eight traditional architectural ingredients: garden, platform, porch, gateway, arch, dome, minaret, and the unification of the whole. Calligraphic and decorative arts also reached new heights as buildings became fantastically ornate. The greatest representative of such art is arguably found at Isfahan, where Shah Abbas presided over an extensive Safavid building program. Famous palaces and mosques of Isfahan include the Ali Qapu and the Hash-Behesht palaces and the Masjid-i-Jami mosque. Persian culture is also justly famous for its bridge architecture, which often featuring multiple, beautifully crafted archways.

Clothing

A common traditional form of dress consisted of a loose white cotton undershirt matched with equally loose drawstring-fastened trousers known as *sherwal,* although in some female fashions these trousers were tapered. Over this an outer gown or coat would be worn. These gowns often featured bright colors and ostentatious patterns and reflected the wealth and statues of the owner. Patterning depended upon tribe or dynasty, but floral and striped motifs were very common, the latter being more popular among the Turkish and Arab peoples rather than the pre-Islamic Persians. Most people wore a sash around the waist as a fashion accessory, and footwear generally consisted of brown or black leather shoes or half boots. Headgear was required, and for men this usually meant a turban or a fezlike hat while for women there was a wide variety of headscarves, wraps, veils, and other head coverings.

Personal Habits

The personal habits and customs of a civilization that persisted for more than 3,000 years are vast in range. One of the best sources of information on early Persian customs is the Greek historian Herodotus, who noted, among other things, that:

> There is no nation that so readily adopts
> foreign customs as the Persians. Thus,
> they have taken the dress of the Medes,
> considering it superior to their own;
> and in war they wear the Egyptian
> breastplate. As soon as they hear of
> any luxury, they instantly make it their
> own: and hence, among other novelties,
> they have learnt unnatural lust from the
> Greeks. Each of them has several wives,
> and a still larger number of concubines.
> Next to prowess in arms, it is regarded
> as the greatest proof of manly excellence
> to be the father of many sons.

The reliability of Herodotus is questionable at times, but his comments do illustrate a perceived adaptiveness in Persian culture that is evidenced by the great array of foreign influences present in Persian, architecture, art, and even military practice. To find more consistent cultural practices, however, it is easiest to look at how Islam shaped later Iranian culture.

Family sits at the root of Iranian society, with the man being the head of the household and the women living protected and, by Western standards, sheltered lives. Favoritism toward family members is not discouraged as in the West, although friendship is also taken extremely seriously, particularly within a business environment. Interactions between men and women are governed by strict rules, and women must always observe Islamic codes of dress, with the head and limbs covered. Mealtimes are family affairs, with the whole family sitting around a table (which may or may not have chairs).

For conservative Muslim Iranians, daily life is structured according to the practical principles of Islam. Most visible is the requirement to pray five times a day at designated times, and during the month of Ramadan all Muslims are required to fast between sunrise and sunset.

Transportation

Until the advent of motorized transport, Persia relied on its horses to provide land transportation. Most horse journeys would have been undertaken riding with goods strapped to the sides of the animals in baskets. However, art from the Achaemenid period also depicts horses pulling light carts or chariots, usually when transporting more affluent members the society.

The Achaemenid era brought one of the great achievements of Persian transportation, the creation on an extensive road network linking the empire together. In total this road network consisted of some 8,000 miles of semipaved surfaces. The greatest of these roads was the so-called Royal Road, built under Darius I. The Royal Road ran 1,677 miles from Susa in the heart of Persia all the way to Sardis in Asia Minor (modern Turkey). The road network was particularly important in facilitating imperial communications. Posting stations were built along the entire route, each station one day's ride from the next. By having couriers at each station, a message could pass along the length of the route in seven to 14 days (it would have taken a single rider three months). The Royal Road in turn formed a section of the Silk Road, a network of overland trade routes that developed over thousands of years linking peoples from coastal China and the southern tip of the Indian subcontinent with the Mediterranean.

Throughout their history the Persians also made extensive use of maritime vessels for long-range journeys beyond the waters of the Persian Gulf, and also for fishing. In the ancient period Persian galleys, two- or three-decked vessels powered primarily by oars, were used for both trade and warfare. The traditional sailing ship of the Arab civilizations of Persia was, and remains in many areas today, the dhow. The dhow is a simple wood-framed vessel that features one or two triangular lateen sails. The design of the sails gave the craft good maneuverability and speed when sailing into the wind, a useful feature in the complicated waters of the gulf.

Other Technologies

Persian culture has always valued intellectual endeavor and inventiveness and has contributed much to the scientific and mathematical fields. Of the latter, the Persian mathematician Muhammad ibn Musa al-Khwarizmi, working in the ninth century C.E., was one of the founders of modern algebra, and 200 years later the scholar Omar Khayyam designed methods of solving cubic equations and quadratic equations. In addition, al-Khwarizmi helped refine the use of Arabic numerals as a system of writing (the system itself was an Indian invention) and helped to spread it throughout the Middle Eastern region and beyond.

Strong mathematical skills aided engineering solutions, and some of Persia's practical inventions have had a fundamental effect on human civilization; the wheel may have been conceived within Persian territory (although Sumer in Mesopotamia, now Iraq, has a strong claim). Windmills seem to have originated in Persia in the seventh century B.C.E. and were used for powering millstones to grind corn and to draw water for irrigation purposes. Many other technologies have been ascribed to Persian origins, from wristwatches to perfume. In most cases it is impossible to be clear about the origins of a particular invention, but it is certain that Persia aided in the transmission to the Middle East and the West of inventions originating in China and India.

The mountains that surround the central Iranian plateau receive a large amount of precipitation, but the streams that flow into the plateau from the mountains dry out or submerge before they penetrate far into the arid interior. To solve this problem the ancient Persians developed a widespread network of underground aquifers for irrigation. These aquifers channeled water from natural underground water reserves in highland areas down to the agricultural terraces of the valleys below. A typical aquifer (or *qanat*) was three to five miles in length and was constructed between 60 and 600 feet below the ground. Some aquifers, however, were more than 40 miles long and 900 feet deep. The aquifer channels themselves were two to three feet in diameter and connected to the surface by a series of vertical inspection and construction shafts spaced at approximately 100-foot intervals along their entire length. They were excavated by small groups of engineers—usually only one person could work in the narrow aquifer channel—and some took decades to complete. The very gently but consistent inclines needed to ensure a constant but not too rapid flow of water were plotted with great accuracy using simple plumb lines and spirit levels.

Art

Painted pottery has been discovered in Iran that dates back to at least the third millennium B.C.E., and in its subsequent history Persia was renowned for its decorative arts. The earliest forms of pottery exhibited simple geometric and linear patterns, but as Persia absorbed more and more cultural influences, the work grew in sophistication and artistry. During the Achaemenid period civic buildings received sumptuous ornamentation accentuated with precious stones from across the empire and ivory work. Pots featured not only painted decoration but also scenes incised into or molded onto the ceramic (representations of animals and plants were popular). Metalworking was equally advanced, with fine, delicate jewelry produced for wealthy patrons and high standards of engraving applied to weapons and drinking vessels.

Another skill for which Persia was renowned was its manufacture of fine carpets and rugs. One of the earliest carpets known, the Pazyryk carpet dating from the fifth century B.C.E., was woven in multiple striking colors and has a border depicting deer and horses. During the early centuries of Islamic rule, Persia sent 600 carpets a year just to the caliph in Baghdad. Persian carpets have retained a reputation for excellence to the present day and continue to be major export product.

Persian art has always reflected the influences of other cultures. During the Hellenistic period, for example, the more dynamic naturalism of Greek art, especially in the rendition of the human form, became apparent in Persian figure sculpture, although with the takeover by the Parthians more traditional and less naturalistic depictions again became fashionable. Possibly the greatest transformation of Persian art, however, and one that has informed all subsequent art to the present day, came with the arrival of Islam. Islam, generally speaking, discourages the depiction of living creatures, and Persian art had to adjust to this new reality. During the Abbasid era ceramic decoration grew more sophisticated, with patterns ranging from simple illustrations of birds and plants through to deeply colored arabesque patterns.

Two of the seminal artistic forms of Islamic Persia were calligraphy and miniature paintings. Calligraphy was used to write lavish copies of the Quran and other documents and had all the emphasis on symmetry and craft seen in other forms of art. The calligrapher's art also became important in building decoration. Miniature painting began in earnest in the 13th century and was principally used to decorate books. These paintings expressed everything from great moments in history to religious themes, love themes, and depictions of nature.

Music

The playing of music in Persia dates back to at least 2500 B.C.E. Unlike much Western music, which relies on a written score, Persian classical music (known as *musiqi-e assil*) has traditionally had an improvised style with the instrumental and vocal improvisation based around agreed scales and melodies. Memorizing these scales and melodies could be a challenging feat, for there were hundreds of them and their rhythmic patterns were extremely complex. The traditional instruments were principally strings and drums. Stringed instruments included various types of lutes such as the *tar*, *tanbur*, and *setar* and harps (although from the Safavid dynasty these lost much influence to the piano), while rhythm came from the *tombak* goblet drum or the *daf* frame drum. There was also a series of woodwind instruments such as the *nay* (an end-blown flute).

While Persian classical music had performed a variety of roles in pre-Islamic Persia, from popular entertainment through to an accompaniment for religious ceremonies, under Islam its practice was officially controlled to varying degrees, and until the 20th century its use was primarily confined to official religious or court use.

Literature

Persia is renowned for its literary output, particularly the excellence of its poetic works. It has given the world much of the epic work of fiction known as *The Book of One Thousand and One Nights* (the exact origins of this collection are much disputed) and other equally rich veins of mythology, folklore, and religious writing. From the sixth century C.E. onward poetry came to the fore, and over subsequent centuries Persian steadily overtook Arabic as the literary language of much of the Middle East and Central Asia. Such was the Persian flair for poetry that everything from engineering texts to medical treatises could be found in poetic form, not just imaginative literature. Writers would often cross multiple genres. The illustrious Omar Khayyam (1048–1131), for example, not only wrote works on mathematics and astronomy but also composed the famous collection of some 1,000 poems known today as the *Rubaiyat*.

A great deal of poetic output was also written under court patronage, and much of this featured tales that exalted leaders and incidents in Persian history. Indeed, Persian literature was central in forming a sense of national identity. The greatest text in this regard is the *Shah-name (The Epic of Kings)* of Abu al-Qasem Mansur (935–1020), who is better known as Firdawsi. This book, 30 years in the writing, was based upon earlier Old Persian texts and charted the history of Persia before the Arab conquest.

Persian poetry went through several stages of evolution. Its handling by Sufi mystics from the 13th century produced some of the most well-crafted examples of the art form, full of longing for unity with the divine. One of the most famous poets of this tradition is Mawlana Jalal ad-Din Muhammad Rumi (1207–73), usually known just as Rumi. Such is the power of his writing that his defining work, the *Masnavi-ye Manavi,* is sometimes referred to as "the Persian Quran."

The quality of Persian writing, and the status of Persian as a literary language, meant that Persian literature had a pronounced impact throughout Asia, and even Mughal India adopted Persian as an official language in the 16th century, a policy only overturned by British colonialism in the 19th century. Indeed, the 19th century in general saw a major shift in Persian writing, as factual prose criticism and analysis came more to the fore and poetry began to be seen as reactionary and in need of modernization.

Religion

The great religion of pre-Islamic Persia was Zoroastrianism, a largely monotheistic faith that emerged around 600 B.C.E. Before that time, according to the little evidence we have, Persian spirituality was essentially polytheistic in outlook, with worship often directed toward natural features such as the sun and water. Animal sacrifice was a common method of making supplication to the gods, and specially appointed priests used intoxicants to attain an understanding of the divine.

Zoroastrianism was a radical break with this type of faith. It was the product of the prophet Zoroaster, who preached the existence of one supreme god, Ahura Mazda, although this did not preclude the existence of other divinities, which were known as *ahuras* (the two other key gods apart from Ahura Mazda were Mithra and Apam Napat). As such, Zoroastrianism was able to preach monotheism while also incorporating many traditional polytheistic beliefs. As time went on Zoroastrianism mutated significantly as each different political dynasty reshaped the faith to its own ends and means and took on new doctrine. The Achaemenids, for example, gave Zoroastrianism concepts of heaven, hell, and judgment. A figure called Ahriman, an evil counterpoint to the light and goodness of Ahura Mazda, was also introduced to Zoroastrianism at a later stage. Underlying all Zoroastrian practices was the principle that right action had to be followed at all times with each person being obliged to demonstrate goodness in action and an avoidance of deceit.

Once Persia came under Muslim Arab control from the seventh century C.E., Islam steadily replaced the existing religious traditions. The country was mainly Sunni in faith until the 17th century. Nevertheless, in the 16th century the Safavid dynasty made Shia the official state religion, and by the 1700s most of the country had converted to Shia. Today, a full 90 percent of Iran's population is Shia and forms one of the largest global enclaves of the Shii faith.

———◆———

Since the 1979 revolution, the history of Iran had been much dominated by troubled international relations. From 1980 to 1988, Iran was locked into a conventional war with its neighbor Iraq, the core of the conflict being a clash over territorial power in the Persian Gulf (*see* IRAQIS: NATIONALITY). That conflict, in which the West largely supported Iraq (the West was acutely fearful of what it saw as the threat of Islamic extremism), cost Iran over half a million dead and billions of dollars of its wealth. U.S.-Iranian relations have also been taut. In November 1979, militant Islamic students took over 60 people hostage at the U.S. embassy in Tehran, and a failed U.S. hostage rescue mission resulted in the deaths of eight U.S. servicemen. In 1988, U.S. Navy forces, responding to the damaging of one of its frigates by Iranian sea mines, destroyed several Iranian military vessels during its attack on an Iranian oil platform, and the accidental shooting down of Iran Flight 655 by the USS *Vincennes,* killing 290 civilians, brought international condemnation.

The Ayatollah Khomeini died in June 1989, and since then Iran has experienced new political tensions between its people and the government, particularly between fundamentalist groups and moderate leaders such as President Mohammed Khatami. Following a period of civic protests and violence, the conservative Mahmoud Ahmadinejad was elected president in 2005. Since then, tensions between the United States and Iran have once again increased, with the United States accusing Iran of attempting to develop nuclear weapons and of fuelling the anti-U.S. insurgency in Iraq. Such frictions have, however, served to maintain a distinctive sense of identity among the Iranians, their self-awareness thriving through opposition and survival.

See also IRANIANS: NATIONALITY

FURTHER READING

Pierre Briant. *From Cyrus to Alexander: A History of the Persian Empire* (Winona Lake, Ind.: Eisenbraun, 2002).

John Curtis, Nigel Tallis, and Béatrice André-Salvini. *Forgotten Empire: The World of Ancient Persia* (Berkeley: University of California Press, 2005).

Marc Van de Mieroop. *A History of the Ancient Near East, ca. 3000–323 B.C.* (Malden, Mass.: Blackwell, 2004).

Josef Wiesehöfer. *Ancient Persia: From 550 BC to 650 AD* (London: I.B. Tauris, 2001).

Phoenicians

The Phoenicians were an ancient people who had a major impact on the commercial and cultural life of the Mediterranean world from the third millennium B.C.E. until the seventh century C.E. The name Phoenician is of Greek origin; it is derived from the word *phoinkes,* which means "red people," a reference to a certain type of dyed cloth commonly exported by the Phoenicians. Historians are less certain about what the Phoenicians actually called themselves, but the most likely possibility is "Kena'ani" meaning "Canaanites," for their territory included the territory of ancient Canaan (*see* CANAANITES). Historians commonly use the word Phoenician to refer to the people of this area after about 1100 B.C.E.

The territory of the Phoenicians was essentially the eastern shore of the Mediterranean Sea, what is today Lebanon and parts of Syria and Israel. Phoenicia also built up an impressive spread of colonies throughout the Mediterranean world at locations as diverse as Portugal, Spain, Gibraltar, Italy, Sardinia, Sicily, Cyprus, Morocco, Algeria, Tunisia, Turkey, and Libya. Although some inhabitants of Lebanon and other countries still regard themselves as Phoenicians, the culture and language were

PHOENICIANS

location:
Eastern Mediterranean, North Africa, southern Europe

time period:
3000 B.C.E. to seventh century C.E.

ancestry:
Unknown

language:
Semitic

essentially dispersed by the seventh century C.E., although the cultural heritage of the Phoenicians in the Middle East and throughout the wider world remains strong.

ORIGINS

The origins of the Phoenician people are unknown. Their extreme antiquity means that they have left few written or pictorial primary sources from their earliest times. Nor should the Phoenicians be thought of as having a single unified cultural identity. "Phoenician" is in many ways a geographical definition rather than an ethnic one. One candidate for a place of origin is the Persian Gulf area, but the strong diversity of historical opinion on the issue of origins suggests that Phoenician territory was populated by migrants from a wide spectrum of regions ranging throughout North Africa and the Middle East.

From about 1100 B.C.E. the Phoenicians began a major period of colonial expansion, founding colonies around the Mediterranean and casting neighboring powers such as the EGYPTIANS and the HITTITES into the economic shade. Phoenician dominance, however, would fade from the sixth century B.C.E. as other imperial powers began to extend their influence over the Mediterranean region. In the sixth century the PERSIANS conquered Phoenicia. The territory was then absorbed by Alexander the Great in the fourth century, after which Hellenistic culture began to overshadow its Phoenician counterpart. Phoenicia's greatest colony, Carthage in North Africa, was destroyed by Rome during the Punic Wars, after which Phoenicia was in turn absorbed by Egypt, the Seleucids, Armenia, the Roman Empire and, finally, the ARABS in the seventh century C.E.

LANGUAGE

One of the earliest forms of Phoenician language was Ugaritic, so-called after the city of Ugarit located on the northern coastline of Phoenicia. This developed into the Phoenician language proper, one of a group of languages that also included Punic (a form of Phoenician particularly concentrated in North Africa), Moabite, Edomite, Hebrew, and Ammonite. All of these languages used a common alphabetic script, and the Phoenicians have been credited with effectively creating the world's first alphabet, an alphabet that went on to form the bedrock of many subsequent alphabets in the Western world and Asia. The alphabet is almost certainly Phoenicia's most significant legacy in the modern world.

Although Punic Phoenician was spoken in parts of the Mediterranean world, particularly North Africa, until the fifth century C.E., Phoenician proper died out during the first century C.E., when it was supplanted by Aramaic, Latin, and Greek.

HISTORY

The Phoenician story begins around 3000 B.C.E., the best estimate for the arrival of the Phoenicians in Canaan. What developed was not a unified nation but a collection of independent coastal cities, ruled by kings and princes, that established active trade relations among themselves and across the wider Mediterranean. These city settlements included Tyre, Sidon, Byblos, Berytus, Ugarit, and Katna, and all exploited their access to the Mediterranean to develop into bustling trade centers. Apart from trade between these cities, the most important destination for Phoenician goods was Egypt. The commercial relationship with Egypt began in earnest during the latter part of the 22nd century B.C.E., after an Amorite invasion of Phoenicia introduced a new spirit of enterprise (see AMORITES). Exports to Egypt during the second millennium B.C.E. included cedar wood, olive oil, dyes, linen and silks, and wines, and in return Phoenicia received gold, copper, corn, and slaves. Through this trade the Phoenicians became known for their exceptional maritime skills, and many Phoenician sailors freelanced by sailing Egyptian trading vessels throughout the Mediterranean.

A potential disruption to Phoenician-Egyptian trade arose in the 18th century B.C.E. in the form of an invasion by the Hyksos people, nomadic warriors from the northeast. The Hyksos took over rule of Byblos and much of Phoenicia and Syria, ejecting the Amorite rulers, and by about 1720 B.C.E. had even conquered Egypt. As it turned out, the Hyksos did nothing but further develop the trade lines throughout the eastern Mediterranean, as doing so enabled them to sustain their own imperial ambitions. Nevertheless, Phoenicia was soon to free itself from Hyksosian overlords. In 1570 B.C.E. the Egyptian prince Ahmose I (1570–45 B.C.E.) launched a war against the Hyksos, a war that was continued by Thutmose III (ca. 1504–1450 B.C.E.). This war eventually pushed the Hyksos out from their Egyptian and Phoenician gains and established Egypt as the dominant power in the Mediterranean. Phoenicia was divided

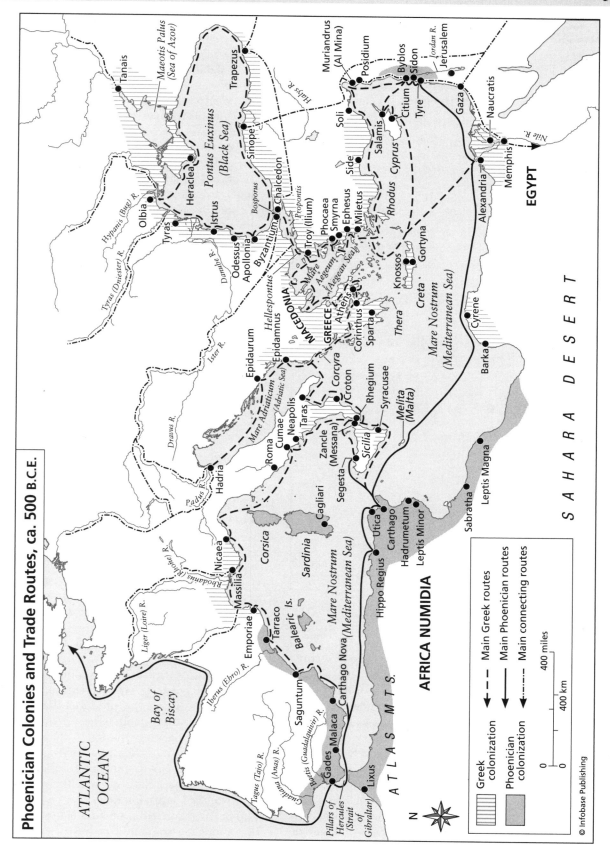

Phoenician Colonies and Trade Routes, ca. 500 B.C.E.

ATLANTIC OCEAN

Bay of Biscay

Liger (Loire) R.
Rhodanus (Rhône) R.
Ister R.
Dravus R.
Padus R.
Danube R.
Tyras (Dniester) R.
Hypanis (Bug) R.
Iberus (Ebro) R.
Tagus (Tajo) R.
Anas R.
Baetis (Guadalquivir) R.
Guadiana R.

ATLAS MTS.

Pillars of Hercules (Strait of Gibraltar)

Lixus
Gades
Malaca
Saguntum
Carthago Nova
Emporiae
Tarraco
Massilia
Nicaea
Balearic Is.
Corsica
Sardinia
Cagliari
Hadria
Roma
Cumae
Neapolis
Taras
Zancle (Messana)
Segesta
Sicilia
Rhegium
Syracusae
Melita (Malta)
Croton
Corcyra
Epidamnus
Epidaurum

Utica
Carthago
Hadrumetum
Leptis Minor
Hippo Regius
Sabratha
Leptis Magna

AFRICA NUMIDIA

S A H A R A   D E S E R T

Mare Nostrum (Mediterranean Sea)
Mare Adriaticum (Adriatic Sea)

MACEDONIA
GREECE
Athens
Corinthus
Sparta
Thera
Creta
Knossos
Gortyna
Cyrene
Barka

Mare Aegaeum (Aegean Sea)

Troy (Ilium)
Phocaea
Smyrna
Ephesus
Miletus
Byzantium
Bosporus
Propontis
Chalcedon
Hellespontus
Apollonia
Odessus
Istrus
Tyras
Olbia
Heraclea
Sinope
Trapezus

Pontus Euxinus (Black Sea)
Maeotis Palus (Sea of Azov)
Tanais

Halys R.

Soli
Side
Salamis
Citium
Rhodus Cyprus
Muriandrus (Al Mina)
Posidium
Byblos
Sidon
Tyre
Gaza
Jerusalem
Jordan R.

Alexandria
Naucratis
Memphis
Nile R.

EGYPT

Greek colonization
Phoenician colonization

Main Greek routes
Main Phoenician routes
Main connecting routes

N

0   400 miles
0   400 km

© Infobase Publishing

Phoenicians time line

B.C.E.

ca. 3000 Migrants settle Phoenician territory.

22nd century Trade relationships develop between Phoenician and Egypt.

18th century Phoenicia is invaded by the Hyksos people.

16th–15th centuries Hyksos are defeated by Egypt, and Egypt takes over Phoenicia, dividing it into three administrative districts.

14th century Phoenicia becomes independent of Egyptian rule, although maintains trade relations.

ca. 1300–1100 Phoenicians begin a period of colonial expansion.

ninth century Assyria begins to exercise increasing control over Phoenicia, and eventually takes over control of the territory from the Phoenician kings.

813 Phoenician colony at Carthage founded.

seventh century The Babylonians invade and occupy Phoenicia.

530s Phoenicia comes under Persian suzerainty.

336 Alexander the Great begins his eastern campaigns, and Phoenicia becomes a Hellenistic colony.

323 Alexander dies, and Phoenicia subsequently passes into the hands of the Seleucids.

146 Carthage is destroyed by Rome at the end of the Third Punic War.

126 Tyre achieves independence from the Seleucids.

C.E.

64 Rome occupies Phoenicia, which becomes part of a new Roman colony called Syria.

193–235 Phoenicia undergoes further political subdivisions as Rome changes the administration of Syria.

sixth century Many Phoenician cities are devastated by earthquakes.

seventh century Phoenicia is occupied by Arab invaders from the east, and Phoenician history effectively ends.

into three Egyptian administrative districts ruled over by individual governors.

Although the Egyptian settlement secured trade relations already established between Phoenicia and Egypt, the 14th century B.C.E. brought a dramatic change in Phoenicia's position. Invasions by peoples such as the Hittites destabilized Egyptian power in the region, and during the century Phoenicia was first lost and then partially regained by the EGYPTIANS. Despite their partial reconquest of Phoenicia, the Egyptians never again established complete control, and by 1300 B.C.E. Phoenicia had essentially regained full independence. Trade relations between Egypt and Phoenicia remained strong, however, and are evidenced by a series of commercial treaties between the two states.

Colonies and Carthage

It was during the second millennium B.C.E. that Phoenicia began to establish itself as a colonial power. It should be remembered, however, that Phoenicia was not a unitary state but a collection of city-states with varying ethnic and "federal" bonds (the presence of a suzerain in Phoenicia often ensured that there was some degree of central planning among all the states and peoples). Nevertheless, such was the efficiency of the Phoenicians that they were able to expand by founding numerous trading colonies throughout the Mediterranean region.

There were various motivations behind this program of colonization. One was that many citizens of Phoenicia had to pay tribute and taxes to the various city-state rulers, and colonization was a way of increasing their commercial wealth to keep pace with such outgoings. The Phoenicians were also aware that other trading powers, particularly the GREEKS, were establishing colonies of their own around the Mediterranean and that Phoenicia would have to follow suit or become uncompetitive. Finally, there was the consideration of overcrowding as the population of Phoenicia expanded and became more physically acquisitive.

The most influential of the Phoenician cities was Tyre, which according to the Greek historian Herodotus was founded in about 1250. Tyre had ascended to power during the later 13th century when raids on the Phoenician coastline had resulted in Aradus, Byblos, and Sidon being entirely or partially destroyed. The city established a colony at Utica in North Africa in about 1100, and many more followed over the next 500 years. In the ninth century Phoenician colonists settled in Cyprus, and other colonies in Malta, Sardinia, and Sicily followed relatively quickly, facilitating improved trans-Mediterranean trade. In total, Phoenicia established some 300 colonies throughout the Mediterranean, Africa, and the Middle East.

By far the greatest of the Phoenician colonies—and also the one that produced the most bloodshed—was that established at Carthage in about 813 B.C.E. Carthage was founded by colonists from Tyre, and was sited some six miles from the modern city of Tunis in Tunisia. The location was a superb choice for maritime trade. It had two large natural harbors, was centrally placed in the Mediterranean, and had easy access to goods sourced from North Africa.

The history of Carthage is a worthy study within itself, for it plots some of the issues that eventually curtailed overall Phoenician power.

By the end of third century B.C.E., it had virtually conquered the whole of the northern coastline of Africa as well as founding colonies in Malta, Sardinia, the Balearic Islands, and mainland Spain. It easily became the economic rival to Tyre, its mother city, and also to some of the other powerful states in the Mediterranean. The fifth and fourth centuries brought regular clashes between Greece and Carthage over colonial possessions, leading to a destructive campaign launched against the Carthaginian mainland by Syracuse in 310 B.C.E. But worse was yet to come. In 264 B.C.E. Carthage was plunged into the First Punic War against the newly emerging power of Rome. With the fighting concentrated mostly around Sicily, the war would lead to over a century of intermittent conflict. Although Carthaginian forces seriously threatened Rome on occasions, eventually Rome's growing power ground down Carthage's resistance. In 149 B.C.E. the third and final Punic War began, and Rome set out to conquer Carthage itself. Three years later the city was captured and virtually razed. Although there was something of a resurrection of Carthage in the first century C.E., it was more of a Roman project, and the city's Phoenician cultural origins had been lost by that time.

Assyrian Invasion

Between the 13th century and the ninth century B.C.E., Phoenicia reigned as one of the commercial engines of the whole Mediterranean region, building this strength through a string of colonies. The ninth century, however, saw Assyria begin to wield increased authority over Phoenician territory as it made periodic military incursions. The result was that successive Assyrian rulers, beginning with Ashurnasirpal II in 868, were able to impose tributes and taxes upon Phoenician cities as a guarantee of their security from Assyrian invasion. Assyrian interference became steadily more aggressive, and Phoenician kings were removed from their thrones as their cities became Assyrian colonies. There was some resistance to Assyrian rule—both Sidon and Tyre either rebelled or resisted (Tyre fell after several sieges)—but ultimately the opposition was overwhelmed and the ASSYRIANS confirmed their ascendancy.

From the Assyrian takeover onward Phoenicia endured successive periods of imperial takeover as one foreign master followed another. The next rulers of Phoenicia were the BABYLONIANS. Concentrated in the southern half Mesopotamia, Babylonia rose as a major Middle Eastern power during the seventh century B.C.E., and by the end of that century it had overwhelmed Assyria and its possessions, including Phoenicia. Babylonian rule was established over Phoenicia between 685 and 636 B.C.E. Again, the Phoenicians did not take occupation by a foreign power lightly. Tyre rebelled against the Babylonian forces of Nebachadnezzar II in 587 and held out under siege conditions for 13 years. In 574 B.C.E., however, the city's resistance finally collapsed and Babylonian power was reasserted.

Babylonia was not able to hold on to Phoenicia for very long. The new power ascendant in the Middle East was the PERSIANS. The Persian leader Cyrus took the Babylonian capital in 539–38 B.C.E. and Phoenicia came under Persian suzerainty shortly after. The Phoenician peoples subsequently became a key element in Persia's maritime resistance against the Greeks, the other great empire in the region at this time. Harsh taxes imposed by the Persians caused rebellions, notably in Tyre and Sidon. These were eventually put down by the Persians, but they gave incidental assistance to Alexander the Great, the Macedonian general who from 336 B.C.E. began an campaign of conquest through Asia Minor and eventually into the Middle East. Tyre resisted Alexander ever after he had defeated local Persian forces. Although the city resisted for eight months, it was finally overpowered and most of its people sent into slavery. Tyre never regained the power and wealth it had previously enjoyed.

During the Hellenistic period Greek culture came to have a much wider influence within Phoenician society. Alexander's generals ruled the cities of Phoenicia following his conquest. After Alexander's death in 323 B.C.E., Phoenicia eventually fell to Seleucus I, although the rule of the Seleucid dynasty was only confirmed after a long period of conflict over Alexander's territories, particular between the Seleucids and the Egyptian Ptolemies. The age of Seleucid rule was reasonably benign for the Phoenician peoples, as Seleucid rulers granted many of the cities a high degree of autonomy to go about their business and continue developing prosperity and trade. Tyre, for example, obtained self-government from the Seleucids in 126.

Roman and Arab Conquest

During the first two decades of the first century B.C.E., Rome was already beginning to extend its empire eastward. It noted with concern, therefore, the threat posed by Tigranes II, the Armenian king who in 83 B.C.E. crushed the last of the Seleucid monarchs and expanded his area of control into much of Phoenicia. From 69 B.C.E. Rome responded by sending military forces against the ARMENIANS, and under the Roman leader Pompey the Seleucids were temporarily restored. In 64 B.C.E., however, Pompey took over all the Seleucid territory directly, incorporating Phoenicia, Syria, and Palestine into a single Roman province that was named Syria (*see* ROMANS).

Roman rule was in many ways the beginning of the end for Phoenician identity. The rule itself, as in much of the Roman Empire, was lightly enforced. In typical Roman style, the Phoenician cities were given a high degree of self-rule, and the granting of Roman citizenship to the inhabitants of Byblos, Sidon, and Tyre fostered great intellectual and commercial confidence. Under the governorship of Herod in the early first century C.E., Berytus—the future Lebanese city of Beirut—also benefited from a major imperial building program that transformed the status of the city throughout the region. The insatiable appetite of Rome for Middle Eastern luxury goods, combined with a high degree of political stability throughout the empire, meant that the Phoenicians could once again indulge in what they did best—trade.

Culturally and politically during this time Phoenician territory was gradually being transformed and reorganized, becoming more distant from what could be classed as traditionally Phoenician. Between 193 and 235 Syria was partitioned into two halves, and those halves were subsequently subdivided during the fifth century, creating new provinces such as Phoenice Prima and Phoenice Secunda, by which time the Roman Empire itself had been split into Eastern and Western Empires.

Other major changes had occurred in Phoenician culture. Probably the most important of these was that Aramaic, Latin, and Greek had steadily supplanted native Phoenician tongues, so by the sixth century Phoenician was increasingly distant from its own ethnic origins. During the same century several of Phoenicia's major cities, including Beirut, were virtually destroyed by earthquakes, and these further weakened the strength of Phoenicia at a time in which the implosion of the Roman Empire under outside forces rendered it critically weakened.

It was under these conditions that Phoenicia succumbed to takeover by an exceptionally forceful religious power expanding from the east—Islam. Islamic expansion had been extremely rapid. The Muslim armies had launched themselves from Medina and Mecca in the 620s, occupying much of the Middle East and North Africa in less than half a century. Jerusalem fell in 634 and in 638 Tyre itself became an Arab possession. The former jewel in the Phoenician crown, Carthage, was destroyed by Arab invaders in 697. The Arab takeover of Phoenicia was effectively the end of the Phoenician story. By this time their language was lost and their cities were ruled by nonindigenous peoples. Culturally the territory had been utterly transformed by nearly 1,000 years of imperial takeovers. Yet there is no denying that the Phoenicians had been central to expansion and development of the Mediterranean as one of the great trading regions of the world.

CULTURE

Economy

The foundation of the Phoenician economy was its maritime trade network, which by 1200 B.C.E. was transporting goods from the Phoenician colonies to the wider world. The trade network meant that goods could be transferred rapidly around the Mediterranean. For example, the journey from Tyre to Rome could be accomplished in around 20 days, while transportation between Carthage and Ostia (near Rome) took a just three to five days. Because of the spread of its colonies and wide access to primary materials, Phoenicia was also a major supplier of consumer goods and construction materials, including timber, wine, woolen textiles, corn, salt, bitumen, glass, copper, and dried fish. It was particularly famous for its purple dye, made from the crushed shells of the *Murex* sea-snail found off the Phoenician coastline. Phoenicia was also in the perfect geographical position to act as a trade intermediary between the western Mediterranean and Mesopotamia, aiding the flow of incense and spices westward. As long as there was no outside interference, these factors produced a particularly strong international economy.

Government and Society

The cities of Phoenicia generally governed themselves on a traditional system of hereditary kingships, the king being assisted by a council of elders to administrate the state. The basis of authority for the kingships was the claim of divine descent, although such claims became more awkward as Phoenician history passed on and outside influences brought their own religious cultures into the Phoenician courts. Marriage alliances between cities served to expand political alliances and monarchical power.

In Phoenicia's later history republican systems often replaced monarchies—testimony to the influence of Greek and Roman systems of government. Tyre itself became republican during the time of Nebuchadrezzar II, with *suffetes* (judges) providing the leadership. Carthage was ordered along similar lines and provided an inspirational model of government for many writers throughout the Western world. Aristotle, for example, wrote in his *On the Constitution of Carthage* (ca. 340 B.C.E.) that:

The Carthaginians are also considered to have an excellent form of government, which differs from that of any other state in several respects, though it is in some very like the Spartan. Indeed, all three states—the Spartan, the Cretan, and the Carthaginian—nearly resemble one another, and are very different from any others. Many of the Carthaginian institutions are excellent. The superiority of their constitution is proved by the fact that the common people remain loyal to the constitution. The Carthaginians have never had any rebellion worth speaking of, and have never been under the rule of a tyrant.

One important point to note about the Phoenician systems of government is that they were often manifestly influenced or even controlled by powerful trading families. In a sense, therefore, Phoenician government and society had a strong thread of meritocracy.

Military Practices

Phoenicia proper, rather than its colonies, was primarily known for its maritime power. Events from the ninth century onward proved that, apart from resisting sieges, the Phoenicians had little capability for dealing with major foreign invasions and often relied on other external powers to eject occupiers. Nonetheless the Phoenician naval forces were extremely significant. For example, much of the Persian fleet in the battle of Salamis in 480 B.C.E. consisted of Phoenician galleys.

Carthage is an exception to the general Phoenician weakness in land forces. Until Carthage's destruction in the Third Punic War the colony boasted one of the most impressive navies in the whole of the Mediterranean, far superior to that possessed by Rome. In terms of its army, Carthage benefited from conscripting large numbers of foreign mercenaries, selecting from the best fighters of North Africa and the Middle East, and even from Celtic Europe and Spain. In terms of cavalry, the Numidians provided the most significant contingent of light horse, backed up by Carthaginian war elephants that were used to smash into enemy ranks with the intention breaking them open.

Tactically, the Carthaginians used a mix of tactics from around the Mediterranean. One of the most popular was the use of the infantry *phalanx*, a close-grouped mass of heavily armored soldiers armed with the extremely long *sarissa* pike. Support came from slingers (typically mercenaries) and javelin throwers. On a strategic level, the Carthaginians were equally sophisticated, striking at enemy weak points rather than seeking out his strengths. Nonetheless, Carthage was unable to resist the exceptional military skills of Rome, and could not prevent its eventual destruction.

Dwellings and Architecture

The earliest examples of Phoenician dwellings and temples tended to be hewn directly out of rock faces and outcrops and finished with masonry blocks. Gradually, however, masonry blocks became the standard system of building construction, and in large-scale buildings the size of the blocks could be very impressive indeed. For example, stone blocks acting as the foundations of the Jewish Temple in Jerusalem, which was built with the help of Phoenician masons during the time of Solomon, measure in some instances up to 25 feet in length and up to 12 feet in depth. Frequently no cement or mortar was used in the construction of a building—the blocks were simply accurately squared off and laid on top one another to form a solid, self-supporting structure. The scale of the construction was, apart from giving an impressive civic scale, important in the Phoenician region, which had to withstand regular earthquakes and needed correspondingly resilient buildings. Buildings were decorated with the usual mixture of pediments, columns, and pilasters, and later the Phoenicians borrowed directly from the architectural styles of the Persians, Greeks, and Romans, eventually adopting the fairly unified Classical style that spread throughout the Mediterranean world.

The Phoenicians were well known for their religious architecture, particularly their temples and shrines. Of the temples, however, few original examples remain within Phoenicia; the most visible examples are to be found in former Phoenician colonies. One of the best examples is the temple of Paphos in Cyprus. This consisted of a large central temple area covering 36,800 square feet and featured a mosaic floor and two roofed aisles, plus a central nave. A large outer wall surrounded the temple itself and the overall impression was one of scale and affluence. On a far smaller scale were the many shrines that dotted the Phoenician landscape. These were often little more than roofed stone cells, although they were frequently decorated with carvings and small pillars and had a resemblance to Egyptian temple design.

Clothing

Clothing for common Phoenicians was very simple—a plain cotton or linen tunic (known as the *shenti*) for men, topped with a conical or cylindrical cap, while women draped themselves in heavy, sleeved gowns that ran from the neck to the feet. For men not wearing caps, the hair and beards were frequently arranged into tight curls.

Higher up the Phoenician social ladder the style of dress was more ostentatious. Cloths and patterns used for the *shenti* or gowns were more luxurious, and upper-class men sometimes wore additional short-sleeved jackets or shoulder mantles. Ornamentation was popular for both sexes. Men wore highly decorated collars, plus whatever armlets, bracelets, and finger jewelry they could afford, while women donned extensive jewelry, including multiple necklaces. These were generally made of glass, rock crystal, gold, silver, or pearl beads. Bracelets were also popular and ranged from wide and heavy gold bands through to more slender, open bracelets terminating in animal head motifs. Earrings tended to be pendulous, some exquisitely crafted with figure designs etched into them.

Personal Habits

Banqueting, wine drinking, and socializing were popular activities. Indeed, unlike many depictions of the ancient world, Phoenician art shows that both men and women sat around banqueting tables, indicating a greater equality in status between the sexes. The depictions also show women playing musical instruments, sometimes in small groups, to entertain menfolk. Women also participated in religious processions.

In terms of leisure pursuits, men who were not out fishing or working in trade sometimes engaged in hunting. The Phoenician homeland had a rich spectrum of Middle Eastern wildlife, and hunting parties would track down and kill everything from antelopes to lions. During the Roman era such hunting parties sought to capture their prey alive so that the animals could be sold for use in the gladiatorial arenas of the Roman Empire.

Transportation

Phoenicia built its economy upon international trade; hence, effective transportation was vitally important to sustaining its wealth. In terms of land transportation, goods were transferred in caravans of wheeled carts pulled by mules, horses, and camels, often over great distances. At sea, however, the Phoenicians deployed far more sophisticated vehicles.

Early Phoenician sailing vessels probably consisted of little more than a relatively short hull powered by a single row of oars down each side and a single square sail. Surviving depictions from the first two millennia of Phoenician history show these boats as rudderless, directed instead by the action of the rowers or the angle of the sail (although many engravings and sculptures show vessels without any form of sail). Goods were either transported within the vessel itself or, in the case of timber, towed behind.

While the earliest Phoenician vessels were short and broad in shape—the Greeks called them *gauloi,* meaning "tubs"—during the first millennium B.C.E. they became sleeker and more powerful, and rudders or paired steering oars were introduced to provide greater maneuverability in treacherous coastal waters. The Phoenicians are credited with being the first civilization to produce keeled ships—a keel provided much greater lateral stability in the water, enabling vessels to make longer voyages through more unsettled waters. A carving from Nineveh, dated to about 700 B.C.E., shows a long two-decked Phoenician galley with two banks of oars on each side (a total of 32 rowers). Sails were also used on these larger ships to provide additional driving power. In military vessels the prow featured a long pointed ram used to stave enemy vessels beneath the waterline. Generally speaking, Phoenician trading vessels were shorter, rounder, and fatter than military vessels. This reflected the need for capacious holds and maneuverability. Military ships relied on speed to survive in combat more than anything. Many trading vessels towed a small boat behind them during their voyages. These served as a form of lifeboat should the vessel find itself in trouble, or was used to ferry crew members from deep waters to the shore.

The Phoenicians are credited with developing techniques of navigation using the stars. By using Polaris (the North Star) and other prominent celestial bodies, plus their intimate knowledge of the direction of prevailing winds and of sea currents, the Phoenicians were able to plot accurate routes over long distances. There is evidence that Phoenician voyagers were making complete circumnavigations of the African continent in the seventh century B.C.E., two thousand years before a European vessel achieved the same feat for the first time.

Other Technologies

While the greatest of all the inventions contributed by the Phoenicians to civilization are undoubtedly the alphabet and certain maritime technologies, these were not the limits of Phoenician inventiveness. Around 1500 B.C.E. they invented glass, a substance that had a seminal impact on the decorative arts. Although small glass beads have been found in Egypt dating from to about 2500 B.C.E., these are usually ascribed to the result of an accidental fusion of sand in heat. The Phoenicians turned glassmaking into a practical industrial skill.

The base technique of Phoenician glassmaking is known as core molding. Sand, limestone, and sodium carbonate were reduced by fire to a molten state, and the molten glass was painted over a core of soft clay, which itself was carved into the shape of the intended vessel. Once the glass had hardened, the clay was then scraped out to leave the glass container. Glass remained an expensive commodity in the ancient world, so this technique of glassmaking was principally used for producing small ointment or perfume bottles, usually for trade on foreign markets.

One other interesting technological advance made by the Phoenicians, possibly in parallel with the Greeks, was in the field of dentistry. As far back as 700 B.C.E., Phoenician dentists were providing their clients with false teeth. In essence what they created was a type of bridgework—false teeth made of wood were tied to natural teeth using gold wire to fill gaps in the mouth.

Art

Phoenician artists are principally regarded for their skill in creating valuable consumer goods, particularly jewelry, and also for their skill in textile manufacture. The Phoenicians famously used the sea-snail *Murex* to create a vivid purple-red dye, which they used expertly in woven fabrics to create luxurious garments that had international renown.

Phoenician graves have revealed a talent for working with precious stones and metals to create small-scale objects d'art. Artifacts recovered include bracelets, rings, amulets, bowls, jewelry boxes, scarabs, and ointment jars. Materials used to make such items included ivory, gold, silver, bronze, copper, and terra-cotta; many of these were inlaid with semiprecious stones. Phoenician decoration crossed the full range of representational art. While some artifacts feature simple patterning, others displayed elaborate depictions of plant and animal life.

Phoenician artists were talented on the small scale but they could also work impressively on larger artifacts. Examples have been found of chairs, thrones, and even complete beds carved entirely, and expensively, out of ivory. Stone stelae—grave monuments—from Phoenician cemeteries are also engraved with religious iconography, sometimes borrowed from other cultures, such as the Greeks or the Egyptians. The motifs on an individual stela were often peculiar to a particular city or community, giving archaeologists a sound clue as to their origins. Carthage seems to have had the most productive output of stelae of all the Phoenician colonies.

Another distinctive Phoenician art form was the terra-cotta mask. These life-sized depictions of human faces showed a great range of age and emotion, from handsome smiling faces to hideous, haggard expressions. Such masks may have been worn during religious ceremonies or placed on the faces of the dead. Suspension holes drilled through many of the masks also indicate that they may have been hung on statues or poles, although their exact function is still not entirely known.

Music

While it is extremely difficult to gain a firm understanding of what Phoenician music sounded like, we do know from engravings and sculpture that music was integral to Phoenician ceremonial and cultural life. Flutes, harps, lyres, and reed pipes of all feature in these depictions suggesting a sophistication in harmony and melody that comes from the use of such instruments together. The Phoenicians were also using musical notation from early in their history. A tablet unearthed from the site of Ugarit has engraved into its surface the notation for a hymn to Nikkal, the moon god's wife. This and other similar discoveries have enabled historians of music to piece together something of the harmonic structures and scales used in Phoenician music.

The available evidence shows that Phoenician music was syncretic in style—it borrowed from the numerous influences of other cultures from the Mediterranean. Hence Egyptian, Greek, Roman, and Mesopotamian attributes are all contained within the Phoenician style of melody and rhythm.

Literature

The principal forms of Phoenician literature were historical inscriptions, narrative poetry, religious and philosophical works, and scientific writings. Extant works are few and far between (most of the surviving material is in the form of short inscriptions), and much historical guesswork is required to fill in some of the gaps. Furthermore, a great deal of what is classed as Phoenician writing was produced in the colonies, particularly Carthage, rather than in Phoenicia proper.

As early as 1000 B.C.E. writers from the principal city-states of Phoenicia recorded the royal lines of succession and detailed major events in the life of each king. Narrative poetry was a far more literary way of envisaging historical or religious narratives, and some substantial works have survived in part to this day. These include the Ugaritic works *The Rapiuma* and *The Epic of Kirta,* written about 1200 B.C.E. One of the earliest Phoenician writers, known through references rather than by the direct survival of his works, was Sanconiatho, who wrote sometime in the 14th or 13th centuries B.C.E. Sanconiatho appears to have documented early Phoenician history and religious thought, and fragments of his writing made their way into the works of later writers such as Philo of Byblos (b. 42 C.E.), who translated Sanconiatho's works into Greek, and Eusebius (ca. 263– 369 C.E.), who quoted passages from Philo's translation.

Various religious and philosophical works have also survived. The most famous and complete of these is the *Baal Cycle*. Written in Ugaritic on clay tablets, the *Cycle* contains a series of stories about Baal (also known as Hadad), the god of storms, agriculture, and fertility. Phoenicia, and also Carthage, produced many works on geography, astronomy, arithmetic, natural history, ethnology, mathematics, and other scientific topics. Hiempsal, Hanno, Mago, and Hamilcar were among the greatest Phoenician writers on these topics. Phoenicia's intellectual enthusiasm had a long-term effect on other Mediterranean cultures, and Phoenician references continue to appear in Greek and Roman works well into the first millennium C.E.

Religion

The indigenous religion of the early Phoenicians centered on the worship of natural features and was embodied in multiple deities. The Phoenician pantheon was extensive but had a smaller group of superior deities. Chief among these gods was El or Baal, who oversaw the cycles of agriculture, and the goddess Ashtarte, the mother deity. The names of gods and goddesses were sometimes different in different cities or communities—Ashtarte, for example, was called Baalat in the city of Byblos. Priests held substantial communal power, thanks to their perceived ability to divine the will of the gods.

The political history of Phoenicia meant that over the millennia its people came into contact with the religious systems of many other peoples, including the Egyptians, Assyrians, Mesopotamians, Greeks, and Romans. Consequently the Phoenician pantheon was constantly morphing and growing with the incorporation of new deities and religious rituals. This may explain why the Phoenicians so readily adopted Christianity in the first century C.E. They are thought to have been among the earliest converts to the new faith in the ancient world. Not all Phoenicians adopted the new religion, however, and paganism prospered alongside Christianity for several centuries, until its official adoption as the state religion of the Roman Empire in the fourth century C.E. The next great religious shift occurred when Islam swept across the Middle East in the seventh century, but by this time Phoenician culture was dying.

———————◆———————

Many people of coastal Lebanon still use the word "Phoenician" to describe their ancestry. Although the modern use of the term may be wistful rather than historically accurate, the Mediterranean world was certainly shaped by Phoenician trade and ideas, and hence the Middle East and Africa are doubtlessly indebted to Phoenician civilization.

FURTHER READING

Sanford Holst. *Phoenicians: Lebanon's Epic Heritage* (Los Angeles, Calif: Cambridge and Boston Press, 2006).

Asher S. Kaufman. *Reviving Phoenicia: The Search for Identity in Lebanon* (London: I. B. Tauris, 2003).

Seymour Gitin. *The Philistines: Neighbors of the Canaanites, Phoenicians and Israelites* (Boston: American Schools of Oriental Research, 2004).

Anthony Strong. *The Phoenicians in History and Legend* (Bloomington, Ind.: 1stBooks Library, 2002).

Glenn Markoe. *Phoenicians* (Berkeley: University of California Press, 2000).

Sabatino Moscati. *The World of the Phoenicians* (London: Phoenix Giant, 1999).

Phrygians

The Phrygians are an ancient people who lived in the highlands of west-central Anatolia. They dominated the region in the era between the collapse of the HITTITES in the 12th century B.C.E. and the rise of the *Lydians* in the seventh century B.C.E. They spoke an Indo-European language closely related to Greek. Their capital was Gordium, which has been excavated beginning in 1950, revealing massive fortifications and an impressive palace, ruins of a city that flourished between the ninth and eighth centuries B.C.E. The Phrygians raised horses and sheep, and their land was rich with timber. They were known for their metalwork and textiles, and famed for their carpets and embroidery. After they were conquered by the Lydians, the Phrygians were Hellenized but reemerged as a distinct culture when their territory was subsumed under the Roman provinces of Galatia and Asia. The Phrygians left a wealth of inscriptions. They had devised an alphabet in the eighth century B.C.E., based on Greek and Semitic alphabets, and approximately 250 texts in that script survive, dating from the eighth century to the third century B.C.E. Apparently Phrygian fell out of use as the language of texts and was used only as a spoken language until it appears again in the first to third centuries C.E. in texts written in Phrygian but with the Greek alphabet. Most of these later inscriptions are curses added to tombstones to warn away anyone who might desecrate the grave. In addition to these inscriptions, another sort of archaeological evidence are grave markers, identifiable as Phrygian because of the typical Phrygian grave motif, a door.

The Phrygians appear in legends well known in the Greek and Roman worlds. According to one legend, the Phrygians were told by an oracle their country would be blessed with peace if they made king the next person who approached the temple of Zeus in a wagon. That person was the peasant Gordius. He was made king and founded the city Gordium. He dedicated his wagon to Zeus and secured it to the temple with an extraordinarily complicated knot, known as the Gordian knot. No one could untie the knot, but, it was thought, whoever could untie the knot would rule all of Asia. For centuries the knot withstood the efforts of everyone who tried it until Alexander the Great arrived and dispatched the knot with a swift stroke of his sword. Another legend, recounted in the Roman poet Ovid's *Metamorphoses,* among other ancient sources, concerns the Phrygian king Midas. The foolish king, who supposedly got his wish that everything he touched would turn to gold only to discover that this magic power also turned his food and drink to precious metal, was probably attributed to the Phrygian king called Mita. Among the ruins excavated at Gordium is a tomb thought to be that of Midas himself.

Peul *See* FULANI.

Pian

The Pian are a subgroup of the KARAMOJONG. They live in northeastern Uganda.

Pogoro (Pogulu)

The Pogoro are a BANTU people of East Africa. The majority of the Pogoro live in Tanzania.

Pogulu *See* POGORO.

Pokomo

The Pokomo people are of both BANTU and OROMO descent. They live along the banks of the Tana River in Kenya.

Pokot

The Pokot inhabit a region that extends from the lands around Lake Baringo in western Kenya in the east to the plains of eastern Uganda in the west. The Pokot are one of the several related groups that make up the KALENJIN and represent roughly 10 to 15 percent of the Kalenjin-speaking people. The Pokot have also been known as the Suk, a term first used derisively by the MAASAI and adopted by the European colonizers of East Africa.

The ancestors of the Kalenjin were highland NILOTES, who began dispersing from their original cradleland at the northernmost tip of Lake Turkana in present-day Ethiopia to East Africa during the first millennium B.C.E. The separate Kalenjin groups such as the Pokot emerged as the highland Nilotes spread out over the region and mixed with people already living there. In the case of the Pokot, the KARAMOJONG and ITESO people were of particular influence on the development of Pokot culture.

Pombo

The Pombo are a subgroup of the KONGO. They live in northwestern Angola and the southeastern Democratic Republic of the Congo. They are a BANTU people.

Pontians

The Pontians were ancient inhabitants of Pontus, a region of northeastern Anatolia bordering on Pontus Euxinus, the Black Sea. At the end of the fourth century B.C.E., after the conquests of Alexander the Great, the independent kingdom of Pontus was established, with its capital at Amasia (the modern city of Amasya, in Turkey, about 50 miles southwest of the Black Sea port, Samsun). While Pontus showed the superficial influence of Hellenic culture, it retained its Persian (see PERSIANS) social structure as a society of feudal lords ruling over villages of heterogeneous peoples. It became a dominant power in Anatolia in the third and second centuries B.C.E. and annexed Sinope (modern Sinope, Turkey, a Black Sea port to the west of Amasia), which became the new Pontic capital from about 183 B.C.E. The Pontic kingdom had conquered neighboring peoples, including, at one point, the Paphlogonians and the PHRYGIANS. The Pontians reached the apex of their power under the rule of Mithradates VI Eupator, who came to the throne in about 115 B.C.E. He was particularly successful at further expanding his realm and posed a serious threat to the Roman Empire. He enlisted the Greek cities in Anatolia and in parts of Greece to unite with him against the ROMANS, and with them, he fought a series of wars against the Roman armies. It was not until 63 B.C.E. that he was finally defeated by the Roman general Pompey, who incorporated Pontus into the Roman Empire, marking the end of the independent kingdom.

Popo See MINA.

Portuguese

Many thousands of people of Portuguese descent live in Africa. They are concentrated in the former Portuguese colonies, such as Angola, Mozambique, and Guinea-Bissau.

Pounou See BAPOUNOU.

Psidians

The Psidians are an ancient people who inhabited the area of southern Anatolia crossed by the Taurus Mountains, a chain running north–south parallel to the Mediterranean coast. Their neighbors included Pamphylia to the south, Phrygia to the northwest, Lycaonia to the northeast, Cilicia to the southeast, and Lycia to the southwest. By the first century B.C.E. Psidian society was organized into small tribes or groups of villages, but also included temples with large estates worked by slaves. The inaccessibility of the terrain and the Psidians' strongly fortified cities protected them from the incursions of conquerors, and they successfully resisted the PERSIANS and the Hellenistic kings. The Romans managed to exercise at least nominal control, with the Roman general Mark Antony installing Amyntas of Galatia as king of Psidia in 36 B.C.E. When King Amyntas died, in 25 B.C.E., most of Psidia was incorporated into the Roman province of Galatia. Over the next century, as the ROMANS reorganized and redrew territorial boundaries, Psidia was incorporated into various provinces. By the second century C.E., the area was urbanized and cities flourished, particularly the metropolis of Sagalassus.

Pullo See Fulani.

Pygmies

The term *Pygmy* has been used, mostly in the past, to refer to a member of the tropical-forest forager groups such as the MBUTI, TWA, AND MBENGA of Central Africa. These people are not black Africans and generally are of short stature, hence the name Pygmy.

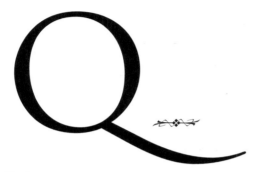

Qajars

The Qajars were the ruling dynasty of Iran from 1794 to 1925, a Turkmen nomadic tribe whose homeland was the area of Azerbaijan (*see* IRANIANS: NATIONALITY). They were Shii Muslims. The first Qajar shah, Agha Muhammad Khan, came to power after the death of the last ruler of the Zand dynasty, which had ruled southern Iran. Agha Muhammad Khan's objective was to reunite Iran, including part of Georgia and the Caucasus, and bring it all under Qajar rule. He established his capital at Tehran, the capital of modern-day Iran, but then a village. In 1796 he was crowned shah. Under Qajar rule, Iran went to war with Russia and suffered major defeats, ceding Georgia and most of the north Caucasus region, and later Armenia and Azerbaijan to Russia. During this era, Britain was also intent on asserting its influence in Iran and neighboring regions, and it virtually controlled the Iranian economy. In 1907 Great Britain and Russia divided Iran into spheres of influence, and in World War I, the country was occupied by British, Russian, and Ottoman troops. Qajar rule never recovered, and the last Qajar shah was deposed in a coup in 1921 led by Reza Shah Pahlavi, whose dynasty ruled until the Islamic Revolution of 1979.

Qara-khanids (Ilek-khanids; Ilig-khanids; Karakhanid)

The Qara-khanids were a Turkic dynasty that ruled in Central Asia from 999 to 1211. Qara-khanid territory was centered on the Tian Shan Mountains (also spelled Tien Shan) in modern-day Kyrgyzstan and Xinjiang, in western China. The area is called Transoxiana, meaning "the land across the Oxus River." The modern name for the Oxus River is Amu Darya. The Qara-khanids rose to power as the Iranian Samanid dynasty disintegrated, which had ruled in Iran and Transoxiana from 874 to 999. Samanid territory was subsequently divided up between the Ghaznavids, who took Khurasan and Afghanistan, and the Qara-khanids, who took Transoxiana, that is, the lands to the north of the Oxus. By the end of the 10th century, the Qara-khanids had converted to Sunni Islam, to which they had been exposed through contact with the Samanids, and some of the early khans were known for their piety. They promulgated the spread of Islam, as among the Kipchak nomads during the 12th century. The Qara-khanid capital was Bukhara, in modern-day Uzbekistan. In contrast to the Samanids, who had a centralized rule, the Qara-khanids ruled as a kind of confederacy, with the Great Khan ruling over the eastern part of the confederation and another khan under him ruling the western lands. Under them was a complicated hierarchy of lower khans and governors, all of them members of the Qara-khanid family. From about 1041, the confederacy was ruled as two distinct khanates, an eastern one and a western one.

Many Qara-khanid rulers distinguished themselves, as, for example, Shams al-Mulk Nasr (r. 1068–80), whose name appears in the

"Mirrors for Princes" literature, a Muslim literary form that provided advice for rulers and cited examples of the pious and just. The wise rule of Shams al-Mulk included public works, such as building new caravanserais, reconstructing the Great Mosque of Bukhara, and the construction of other major buildings. Other rulers were patrons of poets and scholars. A distinguishing feature of Qara-khanid rule is its patronage of Turkish culture, and under their rule the first Turkish Islamic literature appeared. By the end of the 11th century, Qara-khanid power was crumbling, with control first relinquished to the SELJUKS, then, as the Seljuks declined, they came under the rule of the Turkic Qara-kitai confederation, centered in northern China. The Qara-khanids were defeated in 1211 by the Khwarezm-shahs and their dynasty came to an end.

Qara-qoyunlu (Kara Koyunlu)

The Qara-qoyunlu (also known as the Black Sheep confederation) were a tribal confederation of OGHUZ TURKS who dominated areas of modern-day Armenia, Azerbaijan, the southern Caucasus, Iraq, and Iran from the late 14th to the late 15th centuries. Their leader Qara Yusuf (died 1420) established the confederation's independence from the Baghdad and Tabriz-based Iranian Jalayirid dynasty. Later Black Sheep rulers established independence from the Timurids and extended their control over Iraq, parts of Georgia, and central Iran. The Qara-qoyunlu captured Baghdad from the Jalayirid dynasty in 1410.

From 1447, the Qara-qoyunlu became involved in a long-running conflict with the White Sheep confederation, called the AQ-QOYUNLU. Wars between these two tribal confederations lasted until 1451. In 1467 Black Sheep forces suffered a devastating defeat at the hands of the White Sheep. The latter rapidly expanded White Sheep lands, and by 1468 the White Sheep held sway over modern-day Armenia, Azerbaijan, eastern Turkey, Iraq, and western Iran down to the shores of the Persian Gulf and northwards into Khurasan. (See also TURKIC PEOPLES.)

Qashqai (Ghashghai; Kashgai; Kaskay; Qashqa'i, Qashqay)

The Qashqai are a tribal confederacy made up largely of Turkic people but also some other ethnic groups such as Luri, KURDS, and ARABS (see TURKIC PEOPLES). Their territory is centered in Fars Province, in southwestern Iran, the capital of which is Shiraz. Estimates of their numbers vary from 500,000 to 1.5 million, but in any case they make up far less than 1 percent of Iran's population, estimated at nearly 66 million in 2008. The Qashqai are Shii Muslims, as are most Iranians (see IRANIANS: NATIONALITY). They speak Qashqai, a dialect of Oghuz, a Turkic language that they refer to as Turki. Most also speak Persian, an Indo-European language and the official language of Iran.

Although their origins are unknown, most Qashqai themselves believe their ancestors came from Turkestan with the invading armies of the 13th-century conqueror Hulegu or with Tamurlane) in the 14th century. Scholars consider it more likely that they arrived with the great tribal migrations of the 11th century. In any case, they do not appear in the historical record before the 18th century. Their system of tribal government, like that of many Turkish peoples, was based on a ruling family of khans, from whom were drawn the il-khan, the tribal head, and the il-begi, who was the actual ruler. The il-begi was elected from among the close relatives of the il-khan. At various times, particularly in the early 20th century, the Qashqai were united and cohesive and able to exert military and political force, pitting them against the government and outside powers, such as the British in Iran, against whom they engaged during World War I.

Traditionally a nomadic people who herded horses, sheep, camels, and cattle, and moved from summer to winter pastures, their way of life was steadily eroded over the 20th century by government attempts to control them. In 1930 they and other tribes were disarmed by the monarch Reza Shah. After Reza Shah was forced to abdicate in 1941 and was replaced by his son, Muhammad Reza Shah, Qashqai khans who had fled the country returned and tried to resume rule. In 1963 the Iranian government under Shah Reza Pahlavi officially declared tribes not to exist and stripped the khans of titles and privileges, and once again the khans went into exile. When the shah was overthrown in 1979, the Qashqai participated in demonstrations against him, and the exiled Naser Khan and Khusruw Khan returned to Iran. Relations with the new religious regime of Ayatollah Khomeini that had taken control of Iran after the Islamic Revolution soon soured, and in 1980 an army of 600 Qashqai defied the Revolutionary Guard and set up camp in the mountains of Fars. They managed to hold out for the next two years but were finally defeated and their leaders killed or imprisoned.

Qataris: nationality (people of Qatar)

GEOGRAPHY

The modern state of Qatar occupies a small peninsula that protrudes from the larger Arabian Peninsula into the Persian Gulf. This 4,400-square-mile finger of land is arid, flat, and rocky. Its highest point is barely 350 feet above sea level. Qatar is bordered by Saudi Arabia to the south but is otherwise surrounded by the waters of the Persian Gulf. The Hawar Islands, part of the state of Bahrain since the early 20th century and currently the subject of a territorial dispute between Bahrain and Qatar, lie less than two miles off Qatar's western coast. The main island of the neighboring state of Bahrain is about 15 miles away across the Gulf of Bahrain also to the west. Numerous other small islands around the coast of the peninsula are also Qatari territory, and the island of Halul, 30 miles to the east, is an important terminal for oil from the offshore fields belonging to Qatar. A long, narrow inlet of the Persian Gulf, known as Khawr al Udayd, defines part of Qatar's border with Saudi Arabia along the base of the peninsula, although the border in this region is also in dispute. Doha, the capital city and principal port, lies on the east coast of the country. Qatar's other ports and the majority of its industry and population centers also lie along this coast.

The majority of the country consists of very arid desert and receives an average of less than two inches of rain annually. This low rainfall coupled with a scarcity of good freshwater springs severely limits the agricultural opportunities on the peninsula. The little land that is capable of supporting crops such as reeds and spice plants is found along the eastern coast. Today the majority of Qatar's water is derived from the industrial desalination of seawater.

INCEPTION AS A NATION

The Qatari peninsula has been inhabited for millennia, lying as it does on the Persian Gulf trade route between ancient Persia and western Asia. The history of Qatar begins with the domination of the peninsular by the AL KHALIFA and the AL THANI clans of the Bani Utub tribe. These peoples settled in the area after migrating from the arid Najd region of the central Arabian

QATARIS: NATIONALITY

nation:
Qatar; State of Qatar

derivation of name:
From "Qatara," an alternative name for the city of Zubara

government:
Monarchy

capital:
Doha

language:
Arabic is the country's official language, but English is widely used as a second language.

religion:
About 78 percent of the population are Sunni Muslim. Christians make up about 8 percent of the population and the remaining 14 percent follow various faiths, mostly from South Asia.

earlier inhabitants:
Semites

demographics:
Arabs make up 40 percent of the population; Indians, 18 percent; Pakistanis, 18 percent; Iranians, 10 percent. Other South and Southeast Asians as well as Europeans and North Americans make up the majority of the remainder.

Qataris: nationality time line

C.E.

1867 Britain signs a treaty that recognizes Qatar as independent from Bahrain.

1916 Britain and Qatar sign an agreement in which Qatar gives control of its foreign affairs to Britain in return for protection.

1939 Oil is discovered on Qatari territory.

1968 Britain announces its intention to withdraw from its protection agreement with Qatar.

1971 Qatar becomes an internationally recognized independent nation.

1990 Qatari troops take part in the liberation of Kuwait after its invasion and occupation by Iraq.

1995 Prince Hamad bin Khalifa seizes power from his father and begins to institute liberal reforms.

1996 Al Jazeera satellite television station launched in Qatar following the abolition of censorship laws.

1999 The first democratic elections in Qatar since 1971 take place. Female citizens are allowed to vote for the first time in the nation's history.

2003 Qatar allows the U.S. military to site its central command base in Qatar for the duration of the U.S.-led invasion of Iraq.

2003 Voters approve a new constitution that will create a partly elected national parliament. The constitution comes into force two years later.

2005 A joint Qatari-U.S. project is launched to build the world's largest liquefied natural gas plant.

2008 The first government sanctioned Christian church opens in Qatar; Christians are permitted to worship openly for the first time.

Peninsula in the 18th century. By the end of the 18th century the Al Khalifi had also become established on the neighboring islands of present-day Bahrain. An 1867 agreement between the Al Thani of the Qatari peninsula and the British resulted in the end of Al Khalifa power in Qatar. The area was quickly occupied by the Ottoman Empire, however, and it was not until the start of the World War I, when the OTTOMANS withdrew from the area, that Shaykh Abdullah bin Jassim of the Al Thani clan was recognized by the British as the ruler of the area. In 1916 the Al Thani signed an agreement that gave Britain control of Qatari foreign and defense policy in return for protection from their powerful neighbors. This agreement, which made Qatar a British protectorate, was similar to agreements that Britain had signed with other Gulf States in the same era. It marked the start of a close involvement with Britain that was to last for decades.

In 1968 Britain declared the end of its protection agreements with each of the Gulf States, including Qatar. Along with Bahrain, Qatar intended to join with other Gulf States to form a union to be known as the United Arab Emirates (see EMIRATES: NATIONALITY). At the end of the period of negotiation in 1971, however, neither Bahrain nor Qatar had reached a satisfactory agreement with the other gulf emirates. Qatar became an internationally recognized independent state in September 1971.

CULTURAL IDENTITY

As with the peoples of the other Gulf States, the people of Qatar have long been sea traders. Fishing and gathering pearls were the most significant industries for millennia until a downturn in the price of pearls in the early 20th century threatened many Qataris with economic ruin. Large oil reserves were discovered on Qatari territory in the 1940s, and oil production and refining quickly became the cornerstones of a rapidly growing economy. In the 1970s Qatari gross domestic product (GDP) briefly achieved a record growth rate of over 1,100 percent per year thanks to rapidly rising oil prices. Although these growth rates were unsustainable, Qatari society was transformed by the very large sums of money that continued to flow into the country. The discovery of vast natural gas reserves on Qatari territory has guaranteed that the nation will enjoy a buoyant economy for some decades to come. Today Qatar has standards of living that compare with those of any advanced industrialized country.

Education is available for free to all citizens up to the age of 16, and the government is keen to produce a highly educated and technically proficient workforce for the future.

Along with other oil-rich states in the region Qatar has experienced a great influx of foreign nationals who are employed to work in the nation's petroleum, construction, and other industries. About 80 percent of the population of Qatar is made up of foreign workers (known as expatriate workers). Most of these are from South Asia, Egypt, Iran, Palestine, and Jordan. The Qatari government has been criticized for the fact that these temporary workers enjoy few of the benefits available to citizens, even if they have lived and worked in the country for several decades.

The overwhelming majority of the citizens of Qatar, as well as the foreign workers who live there, are Muslim. Qatari law and government are based on the principles of Salafism, which is a Sunni interpretation of Islam that has been popular in the Arabian Peninsula since the 1920s. The movement began in the 18th century in Qatar's large and powerful neighbor, Saudi Arabia. Salafism, which is also sometimes known as Wahhabism, has as its central belief the idea that Islam was at its most perfect during the time of the prophet Muhammad and his immediate descendents. Salafism teaches that the changes to Islamic tradition and law that have occurred in the centuries since that time are the result of flawed human reasoning and should be abandoned. For this reason, Salafism is often seen as a very conservative form of Islam. The influence of Salafist ideas on Qatari society has meant that its laws have generally been less liberal that those of other Gulf States. Until recently public dress codes for men and women were strictly enforced, and although these have now been relaxed a little, almost all Qatari women still wear an *abaya* in public. The *abaya* is the traditional, black form of the *hijab* worn by many Muslim women. Qatari women are, however, legally permitted to drive, unlike Saudi Arabian women.

In 1995 Prince Hamad bin Khalifa became emir of Qatar by forcibly deposing his father. Since that time he has introduced a series of reforms designed to liberalize Qatari society and to make politics more open. As a result of these reforms, a new constitution came into force in 2005, and female citizens were allowed to vote for the first time in 1999. The introduction of greater freedoms for the media contributed to the establishment of the Al Jazeera

The Aspire Tower, a 1,050-foot-high structure built in the city of Doha, Qatar and completed in 2007. The uncompleted tower was the focal point of the 2006 Asian Games held in Doha.

satellite television station in Qatar in 1997. Al Jazeera attracted international attention when it became the only television station allowed to report from inside Taliban-controlled Afghani-stan in the late 1990s and the first to broadcast statements made by al-Qaeda leader Osama bin Laden following the start of U.S.-led military action in Afghanistan in 2001. Al Jazeera has become very popular across the Arabic-speaking world because it is seen as an alternative to the other major international news channels based in the United States or western Europe.

Further Reading

Frederick F. Anscombe. *The Ottoman Gulf: The Creation of Kuwait, Saudi Arabia, and Qatar* (New York: Columbia University Press, 1997).

Lisa McCoy. *Qatar* (Broomall, Penn.: Mason Crest Publishers, 2008).

H. Rahman. *The Emergence of Qatar: The Turbulent Years, 1627–1916* (London: K. Paul, 2005).

Rosemarie Said Zahlan. *The Creation of Qatar* (London: Croom Helm, 1979).

Qays

Qays (Qays Aylan, sometimes called Mudar) is a designation that came into use after the coming of Islam, referring to a group of northern Arab tribes. Their rivals were the southern Arab tribes, grouped together as Yemen (Yaman), also called Kalb. The two groups—Qays and Yemen—which each based their group's identity on a purported shared ancestry, became the opposing political parties that dominated the era of the Umayyads (661–750), the first dynasty to rule after the four Rightly Guided Caliphs who immediately succeeded the prophet Muhammad. During this period the Muslim community was rapidly expanding and different groups were vying for power. These associations based on claimed kinship provided a cohesive base of shared interest. Scholars have suggested that the primary features distinguishing these groups were that Qays advocated expansionist policies for the Muslim polity, while Yemen supported maintaining stable, defensible frontiers and assimilation of non-Arabs.

With the coming to power of the Abbasid dynasty (750–1258), little more was heard of Qays and Yemen until the names surface again in connection with rivalries among powerful families in Ottoman Palestine and Lebanon. The OTTOMANS were the Turkish dynasty that came to power in Anatolia in the 15th century and grew to become a world power, rivaling the West for many centuries until it was dismantled in 1922 in the aftermath of World War I. In this context of Palestine and Lebanon, the fact that these alliances were largely political became clear, in that some who claimed affiliation with one party or the other were not Arab at all but instead were CIRCASSIANS, KURDS, or other non-Arabs. After a battle in 1711 in which the Yemen were utterly routed, the nomenclature disappeared and the powerful families of Lebanon no longer identified themselves as one faction or the other but instead went by their own names.

In Palestine, the Qays/Yemen rivalry is recorded as early as the 14th century. In the 16th century, regions of Palestine allied themselves with these opposing factions and conflict erupted frequently. In the 18th and 19th centuries, wars between Qays and Yemen groups were fought mainly in the cities of Nablus and Jerusalem. As in Lebanon, these were conflicts between rival families, but they were defined in terms of Qays versus Yemen, and the people of the area—townspeople, farmers, and BEDOUIN—declared their affiliation with one or the other. This extended to the Christians as well as Muslims.

As the Ottomans were able to assert their rule more effectively in the second half of the 19th century, these factional wars subsided. Nevertheless, some symbols of affiliation persisted in local customs, particularly those observed in rural areas. The Qays was identified with the color red, and the Yemen with white, and these colors were used in the different groups' flags, their clothing, women's veils, and especially for bridal veils and canopies. There was often intermarriage between the two tribes, but intermarriage necessitated taking special steps. For instance, if a Qays woman married a Yemen man, she could not move to her husband's house in Yemen territory dressed in red. She would have to either conceal her red clothing under something white or change into white clothing at the border.

Qimant

The Qimant are closely related to the Agaw and live mostly in western Ethiopia.

Qizilbash

The Qizilbash are a Twelver (Imami) Shii group who form an influential minority in Afghanistan. Most live in urban centers including Kabul, Herat, and Kandahar. They speak Dari, a Southwest Iranian language related to Persian. Estimates of their population vary widely, from 50,000 to 200,000. One of the reasons exact numbers are difficult to obtain is that some may identify themselves as Sunni PASHTUNS, since Shii belief allows *taqiyya*, or "dissimulation," in order to avoid religious discrimination. The Qizilbash are a highly literate group who often hold high positions in the government and in the professions. The group maintains contact with the Shii world outside Afghanistan, through pilgrimages to the Shii holy sites of Karbala, in Iraq, and Mashhad, in Iran. The name Qizilbash comes from the Turkish, meaning "red-head," and dates from the period of Safavid rule of Iran and parts of what is today Afghanistan (1501–1722), which established Twelver Shia as the state religion of Iran. Under the Safavids, members of this particular religious sect wore distinctive red hats with twelve gores, symbolizing the Twelve Imams. The Ottoman Turks called them "red-heads" as a term of disdain, but those to whom the term was applied adopted it themselves as a point of pride. The Qizilbash of Afghanistan are traditionally identified as the descendants of the garrison left to rule the area by Nadir Shah, a Safavid ruler who passed through the region in 1738 during his campaign in India. Their power and influence was cause for resentment among the majority Sunni Pashtun, and tense relations were exacerbated when the Qizilbash allied with the British during the Anglo-Afghan War (1838–42). During the war of 1891–93 waged by the Afghan emir Abd al-Rahman against the HAZARAS, another Shii Afghan minority, all Shii were declared infidels. Abd al-Rahman accused the Qizilbash of aiding the Hazaras and used that as a pretext for seizing their property and persecuting them.

Quraysh (Qoreish)

Quraysh is the tribe of Muhammad, the prophet of Islam. The tribe traces its ancestry to the prophet Abraham, through his son Ishmael (Ismail, in Arabic), and their special status in Islam is supported by the claim of Quranic scholars that the Quran was revealed in the language of the Quraysh. In the late sixth century C.E., when Muhammad was born, this northern Arab tribe was centered in the city of Mecca, which was to become the holiest city of Islam.

The leading figures of the tribe were prosperous traders, dominating the East African, Indian Ocean, and Mediterranean trade routes. With the coming of Islam and its rise to dominance, many members of the Quraysh became Muslims and held positions of prestige and status in the Muslim community. When Muhammad died, his father-in-law, Abu Bakr became caliph, or successor, to Muhammad as the political leader of the Muslim community, as it was thought that only a man of the Quraysh would be able to maintain unity among the Muslims. Likewise, the three other caliphs who followed Abu Bakr, who together are known as the Rightly Guided Caliphs, were all of the Quraysh, as were the rulers of the subsequent two dynasties, the Umayyads (661–750) and the Abbasids (750–1258).

While the Quraysh were central to the success of Islam, they were also its main detractors. They had been guardians of the Kaaba before Islam, when it was the center of pagan worship. The Kaaba, now the focal point for Islamic worship, is revered as having been built by the prophet Abraham, and it houses the Black Stone, the meteorite sent by God. But when Muhammad began preaching his message, many of the Quraysh clung to the old religion and to the status and wealth their position as protectors of the Kaaba brought them. Some accused Muhammad of being an imposter and of preaching a false religion, and ultimately it was persecution at the hands of the Quraysh that caused Muhammad and his followers to flee Mecca for Medina in 622, the pivotal event of Islam, known as the Hijra, or "migration." Nevertheless, Muhammad tried to convert some of his relatives, and many of the prominent early converts were members of this tribe. In modern times, there are still Quraysh living as nomads in the vicinity of Mecca, and the key to the Kaaba is safeguarded by a clan, or subgroup, of this tribe, the Shayba.

Rabai

The Rabai are one of the nine closely related groups that make up the MIJIKENDA. The Mijikenda mostly inhabit coastal regions of Kenya.

Rabiah (Rabia)

Rabiah is a name that frequently appears in tribal names of pre-Islamic (pre–seventh century) Arabia and Yemen. Rabiah is associated with Mudar, as groups of tribes descending from a common ancestor, with the two sons Rabiah and Mudar as progenitors of different lineages of North Arabian tribes. Because the genealogy given in the early histories is confused, it is difficult to tell whether the tribes existed or were an idealized ancestry. In the medieval histories, the Rabiah, along with the Mudar, are said to have been ruled by the Himyar kingdom of the Yemen, which was overthrown by the ABYSSINIANS in about 340 C.E.. Sometime before the advent of Islam in the early seventh century, the Rabiah and the Mudar migrated north into Iraq, where Diyar Rabiah, "the abode of the Rabiah," was established along the Tigris and Diyar Mudar along the Euphrates. Before Islam, the Rabiah were largely Christian, but by the early years of the Muslim state, they had become an important contingent in the Muslim armies.

Randili

The Randili are one of the nine main subgroups of the OROMO. They live in Ethiopia.

Rangi

The Rangi are a BANTU people living primarily in central Tanzania.

Rapulana

The Rapulana are one of the subgroups of the ROLONG, a TSWANA people of southern Africa.

Rashid

The Rashid are an important family of the Abda clan of the SHAMMAR, a group of nomadic tribes of north-central Saudi Arabia and parts of Syria and Iraq. The Rashid, Sunni Muslim ARABS, whose homeland is Najd, in north-central Saudi Arabia, contended with the Saud dynasty for control of that area in the 19th century. The SAUD had first risen to prominence in the mid-18th century as the military-political arm of the radical Muslim reformer Muhammad ibn Abd al-Wahhab. Saud-Wahhabi power waxed and waned from its beginning until the early 20th century and the founding of the Kingdom of Saudi Arabia in 1932. Meanwhile the Rashid, who were the ruling nobility of the Shammar, had established their own emirate centered on the oasis Haail, north of Riyadh, the Saud base of power. The Rashid emirate in Haail lasted from 1836 until 1921. The Rashid were able to rally the Shammar behind them to counter the growing power of the Saud-Wahhabi forces and to present a united front against incursions from the Ottoman Empire (*see* OTTOMANS).

The Rashid reached the height of their power under the leadership of Muhammad ibn Rashid, who ruled from 1872 to 1897 and extended his territory north into modern-day Syria and Iraq, and south to what is today Oman and southern areas of the Red Sea coast. He expelled the Saud from Najd and sent them into exile in Kuwait. Rashid forces included not only Shammar tribesmen but also the emir's slaves and conscripts. But just as the Saud had had difficulty in maintaining control over a large and relatively inaccessible area, the Rashid, too, could not hold on to distant territories. The turning point came in 1902 when Abd al-Aziz ibn Saud returned to Riyadh, from which his family had been evicted by the Rashid some 12 years earlier, and killed or captured the Rashidi rulers and declared himself ruler. It has been suggested that one of the reasons the Rashid were ultimately unsuccessful was that they were seen as asserting the control of one tribal confederation—the Shammar—over other tribes, while the Saud conquered under the banner of religious reform without respect to tribal affiliation. By 1921 the Rashidi emirate had been incorporated into the Saud, and ultimately, the Kingdom of Saudi Arabia (see SAUDI ARABIANS: NATIONALITY).

Ratlou

The Ratlou are one of the four main subgroups of the ROLONG. The Rolong are a TSWANA people of Southern Africa.

Rega See LEGA.

Reizegat

The Reizegat are one of the main BAGGARA subgroups. The Baggara are a Sudanese people of BEDOUIN and black African descent.

Rendille

The Rendille are a Cushitic people closely related to the SOMALIS (see Cushites). They live in northern Kenya.

Reshawa (Bareshe; Gungawa; Reshe)

The Reshawa live along the banks and on the islands of the Niger River in northwestern Nigeria.

Reshe See RESHAWA.

Ribe

The Ribe are one of the nine closely related groups that make up the MIJIKENDA. The Mijikenda mostly inhabit coastal regions of Kenya.

Rolong

The Rolong are one of the main subdivisions of the TSWANA people of southern Africa. Rolong peoples can be found living in many parts of Botswana as well as neighboring regions of South Africa.

The Rolong claim descent from a founding ancestor called Marolong, who is thought to have lived around 1300. They are one of the many powerful SOTHO-Tswana clans that emerged after the end of the first millennium. The Rolong became one of the most powerful of the western clans, dominating a region that extended from the Kalahari Desert in the north to the Vaal River in the south. They kept large herds of cattle and controlled access to local sources of iron ore. By the 18th century, the Rolong had established a powerful kingdom, the most famous ruler of which was Tau, who is still remembered as a great military leader. The four main subdivisions of the Rolong—the RATLOU, TSHIDI, RAPULANA, and SELEKA—each claim descent from one of Tau's four sons. The THLAPING are a Rolong people who separated from the main group during Tau's reign and established a powerful independent state.

Roma (singular, Rom; Romany, Dom, Domi, Domari; pejorative terms Gypsy, Gipsy, Arabic Nawar, Persian Koli)

The Roma are a traditionally nomadic people thought to be of Indian origin, most of whom speak the language of the country in which they reside along with Romany, an Indo-European language of the Indic branch, or one of its dialects such as Domani. Their population is mainly concentrated in eastern Europe, although there are Roma communities around the world, with population estimates varying wildly, from 2 million to 40 million worldwide. Arriving at accurate numbers is complicated by the fact that the Roma are either not counted or, anticipating discrimination, they disguise their ethnicity. They are thought to have left India in a series of migrations that brought them to Iran by the 11th century C.E., southeastern Europe by the beginning of the 14th century, western Europe by the 15th century, and on every inhabited continent by the 20th century.

There are substantial Roma communities in the Middle East and North Africa, with the largest in Egypt, estimated at perhaps 1 million. In Egyptian Arabic, they are called Dom or Ghagar, which is a term of insult, and many live literally at the edges of society—in the City of the Dead, an enormous cemetery against the Muqattam Hills in Cairo, an area that has long attracted the poor in a badly overcrowded city with housing resources strained to breaking. Some Egyptian Roma are metalworkers, some are entertainers—musicians, dancers, or storytellers—and some, as a last resort, are beggars. Other countries with large Roma populations include Turkey and Syria. Across the region, Roma live a variety of lifestyles and earn their living in a variety of ways. Some work as migrant farmhands, as in Jordan and Lebanon, while others live sedentary lifestyles, as in Syria, where some are metalworkers, carpenters, or construction workers. Most at least ostensibly practice the religion of the country in which they live, which, in the Middle East, is Islam. Roma everywhere are often victims of discrimination and suffer from lack of access to education and employment. Many countries are making efforts to improve these conditions.

Romans

The Romans were identified with a specific city, Rome, which was traditionally founded during the eighth century B.C.E. by peoples principally from the territories of Etruria and Latium, in what is today west-central Italy. A subsequent growth in Roman power, especially during the second and first centuries B.C.E., saw Rome first take over the rule of Italy, then develop one of the largest empires the world has ever seen. This empire, by the end of the second century C.E., stretched from Britain in the west to Assyria in the east, and the number of people classed as Romans was widened by the granting of citizenship rights, even to peoples living outside Italy itself; there was a great extension of citizenship throughout the empire in 212 C.E. under Caracalla for example.

ORIGINS

In popular myth Rome, the city of the Romans, was founded in 754 B.C.E. by Romulus and Remus, twin brothers who were abandoned at birth yet suckled by a she-wolf. When they reached adulthood, having been discovered and brought up by a local shepherd, Romulus laid the foundations for what would become the city of Rome. In reality, Etruscan peoples began developing Rome in the eighth century B.C.E., and by the end of the sixth century B.C.E. the last Etruscan king had been ejected and Rome was a republic. Because of Rome's subsequent imperial expansion across the Mediterranean and further east, the Romans had a profound effect on the history and culture of Africa and the Middle East, despite not being indigenous to these regions.

LANGUAGE

The Romans spoke Latin, a language that developed possibly from around the sixth century B.C.E., building upon Greek influences, and was well established by the third century B.C.E. Early Latin developed into the more literary Classical Latin by the turn of the millennium, as well as the more common Vulgar Latin used by people in everyday speech. Latin as a living language effectively died out by the seventh century C.E.

HISTORY

The history of the Romans in the Middle East and Africa is a vast tale spanning several centuries, so a relatively brief overview is all that is possible here. The expansion of Roman power around the Mediterranean during the third century B.C.E. brought Rome into conflict with the great African power of Carthage, whose territory roughly occupies that of modern Tunisia. Rome subsequently fought three major and prolonged conflicts against Carthage (known as the Punic Wars) that eventually saw Carthage lose its possessions in Spain, Sicily, Corsica and Sardinia. At the end of the Third Punic War (149–146 B.C.E.) Carthage itself was invaded and defeated by the Romans, who termed their new province "Africa."

The annexation of Africa eventually brought Rome into conflict with a former ally and Africa's neighbor, Numidia. War against Numidia's king Jugurtha resulted in some significant defeats for Rome, but she eventually rallied—Numidia was defeated and Jugurtha was executed in 104 B.C.E. From this time Roman power and cultural influence over Numidia would be strong, and during the first century B.C.E. the territory became temporarily the province of "Africa Nova." Nor would Numidia be the last African nation to fall under the Roman shadow. In 74 B.C.E., Cyrene, a territory within present-day Libya, was taken over as a Roman province during a general Roman effort to clamp down on piracy in the Mediter-

ROMANS

location:
Middle East and North Africa

time period:
Second century B.C.E. to ninth century C.E.

ancestry:
European

language:
Latin (Indo-European)

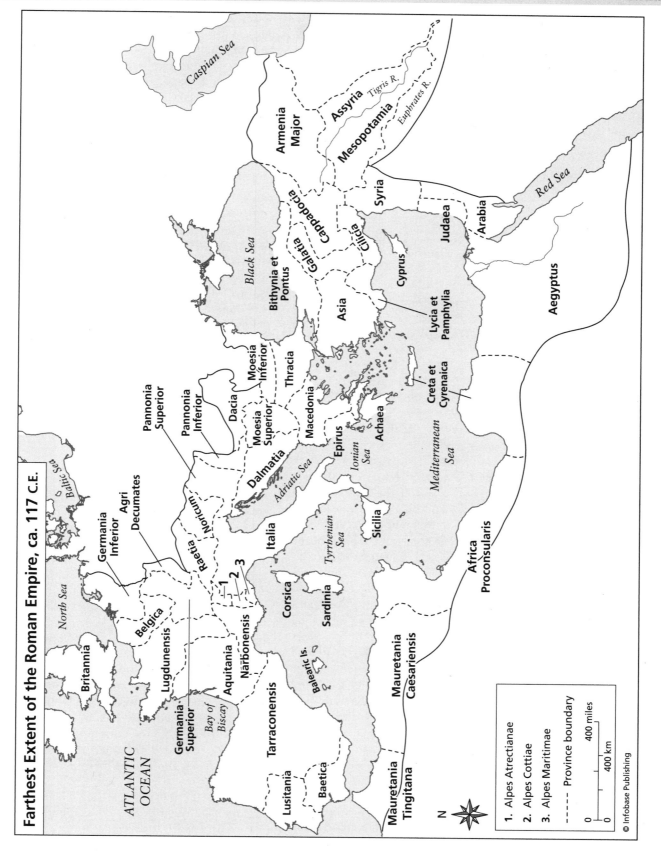

Farthest Extent of the Roman Empire, ca. 117 C.E.

Caspian Sea

Assyria

Tigris R.

Mesopotamia

Armenia Major

Euphrates R.

Red Sea

Cappadocia

Syria

Arabia

Judaea

Galatia

Cilicia

Cyprus

Black Sea

Bithynia et Pontus

Asia

Lycia et Pamphylia

Aegyptus

Baltic Sea

Moesia Inferior

Thracia

Creta et Cyrenaica

Pannonia Superior

Pannonia Inferior

Dacia

Moesia Superior

Macedonia

Mediterranean Sea

Germania Inferior

Agri Decumates

Raetia

Noricum

Dalmatia

Epirus

Achaea

Ionian Sea

North Sea

Belgica

Italia

Adriatic Sea

Sicilia

1

2

3

Corsica

Sardinia

Tyrrhenian Sea

Africa Proconsularis

Britannia

Lugdunensis

Aquitania

Narbonensis

Germania Superior

Bay of Biscay

Balearic Is.

Mauretania Caesariensis

ATLANTIC OCEAN

Tarraconensis

Lusitania

Baetica

Mauretania Tingitana

N

1. Alpes Atrectianae
2. Alpes Cottiae
3. Alpes Maritimae

- - - Province boundary

0   400 miles

0   400 km

© Infobase Publishing

Romans time line

B.C.E.

149–146 Third Punic War. Carthage is invaded and defeated by the Romans, and becomes the Roman province "Africa."

74 Cyrene made a Roman province.

67–64 Rome takes over Cicilia and Syria.

63 Rome captures Jerusalem and annexes Palestine.

30 Rome annexes Egypt.

C.E.

6 Judaea is made a Roman province.

second century Rome brings a succession of countries under its imperial wing. By the end of the century its Middle Eastern and African acquisitions include Mauretania, Numidia, Cyrenaica, Egypt, Arabia, Judaea, Phoenicia, Syria, Mesopotamia, and Assyria.

fourth century Rome is split between Western and Eastern Empires, the latter centered upon Constantinople.

seventh–ninth centuries The Romans lose their eastern and African possessions to the Persians then the Arabs.

ranean. Cyrene had previously been under the control of Ptolemaic Egypt, the greatest of all the African powers but one that would also become a Roman acquisition following the victory of Octavian (the future Augustus) over Mark Anthony and Cleopatra at Actium in 31 B.C.E. Egypt subsequently became the emperor's own personal province and set the pattern for the complete Roman domination of North Africa. By 44 C.E., the whole northern coastline of the African continent was in Roman hands.

While Rome was extending its influence over North Africa, it was also expanding into the Middle East. As part of its antipiracy campaign, Rome annexed Syria in 64 B.C.E., having consolidated neighboring Cilicia in three years previously. The greatest expansion in Rome's Middle Eastern power, however, began with the reign of the emperor Augustus in 27 B.C.E. and ran for the next two centuries. During this period Rome acquired the provinces of Arabia, Judaea, Phoenicia, and Coele, or what is today the entirety of Israel/Palestine, Jordan, Lebanon, and Syria and some of western Saudi Arabia. Further north, second-century C.E. conquests included Mesopotamia, Armenia, and Assyria.

As history now knows, the Roman Empire, great as it was, began a steady collapse from the later third century C.E. The collapse would take a long time, although Romanization was maintained by the Byzantine Empire centered

on Constantinople until that city was taken by the TURKS in 1453. During the period when the Western Empire was at its height of power and confidence, its rule over large portions of Africa and the Middle East brought mixed blessings. There is no denying that Roman control over the provinces could be autocratic and occasionally extremely violent, but equally the Roman Empire brought a large measure of peace to provincial peoples, a peace that was maintained for the best part of two centuries.

CULTURE

Economy

The spread of the Roman Empire undoubtedly spread greater prosperity throughout the Middle East and Africa, the empire providing both an infrastructure to maritime and land trade routes (such as through the development of port facilities and the building to better roads) and through opening more international markets to traders. Maritime trade was by far the fastest and most profitable way of moving goods around the empire. The journey from Carthage to Ostia near Rome took a mere six days, while even the lengthy journey from Caesarea in Judea through to Rome itself could be managed in 20 days.

Rome itself, which rose to have a population of some 1 million people, had an insatiable greed for overseas goods. From North Africa flowed marble, timber, and copper used in Rome's building projects, while linen yielded luxury bedding and clothing (North Africa was also a major exporter of olives). From the eastern border of the Mediterranean came wine, glass, dyes, wool, and textiles, plus precious metals and spices imported from overland routes further to the east. The Middle Eastern and African provinces also provided many thousands of exotic animals destined for display or butchery in the arenas of Rome or other imperial cities.

Yet the provinces themselves also benefited from the greater ease of trade—Egypt, for example, received wine, metals, horses, and ceramics from other imperial lands. All this trade traffic was aided by Rome's imposition of a single currency throughout many parts of the empire.

The provincial exports, it should be noted, were often delivered as part of taxation rather than trade. Roman tax impositions on the provinces were never light, but neither were they heavy enough to cripple the economy or breed too much rebellion. Taxes were paid in

The facade of the Celsus Library in the ruined ancient Greek city of Ephesus (close to the modern Turkish town of Selçuk). Built to commemorate the Roman governor of the region in 135 C.E. the building was later destroyed but the facade was reconstructed in the 20th century.

either fixed sums of silver based on the value of a harvest, or in kind through goods. Although corruption in tax collection doubtless existed in some measure, from the time of Augustus there was greater accountability in tax collection appointments and procedures, hence less room for collectors to line their pockets or dangerously alienate the locals.

Government and Society

The Romans were fairly enlightened when it came to matters of government over the provinces. Roman governors and officials were put in place, but the Romans also left as much of the local administration and law in place as possible. Strabo, for example, in his *Geography* explains that some of the "native magistrates" in Alexandria were allowed to continue in service after the Roman takeover—they included the

"Expounder of the Law," the "Writer of the Records," the "Chief Judge." and the "Commander of the Night Guard." Allowing such local functions to continue was essential if Rome was to maintain a smooth administration of such a large and diverse Empire.

The Romans' attitude toward local people could, of course, vary according to the restlessness of the province. While provinces such as Africa were governed with relative calmness, the Middle East could be far more explosive, resting as it did on religious fault lines. Between 66 and 73 C.E., for example, a Jewish revolt against Roman rule resulted in a hideously bloody war that saw the revolt finally crushed with hundreds of thousands of dead and the Temple of Jerusalem destroyed (in 70) (*see* JEWS). Rome would offer its eastern and African provinces the carrot of good trade conditions, but at the same time wield the stick of military deployments. Local peoples might have to garrison Roman troops, and Rome also created many frontier defenses to protect its provinces from dangers without. Under the Emperors Trajan (r. 98–117) and Hadrian (r. 117–138), for instance, Syria received dozens of fortifications around its borders, although these defenses were only partially successful in preventing incursions from foreign armies.

The Romans living in the Middle Eastern and African provinces certainly borrowed some culture influences from the indigenous peoples, but Roman culture was held as supreme over all other forms, and local peoples were encouraged to obtain favored status with the Romans. Some communities could even achieve exemption from taxation and did not have to quarter Roman troops.

Military Practices

Rome was undoubtedly a leader in military power during the imperial period, its military might resting on a system of disciplined legions, highly motivated to succeed in battle. Generally speaking, the Romans would have preferred to keep their armies undiluted with foreign mercenaries or conscripts, but some troops from the African and Middle Eastern provinces were conscripted. Later, however, the *auxilia* troops came to constitute around half of Roman forces. *Auxilia* were provincial conscripts (although only Roman citizens were allowed into the legions) who became hugely significant to Roman military muscle. High-quality spearmen and archers were recruited as *auxilia,* including archers from Syria and Nabataea (what is now southern Jordan) and a variety of spearmen and slingers. Rome also became hugely reliant upon *auxilia* for cavalry, and the cavalry skills of the east were particularly utilized.

Architecture

Architecture was one of the greatest Roman exports to the provinces, particularly in the form of ceremonial and civic buildings. Between the first and third centuries C.E., for example, the Romans constructed the vast temple complex of Baalbek in Syria, a work to rival even the Athenian Parthenon in splendor and scale. The Jupiter Temple alone featured 54 columns surrounding its central sanctuary. Almost every town in the empire also received an amphitheater to host plays and games. The amphitheater in Alexandria had a 138-foot-wide auditorium and could seat thousands of people, and it re-

mained in use until the seventh century. Although the Romans brought with them their own forms of civic architecture, they in turn were influenced by indigenous styles. Columns, sculpture, and frescos took on eastern iconography and mannerisms, depicting scenes of, for example, African wildlife or palm leaf motifs.

Although the Middle Eastern and North African cities were often in a highly developed state when the Romans took over, the Roman imperial energy accelerated their general urbanization. A good example is Leptis Magna in the Roman province of Africa. Under Septimus Severus (r. 193–211) this city was adorned with Roman state architecture, including a basilica, a forum, and colonnaded streets, plus a great bathhouse adorned with hunting scenes. Many other cities such as Palmyra, Alexandria, Carthage, and Utica received similar displays of grandeur.

Religion

Rome exported its religion as well as its people and goods to the provinces. The large number of temples built throughout Africa and the Middle East, however, testify not only to the influence of Roman gods such as Jupiter and Mars but also to the cult of emperor worship established from the time of Augustus onward. The demand for emperor worship varied according to the emperor on the throne. Generally speaking, most Roman emperors had a good degree of tolerance toward foreign faiths, and allowed their unobtrusive practice as long as they did not challenge the Roman hegemony. Yet should a challenge arise, the consequences could be brutal, as with Judaism. Judaism and, later, Christianity were direct affronts to Roman religion because their monotheism denied the polytheistic Roman system, and hence the value of emperor worship itself.

Palestine became a battleground for the religions. Jews came under several degrees of persecution by the Romans and under the emperor Nero (r. 54–68) Christians also received ruthless treatment. It is a testament to the strength of the young faith that Christianity would eventually become one of Rome's state religion from the rule of Constantine (r. 306–337).

◆

Rome was one of the seminal influences over the cultural development of Europe and Asia, and its legacy in architectural terms alone is still highly visible throughout Africa and the

Middle East. Yet although the grand symbols of Roman power are most visible, millions of Roman émigrés lived their lives in the provinces quietly as traders and farmers. Although the Roman Empire would eventually collapse, often with brutal political and social circumstances, it is almost undeniable that Rome exported as many benefits to its provinces (as long as they were compliant) as problems.

Ronga

The Ronga are a subgroup of the Central African TONGA people. They are concentrated in southern Mozambique.

Rongo

The Rongo are considered to be a part of the SUKUMA people and live in Tanzania.

Rozvi (Rozwi)

The Rozvi are a subgroup of the SHONA of Zimbabwe. The Rozvi founded a powerful empire, the Rozvi Empire, or Changamire State, which dominated the region in the late 17th and 18th centuries. It was destroyed by NGUNI invasions in the early 19th century.

Rozwi *See* ROZVI.

Rufiji

The Rufiji are a BANTU people of East Africa. They live between the Rufiji and Kilombero Rivers.

Ruhaya *See* HAYA.

Rukuba

The Rukuba, or Bache as they sometimes call themselves, make up a small ethnic group living on the highlands around the town of Jos in central Nigeria. Their language (also called Rukuba) is a BANTU language.

In the 18th century or earlier, the Rukuba migrated from Ugba some 37 miles north to their present location on the Jos plateau. There they set up several chiefdoms centered on separate villages. Rukuba society as a whole is made up of a federation of such chiefdoms. Historically, the chief held a semireligious position, and if things were going badly, he would be held to blame and deposed.

Marriage in Rukuba society is unusual in that a Rukuba woman can marry more than once, and she is considered to be married to all her husbands even though she will live with only one at a time. A man might have more than one wife living with him at any time. Any children belong to the husband the mother claims is the father.

Ruwallah (Jelas; Roala; Ruwayla; Ruweilah; Rwala)

The Ruwallah are a large and powerful Arab tribe whose homeland is the northern deserts of modern-day Saudi Arabia and parts of Syria and Jordan. Traditionally nomads, they moved with their animals (mainly camel herds) in the desert to the east of Medina, Saudi Arabia. A migration brought them north into Syria by the early 18th century. Around 1800 a second wave of migration brought the Ruwallah to Syria again and to Mesopotamia (modern-day Iraq). Observers in the early 20th century describe them as camel herders. They also hired themselves out to guide and protect caravans, and they journeyed to the markets of Syria and Egypt, where their camels were in demand. In the 19th century and until the First World War, the Ruwallah were the most powerful of the ANIZAH tribes. They asserted and maintained their independence from the Wahhabis, the reformist Muslim religious group allied with the clan of Ibn Saud, who first came to power in the mid-18th century, and from the Ottoman forces, who then controlled the Arabian Peninsula. Nevertheless, they were to lose much of their economic strength because, with the opening of the Suez Canal in 1870 and the north–south Hijaz Railway in 1908, their camels were no longer in demand. After World War I, when the British and the French controlled Syria and Jordan, the status of the Ruwallah as Syrian or Saudi came into question. Many Ruwallah migrated north to Syria in the summer, and they were determined to be Syrian. Those who stayed in Saudi Arabia and paid taxes there were Saudi citizens. From the establishment of the Saudi state in 1932 (*see* SAUDI ARABIANS: NATIONALITY) to the mid-1950s and later, as oil wealth increased, many Ruwallah joined the Saudi National Guard or worked in the oil industry. Today they can be found in the military, government, the professions, and business. They continue to be a politically influential group Saudi Arabia, Jordan, and Syria.

Rwandans: nationality (people of Rwanda)

RWANDANS: NATIONALITY

nation:
Rwanda; Republic of Rwanda

derivation of name:
Unknown

government:
Republic

capital:
Kigali

language:
The country's official languages are Kinyarwanda, English, and French. Kiswahili is widely used in commerce.

religion:
About 94 percent of the population are Christian (Roman Catholic, 57 percent; Protestant, 26 percent; and Adventist, 11 percent). Muslims make up 5 percent of the population.

earlier inhabitants:
Unknown

demographics:
Hutus make up 84 percent of the population, Tutsis 15 percent, and Twa 1 percent.

GEOGRAPHY

Rwanda is a small landlocked nation in east central Africa. It has an area of about 10,200 square miles and is bordered by four other nations. Rwanda's northern border meets Uganda; Tanzania lies to the east; Burundi to the south; and the Democratic Republic of the Congo to the west. Much of Rwanda's border with the Democratic Republic of the Congo is formed by Lake Kivu.

Rwanda is a mountainous country lying on the eastern edge of the Great Rift Valley, a geological feature that marks the junction of several of the earth's tectonic plates. Lake Kivu is one of a series of lakes that owe their existence to this great fault line in the earth's surface. The land rises gradually from relatively flat plains in the east along the border with Tanzania to a central mountain plateau that marks the continental divide between the drainage basin of the Nile River in the east and the Congo River in the west. From the top of this mountain crest the land drops steeply to the shore of Lake Kivu. A range of volcanic peaks known as the Virunga Mountains extends from the northeast corner of the country into the neighboring Democratic Republic of the Congo. Most of Rwanda is at least 3,300 feet above sea level, and the central plateau rises to more than 6,000 feet. Rwanda's highest point, the 14,830-foot-high peak of Mount Karisimbi, is part of the Virunga Mountain range.

The major watercourses of the region flow along Rwanda's borders. Rwanda's western border with the Democratic Republic of the Congo south of Lake Kivu is demarcated by the Ruzizi River, which connects Lake Kivu to the much larger Lake Tanganyika further south. The Kagera (Akegra) River, a tributary of the Nile River, flows along much of Rwanda's border with Tanzania.

Rwanda is the most densely populated country in Africa. Prior to the interethnic conflicts of the early 1990s it was primarily rural, but since that time the population has rapidly shifted toward the urban centers. Rwanda's capital city, Kigali, is situated close to the geographical center of the country. Other important cities include Butare in the south, which is home to the University of Rwanda; Cyangugu at the southern end of Lake Kivu, which is an important transport link to central Africa; and Gitirama, which is situated close to Kigali and is Rwanda's second-largest city.

INCEPTION AS A NATION

The history of Rwanda is closely linked to that of Burundi, its southern neighbor (see BURUNDIANS: NATIONALITY). The two countries share a very similar culture and were administered as a single entity known as Ruanda-Urundi until independence in 1962.

The earliest known inhabitants of the area of present-day Rwanda and Burundi were the Twa, a forest-forager people who are also found around Lake Tumba in present-day Zaire and also in Burundi and Uganda (see MBUTI, TWA, AND MBENGA). The Hutu people migrated into the area between the seventh and 11th centuries and largely supplanted the Twa. At some time during the 15th century the ancestors of the modern Tutsi people also began moving into the area. The Tutsi founded powerful kingdoms and virtually enslaved the existing Hutu population. By the 18th century a single kingdom under the rule of a Tutsi aristocracy controlled much of the area (see HUTU AND TUTSI).

At the Berlin Conference of 1884–85, European nations partitioned Africa into a series of spheres of influence assigned to each of the powers that had an interest in establishing colonies on the continent. Germany was assigned a portion of East Africa that included the territories of present-day Tanzania, Burundi, and Rwanda. By 1899 Germany had brought the area under its control and Rwanda had become part of the colony of German East Africa. In 1919, following Germany's defeat in World War I, Rwanda and Burundi were assigned to the control of Belgium by the League of Nations (the forerunner of the United Nations). Following World War II Rwanda's status changed again when it became a United Nations trust territory, although it remained under Belgian administration. In July 1962 both Burundi and Rwanda became fully independent. Rwanda's first president was Gregoire Kayibanda.

CULTURAL IDENTITY

During colonial rule from the late 19th to the mid-20th centuries a rigid system of social stratification emerged in Rwanda and Burundi that has had violent repercussions to the present day. The three ethnic groups involved are the Tutsi, the Hutu, and the Twa. Although the Hutu made up the great majority of the population, it was the Tutsi who formed the ruling

Rwandans: nationality time line

C.E.

15th century Tutsis migrate into present-day Rwanda and establish ascendancy over the Hutu.

1890 Rwanda becomes part of German East Africa.

1916 Belgian forces occupy Rwanda.

1923 Rwanda becomes a League of Nations mandate territory under Belgian administration.

1946 Rwanda becomes a United Nations trust territory under continued Belgian administration.

1957 Hutus form political parties and demand majority rule.

1959 Tutsi King Kigeri V and thousands of Tutsis forced into exile following interethnic violence.

1961 Rwanda becomes a republic.

1962 Rwanda becomes independent with Gregoire Kayibanda as president.

1963 Tens of thousands of Tutsis killed following Tutsi rebel incursions across the Rwandan border from Burundi.

1973 Kayibanda deposed in a military coup led by Juvenal Habyarimana.

1978 Habyarimana elected president under a new constitution.

1988 Fifty thousand Hutus seek refuge in Rwanda following interethnic violence in Burundi.

1990 The mainly Tutsi Rwandan Patriotic Front (RPF) invades Rwanda from bases in Burundi starting a civil war.

1993 Habyarimana's government signs a power-sharing agreement with Tutsi rebels.

1994 Habyarimana and the president of Burundi killed in a plane crash suspected to be assassination. RPF launches a new offensive. Hutu extremists and elements of the Rwandan military massacre 800,000 Tutsis and moderate Hutus then flee to neighboring Zaire along with 2 million refugees.

1995 United Nations tribunal begins charging persons responsible for the 1994 massacres.

1996 Zairian government forces attack Hutu refugee camps in Zaire.

1997 Rebels backed by Rwanda and Uganda depose President Mobutu Sese-Seko of Zaire. Laurent Kabila becomes president of Zaire (renamed the Democratic Republic of Congo).

1998 Rwanda backs rebels attempting to depose Laurent Kabila after Congo fails to expel Hutu extremists.

2000 Paul Kagame is voted president by ministers and parliament.

2002 Rwandan troops withdraw from the Democratic Republic of Congo.

2003 Kagame wins presidential elections

2006 UN tribunal issues an arrest warrant for President Kagame alleging his involvement in the assassination of Habyarimana.

2007 Rwanda and the Democratic Republic of Congo sign a peace agreement in which the DRC undertakes to extradite Hutus involved in 1994 massacres.

2008 Arrest warrants are issued for 40 Rwandan army officers accusing them of genocide.

class. The Twa, who have been a tiny minority for many centuries, lived outside of the mainstream of the Tutsi-Hutu economic and social structure. Although all three groups, and particularly the Tutsi and Hutu, share almost exactly the same culture, they were regarded as ethnically and racially distinct by the European colonial authorities. First the Germans and later the Belgians deliberately strengthened the power of the Tutsi minority and encouraged the idea that they were distinct from the Hutu majority. The end of colonial rule precipitated a situation in which the majority Hutus anticipated a greater share of power, and tensions had already begun to rise before the final declaration of independence.

An armed Rwandan woman

In 1957, five years before independence, Hutu political parties began to form, calling for the abolition of the Tutsi monarchy and a greater voice for the majority in governing the country. By 1959 interethnic tensions resulted in a Hutu revolution that caused the Tutsi king and tens of thousands of other Tutsi to leave the country to seek refuge in Uganda and Burundi. In 1961 Rwanda was declared a republic, and at independence in 1962 it was a Hutu, Gregoire Kayibanda, who became the country's first president. In 1963 Tutsi rebels launched an invasion of Rwanda from bases in Burundi that was defeated by government forces. Reprisals were carried out against Tutsi still living in Rwanda that resulted in the deaths of more than 10,000 people and forced many more Tutsi to flee the country.

Hutu-Tutsi violence flared again in the early 1990 when a large force of exiled Tutsi in Uganda calling themselves the Rwanda Patriotic Front (RPF) invaded Rwanda intent on overthrowing the Hutu government. A series of peace talks and the intervention of forces from European countries failed to stop the violence. Tutsi rebels continued to cross the border into Rwanda from surrounding countries, and the Hutu military continued to kill and harass Tutsi living inside the country. In 1994 the situation became critical when two Rwandan politicians were assassinated and a plane returning the presidents of both Rwanda and Burundi from a peace conference was shot down by a missile. Encouraged by radical politicians, a general massacre of the Tutsi began in Rwanda. The army and bands of Hutu militias armed with primitive weapons set about systematically killing and maiming any Tutsi they could find. By July 1994 hundreds of thousands had been killed and hundreds of thousands more had fled the country. Moderate Hutu politicians, including the prime minister, and Hutu civilians were also killed.

As the massacre was taking place the advance of the RPF rebels into Rwanda continued. The RPF had occupied Kigali and established control over much of the country by the end of 1994. As they advanced the Hutu military and militias retreated into the Democratic Republic of the Congo (at that time known as Zaire) along with more than a million Hutu civilians. The RPF established a new government in Rwanda based around a constitution intended to eliminate the ethnic tensions of the past. The first president of the new regime was a Hutu. Tens of thousands of Hutus suspected of involvement in the massacre were arrested and interned. A series of trails intended to produce a just settlement to the national trauma of the massacre dragged on for years after the event.

By 1996 the Hutu refugee camps in Zaire (later the Democratic Republic of the Congo) had become a training ground for Hutu paramilitaries whose aim was to return to Rwanda and overthrow the RPF government. The Rwandan and Ugandan governments intervened in the internal politics of Zaire by supporting the Zairian rebel leader Laurent Kabila, who quickly overthrew the dictatorial leader Mobuto Sese-Seko. The failure of Kabila's new government in the renamed Democratic Republic of the Congo to eject the Hutu paramilitaries led to a second Rwandan- and Ugandan-backed rebellion against Kabila. Zimbabwe, Namibia, and Angola sent troops to aid Kabila. The conflict quickly escalated as the armed forces of six nations fought over the Congo's political future and mineral wealth. The war fought in the Democratic Republic of the Congo continued until 2002 and cost 3 million lives. It has been described as Africa's First World War and is certainly the most devastating war to have occurred on the continent (*see* CONGOLESE [DEMOCRATIC REPUBLIC OF THE CONGO]: NATIONALITY).

In Rwanda the repercussions of the events of 1994 have continued to dominate the political scene. The country returned to democracy in 2003 with the first presidential and parliamentary elections since 1994. Paul Kagame, the RPF leader, won the presidency, and the RPF secured a large majority in the national assembly. In the same year a constitution that specifically outlaws the incitement of ethnic violence was also approved by a large majority of the electorate. In 2005 tens of thousands of prisoners held since 1994 were released after confessing to involvement in the massacre, and in 2006 the administrative regions of the country were reorganized with the aim of creating ethnically diverse regions to replace the old ethnically divisive regions.

Mutual suspicion between the Hutus and Tutsis ingrained over centuries has made it extremely difficult for Rwandans to develop an inclusive sense of national identity. These ethnic rivalries are not restricted within the borders of Rwanda. A very similar standoff exists in neighboring Burundi and in the Ugandan–Rwandan border region. For decades, hundreds of thousands of Hutus and Tutsis have been forced to flee across the Burundian–Rwandan border and back again as ethnic violence has waxed and waned in both countries. As a result many Rwandans still feel much closer ties to the wider transnational community of their ethnic groups than they do to their nation.

FURTHER READING

Christina Fisanick. *The Rwanda Genocide*. At issue in history (San Diego: Greenhaven Press, 2004).

Mahmood Mamdani. *When Victims Become Killers: Colonialism, Nativism, and the Genocide in Rwanda* (Princeton, N.J.: Princeton University Press, 2001).

Linda Melvern. *Conspiracy to Murder: The Rwandan Genocide* (London: Verso, 2004).

Aimable Twagilimana and Learthen Dorsey. *Historical Dictionary of Rwanda* (Lanham, Md.: Scarecrow Press, 2007).

Jan Vansina. *Antecedents to Modern Rwanda: The Nyiginya Kingdom*. Africa and the diaspora (Madison, Wisc.: University of Wisconsin Press, 2004).

S

Sabaeans

The Sabaeans are an ancient Semitic people (*see* SEMITES) of the southwestern Arabian Peninsula (modern-day Yemen) and the earliest attested civilization of Arabia. Theirs is the land of the biblical Sheba, and their civilization is conservatively dated from about 750 B.C.E. to 115 B.C.E., at its peak extending to all of South Arabia. The Sabaean civilization ceased as an independent polity in the third century C.E. when it was brought under the rule of the Himyarites, who originated to the south of Sabaean territory.

The Sabaean capital was Marib, east of Sanaa, the modern-day capital of Yemen. The city was known for its great dam, described in medieval texts as a great feat of engineering, and restored by the Himyarites in the sixth century C.E. The Sabaeans are mentioned by the Greek writer Theophrastus (d. 288 B.C.E.) in his *Enquiry into Plants*. The Sabaean homeland, unlike much of the peninsula, is verdant, and it sits on trading crossroads that have been well traveled since ancient times. The Sabaeans' most important export was incense, in great demand in ancient times for use in religious ceremonies and for other purposes. Sabaean trade routes included overland routes north, through Mecca and the Nabataean city of Petra in modern-day Jordan, and from there, west to Egypt or north to Syria and Mesopotamia. Abundant records of this civilization, dating from as early as the eighth or ninth century B.C.E., are preserved in inscriptions, or epigraphy, on stone or metal.

Sabaot

The Sabaot are a subgroup of the KALENJIN people. The majority of the Sabaot live in the western highlands of Kenya.

Sadama (Sadamo)

The Sadama are a Cushitic people who live in southwest Ethiopia near Lake Abaya (*see* CUSHITES). They are closely related to the OROMO people. There are two main Sadama subgroups: the YAMARICO and the ALETA, who live south of the Gidabo River. Each group claims descent from a different ancestor. As well as these lineage-based divisions, there are other subgroups that are largely based on the region a group inhabits or the religion its members follow.

The majority of the Sadama practice the Sadama religion, which involves a belief in a creator god called Magano and the showing of reverence to ancestors. Many followers are also Christian. About 10 percent of the Sadama are Muslim, and the members of the TAMBO, GARO, and ALABA subgroups mostly follow Islam. In recent decades a new religion called Wando Magano has fast been gaining converts. It brings together elements of the Sadama religion, Christianity, and Islam.

Sadamo *See* SADAMA.

Safwa (Guruku; Mbila)

The Safwa are a Tanzanian people.

Sagala *See* KAGURU.

Sagara (Saghala)

The Sagara are a part of the ZARAMO and live on the coastal lowlands of Tanzania.

Saghala *See* SAGARA.

Saharawis (Western Saharans)

The inhabitants of the coastal deserts of what is now Western Sahara are collectively referred to as the Saharawis. The Saharawis are MOORS of mixed Berber, Arab, and black African descent (*see* BERBERS; ARABS). They speak a dialect of Arabic known as Hassaniya. The Saharawis were once a nomadic people, but since the 1950s the majority have settled in the towns and villages and become farmers or traders. Today, many Saharawis live in refugee camps in Algeria.

During the European scramble for Africa at the end of the 19th century, the Spanish took Western Sahara. The Spanish were not much interested in the area itself; they wanted it mostly so that they could protect the Canary Islands off its shores in the Atlantic Ocean. Much of the desert regions remained out of their control well into the 20th century, and the area became a refuge for people fighting the French expansion into Mauritania and Morocco. When Spain withdrew from the area in 1976, it was divided between Mauritania and Morocco. Mauritania withdrew from Western Sahara three years later, however, and Morocco annexed the entire territory. The Saharawis embarked on a campaign of resistance to Moroccan rule, forming the Polisario movement in 1973. A referendum on independence for Western Sahara has been promised since 1997, but continuing disagreements between the Moroccan government and Polisario have repeatedly delayed the process.

Saho (Shiho; Shoho)

The Saho are a group made up by peoples including AFAR, TIGRE, and ARABS who are united by the Saho language. The majority live in coastal northern Ethiopia and coastal Eritrea.

Sahwi *See* SEFWI.

Sakalava

The Sakalava are one of Madagascar's larger ethnic groups.

Sakas (Indo-Scythians)

Sakas, whose name means "Scythian," refers to two dynasties of satraps, or governors, who ruled in northwest India. Their language was Sanskrit. The longer-lasting dynasty of satraps was founded by Chastana, whose rule is known in Indian history as the era of Saka.

Sakon

The Sakon are part of the KRU cluster of peoples. The Kru are one of the largest ethnic groups in Liberia.

Samburu (Lokop; Sampur)

The Samburu are a MAASAI people of Kenya.

Samo

The Samo people are closely related to the MANDING. They live primarily in northwestern Burkina Faso.

Sampur *See* SAMBURU.

San

Along with the historical KHOIKHOI people, San-speaking peoples make up the KHOISAN grouping of eastern Namibia, western and central Botswana, and bordering parts of South Africa. Distinct San groups include the KUNG of northeastern Namibia and the Khwe, who live in the central Kalahari Desert in Botswana.

The San were the first known inhabitants of southern Africa, where they lived in widely scattered bands at least 20,000 years ago. Many beautiful rock paintings in the region have provided important clues to their history. The Khoisan are not black Africans but make up a unique "racial" category of their own. Historically, the San were predominantly hunter-gatherers. The Khoikhoi were San peoples who adopted pastoralism in favor of a hunter-gathering lifestyle. Over many hundreds of years, these people retreated or were absorbed as other ethnic groups (such as the BANTU) migrated into the area and few direct descendants remain. The San were once referred to as Bushmen, an offensive term that has now fallen largely out of use.

Sandawe

The Sandawe live in the northern regions of Tanzania's central highlands. The districts they

SÃO TOMÉANS: NATIONALITY

nation:
São Tomé and Principe; Democratic Republic of São Tomé and Principe

derivation of name:
Named for the islands of São Tomé (Saint Thomas) and Principe (Prince), which were first named by Portuguese explorers in the 15th century C.E.

government:
Republic

capital:
São Tomé

language:
Portuguese in the country's official language. Many people speak a creole language derived from Portuguese and the West African languages spoken by slaves and contract laborers brought to the islands over centuries.

religion:
More than 80 percent of the population are Christian, with the overwhelming majority of these professing Roman Catholicism. About 20 percent follow no recognized faith.

earlier inhabitants:
There were no inhabitants before Portuguese colonization.

demographics:
São Toméans may belong to one of several social groups including *mesticos* (mixed African-European heritage), *forros* (descendants of freed slaves), *servicias* (contract laborers from West Africa), *angolares* (descendants of Angolan slaves), and Europeans.

inhabit include Mbulu, Singida, Iramba, and Kondoa, which cover the plateau south of lakes Eyasi and Manyara in northern Tanzania.

Together with the HADZA, the Sandawe are perhaps the last-remaining descendants of East Africa's first human inhabitants. The original human inhabitants of southern and East Africa were the ancestors of the modern-day KHOISAN people. The Khoisan are not black Africans but make up a unique "racial" category of their own. They are historically associated with hunter-gatherer lifestyles and distinctive for their short stature and use languages that contain clicking and popping sounds. Over many hundreds of years, as other groups migrated into the area, most Khoisan people retreated or were absorbed by the incoming communities. The Sandawe and sometimes the Hadza are counted as the Khoisan's only direct descendants remaining in East Africa today.

Sanga *See* SANGO.

Sango (Bosango; Sanga)

The Sango live in a region that includes the Central African Republic, the Republic of the Congo, the Democratic Republic of the Congo, and Chad. Sanga is the national language of the Central African Republic.

São Toméans: nationality (people of São Tomé and Principe)

GEOGRAPHY

The nation of São Tomé and Principe consists of two small islands located in the Gulf of Guinea off the west coast of the continental mainland of Africa. São Tomé, the larger of the two islands, is approximately 30 miles long and 18 miles wide; Principe, the smaller island, is just 13 miles long and 9 miles wide. Together they have an area of about 385 square miles. The island of Principe, which is marginally closer to the mainland, is about 225 miles from the coast of the nation of Gabon; the island of São Tomé, the more southerly of the two, lies just north of the equator.

São Tomé and Principe Island are formed from the remnants of a chain of extinct volcanoes. Both islands are mountainous with narrow plateaus along their coasts. The highest point on São Tomé is 6,640 feet above sea level, and the highest peak on Principe is 3,010 feet above sea level. Steep hills, ravines, and heavy tropical forest cover characterize the interior landscapes of both islands. Agriculture and the majority of the population are restricted to the narrow coastal plateaus.

About 95 percent of the population of the country lives on São Tomé Island. The capital city, also named São Tomé, is near the northern tip of São Tomé Island and is home to about one third of the population. Santo Antonio, the principal town of Principe Island, has a population of less than 2,000.

INCEPTION AS A NATION

When Portuguese explorers landed on the islands in 1471, they were uninhabited and had probably never had an indigenous population. The first Portuguese settlers arrived in the 1480s, but their colony foundered because they were unable to produce food in the unfamiliar conditions and climate. Despite these early setbacks, more settlers arrived early in the 1500s and the colonization of the islands grew slowly from these first groups. It was the policy of the Portuguese government of the time to forcibly relocate convicted criminals and orphans to its colonies, and these made up a significant proportion of the early settlers. A group of 2,000 Jewish children who had been taken from their parents by the government to ensure that they were raised as Christians were among those sent to the islands. Government officials and traders also traveled to the islands and imported slaves from the mainland to work their plantations.

Little changed in the tiny colony for the first 400 years of its existence. The islands became first an important center for the production of sugar and the transshipment of slaves from the west coast of Africa to the Americas and, later, a center for the production of cocoa and coffee. In 1951 São Tomé and Principe became an overseas province of Portugal. During the 1960s a nationalist movement known as the Movement for the Liberation of São Tomé and Principe (MLSTP) began to agitate for independence from Portugal, and in 1974 the fall of the dictatorial government of Portugal led to independence negotiations. São Tomé and Principe achieved independence in July 1975, with Manuel Pinto da Costa as the nation's first president.

CULTURAL IDENTITY

São Tomé and Principe's cultural development was quite different from that of the nations of

São Toméans: nationality time line

C.E.

1471 Portuguese explorers land on the uninhabited islands of São Tomé and Principe.

16th century São Tomé settled by Portuguese colonists. Slaves of original settlers are freed.

19th century Cocoa and coffee introduced to the islands and soon become the colonies' chief exports. Descendants of slaves imported after 16th century freed.

1951 São Tomé and Principe becomes an overseas province of Portugal.

1960 Independence group Movement for the Liberation of São Tomé and Principe (MLSTP) formed.

1974 Portuguese government deposed. Negotiations for São Tomé and Principe independence take place between new Portuguese government and the MLSTP. Many Portuguese leave the islands.

1975 São Tomé and Principe achieves independence.

1978 Government requests intervention of Angolan troops to suppress a coup attempt.

1990 A new constitution legalizes opposition parties.

1991 First open multiparty elections take place; the MLSTP loses its majority and Miguel Trovoada is elected president.

1995 President Miguel Trovoada deposed in a bloodless coup but reinstated after a few days following international pressure.

2003 Government of President Fradique de Menezes deposed by a coup while the president is away from the country. De Menezes is reinstated after a week following negotiations with coup leaders.

2004 A law intended to protect expected oil revenues from corruption is approved.

2005 International oil companies conclude agreements with São Tomé and Principe government in conjunction with Nigerian government for extraction rights in the Gulf of Guinea.

2007 Ninety percent of São Tomé and Principe's foreign debt is canceled by the International Monetary Fund.

mainland West Africa. In part this was due to the colony's isolation but also to the fact that there was no indigenous population when the first European settlers arrived. At first there were three distinct social groups on the islands. The free white settlers who owned the plantations or worked for the government; the white deported criminals and orphans forcibly relocated by the Portuguese (known as *degredados*); and the African slaves imported from West Africa. Degredados were encouraged by royal charter to take African slaves as their wives in order to boost the population, and early in the 16th century all slaves belonging to the first settlers and the children of those slaves were freed. The effect of these measures was to create a large, free, mixed-ancestry and African population that formed the core of São Toméan culture. In the 19th century later generation of slaves, most of whom had originated in Angola, were also freed. Many of these remained tied to the plantation system however. The descendants of the freed slaves were referred to as *forros*, and a small subgroup of these (the descendants of those slaves freed in the 16th century) had considerable wealth and political influence.

Although slavery on the islands officially ended in 1869, slavelike conditions continued for the majority of the colony's plantation workers. In the first decade of the 20th century there was an international outcry at the labor conditions endured by "contract" laborers on São Tomé's plantations. Although some reforms were made, the oppressive conditions continued well into the 1950s and contributed to the nascent independence movement on the islands. The nation's small size made it extremely difficult for the rebels to conduct a military campaign against the colonial administration, and the Movement for the Liberation of São Tomé and Principe (MLSTP) spent much of the 1960s and early 1970s in exile in Gabon until the Portuguese government recognized their authority in 1974.

Democratic government was not established in the island nation until the late 1980s, and its first democratic election did not take place until 1991. Political unrest during the 1990s led to frequent changes of leadership and two military coups. Since that time the gradual decline in the economic importance of the cocoa and coffee plantations has led to increased social mobility within the country, and the social distinctions that were fixed during the colonial period have eroded.

The discovery of large oil reserves in the Gulf of Guinea has presented São Tomé and Principe with a new opportunity for economic stability. In 2005 São Tomé and Nigeria signed the first in a series of joint agreements with international companies over rights to locate and extract oil. The government in São Tomé also established a joint military commission with Nigeria in 2007 to protect their mutual oil interests in the Gulf of Guinea. Together with the cancellation of 90 percent of São Tomé and Principe's foreign debt by the International Monetary Fund, also in 2007, these developments represent the country's best hope for stability and economic development in the future.

FURTHER READING

Robert Garfield. *A History of São Tomé and Príncipe Island, 1470–1655: The Key to Guinea* (San Francisco: Mellen Research University Press, 1992).

Tony Hodges, and M. D. D. Newitt. *São Tomé and Príncipe: From Plantation Colony to Microstate* (Boulder, Colo: Westview Press, 1988).

Gerhard Seibert. *Comrades, Clients and Cousins: Colonialism, Socialism and Democratization in São Tomé and Principe.* African Social Studies Series, 13 (Leiden, Netherlands: Brill, 2006).

Caroline Shaw. *São Tomé and Príncipe* (Oxford, U.K.: Clio, 1994).

Sapei *See* SEBEI.

Sar

The Sar are a subgroup of the SARA. They live in southern Chad.

Sara

The name Sara refers to the non-Muslim people of southern Chad who speak similar languages and form the largest ethnic grouping. Outsiders often use it to refer to several groups as one unit when they are, in fact, distinct ethnic groups themselves. The main peoples that make up the Sara are the KABA, NAR, SAR, GULAY, NGAMBAY, and MBAY. The largest Sara subgroup is the Ngambay, followed by the Gulay and then the Sar. The Sara language group is a Central Sudanic Nilo-Saharan language.

The Sara are also called the KIRDI—a name used by Muslims to refer to non-Muslims—originally by people such as the BAGIRMI, who frequently raided the Sara for slaves in the 19th century. The balance of power was tipped after the colonial era, however, which transformed Sara society. Being settled farmers living in the more fertile south of Chad, the Sara bore the brunt of colonial policies—the introduction of a cash economy and forced labor, for example—but they also had greater education opportunities. As a result, in present-day Chad most government and other official posts are filled by southerners such as the Sara. The religious, economic, and social differences between northerners and southerners have led to tensions and, at times, war between northerners and southerners.

Saracens

Saracen is a term used to refer to ARABS or Muslims, including TURKS, especially during the Crusades, the religious wars largely aimed at taking back Jerusalem and other holy places from Muslims, which began with the call to war given by Pope Urban II in 1095 and lasting into the 15th century. The word appears in Classical and Western sources but is not a term Arabs or Turks used to refer to themselves. While the derivation of the word is controversial, one often cited possibility is that the word derives from the Greek *sarakenos,* which itself may come from Arabic *sharqi,* meaning "eastern." More likely the term originally denoted a people from a region of northwest Arabia, mentioned in the first century C.E. by Dioscorides, the physician known for his catalog of plants and their medicinal uses, and by the encyclopedist Pliny the Elder, and in the second-century C.E. *Geography* of Ptolemy. By the fourth century, Christian church historians were using the word with pejorative connotations to refer to the Arabs, whom they considered descendents of Ishmael, the son of the prophet Abraham with his concubine Hagar. During the Middle Ages in Europe, the term as denoting Arabs or Muslims was popularized by epic poems about the Crusades, the *chansons de geste,* or "songs of deeds," composed in Old French and set in the time of Charlemagne, who is depicted as the champion of Christendom, or later figures. The term has survived in European languages into modern times.

Sasala (Isala; Sisala)

The Sasala are a people of northern Ghana.

Sassanians

The Sassanians were the peoples of the third, or second "Great," Persian Empire known as the Sassanid Empire that existed from 226 to 651. They emerged from the preceding Parthian dynasty, and were succeeded by a Persian Islamic state. The core territory of the empire was Iran, and at its territorial height it stretched from the eastern edge of modern Turkey to what is now western Pakistan, occupying the territory between the Roman Empire and, from the mid-fourth century, the Hepthalites, or White Huns (*see* PARTHIANS; PERSIANS; ROMANS).

ORIGINS

The name Sassanian comes from Sassan, the Great Priest of the Temple of Anahita, an Iranian shrine cult. The son of Sassan, Ardashir I, was the founder in 226 C.E. of what became the Sassanid Empire. The context was a power struggle in the upper ranks of the Parthian Arsacid Empire, which Ardashir took advantage of by ousting the Arsacid client ruler of Persis (modern Fars Province in southern Iran) and establishing himself as ruler.

The Sassanid Empire was predominantly ethnically Persian, and its social structure was designed to concentrate power based on ethnicity, with a class system determined by birthright with a few rare exceptions.

LANGUAGE

The spoken language of the Sassanians was Middle Persian, also know as Parsik or Parsig, from which the name for modern Persian—Farsi—is derived.

The official written script is known as Pahlavi, adopted from the Aramaic alphabet and modified from the form being used by the Arsacids at the time of the inception of the Sassanid Empire, also known as Northwest Pahlavi. The Sassanian form is also known as Southwest Pahlavi—Middle Persian in its spoken form. Arsacid Pahlavi appears to have been used throughout the Sassanian Empire, and it is likely a great deal of absorption took place until, by the end of the Sassanid Empire, only Southwest Pahlavi (Middle Persian) is referred to in the documentary record.

HISTORY

Ardashir I's establishment of local rule in Parsis was followed by series of rapid expansions into the territory of the regional overlord, Artabanus V, whose defeat at the battle of Hormizdeghan effectively ended Parthian rule in Persia. After becoming sole ruler, Ardashir I appointed himself *shahanshah,* "King of Kings" (with his wife being "Queen of Queens," or *banebshenan*). These remained the titles for Sassanian monarchs until the end of the empire.

For the majority of the empire's history, the Sassanids and Romans were either directly at war or in a state of uneasy truce. The reign of Ardashir's son Shapur I was involved in campaigns against the forces of Roman emperors Gordian and Valerian, with the defeat of the former and the capture and lifetime imprisonment of the latter in 260 C.E. In 337 Shapur II broke a 40-year peace treaty to war with the Romans, expanding Sassanian lands into Armenia and Mesopotamia. Following the siege of Singara in 344 C.E. he renegotiated peace with Constantius II after a long campaign that had ended in stalemate and the death of the Roman emperor Julian in battle.

In 324 Emperor Constantine had adopted Christianity into the Roman Empire, fueling tensions between the state religion—Zoroastrianism—and Christianity within the Sassanid Empire. Under Shapur II, the Christians suffered. However, religious tolerance varied according to the monarch of the time—for example, by the rule of Yazdegerd I (r. 399–421), a time of relative peace and prosperity, Christians were again tolerated.

Bharam V's reign (421–438) is one associated with political and cultural accomplishment. In 427 he crushed an invasion by the newly expansionist Hepthalites. Seeking approval at home, he pursued the popular measure of persecuting religious minorities, including the Christians. Failing to secure their extradition to the Roman Empire, he forged a peace settlement with Constantinople on the terms that the Sassanians would tolerate Christians if the Romans tolerated Zoroastrians on their own soil. Due to his popular successes and flamboyant nature, Bharam V has become a favorite subject of Persian art and literature.

The threat of the White Huns permeated the reign of Bharam's successors until in 484 the Shananshah Feruz and many of his noble-

SASSANIANS

location:
Persia (centered on modern Iran)

time period:
226 to 651 C.E.

ancestry:
Parthian; Persian

language:
Middle Persian

men were killed in battle. During the subsequent period of instability the Hepthalites captured royal treasures and demanded tribute, and in capitulating the Sassanid monarchy undermined its own public support. This fueled rebellion led by a priest called Mazdak, who called for social equality and the redistribution of material wealth. The new king, Kavadh I, attempted to appease both revolutionaries and the nobility by initiating a program of cautious reform—the ruling class responded by deposing and imprisoning him. After two years in the "Castle of Oblivion," he escaped and fled east, where the Hepthalites—happy for a Sassanid king to be in their debt—gave him an army. Kavadh returned to Ctesiphon, retook the throne, secured peace with the Hepthalites, and renewed war on the Byzantine Empire.

It is Kavadh's son, Khosrau, who takes the most celebrated title of *anushirvan,* or "immortal soul." He instigated a number of lasting social reforms, including improvements in communications (canals and roads), reformed taxation, and improved urban water supplies. Despite reaffirming Zoroastrian doctrine while consolidating the rigid social class system, he encouraged tolerance of other religions, and members of the Roman Academy of Athens were allowed to enter and leave the Sassanid Empire without persecution.

Khosrau broke the "eternal peace" settlement with the Byzantine Empire in 540 on the grounds of a rejected demand for Byzantine territory bordering the Black Sea. Despite a bribe of 400,000 gold coins from Emperor Justin I, Khosrau kept the war going for three years before accepting peace to concentrate on subduing his father's onetime allies, the White Huns. Sometime between 557 and 560, his forces finally destroyed the Hepthalites as a political opponent.

Justin's successor, Justin II, soon ceased tribute payments to the Sassanians and declared war, spurred on by an uprising in Armenia. This proved disastrous for Justin's empire. In 573 the Byzantine city of Dara, among others, had fallen to Persian forces and tribute payments had recommenced.

However, further war with the Byzantine Empire was not long in coming. Khosrau

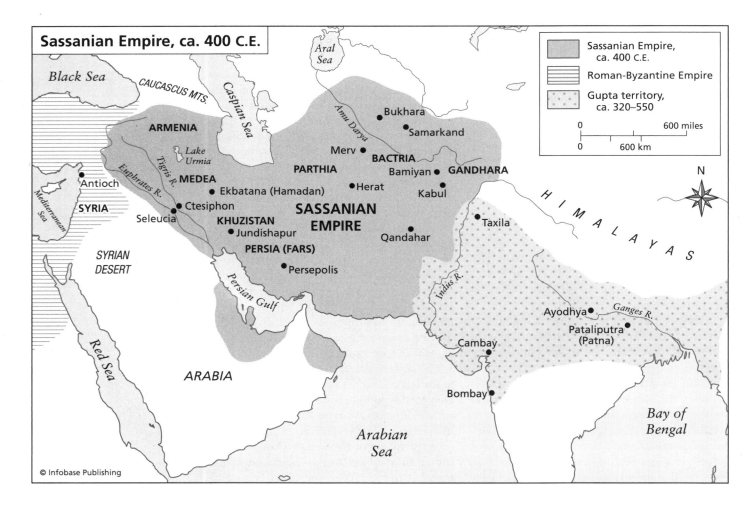

Sassanian Empire, ca. 400 C.E.

I's death in 579 sparked a struggle for succession that eventually placed his son's son on the throne. Khosrau II became king with military assistance from Maurice, the new Byzantine emperor, and when Maurice was deposed and executed during a mutiny led by a man called Phocas, Khosrau II took the opportunity to declare war once again on Constantinople, launching a major offensive in 602.

In a territorial sense, this campaign was a success. The Sassanid Empire soon had control of land stretching from eastern Anatolia (modern Turkey) to Egypt—this was the largest extent of the Sassanian Empire throughout its history. However, the expansion was untenable because it was based on unsustainable social and military practices. Khosrau II was a cruel and intolerant ruler, and his imposition of heavy taxation to pay for this military exploits fomented much resentment at home. Despite this revenue, he had overstretched his military resources. Emperor Heraclius, Phocas's successor as of 610, soon took advantage of this situation with a string of successful moves against the Persians.

In 627 Heraclius landed his forces on the coast of the Black Sea and marched upon the Sassanid capital. This army encountered the bulk of Khosrau's Persian forces on route, and after a day of fighting now known as the Battle Of Nineveh, Khosrau's army was destroyed. Four days after fleeing from the advancing Byzantine forces, Khosrau was executed by his own generals.

The newly crowned Khavad II signed a treaty returning territory to Constantinople that including Egypt and Palestine, and peace was again declared between the Sassanians and Romans. When Khavad died after just a year, a series of bloody struggles took place to decide who would take the throne, and without strong leadership or law enforcement, the empire fragmented—cities and regions seceded from Sassanid rule and its economy subsequently collapsed. When the Islamic Arab Caliphs started their attacks from 634, the Sassanians were in poor shape to offer long-term resistance, and within five years their lands had been absorbed into the first Iranian Islamic state.

CULTURE

The Sassanian economy was underpinned by agricultural production. Sassanian foreign policy heightened the importance of arms manufacture and stimulated extensive mining and metalworking, the former on the fringes of the

Sassanians time line	
C.E.	
226	Ardashir I establishes local rule in Parsis.
260	Shapur I defeats and captures Roman emperor Valerian.
324	Constantine the Great officially adopts Christianity into the Roman Empire.
337–344	Shapur II breaks peace treaty to expand into Roman territory; peace renegotiated with Constantius II.
399–421	Rule of Yazdegerd I
421–438	Rule of Bharam V
484	Feruz killed in battle; Hepthalites plunder Sassanid territory; monarchy establishes peace at expense of public support, fueling rise of Mazdak.
496–531	Reign of Kavadh I
531–579	Reign of Khosrau I
557–560	Sassanians destroy Hepthalite Empire
602	Khosrau II launches offensive on Byzantine Empire that leads to overextension of Sassanian military forces.
627	Heraclius sends forces into Persia and destroys bulk of Sassanid army at Battle of Nineveh; Khosrau flees and is executed.
651	Sassanid Empire is fully absorbed into Persian Islamic state.

empire where ores could be found. Although government was centralized, production was largely in the hands in private entrepreneurs who fitted into the Sassanian system of taxes, levies, and custom duties. Rather than directly controlling local production via state employees, the Sassanian ruling class supported economic growth by feeding resources such as skilled labor into regions they wished to economically stimulate. Sassanian rulers took direct control only in large-scale projects that were beyond the financial reach of individuals, such as Khosrau I's canal-engineering project. The power invested in local manufacturers fostered the development of both craft guilds and revolutionary proletariat organizations, with the power to encourage the monarchy to seek their approval.

Society was stratified, with the *Shahanshah* and *Banebshenan* on the top tier. Directly under them came the *shahrdar,* or provincial rulers. The Sassanian bureaucracy included the *bozorg farmadar* (head chancellor) and the heads of the Zoroastrian priesthood and of the traders. This ruling class was reinforced with ethnic identity, as membership of these upper tiers of society was dependent on being of the Parthian or Persian nobility, with very few exceptions. Below them came the lower ranks of the bureaucracy,

Khosrau I: Ruler of the Sassanians

Khosrau I is the most celebrated and best-known ruler of the Sassanian Empire, ruling from 531 to 579 C.E. as the 20th Sassanian monarch. Elsewhere in the world he is known under the name of Anushirvan, or Anushirvan the Just. His reign is associated with reform, innovation, and an intensification of documentary sources and record keeping.

Khosrau's foreign policy continued the age-old struggle against the Byzantine Empire and threats from the east, with a broken peace settlement with the Romans allowing him to invade Syria, sack Antioch, and relocate its inhabitants after 540. The end of his reign saw him in the middle of negotiations for another peace settlement after an opportunistic war to support a revolt in Byzantine territory. To the east, he temporarily allied the Sassanid Empire with the Turks, and this allowed him to destroy the Hepthalites around 560.

Khosrau's political and social reforms were substantial and had long lasting positive effects. His taxation policy was, for the first time, based on property and not produce. He reformed the Sassanian army, changing the support system for the knights so they were equipped and financially supported directly by the central government, thus taking military power from the landed elite and placing it in the hands of the bureaucracy and the throne. His urban redevelopment programs also improved the empire's communications and stimulated trade.

A great deal of what is known about the Sassanian Empire was documented during Khosrau's reign thanks to the renewed vigor of the bureaucracy and of literature during this period. Many world texts were translated into Pahlavi. As with political reform and religious tolerance, the support of artistry was highly dependent on the wishes of the current ruler, and under Khosrau all branches of art appear to have flourished. External cultural influences were adopted and encouraged—for example, it is around this time that chess was first brought into the empire from India.

The danger of Khosrau's reign from a historical perspective arises because of its illustrious nature. The king's almost mythical status in Persian history may have led to various political and cultural achievements occurring outside his reign gradually being shifted into it through inaccuracy or aggrandizement. However, hard it is to overemphasize his impact on the empire and on the succeeding Muslim states in Iran, much of his consolidation work was soon undone by Khosrau II, who sowed the seeds of the empire's demise.

siege weapons were used for assaults on cities and fortifications.

Trade links were vital to the economy because of the extensive production of finished goods from imported raw materials, such as the weaving of imported Chinese silk. This made foreign policy of maintaining the security of the trade route to China of paramount importance. Sassanian finished fabrics were highly elaborate and sought after; silk and woolen textiles were exported, along with skins and leather. Other imported goods such as paper and spices were redistributed along trade routes by merchants. Sassanian coinage itself, the silver *drahm,* became an exportable commodity and was even used in the Muslim state that followed the end of the Sassanid Empire.

The Sassanian Empire is seen as a time of enormous cultural achievement in the history of Persia and the progenitor for the development of the styles of Muslim art. Sassanian cultural material was distributed eastward into India and China and westward as far as Spain. The Sassanian textiles that have survived to the present day are among the most treasured in the world, utilizing elaborate and intricate designs. Sassanian metalwork was also a field for celebrated creative expression, often with designs glorifying the ruling dynasty and its military power.

Sassanian architecture was informed by earlier Parthian modes but developed its own distinctive style, utilizing large brick walling and molded or carved stucco, and in turn informing and influencing many later Iranian architectural styles.

Although the Sassanians had enjoyed 400 years of political, military and cultural success, in later years they had come at a heavy cost. The ruinous rule of Khosrau II accelerated the increasing precariousness of Sassanid rule and left the empire fatally vulnerable. Despite ceasing to exist as a unified people beyond 651 the Sassanid Empire left a lasting mark on the development of many world civilizations, including Iranian Muslim society, which could directly draw on the rich cultural resources that remained after the second Great Persian Empire had collapsed.

FURTHER READING

Elton L. Daniel. *The History of Iran* (Westport, Conn.: Greenwood Press, 2001).

David Nicolle. *Sassanian Armies: The Iranian Empire Early 3rd to Mid-7th Centuries A.D.* (Stockport, U.K.: Montvert, 1996).

the warriors and the commoner class. The class system and governmental hierarchy was also supported by the state religion, Zoroastrianism. This form of the religion was subtly different to Zoroastrianism elsewhere, as it was altered to reinforce Sassanian cultural identity. Madzean interpretations of this form of Zoroastrianism led to the development of Iranian cosmology.

The Sassanid army, or *spah,* was based around the use of cavalry. The two primary cavalry units were called the *clibanarii* and the *cataphracts.* The influence and dependence on these cavalry, the *cataphracts* in particular, would later be adopted as the template for the European medieval feudal caste of knights on horseback. Archers and infantry supported the cavalry during open battle, and sophisticated

Saud (Al Saud, Suud, Saaud)

Saud is the ruling family of the Kingdom of Saudi Arabia (see SAUDI ARABIANS: NATIONALITY). They are Arabic-speaking Sunni Muslims. The ancestral homeland of the Saud is the north-central desert of the Arabian Peninsula, the area called Najd. Members of the Al Saud clan were landholding merchants, and in the mid-18th century C.E., when they first rose to prominence outside their own region, they ruled the small town of Diriyya, in Najd. During this time, the Saud made a crucial alliance that was to have far-reaching consequences. Muhammad ibn Abd al-Wahhab had begun preaching a fiery brand of Islamic reform, aimed at ridding Muslim religious practice of everything he deemed corrupt and contrary to "pure" Islam. Muhammad ibn Saud took up his cause and provided the military-political support to spread the doctrines of Wahhabism. The alliance took the rule of Saud and the religion of the Wahhabis to most of northern Arabia, and their forces managed to take Mecca and Medina.

This incursion into the holy cities set off alarms in the Ottoman Empire (see OTTOMANS), which had controlled the coastal areas of the peninsula, including Mecca and Medina, although the empire had not managed to penetrate the interior. The Ottomans retook Mecca and Medina in 1813 and pushed the Wahhabis back into central Arabia, where they remained for most of the 19th century. During this time, the Saud were also contending with the al-Rashid clan, of the SHAMMAR tribe, for control of central Najd, and particularly the city of Riyadh, which the Saud had taken by 1792 and made their home base. But in 1890, when Abd al-Aziz ibn Saud, who was to become the founder of the Kingdom of Saudi Arabia, was 10 years old, the Ottoman-backed Rashid drove the Sauds out of Riyadh. Ibn Saud was to take the city back in 1902, and it was to become the capital of the modern country.

Over the next 30 years, ibn Saud consolidated his control over Najd, and by 1924 he was again threatening the cities of Mecca and Medina, ruled by the Hashemite (see HASHEMITES) sharif Husayn, whose sons were installed by the British in the aftermath of World War I and the dissolution of the Ottoman Empire, as rulers of Transjordan (modern-day Jordan) and Iraq. Meanwhile, ibn Saud enlisted a core group of Wahhabi supporters, the Ikhwan, or "Brothers," to abandon nomadism and take on agriculture instead. Thus they became much easier to control and they formed the backbone of Ibn Saud's campaign to unite most of the Arabian Peninsula under his rule as the Kingdom of Saudi Arabia, established in 1932.

Meanwhile, Western countries had become interested in the possibility of oil in the region, and in 1933, Ibn Saud granted exploration rights to Standard Oil of California, establishing a lasting and many-faceted relationship with the United States. A joint company was eventually formed, the Arabian American Oil Company (Aramco, which was to become the Saudi Arabian Oil Company, or Saudi Aramco, in 1980, when the Saudi government acquired 100 percent of its assets). In 1938 the first oil was struck in the eastern area of Jabal Dhahran, thrusting the country—and the Saud—headlong into the 20th century. This region, which had depended largely upon the date palm and the camel to eke out a meager existence, was now on the way to enormous wealth under the close control of the ruling Sauds. The strict Wahhabi society was now host to an influx of American and other foreign workers and their families, and later American troops. Exposure to and interdependence with the West, welcome or not, was to become a central issue for the Saud dynasty, one that has continued to reverberate.

Saudi Arabians: nationality (Saudis, people of Saudi Arabia)

GEOGRAPHY

The Kingdom of Saudi Arabia is a large nation situated on the Arabian Peninsula. The territory of Saudi Arabia covers about 80 percent of the peninsula and is bordered to the south by the United Arab Emirates, Oman, and Yemen. In the north Saudi Arabia borders Kuwait, Iraq, and Jordan. Qatar also borders Saudi Arabia at the neck of the Qatar Peninsula, which protrudes into the Persian Gulf from the main body of the Arabian Peninsula. Saudi Arabia has long coastlines on both the Persian Gulf and the Red Sea. In total it has more than 1,600 miles of coast. The Kingdom of Saudi Arabia has an area of approximately 860,000 square miles. The exact figure is unknown because Saudi Arabia's borders with Oman and the United Arab Emirates have never been precisely demarcated.

In the west Saudi Arabia's Red Sea shore is backed by a range of mountains that parallel the coast and stretch almost unbroken from north to south. North of the city of Mecca these mountains are lower, ranging from 2,000 to 7,000 feet

---

SAUDI ARABIANS (SAUDIS): NATIONALITY

nation:
Saudi Arabia; Kingdom of Saudi Arabia

derivation of name:
Named for the House of Saud, the country's ruling family.

government:
Monarchy

capital:
Riyadh

language:
Arabic

religion:
100 percent of the country's citizens are Muslim. Between 80 and 85 percent of these are Sunni Muslims; the remaining 15 to 20 percent are Shii Muslims.

earlier inhabitants:
Bedouin; Semites

demographics:
About 90 percent of the country's citizens are Arabic; the remaining 10 percent have Afro-Asian roots. Up to 25 percent of the population are immigrant workers from other Arab countries, South and Southeast Asia.

or less in height, and abut the sea with coastal plains in just a few places. South of Mecca the mountains are higher and more rugged, with some peaks reaching almost 10,000 feet. Also south of Mecca there is an almost continuous coastal plain known as the Tihamah region, which lies between the western slopes of the mountains and the sea. The Tihamah plains are about 40 miles wide on average and rise to the generally steep western slopes of the mountains that separate them from the country's interior. The area receives significant but unpredictable rainfall and has some value as agricultural land. There are no large natural harbors along Saudi Arabia's Red Sea coast, but the country's second-largest city, Jeddah, is situated here. Jeddah is the primary disembarkation point for Muslim pilgrims making the journey to Mecca, which lies about 45 miles inland. The western coastal strip and its mountains from Mecca and Medina northward are known collectively as the Hijaz region. The southern coastal area, including the Tihamah plains and the mountains behind then, is known as Asir.

East of Saudi Arabia's coastal mountains lies the great Najd plateau, which constitutes the majority of the country's interior. The eastern slopes of the coastal mountains are gentler than their western slopes and merge slowly into the rocky, heavily eroded plains of the Najd. Overall, the entire plateau has a gentle but consistent incline from east to west. In the west it has an average altitude of 4,000 feet, falling to 2,400 feet at its eastern limit. The Najd is interspersed with numerous isolated sandy deserts and small mountainous uplands. There are no permanent natural watercourses in Saudi Arabia but the Najd is crossed by many ancient river valleys, known as *wadis*, which sometimes carry short-lived rivers after heavy rainfall in the mountains. Bisecting the Najd plateau from north to south, about halfway between the east and west coasts, is an abrupt escarpment known as Jebel Tuwaiq. The western side of this escarpment rises 800 feet almost vertically from the plain. Many oases are located in the vicinity of Jebel Tuwaiq, and much of the population of the interior of the country is clustered around these vital water sources. The capital city, Riyadh, is located in this area. Saudi Arabia's eastern coast (on the Persian Gulf) is very low lying and barren. In many places sand- or gravel-covered plains give way to salt marshes with no clear shoreline. The coastal waters are shallow, and many shoals and reefs extend far into the sea.

The great majority of Saudi Arabia and the entire Arabian Peninsula are arid, but the southern portion of the country is dominated by one of the world's most arid deserts, the Rub al-Khali (or Empty Quarter). One of the largest sand deserts in the world, the Rub al-Khali stretches 600 miles from east to west and 300 miles from north to south. Although the majority of the desert is within Saudi Arabia, it also covers large parts of the neighboring countries of the United Arab Emirates, Oman, and Yemen.

INCEPTION AS A NATION

Little detail is known about the history of the peoples of the central Arabian Peninsula prior to the rise of Islam in the seventh century C.E. Archaeological and linguistic evidence suggests that there were several waves of migration from the Arabian Peninsula into surrounding territories beginning at some time before the middle of the third millennium B.C.E. Some historians believe that the expansion of Akkadian culture into an imperial power from around 2400 B.C.E. followed an influx of peoples speaking a Semetic language from the Arabian Peninsula into Mesopotamia (see AKKADIANS). Other migrations in the same era may have brought people from the Arabian Peninsula into the Levant. These migrations are thought to have occurred because of the increasing desertification of the interior of the peninsula, a process that began about 12,000 years ago and continues to the present day.

Numerous kingdoms and civilizations are known to have thrived on the Arabian Peninsula prior to the Islamic era, but these were almost exclusively restricted to its coastal perimeter and consequently belong largely to the histories of Yemen, Oman, the United Arab Emirates, and Qatar. The history of modern Saudi Arabia begins with the emergence of the Muslim faith in the seventh century C.E. Muhammad, the revealed of Islam, was born in the city of Mecca in 570, and it was there that he began to preach in around 610. Following years of persecution and hostility from local tribes, Muhammad and his followers migrated to the city of Medina (then known as Yathrib), where he united many of the local peoples and formed the core of the first Muslim polity. Muhammad's followers rapidly extended their influence across much of the Arabian Peninsula from Medina. By the time of Muhammad's death in 632, the majority of the peoples of the peninsula had been converted to Islam.

In the decades after Muhammad's death Arab armies dedicated to spreading Islam rapidly conquered much of the Middle East and North Africa. By 750 Muslim armies had established an empire that stretched from the Atlantic coast of Morocco in the west to the Indus River in the east and from the Black Sea in the north to the southern tip of Arabia. In the intervening time, however, the political center of the Arab Muslim world had moved from Arabia to Damascus in Syria. The capital of the Caliphate subsequently moved to Baghdad then to Cairo and finally, under the OTTOMANS, to Istanbul. The Arabian Peninsula remained culturally important throughout these centuries of change, and Mecca and Medina remained the two most important holy cities in Islam, but it had ceased to be the source of the caliphate's rulers within a century of Muhammad's death.

In 1744 Muhammad ibn Saud founded the first modern Saudi state centered in the city of Diriyah, now a suburb of modern Riyadh. Muhammad ibn Saud, the founder of the Saud dynasty (or House of Saud), which rules Saudi Arabia to the present day, was inspired by the religious teachings of Muhammad ibn Abd al-Wahhab to establish a new kind of Islamic kingdom. Abd al-Wahhab preached that Islam had become corrupt in the centuries since Muhammad's death and that Muslims should return to the practices of the time immediately following his death. Prince Saud set out to implement these teachings among his own people and to spread them by military conquest across the entire Muslim world. The armies of the first Saudi Kingdom subdued the Najd by the end of the century, and in 1802 seized control of the western coast of the peninsula including the holy cities of Mecca and Medina. The Ottomans had previously held these important sites for more than 300 years and their loss was a serious embarrassment. A major Ottoman expedition was launched from Egypt, which rapidly retook the Mecca and Medina and then pushed into the interior of Arabia. Diriyah fell to the Ottomans in 1818.

Despite this crushing defeat, however, the House of Saud quickly reestablished itself. The second Saudi Kingdom is regarded as having been founded in 1824 when the House of Saud reconquered Diriyah from the Ottomans' Egyptian forces. This second state was less expansionist that the first but did establish control over much of the Najd and the east of the peninsula. It built its capital in Riyadh. Throughout the second half of the 19th century the

---

Abd al-Aziz Ibn Saud: The founder of the modern Saudi state ~~~

Abd al-Aziz Ibn Saud, or Ibn Saud as he was popularly known in the West, was the first monarch of the modern Kingdom of Saudi Arabia. He played an active role in the establishment of the kingdom, ruled through the turbulent period of World War I and World War II, and lived to see the beginnings of the economic transformation of the nation that came with the discovery and exploitation of its oil reserves.

Abd al-Aziz Ibn Saud was born in 1878 the son of Abd al-Rahman ibn Faysal, who was the last ruler of the second Saudi state. In 1890 the future king was forced into exile in Kuwait, then part of the Ottoman Empire, with the rest of his family when the al-Rashid clan defeated the second Saudi state and captured its capital, Riyadh. At the age of 24 Ibn Saud led a raid into al-Rashid territory that culminated in a daring recapture of Riyadh (1902). Rallying behind Ibn Saud's charismatic leadership, the al-Saud clan and their allies rapidly conquered a large area of the Najd region.

Ibn Saud's ambition to unite the entire Arabian Peninsula under his rule took many years to come to fruition. In 1915 he entered into a protection agreement with the British, who supplied him with arms and funds in return for a promise not to attack their interests in the Persian Gulf or the territory of Husayn ibn Ali, an ally of the British who held the Hijaz region in which the Islamic holy cities of Mecca and Medina are located. Husayn ibn Ali's involvement in the Arab Revolt of World War I weakened him financially, and in 1924 Ibn Saud besieged Mecca and forced his abdication and exile. Ibn Saud proclaimed himself king of the Hijaz in 1926, king of the Najd in 1927, and in 1932 consolidated both territories into the Kingdom of Saudi Arabia with himself as monarch.

During the decades of struggle that preceded the establishment of the Kingdom of Saudi Arabia, Ibn Saud made use of two interrelated religious and social movements: Wahhabism and the Ikhwan. The Wahhabis, who refer to themselves as Muwahhidun, were a reformist Islamic sect that had been associated with the House of Saud since the 1740s. The Ikhwan (Arabic for 'brothers') were a Wahhabi militia made up of Bedouin Arabs who formed the main strength of Ibn Saud's forces. Ibn Saud later came into conflict with elements of the Ikhwan when he forbade them from raiding into neighboring states, but Wahhabism itself was established as the faith of the new kingdom and continues to dominate Saudi Arabia to the present day.

Once established as king, Ibn Saud concentrated on quelling long-standing conflicts between clans and continued the Ikhwan policy of encouraging nomadic groups to settle in permanent towns and villages. It was his ambition to establish Saudi Arabia as a modern industrialized state while remaining faithful to the tenets of Wahhabism. To this end Ibn Saud allowed American oil companies to search for and exploit Saudi oil, recognizing the need for trade revenues, but also tackled the banditry that had plagued the pilgrimage sites of the Hijaz for centuries.

Since Ibn Saud's death in 1953, every subsequent king of Saudi Arabia has been one of his sons; he is believed to have fathered more than 50 children.

Saudi Kingdom fought the Al Rashid Kingdom, which was centered in the north of the Najd. At the Battle of Mulayda in 1891 the Saudis were defeated and their territories came under the rule of the House of Al Rashid for a time.

The House of Saud reemerged for a third time in 1902 when it once again captured their former capital, Riyadh, from the Al Rashid. A long period of conflict followed in which the

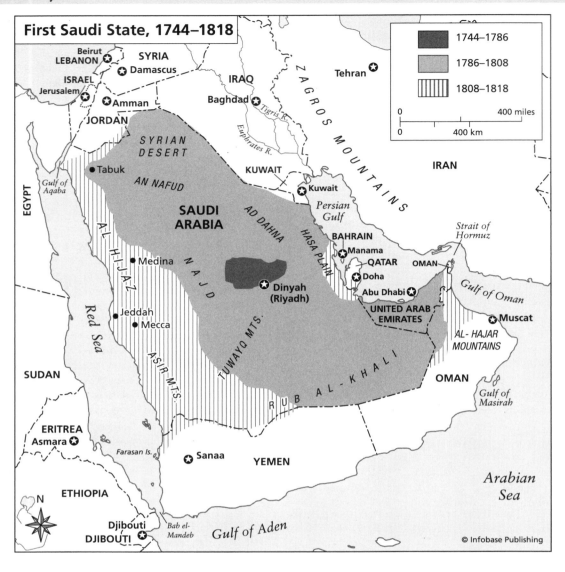

First Saudi State, 1744–1818

Legend:
- 1744–1786
- 1786–1808
- 1808–1818

0   400 miles
0   400 km

© Infobase Publishing

Saudis slowly established control over much of the territory of present-day Saudi Arabia. By 1922 control of the Najd had been reestablished, and in 1925 the western coast, including the important prizes of Mecca and Medina, was also conquered. By this time the Ottoman Empire had come to an end following its defeat in World War I. Prince Abd al-Aziz bin Abd al-Rahman bin Faysal bin Turki bin Abdallah bin Muhammad al-Saud (known as Ibn Saud in the West or Abd al-Aziz for short), who had led the House of Saud to victory, was proclaimed king of a unified Kingdom of Saudi Arabia in September 1932, marking the foundation of the modern state of Saudi Arabia.

CULTURAL IDENTITY

Saudi Arabian culture is dominated by Islam. There is a strong tradition of egalitarianism in Saudi culture, which draws directly on the Islamic principal of *ummah* (meaning "community"). According to this principle a person's identity as a Muslim takes precedence over race, ethnicity, and nationality, and these other factors should never form the basis for social, economic, or legal differentiation. In a country that is 90 percent Arab and effectively 100 percent Muslim, this rarely causes a problem. On the other hand, distinctions in social status have certainly been made traditionally with reference to ancestry. The most prestigious social group is made up of those who are recognized as being able to trace their lineage to the family of the prophet Muhammad. Other families claim descent from the eponymous founders of the ancient Arab tribes. At the lowest level of prestige is the claim to Arabian descent rather than descent from outside the Arabian Penin-

Saudi Arabians: nationality time line

C.E.

1744 First Saudi state founded by Prince Muhammad ibn Saud.

1802 Muhammad ibn Saud captures the holy cities of Mecca and Medina.

1818 Ottoman forces crush the first Saudi state.

1824 Second Saudi state founded by Turki ibn Abdallah ibn Muhammad.

1891 House of Al Rashid defeats the second Saudi state at the Battle of Mulayda.

1902 Abd al-Aziz al-Saud recaptures the old Saudi capital of Riyahd from the Al Rashid.

1925 Abd al-Aziz captures the cities of Mecca and Medina.

1932 Foundation of the modern Kingdom of Saudi Arabia with Abd al-Aziz as king.

1938 Oil is discovered in Saudi territory.

1953 King Abd al-Aziz dies and is succeeded by his eldest son Saud bin Abd al-Aziz al-Saud.

1960 Saudi Arabia becomes a founding member of the Organization of Petroleum Exporting Countries (OPEC).

1964 King Saud is deposed by Prince Faysal bin Abd al-Aziz al-Saud.

1973 Saudi Arabia leads a cessation of oil exports to Western nations that support Israel in the Arab-Israeli War (also known as the Yom Kippur War).

1975 King Faysal is assassinated by his nephew Faysal bin Musaid bin Abd al-Aziz. Faysal's brother, Khalid bin Abd al-Aziz al-Saud, takes the throne.

1980 Saudi government takes full control of the Arabian American Oil Company (Aramco), which has been U.S.-owned until this time.

1982 King Khalid dies and is succeeded by Prince Fahd bin Abd al-Aziz al-Saud.

1990 Saudi Arabia allows troops from the United States and other non-Muslim nations to deploy on its territory in preparation for the campaign to liberate neighboring Kuwait from Iraqi occupation.

1992 King Fahd adopts the Basic Law of Government in which the Quran is cited as the nation's constitution. A Consultative Council is set up.

2002 Saudi Arabia refuses permission for U.S. forces to launch attacks on Iraq from Saudi territory. U.S. troops are withdrawn from the country the following year.

2003 Suicide bombers kill 35 people in attacks on compounds for Western residents. Seventeen others are killed in other attacks the same year.

2004 Militants attack foreign workers at an oil company compound. American and British citizens are abducted and killed. The U.S. embassy in Jeddah is attacked. Car bombs explode in Riyadh.

2005 Nationwide municipal elections held. King Fahd dies and is succeeded by Prince Abdullah bin Abd al-Aziz al-Saud.

2007 Four French citizens are killed in a terrorist attack. The religious police are banned from detaining suspects.

sula. The traditional nomadic peoples of the Arabian interior are regarded as the "purest" representatives of Arab identity (*see* ARABS), and there is a great deal of emphasis in Saudi society on the preservation and perpetuation of symbols from this heritage. Ancient mosques and other buildings have been painstakingly restored or reconstructed, traditional motifs are incorporated into even the most modern buildings, and re-creations of traditional BEDOUIN tent dwellings are frequently displayed in hotels and museums or enjoyed by Saudis who want to reconnect with their cultural roots in the desert.

In part the Saudis' preoccupation with the relics and symbols of their past is a reaction to the very rapid transformation of their country that took place in the second half of the 20th century as a result of the massive influx of revenue from the export of oil. Geologists from the United States discovered oil in Saudi territory in the 1930s, but large-scale extraction did not begin until after World War II. Production rose dramatically in the 1960s and revenues rose greatly in the 1970s, revolutionizing the Saudi economy. In 50 years Saudi Arabia was transformed from a poor developing nation into one of the richest nations on earth. Saudi Arabia has the world's largest proven oil reserves (amounting to almost a quarter of proven reserves worldwide), and the export of oil accounts for about 75 percent of government revenues. The influx of oil wealth has brought great change to Saudi society. In the 1950s the majority of the population lived a nomadic lifestyle, but by the end of the century 95 percent were settled in newly constructed towns and villages. This population has also grown dramatically from around 4 million in 1960 to more than 27 million in 2006. Between 5 and 6 million of those residing in the kingdom are non-nationals, the great majority of them from other Arab countries or from South and Southeast Asia. These immigrants are attracted by employment in the service, construction, and oil industries. In general they are banned from holding or applying for Saudi citizenship and are required to return to their country of origin if they are not working. Oil wealth has brought universal education, universal public health care, and world-class infrastructure to the Saudis. These benefits are not generally extended to foreign workers, however. Saudi Arabia's powerful economy gives it great political leverage in the Arab world and considerable influence on the world stage. An example of this power came in 1990 and 1991 when Saudi Arabia expelled 800,000 Yemeni workers from its territory because of the Yemeni government's failure to support the U.S.-led liberation of Kuwait from Iraqi occupation. The impact on Yemen's economy was devastating. In recent decades the Saudi government has made considerable efforts to diversify the country's economy, including plans to construct six entirely new industrial cities.

The House of Saud has had a long relationship with the strand of Islam founded by Muhammad ibn Abd al-Wahhab in the 18th century. Abd al Aziz, the founder of modern Saudi Arabia, revived this relationship in the first decades of the 20th century, and Abd al Wahhab's teachings became very popular across the Arabian Peninsula from the 1920s. The branch of Sunni Islam that follows Abd al-Wahhab's teachings is commonly known as Salafism. It is also sometimes known as Wahhabism, a term that was originally used derogatively by its opponents. Followers of Salafism refer to themselves as *muwahidun* (meaning "unitarians"). Salafism has as its central belief the idea that Islam was at its most perfect during the time of the prophet Muhammad and his immediate descendents. Salafism teaches that the changes to Islamic tradition and law that have occurred in the centuries since that time are the result of flawed human reasoning and should be abandoned. For this reason, Salafism is often seen as a very conservative form of Islam. The Quran is regarded as the constitution of Saudi Arabia, and the kingdom's legal system is strictly based on sharia religious law. Saudi Arabia and neighboring Qatar are the only two nations in which Salafism is the dominant form of Islam.

The influence of Salafist ideas on Saudi society has meant that its laws and customs have generally been less liberal that those of other Muslim Arab states. Restrictions on the role of women in society are one of the clearest examples of this tendency. Women are not permitted to interact with males outside of their immediate family, may not appear in public unveiled, may not work in an occupation where they will come into contact with unrelated males, may not travel abroad without an appropriate male escort, and may not drive on public roads. In addition, a woman's testimony is permitted in court only if there were no male witnesses and is given far less weight than testimony provided by a man. In some cases women who have made accusations of rape have themselves been convicted of transgressing the law against associating with unrelated males. While these restrictions are less rigidly enforced today than they have been in the past, the role played by women in the economic and political life of the country remains disproportionately small. The Saudi legal system also permits the use of capital and corporal punishment, including amputation and lashings. These and other issues, including restrictions on freedom of religion and freedom of speech and the persecution of homosexuals, have attracted serious and widespread criticism from numerous international human rights organizations.

The shrines at Mecca and Medina are important in Saudi society, and the Saudi government sees the protection of these sites as one of its most important duties. Every year about 2 million Muslims from all over the world take part in the pilgrimage to Mecca known as the hajj. The Saudi government has spent a great deal of money improving the infrastructure of the city to support these millions of visitors, although the pilgrims are themselves an important source of income for the city and the wider region. Non-Muslims are forbidden from entering the city.

Saudi Arabia is effectively governed by an absolute monarchy. The 1992 Basic Law of Government states that the country's rulers must be the sons or grandsons of the first king Abd al Aziz. The monarch appoints the members of a Council of Ministers, which includes a prime minister, and it is this body that drafts legislation with the approval of the king. There is also a 150-member Consultative Assembly whose members are also royally appointed. Saudi Arabia held limited elections in 2005 when male Saudis were given the opportunity to vote in elections to appoint half the members of municipal councils. Women were not permitted to vote or to stand for election. There is increasing pressure within Saudi society for democratization, but no plans for radical change in the structure of government have been announced. Justice is dispensed by a network of religious courts, and judges are appointed by the king on the recommendation of the Supreme Judicial Council. In the first decade of the 21st century Saudi Arabia has faced a growing internal security problem. The majority of those who carried out the September 11 attacks on the United States in 2001 were Saudi citizens, and a number of militant Islamic organizations are believed to exist inside Saudi Arabia or to be funded by Saudi citizens. The government faces a difficult challenge as it comes under pressure from one section of society to liberalize and from another conservative section of society to maintain or strengthen traditional values and customs.

Saudis adhere to a strict Muslim dress code intended to promote modesty, especially for women. Men traditionally wear ankle-length wool or cotton shirts (known as a *thawb*) and checked or plain headscarves (*kaffiya* or *ghutra*) held in place with a cord. In private women wear similar gowns, often decorated with traditional motifs, but in public they are required to wear an overgarment known as an *abaya* or similar dress that covers them completely apart from the head, hands, and feet. Women are also required to wear a headscarf and a veil in public. *Abayas* are traditionally black, while men's clothes are often white or very pale in color. The Islamic proscription against the consumption of pork and alcohol are also strictly enforced in Saudi society.

FURTHER READING

Madawi al-Rasheed. *Kingdom Without Borders: Saudi Arabia's Political, Religious and Media Frontiers* (London: C. Hurst, 2008).

Mohammed Ayoob, and Hasan Kosebalaban. *Religion and Politics in Saudi Arabia: Wahhabism and the State* (Boulder, Colo: Lynne Rienner Publishers, 2009).

Wayne H. Bowen. *The History of Saudi Arabia* (Westport, Conn: Greenwood Press, 2008).

Nicholas Buchele. *Saudi Arabia* (London: Kuperard, 2008).

Mark Weston. *Prophets and Princes: Saudi Arabia from Muhammad to the Present* (Hoboken, N.J.: Wiley, 2008).

Sea Peoples

"Sea Peoples" is a term used to define a number of population groups in the eastern Mediterranean at the end of the Late Bronze Age (1600–1100 B.C.E.) who formed alliances to attack Mediterranean civilizations, most notably Egypt during the 13th and 12th centuries B.C.E. The term originates in a translation of the Great Karnak Inscription from the reign of Egyptian pharaoh Merenptah (1213–03 B.C.E.) referring to "the foreign peoples of the Sea" as an overarching term for this confederacy of raiders (*see* EGYPTIANS). The Egyptologist Gaston Maspero coined the term "Sea Peoples" in 1881.

Historical evidence for the Sea Peoples is fragmentary, primarily consisting of the records of eastern Mediterranean civilizations in conjunction with modern archaeological findings. The records that have survived explicitly refer to the peoples of the Shardana, Shekelesh, Teresh, Lukka, Ekwesh, Denyen, Tjeker, Peleset, and Weshesh. Since these names come from an incomplete documentary record, other Sea Peoples probably also existed whose identities are lost to us. The Sea Peoples are associated with the eastern Mediterranean—the shores of the Aegean and eastward along the lands of the Middle East, and south to the coast of Egypt. A number of theories also associate particular groups with northern Syria and Sicily.

ORIGINS

Because of the scarcity of documentary and archaeological evidence, the origin of the Sea

SEA PEOPLES	
location:	Eastern Mediterranean
time period:	1600 to 1100 B.C.E.
ancestry:	Anatolian; Mycenaean (primary theories)
language:	Anatolian (such as Luwian) and Mycenaean dialects postulated.

Peoples is a contentious issue. Around the time they first appear in force in the Egyptian records, the cultures of the eastern Mediterranean en masse were experiencing a period of turmoil after centuries of relative stability. The Egyptian-controlled Levant (modern Middle Eastern states bordering the Mediterranean) was in tumult. In Anatolia (modern-day Turkey), the Hittite Empire collapsed (*see* HITTITES). The Mycenaean palace complexes of Greece were abandoned or destroyed (*see* GREEKS). Archaeological evidence of widespread destruction has also been uncovered in Cyprus.

The appearance in the records at this time of the Sea Peoples has led to the postulating of a number of theories associating them with the collapses; either as raiders or as victims, part of the displaced populations. It seems likely that the collapse of these Mediterranean Late Bronze Age civilizations in the 13th–12th centuries B.C.E. was primarily the result of a combination of internal economic and political instabilities, aggravated by raiding and possibly natural disaster, and it would be misleading to identify invading raiders solely as the prime mover for this collapse.

From etymological and archaeohistorical evidence, the following origin theories have been postulated for individual groups of the Sea Peoples.

Because of their name, the Shardana (also known as Sherden) have become associated with Sardinia, but archaeological and genetic evidence points to their origins being in Anatolia or possibly northern Syria, with their presence in Sardinia at a later date accounting for the similarity in naming. Similarly, the Shekelesh are later associated with the Sikel people of Sicily and mainland Italy. The nature of archaeological findings associated with the Sikels, compared with mainland Greece cultures, show little correlation. It has therefore been suggested that the Shekelesh were originally from Anatolia or the Levant rather than Mycenaean Greece, despite a lack of references to them in the records of the Anatolian Hittite culture. The Ekwesh people have been associated either with the ancient Anatolian kingdom of Ahhiyawa, or the Mycenaean Achaeans, the invading Greek forces of Homer's *Iliad*. It is thought the Teresh were originally Anatolian, as were the Lukka, most likely coming from the Carian coastline or Lycia in Western Anatolia.

The other recorded Sea Peoples may have been labeled under a misnomer—the fact that they attacked from the land has been interpreted as suggesting they were uprooted farmers searching for new territory to settle in. Of these, the Denyen may have come from northern Syria, the TJEKKER perhaps from The Troad (northwestern Anatolia), and the Peleset, who are associated with the later Philistines, also from Anatolia.

These conclusions are tentative, controversial, and continually under review.

LANGUAGE

The lack of documentary evidence has thwarted attempts to definitively identify the languages used by the Sea Peoples. However, inferences can be drawn from geographic or ethnographic associations. In *The Language of the Sea Peoples,* Fred Woudhuizen concludes that many of the Sea Peoples appear to be Anatolian in origin and that a linguistic connection can be made between their Late Bronze Age languages and Early Iron Age Luwian population groups from Anatolia (*see* LUWIANS). Therefore, it is postulated that some of the Sea Peoples spoke a Luwian dialect closely related to Hittite.

HISTORY

The primary documentary sources for information about the Sea Peoples are inscriptions and letters from ancient Egypt. The Shardana and Lukka are referenced in the Amarna Letters (cuneiform administrative tablets) of the 14th century B.C.E. From the reign of pharaoh Ramesses II a number of stelae (inscribed funerary monuments, singularly called *stele*) recall successfully repulsed attacks on the Nile Delta by the Shardana. Some of these raiders had been absorbed into the Egyptian forces by the time of the Battle of Kadesh between Egypt and the Hittite Empire in 1274 B.C.E.

The Victory or Israel stele of pharaoh Merenptah (1213–03 B.C.E.) refers to a battle against an alliance of raiders known as the Nine Bows, led by a king of Libya. These raiders are described on the Great Karnak Inscription as including the Sherden (Shardana), Ekwesh, Lukka, and Teresh. The raids against Egypt are recorded as unsuccessful, although it is possible this is a misrepresentation, since soon after the attacks Egypt went into a domestic decline almost to the point of civil war.

The second major wave of attacks by the Sea Peoples on Egypt occurred during the time of Ramesses III in the Twentieth Dynasty of Egypt (early 12th century B.C.E.). These attacks are documented on this pharaoh's mortuary temple reliefs at Medinet Habu near modern Luxor. The attacks took the form of at least three separate invasions. The Peleset and Tejeker are recorded as being involved in the first attack, and also appear in the second, along with the Shekelesh, Denyen, and Weshesh. All these groups were involved in the third invasion. The invaders of the second attack are again referred to as the alliance of the Nine Bows, as during the reign of Merenptah. All three campaigns are recorded as Egyptian victories.

A number of letters discovered in the ruins of the Syrian coastal city of Ugarit discuss the threat of an attack by the Sea Peoples, along with a final undelivered letter that talks of an invasion being under way. Shortly afterwards this thriving city was destroyed, never to be resettled. Around the same time, the Hittite capital of Hattusa was also razed, prompting the collapse of the Hittite Empire; however, it is now generally believed that the Sea Peoples were not directly involved and that the invading forces were from inland and were possibly the Kashka, long-term rivals of the Hittites who had plundered Hattusa previously.

Similar-scale destruction was wrought across the Levant at this time, although apparently largely sparing the population centers of the PHOENICIANS, which has led some scholars to postulate that the raiders found them useful in some way, so sparing them. The key Mycenaean palatial city-states of Greece also collapsed around this time, with destruction and population dispersal. The end of these Anatolian and Mycenaean civilizations, combined with evidence of destruction in the Levant and in Cyprus, have lead to theories that primarily attribute these collapses to invasion by the Sea Peoples. The fall of Mycenaean Greece has also been associated with invasion from the Dorian people from north of Greece.

These collapsing civilizations do, however, seem to have already been in a precarious position. For example, Mycenaean city-states consisted of relatively large populations overdependent on their central bureaucracies and therefore economically vulnerable to change, such as that brought by natural disaster. No great military attack would have been required to unbalance these states. It has been posited by many, including Eliezer Oren, that the collapse of both the Hittite and Mycenaean civilizations directly created the displaced Sea Peoples, Greeks, and Anatolians alike who became united in a search for stable new territories to settle.

Sea Peoples time line	
B.C.E.	
mid-14th century	"Armana Letters" composed.
1600–1100	Late Bronze Age (Near East)
1279–13	Reign of Ramesses II in Egypt
1277	Ramesses II's forces face Shardana raiders.
1274	Battle of Kadesh; Egypt and Hittites clash.
1213–03	Reign of Merenptah in Egypt.
1208–07	Merenptah's forces face the 'Nine Bows' alliance.
ca. 1200	Hittite capital Hattusa destroyed.
1195	Ugarit destroyed.
1186–55	Reign of Ramses III in Egypt
1186, 1178, 1174	Ramesses III faces attacks from Sea Peoples (in 1178, the 'Nine Bows').

Beyond large-scale invasion theories, the Sea Peoples are associated with the settlement of a number of eastern Mediterranean communities. The physical evidence of the Philistines of this period shows a break in continuity, and this has been interpreted as a replacement of the local population with Sea Peoples, possibly the Peleset from mainland Greece or the Pelasgians from Greece and Crete. A change in indigenous pottery styles to those similar to Mycenaean ware has been seen as supporting the theory that these Sea People originated in Greece, although this stylistic change is seen in the archaeology later than the evidence for population disruption.

The Sea Peoples have also come to be associated with Homer's depiction of Troy, the legendary city-state destroyed sometime near the end of the Mediterranean Bronze Age. A theory offered by Eberhard Zangger is that the Trojan War is a depiction of the tradition of struggle between the Anatolian Sea Peoples and the Mycenaean states, the latter seeking to restrain the former's territorial expansion. On the other hand, name associations have been used to tie some of the Sea Peoples to historically known Greek groups, such as the similarity between "Ekwesh" and the Greek "Achaeans" mentioned in the *Iliad* as participating in the assault on Troy.

CULTURE

There is little direct evidence of the culture of the Sea Peoples. The descriptions that reach us through Egyptian records naturally concen-

Ramesses III: A difficult reign ～～

Ramses III was the second pharaoh of the Twentieth Dynasty of ancient Egypt, corresponding approximately to the years 1186–1155 B.C.E. His reign saw a decline in the economic fortunes of Egypt that would lead to the end of the Twentieth Dynasty as the Egyptian ruling class. This decline is related to a number of factors, the most notable of which is the expensive ongoing struggle against the raiders known as the "Sea Peoples" midway through this period. Climatological evidence dating to around 1159 B.C.E. has pointed toward the eruption of the Icelandic volcano Hekla III, and it is believe this event contributed to crop failures in Egypt at a time when the economy was already weakened from supporting the military campaigns and temple complex construction programs of Ramesses III. His final years saw an attempt upon his life now known (from a recovered papyrus document) as the Harem Conspiracy. He died at age 65 and was mummified—his body was discovered in 1886. The title of pharaoh passed to his son, Ramesses IV.

The mortuary complex of Ramesses III is known as Medinet Habu, located on the western bank of the river Nile near Luxor. This complex is the source for the primary documentary evidence about the Sea Peoples. Designed to portray the splendor of the pharaoh's reign as comparable to that of Ramesses II, the temple was decorated with texts and reliefs depicting the key events of his rule, including the Egyptian campaigns against the invading Sea Peoples.

The use of the Medinet Habu inscriptions as a primary source of evidence for the investigation of the Sea Peoples is not without its problems. The growing civil strife attested to in other documentary records is entirely absent, as is any reference to the crop failures associated with the eruption of Hekla III. It can therefore be assumed that the inscriptions chose to ignore the more negative aspects of Ramesses III's reign and are not a complete and objective record. Furthermore, some modern scholars have suggested that the Sea People campaigns, rather than being three major united attacks against Egypt, may be a string of semi-united skirmishes, and that the unity of the raiders under one banner may have been overestimated or falsely portrayed. Nevertheless, Medinet Habu remains the primary contemporary account and the foundation of what we know about these displaced peoples of the late Mediterranean Bronze Age.

trate on military characteristics. At Medinet Habu, the Shardana are depicted as wearing three-horned helmets with the middle horn affixed with a small ball. In their hands they carry large shields and swords of the Bronze Age Naue II type—a single bronze casting with attachments to the base of the tang to make the haft. Swords of this type were found in the ruins of Ugarit. In a similar fashion, the Shekelesh are shown in cloth headdresses with medallions on their chests, carrying two spears and a round shield.

Because of the associations outlined above, it will be useful to give broad outlines of the primary Anatolian and Greek cultures and the development of the Philistine people, as these may give a broad context for the cultural nature and development of the Sea Peoples.

The Hittites of Anatolia occupied lands rich in natural resources and it is believed that they were among the first peoples in the Mediterranean to employ ironworking and to have a government based around a constitutional monarchy. They also had a system of laws inherited from the BABYLONIANS. Because of the political instability of the region, trade would have been a less effective method of supporting their agricultural economy than the material gains arising from territorial expansion.

Based on the example of Pylos from the southern Peloponnesus of Greece, the Mycenaean city-states appear to have been monarchies, underpinned by a warrior ruling class and a specialized mercantile class. They were usually housed in well-fortified towns, sometimes surrounding a palace complex, and used the Linear B script, derived from the Linear A language used by the Minoans. The economy was founded on agriculture and pottery and textile production, and the movement of these goods through far-reaching trading networks.

The archaeological evidence from the seaport of Ashkelon suggests that some of the early pottery of the Philistines contained Mycenaean influences, lending credence to the idea that these were settling Sea Peoples. The name Pelasgians, a reference in Greek records to previous inhabitants of Greece and the Aegean, has also been equated with that of the Philistines, as has the Sea People name Peleset. Israeli archaeological work in the remains of five Philistine cities has established that Philistine structural remains are comparatively advanced, suggesting greater cultural and technological complexity than their neighbors. Their cities were governed by a ruling hierarchy, and appear to have held a regional monopoly on iron smelting.

Beyond the end of the piecemeal documentary evidence for the Sea Peoples, what we know is surmised from archaeological evidence and analogy. What we know is that the end of the eastern Mediterranean Bronze Age saw large movements of populations, including some that turned to raiding and have subsequently been termed the Sea Peoples. Their alliances, including that of the "Nine Bows," appear to have been temporary, and today their impact on the development of Mediterranean civilizations remains a subject of lively controversy.

FURTHER READING

Eliezer D. Oren, ed. *The Sea Peoples and Their World: A Reassessment* (Philadelphia: University of Pennsylvania Press, 2000).

N. K. Sandars. *The Sea Peoples: Warriors of the Ancient Mediterranean* (London: Thames and Hudson, 1987).

Frederik Christiaan Woudhuizen. *The Language of the Sea Peoples* (Amsterdam: Najade Press, 1992).

———. "The Ethnicity of the Sea Peoples." Ph.D. diss. Erasmus Universiteit Rotterdam, 2006.

Eberhard Zangger. "Who Were the Sea People?" *Saudi Aramco World* 46, no. 3 (May/June 1995).

Sebei (Sapei)

The Sebei live on the northeastern slopes of Mount Elgon, Uganda. They are a KALENJIN people and are related to the MAASAI.

Sefwi (Sahwi)

The Sefwi are closely related to the ANYI and BAULÉ people. They live primarily in western Ghana.

Seleka

The Seleka are one of the four main subgroups of the ROLONG. The Rolong are a TSWANA people of Southern Africa.

Seljuks (Saldjuks; Seldjuks; Seljuk Turks)

The Seljuks were a Turkic dynasty from central Asia who led a confederation of tribes that conquered large areas of the Middle East and Anatolia (eastern Turkey) in the 11th and 12th centuries C.E. The Seljuks were a prominent clan of the OGHUZ TURKS who lived northeast of the Aral Sea, to the north of the Jaxartes River (Syr Darya River) in modern south Kazakhstan. The patriarch and namesake of the clan, Seljuk, lived in the mid-10th century, and it was his grandsons, Tughril Beg and Chagri Beg, who founded a Sunni Muslim empire that stretched from central Asia through Iran and Iraq to Syria, Palestine, and Anatolia.

ORIGINS

As early as the eighth century Turkic tribes from the Altay Mountains and surrounding regions (Mongolia, Kazakhstan, northwest China) began to migrate as a result of intertribal warfare. These Turkic tribes also raided other territories for plunder and to acquire pasture for their horses and sheep (*see* TURKIC PEOPLES). As a result of these migrations, by the 10th century the Oghuz Turks were pasturing their animals in the region northeast of the Aral Sea. The Oghuz were forced to migrate southward at the end of the 10th century because of pressure from other Turkic tribes also moving down from the north. After spending a few years in the region of Bukhara (Uzbekistan), where they converted to Sunni Islam, they moved on to settle in the Khurasan area of northeast Iran in 1025. Here the grandsons of Seljuk and other tribesmen were invited to serve as mercenaries in the army of Mahmud of Ghazni, the ruler of the Ghaznavid Empire, which at that time held much of Afghanistan, Iran, and northern India. Meanwhile, many more Oghuz migrated south to join their tribesmen in Khurasan. In 1037 Tughril Beg and Chagri Beg gathered an army and led an uprising against the Ghaznavids. They quickly conquered Khurasan and its chief city, Nishapur, and in 1040 they completely defeated the Ghaznavid army at the Battle of Dandanqan.

After consolidating power in Khurasan, Tughril left his brother Chagri in charge of the region and headed west with his main force. In 1055 Tughril conquered Baghdad, which was then the capital of the Buyid dynasty, which controlled most of Iran and Iraq (*see* BUYIDS). The Abbasid caliph had been a virtual hostage of the Buyid princes before the Sunni Seljuks arrived. Tughril and the Seljuk armies liberated the caliph Abdullah al-Qaim and reestablished his influence as spiritual leader over their growing empire. In exchange for promoting the caliph's spiritual authority over the empire, however, Tughril insisted on being acknowledged as the supreme military and political leader by the caliph. Al-Qaim subsequently proclaimed Tughril the "sultan of the east and west" and was thereafter protected and promoted by the Seljuks as the rightful spiritual leader of the Muslim world. The reestablishment of Sunni caliphal authority under Tughril, as well as the appropriation of the remaining territories in Iraq and Iran in the next few years by the Seljuks, was a major blow to Shii Islamic political ascendancy and is one of the reasons why most of the Middle East is Sunni Muslim today.

LANGUAGE

The Seljuks spoke Oghuz Turkic, one of many Turkic dialects. However, the Seljuk leadership and military had already begun using the Persian language while living among the Ghaznavids in Khurasan. Throughout the period of Seljuk imperial expansion the rulers of the Seljuks used Persian in government and

---

SELJUKS

location:
South Central Asia; the Middle East; Anatolia

time period:
11th to 12th century C.E.

ancestry:
Central Asian Turkic tribe living near the Aral Sea in the 10th century.

language:
Oghuz Turkic; and Persian in government

Seljuks time line

C.E.

990–1020 Oghuz Turks, including the clan of Seljuk, migrate southward from the Aral Sea to the area surrounding Bukhara, where they convert to Islam.

1025 The Seljuk clan move further south into the Khurasan region of northeast Iran and serve as mercenaries in the Ghaznavid army.

1040 Tughril Beg and Chagri Beg lead a rebellion that defeats the Ghaznavids at the Battle of Dandanqan.

1055 Tughril Beg takes Baghdad and is named "sultan of the east and west."

1063–72 Reign of Alp Arslan

1071 At the Battle of Manzikert the Seljuks defeat the Byzantines and begin to populate Anatolia.

1072–92 Reign of Malikshah

1092 Nizam al-Mulk, the great Seljuk vizier, and Sultan Malikshah are assassinated.

1092–94 Family strife between Seljuk rulers characterizes the gradual decline and fragmentation of the Seljuk Empire into smaller units.

1194 The last Seljuk sultan is defeated by the Khwarezmian Empire of Iran.

sponsored the writing of Persian literature. But the great numbers of Turkic nomads, herders, and raiding bands whose migration westward coincided with the rise of the Seljuks spoke Oghuz Turkic or other Turkic dialects and continued to do so. A century later, when the Mongols, another Turkic people, overran much of the Middle East and Central Asia, they brought still more Turkic-speaking soldiers and migrants into the region.

Turkic is a subfamily of the Altaic language family, which includes the Turkic, Mongolian, and Tungusic subfamilies. In modern times Turkic languages are spoken by peoples from the Mediterranean Sea all the way to northwest China. Osmanli, or modern Turkish, is spoken in Turkey and parts of the Balkans and is descended from the language of the Seljuks who first conquered Anatolia. In addition, Azeri (spoken in Azerbaijan); Turkmen (spoken in Turkmenistan and Central Asia); Uzbek, Kazakh, Kyrgyz (Central Asian languages); and Tatar and Uygur (Central Asian and Northwest Chinese languages) are all Turkic languages in use today.

HISTORY

The Seljuk victory in Iran and Iraq opened the way for many waves of nomadic Turkic tribes to migrate westward through Iran. These groups often raided the territories of the Fatimids of Syria and the Byzantines of Anatolia and Armenia. The elements that carried out these raids were not usually directed or even under the direct authority of the Seljuk sultans, but their attacks antagonized the Fatimids and the Byzantines and often resulted in retaliatory skirmishes with the Seljuk armies.

Chagri Beg died in 1060 and his son Alp Arslan took over the administration of the eastern part of the Seljuk Empire centered around the Khurasan area. In 1063 Chagri's brother Tughril also died, and Alp Arslan moved west and consolidated the territory of the former Buyid Empire and the province of Khurasan under his rule.

The next step in the territorial expansion of the Seljuks occurred as a result of an encounter with the Byzantine armies. Concerned about Turkic nomads who were increasingly encroaching on Byzantine territories, the Byzantine emperor Romanos I brought out his army to meet Alp Arslan and the Seljuks at the Battle of Manzikert on the eastern borders of the Byzantine Empire in 1071. Romanos suffered a catastrophic defeat at the hands of the Seljuks and was captured in the battle. The chaotic political situation within the Byzantine Empire that followed this defeat and the empire's unwillingness to confront the Seljuks a second time meant that Turkic raiders and nomadic herders were free to settle in Anatolia in increasing numbers.

The Seljuks did not directly occupy Anatolia after their defeat of the Byzantine armies, but they encouraged other Oghuz tribes to migrate into the region. In this way Alp Arslan provided an outlet for the territorial ambitions of the Turkic peoples constantly migrating into the region from the east while keeping the inevitable political wrangles that resulted from the expansion out of his empire. Two independent Turkic dynasties arose in Anatolia, a rival group of Seljuks (the Rum Seljuks), who made their capital in the city of Konya, and a group called the Danishmendids, who settled in central and eastern Anatolia. The permanent settlement of Anatolia by thousands of Turkic migrants in the 11th and 12th centuries represented a huge demographic change for the region, and their impact on the culture and religion of the area has persisted to the present day. The encroachment of these Muslim tribes into the territory of the Christian Byzantine Empire, and especially their close proximity to the ancient capital city of Byzantium situated on the Bosporus, had a great psychological impact on Christian medieval Europe. It was a primary motivation for organizing the First Crusade (1096–99).

After Alp Arslan died in 1072, his son Jalal al-Dawlah Malikshah took the throne of the Great Seljuk Empire and continued to expand its territory. Tughril Beg, Alp Arslan, and Malikshah are collectively referred to as the Great Seljuk Sultans because during their reign the Seljuk Empire was unified and expanded throughout the Middle East. Both Alp Arslan and Malikshah benefited from the council and administrative prowess of Nizam al-Mulk, who served both sultans as vizier, or political advisor. One of Nizam al-Mulk's legacies was the establishment of a group of madrasas in Iran and Iraq. Madrasas, or Islamic colleges that teach Muslim law and theology from the Sunni perspective, were a novel development of this period. An important function of Nizam al-Mulk's madrasas (collectively known as the Nizamiyya) was to counter Shii ideas and theology disseminated from Egypt, which was then under the control of the Fatimid dynasty. In 1092 members of the Shii Ismaili Nizari sect, commonly known in the west as the ASSASSINS, killed both Malikshah and his vizier Nizam al-Mulk (*see* ISMAILIS). Following the death of Malikshah, the empire disintegrated into fragments ruled by various members of the Seljuk family. Theoretically all of these local rulers owed allegiance to subsequent holders of the title Great Sultan, who continued to hold court in Khurasan, but the sultan's power became increasingly symbolic rather than actual as time past. The most important of these later regional Seljuk monarchies were in the Kerman region of Iran, the Hamadan region of Iraq, in Syria, and the Seljuks of Rum in Anatolia.

CULTURE

The Turkic peoples originated on the steppe lands of Central Asia. These are the vast semiarid grassy flatlands that dominate much of Central Asia and southern Russia. The steppe can support a nomadic lifestyle that involves the herding of large flocks of animals but it is not sufficiently fertile for the production of grain crops. The Turkic tribes that occupied these areas were nomadic herders of horses, sheep, goats, or camels, depending on local conditions. They were renowned for their ruggedness, their fierceness in battle, and their expertise as horsemen and archers. Their nomadic lifestyle precluded the building of cities or the development of sophisticated art or technology,

Alp Arslan: The Seljuk Lion

Alp Arslan was the second sultan of the Seljuk dynasty. Muhammad ibn Daud, the name he adopted on converting to Sunni Islam, was born in about 1026. He received the honorific name Alp Arslan, meaning "valiant lion" in Turkish, in recognition of his numerous military victories. Alp Arslan's conquests at the cost of the Byzantine Empire reestablished Muslim control of the Middle East following the decline of the Abbasid caliphate.

Alp Arslan's father, Daud Chagri Beg, was the military commander of the Khurasan province of eastern Iran. Alp Arslan inherited this position after his father's death in about 1059. Alp Arslan's uncle, Tughril Beg (ca. 990–1063), had conquered Baghdad, the traditional capital of the caliphate, in 1055 and had been named "sultan of the east and west" by the caliph. Prior to this the Buyid dynasty had ruled the empire as sultans and reduced the hereditary position of the caliph to little more than that of a religious figurehead. By naming Tughril Beg as sultan, the caliph bestowed on him effective control of the entire territory of the caliphate, and it was this position that Alp Arslan inherited when his uncle died in 1063.

As sultan Alp Arslan campaigned successfully in Georgia, Armenia, and Transoxiana. In 1070 he took the Syrian city of Aleppo, extending his territories to the Mediterranean coast. Seljuk elements and other Turkic groups that had long been raiding into Byzantine territory in Anatolia (present-day Turkey) provoked a major confrontation between Byzantine forces and Seljuk forces at the Battle of Manzikert in 1071. Alp Arslan's devastating victory in this battle opened Anatolia to waves of Turkic settlement and marked the beginning of the end of the Byzantine Empire. The Byzantine emperor Romanos IV was captured during the battle and famously freed by Alp Arslan.

Alp Arslan's military prowess greatly expanded the area of his empire, but it was his Persian vizier, known as Nizam al-Mulk, who is credited with successfully administering these territories and establishing a system of government that was to persist for centuries. Nizam al-Mulk held the powerful position of vizier throughout the reign of Alp Arslan and that of his son and successor, Jalal al-Dawlah Malikshah (r. 1072–92). One of his lasting innovations was the establishment of centers of higher education, known as Nizamiyya schools, which were among the first higher education institutions in the Muslim world. Nizam al-Mulk was also acknowledged as a prominent scientist and poet and is regarded today as one of the leading figures in early Persian literature.

Alp Arslan died in 1072, within a year of his greatest victory. According to traditional accounts a captive inflicted a fatal wound on the sultan while he was campaigning in Central Asia near the Oxus River.

however. The ninth-century Persian writer al-Jahiz complained that the Turks were "uninterested in craftsmanship or commerce, medicine, geometry, fruit-farming, building, digging canals, or collecting taxes… they care only about raiding, hunting, horsemanship, skirmishing with rival chieftains, taking booty, and invading other countries."

Government and Society

Although the Seljuks conquered the ancient city of Baghdad under Tughril Beg in 1055, it did not become their administrative center.

A painted plaster figure from 12th-century Iran. It is thought to depict an individual from the Seljuk court and may have served a ceremonial purpose.

The Great Sultans regularly shifted their capital from Nishapur to Rayy to Isfahan and sometimes held court from a military camp as they went from place to place.

The Seljuks made a significant change to the political situation in the Middle East by ratifying a new power-sharing arrangement between the Sunni caliph and the political and military leader, the sultan. Sunni Muslims had regarded the caliph of Baghdad as the "Commander of the Faithful," the leader of Muslims on earth and the political (although not the prophetic) successor of the prophet Muhammad since the Abbasid period (beginning 750). However, the actual power of the caliph had been drastically reduced under the reign of the Shii Buyid dynasty, who did not respect the caliph's claim to be the successor to the prophet Muhammad.

When the Seljuks took Baghdad from the Buyids, they portrayed themselves as the liberators of the caliphate. At the same time, Tughril, the Seljuk leader who had conquered Baghdad, demanded that the caliph Abdullah al-Kaaim acknowledge him and his successors as the supreme military and political rulers of the Sunni Muslims. The title "sultan" was first officially used by the Seljuks to describe a supreme political ruler who supported the caliph, the supreme spiritual leader. The title of sultan, as well as the system of separating the powers of political and spiritual leadership in Islam, was subsequently followed by other Muslim dynasties across the Middle East and in India.

Weaknesses of Government

One of the most striking aspects of Seljuk history is the relatively short period in which the large territory they had conquered held together as a viable state or empire. The Seljuk Empire was a unified and expanding entity for only about 60 years before it began to fragment. The Seljuks went from being nomadic herders and raiding warriors to the rulers of large settled populations and agriculturally based economies in a very short period of time. It is argued by some scholars that their nomadic background ill-equipped them for governance over parts of the world that were some of the most technologically and culturally advanced of the time. Other dynasties and empires created by Turkic peoples, such as the Ghaznavids and the Mongols, were similarly short-lived.

As the Seljuk sultans tried to consolidate their territorial gains in the 11th and 12th centuries, nomadic cultural traditions were sometimes a hindrance to the building of a stable polity or economy. Scholars have identified three important Turkic traditions as the chief obstacles to the building of a politically stable state: the *iqta,* a system of land grants to leading members of the ruling family; the tradition of the *atabeg,* or "tutor to the prince"; and the lack of a fixed system of succession.

The *iqta,* or appanage, system was part of a Seljuk system of governance that placed power in the hands of a ruling family as opposed to one supreme ruler. The leading member of the ruling family was obligated to delegate lands to other family members, who would administer these territories on behalf of the sections of the tribe they represented. Land grants of this kind were given to brothers, uncles, cousins, and nephews of the Seljuk sultans. The terms of an *iqta* land grant specified that the trustee could

The Kharraqan towers are two 11th-century mausoleums built for Seljuk princes in northern Iraq.

collect taxes from that territory in order to support his own needs. In exchange, the trustee was required to provide the sultan with a number of soldiers, who were also supported from the land grant. Originally, lands granted in this way did not become the private property of the assignees. The land could be reassigned or the grant revoked by the sultan. However, as the unity of the Seljuk Empire weakened after the death of Malikshah in 1092, many *iqta* holders came to regard themselves as the rightful owners of the lands that had been granted to them or their predecessors. This dissipation of land ownership, and the authority that went with it, contributed to the fragmentation of the empire in the 12th century.

Another cultural institution, that of the *atabeg* or "tutor to the prince," made it difficult for the Seljuk sultans to keep their empire unified. An *atabeg* was a tutor or regent whose duty was to educate and train a young Turkic prince. Tribal custom dictated that in the event of the youth's death, the *atabeg* could legitimately marry the youth's mother and assume control of his property and land. This cherished tribal institution encouraged the fragmentation in the Seljuk Empire because it led to the creation of more and more independent principalities.

The lack of a clear mechanism for the inheritance of power was another problem that had its roots in the Seljuks nomadic past. In nomadic Turkic tribes leadership could pass to any capable male relative of the leader who had died; it did not automatically pass from father to son. This lack of a fixed system of succession is perhaps the principal reason that the Seljuks and other Turkic dynasties were not able to maintain large territorial empires. The death of an imperial leader almost always resulted in a protracted power struggle between members of his family. Even in times of relative prosperity and stability there was no certainty about succession. These struggles were rarely resolved by the emergence of a clear winner and often resulted in the fragmentation of territory between family members.

The hereditary succession of the title of sultan from Chagri Beg to his son Alp Arslan, and

SEMITES

location:
Arabia, Syria-Palestine,
Mesopotamia, Abyssinia,
modern day Diasporas.

time period:
Prehistory to present day

ancestry:
Semitic

language:
Semitic

then to his son Malikshah, was unusual and aroused the indignation of many members of the Seljuk family. Following Malikshah's succession, several powerful members of the ruling family raised armies and prepared to rebel, but the sultan was able to redirect their ambitions into the conquest of new territories. It was only because the three Great Seljuk Sultans were successful in circumventing nomadic traditions in this way that they were able to build such a vast territorial empire.

Military Practices

Like their fellow Turkic people the Mongols, who would conquer the Middle East in the 13th century, the Seljuks were adept at cavalry warfare and utilized mounted archery as an important part of their tactics. Unlike European armies of the time, the Seljuks avoided pitched battles in which two armies confront each other head-on. The Seljuks preferred to harass an enemy with repeated skirmishes, volleys of arrows, and feigned retreats.

The Seljuk army was made up largely of slave soldiers from various regions and ethnic groups in much the same way that Turkic people themselves had been used as military slaves by Arab and Persian Muslim dynasties in the ninth and 10th centuries. Slaves who were trained from childhood for military service were referred to Mamluks, from the Arabic word meaning "owned." Mamluks could achieve rank, status, and power as the servant of a Muslim dynastic ruler.

◆

Today it is possible to travel by land from the Mediterranean Sea to northwest China and meet with speakers of Turkic languages along the entire route. Scholars debate whether the Turkic Seljuks, and later the Turkic Mongols, contributed to the Middle East culturally or whether they brought little more than war and economic chaos. The fact remains, however, that the vast numbers of Turkic nomads who followed the invading armies from the 11th to the 14th centuries brought widespread and lasting change to the ethnic landscape of the Middle East.

Generally, the Turks who came to this region under the Seljuk expansion continued their culture and way of life from the 11th century, through the Mongol invasions of the 13th century, and from the establishment of the Ottoman empire (late 13th century) to the end of World War I. The Seljuk sultanate of Rum not only was responsible for a sustained resettlement of thousands of Turks in Asia Minor, changing the language and demography of the region, it also corresponded geographically to the actual boundaries of the modern state of Turkey. For this reason Turkish nationalists in the early 20th century chose to emphasize the role of the Seljuk Turks as the founders of their ethnic and national heritage, seeing a continuity from the 11th century down to modern times.

FURTHER READING

Claude Cahen and P. M. Holt. *The Formation of Turkey: The Seljukid Sultanate of Rūm: Eleventh to Fourteenth Century* (Harlow, England: Longman, 2001).
John Freely. *Storm on Horseback: The Seljuk Warriors of Turkey* (London: I. B. Tauris, 2008).

Semites (Shemites)

Conventionally, some would say hypothetically, the Semites are a prehistoric people from whose homeland a series of waves of migrations took place throughout history to various areas of the Near and Middle East, and from whom the various branches of Semitic peoples are said to originate. The name "Semites," together with the older form "Shemites" is derived from the 10th chapter of the Hebrew Bible's book of Genesis. This chapter provides a genealogy of the descendants of Noah and his three sons: Ham, Shem (Sem), and Japheth. In the list of the descendants of Shem, the names Aram, Asshur, Eber, and Jokhtan are mentioned respectively as the fathers of the ARAMAEANS, the ASSYRIANS, the Hebrews, and the pure ARABS. Hence, these peoples are often named "Semitic" by virtue of their supposed common ancestor.

In 1781 the German historian August Ludwig von Schlözer first used the term "Semitic" in terms of language to refer to the close relationship between the Arabic, Aramaic, Assyrian, Babylonian, and Hebrew languages, although this relationship had been recognized for well over 200 years in the West and for much longer in the East. While the affinity between the Semitic languages is clear and undisputed among scholars, the idea of an ethnic or racial affinity between the so-called Semitic peoples remains an area of controversy, and many scholars feel that the term Semitic should be confined solely to linguistics.

On the basis of their languages however, Semitic peoples are divided into a number of groups including the Babylonian-Assyrian or Eastern Semites; the Western Semites, including the Aramaeans and the Canaanite Hebrews and PHOENICIANS; and the Southern Semites, with two subgroups: the Arabian Semites and the Ethiopic Semites. The terms Proto-Semites and Proto-Semitic are often used to refer to the early Semites and their language before their differentiation into the various Semitic peoples and languages.

ORIGINS

There are a number of theories as to the location of the original homeland of the Semites. These include Africa, Arabia, Armenia, Mesopotamia, and Syria-Palestine. The most generally, but by no means exclusively, accepted hypothesis is that the original homeland of the Semites was the Arabian Peninsula. The Semitic traditions, the historical sources, and ethnological data all point to Arabia as being the place from where the various Semitic peoples radiated. Arabia also constituted what is known as a "sheltered area" with limited communication with the outside world and fewer external influences upon its language and people than other areas of the Semitic region. Hence, the nomadic BEDOUIN way of life and the Arabic language remained relatively untouched and preserved in the Arabian Peninsula for long periods of time. It is also considered to be a law of history that peoples who practice agriculture do not revert to nomadic ways of life. Therefore, there are some who take the original Semites to be none other than the Bedouin of Arabia, groups of whom, for various reasons, throughout history migrated north, northeast, and south to more settled areas where they went on to assimilate with other civilizations as well as establishing those of their own.

According to some, the earliest wave of Semitic migrations from the Arabian Peninsula took place between the ninth and third millennia B.C.E. toward Syria in the north and toward the valley of the two rivers of Mesopotamia, the Euphrates and the Tigris, in the east. Certainly the existence of a Semitic people is historically attested in the Mesopotamian region from the beginnings of the fourth millennium B.C.E., and princes with Semitic names appear in the Sumerian king list for the period after the flood of around 2900. In about 2350 B.C.E., a Semitic people, who had been in the area of southern Mesopotamia for some time pursuing a traditional pastoral existence, succeeded in overthrowing the non-Semitic Sumerian kingdom

of king Lugal-Zaggi-Si and establishing in its place the Akkadian dynasty centered around the city state of Akkad after which the dynasty was named (*see* AKKADIANS; SUMERIANS). This dynasty lasted for around two centuries until it was overthrown by an influx of Gutians from the Zagros Mountains to the east.

Other migrations of Semitic peoples from Arabia include the Aramaeans in about 2500 B.C.E. (although some Eastern scholars date the migrations of the Aramaeans to much earlier, beginning around 9000 B.C.E.), the Hebrews in about 1400 B.C.E., the Ethiopians (*see* ETHIOPIANS) before about 500 B.C.E., and the Islamic Arabs beginning in the mid-seventh century C.E.

Apart from that of the Arabs, whose migrations were for reasons of territorial expansion fueled by a newfound religious confidence, two possible reasons are given for these migrations, the first of which is the climatic crisis of 6500–3500 B.C.E., making conditions in the Arabian Peninsula desert harsher and so driving groups of people to seek alternative places to live. The second reason is the natural pull that life in these more settled and fertile areas exerted upon the nomadic Bedouin, attracting them to migrate and settle there.

LANGUAGE

In the 19th century scholars set about studying and classifying the Semitic languages with renewed vigor. They launched these studies subsequent to a wider recognition of the relationship between the Arabic, Aramaic, Hebrew, and Ethiopic languages, and after archaeological discoveries throughout the Semitic region that included, in the 1840s and 1850s, the discovery and deciphering of a hitherto unknown Semitic language, Akkadian. Their efforts led them to posit the idea of a Proto-Semitic language at the head of the entire Semitic language grouping based on the analogy of the Proto-Indo-European language. Attempts were made to reconstruct this language based on the common features of the languages for which data were available. The results of the reconstruction of this hypothetical language remain the only real source of information about the original peoples of the Arabian Peninsula before their migration and differentiation.

According to linguists, the Proto-Semitic language had 29 consonants (Arabic and Hebrew with 28), many of which were glottalized, three short vowels (*a, i, u*), and three long vowels (a, i, u), which remains the vowel system of Arabic. Nouns were either of masculine or feminine gender with a marker (-at or -t) for the feminine, and there were three grammatical cases for nouns—nominative (for the subjects of sentences and the predicates of nominal sentences), accusative (for the direct objects of verbs and other adverbial forms), and genitive (following prepositions or for possessive constructs). The Semitic languages in general exhibit most of these and a number of other common features, including a triconsonantal root structure, emphatic or glottalized consonants, the use of prefixes, suffixes, and infixes, the use of gender for nouns, the presence of nominative, accusative, and genitive grammatical cases, and, in several languages, the use of vocalization to indicate short vowels, only the long vowels being normally written.

The Semitic languages are divided into a number of groups. The East Semitic grouping has one member in Akkadian, the earliest recorded Semitic language, which was used in Mesopotamia from 2500 to 600 B.C.E. and branched, from about 2000 B.C.E., into Assyrian and Babylonian. Archaeological discoveries in Mesopotamia have unearthed a large number of clay tablets containing inscriptions in Akkadian written in wedge-shaped or cuneiform characters, a writing system based on ideograms, which was borrowed from the Sumerians. West Semitic is subdivided into North-West Semitic and South-West Semitic. The former includes Aramaic, a language spoken in Syria-Palestine beginning around the first millennium B.C.E. Between the seventh and fourth centuries B.C.E., Aramaic was the lingua franca of the Babylonian and Persian empires, and parts of the Jewish Bible such as the book of Daniel were written in Aramaic. Later forms of Aramaic are usually divided into Eastern and Western. Eastern Aramaic includes Syriac and Mandaean, and Western Aramaic was the language spoken in Palestine at—and for some centuries after—the time of Christ. To the North-West Semitic grouping also belongs Canaanite, represented by Hebrew, the earliest form of which is that of the Jewish Bible beginning about 1200 B.C.E., and Phoenician (Punic), the language spoken between 1000 B.C.E. and 200 C.E. in the Phoenician cities of Sidon and Tyre, and in the Phoenician colonies such as Carthage in North Africa. South-West Semitic languages are made up of Arabic, the earliest attested manifestation of which takes the form of inscriptions probably dating back to the eighth century B.C.E., and Ethiopic, the oldest form of which is Geez, the language of the Abyssinian kingdom of Axum, which flourished in the first centuries of the common era, but also includes Amharic, Tigrynia, and TIGRE.

Several of these languages continue to be spoken to the present day, including Arabic, with up to 200 million speakers; Amharic, one of the official languages of Ethiopia (with a significant community of speakers in Israel), at over 17 million; Ivrit, the modern form of Hebrew, one of the official languages (the other being Arabic) of Israel, at nearly 9.5 millions; and Tigrynia, official language of Eritrea and one of the official languages of Ethiopia with over 5 million speakers. Dialects of Aramaic represented by modern versions of Syriac are still spoken by some small communities, notably the Turoyo dialect of Tur Abidin in eastern Turkey, and some forms of Syriac are still used as liturgical languages in several denominations of churches throughout the Middle East.

HISTORY

Since the early Semites dwelt in the period of prehistory before written records began and left no civilizations behind them, nothing concrete is known of their history. (For the histories of the various differentiated Semitic peoples *see* the relevant entries.)

CULTURE

It is possible to gain a certain amount of insight into many aspects of the lives of the Proto-Semites based on information we have about Bedouin life in the Arabian desert, which remained, until only very recently, unchanged for many centuries. Further, the reconstruction of the Proto-Semitic language has afforded us the closest thing we have to an encyclopedia of early Semitic life and culture.

The early Semites of the Arabian Peninsula were either fully nomadic, dependant upon the camel (if one accepts the hypothesis that the camel had been domesticated by this time), or seminomadic, pursuing a pastoral existence herding flocks of sheep and goats from pasture to pasture, oasis to oasis, and well to well. There were probably a number of settled tribes in areas in which agriculture was sustainable, and reconstructed linguistic evidence shows that the cultivation of several types of grains may have taken place, including barley, millet, and wheat, together with fruits such as grapes. Society was based on the bonds of tribe and family and was largely patriarchal, with limited polygamy practiced. Marrying outside the tribe would have been rare and frowned upon. Each tribe would have had a leader, who also may have acted as a judge in disputes, and who would probably have been elected by a council of the elder members of the tribe, but the idea of princes and kings may also not have been unknown to the early Semites. The tent, perhaps made out of animal hair, which may have been waterproofed with bitumen, would have been the standard dwelling, although linguistic evidence suggests that some people at least may have lived in houses with doors with some basic furniture. They would have kindled fires for warmth at night and to cook their food and help keep wild animals at bay.

The early Semites knew of archery, and the bow and arrow as well as the spear or lance would have been used for hunting and for self-defense. They may also have known about mining and the extraction of metals from their ores by smelting, since there are Proto-Semitic words for smelting and for coal. However, the only word relating to specific metals that can be reconstructed is that relating to silver (*kasp*), which, in Chadic, can actually mean "iron," and there were no specific terms for gold, copper, or lead. A term used for iron (*parzill*) is reckoned to be a non-Semitic word.

Terms relating to religious sensibilities are attested among the early Semites, and the concept of the holy was recognized, as well as ritual practices such as sacrifice and anointing. As with the majority of the pre-Islamic Arabs, the early Semites were polytheistic, attributing divinity to natural phenomena such as trees, plants, rocks and water, as well as the sun, moon, and stars, although historians many have speculated about the desert dwellers' natural inclination toward monotheism. The early Semitic word for "god," *vl*, later became *El*, the supreme god of the CANAANITES as well as being at the root of the Hebrew *Elohim* and Arabic *Allah*, both of which refer to one supreme god.

FURTHER READING

Gil Anidjar. *Semites: Race, Religion, Literature* (Stanford, Calif: Stanford University Press, 2008).

George A. Barton. *Semitic and Hamitic Origins: Social and Religious* (Philadelphia: University of Pennsylvania Press, 1934).

Sabatino Moscati. *Ancient Semitic Civilizations* (London: Elek Books, 1957).

———. *The Semites in Ancient History: An Inquiry into the Settlement of the Beduin and Their Political Establishment* (Cardiff: University of Wales Press, 1959).

Kees Versteegh. *The Arabic Language* (Edinburgh: Edinburgh University Press, 1997).

Sena (Chisena)

The Sena are a large ethnic group living in the border region of Malawi and Mozambique.

Senegalese: nationality (people of Senegal)

GEOGRAPHY

Senegal is a nation on the western extremity of Africa. It has an area of approximately 197,000 square miles and is bordered by five other countries. Mauritania meets Senegal's north and northeast borders, Mail lies to the east, and Guinea and Guinea-Bissau lie to the south. The Gambia is surrounded on three sides by Senegal and forms a finger of land that stretches deep into the territory of Senegal along the length of the Gambia River. Senegal's coastline extends for 330 miles along the Atlantic Ocean, although it is interrupted by the 50-mile-long coastline of Gambia.

The northern coast of Senegal is dominated by sand dunes that give way to a dry sandy plain that extends deep into the interior of the country. The southern coast is characterized by muddy estuaries, and the southern portion of the country, south of the Gambia, is more heavily forested than the north. The northeast corner of Senegal is semidesert, although a narrow corridor of more fertile land extends along the length of the Senegal River, which flows along much of the country's northern and eastern border. A range of hills rises in the southeast corner of the country, although none reach an altitude of more than 2,000 feet.

Senegal's capital, Dakar, is situated on the Cape Verde peninsula, which is the westernmost part of mainland Africa. Touba, Senegal's second-largest city, is situated about 100 miles inland from Dakar and is a significant religious center for the country's Muslims. Saint-Louis on the northern coast of Senegal at the mouth of the Senegal River and close to the border with Mauritania is one of the country's oldest colonial cities and was the capital of the French colony of Senegal until 1960.

INCEPTION AS A NATION

Archaeological evidence indicates that the valley of the Senegal River was inhabited in the prehistoric period. From the 10th century C.E.

SENEGALESE: NATIONALITY

nation:
Senegal; Republic of Senegal

derivation of name:
Named for the Senegal River

government:
Republic

capital:
Dakar

language:
French in the country's official language. The most widely spoken indigenous languages are Wolof, Pulaar, Jola, and Manding.

religion:
About 94 percent of the population are Muslim, 5 percent are Christian (predominantly Roman Catholic), and the remaining 1 percent follows indigenous faiths.

earlier inhabitants:
Unknown

demographics:
The largest ethnic group are the Wolof, who make up 43 percent of the population. Other significant groups include the Pular (24 percent), Serer (15 percent), and Diola (4 percent). The remaining 14 percent is made up of numerous smaller groups including the Manding, Soninke, Tukulor, Fulani, and Bambara.

trade routes between West Africa and the cultures of the Mediterranean coast to the north (including Egypt) were well established and the peoples who lived in the area of the Senegal River were in close cultural contact with the Muslim world of North Africa. By the middle of the 14th century Senegal was part of the large and powerful West African Mali Empire, which stretched from the Atlantic coast of present-day Mali and Senegal as far inland as Gao on the Niger River. As the Mali Empire declined in the second half of the 14th century, the WOLOF Empire developed in the north of present day Senegal and persisted in one form or another until the 1890s. When Portuguese explorers first reached the coast of Senegal in the 1440s, the Wolof state of northern Senegal was at the height of its power. The Portuguese developed a lucrative trade in gold and slaves along the Sen-

egalese coast during the second half of the 15th century, and traders from other European nations also established a presence during the 16th century. The rulers of the Wolof state became wealthy from this trade and used their wealth to strengthen their power in the region. By the 17th century, however, the coastal regions of Senegal had become largely independent of the Wolof state, and its power began to decline as it lost control of trade with the Europeans.

Gorée Island just off the coast of Cape Verde Peninsula was first used a trading base and resupply port by the Portuguese in the 15th century. During the 16th century it was captured by the Dutch, and during the 17th century by first the British and then the French in the 1670s. During this period Gorée Island became one of the largest transshipment points for slaves from West Africa. It remained a center for the trade

---

Senegalese: nationality time line

C.E.

12th–14th centuries Area of present-day Senegal ruled by the Wolof Empire.

1440s Portuguese explorers and traders reach the mouth of the Senegal River.

1659 Saint-Louis founded by the French at the mouth of the Senegal River.

1756–63 Britain takes control of French settlements in Senegal, forming the colony of Senegambia.

1816 France regains control of Senegal from the British.

1895 Senegal becomes part of French West Africa.

1946 Senegal becomes part of the French Union.

1958 Senegal becomes an autonomous republic within the French Community.

1960 Senegal becomes independent as part of the Mali Federation. The Mali Federation dissolves and Senegal becomes a single independent republic with Leopold Senghor as president.

1962 Unsuccessful coup attempt

1966 Senghor's Senegalese Progressive Union becomes the only legal political party.

1978 Multiparty system adopted.

1981 Senghor resigns as president. Abdou Diouf becomes president.

1982 Senegal and Gambia form the Senagambian Confederation.

1988 Diouf elected to a second term as president.

1989 Senagambian Confederation dissolved.

1993 Diouf elected to a third term as president.

2000 Abdoulaye Wade defeats Diouf in presidential elections.

2004 Government signs peace accord with secessionist Casamance Movement of Democratic Forces (CMDF).

2006 Government forces launch an offensive against a CMDF faction in the southern Casamance province.

2007 Wade wins a second term as president. Opposition parties boycott parliamentary elections.

2008 Former Chadian leader Hissene Habre goes on trail for human rights abuses in Senegal.

Senegalese troops serving with the French Army in Europe during World War I

until France finally abolished slavery in all of its colonies in the 1840s. The city of Dakar grew up on the coast of Cape Verde as a direct result of the economic importance of Gorée Island. In the 1650s the French established another colony on the uninhabited island of Ndar at the mouth of the Senegal River in the north of the country. This settlement became the heart of the French city of Saint-Louis, which was the center of French colonial activity in West Africa for the next three centuries.

The 19th century brought fierce competition between the European colonial powers for control of Africa, and France concentrated on expanding its possessions in West Africa farther inland. Senegal was proclaimed a French possession in 1840, and the indigenous peoples of the Senegal River valley were subjugated in a series of French military campaigns during the 1850s and 1860s. In 1895 France created the federation of French West Africa, which incorporated the colonies of Senegal, French Sudan

(present-day Mali), French Guinea (present-day Guinea), and Ivory Coast into a single administrative unit. French West Africa was later expanded to include all of France's colonial possessions in West Africa, and its administrative capital was relocated from Saint-Louis to Dakar.

In 1946, following World War II, the French government reorganized all of its foreign colonies under a new organization known as the French Union. Under the French Union all peoples living within the former French colonies were granted French citizenship and a greater degree of local administration was encouraged. In 1958 the French Union was replaced by the French Community, which gave a large degree of autonomy to the former colonies with the understanding that France would not oppose their eventual evolution toward full independence. In 1959 French Sudan (present-day Mali), Senegal, Dahomey (present-day Benin), and Upper Volta (present-day Burkina Faso) drew up a constitu-

Leopold Sedar Senghor: The Poet President

Leopold Sedar Senghor was the first president of independent Senegal and was elected to the office four more times, holding the post for 20 years. He is credited with overseeing one of the most successful and peaceful transitions from colonial rule to independence in Africa and is also acknowledged as one of the continent's leading literary figures and political thinkers of the 20th century.

Leopold Sedar Senghor was born in 1906 in the small coastal town of Joal about 60 miles south of the capital Dakar. His father, a moderately wealthy businessman, was a Serer (one of the smallest ethnic groups in Senegal) and a Catholic (about 95 percent of Senegalese are Muslim). Senghor excelled at school in Dakar and was offered an opportunity to study in France, which he took up in 1928. After graduating from the University of Paris in 1935, Senghor held university teaching positions in Tours and Paris until the outbreak of World War II in 1939. Volunteering for the French army in 1939 he was captured by the Germans in 1940 and spent two years in prisoner-of-war camps in France until being released on medical grounds in 1942. Senghor then returned to teaching, becoming head of the linguistics department of the École Nationale de la France d'Outre-Mer (the National School of Overseas France), an institution for the education of colonial administrators.

Before World War II Senghor began to gain recognition as a leading poet in the French language. Along with other African intellectuals living in France he developed the concept of "négritude," a reaction to racist attitudes then prevalent in France and the rest of Europe that emphasized the cultural achievements of Africans. After World War II, with the reorganization of France's colonial territories into the French Union, Senghor became involved in African politics as an elected representative for Senegal in the French National Assembly. He also served on the commission that drew up the constitution of the Fifth French Republic, which was inaugurated in 1958.

Leopold Senghor was the president of the short-lived Mali Federation and became president of Senegal when that union collapsed in 1960. As president Senghor initially quarreled with his prime minister and oversaw the strengthening of his presidential powers and the banning of all political parties other than his own Senegalese Progressive Union in 1966. Senghor retained close ties with the former colonial power, France, and rejected the Marxist ideologies adopted by some other heads of state in newly independent African states. Senghor became a leading theorist and proponent of African socialism—a political philosophy that aimed to integrate socialist ideals with traditional African lifestyles and economic systems. African socialism became a very influential political philosophy in the 1960s and 1970s, and Senghor was widely regarded as one of its guiding authorities.

Leopold Senghor's regime was popular but not without opponents. Some elements of Senegalese society objected to the continuation of close ties with France and with the president's reliance on French political advisors. Many social inequalities that had become established under colonial rule were not addressed, and a limited form of multiparty politics was not introduced until 1978. Retrospectively, however, Leopold Senghor's presidency is widely regarded as having successfully negotiated a perilous path between the kind of radical economic and social policies that blighted other newly independent African nations and the dangers of alienating the populace by allowing the former colonial power too much influence.

Leopold Senghor stepped down from the presidency in 1980, before the end of his fifth term, and retired to live in France. He was elected to the Académie française, the preeminent authority on the French language, in 1983 becoming the first African in history to hold such a position. Senghor died in France in 2001 and was buried in Dakar.

tion for the establishment of a unified state to be known as the Mali Federation. Although the Mali Federation achieved independence from France as a single nation in June 1960, political differences caused it to break up within two months. Senegal withdrew from the federation and declared its independence in August 1960. Leopold Senghor was elected as the nation's first president a short while later.

In 1982 Senegal entered into an agreement with the Gambia to form the Senegambian Confederation. This attempt to unify the economies and armed forces of the two nations came to an end when Gambia voluntarily withdrew from the confederation in 1989.

CULTURAL IDENTITY

Senegal is widely regarded as a paradigm of political and economic stability in a continent that has been plagued by violence and economic underperformance in the period following the end of colonial rule.

Following a constitutional crisis in the first two years of independence, the powers of the presidency were strengthened and Leopold Senghor, leader of the Socialist Party of Senegal (SPS), was retained in office. Senghor was reelected in 1968, 1973, and 1978. From 1966 to 1976 the SPU was the only legal party, and when Senghor stepped down in 1981, he was replaced by his protégé, Abdou Diouf. The SPS remained in power under the leadership of Diouf until 2000, when Diouf was defeated in presidential elections by Abdoulaye Wade of the Senegalese Democratic Party. The peaceful transfer of power to the Democratic Party after 40 years of rule by the SPS was regarded as a major triumph of the democratic process.

Despite its admirable record of political stability, Senegal has not been completely free from conflict in the half century since independence. The region of Senegal south of the Gambian enclave known as Casamance, for the Casamance River, has always been culturally and politically isolated from the main body of the country in the north. From the early 1980s until the early 2000s, a separatist movement fought a low-level campaign against government troops in the region. There have also been periodic limited clashes across the northern border with Mauritania over the issue of grazing rights for the seminomadic pastoralists who live there.

Three ethnic groups dominate the north of the country: the Wolof (who account for almost 45 percent of the population), the Pular, and the SERER. The LEBU, smaller group, are concentrated around Dakar. In the south the Diola are a small but politically influential group in the Casamance region. The Manding live primarily in the southeast of the country, and the FULANI are scattered throughout the nation but are more prevalent in the arid eastern quarter. There is little history of interethnic conflict in Senegal, although the peoples south of the Gambian enclave were historically less strongly influenced by Islam and have a culture that is recognizably distinct from the Wolof-dominated north. The Casamance has always been sparsely populated compared to the north, however. The strength of national identity in Senegal is often attributed to a long history of shared identity under colonial rule, the dominance of the majority Wolof culture, and the long-established influence of Islam.

Since the 1960s Senegal, and especially Dakar, has been an important center for the promotion of indigenous African culture and history. The first World Festival of Negro Arts, held in Dakar in 1966, was one of the first international events to bring African artists and artists of African heritage from the United States and Europe together. The Fundamental Institute of Black Africa, also in Dakar, is an important museum that holds an extensive collection of ethnographic art from across West Africa. Leopold Senghor, Senegal's first president, was an internationally renowned poet, philosopher, and statesman and did much to promote the culture of Senegal internationally. Other well-known Senegalese cultural figures include the writers Birago Diop and David Diop, and the movie director Ousmane Sembene.

FURTHER READING

Elizabeth L. Berg. *Senegal* (New York: Marshall Cavendish, 1999).

Sheldon Gellar. *Senegal: An African Nation between Islam and the West 2d ed.* (Boulder, Colo.: Westview Press, 1995).

Eric Ross. *Culture and Customs of Senegal* (Westport, Conn: Greenwood Press, 2008).

Janet G. Vaillant. *Black, French, and African: A Life of Leopold Sedar Senghor* (Cambridge, Mass.: Harvard University Press, 1990).

Senufo

The Senufo are one of the larger ethnic groups of West Africa. Numbering more than 3 million, they can be found living in a region bordered by the Bani River to the north, the Bagoe River to the west, and the Black Volta River to

the east. This places them in the countries of Mali, Burkina Faso, and Ivory Coast. Various Senufo subgroups exist, such as the Fodonon of Lataha, Kulebele, and Tyebara of Korhogo. The vast majority of Senufo people are what is known as Southern Senufo, nearly a quarter of whom are Muslim.

Like the MENDE of Sierra Leone and Liberia, in the past many Senufo men belonged to the Poro secret society. The organization of these groups differed from village to village, but they all aimed to teach boys becoming men how to behave. Poro were powerful regulatory forces in society. They laid down rules, sanctioned acceptable behavior, punished or prohibited unacceptable behavior, and generally provided social and cultural unity to the Senufo. In recent decades, however, more and more Senufo are adopting Islam, and the influence of the Poro societies has diminished.

Serer

The Serer are one of Senegal's largest ethnic groups. They inhabit the rolling plains of Cayor, Baol, and the town of Nioro du Rip, mostly in the regions to the south and west of Dakar, the capital city. Smaller numbers of Serer people live in Gambia and Guinea-Bissau. The majority of the Serer are farmers, cultivating groundnuts and millet. The Serer language is closely related to that of the TEMNE and WOLOF peoples as well as Fulfulde, which is spoken by the FULANI.

Together with the Wolof, the Serer were the primary inhabitants of the Wolof Kingdom, and later empire, which became powerful in the 15th century. The Wolof introduced the Serer to Islam, which was at first violently resisted. Since the 19th century, however, Islam has spread increasingly rapidly among the Serer. By the early 1990s, more than 80 percent of the Serer were Muslim.

Seychellois: nationality (people of the Seychelles)

GEOGRAPHY

The Republic of the Seychelles is a small nation that consists of an archipelago of more than 100 islands in the Indian Ocean. The islands of the Seychelles lie about 1,000 miles east of the coast of Kenya. The exact number of islands in the archipelago is unknown, with estimates ranging from 115 to 155; the great majority of these are very small and completely uninhab-

SEYCHELLOIS: NATIONALITY

nation:
Seychelles; Republic of Seychelles

derivation of name:
Named for Jean Moreau de Séchelles—minister of finance under King Louis XV of France

government:
Republic

capital:
Victoria

language:
English is the country's official language. The Seychellois Creole is the lingua franca spoken by 92 percent of the population.

religion:
About 93 percent of the population are Christian and about 75 percent of these are Roman Catholics. Other Christian denominations include Anglicans and Seventh-Day Adventists. Hindus make up about 2 percent of the population, Muslims about 2 percent, and other groups the remaining 1 percent.

earlier inhabitants:
Uninhabited

demographics:
99 percent of the population have mixed French, British, African, Indian, Chinese, and Malagasy ancestry. There are small groups of Europeans, Arabs, and North Americans.

Seychellois: nationality time line

C.E.

1502 Portuguese explorer Vasco da Gama visits the Seychelles.

1609 British explorers land on the island.

1756 France claims sovereignty.

1768 First French settlements

1794 Britain seizes control of the island. Administration is from Mauritius.

1903 The Seychelles become separately administered British colony.

1948 First local elections to the Legislative Council

1964 Seychelles People's United Party (SPUP), led by France Rene, and the Seychelles Democratic Party (SDP), led by James Mancham, founded.

1976 Seychelles become independent, with Mancham as president and Rene as prime minister.

1977 Rene deposes Mancham in a coup and establishes a one-party state.

1981 Attempted coup by South African mercenaries

1982 Attempted military coup prevented by Tanzanian troops.

1991 Multiparty system reinstated under a new constitution.

1993 Rene wins first multiparty presidential elections.

1998 Rene wins a second term as president.

2001 Rene wins a third term as president.

2004 Rene retires and is replaced by former vice president James Michel.

2006 Michel wins presidential elections.

ited. Geologically the islands are of two distinct types. The central spine consists of mountainous granite islands, but surrounding this core are dozens of flat coral islands. Altogether the islands of the Seychelles have an area of approximately 118 square miles. Mahé, the largest island, has an area of about 60 square miles and the 2,990-foot-high peak of Mount Seychellois, the highest point in the nation. The second-largest island, Praslin, has an area of about 15 square miles. Taken together the two islands of Mahé and Praslin account for almost 65 percent of the total area of the country. About 80 percent of the population lives on Mahé Island, many of these in the nation's capital, Victoria, which is situated around a natural harbor on the northeast of the island.

INCEPTION AS A NATION

It is likely that Arab sailors or the ancestors of the MALAGASY were the first to visit the islands of the Seychelles, but when the Portuguese explorer Vasco da Gama visited them in 1502, they were uninhabited. The crew of a British vessel made the first recorded landing on the islands in 1609. Indian Ocean pirates used the islands as a safe haven during the 17th and 18th centuries. In 1756 France was the first nation to lay claim to them and, in 1768, the first to establish a settlement there. During the Napoleonic Wars (1794–1812) Britain seized control of the Seychelles, and they remained a British colonial possession until independence in 1976.

Following the end of the slave trade in the mid-19th century, many of the slave-owning landowners on the islands migrated to the African mainland, while thousands of freed slaves moved to the islands to seek work. Laborers from India and other parts of South and Southeast Asia were also imported during the second half of the 19th century, adding to the islands' already diverse ethnic mix.

In 1903 the islands ceased to be administered from Mauritius and became an independent crown colony. The first local elections to the Legislative Council were held in 1948, and in 1967 a new constitution vested authority in a governor appointed by the British government and a locally elected governing council. Further constitutional amendments in 1970 gave the Seychelles greater autonomy, and full independence was granted in June 1976. At independence the Seychelles were governed by a coalition, with James Mancham as president and France Rene as prime minister.

CULTURAL IDENTITY

The first decade of the Seychelles' independence was punctuated by political instability. The Seychelles People's United Party (SPUP), led by Prime Minister France Rene, had been the leading voice for independence in the early 1970s, while the Seychelles Democratic Party (SDP), led by President James Mancham, had advocated continued close political ties with Britain. Less than a year after independence Mancham was deposed in a bloodless coup and Rene installed in his place as president. Rene transformed the Seychelles into a one-party state with the newly constituted Seychelles People's Progressive Front (SPPF) as the only legal political organization. In 1981 a group of South African mercenaries attempted a coup that is believed to have had the reinstatement of Mancham as its aim, but this failed. A second attempted coup in 1982 was prevented by Tanzanian troops deployed in the Seychelles following the 1981 incident.

Opposition Seychellois groups in exile campaigned for electoral reform and an end to

Rene's regime throughout the late 1980s and gained considerable international support. In 1991 Rene instigated a constitutional review, and the country's first multiparty elections since independence were held in 1992. Many opposition leaders returned from exile, including Mancham, and there was a period of national reconciliation during the electoral process. Rene, continuing to enjoy popular support, won three more presidential terms before finally retiring in 2004. The SPPF has also remained the largest party in parliament, although its majority has steadily declined since 1992.

Seychellois society remains stratified according to ethnic origin. Having evolved from a social system in which mostly African slaves (and later indentured workers) were employed on white-owned plantations, modern Seychellois tend to regard people of lighter skin tone as having higher status than people of darker skin tone. The islands' small Chinese and Indian communities, who have traditionally worked as shopkeepers and traders, stand somewhat outside this gradation of rank. While the predominantly white political and economic elite of the islands has retained much of their European culture and the predominantly black lower classes have formed a distinct culture of their own, there is also a supraculture that binds all the Seychellois together into a relatively peaceful and tolerant society. In the first decade of the 21st century, traditional distinctions based on ethnic origin are slowly breaking down as the Seychelles becomes part of the global economy, particularly through its tourism industry, which has brought large multinational employers to the country and new opportunities for all Seychellois.

FURTHER READING

James R. Mancham. *Paradise Raped: Life, Love, and Power in the Seychelles* (London: Methuen, 1983).

William McAteer. *Rivals in Eden: A History of the French Settlement and British Conquest of the Seychelles Islands, 1742–1818* (Lewes, Sussex, U.K.: Book Guild, 1991).

William McAteer. *To Be a Nation: Being the Third Part of The History of Seychelles, 1920–1976* (Mahé, Seychelles: Pristine Books, 2008).

Deryck Scarr. *Seychelles Since 1770: History of a Slave and Post-Slavery Society* (Trenton, N.J.: Africa World Press, 1999).

Shambaa

The Shambaa are a cluster of closely related ethnic groups, including the SHAMBALA, the PARE, and the BONDEI, who inhabit the coastal lowlands of Tanzania. The majority of the Shambaa are Muslim.

Although they are what is known as an Eastern BANTU people, the Shambaa are descended from both Bantu and Cushitic ancestors (*see* CUSHITES). Early in the first millennium C.E., Bantu speakers migrating into East Africa from Central Africa mingled with Cushitic peoples who had already moved into that region. Interaction between the two cultures led to the development of the Shambaa and other groups such as the KIKUYU. At first the Shambaa's ancestors lived in widespread, independent settlements. After experiencing MAASAI raids in the early 18th century, however, the different family-based groups began to form closer political unions. Under Mbegha, who perhaps came from areas in western and central Tanzania that had already established chieftaincies, the Shambaa began to develop a powerful centralized state. Ruled by a group known as the Kilindi, the Shambaa kingdom reached its height in the 19th century under the famous Kimweri ye Nyumbai.

Shambala

The Shambala are a subgroup of the SHAMBAA. The Shambaa inhabit the coastal lowlands of Tanzania.

Shammar

The Shammar are a group of nomadic tribes now living in Saudi Arabia, Syria, and Iraq. In oral tradition they trace their origins to Yemen, in the southwestern Arabian Peninsula, to the ancient Yemeni king Shimmar ibn al-Amluq. While the precise date of their migration north is not known, their oral narratives put them in the area called Jabal ("mountain") Shammar, in north-central Saudi Arabia, in the 16th century C.E. In the 18th century some members of the tribe migrated farther north, to the area between the Tigris and the Euphrates Rivers, in modern-day Iraq, and they are known as northern Shammar. Those who remained in Jabal Shammar, referred to as southern Shammar, are divided into four tribes: Abda, Sinjara, Aslam, and Tuman. A British Foreign Office report from 1868 gives the branches of Shammar as Faddagha, Tayy, Ubayd, and Utayba. The Shammar chiefs came from the family of Al Rashid, who ruled from the oasis of Hail, 250 miles northeast of Medina. Some northern Shammar became Shii Muslims, like many of their neighbors, while those in the Shammar area itself were and remained Sunni.

In the 19th and early 20th centuries the Shammar were at the height of their power, with a population estimated at between 150,000 and 200,000, and they controlled most of central Arabia. Their territories were crossed by heavily traveled trade routes, and this was an important factor in their rise to power. When the Wahhabis, fanatical Muslim reformers, came to power in central Arabia in the mid-18th century, caravans trying to avoid Wahhabi territory would instead travel via the Shammar oasis of Hail, providing income and prestige for the Shammar and the Al Rashid, their leaders. In 1902, Ibn Saud, who was to found the ruling dynasty of Saudi Arabia and who was allied with the Wahhabis, returned from exile in Kuwait and recaptured the city of Riyadh from the Rashid leaders of the Shammar and drove them out of Hail. While some of the Shammar fled to join their northern compatriots, most remained in central Arabia and accepted, to varying extents, the dominance of the Saudis. Ibn Saud abolished tribal territories in 1925, and with that, the Shammar lost their exclusive rights to lands on which to graze their herds. Eventually they were forced into sedentary living and lost their autonomy.

Shamya *See* SINYAR.

Shanga *See* SHANGAWA.

Shangawa (Shanga)
The Shangawa live on and around the islands and banks of the Niger River near the Nigerian city of Shanga in the northwest of the country. They were once part of the SONGHAY Empire.

Sherbro (Southern Bullom)
The Sherbro live along the coast of Sierra Leone. They are increasingly being absorbed by the MENDE.

Shiho *See* SAHO.

Shikongo (Bashikongo)
The Shikongo are part of the KONGO peoples. They live in coastal regions of northwestern Angola and the southeast of the Democratic Republic of the Congo.

Shilluk
The Shilluk are NILOTES who live in southern Sudan, along the White Nile River.

ORIGINS
According to Shilluk history, their Nilotic ancestors began to migrate into their present-day location roughly 400 years ago. Much of Shilluk history is preserved orally, through legends and stories, and goes back hundreds of years.

LANGUAGE
The Shilluk speak a Nilotic language, which is also called Shilluk.

HISTORY
With its ethnic and religious diversity, Sudan has suffered internal conflict for many years. Like the Sudanese DINKA, NUER, NUBA, and many other southern groups, the Shilluk are non-Muslim minorities in a country in which Muslim ARABS from the north dominate the government. In 1983, the imposition of sharia (Islamic holy) law triggered the outbreak of civil war between north and south Sudan that continued until 2002.

In 1989 at least 700 Shilluk—mostly farmhands working roughly 100 miles north of Kodok on the White Nile—were massacred by an Arab militia that had been armed by the Sudanese government.

CULTURE
The majority of Shilluk are pastoralists who combine the herding of cattle, sheep, and goats with growing crops. Beans, corn, millet, sesame, and pumpkins are common food crops, and tobacco is grown both to use and to sell. Because the Shilluk live along the banks of the White Nile River, fishing is an important activity for them, and fish are an important supplement to the diet. Shilluk fishermen intensively exploit the Nile waters for fish, which are caught with nets or specially designed fishing spears. Infrequent hunting parties are arranged by Shilluk men, though only smaller mammals—certain antelopes and gazelles, for example—are caught. In the past, hippopotamuses were hunted by the Shilluk, but they are now protected by law.

Government and Society
The Shilluk are divided into about 100 clans or groups, each with a common ancestor or ances-

The palace of the Shilluk *reth*, or king, stands on an artificial mound of earth.

tors. The clans are scattered throughout various villages. Each village has an original or founding family called a *diel*. Each village has a chief, who is usually a member of the *diel*, subject to approval by the Shilluk king, or *reth*. The Shilluk *reth* is a living symbol of Shilluk history and culture and is thought to be possessed by the spirit of Nyikang—the first Shilluk king and Shilluk culture hero. Nyikang is closely associated with the Shilluk religion. The *reth*, therefore, is sometimes described as a divine king. Indeed, the *reth*'s role is more religious than political. He is the central figure who unites the Shilluk into a people. His subjects believe he is the reincarnation of the legendary Nyikang and that his good health ensures their prosperity. The *reth* resides at Kodok, formerly known as Fashoda. Since 1956, the *reth* has had the status of magistrate within the Sudanese judiciary.

Many traditions surround the ceremony of electing a new *reth*. The new ruler must be the son of any former king who can win the support of the people. The successful candidate is chosen by the two paramount chiefs. An electoral college of 14 other chiefs has to approve their choice. There follow ceremonies at which effigies of Nyikang and his son Dak are paraded. Finally, the new king is enthroned, when it is believed that the spirit of Nyikang enters him.

Religion

Although a tiny minority of Shilluk people have converted to Islam, the vast majority adhere to the Shilluk religion. The Shilluk religion is centered around a creator god known as Juok. Nyikang is considered to be the intermediary between an individual and Juok. Whereas Nyikang founded the Shilluk people, it was Juok who created the world and who continues

to maintain it. Also, whereas Nyikang is represented by a human—the *reth*—Juok is not.

The Shilluk have a wealth of stories about Nyikang. According to one legend, Nyikang came from the south sometime in the 1500s accompanied by his warrior son, Dak, and their followers. Using his powers, Nyikang helped his followers cross the crocodile-infested waters of the White Nile. Another legend says that Nyikang's mother was a crocodile, which may explain his power over these guardians of the river. Nyikang's mother is associated with rivers and river creatures, and offerings are left for

Shilluk time line

C.E.

ca. 1000 Nilotic peoples are known to be settled in region to the far southwest of the Bahr al Ghazal River.

ca. 1500s Nilotic ancestors of Shilluk migrate into present location along banks of White Nile.

1684 Shilluk attacks on Arab settlements

1821 Trade routes opened from north to south Sudan, leading to a reduced southern population through disease and slave trading.

1840s–50s Arab slave trade at height in Shilluk territory; Shilluk are targeted by slave raiders.

1898 Britain and Egypt jointly colonize Sudan.

1955–72 First Sudanese civil war between north and south

1956 Sudanese independence

1972 End of first Sudanese civil war; south granted regional autonomy.

1983 Sudan adopts sharia (Islamic holy) law against wishes of mainly non-Muslim south; civil war breaks out again.

1989 More than 700 Shilluk massacred at Jebelein.

2002 End of Sudanese civil war between north and south

her on riverbanks. In another legend, Nyikang fought with the Sun, which had gained possession of one of his cows, and drove it back into the sky. When the rains come at the end of the dry season, Nyikang is said to be overcoming the sun and bringing much-needed water to the thirsty land.

See also SUDANESE: NATIONALITY.

FURTHER READING

Wilhelm Hofmayr and P. Banholzers. *The Shilluk: History, Religion and Life of a Nilote Tribe* (Oxford: Bodleian Library, 1980).

Diedrich Westermann. *The Shilluk People: Their Language and Folklore* (Westport, Conn.: Negro Universities Press, 1970).

Shirazi (Mbwera)

The Shirazi are descended from Persian, Arab, and African ancestors. They inhabit the islands off the northeast coast of Tanzania.

Shoho *See* SAHO.

Shona

The lands of the Shona people cover most of Zimbabwe and extend into Mozambique; there are also Shona populations in South Africa, Botswana, and Zambia. They are the dominant ethnic group in Zimbabwe, where the Shona make up about 70 percent of the total population. Around 500,000 Shona people live outside Zimbabwe, mainly in neighboring countries.

ORIGINS

The Shona are descended from Iron Age BANTU-speaking farmers who settled on the Zimbabwe plateau in around 200 C.E. Little is known of these early settlers except that they worked with iron. From about the 10th century, however, the Shona civilization that had developed in the area became adept at working with gold and copper, both of which were found on the plateau, and traded those metals with coastal cities. The people who ruled this trade became the wealthy elite, whose graves were later found to contain gold ornaments and imported beads and cloth.

LANGUAGE

The Shona language is also called Shona and is one of the most widely-spoken of the Bantu languages. It is spoken not only by the Shona but also, as a second language, by many other people in Southern Africa. Many Shona also speak English—a legacy of colonialism.

HISTORY

From around the late 1100s, the Shona began to construct impressive dry-wall enclosures (built without mortar) serving as palaces and called *zimbabwes* (literally, "stone houses"). This building system was perfected at the site of Great Zimbabwe (south of modern Masvingo) from the 1300s onward. Great Zimbabwe had been abandoned as a palace by the Shona kings by the end of the 15th century, but it continued as a religious and ceremonial site. The capital was moved north to the area around the Zambezi River. This marked the beginning of a new Shona dynasty, the Mwene Mutapas. The first Mwene Mutapa was Nyatsimba Mutota, who conquered territory from the Kalahari Desert to the Indian Ocean. After the death in 1480 of his successor, Matope, the kingdom split, the southern part being dominated by the ROZVI peoples, a Shona subgroup.

When the Rozvi Empire finally collapsed in the early 19th century, over a hundred small Shona states took its place. Many of these were disrupted after 1820 as a result of the wave of emigration emanating from Shaka's Zulu Mfecane expansion. This brought the NDEBELE people into southern Zimbabwe. It was the Ndebele who gave these many groups the name "Shona." Previously, each group was known by its own name, even though they were all Shona-speaking peoples.

After 1850 most of the area was colonized by the British and renamed Southern Rhodesia, for the British imperialist and colonial administrator Cecil Rhodes. In 1965 the white population declared independence from British rule as Rhodesia. After a prolonged civil war, full independence and majority rule were negotiated in 1980.

CULTURE

The majority of the Shona people earn their living from agriculture. The staple food crop is corn; other cereal crops include wheat, millet, sorghum, and barley. Other important food crops include vegetables, fruit, cassava, and soybeans. Sugar, cotton, and tobacco are the main cash crops. The Shona also raise cattle, goats, sheep, pigs, and poultry.

During the colonial period and the following era of white rule, the most fertile farming land in present-day Zimbabwe was taken

SHONA

location:
Zimbabwe, Mozambique, South Africa, Botswana, and Zambia

time period:
Third century C.E. to present

ancestry:
Bantu

language:
Bantu (Niger-Congo)

by white settlers. As a result, many Shona lost their land. Even today, despite official land resettlement schemes, the Shona suffer the legacy of these policies. Land shortages combined with recurring drought mean that few are able to support themselves by agriculture alone. Instead, they have to supplement their income by working in nearby towns. In Zimbabwe, many Shona work in mining, where over 40 different minerals are exploited. Gold is the most important mineral and has been mined by the Shona for many hundreds of years. Other important minerals mined are nickel, coal, copper, and iron.

Government and Society

Before colonialism, Shona society was organized into chiefdoms, each led by a hereditary chief. This man would be responsible for land distribution and would judge disputes. Historical records report that most societies were basically egalitarian and chiefs were not markedly more wealthy than their subjects. The authority of the chiefs is still recognized, but they no longer have any real political power. Instead, they now perform the more socially oriented function of maintaining and preserving Shona culture and values.

Most Shona have only one marriage partner. An important part of marriage arrangements is the bride-wealth, which is given by the groom to the bride's family. Previously, this sum was in cattle but it is now more likely to be cash. Alternatively, some sort of service can be provided instead of cash. The families of well-educated girls normally demand a higher amount. If a couple divorces, a negotiable proportion of the original bride-wealth has to be repaid.

Religion

With colonialism came Christian missionaries. Although they made little headway at first, over a quarter of all Shona are Christians today. The majority are members of independent churches established, attended, and controlled largely by Africans, not by Europeans. Also, the Shona religion is still widely followed and remains a vital force in Shona society.

The Shona religion involves the recognition of a supreme god, referred to in historical documents as Murungu but more commonly called Mwari today. A major part of the Shona religion involves ancestral spirit cults. The spirit of an ordinary person is known as a *mudzimo* while that of someone more influential as *mhondoro*. *Mhondoro* spirits provide the link between

mortals and Mwari. When they possess a medium, they can intercede with Mwari on behalf of the people on ethical as well as practical matters such as predicting rainfall. Harmful spirits called *ngozi* are thought to cause evil, and they can be the spirits of people who were murdered. *N'anga* are religious and medical practitioners who both heal illnesses with herbs and diagnose evil forces at work through various means of divination.

The incoming religion of Christianity and the already present Shona religion have each altered in response to the presence of the other. Many of the independent churches incorporate so-called traditional beliefs about healing into their form of Christianity, so that the Holy Spirit is believed to heal through possession; in turn, the Shona religion has developed a traditional creation story that was not in existence before colonialism.

See also ZIMBABWEANS: NATIONALITY.

FURTHER READING

D. N. Beach. *The Shona and Zimbabwe, 900–1850: An Outline of Shona History* (New York: Africana Publishing Co., 1980).

Shona time line

C.E.

200s Bantu-speaking peoples begin to arrive in Southern Africa.

900s Bambandyanalo/Mapungubwe trading center on Limpopo River.

1000s Major Iron-Age settlement, Leopard Kopje, built.

1100–1300 Bambandyanalo/Mapungubwe at its height.

1100s Great Zimbabwe building begins.

1300s–1400s Great Zimbabwe reaches height; wealth boosted by gold trade.

1480 Mutapa Empire breaks up; Rozvi dynasty emerges; by 1500 Great Zimbabwe abandoned; Shona civilization moves north to create Mutapa Empire.

1700s Rozvi Empire fragments.

1890 Cecil Rhodes's British South Africa Company establishes colony of Southern Rhodesia.

1896 Shona and Ndebele at war with British colonizers

1923 British government takes control of Southern Rhodesia; white immigration encouraged.

1965 Illegal white-minority rule established in Southern Rhodesia as Rhodesia.

1967–75 Guerrilla war fought against white Rhodesians.

1980 End of white-minority rule in Rhodesia, which is renamed Zimbabwe

See also ZIMBABWEANS: NATIONALITY

D. N. Beach. *The Shona and Their Neighbours* (Oxford, U.K.: Blackwell, 1994).

Paul Berliner. *The Soul of Mbira: Music and Traditions of the Shona People of Zimbabwe* (Berkeley: University of California Press, 1978).

Solomon M. Mutswairo. *Introduction to Shona Culture* (Zimbabwe: Juta, 1996).

Shope (Chope)

The Shope live in southern Mozambique, a country where they are considered to be among the earliest known inhabitants.

Sia

The Sia are closely related to the Manding. They live primarily in Mali and Burkina Faso.

Sidonians

Sidonians are the ancient people of Sidon, a city on the coast of modern-day Lebanon in the eastern Mediterranean. The Sidonians are often also termed Phoenicians in classical Greek texts, such as the *Iliad* and the *Odyssey*, and in the Old Testament. The city of Sidon was founded in the third millennium B.C.E., and by the second millennium it was a flourishing city. Athens was a major trading partner, and Hellenic civilization was a strong influence. Sidon was particularly known for its glass blowing and for purple dyes. The city and its people were ruled by, among others, the Assyrians, the Babylonians, Persia, Alexander the Great, the Ptolemys of Egypt, and the Romans. During the era of the Crusades (late 11th century until roughly the 14th century), the city was won and lost by the Crusaders and destroyed and rebuilt. The city flourished under Ottoman rule and in the late 18th century was used by the French as a port for the Syrian city of Damascus. In modern times, the city has yielded some important archaeological artifacts dating from the Phoenician era, and two Crusader castles still stand.

Sierra Leoneans: nationality (people of Sierra Leone)

GEOGRAPHY

The Republic of Sierra Leone is a coastal nation in West Africa. It has an area of approximately 28,000 square miles and borders two other countries; Guinea surrounds Sierra Leone to the north and east, and Liberia meets its southern border. Sierra Leone's coastline extends for 250 miles along the Atlantic Ocean. The Banana and Turtle Islands, which lie just off Sierra Leone's coast, are also part of its territory, as is the large island of Sherbro and numerous smaller islets.

Geographically, Sierra Leone consists of three broad zones running roughly parallel with the coast. The Atlantic shore is a mixture of sandy beaches and mangrove swamps extending inland to a broad low-lying coastal plain. The one exception is a small mountainous peninsula, known as the Sierra Leone Peninsula, which extends into the Atlantic Ocean in the northwest corner of the country. The mountains of the Sierra Leone Peninsula reach a maximum elevation of about 2,900 feet. East of the coastal plain is a zone of forested hills, which rise onto the inland plateau that forms the eastern segment of the country. The plateau has an elevation of between 1,000 and 2,000 feet, but there are a few isolated peaks in excess of 6,000 feet. The Loma Mountains, in the extreme east of Sierra Leone close to the border with Guinea, include the 6,390-foot peak of Mount Loma (also known as Mount Bintimani). Numerous rivers flow from the upland east toward the western coast.

Sierra Leone's capital city, Freetown, is situated on the northern tip of the Sierra Leone Peninsula. The peninsula and a natural inlet in the coast to its east form the largest natural harbor in West Africa and one of the largest natural harbors in the world. Freetown has been a center of West African maritime trade for centuries thanks to its exceptional anchorage. About a quarter of Sierra Leone's population lives in Freetown. Other major settlements include Bo, a former colonial administrative center in the center of the country, and Kenema, a town in the southeast. Both Bo and Kenema were situated on the railroad link traveling south and east of Freetown, but this line was closed in 1974.

INCEPTION AS A NATION

The early history of Sierra Leone is largely unknown, but archaeology has established that peoples using iron tools were present in the area by about 800 C.E. and that agriculture was being practiced on the coastal plains by about 1000. The history of modern Sierra Leone begins with the first European exploration of the coast. In 1462 Portuguese explorers named the mountains of the peninsula on which Freetown was later founded the Serra de Leão (or "Lion Moun-

SIERRA LEONEANS: NATIONALITY

nation:
Sierra Leone; Republic of Sierra Leone

derivation of name:
From the Portuguese name Serra de Leão (Lion Mountain)

government:
Constitutional democracy

capital:
Freetown

language:
English is the country's official language, but Krio (language of the Sierra Leone Creoles) is the nation's lingua franca. Mende is the principal tongue of the south, Temne of the north.

religion:
About 60 percent of the population is Muslim; indigenous faiths are followed by about 30 percent; and Christians constitute 10 percent.

earlier inhabitants:
Unknown

demographics:
Mende and Temne peoples make up about 60 percent of the population (30 percent each). Other groups include the Limba (10 percent), the Kono (9 percent), the Manding (6 percent), and Sierra Leone Creoles (5 percent). The remaining 10 percent include peoples from about 15 other West African ethnic groups as well as small groups of Sierra Leonean–Lebanese and Europeans.

Sierra Leoneans: nationality time line

C.E.

1787 Freetown colony established by British abolitionists; former slaves from Britain, Canada, and Jamaica are the first colonists.

1807 Britain outlaws the transatlantic slave trade.

1808 Freetown comes under direct British administration.

1896 Britain declares a protectorate over Sierra Leone.

1898 Bai Bureh, leader of the Temne people, leads a revolt against British taxation.

1954 Milton Margai becomes Sierra Leone's first elected prime minister.

1961 Sierra Leone become an independent nation.

1967 Newly elected Prime Minister Siaka Stevens removed from power in a military coup.

1968 Siaka Stevens returned to power following two further coups.

1971 Sierra Leone becomes a republic, with Stevens as its first president.

1971–73 Guinean troops deployed in Sierra Leone to support Stevens's government.

1978 Sierra Leone becomes a one-party state. A referendum supports the adoption of a constitution in which Stevens's All People's Congress (APC) becomes the only legal political party.

1985 Joseph Saidu Momoh installed as new president following Stevens's retirement.

1991 Revolutionary United Front (RUF) guerrillas seize control of towns close to Sierra Leone's border with Liberia; start of civil war.

1992 Momoh deposed in a military coup led by Valentine Strasser.

1996 Strasser deposed in a military coup. Ahmad Tejan Kabbah elected president.

1997 Kabbah deposed in a military coup led by Johnny Paul Koroma. Armed Forces Revolutionary Council (AFRC) set up; constitution suspended; political parties outlawed.

1998 United Nations–sanctioned Economic Community of West African States Monitoring Group (ECOMOG) forces, led by Nigeria, take control of Freetown. Kabbah returns to government.

1999 Major battle for control of Freetown between ECOMOG forces and RUF rebels ends in rebel defeat.

2000 Hundreds of ECOMOG troops captured by rebels. British forces subdue rebels. RUF leader Foday Sankoh arrested.

2002 Disarmament of rebels complete; civil war ends. Kabbah wins presidential elections.

2006 Former Liberian president Charles Taylor arrested in Nigeria and brought before Sierra Leone's Special War Crimes Court.

2007 Ernest Bai Koroma of the APC wins presidential elections.

---

tain") and noted the presence of the exceptional natural harbor that they overshadowed. In the 1670s British slave traders established a base on Bunce Island, which lies at the mouth of the Sierra Leone River estuary about 20 miles from the site of modern Freetown. For the next 130 years Bunce Island became one of the most important transshipment points for the transport of slaves from West Africa to British territories in the Caribbean and North America.

In the late 18th century political pressure for an abolition of the slave trade began to grow in Britain. As a response to anti-abolitionist claims that black Africans were incapable of administering themselves, abolitionists determined to establish a colony of former African slaves in Africa. In 1787 a group of former slaves collected from the streets of London were sent to the Sierra Leone Peninsula to set up such a colony, which was named Freetown. These first settlers were soon joined by former slaves from Canada, who had gained their freedom by fighting for the British in the American War of Independence, and by former slaves from Jamaica.

Poor preparation, unfamiliar conditions, and aggression from indigenous peoples almost destroyed the initial Freetown settlement, but the colony persisted and grew in strength after the abolition of the slave trade.

In 1807 Britain outlawed the slave trade and Freetown became the base from which British naval ships enforced the ban along the West Coast of Africa. Africans released from illegal slave traders were usually brought to Freetown and added to the population of the colony. The Freetown colony came under the direct protection of the British government in 1908 and was slowly expanded in subsequent years through treaties with the leaders of indigenous peoples and purchases of land. Although many of the former slaves who were settled in Freetown were of West African origin, they came from a large number of diverse ethnic backgrounds. Since there was little possibility for them to return to their original homes, most stayed in the colony and became part of a bewilderingly complex ethnic mosaic that gradually formed its own cultural identity. The descendants of these settlers became known as Sierra Leone CREOLES (or Krios)

In 1896 Britain declared a protectorate over a wide area corresponding to the present-day territory of Sierra Leone, although this was administered separately from the Freetown colony. By this time other former slave colonies had been established along the coast, notably on Sherbro Island. The indigenous peoples of the area opposed British rule, particularly the imposition of taxes, and organized a series of rebellions. The most notable of these was under Bai Bureh, the leader of the TEMNE people, in 1898.

The early 20th century was generally peaceful in British-ruled Sierra Leone. Commercial exploitation of the interior was facilitated by the construction of a railroad, and the British and Sierra Leone Creoles steadily exerted their authority over the entire country from their strongholds on the coast. A constitution adopted in 1924 provided for a Legislative Council with limited powers and a second, adopted in 1951, allowed for more general, but not universal, suffrage, resulting in a Creole majority on the council. The Legislative Council was abolished in 1957 to be replaced by a House of Representatives consisting of elected members, and in 1958 the House elected Milton Margai as Sierra Leone's first prime minister. Sierra Leone achieved full independence in April 1961 as a Commonwealth Nation, with Milton Mar-

gai continuing to serve as prime minister. The country became a republic in 1971.

CULTURAL IDENTITY

Sierra Leone's postindependence history has been chaotic and bloody. Between 1967 and 1990 there were three military coups, numerous changes of government, and a series of violent political demonstrations and rebellions. In 1978 Sierra Leone became a one-party state, the only legal party being the All People's Congress (APC), and in 1985 Joseph Saidu Momoh became the country's president. Momoh's rule was characterized by increasingly serious abuses of power, including widespread corruption and the violent suppression of political opposition. A rebel group calling itself the Revolutionary United Front (RUF) began an insurgency against the government in 1991 by attacking and occupying villages close to Sierra Leone's eastern border with Liberia. Momoh's regime proved unable to prevent the rebels from gaining ground, and he was deposed in a military coup in 1992 that established the National Provisional Ruling Council (NPRC) as Sierra Leone's executive body. The NPRC had no more success than Momoh at containing the rebellion, and the RUF quickly took control of the Kono District of eastern Sierra Leone and its commercially important diamond mines.

Conflict between the RUF and successive governments in Freetown continued for more than 10 years until 2002. Sierra Leone's civil war was one of the most brutal and destructive wars in African history. Tens of thousands of people were killed, many of them noncombatants, and as many as 2 million people (a quarter of the population) were displaced from their homes. The RUF rebels were notorious for their practice of amputating the limbs of civilians in captured towns, although both sides committed atrocities and made extensive use of child soldiers in frontline fighting. Various other armed groups became involved in the fighting including the forces of Liberian rebel leader Charles Taylor (*see also* LIBERIANS: NATIONALITY), troops from Guinea, private military contractors from South Africa, and the combined forces of the Economic Community of West African States Monitoring Group (ECOMOG)—a multilateral peacekeeping force formed from the militaries of Nigeria, Ghana, Guinea, Gambia, Liberia, Mali, Burkina Faso, and Niger. Although the war began as an attempt to overthrow the government of President Momoh, the potential wealth to be gained from control of Sierra

Leone's diamond mines became the leading motivating force for its continuation. The illegal trade in diamonds from Sierra Leone (often referred to as the trade in "blood diamonds") provided much of the funding for the activities of rebel groups both within Sierra Leone and across the border in Liberia. Sierra Leone's civil war was ended by the intervention of British troops in 2000 and the capture of the leader of the RUF by government forces.

The civil war crippled Sierra Leone, leaving tens of thousands physically mutilated, millions displaced, and thousands of former child soldiers psychologically traumatized. The country's economy was devastated, and Sierra Leoneans become one of the world's most impoverished peoples during the course of the war. Lawlessness and banditry had become commonplace by the closing stages of the conflict. Since 2002 a Truth and Reconciliation Commission has attempted to gather evidence against those responsible for the worst atrocities, and former President Charles Taylor of Liberia has been put on trial by Sierra Leonean authorities for war crimes.

There are between 15 and 20 ethnic groups in Sierra Leone, depending on methods of categorization. The two largest are the MENDE and Temne people, each accounting for about 30 percent of the population. The Mende predominate in the south and east of the country while the Temne are most numerous in the north. The great majority of the Temne are Muslim. The majority of Mende are Christian. Other significant ethnic groups include the LIMBA, who also live in the north; the KONO, who give their name to the diamond-rich eastern province; and the Manding, who are the descendants of the people of the medieval Mali Empire. The Sierra Leone Creoles, the descendents of the freed slaves who founded the Freetown colony, make up about 10 percent of the population and are restricted largely to modern Freetown. Sierra Leone is also home to an unusual cultural group known as the Sierra Leonean-Lebanese. These are the descendants of LEBANESE settlers who began arrived in Sierra Leone in the 1890s. The first Lebanese to settle in Sierra Leone were Maronite Christians (see MARONITES), although later groups tended to be Muslims. The Lebanese were among the first foreigners to become involved in Sierra Leone's diamond export trade when deposits were first discovered in the country in the 1930s. Today they make up about 2 percent of the population. Perhaps surprisingly, given Sierra Leone's violent his-

An ornate ivory vessel created by a Sapi artist. The Sapi were a people of the coastal region of Sierra Leone who traded with Portuguese explorers in the late 15th century.

tory, ethnic and religious differences have rarely been the source of conflict. During the civil conflict the warring militias paid little attention to the ethnic background of their victims. Power and wealth were the main motivating factors rather than any attempt to gain political autonomy for particular ethnic or religious groups.

Since 2002 Sierra Leone has gradually been recovering from the effects of its civil war. The democratic system that has been in place since the 2002 elections has delivered substantively representative government, and efforts have been made to tackle the endemic corruption that was one of the leading causes of the war, particularly in the diamond industry. The last United Nations peacekeeping troops left the country in 2005, and elections in 2007 brought a peaceful transfer of power from the ruling party to the former opposition for the first time in decades.

FURTHER READING

Joe A. D. Alie. *A New History of Sierra Leone* (New York: St. Martin's, 1990).

Margaret Binns. *Sierra Leone* (Oxford, England; Santa Barbara, Calif.: Clio Press, 1992).

Greg Campbell. *Blood Diamonds: Tracing the Deadly Path of the World's Most Precious Stones* (Boulder: Westview Press, 2002).

C. Magbaily Fyle and Cyril P. Foray. *Historical Dictionary of Sierra Leone* (Lanham, Md: Scarecrow Press, 2006).

John-Peter Pham. *The Sierra Leonean Tragedy: History and Global Dimensions* (New York: Nova Science Publishers, 2006).

Tanja Schümer. *New Humanitarianism: Britain and Sierra Leone, 1997–2003*. Palgrave studies in development (Basingstoke; UK: Palgrave Macmillan, 2008).

Sihanaka

The Sihanaka are a MADAGASCAN PEOPLE who live inland in the northern half of the island.

Siku

The Siku are part of the KRU cluster of peoples. The Kru are one of the largest ethnic groups in Liberia.

Sinyar (Shamya)

The Sinyar live on and either side of the border between Sudan and Chad.

Sisala *See* SASALA.

Sisi

The Sisi are one of the many TEKE groups. The Teke live in Gabon, the Republic of the Congo, and the Democratic Republic of the Congo.

Soga (Basoga; Lukenyi; Lusoga)

The Soga live in southeastern Uganda, where they are one of the larger ethnic groups.

Sogdians (al-Sughd; Soghdians)

Sogdians are an ancient people of Central Asia whose homeland was called Sogdiana, in modern-day Uzbekistan. They were an Iranian people who continued to practice Zororastrianism up into classical Islamic times. Their earliest settlements can be dated to between 1000 and 500 B.C.E. They were ruled by the ancient Iranian dynasty of the ACHAEMENIDS and later were conquered by Alexander the Great. In the second century B.C.E. they were invaded by the ŚAKAS, an ancient Iranian dynasty, and Yueh-chih peoples, who ruled in Bactria and India from about 128 B.C.E. until about 450 C.E. Despite these invasions, the Sogdians remained a prosperous civilization, and their major cities of Samarkand and Bukhara flourished. In pre-Islamic times as well as in the Islamic era, Sogdian merchants were frequent travelers along the Silk Road to the far reaches of northern China and established colonies there, as recorded in both Chinese and Islamic histories. Under the Samanid dynasty (874–999), a Muslim Persian dynasty that ruled over much of Central Asia, Sogdian lands were an important center of Muslim culture and remained so until the Mongol invasions of the 13th century.

Solongo (Basolongo)

The Solongo are one of the larger KONGO subgroups. They live in northwestern Angola and the southwest of the Democratic Republic of the Congo.

Somalis: nationality (people of Somalia)

SOMALIS: NATIONALITY

nation:
Somalia

derivation of name:
From the Somali people

government:
Transitional

capital:
Mogadishu

language:
Somali is the country's official language. English, Italian, and Arabic are spoken by sections of the population.

religion:
About 99 percent of the population are Sunni Muslim; there is a very small Christian minority.

earlier inhabitants:
Cushitic peoples

demographics:
About 85 percent of the population is Somali. Other East African peoples and a small number of Arabs make up the remaining 15 percent.

GEOGRAPHY

Somalia is a coastal nation in East Africa. It is situated on a large peninsula commonly known as the Horn of Africa (or the Somali Peninsula), which protrudes from the east coast of Africa immediately south of the Red Sea and the Gulf of Aden. Somalia has an area of approximately 246,000 square miles and borders three other nations: Djibouti meets Somalia's border in the extreme northwest of the country, Ethiopia lies to the west, and Kenya to the southwest. Somalia has about 1,900 miles of coastline. Its north coast is on the Gulf of Aden (part of the Arabian Sea), while its east coast extends along the Indian Ocean. Several regions in the north of the country are effectively self-governing but do not constitute internationally recognized national entities.

Somalia's northern coast is backed by a narrow semi-arid coastal plain known as the Guban, which is in turn backed by the Karkaar Mountains. The Karkaar range begins in neighboring Ethiopia and extends from west to east across the northern portion of the country, ending at the most easterly point of the peninsula in sheer cliffs. Mount Shimbiris, the highest peak in Somalia at a little over 8,000 feet, is part of the Karkaar Mountains. Southwest of the mountains is an extremely arid central plateau with an elevation of about 2,000 feet. Numerous eroded gullies cross this plateau, but there are no year-round watercourses.

Toward the southeastern coast the land declines onto a broad plain that is bisected

Somalis: nationality time line

C.E.

seventh century Muslim sultanate of Adel founded on Somalia's northern coast.

16th century Sultanate of Adel defeated by Ethiopian and Portuguese forces and disintegrates into smaller states.

1860s France establishes a presence on Somalia's northwest coast (present-day Djibouti).

1887 Britain established the British Somaliland protectorate in northern Somalia.

1889 Italy establishes the Italian Somaliland protectorate in the south of the country.

1936 Italy captures Somali-speaking portion of Ethiopia and combines it with Italian Somaliland to form Italian East Africa.

1940 Italy captures British Somaliland.

1940 Britain retakes British Somaliland and captures Italian Somaliland.

1948 Britain cedes Somali-speaking Ogaden region to Ethiopia.

1950 Italian Somaliland becomes a United Nations trust territory under Italian administration.

1956 Italian Somaliland granted autonomy and renamed Somalia.

1960 Former Italian Somaliland and British Somaliland united as the independent nation of Somalia.

1963–64 Border disputes with Kenya and Ethiopia

1969 Muhammad Siad Barre takes power after a coup.

1970 Barre declares Somalia a one-party socialist state.

1974–75 Serious drought in Somalia

1977–78 War with Ethiopia over control of the Ogaden region; Somalia defeated by Soviet-backed Ethiopian forces and Cuban troops.

1991 Barre overthrown; United Somali Congress (USC) forms government in Mogadishu. USC splits to form two warring factions. Former British Somaliland declares independence as the Republic of Somaliland.

1992 Widespread famine as warring factions disrupt agricultural production. U.S.-led United Nations Task Force deployed to safeguard relief efforts.

1993 Pakistani and U.S. troops killed in interclan fighting.

1995 United Nations peacekeeping forces leave Somalia.

1998 Northeast territory declares autonomy as Puntland.

2000 Transitional Federal Government (TFG) established after peace conference in Djibouti.

2006 Widespread fighting for control of the south between the Islamic Courts Union (ICU) and TFG forces. ICU defeated with the help of Ethiopian troops.

2007 United Nations authorizes deployment of African Union peacekeeping troops in Somalia. Conflict between Islamist insurgents and government forces displace more than 300,000 Somalis.

2008 United Nations votes to allow national navies to enter Somali territorial waters to conduct operations against pirates.

---

from north to south by the country's two most important rivers. The Shebelle River rises in the highlands of Ethiopia and flows southeast through Somalia toward the Indian Ocean. A few miles from the coast, however, the course of the river turns sharply southwest and parallels the line of the coast until it joins the Jubba River. The Shebelle River is seasonal—its waters flow only as far as the Jubba after heavy rains, which come between March and May if at all. The Jubba River also rises in Ethiopia and flows southeast through Somalia toward the Indian

Ocean. The Jubba is Somalia's only permanent watercourse, but it is not navigable for most of its length. The plains between the Shebbelle and Jubba Rivers are low-lying and agriculturally productive. The area between the Jubba River and the border with Kenya is productive pastureland. Both areas are prone to flooding.

The country's capital city, Mogadishu, is situated on the southeast coast close to the terminal southwest bend in the Shebelle River. It is estimated that about a third of Somalis live in urban areas, the great majority of these in Mogadishu, but the extreme confusion produced by Somalia's civil war makes accurate figures difficult to compile.

INCEPTION AS A NATION

The first recorded evidence of the inhabitants of the area known today as Somalia comes from a first-century C.E. Greek text that describes trading opportunities in the Red Sea and the Arabian Sea. The Romanized writer of the text (known as the *Periplus of the Erythraean Sea*) describes a series of port cities along the northern and southeastern coast of the Somali Peninsula and three coastal kingdoms; the Himyarite Kingdom in the vicinity of present-day Djibouti, the Hadhramaut Kingdom on the tip of the peninsula, and the Bazrangid Kingdom in the vicinity of present-day Mogadishu.

Trade between the Somali Peninsula and the Arabian Peninsula has taken place for thousands of years, as has the exchange of cultural ideas. Islam arrived in Somalia from the Arabian Peninsula in the seventh century, and Somalia has been a predominantly Muslim nation from that time. Relations with its predominantly Christian neighbor, Ethiopia, remained peaceful for centuries thanks in large part to a prohibition against attacking Ethiopia issued by the prophet Muhammad, some of whose early followers were granted asylum in Ethiopia after they migrated there to escape persecution in Arabia (*see* ETHIOPIANS: NATIONALITY). In the 14th century Ethiopia extended its territory into parts of northern Somalia, but these areas remained Muslim. In the 16th century Ahmad ibn Ibrihim al Ghazi, the ruler of the Sultanate of Adel, a Muslim province of the Ethiopian Empire, rebelled against Ethiopian rule and created a state that encompassed large areas of Ethiopia and present-day Somalia. Ghazi was prevented from conquering the whole of Ethiopia and forcibly converting its inhabitants to Islam only by the intervention of Portuguese troops. Other powerful states that arose within the territory of present-day Somalia were the Ajuuraan Kingdom, which ruled the area around Mogadishu and the valley of the Shebelle River between the 14th and the 17th centuries, and the Kingdom of Majeerteenia, which was established on the tip of the Somali Peninsula from the mid-18th century and survived until the beginning of the 20th century.

European interest in the Somali Peninsula became critical in the second half of the 19th century. With the opening of the Suez Canal in 1869, the Horn of Africa and the southern tip of the Arabian Peninsula became strategically important because they overlooked the approaches to the Bab al Mandeb Strait (also known as the Mandab Strait) at the southern end of the Red Sea. Britain had already established a presence in Aden, on the north side of the Arabian Sea, in 1839 and wanted to control the Somali port of Berbera on the south side as well. From 1884 to 1886 Britain signed a series of protection agreements with local rulers along the northern coast of the Somali Peninsula that led to the establishment of the British Somaliland Protectorate in 1887. The French established French Somaliland in the area of present-day Djibouti at the same time (*see* DJIBOUTIANS: NATIONALITY), and in 1889 Italy seized southern Somalia, naming it Italian Somaliland.

Britain took little interest in its Somaliland protectorate, regarding it as a supply point for its Aden colony, but from 1899 it faced one of the most determined and protracted local rebellions in the history of British imperialism. Muhammad Abdullah Hasan, a Muslim scholar, led a rebellion and a wider war against Ethiopia that continued until 1920. The rebellion was finally ended by a series of bombing campaigns against centers of resistance that led to Abdullah Hasan's death. By this time, however, up to a third of the population of British Somaliland had been killed in the fighting or had starved as a result of the disruption caused by the conflict. Britain invested very little in infrastructure during these two decades, while the Italians in southern Somalia made considerable investments as they sought to establish an agriculturally productive colony over the same period. This imbalance led to the dominance of the south in the postindependence period and can be seen as one of the causes of the later Somali civil war.

At the beginning of World War II Italian forces briefly conquered British Somaliland, uniting the future territory of Somalia under one administration for the first time, but Britain rapidly reversed the situation by recapturing British Somaliland and overrunning Italian Somaliland by the end of 1941. In 1948 Britain ceded the Ogaden region, which had been captured from Ethiopia by the Italians, to Ethiopia, but British administration in the rest of Italian Somaliland continued until 1950 when the United Nations declared that the territory would return to Italian administration for a period of 10 years, after which it would become independent. With the help of United Nations funding, the 1950s were a period of considerable economic growth for southern Somalia, and a mature indigenous political culture became established under the assurance of eventual independence. The same was not true in British Somaliland, where economic development was sluggish and political parties had to fight for similar assurances from the British government.

British Somaliland gained full independence on June 26, 1960, and Italian Somaliland on July 1 of the same year. The two territories immediately united to become the Somali Republic and the following year held elections in which Aden Abdullah Osman Daar became the nation's first president.

CULTURAL IDENTITY

Somalia's development was hampered by two critical issues from the moment of independence—the great economic and cultural disparity between the north and the south, and the issue of sovereignty over the Ogaden region. The British ceded Ogaden to Ethiopia in 1948, but it had been a source of contention between the two nations for centuries before this date. Traditionally, the majority of the population was Muslim and ethnically Somali. Wars had raged over this desolate terrain many times as Muslim kingdoms pushed west into Ethiopia or as Christian Ethiopian kings pushed east toward the sea. From its inception the Somali government supported the concept of a "Greater Somalia," which would see the Somali-majority regions of Djibouti, Ethiopia, and Kenya conjoined with the existing Somali state. Intermittent border clashes with Kenya and Ethiopia began almost immediately and continued for many years. In 1975 the Somali government stated its formal support for the Western Somali Liberation Front, a rebel group that had been conducting an independence campaign in the Ogaden region against the Ethiopian government for several years. In 1977 Somali forces invaded the Ogaden

A Somali boy leading a heavily laden camel

and made rapid progress into Ethiopian territory. The tide of the war was turned, however, when the Soviet Union switched its support to Ethiopia and provided the government with large amounts of weapons and funding. The following year Somali forces were forced out of Ethiopia by the newly equipped Ethiopian forces and a large contingent of Cuban troops deployed to support the country's communist government. The war had a negative effect on Somalia's economy and increased discontent with the government of Siad Barre.

Siad Barre had come to power in 1969 as the result of a military coup. He established a one-party state headed by the Supreme Revolutionary Council (SRC) and implemented an economic ideology known as "scientific socialism." Barre's regime nationalized many foreign companies, formed compulsory construction gangs from the ranks of the unemployed, and initiated a national literacy program based around the adoption of a new Latin script for the Somali language. Severe drought conditions, which struck Somalia in 1973 and 1974, precipitated a national emergency and heightened discontent at the perceived inefficiency of the government. Somalia's defeat in the Ogaden War in 1978 and incursions into Somali territory by Ethiopian troops in 1982 added to the political turmoil. By the late 1980s several rebel groups had emerged in Somalia. Some were backed by the Ethiopian government, and many shared similar secessionist aims. Among the armed groups active in Somalia at the time were the Somali Salvation Democratic Front (SSDF), the Somali Democratic Alliance (SDA), the Somali Democratic Movement (SDM), the Somali National Movement (SNM), the Somali Patriot Movement (SPM), and the United Somali Congress (USC). All of these groups were essentially clan based, led by a local clan leader, and brutally violent. Government forces were equally ruthless, leading to great disruption and suffering among the populations of affected areas.

After years of almost continuous small-scale conflict, Barre was forced from office and fled the capital city. The forces of the United Somali Congress (USC) occupied Mogadishu and set up a de facto government, but this rapidly fragmented into two rival camps. The USC was made up of members of the HAWIYE clan, one of the largest subgroups of the Somali people and the predominant ethnic subgroup of southern Somalia and neighboring northeast Kenya. Although the USC had taken the capital, they failed to reach agreement with other rebel groups that were strong in other parts of the country. The Somali National Movement (SNM), the political wing of the ISAAQ clan, held northwest Somalia (roughly the area of the former British Somaliland) and declared an independent state known as the Republic of Somaliland in May 1991, although this was not internationally recognized. The lack of an effective central

government and the continued depredations of rebel groups in other parts of the country led to a complete breakdown of public services and massive disruption to agriculture. By the end of 1992 hundreds of thousands of Somalis had died or migrated across the country's borders. Efforts by the international community to supply food aid were hampered by the activities of armed groups that appropriated the supplies for themselves. The United Nations sanctioned the deployment of a large U.S.-led multinational force to safeguard relief operations late in 1992, and by early 1993, 34,000 troops were in place in Somalia.

The presence of the United Nations Task Force reduced violence in the country for a time, but in the absence of a central government structure, a plethora of local armed groups soon began to reemerge. In Mogadishu the two USC factions, one led by Ali Mahdi Muhammad and the other by Muhammad Farrah Aideed, continued to struggle for control. UN Task Force troops were drawn into the conflict, resulting in the deaths of 23 Pakistani soldiers and 18 U.S. soldiers in 1993. U.S. forces withdrew from the country in 1995, and Mogadishu immediately descended into chaos as the USC factions fought inconclusive battles for control of the capital. In 1998 the Somali Salvation Democratic Front (SSDF) declared the autonomy of the northeast portion of the Somali Peninsula under the title of Puntland. At the end of the 20th century, Somalia had effectively been split into four separate entities: Puntland in the northeast, the Republic of Somaliland in the northwest, and the two areas of southern Somalia controlled by the opposing USC factions—Aideed south of Mogadishu and Ali Mahdi north of Mogadishu.

Peace talks held in 2000 succeeded in establishing a Transitional Federal Government (TFG) that was intended to stop the fighting in the south and negotiate with the Republic of Somaliland and Puntland for a long-term solution to the de facto division of the country. The leaders of the various Somali rebel groups were Muslim, as is most of the population of Somalia, but their political aims had been largely secular. Following the collapse of the state's institutions in 1991, a network of sharia-based Islamic courts that had grown up throughout southern Somalia came to represent the only widely accepted judicial system in the country. The leaders of these courts formed a political union in 1999, known as the Islamic Courts Union (ICU), and combined their security forces to form a powerful new militia. From 2000 the ICU opposed the newly established TFG and set about trying to establish a fundamentalist Muslim state. By 2006 they controlled much of southern Somalia, but a series of defeats at the hands of TFG forces and Ethiopian troops removed them from power early in 2007. Since 2007 the ICU has conducted a guerrilla war against the government, particularly through its militant youth wing known as the Hizbul Shabaab (or the Shabaab).

Somalia ceased to exist as a unified national entity in 1991, although the independence of the various autonomous regions that have subsequently formed within its territory have not been internationally recognized and a federal structure that reunites them as part of a single state may yet emerge. At the present time there is no national cultural identity to speak of. The Somali people retain a sense of ethnic identity, but this extends beyond the borders of Somalia into Djibouti and parts of Ethiopia and Kenya and has been severely strained by decades of conflict between rival clan groupings.

Somali society is clan based; families traced through the paternal line form the basic social and political units. Traditionally Somalia's clans have been divided into two groups, a group of "noble" clans known collectively as the Samaal, and a less prestigious group known as the Saab. The largest Samaal clans are the DAROD, Isaaq, Hawiye, and DIR, while the largest Saab clans are the Rahanweyn and the DIGIL. Each clan has numerous subclan divisions. A group of occupational clans made up a third tier of traditional Somali society, and their members were excluded from marrying into the other clans. They lived in separate settlements and engaged in occupations such as metalworking or tanning that were passed from father to son. The Samaal were traditionally nomadic pastoralists, while the Saab were traditionally sedentary farmers. Political affiliation in modern Somalia is almost exclusively clan based, and the civil war that has ravaged the country since 1991 has been conducted between militias loyal to particular clans or subclans.

Islam has played a role in Somali society since the seventh century, although it probably did not became the faith of the majority until the 10th or 11th century. After independence in 1960 the norms of secular government established under colonial rule continued. Somalis practiced a fairly liberal form of Islam that did not preclude public entertainment such as music and cinemas. Women played a traditional role in society according to Muslim precepts but were not generally required to be veiled and were not completely excluded from economic life. During the regime of Said Barre from 1970 to 1991, the influence of Islam was diminished as the government sought to subordinate traditional ways of life to a vision of a socialist secular society. The collapse of central government in 1991 brought a resurgence in faith and traditional clan-based life, since these were the only institutions capable of providing social support. A fundamentalist Muslim regime ruled southern Somalia in the early 2000s, and since its collapse in 2007, numerous attacks against the authorities had the aim of undermining the secular government.

FURTHER READING

Mohamed Diriye Abdullahi. *Culture and Customs of Somalia* (Westport, Conn: Greenwood Press, 2001).

Hussein Mohamed Adam. *From Tyranny to Anarchy: The Somali Experience* (Trenton, N.J.: Red Sea Press, 2008).

I. M. Lewis. *Understanding Somalia and Somaliland: Culture, History, Society* (New York: Columbia University, 2008).

Shaul Shay. *Somalia between Jihad and Restoration* (New Brunswick, N.J.: Transaction Publishers, 2008).

Somba (Tamberma)

The Somba live in northwestern Benin and neighboring parts of Togo. They are sometimes classified as an EWE people; their language is a part of the MOLE-DAGBANE group.

Songhay

The Songhay people emerged as a distinct ethnic group under the influence of the historic Songhay Empire, which was one of the most powerful precolonial West African states. Today roughly half of the Songhay people live in eastern Mali, while the other half live in western Niger, where they are one of the largest ethnic groups; a small minority live in northern Benin. Their language, also called Songhay, is used by traders over a large area of West Africa. The Songhay language is a Nilo-Saharan language. The Songhay religion has been Islam for many centuries.

The Songhay state was founded in about 750 C.E. on the Niger River on an important trade route. The capital was on the Niger River at Gao, which is still a major Malian city today. From about 1240 to the 1340s Songhay was part of the Empire of Mali, but under Sunni Ali (r. 1464–92) Songhay became the most powerful empire in West Africa, absorbing much of Mali's lands. Askia Muhammad (r. 1493–1528) extended the boundaries of Songhay to their utmost, and Songhay remained powerful until it was conquered by the Moroccans in 1591.

Songye

The Songye are a subgroup of the LUBA peoples of Central Africa. The Songye inhabit a region in the southeast of the Democratic Republic of the Congo, concentrated around the town of Kabinda and are also dispersed mainly between the Lubufu and Lomami Rivers. Other Songye groups, such as the Bangu-Bangus, also live in the Democratic Republic of the Congo.

According to oral histories, the Songye were the founders of the powerful Luba Kingdom, which covered the lands between the Lubilash and Lualaba Rivers. The Songye are said to have migrated into this region from the north, led by their *kongolo* (king), and they settled on the Lubilash River. The first *kongolo* married the queen of the local people, the Kalundwe, founding the Luba kingdom. The Luba kingdom reached its height under Songye rulers, but they were displaced by the Kunda (who also migrated into the region from the north) sometime in the 15th century.

Soninke

The Soninke are a large ethnic group of well over 2 million people who are widespread in many countries of West Africa. The largest Soninke communities can be found in Mali, Burkina Faso, and Ivory Coast, and smaller numbers live in Guinea-Bissau, Senegal, Gambia, Guinea, and Mauritania. The Soninke language belongs to the MANDÉ language group, but most Soninke speak the language of the people they live among instead of Soninke (or Azer).

The Soninke people were the citizens of the historic state of Ghana, which lay to the north of the Senegal and Niger Rivers in what is now western Mali and southern Mauritania. The Soninke eventually overthrew the Maga, the people who founded the state. By the 1200s, Ghana had grown powerful from the trade in gold mined by the Soninke and by salt, and it controlled the West African ends of the trans-Saharan trade routes.

Soso *See* SUSU.

Sotho (Basotho)

The Sotho are one of the principal BANTU-speaking peoples of southern Africa. The majority of the Sotho live in South Africa, but they also make up the majority of the population of the nation of Lesotho (*see* BASOTHO: NATIONALITY). In South Africa about 2.5 million Northern Sotho live in northern and eastern Transvaal province, and a further 2 million Southern Sotho live in the Orange Free State.

ORIGINS

The Bantu-speaking ancestors of the Sotho originated in present-day eastern Nigeria. There, over 2,000 years ago, they developed a way of life based on farming and ironworking. These people gradually spread southward, and by about 1000 c.e. they had settled on the Highveld—the high arid plains to the west of the Drakensberg Mountains—and in the valleys of the Orange, Vaal, and Tugela Rivers. They slowly absorbed the existing population, the KHOISAN, adopting many aspects of their culture including elements of their languages and many of their musical instruments. By about 1400, the Sotho had established their main clans (several families who share the same ancestor or ancestors). Each clan adopted an animal, such as a wildcat, porcupine, or a crocodile, as its symbol, or totem. Groups of these clans eventually came together to form the three major divisions of the Sotho people: the Northern Sotho, the Southern Sotho, and the TSWANA (or Western Sotho). The Tswana are now generally viewed as a separate ethnic group from the other Sotho peoples.

LANGUAGE

Northern Sotho (or Sesotho sa Leboa) is spoken in South Africa, and the closely related Sesotho in Lesotho.

HISTORY

During the 17th century, the PEDI group of clans became dominant among the Northern Sotho and established the Bapedi Empire, which lasted for over 200 years. During the same period, the Southern Sotho were living in an age of relative peace and prosperity. This was to last until the 1820s, when the lives of all the Sotho peoples were disrupted by the Mfecane—two decades of invasion, warfare, and famine triggered by the ZULU upheavals east of the Drakensberg Mountains. After the Mfecane, the Bapedi lands were taken over by AFRIKANERS, or Boers. This region (now Transvaal) eventually became part of South Africa. The introduction of apartheid in 1948 made the Northern Sotho third-class citizens in their own land. In 1959 the South African government attempted to divide the black population from the whites by creating homelands, or Bantustans, in which black people were forced to live. The Northern Sotho were allocated a number of separate regions within Transvaal, collectively known as the Lebowa homeland.

In the south, the only people to resist the Mfecane were some members of the Kwena (Crocodile) clan, led by their chief Moshoeshoe I, who was able to unify the Southern Sotho clans and establish the Basuto Kingdom. After losing about two thirds of his country's arable land to the Afrikaners' newly formed Orange Free State, Moshoeshoe requested British protection. In 1868 the country became the British protectorate of Basutoland, which remained a British colony until it gained independence in 1966 as Lesotho.

The abolition of apartheid laws in 1991 gave all South African citizens equal rights. In 1994 the Land Rights Bill—designed to help people in South Africa regain land lost since 1913 because of unjust laws—was introduced.

CULTURE

The Sotho have a long history of agriculture. Until the late 19th century, they accumulated wealth in the form of cattle and exported grain to other parts of southern Africa. But since then, a large proportion of the able-bodied men have become migrant laborers who leave their homes to work in the gold, diamond, and coal mines and other industries of South Africa. In the rural areas, the women they leave behind have to raise the children and tend the farms, often single-handedly. They raise cattle, sheep, goats, and pigs; corn, sorghum, wheat, and vegetables are grown, but farming is hampered by overgrazing and soil erosion. Most depend on the money the men send back to them. Many people have left the land to live in the lowland towns that serve as temporary homes for migrant workers on their way to and from the mining and industrial areas of South Africa. Typical of these "camp towns" are those along the northwestern and western borders of Lesotho, including Teyateyaneng, Leribe, Mafeteng, and the capital, Maseru.

The Sotho have a rich culture of poetry, song, dance, and storytelling. This includes *lithoko,* or praise poems; *lifela,* songs describ-

---

Sotho time line

C.E.

200s Bantu-speaking peoples begin to arrive in Southern Africa.

by 1400 Emergence of Sotho clans

1600s–1800s Bapedi Empire of Northern Sotho Pedi clan

1819–1839 Mfecane: period of mass migrations and wars; Boers colonize Northern Sotho.

1824 Moshoeshoe founds Basuto Kingdom.

1851–52 Sotho-British wars I and II: British withdraw from Sotho land.

1855 Height of Basuto Kingdom

1858 Basuto at war with Boers

1860–67 Sotho and Venda drive Boers south of Olifants River.

1865–68 Basuto at war with Boers; Basuto made a British colony.

1880–81 "Gun War": Sotho rebel when British try to disarm them.

1907 Nationalist movements emerge; Progressive Association formed.

1913 South African Sotho restricted to inadequate "native reserves."

1966 Basuto independent as Lesotho (a constitutional monarchy).

See also Basotho: NATIONALITY

---

ing the life of migrant laborers; and *tumellano,* in which large groups of people sing together in harmony.

Government and Society

The main social levels of Sotho society are clan groups, individual clans, lineages, and families. The members of each clan share a common name referring to the originator or founding father of that clan. Within each clan are lineages. Several lineages comprise a clan. The lineages are divided into families, and groups of families live together in villages.

The Sotho are now ruled by democratic central government structures, and so while the traditional hierarchy of chiefs has lost much of its power, it still survives as a social force. At the top of the hierarchy is the paramount chief or king, and below him are the chiefs, subchiefs, and headmen. Chiefs exercise their powers in consultation with all the adult males of their areas and reach their decisions at *pitsos* (public meetings) held in their *kgotlas* (courts or meeting places).

Religion

The majority of Sotho are now Christians, but many still follow the Sotho religion, which they share with the Tswana. The souls of the dead

SOUTH AFRICANS: NATIONALITY

nation:
South Africa; Republic of South Africa

derivation of name:
Geographical location

government:
Republic

capital:
Pretoria (administrative capital)

language:
South Africa has 11 official languages: Afrikaans (13 percent), English (8 percent), Southern Ndebele, Northern Sotho (9 percent), Sotho (8 percent), Swati, Tsonga (4 percent), Tswana (8 percent), Venda, Xhosa (18 percent), and Zulu (24 percent), the remaining 8 percent speak various African and Asian languages. Many people are bi- or trilingual.

religion:
About 80 percent of the population are Christian, the largest denominations being Zion Christian (11 percent), Pentecostal (8 percent), Catholic (7 percent), Methodist (7 percent), and Dutch Reformed (7 percent). About 2 percent of the population are Muslim. 15 percent profess no faith.

earlier inhabitants:
Khoisan; San

demographics:
According to government methods of ethnic differentiation 79 percent of the population are black African, 9.5 percent are white, 9 percent are "colored," and 2.5 percent are Indian or Asian.

are believed to have the power to influence the lives of the living, and the Sotho make offerings to these *badimo* to thank them for their help or to ask them for assistance.

The Sotho also have professional alternative medical practitioners who employ a wide range of herbal medicines and rituals to cure diseases, bring good luck and fertility, and protect people from misfortune. South African health authorities have come to recognize the value of these health workers. Instead of trying to obliterate such practices, which were scorned under apartheid, the government has tried to incorporate them into the official health system at the community level. Workshops and courses are provided to give them a wider health-care education.

See also BASOTHO: NATIONALITY; SOUTH AFRICANS: NATIONALITY.

FURTHER READING

The Sesotho Speaking People. A Cultural Image of South Africa, 6 (Alberton, South Africa: Lectio Publishers, 2006).
The Setswana-Speaking People. A Cultural Image of South Africa, 7 (Alberton, South Africa: Lectio Publishers, 2006).

Sotho–Tswana complex

A large proportion of Southern Africa's population is made up of people of SOTHO or TSWANA descent. These two closely related groups share a common origin in the early Iron Age population of South Africa. By the 15th century large numbers of Sotho-Tswana settlements extended over much of what is now the Highveld of northern South Africa. By the 16th century a large number of Sotho-Tswana states had emerged, and these and their dominant lineage groups developed into the different Sotho and Tswana groups and subgroups recognized today.

South Africans: nationality (people of South Africa)

GEOGRAPHY

The Republic of South Africa is a large nation occupying the southern tip of the African continent. It has an area of approximately 471,000 square miles and borders six other countries. Four nations meet South Africa's borders on the north; from west to east these are Namibia, Botswana, Zimbabwe, and Mozambique. Lesotho is entirely enclosed by the territory of South Africa, and Swaziland lies on the country's northeast border surrounded by the territory of South Africa on one side and Mozambique on the other. South Africa's coastline extends for 1,740 miles along the South Atlantic Ocean in the west and the Indian Ocean in the east. South African territory also includes two small islands in the Indian Ocean known as Prince Edward Island and Marion Island (together called the Prince Edward Islands). They are situated about 1,100 miles southeast of Port Elizabeth on the coast of mainland South Africa. South Africa is divided into nine provinces: Northern Cape Province occupies the northwest corner of the country; Western Cape Province and Eastern Cape Province extend along the Atlantic and Indian Ocean coast in the south; KwaZulu-Natal Province also extends along the Indian Ocean coast as far as the country's border with Mozambique; Mpumalanga Province and Limpopo Province occupy the northeast corner of the country, meeting the borders of Mozambique and Swaziland; North West province extends along the northern border with Zimbabwe; and Free State Province and Gauteng Province are in the country's interior.

The geography and topography of South Africa are extremely varied. Simplistically the country has three topographical zones: a narrow low-lying coastal zone that extends around the entire coastline; a largely flat highland plateau that rises from the coastal zone as a mountainous escarpment (known as the Great Escarpment); and a mountainous band that extends from northeast to southwest across the eastern half of the interior (running through Swaziland). The interior is dominated by the great expanse of the highland plateau, which rises steadily from west to east culminating in the Drakensberg Mountains. South Africa's highest point, the peak of Mount Injasuti at 11,180 feet, lies in the Drakensberg Mountain range on the border with the mountainous country of Lesotho. Much of the plateau is covered by grass prairie, known locally as the veld. The coastal margins in the west and south are very fertile and are famous for their plantations of citrus fruits and grape vines. Two of Africa's most arid regions, the Namib Desert and the Kalahari Desert, intrude into northern parts of South Africa. The southern fringes of the Namib Desert, which extends along the Atlantic Coast of neighboring Namibia, protrude into the extreme northwest corner of South Africa. The Kalahari Desert, which covers most of neighboring Botswana, impinges on the central northern region of the country. Generally South Africa is more arid in the northwest and less arid in the east. On the eastern side of the Drakensberg Mountains the land falls in a series of rolling fertile hills toward the nation's Indian Ocean coast, which features lush subtropical vegetation.

The country's two major rivers are the Orange and the Limpopo. The Orange River rises in Lesotho and flows westward through South Africa for more than 1,300 miles before emptying into the Atlantic at Alexander Bay. For the last 340 miles of its course the Orange River marks the international boundary between South Africa on its southern bank and Namibia on its northern bank. The Vaal River, a major tributary of the Orange River, also rises in the Drakensberg Mountains and follows a more-or-less parallel but more northerly course to the Orange before the two rivers reach their confluence near the city of Kimberley. The Limpopo River flows along the northeast border of South Africa, dividing it from Botswana and Zimbabwe. Numerous short, fast-flowing rivers flow from the mountainous escarpment that surrounds the central plateau toward the sea.

The northwest sector of South Africa is very sparsely populated; the great majority of South Africans live in the eastern half of the nation. The most densely populated areas lie along the southern and southeastern coasts and around the major urban centers of the interior. South Africa's largest city, Johannesburg, is situated in the northeast and is the nation's economic and industrial center. The country has three capitals. Pretoria is the administrative or executive capital (housing the seat of the national government). Cape Town is the legislative capital. Bloemfontein is the judicial capital. Pretoria is situated about 30 miles north of Johannesburg in the northeast, Cape Town lies on the coast in the extreme southwest, and Bloemfontein is situated close to the country's geographical center. Other large cities include Durban and Port Elizabeth, both of which lie on the Indian Ocean coast. According to official figures about 50 percent of the population live in urban areas.

INCEPTION AS A NATION

The earliest known inhabitants of the territory that is today South Africa were SAN and Khoi peoples. BANTU-speaking peoples migrated southward into the region from the 15 century or earlier. These were the ancestors of the NGUNI- and TSWANA-SOTHO-speaking ethnic groups that make up much of South Africa's population today: the ZULU, XHOSA, SWAZI, TSONGA, Botswana, and BASOTHO peoples (*see* BOTSWANANS: NATIONALITY).

Shortly after this migration began, Europeans also established their first footholds along the coast. Portuguese explorers had rounded the southern tip of Africa late in the 15th century and visited locations on the coast, but it was the Dutch who established the first permanent settlement in 1652. The Dutch East India Company's Cape Colony, established on the site of modern Cape Town, was to become a vital resupply station for vessels making the long journey from Europe to India. In the decades after its establishment, Dutch settlers rapidly established themselves in the territory surrounding Cape Town, displacing the nomadic inhabitants. Other settlers pushed inland to seek pasture for their cattle, further undermining the existing culture and way of life of the indigenous inhabitants. Dutch settlers encountered their first serious resistance along the Great Fish River as their eastern expansion met the western expansion of the Xhosa people. A series of wars (known as the Cape Frontier Wars or the Xhosa Wars) were fought along this natural boundary between 1779 and 1879. Britain seized control of the Cape Colony in 1795, and the territory was officially ceded to Britain in 1814 under the terms of the Treaty of Vienna. With the introduction of regular troops to defend the colony, the Xhosa were repeatedly defeated and pushed back until all of their territory fell under British control.

Conflict between the descendents of Dutch settlers in the Cape Colony (known as BOERS) and British authorities led to a mass migration of Boers out of the colony and into the lands to the east in the 1830s. Known as the Great Trek, this migration led to the foundation of several Boer states beyond the borders of the Cape Colony. The Boers who undertook these migrations were known as Voortrekkers. Boer Voortrekkers created more than a dozen states in this period; some were established through negotiation with local Bantu-speaking peoples, others through warfare. Many of these states were short-lived but others were more successful.

The Natalia Republic was established in the territory between present-day Lesotho and the Indian Ocean in 1839 and survived until 1843, when it was annexed by Britain (and renamed Natal). Voortrekkers migrated once again out of British-controlled Natal, helping to establish the Orange Free State in the territory between

South Africans: nationality time line

C.E.

Fourth to 15th century Bantu-speaking peoples migrate into southern Africa from the north.

1480s Portuguese explorers sail around the southern tip of Africa.

1497 Portuguese explorer Vasco da Gama visits the coast of present-day Natal.

1652 Dutch East Indian Company establishes a permanent settlement on the site of present-day Cape Town.

1795 Britain seizes the Dutch Cape Colony.

1814 Cape Colony formally ceded to Britain.

1816–26 Shaka Zulu creates a Zulu Empire in southern Africa.

1835–40 Boers migrate from Cape Colony on the Great Trek and found the Orange Free State, Transvaal, and Natalia.

1843 Britain annexes Natalia (later Natal).

1877 Britain annexes Transvaal.

1879 Final defeat of the Zulus by the British in Natal.

1880–81 First Anglo-Boer War. Transvaal Boers rebel against British rule; Transvaal restored as an independent republic.

1899–1902 Second Anglo-Boer War. Transvaal and the Orange Free State become self-governing British colonies.

1910 Union of South Africa formed from Cape Colony, Natal, Transvaal, and the Orange Free State.

1912 Native National Congress founded. Later renamed the African National Congress (ANC).

1914 National Party (NP) founded by Afrikaner nationalists.

1931 British parliament gives up the right to legislate over South Africa.

1948 Apartheid era begins as NP comes to power.

1950 Group Areas Act introduced to classify the population according to "race."

the Orange and Vaal Rivers and the Transvaal in the territory north of the Vaal River. Britain and the other major powers recognized the independence of both Transvaal and the Orange Free State, but Britain's continued ambitions in the area were heightened when large deposits of gold, diamonds, and other valuable minerals were discovered there.

Tension between the British and the Boers led to two Anglo-Boer Wars, the first of which began in 1880 when Britain attempted to annex Transvaal and ended in 1881 with Britain's defeat. The Second Boer War began in 1899 following British attempts to destabilize the Transvaal government by demanding equality for the large numbers of British setters who had been attracted there by the gold and diamond fields. The war began with preemptive strikes by irregular Boer troops into British-controlled Natal. Despite early successes, the Boers could not match the resources of the British Empire in

the long term and were finally defeated in 1902. In order to defeat the highly mobile Boer guerrillas the British adopted tactics that resulted in thousands of civilian deaths, including a scorched-earth policy intended to deny food supplies to the fighting Boers and a policy of interning thousands of Boer civilians in "concentration camps" to prevent them from giving aid to the fighters. An estimated 25,000 Boer civilians died in the conflict, largely as a result of starvation and disease. Following the Boer's defeat, Britain annexed the Orange Free State and Transvaal, transforming them into self-governing colonies within the British Empire.

In 1910 the British colonies of Cape and Natal and the former Boer republics of Transvaal and the Orange Free State were joined together to form the Union of South Africa. This new state was self-governing, having a bicameral legislature, but remained under ultimate British authority until 1931, when the British

1960 Sixty-nine black demonstrators are killed by security forces at Sharpeville (known as the Sharpeville Massacre). ANC is banned.

1962 South Africa becomes a republic and leaves the Commonwealth.

1964 ANC leader Nelson Mandela is sentenced to life imprisonment on charges of sabotage.

1970s Three million South Africans forcibly resettled in black "homelands."

1976 Six hundred people are killed in antigovernment demonstrations beginning in the Soweto township.

1984–89 Frequent revolts in black townships cause the government to declare a state of emergency.

1989 President Pieter Willem Botha replaced by Frederik Willem de Klerk. Public facilities are desegregated; de Klerk meets Nelson Mandela to discuss reform.

1990 Mandela and other ANC leaders released. ANC relegalized.

1991 Apartheid legislation repealed. Widespread fighting between ANC and Zulu Inkatha movement supporters.

1994 ANC wins the nation's first nonracial elections. Mandela becomes president with F. W. de Klerk as vice president in a Government of National Unity.

1996 Truth and Reconciliation Commission established. NP withdraws from Government of National Unity.

1999 ANC wins national elections. Thabo Mbeki replaces Mandela as president.

2003 Government initiates a major program to address South Africa's serious AIDS epidemic.

2004 ANC wins national elections with a large majority. Mbeke begins second term as president.

2005 Government committee recommends changing the name of the city of Pretoria to Tshwane.

2006 South Africa becomes the first African nation to sanction same-sex marriages.

2007 Major strike among public sector workers. Jacob Zuma becomes president of the ANC.

2008 Economic migrants from Zimbabwe, Malawi, and Mozambique are targeted in nationwide violence resulting in dozens of deaths.

parliament gave up the right to pass legislation governing its people. For the next 30 years the Union of South Africa retained Britain's monarch as its head of state with a governor-general acting as the monarch's representative, although effective power was in the hands of the elected prime minister of the union. In 1960 South African voters elected to remove the British monarch as head of state, and the country became the Republic of South Africa in May 1961.

CULTURAL IDENTITY

Modern South Africa is a nation of great cultural diversity. In the 2001 census respondents had the opportunity to assign themselves to one of five ethnic groupings: Black African, White, Colored, Indian or Asian, and Other. The simplicity of this formula disguises the fact that there is great cultural and ethnic diversity within these classifications. Black Africans

for example, who make up about 80 percent of the population, belong to numerous culturally distinct groups including Zulu, Xhosa, Basotho (or South Sotho), Bapedi (or North Sotho), VENDA, Tswana, Tsonga, Swazi, and NDEBELE. The Whites, who make up about 9 percent of the population, also have diverse ethnic backgrounds, including Dutch, Portuguese, German, Huguenot French, English, Scottish, and Irish. Linguistically the white population is further divided into those who speak Afrikaans and those who speak English as their first language. The term "Colored" is still widely used in South Africa to refer to people whose ancestors include Whites, black Africans, Asians, or people from other ethnic groups. They represent an extremely diverse admixture of ethnicity that makes up about 9 percent of the population. In Western Cape Province, for example, there are a culturally distinct CAPE COLORED AND CAPE MALAY populations whose ancestors were pre-

Nelson Mandela: Symbol of Opposition

Nelson Mandela, a leading activist in the African National Congress (ANC) who spent 27 years in prison because of his opposition to South Africa's system of apartheid, became the country's first black president in 1994 and one of the most widely respected statesmen of the late 20th and early 21st centuries.

Mandela was born in 1918 in what was then known as South Africa's Cape Province (his birthplace is in the Eastern Cape Province today) and named Rolihlahla Dalibhunga. His English name "Nelson" came from a childhood teacher, and his surname "Mandela" came from his grandfather. Mandela was related by birth to the traditional ruling family of the THEMBU people, and his great-grandfather had been *inkosi* (king) of the Thembu in the early 19th century. His father died when Mandela was nine, and from this time was raised by Jongintaba Dalindyebo, the acting regent of the Thembu.

Joining the ANC is 1943, Mandela founded and became president of the ANC Youth League. In 1952, having qualified as a lawyer, Mandela opened a law firm in Johannesburg with his friend Oliver Tambo. Both campaigned against the apartheid policies instituted by the National Party government that had come to power in 1948, activities that led to his arrest for high treason on 1956. Although the charges were dropped after a four-year-trial, the security forces continued to persecute Mandela and hundreds of other ANC activists. In 1960 the ANC was declared illegal by the government, and security forces killed 69 black protesters in Sharpeville. In hiding, Mandela decided that peaceful opposition to apartheid could not succeed, and in 1961 he became the leader of the ANC's armed wing Umkhonto we Sizwe (Spear of the Nation), which carried out bomb attacks against military and government targets.

Mandela was captured and arrested in 1962 and sentenced to life imprisonment in 1964 for his part in the ANC's bombing campaign. For the first 18 years of his time in prison Mandela was incarcerated in harsh condition on Robben Island along with hundreds of other political prisoners. In 1982 he was moved to a mainland prison along with other senior ANC leaders, and in 1985 secret meetings were held between Mandela and government officials, during which Mandela refused to renounce armed struggle in return for his freedom. Other meetings between Mandela and official representatives followed as the National Party government, under great international pressure, began to make tentative moves toward reform. When Frederik Willem de Klerk replaced the ailing stalwart of apartheid, Pieter Willem Botha, as president in 1989, South Africa moved rapidly toward change. Mandela was released from prison in 1990 and in 1991 was elected president of the newly relegalized ANC. In recognition of his part in the dismantling of apartheid, Mandela was awarded the Nobel Peace Prize, along with F. W. de Klerk, in 1993.

During his 27 years in prison Mandela became a powerful symbol of the ongoing struggle against apartheid. He was met by huge rejoicing crowds on his release, and his popularity translated into overwhelming support for the ANC in South Africa's first nonracial elections held in 1994. As the leader of the ANC, Mandela became president. During his five-year term as president, Mandela concentrated on rebuilding South Africa's international image and promoting conciliation between the country's white minority and black majority. His perceived success in these endeavors coupled with his great personal charm elevated him to the status of one of the world's most loved and admired statesman. Since his retirement from party politics in 1999, he has continued to be active in national and international issues, including attempts to tackle South Africa's AIDS epidemic.

dominantly Dutch and from one or more of the many African and Asian groups used as slaves in the early history of the Cape Colony. In other parts of South Africa Colored people have different backgrounds. In KwaZulu-Natal, for example, Coloreds usually have British and Zulu ancestry. Many Cape Coloreds speak Afrikaans as their first language, but other groups speak English or Bantu languages. The Indian or Asian group, which make up about 2.5 percent of the population, is equally diverse, including people with Indian, Chinese, Sri Lankan, Bangladeshi, Burmese, Nepalese, Iranian, or any one of many other Asian ethnicities.

Today a South African's ethnicity is essentially determined by the traditional identity of his or her family and personal choice and has no impact on the individual's legal status. For much of the history of South Africa, however, this was not the case. The stratification of society into White, Non-White, and Colored groups began in the earliest colonial period, with Whites enjoying full economic and political freedoms, Coloreds having less freedom, and Non-Whites living with very few freedoms or in a state of slavery. This was the case in most of colonial Africa, but unlike much of the rest of Africa the situation did not change when the country became independent. In the postwar period South Africa became internationally notorious as a nation in which strong policies of racial segregation were the dominant form of social stratification. Apartheid (the Afrikaans word for "apartness") was the name given to South Africa's policy of racial segregation, discrimination, and white domination that was in force from 1948 to 1991.

By the time apartheid was officially introduced, racist policies had been practiced for over 300 years in South Africa. The Dutch who settled on the Cape in the 17th century soon established semislave relationships with the local KHOIKHOI population—whose way of life became dependent on Afrikaner (the name the Dutch settlers later adopted) employment (*see* AFRIKANERS). The Boers (the Dutch word for farmers) then began to import slaves from other parts of Africa and from Asia to provide cheap labor for building and farming work.

In the 19th century Britain outlawed slave trading, though existing slaves could still be kept legally. When in 1820 about 4,000 Britons settled in the Cape Colony, they were unable to purchase slaves legally, and with no free labor available, the new settlers set about wresting the Afrikaners' slaves from them by decreeing that nobody, of whatever color, could be forced into service. This was followed by the abolition of slavery throughout the British Empire in 1833. Combined with other changes, this threatened to destroy the Afrikaners' lifestyle, and in 1836 they began to trek to the interior of Africa where they planned to live unhampered by British bureaucrats. The Afrikaner republics that were set up en route of this Great Trek had as the bases of their constitutions the right of Afrikaner self-determination and the "right" to rule the "natives."

Over the years the Afrikaners—who were mainly farmers or, later, part of the underclass of urban workers—came to resent the British, who dominated the lucrative mining industry, skilled professions, the military, and the civil service. Indeed, the strident Afrikaner nationalist sentiment that emerged had developed largely as a result of British imperialism and domination. This nationalism was turned on the black population in force after the National Party (NP)—formed in 1912 to further Afrikaner interests—came to power in 1924.

In 1934 the NP merged with another party to form the United Party, which addressed the interests of both English speakers and Afrikaners. The remnants of the NP were resurrected by the Broederbond (an influential, secret nationalist Afrikaner society) and other Afrikaner extremists led by Dr. Daniel François Malan. This "purified" National Party came to power in 1948, promising to create apartheid. Malan promised to send all black people to reserves, run a white-only economy, and "to save civilization from black hordes"—a task he claimed to be ordained by God. This message appealed to many white industrial workers who feared competition from the black majority for their jobs. Apartheid was also welcomed by the mine owners and white farmers, as it allowed them to maintain the profitable status quo. In order to provide themselves with cheap labor, mine owners had long been employing black workers and installing them in cramped, single-sex barracks.

Apartheid was different from the racial segregation practiced historically in South Africa because it was enshrined in, and enforced by, the law. Under J. B. M. Hertzog the Ministry of Native Affairs (created in 1910 and later known as the Ministry of Bantu Affairs) began drafting some of the laws and policies that formed the framework of apartheid. Although many racist policies were in place before 1948, after this date they were extended and enforced to a greater extent. At the heart of apartheid was the denial of voting rights to all but the white population. Like other policies, disenfranchisement had a long history. The first Afrikaner republics of the 1800s had allowed only Afrikaner men to vote. Also, the British passed a law to deny black people the right to vote outside the Cape. Within the Cape, few could meet the strict educational and financial requirements needed to qualify for suffrage. Indian and "Colored" voters were given separate houses of representation in 1983, but in a ratio that ensured continued white domination. In protest, many did not exercise their right to vote.

Relocation policies aimed to limit the number of black people staying overnight in "white" towns and to segregate people within urban areas. After the 1913 Native Land Act, black South Africans were allowed to buy or rent land only in "native reserves." Over 60 percent of the population was restricted to living in only 7.3 percent of the land (later increased to 13 percent). Denied access to land, black South Africans had to work for the white population, who needed their labor on farms, in towns, and in the mines. The 1948 Group Areas Act created separate residential and business areas for each officially designated race into which people could be forcibly moved. By the 1960s it was obvious that the reserves were unviable; they were overpopulated and underresourced, and starvation was widespread. Nevertheless, in 1959 the 260 reserves were organized into several homelands, or Bantustans. Despite segregationist policies, 60 percent of the black population lived in "white" areas in 1948. Between 1960 and 1983, however, over 3 million people were evicted to live in the homelands.

Color bars prevented the majority of South Africans from doing many things, such as working as skilled professionals. Unofficial color bars had long been in existence in the mining industry, for example. White workers filled supervisory and skilled positions while black workers were left to do the lower-paid manual jobs. When the mines tried to promote black workers to supervisory positions in 1922—simply to save money on wages—strikes and demonstrations by white miners nearly caused a civil war. Two years later the NP came to power with the support of the white-only trade unions and immediately legalized color bars.

In 1955 the Bantu Education Act was passed. After this date, many students were denied the right to a high-standard academic education. Instead, a poor-quality education was provided as approved by the Department of Native (Bantu) Affairs. Schools that refused to conform were closed down and reluctant teachers fired.

Under the Population Registration Act introduced in 1950, every South African was required to register and be classified by "race," which would then be stamped in his or her identity pass. This was then used to determine, for example, where people could live, what job they could do, and whom they could marry. The official recording of ethnicity for the purposes of restricting work and travel had a long history. The first pass law—the Hottentot Code—was introduced by the British to the Cape Colony in 1809. It required that all Khoikhoi have a fixed place of abode and a pass with an employer's stamp if they needed to travel. This law forced the Khoikhoi to work for the Afrikaners in order to get a pass. Although repealed a few years later—in order to create a mobile supply of workers for the British settlers—it was the first of many similar laws. Pass laws gave the authorities power to restrict people's access to towns, send others back to homelands, and ensured the supply of labor to the white population.

Wealthy and heavily armed, South Africa was able to dominate neighboring countries—the front-line states in the fight against apartheid—in order to protect its own policies. Intimidation, sabotage, military action, and subversion were all used to destabilize the regimes that South Africa found threatening and prop up those that supported it—the illegal white-minority regime in Rhodesia (present-day Zimbabwe), for example (*see also* ZIMBABWE-ANS: NATIONALITY). Using the excuse of trying to eliminate its enemies' guerrilla bases, South Africa invaded many front-line states. Angola was invaded, bombed, and—along with Mozambique—subjected to a prolonged civil war due, in part, to South Africa's funding of rebel groups (*see also* ANGOLANS: NATIONALITY and MOZAMBICANS: NATIONALITY). Other East and Central African countries suffered from these problems through the influx of refugees from war zones. Namibia was illegally occupied by South Africa (as South West Africa) until 1990 and a form of apartheid was introduced there (*see also* NAMIBIANS: NATIONALITY). South Africa easily pressured Lesotho and Swaziland, which are economically reliant on the goodwill of South Africa, into supportive roles (*see also* LESOTHO: NATIONALITY and SWAZI: NATIONAL-ITY). Border blockades were often used to force Lesotho's policies into line.

Opposition to apartheid was widespread, involved people of all colors, and took many forms. The first organized resistance was led by Mohandas Karamchand Gandhi, an Indian lawyer, who came to Natal in 1893 and stayed until 1914. Using nonviolent methods and recourse to the law, Gandhi was an inspiration to later movements. The South African Native National Congress, which became the African National Congress (ANC) in 1923, was formed in 1912. Its first leaders—John L. Dube, president, and Sol Plaatje, secretary—attempted to effect changes by appealing to Britain and challenging unjust laws in court. The government's refusal to reform, however, led to the development of more militant methods. The ANC really became a mass movement only in 1944 with the founding of the ANC Youth League by Anton Lembede. His colleagues included Nelson Mandela, Walter Sisulu, and Oliver Tambo.

One of the first examples of successful mass political mobilization was the Defiance Campaign of 1952. With Indian and other groups and using trained volunteers, the ANC orchestrated local defiances of unjust laws all over the country. The campaign was called off after outbreaks of violence occurred. Reprisals by the government were often severe. Police powers were increased to deal with the growing unrest caused by apartheid. Torture and informers were widely used, and many people died in police custody. More "humane" methods included banning and issuing restraining orders against political activists to halt their activities.

In 1961, as president of the ANC, Tambo left South Africa to open overseas offices of the ANC. From Lusaka, Zambia, he organized guerrilla forays into South Africa and raised funds. In the same year, Mandela formed the Umkonto we Sizwe (Spear of the Nation) movement, which was to perform sabotage on economically important facilities in order to pressure the government into talks. The initial result was that Mandela and Sisulu, among others, were imprisoned for life in 1964.

Large-scale uprisings led by the schoolchildren of Soweto (the southwestern townships of Johannesburg) followed the 1976 announcement that Bantu education would be in Afrikaans. Protests escalated and strikes brought Johannesburg to a standstill. Police response was harsh, and by the end of the year over 500 people, including many children, had been killed. Most opposition leaders were committed to nonviolent methods (Desmond Tutu won the Nobel Peace Prize in 1984 for his nonviolent campaigning), but this practice was sometimes ignored by others. Apartheid policies of segregation, not only by race but also by ethnic group, led to outbreaks of what came to be called "black-on-black" violence—though many incidents were incited by government agents. Although Chief Buthelezi's Zulu Inkatha movement (originally formed in 1928 and reconvened in 1975) and Mandela's Umkonto were mutually supportive, their members often clashed.

Deaf to moral arguments, economic reasons for the government to end apartheid brought matters to a crisis point. Even before the 1948 elections, serious drawbacks to segregationist policies had become obvious. The government soon discovered that labor provided by the excluded majority was vital for the fastest-growing sector of the economy: manufacturing industries. This labor force also needed to be educated and mobile enough to be efficient—impossible within apartheid. Employers, especially in construction, often had to ignore color bars just to fill vacancies. After the 1970s Soweto uprisings, foreign investment halted, capital flowed out of the country, house prices and the share market slumped, and businesses collapsed. In many ways, apartheid did not make economic sense. Pressure at home and from abroad was also making the system increasingly unworkable. As increasing numbers of African and Asian countries joined the United Nations, calls for sanctions against South Africa grew. Antiapartheid movements had been arguing for sanctions for years, and in 1985 many international banks paid heed. Loans were not renewed and the promise of future ones withdrawn. In 1990 Mandela was released from prison, and in 1991 all apartheid legislation was repealed. Finally, in 1994 the first nonracial elections were held in South Africa and Mandela was elected president.

The transition from apartheid to majority rule in South Africa was a difficult process, and the social legacy of apartheid will continue to impact South Africans for decades. In the period immediately following the end of apartheid, there was a widespread feeling among the black African community that the people who had instituted and perpetuated apartheid should be prosecuted for crimes against humanity. Instead of immediately prosecuting former government officials, however, the new government established a Truth and Reconciliation Commission in 1996, the purpose of which was to give victims of violence the opportunity to present their testimony publicly and also to encourage perpetrators of violence to describe their own activities. The commission had the power to grant amnesty from prosecution to anyone providing testimony. A central goal of the commission was to encourage recognition that illegal or immoral acts had been committed not only by the government but also by their opponent, including the ANC. Of the more than 7,000 witnesses who petitioned, amnesty was granted to 849 individuals. The commission's final report, delivered in 1998, criticized both sides in the conflict for committing atrocities. While this conclusion, and the granting of amnesty to the perpetrators of violence, angered many South Africans, the commission was generally acknowledged as playing a vital role in the country's transition and in forestalling the potential for retributive violence. It has since been adopted as a model in other nations emerging from periods of internal violence.

Neither the initial expectations among black Africans of an imminent economic and social miracle nor the initial fear of bloody reprisals among whites came to fruition. The transition to a new constitution, adopted in 1997, did not resolve the uncertainty and confusion that followed such a radical change in the country's political structure. This uncertainty contributed to a downturn in the economy, which was further damaged by a massive increase in reported crime. An epidemic of robberies, assaults, kidnappings, and murders struck the country's urban areas, leading to the widespread establishment of vigilante groups (particularly among whites) and a dramatic fall in foreign investment and tourism. Despite the increase in criminal violence, political violence has not been a significant feature in the elections that have taken place under the new constitution. Mandela stepped down from the presidency in 1999 after serving one term and was replaced by Thabo Mbeki. The ANC won large majorities in the elections of 1999 and 2004, and although both of these elections were judged to be free and fair by international observers, the ANC's dominance of South African politics has raised concerns that South Africa could become a de facto one-party state.

Since 1994 all traces of the legal framework of apartheid have been erased, but the economic situation of most black Africans and many Coloreds remains dire. Despite losing their political supremacy, whites continue to enjoy the status of an economic elite, with average annual incomes far in excess of those earned by other groups. Successive ANC governments have faced criticism for not directly intervening to redress economic disparities, while they claim in response that such actions could damage the economy irrevocably. Culturally, the new regime has avoided attempting to impose a predetermined template for national identity, hoping instead that a new South African identity will emerge naturally from the free interaction of the nation's many and various cultural groups. Despite decades of oppression by the state, most black South Africans identify primarily with their nation and with their ethnic group second. Whites also have a strong sense of South African national identity, as do Coloreds, many of whom refer to themselves as Afrikaners today.

FURTHER READING

Iris Berger. *South Africa in World History* (New York: Oxford University Press, 2009).

John Carlin. *Playing the Enemy: Nelson Mandela and the Game That Made a Nation* (London: Atlantic, 2008).

Robert C. Cottrell. *South Africa: A State of Apartheid* (Philadelphia: Chelsea House, 2005).

T. R. H. Davenport and Christopher C. Saunders. *South Africa: A Modern History* (Hampshire, U.K.: Macmillan, 2000).

Nelson Mandela. *Long Walk to Freedom: The Autobiography of Nelson Mandela* (Boston: Little, Brown, 1994).

Martin Meredith. *Diamonds, Gold, and War: The British, the Boers, and the Making of South Africa* (New York: PublicAffairs, 2007).

Alfred T. Moleah. *South Africa: Colonialism, Apartheid and African Dispossession* (Wilmington, Del: Disa Press, 1993).

Mueni wa Muiu. *The Pitfalls of Liberal Democracy and Late Nationalism in South Africa* (New York: Palgrave Macmillan, 2008).

Robert Ross. *A Concise History of South Africa* (Cambridge, U.K.: Cambridge University Press, 1999).

Leonard Monteath Thompson. *A History of South Africa* (New Haven, Conn.: Yale University Press, 1990).

Nigel Worden. *The Making of Modern South Africa: Conquest, Segregation, and Apartheid* (Oxford, U.K.: Blackwell, 1994).

South Mugirango

The South Mugirango are one of the main subdivisions of the GUSII. The Gusii are a large ethnic group of western Kenya.

Southern Bullom   *See* SHERBRO.

Sudanese: nationality (people of Sudan)

GEOGRAPHY

The Republic of the Sudan is a large country in East Africa. With an area of approximately 967,500 square miles, it is the largest nation on the African continent. Sudan has borders with nine other countries and a coastline on the Red Sea. Egypt meets Sudan's border to the north; Libya to the northwest; Chad and the Central African Republic to the west; the Democratic Republic of the Congo, Uganda, and Kenya to the south; and Ethiopia and Eritrea to the east. Sudan's coastline stretches for 530 miles along the western shore of the Red Sea.

The majority of Sudan's territory consists of a single low-lying plain that stretches from north to south and west to east across·the entire nation. Low hills are found along the southern and southwestern borders and in a strip that runs parallel to the coast. Sudan's only significant upland region is the isolated volcanic massif known as the Marrah Mountains in the extreme west of the country lying close to the border with Chad. The country's highest point, however, is the 10,456-foot-high peak of Mount Kinyeti, an isolated mountain that lies in the extreme south of the country on the border with Uganda. A range of dome-shaped hills known as the Nuba Mountains interrupts the rolling Sudanic plain in the south-central region of the country, but their greatest elevation is only about 3,000 feet.

Sudan's most prominent geographical feature is the Nile River, which forms from the confluence of the Blue Nile River and the White Nile River in the central region of the country. The Blue Nile rises in neighboring Ethiopia and flows from south to north through the eastern portion of Sudan. The White Nile rises in neighboring Uganda and flows from south the north through the southern and central portion of Sudan before it is joined by the Blue Nile near the city of Khartoum.

Three distinct climatic zones are found within Sudan. The south has a long rainy season (from April to December) and features dense tropical woodlands and swamps. The semidesert Sahel region forms a belt across the central third of the country and experiences a shorter, less reliable, rainy season from July to September. The north is dominated by desert, although it is bisected by the fertile valley of the Nile River.

Nubian pyramids in Sudan built for the Nubian rulers of the Kingdom of Meroë between ca. 300 B.C.E. and 300 C.E.

About 60 percent of the population lives in the north, an area with a distinct Arabic-speaking Muslim culture. All of Sudan's major urban centers are found in the north-central part of the country close to the confluence of the White Nile and the Blue Nile or further downstream on the Nile River. The arid northwest is very sparsely populated. Sudan's capital, Khartoum, is situated at the confluence of the White Nile and the Blue Nile and is divided from the cities of North Khartoum and Omdurman by the Blue Nile and the White Nile respectively. Taken together these three cities represent the largest urban concentration in Sudan, although Omdurman is actually the largest individual city in the country.

INCEPTION AS A NATION

The ancient EGYPTIANS referred to northern Sudan as Cush, a territory rich in gold and iron and centered around the southern extremities of the Nile Valley in much the same way as their civilization straddled the northern part of the Nile's course. The histories of ancient Egypt and northern Sudan were closely interwoven for centuries as Egyptian power advanced and ebbed along the upper Nile. During the New Kingdom Period (ca. 1570–1100 B.C.E.), Egypt's power over Cush reached its greatest extent as the territory as far south as the site of modern Khartoum became an Egyptian province governed by a viceroy. During this period Egyptian culture became firmly established in Cush. Temples built to the Egyptian gods remained in use until the arrival of Christianity a thousand years later, the Egyptian language was used extensively, and the nobility adopted Egyptians patterns of life.

At the end of the New Kingdom Period Egypt subsided into an era of civil war and disunity. By 750 B.C.E. the city of Napata (situated about 250 miles north of present-day Khartoum) had established itself as a powerful center of trade and began to assert its military might on the fragmented kingdoms of Egypt. The rulers of Napata formed a dynasty that ruled upper Egypt for a century and the entire Nile Valley for several decades until they were forced into retreat by the ASSYRIANS in the mid-seventh century B.C.E.

In the sixth-century B.C.E. the rulers of Cush were forced by a resurgent Egypt to relocate their capital to Meroë, a city about 125 miles downstream from present-day Khartoum. From this time the development of Cush and Egypt began to diverge. Egypt came under Assyrian, Greek, and finally Roman power while Meroitic Cush retained its independence and continued trading down the Nile to the Mediterranean. Cush retained much of the culture of ancient Egypt. Its rulers retained the pharaonic traditions of erecting pyramids and recording their achievements on monumental stelae using a system of hieroglyphs derived from the Egyptians.

Meroitic Cush ceased to exist as a separate state in the fourth century C.E. when it was conquered by the Ethiopian kingdom of Axum. Christian missionaries who arrived in northern Sudan in the sixth century described three kingdoms along the Nile at that time. The northernmost kingdom, known as Nobatia, had its capital at Faras (the ruins of which were submerged beneath the waters of Lake Nasser as a result of the construction of the Aswan High Dam in the 1960s). The middle kingdom,

Sudanese: nationality time line

B.C.E.

ca. 750 Rulers of Cush (modern north Sudan) establish rule over upper Egypt.

ca. 590 Egypt captures the Cushitic capital of Napata. Cushitic rulers move their capital south to Meroë.

third–second centuries Meroë is the center of a powerful Cushitic kingdom.

C.E.

ca. 350 Meroë conquered by Axumite Empire.

sixth century Coptic Christianity introduced to northern Sudan.

650s Advance of Muslim Arabs into northern Sudan from Egypt halted by Sudanese resistance.

16th century Muslim kingdom of Sennar established in northern Sudan.

1820s Egyptian Ottoman forces advance into Sudan and conquer the north of the country.

1880s Religious leader Muhammad Ahmad leads a rebellion against Egyptian rule, establishing a Mahdist state in northern Sudan.

1889 Anglo-Egyptian forces invade Sudan, dismantle the Mahdist state, and establish Anglo-Egyptian administration.

1955 Antigovernment insurgency begins in southern Sudan

1956 Sudan becomes independent as the Republic of Sudan.

1958 A military coup brings General Ibrahim Abboud to power.

1964 Abboud's military dictatorship overthrown and a parliamentary government established.

1969 A military coup brings Jafar Numayri to power. Anyana Rebellion brings renewed violence in the south.

1972 Numayri concludes a peace agreement with southern rebels. Southern Sudan becomes self-governing.

1985 Fighting resumes in the south after Numayri attempts to introduce Islamic law to the region. Sudan People's Liberation Movement (SPLM) leads the rebellion. Numayri deposed in a military coup.

1989 Second military coup brings Umar al-Bashir to power.

1993 Umar al-Bashir appointed president of a one-party state.

2000 Opposition parties boycott presidential elections. Al-Bashir elected to another five-year term.

2002 SPLM and Khartoum government agree to a cease-fire.

2003 Sudan Liberation Movement (SLM) and Justice and Equality Movement (JEM) begin an antigovernment rebellion in the Darfur region of western Sudan.

2004 Government forces launch operation in Darfur to quell the rebellion. United Nations reports that Janjaweed militias are massacring civilians in Darfur.

2005 Government and SPLM sign a peace accord. Autonomous government set up in the south. United Nations accuses Khartoum government and militias of systematic human rights abuses in Darfur.

2008 United Nations peacekeeping force deployed in Darfur. National census begun in preparation for future elections.

known as Muqurra, had its capital at Dunqulah (about 90 miles south of the modern city of Dunqulah); and the most southerly kingdom, Alwa, was centered on the city of Soba close to modern Khartoum. The rulers of these kingdoms became Coptic Christians during this period (*see* COPTS).

Islam arrived in northern Sudan in the 650s as Arab forces raided south from their recently conquered Egyptian territories. The Arab advance met strong resistance from the Christian kingdoms of northern Sudan. This, combined with the relative poverty of the region, induced the ARABS to conclude a peace and to halt their advance. During the ninth and 10th centuries the Christian kingdoms of northern Sudan reached the peak of their power, but they were isolated from the rest of the Christian world by intervening Muslim-held territory, and Islamic culture gradually began to dominate through trade and Arab settlements. By the 14th century the Christian kingdoms had essentially ceased to exist and a patchwork of small polities, many of them primarily Muslim, had emerged in northern Sudan. In the 16th century a powerful Muslim state known as the Kingdom of Sennar developed in northern Sudan.

Ottoman rule came to northern Sudan in the 1820s (see OTTOMANS) in the form of an invasion by Egyptian forces. Ottoman Egypt claimed sovereignty over the entire area of modern Sudan for much of the 19th century, although its rule was never firmly established in the south. There, swamps and thick forests made travel and administration extremely difficult and Muslim culture was resisted by the powerful kingdoms based in present-day Uganda (see UGANDANS). Egypt's involvement in Sudan became strongly influenced by Britain's involvement in Egypt during the second half of the 19th century. British and French influence in Egypt grew significantly after the completion of the Suez Canal in 1869. By 1877 the European powers had enough influence to dethrone the khedive (ruler) of Egypt, Ismail Pasha, and install his more pliable son in his place. In 1874 Major General Charles George Gordon, a British officer, had been appointed by the khedive to develop transportation links in the south of Sudan and was soon named governor of the entire province.

French and British administrators were already serving in the Egyptian government at this time as part of international agreements involving the security of the Suez Canal and the resolution of Egypt's substantial foreign debts. Britain used its position in Egypt to suppress the slave trade that still flourished in East Africa at that time. Southern Sudan was one of the main sources of slaves, and General Gordon was closely involved in curtailing the activities of slave traders from the north of Sudan. The result was a powerful uprising among the north Sudanese led by Muhammad Ahmad ibn as Sayyid Abd Allah (1844–85), a Muslim religious leader who proclaimed himself the proph-

esized Mahdi, or redeemer of Islam. Many of the tribes involved in slave trading supported Muhammad Ahmad because he promised to end Egyptian and British involvement in the region. In 1881 Muhammad Ahmad declared a holy war against the occupying Egyptian forces and rapidly formed a large army that repeatedly defeated Egyptian troops. The British government ordered Egypt to withdraw its forces from Sudan in 1884 and General Gordon was once again appointed to carry out the task. Before Khartoum could be evacuated, however, Muhammad Ahmad's forces besieged the city and captured it in January 1895. General Gordon was among the 7,000-strong garrison massacred by Ahmad's warriors.

Although Britain had advised a withdrawal from Sudan, the sensational death of General Gordon led the government to conclude that Muhammad Ahmad's movement could not be allowed to continue in case it expanded to threaten other colonial territories. In 1896 a retrained and reequipped Anglo-Egyptian army under British officers invaded the Mahdist state that had been founded after the fall of Khartoum. By the end of 1898 the Mahdists had been defeated and Britain established an Anglo-Egyptian administration over the whole of Sudan that was to persist until Sudanese independence in 1956.

Until 1896 Britain had regarded the administration of Sudan as an Egyptian matter, although Egypt itself was a British protectorate from 1882. After the involvement of British forces in the war against the Mahdists, however, the new system of Anglo-Egyptian administration involved closer British involvement in the affairs of Sudan. This was considered necessary by the British government to counter the ambitions of France and Belgium in the region of the headwaters of the Nile River.

When Egypt's King Farouk was deposed in 1952, it became clear that Britain's already tenuous hold over Egypt was coming to an end. In 1953 Britain and Egypt agreed to initiate a three-year transitional period that would end with Sudan's independence. The Republic of Sudan was declared in January 1956 under a parliamentary government that had been elected in 1954 with Ismail al Azhari as its first prime minister.

CULTURAL IDENTITY

In the 1920s Britain had divided Sudan into northern and southern administrative regions in recognition of the very different cultures that predominated in the north and the south. The north was Islamic, spoke Arabic, and had strong historical ties with Egypt and the north, while the south was Christian or animist and had stronger links with the peoples of the Great Lakes region to the south. In 1943 Britain began preparing north Sudan for independence as a separate state and envisaged south Sudan's fate as being coincidental with the future of Britain's other possessions in East Africa. After World War II, however, Britain reversed this decision and reintegrated the north and south under a single administrative authority in the north. In 1948 a Legislative Assembly for the whole of Sudan was established in Khartoum. The south was woefully underrepresented in the assembly, and its business was carried out in Arabic rather than English, the language that local administrators from the south had been trained in. When Sudan was granted autonomy under its own parliament in 1953, fewer than 10 of the hundreds of administrative positions vacated by the British went to Sudanese from the south. The Khartoum government was committed to instituting a federal system on the advent of independence that would give the south considerable autonomy, but these promises were not kept. A rebellion by army officers in the south, which began in 1955, marked the opening phase of a civil war that was to seriously hamper Sudan's development for decades to come.

In the two years after independence, power changed hands several times in the midst of an economic crises precipitated by poor cotton harvests, and in November 1958 General Ibrahim Abboud seized control of the government, instituting a military dictatorship and banning all political parties and trade unions. During Abboud's regime the outlawed political parties joined to form the United Front (UP) and the Professional Front (PF), the latter composed primarily of doctors, teachers, and lawyers. Their combined opposition forced Abboud to resign in 1964, and his regime was replaced by a parliamentary system. The new government was poorly organized, however, and weakened by the continuing civil war in the south.

In 1969 the military again took control under Jafar Numayri. Concurrent with the change of regime was a major escalation in the civil war known as the Anyana Rebellion. The Anyana was a southern rebel army formed by a coalition of Lotuko, MADI, Bari, ACHOLI, Zande, and DINKA fighters. The renewed vigor of southern claims for autonomy forced the government into negotiations, and a cease-fire was agreed to in 1972 as the first step in promised moves toward self-rule for the south. At the same time as promising a degree of freedom for the south, however, Numayri moved to institute a one-party state in the north and repressed political opposition. A period of economic recovery in the 1970s foundered in the mid-1980s when drought and a huge influx of refugees from wars in neighboring Chad and Ethiopia taxed the country's resources. A series of failed assassination and coup attempts, many allegedly funded by Libya, demonstrated the general dissatisfaction of the general population with Numayri's government. An attempt by Numayri to impose Islamic law in the south in 1985 brought about a rekindling of the civil war, which had been largely dormant for over a decade.

The army deposed Numayri in 1985 and ruled for the following four years, until the Revolutionary Command Council (RCC), under the leadership of Umar Hassan Ahmed al Bashir, took control. The RCC immediately declared a state of emergency. It abolished the National Assembly, disbanded political parties, trade unions, and newspapers, and banned strikes, demonstrations, and all public gatherings. Although the military government was disbanded in 1993, General Bashir remained in power as president.

Conflict between the north and south that had reemerged in 1985 continued throughout the 1990s despite numerous peace talks. The Sudan People's Liberation Movement (SPLM) and its military arm, the Sudan People's Liberation Army (SPLA), waged a continues guerrilla war against government forces until a cease-fire was finally agreed to in 2002 and a final end to hostilities in 2005.

Even as Sudan was emerging from one period of civil war, however, a second was beginning. In 2003 rebel groups in the western Darfur region of Sudan, principally the Sudan Liberation Movement (SLM) and the Justice and Equality Movement (JEM), began an armed campaign against the government in Khartoum, accusing them of ignoring the economic development of the west and of oppressing the area's "non-Arab" population. In the context of Sudan, "Arab" refers to the peoples of northern Sudan and the Nile Valley who are descended from the indigenous peoples of ancient Cush as well as Egyptian Muslims and Arabian Arabs who settled in the area from the sixth century C.E. In the same context, "non-Arabs" are peoples of the west and south who are culturally closer to the peoples of Central and East Africa. The ensuing war in Darfur killed between 200,000 and 400,000 people in five years and displaced as many as 2.5 million persons. Forces on both sides committed atrocities, but the so-called Janjaweed militia became particularly notorious for committing mass rape and massacring the inhabitants of refugee camps. The term "Janjaweed" is used collectively to refer to armed raiders from many different tribes rather than to a specific group. However, they have in common the fact that they are drawn from the nomadic Arab peoples of the north of the region and that they are believed to act, at least in part, under the orders of the Khartoum government. The SLM and JEM rebels draw their support from the sedentary population that traditionally farms the marginal agricultural lands around the base of the Marrah Mountains. Conflict between farmers and nomadic pastoralists has been endemic to Darfur for centuries, but the increasing desertification of the region has exacerbated the problem by forcing the nomadic peoples further into the traditional territory of the sedentary peoples. Since 2004 Janjaweed elements have also been widely accused of mounting attacks across the border into Chad and are regarded as a contributing factor in the outbreak of civil war in Chad in 2005.

Modern Sudan cannot be said to have a national identity, and in that sense no one cohesive group can be said to constitute the Sudanese. Almost 50 years of intermittent war between the Muslim north and the Christian or animist south has left a north–south divide that is as evident today as it was at independence. Within these distinct regions considerable unity has been achieved between their many different ethnic groups through the years of north–south conflict, but the south remains committed to autonomy and the north continues to operate as an essentially separate state. The conflict in Darfur, which has brought great suffering and economic hardship to the west of the country, is another factor precluding the development of a national identity. Modern Sudanese identify primarily with their traditional ethnic groupings, many of which cross the country's borders, rather than with a nation-state. There are thought to be hundreds of distinct peoples within Sudan's borders speaking dozens of languages. Many of the smallest ethnic groups have become submerged in other larger groups through displacement during the country's many conflicts, but Sudan is still regarded as one of the most ethnically diverse nations in Africa. The majority of this diversity is found in the south, where there are many more individual groups than in the more culturally homogenous north.

FURTHER READING

Don Cheadle and John Prendergast. *Not on Our Watch: The Mission to End Genocide in Darfur and Beyond* (New York: Hyperion, 2007).

Robert O. Collins. *A History of Modern Sudan* (Cambridge, U.K.: Cambridge University Press, 2008).

M. W. Daly. *Darfur's Sorrow: A History of Destruction and Genocide* (Cambridge, U.K.: Cambridge University Press, 2007).

Ibrahim Elnur. *Contested Sudan: The Political Economy of War and Reconstruction* (New York: Routledge, 2008).

Kwame Essien and Toyin Falola. *Culture and Customs of Sudan* (Westport, Conn: Greenwood Press, 2008).

Julie Flint and Alexander De Waal. *Darfur: A New History of a Long War* (London: Zed Books, 2008).

William R. Jeffries. *The Darfur Crisis* (New York: Nova Science Publishers, 2008).

R. S. O'Fahey. *The Darfur Sultanate: A History* (New York: Columbia University Press, 2008).

Gérard Prunier. *Darfur: The Ambiguous Genocide* (Ithaca, N.Y.: Cornell University Press, 2005).

Brian Steidle and Gretchen Steidle Wallace. *The Devil Came on Horseback: Bearing Witness to the Genocide in Darfur* (New York: PublicAffairs, 2007).

Sudanis

The Sudanis, or the "Black Moors," are one of the two main subgroups of the MOORS Mauritania. They are descended from black African peoples such as the FULANI, SONINKE, TUKOLOR, and WOLOF.

Sudayr (Sudair)

The Sudayr are a Sunni Muslim Arab clan of the Dawasir, whose homeland is the northern area of Najd, in north-central Saudi Arabia. They are one of the most prestigious clans of the Dawasir, and since the 19th century C.E. have been closely associated with the SAUD, the ruling dynasty of the Kingdom of Saudi Arabia, through intermarriage and other affiliations. In the 1970s seven royal princes, all sons of Abd al-Aziz ibn Saud, the founder of the kingdom, and a Sudayri mother, rose to the highest levels of government office, including governor of Riyadh and minister of defense. Western observers dubbed the brothers "the Sudayri Seven." One of them became King Fahd, who ruled the kingdom from 1982 until his death in 2005.

Suk *See* POKOT.

Suku

The Suku inhabit a region in the southwest of the Democratic Republic of the Congo called Kwango for the Kwango River, which runs through it before becoming the Cuango River in Angola. The Suku language, also called Suku, is a Bantu language closely related to KONGO.

In the 17th century the LUNDA Empire was conquering lands in the southwest of the modern-day Republic of the Congo, and refugees from the Lunda invasions established the Suku Kingdom. The king was known as the Yaka of Minikongo, and hence the Suku were once known as the Yaka of Minikongo to differentiate them from the Yaka proper, who inhabit lands to the south of the Suku. In the 19th century the Suku profited as intermediaries of the trade in oil, raffia, cloth, beads, and guns. The carving up of Africa by European colonialists, however, brought an end to this trade, and Sukuland became an economic backwater.

Sukuma

The Sukuma are closely related to the NYAMWEZI people. The Sukuma live in lands to the north of the Nyamwezi in west-central Tanzania, covering the regions of Shinyanga and Mwanza. In fact, *sukuma* literally means "north" in the Nyamwezi-Sukuma language. The languages Sukuma and Nyamwezi are sometimes considered to be two closely related BANTU languages, but they are really several different dialects of the same language. Despite their many similarities and ties, the Sukuma and Nyamwezi are two distinct ethnic groups.

Like other Bantu peoples of what is now western and central Tanzania, the Sukuma formed semi-independent, self-governing units called *ntemi*. The *ntemi* system of political organization was in use by the Sukuma and Nyamwezi people by the 14th century, and it was adopted by other peoples in the region who came into contact with them.

Sumerians

Along with Egypt and the settlements in the Indus River Valley, Sumer was one of the earliest known cultures to develop the characteristics of an organized society. Theirs was one of the world's first civilizations. The Sumerians were the first people known to have invented an all-purpose system of written communication. Consequently their civilization is the earliest for which we have written records. The earliest of these records date from the fourth millennium B.C.E.

The Sumerians lived in present-day southern Iraq. The term *Sumerian* (from the word "Shumeru," the Akkadian name for the region) was first used by the AKKADIANS, a Semitic group from northern Mesopotamia who eventually assimilated into Sumerian culture (*see* SEMITES). The Sumerians themselves never used this term, calling themselves instead "sa gi ga," which can be roughly translated as "black-headed people." There is some debate as to whether this term was meant figuratively or whether it referred to some distinctive physical characteristic of the Sumerians. The fact that the Sumerians spoke a language totally unlike those of other Mesopotamian peoples makes it likely that the term may have been misinterpreted over the millennia. As such, the more recent Semitic term "Sumerian" has been generally adopted for the purpose of describing these ancient people.

The land that was to become Sumer was initially settled by farmers known as Ubaidians. Their exact origins are as yet unknown. Gradually, Semitic tribes from the surrounding areas migrated to the region and assimilated into Ubaidian society. Sometime around 3250 B.C.E. the people who became known as the Sumerians also migrated into the region from an unknown area. These new people spoke a language totally unlike any other known language from the time period, and had a unique culture. The Ubaidian, Semitic, and Sumerian elements of this new lower Mesopotamian society eventually combined through intermarriage and assimilation. They formed a complex society that fostered the world's first functional law code, the first coherent writing system, and some of the most powerful, competitive, and successful city-states of the ancient world, including Kish, Ur, Eridu, Nippur, and Lagash.

The decline of Sumer as an independent civilization is thought to have begun in the third millennium B.C.E. after a series of devastating attacks and rapid, large-scale migrations to the north. The region eventually became Babylonia under the influential Semitic leader King Hammurabi (ca. 1795–50 B.C.E.) In time,

SUMERIANS

location:
Southern Iraq, near the Persian Gulf

time period:
5300 to 2000 B.C.E.

ancestry:
Ubaidian; Semitic

language:
Sumerian

Sumerian cuneiform from the 26th century B.C.E.

the area became home to several other peoples, including the ASSYRIANS, who were heavily influenced by the culture and practices of the Sumerian civilization that had preceded them.

ORIGINS

While the exact origin of the first Sumerian people is still unknown, it is widely accepted that they most likely came from the Indus River valley or from the Euphrates River valley. Excavations in the Indus River valley have unveiled a large number of artifacts from an extremely ancient civilization that is very similar to what is known of Mesopotamian Sumer. Although southern Mesopotamia and the Indus River valley are about 1,500 miles apart, identical stamp seals have been found at excavations of both sites, along with figurines and architecture in the Indus River valley that practically mirror those found in lower Mesopotamia dated from the time of Sumerian predominance. This could be attributed to extensive trade between the two regions, but it is also possible that the Sumerian people originally came from the Indus River valley area and migrated south.

It has also been suggested that the Sumerians may have come from the Elamite mountain range, which lies to the east of Sumeria in present-day Iran. The prominence of mountains as symbols in Sumerian literature and art has led some scholars to suggest that the Sumerians may have originated in a mountainous area. Innumerable statues and other representations of Sumerian gods depict deities as standing or living on mountains, which connotes a familiarity with and a reverence for mountains. Adding weight to this theory is the fact that early Sumerian architecture is based on a type of timber construction that would have required access to wooded highlands. There were no such areas within ancient Sumeria but there were in the Elamite region.

More than one Sumerian origination legend states that there was an influx of people from the sea at a very early point in Mesopotamian history. That group of people could plausibly be the Sumerians themselves, though a lack of corroborative evidence makes it difficult to say for sure. The greatest credit to this theory is the relative proximity of the oldest city in Sumer to the Persian Gulf. Eridu, which is the earliest known settlement in lower Mesopotamia, is less than 100 miles away from the Gulf. Many historians have suggested that this

Detail of a fragment from the Stele of the Vultures erected ca. 2600–2500 B.C.E. to commemorate the victories of the Sumerian King Eannatum and discovered by archaeologists near the ancient city of Lagash in southern Iraq.

nearness makes a prehistoric seaborne arrival to Sumer plausible.

LANGUAGE

The Sumerian language is totally isolated, meaning that it has no apparent roots in any known language family from its time. Although the Sumerian language was eventually superseded by the Akkadian language as a means of day-to-day communication, Sumerian continued to be used through subsequent periods of Mesopotamian history in sacred rites and literature. The language became totally extinct by the second century C.E. and was not rediscovered until the 19th century, when excavations in southern Iraq uncovered evidence of a society that predated the Babylonian Empire.

Written Sumerian is divided into five chronological periods: Archaic Sumerian (3100–2600 B.C.E.), Classical Sumerian (ca. 2600/2500–2300/2200 B.C.E.), Neo-Sumerian (ca. 2300/2200–2000 B.C.E.), Late Sumerian (ca. 2000–1800/1700 B.C.E.), and Post-Sumerian (ca. 1800/1700–100 B.C.E.). Archaic Sumerian texts are limited mostly to business and municipal records, with some instances of written exer-

cises for educational purposes. Classical Sumerian findings extend to records of area rulers in addition to legal and public records. Sumerian writings from this period were the first to be translated by modern experts.

In 1835 English archaeologist Henry Rawlinson and his team of Persian and Kurdish workers discovered a steep cliff face covered in ancient inscriptions outside of the city of Kermanshah in western Iran. The rock is now known to have been created by the Persian king Darius I in the fifth century B.C.E. after Babylon has been conquered and made part of the Persian Empire (*see* PERSIANS). The rock is covered in inscriptions in three different languages. One of these was known to be Old Persian, but the other two cuneiform languages were then unknown. Rawlinson was able to successfully decipher a substantial amount of the text.

Until that time, it had been believed that the Babylonians had pioneered cuneiform writing. It was a significant discovery when it became apparent that many of the cuneiform writings on Behistun Rock were not from a Semitic language. Sumerian civilization was finally unveiled after millennia of total obscurity. It became obvious that a much older pre-Babylonian civilization must have started the practice of cuneiform writing. The BABYLONIANS and subsequent Mesopotamian peoples had simply followed a preexisting example. When ancient Lagash (near the modern city of Telloh) was excavated, these ideas were verified. The figures and bas-reliefs found on the site were very different from Babylonian representations. In addition, written tablets found at the site revealed a history stretching back far beyond that of Babylon.

What makes the Sumerian language so significant is that it is the earliest known written language in the world. Subsequent Mesopotamian languages such as Akkadian and Elamite adopted the Sumerian example, as did totally separate Indo-European languages such as Hittite. There is still much debate about the relationship of the Sumerian language with other known languages. As far as can be discerned with the evidence that is available, it seems that Sumerian is an isolated language. However, it has been hypothetically linked to a number of somewhat comparable language families such as Dravidian, Uralic, and Tibeto-Burman. It seems most likely that if there is any relation at all, it will be to more expansive groups such as Nostratic or Caucasian.

HISTORY

The history of Sumer is usually divided into seven major periods: the prehistoric Ubaid and Uruk periods, the Early Dynastic period (which includes four distinct subperiods), the Lagash dynasty, the Akkad dynasty, the Gutian period and Sumerian Renaissance, and the Ur III period.

Ubaid Period

The prehistoric nature of Sumer has been somewhat difficult to discern, but historians have made educated guesses based on findings at the al-Ubaid archaeological site near the ancient city of Ur in southern Iraq. At al-Ubaid grave sites were found that belonged to the earliest known inhabitants of the area, the Ubaidians. These workers of the land were the first permanent settlers in the area that became Sumer. They made important advances in agriculture and established many of the early trade routes that eventually became invaluable to the entire Mesopotamian region. They lived in large communities dotted with primitive but effective mud-brick homes and prominent municipal temples. Advanced pottery, masonry, and metalwork have been found in the Ubaidian ruins, showing a trend toward specialized labor and developing culture. It is also clear from studying the grave sites that during the Ubaidian period this region began to experience the first hints of social stratification. Some Ubaidians were buried along with considerable riches, while others were buried with next to nothing. The Early and Middle Ubaid periods (ca. 5300–4500 B.C.E.) saw the settlement of the area and the rapid development of agricultural methods that enabled and encouraged permanent settlers. In the Classic Ubaid period (ca. 4500–4000 B.C.E.), the region experienced its first boom of urbanization.

Uruk Period

The next major period in pre-Sumerian history was the Uruk period. By this time (ca. 4000 B.C.E.), increasingly extensive Mesopotamian trade routes had made lower Mesopotamia a bustling collection of city-states where local governments kept watch over citizens and utilized specialized laborers. This period brought the dawn of mass production, evidenced by large amounts of disposable single-use bowls found in ruins carbon-dated to this time period. In the Uruk age, the use of slaves became prevalent, and competition between the city-states of Sumer began to rapidly escalate. By this time, the once-small communities had become lively city-states with organized governments. The city of Uruk itself, located south of modern Baghdad, was the first major city-state of Sumer. The first real city in Mesopotamia, Uruk was centered on the Anu and Eanna temples. This civic structure was a sign of the future in Mesopotamia: All of the subsequent city-states that formed had religious districts at their centers.

Early Dynastic Periods

Almost everything that is now known about this mostly undocumented period is derived from a manuscript known to modern scholars as the Sumerian King List, a Sumerian-language document that is the chief source of knowledge about the rulers of the third millennium B.C.E. The document lists all of the Sumerian kings from before an event described as "the Great Flood" and up until about 1730 B.C.E.

The King List includes three major dynastic periods: Early Dynastic I, Early Dynastic II, and Early Dynastic III. The first period is largely unaccounted for, as it reaches past the 26th century in recorded dates. The kings listed

Sumerians time line

B.C.E.

5300–4000 Nomadic farmers known as Ubaidians settle in lower Mesopotamia; advanced agricultural methods promote long-term settlement and Sumer begins to rapidly urbanize; the plow is invented.

4000 Uruk becomes first major city-state in world; organized government and mass production are born in Sumer, as well as the earliest known cuneiform writing system.

2457 King Eannatum of Lagash conquers all of Sumer, creates first known empire in the world.

2334 Sargon of Akkad comes to power; he is the first leader known to have attempted the conquest of the known world; first Semitic ruler of Sumer.

2250 Akkadian Empire comes to an end at hands of Gutians; there is a large-scale migration out of southern Mesopotamia into the north in search of better soil; Sumerian civilization goes into decline.

2150 Short Sumerian Renaissance with the Third Dynasty of Ur ends only 150 years later; sharp shift in population and many foreign influences gradually phase out Sumer as an independent civilization.

1900 Lower Mesopotamian city of Babylon begins to gain power; within 200 years it is the largest city in the world.

in this period are credited as having extremely long reigns, each about 3,600 years. This obvious exaggeration lends to the hypothesis that some of these kings were probably legendary rather than real.

The second early dynastic period includes the first dynasties of the city-states of Kish, Uruk, and Ur. Most notably, the first dynasty of Uruk includes the name of Gilgamesh. The most famed piece of literature to have survived from ancient Sumer, *The Epic of Gilgamesh*, describes the semilegendary reign of this early Sumerian king.

The third period in the King List has the longest time span and includes the second and third dynasties of Ur, the second, third, and fourth dynasties of Kish and Uruk, the Akkadian period (which started with the reign of the famed King Sargon), the relatively short-lived Gutian period, and ends with the Amorite dynasty of Isin.

Lagash Dynasty

The dynasty of Lagash is chiefly known for the reign of Eannatum of Lagash, who ruled one of the first empires in recorded history. It is directly because of Eannatum's time in power that nearly all of Sumer was placed under the control of Lagash, which became the largest city in the world at the time. The rival city-states of Kish, Larsa, Ur, Uruk, and Umma were all under Eannatum's rule, in addition to territories acquired in Elam and Persia. Eannatum was eventually overthrown by rivals from Umma, adding animosity to the long era of intense rivalry between Lagash and Umma. The Lagash dynasty was the last time for over 200 years that a ruler of Sumerian ethnicity would be in command. After this period, the Akkadians rose to power, and independent Sumerian civilization came to an end.

Akkad Dynasty

The Akkad dynasty marks a turning point in Sumerian history at which the Semitic peoples of lower Mesopotamia came into power and Sumerian culture as a distinct entity started to disappear. Though there were a few less notable Semitic rulers before his time, Sargon of Akkad is credited with being at the helm of the Akkadian Empire at its greatest extent. While it is not clear how exactly Sargon reached his position of power, it is apparent that his empire was built quickly and efficiently. After attacking and conquering the city-states of Uruk, Ur, Lagash, and Umma, Sargon appointed Akkadian governors and made Semitic Akkadian the official language of Sumer. The Akkad dynasty lasted for about 200 years, and ended abruptly with the short reign of Shar-kali-Sharri, who was attacked and overthrown by the Gutians.

Gutian Period and Sumerian Renaissance

The Gutian period, which marked a brief Sumerian renaissance, began when the Central Mesopotamian-based Guti people took hold of Sumer during a series of brutal attacks. After the Guti invasion there is a brief period of historical silence from which there are no known records made by any kings or leaders. It is not known whether this period was obscured by the loss or destruction of public records or whether it was simply a period of chaotic anarchy in the wake of the devastating coup. The Guti ultimately appointed Gutian kings, but their 125-year dynasty seems to have been one of little artistic expression or public record keeping.

The Guti eventually absorbed into Sumerian culture, worshipping Sumerian gods and appointing Sumerian leaders to civic positions, leading to the restoration of Sumerian cultural predomination. Despite being conquered by two foreign influences, Sumerian society was still prevalent. By this time, however, Sumer had become a land of mixed ethnicity. The Guti and the Sumerians had frequently intermar-

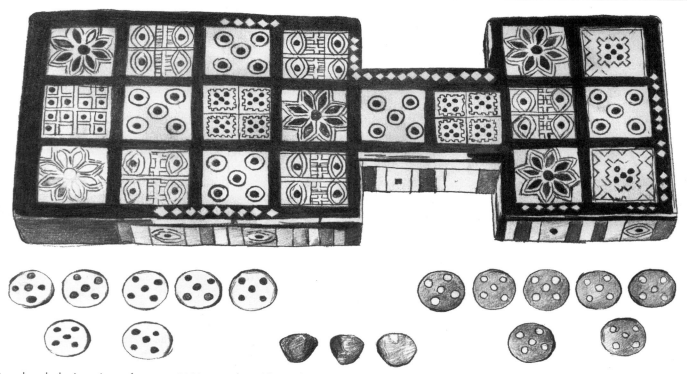

Board and playing pieces from ca. 2600 B.C.E. found by archaeologists at the site of the ancient Mesopotamian city of Ur.

ried, and the assimilation process was already nearly complete.

Ecologically, the agricultural prospects of Sumer were rapidly diminishing. Because of rising salinity levels and increased aridity, Sumer was no longer the fertile country it had once been. As a direct result, there was large-scale migration out of southern Mesopotamia into the North Country in search of better growing conditions. Even in its period of resurgence, Sumer was fading.

Ur III Period

The Third Dynasty of Ur came to power after the collapse of the Akkadian Empire and the subsequent Gutian period, which led to the beginning of the Sumerian Renaissance. The weak leadership of the Guti and their rapid absorption into Sumerian society cut their reign short, and Sumerians came back into power for a short time. Around 2050 B.C.E., Ur-Nammu of Ur came to control all the city-states in his vicinity and ushered in a golden age of Sumerian cultural rebirth. There is not much documentation available to clarify what happened during this period, but it is clear that the government was becoming more centralized. The city-states were continuing to build important relationships, and trade around the Persian Gulf was flourishing.

Decline

Sumer was facing pressure from the west and the east from the AMORITES and the ELAMITES respectively. The most prosperous city-states in Sumer were gradually conquered by these foreign influences. Two hundred and fifty years of violent warfare followed the decline of the Third Dynasty of Ur, and by 1750 B.C.E. the previously insignificant city of Babylon had been established as the capital of Mesopotamia under the rule of King Hammurabi I. Sumerian prevalence had come to an end.

CULTURE

Between the end of the First Dynasty of Ur and the Sumerian Renaissance, the period of intense war between the city-states led to the solidification of political thought and civil law. Although the famous Code of Hammurabi was recorded around 1900 B.C.E., after Sumer had disappeared, it is clear that the code was based upon the examples of the Sumerians, much like nearly every other aspect of Babylonian civilization. In fact, Hammurabi's law code is faithfully based upon an earlier code drawn up by King Dungi of the Third Dynasty of Ur in the last golden age of Sumer. The main contrasts between the Sumerian law codes and those of Babylonia are that the new empire had a considerably larger scope and significantly stricter penalties for offences committed against the family unity.

Class System and the Law Code of Hammurabi

King Hammurabi I was the first king of the Babylonian Empire. Having conquered Sumer and Akkad, Hammurabi's Babylon became the cultural and civic core of all of Mesopotamia. Hammurabi's famous law code sheds a great deal of light on ancient Mesopotamian society. The document, essentially the codified version of earlier Sumerian laws, is the best resource for interpreting Sumerian standards.

The Code of Hammurabi clarified a distinctly stratified social environment that had obviously existed in Sumer for quite some time. The populace consisted of three social classes: the patrician *amelu* order, which included religious and government officials as well as soldiers; the free but lesser middle *mushkinu* class, which included merchants, teachers, farmers, and specialized as well as unspecialized laborers; and, finally, slaves.

Legally, these classes were treated very differently. Any offences against *amelu* were punished with much harsher sentences than those against a middle-class citizen or a slave. If a nobleman was accidentally killed, the guilty would be required to pay a large monetary sum to the victim's family. If the same person were to accidentally kill a middle-class merchant, he or she would be forced to pay a much smaller sum. *Amelu* were punished more severely than *mushkinu* for the same offences. If an *amelu* caused physical injury to someone socially superior to him, he would be held to the "eye for an eye" standard. If it were the other way around, the *mushkinu* would only be fined. The law code differentiated between *amelu* and *mushkinu* only in personal matters. When it came to property, both classes were treated equally.

Slaves in Sumer were given a number of opportunities, although they were by no means on equal ground with the patrician and middle classes. A slave could challenge his sale in court, own his own business, receive loans, and even buy his own freedom. Conversely, slaves had few other legal rights. If a slave was caught trying to run away, he could be beaten. If he struck his master, his ear could be cut off.

Civil Law

Every aspect of municipal existence was documented in Sumer. Whether engaging in a monetary transaction, loaning money, writing up contracts, getting married, adopting a child, getting a divorce, or filing a grievance against another citizen, every public transaction or process had to be recorded. If there were any type of disagreement, these documents would be used as evidence. The Sumerians housed both a civic and ecclesiastical court. Every temple was alternatively a legal court, and both religious officials and appointed secular judges were qualified to make judgments.

The judicial systems of ancient Sumer and the modern world share a great deal in common. If a citizen had a complaint, he or she would seek the services of a *mashkim,* a type of mediator who would try to settle the case between the two parties without necessitating court and the full legal process. If the case could not be settled in this manner, or was outside of the *mashkim's* scope, the case would go to court. Up to four paid judges would hear the case from the plaintiff and the defendant. Witnesses gave their evidence under oath and previous examples were studied to determine a judgment. Once the judgment was made, sentences were irreversible. Court-appointed constables were responsible for implementing the sentence, whether it was collecting a fine or exacting an equal physical punishment. The "eye for an eye" doctrine was prevalent in Sumer in cases of physical injury, and capital punishment was used in severe cases. The entire legal proceeding and the subsequent sentencing were meticulously recorded by court scribes.

Marriage and Family Life

Women in ancient Sumer enjoyed a good number of rights compared to other ancient civilizations. It is clear that unfaithfulness in marriage was not tolerated by the law, and in general the legitimacy of the marital bond was firmly defended. Marriages were always prearranged by the respected elders of the family. The prospective groom would give his future wife a monetary engagement gift for which he would be doubly reimbursed should his bride have second thoughts before the wedding. After this, the punishment for infidelity as well as the rules for divorce were explained and detailed in writing.

Within a marriage, the wife was allowed to own her own slaves and have her own business, and she was the sole proprietor of her husband's estate should he be absent, unless the two had a mature son. When a married man died, his widow received as large a share of his estate as any of their children, and she would again be in sole possession of her dowry. However, carrying on the bloodline was clearly of utmost importance. A Sumerian woman's position in the home was chiefly that of child bearer, and secondarily as a wife. A man could sell his wife into slavery in order to pay a debt and could divorce her for the slightest reason. A woman had to go through a significantly longer and more difficult process to get a divorce, and by the time of the Third Dynasty of Ur, adultery on her part was punishable by drowning. Furthermore, if she was unable to bear children, she could be divorced, her marital rights would be stripped away, and her husband was legally allowed to utilize the services of concubines or a second wife. If a man did take a second wife, however, he was obligated under law to care for the first wife and keep her in his home. Additionally, the new wife was considered legally subservient to the first. If a woman was not physically barren but simply refused to bear children, she could be sentenced to death by drowning.

Children in Sumer were seen as totally subservient to their parents. Parents could disown their children and strip them of their inheritance as they pleased. They could be sold temporarily and permanently as slaves to pay debts. As a general rule, property was passed down to the children. The law outlined the fair division of an estate among children. Under the "Law of Nisaba and Hani," a son had the right to withdraw his share of his father's inheritance before his father passed away. The payment would be recorded and archived, and the son would have no longer have any claim on his father's assets.

Religion

Religion was an important part of Sumerian life. Sumerians believed that humans were created for the sole purpose of serving the many gods of their polytheistic religion, and their most important cities were always centered on huge ziggurats, which are elaborate multilevel temples. The Sumerians practiced a polytheistic religion with a large number of gods, both public and personal.

The four main gods of Sumerian religion were the water god Enki, the earth god Ki, the air god Enlil, and the god of heaven, An. It was believed that these gods were the authors of the laws and ethics that governed society. Everyone was required to abide by these rules, but it was also generally accepted that sin, moral decay, and difficult times were an inevitable part of the human experience. For these periods of

A Sumerian alabaster figure dating from ca. 2700 B.C.E.

time, each family was said to be provided for by a personal god who acted as an intermediary between the family and the major gods.

Each city also had a patron god. The major gods themselves were seen as far too busy to bother with everyday trifles. It is believed that most of the local gods were historical figures that became deified after performing services to the community or through their influential leadership. There are many references to "gods" living among their subjects in the city temples, eating earthly meals, and marrying human women. Each Sumerian city-state had a central ziggurat staffed by priests and priestesses, musicians, and various other temple officials.

Many religious festivals happened throughout the year, and ritual sacrifices were performed at the temple. Each month, the Sumerians celebrated with feasts dedicated to the gods, and each new year was marked with large-scale public celebrations.

Military

The long period of civil wars between the city-states of Sumer helped hone military practices that influenced later Mesopotamian societies as well as other worldwide heirs to Sumerian civilization. Much of the evidence for Sumerian military practices comes from a Sumerian military monument known as the Stele of the Vultures that was found in southwestern Iraq in the 20th century. Although it is now in fragments, the stele was originally a tall stone monolith that detailed the victory of King Eannatum of Lagash over the city-state of Umma in or around 2450 B.C.E. This battle was just the first of many violent clashes between Lagash and Umma.

The stele depicts Eannatum leading his spear-carrying infantrymen into battle in a phalanx formation. This is one of the earliest depictions of this formation, which eventually became associated with classical Greek civilization. The phalanx is a rectangular formation in which spear-carrying infantrymen create a dense block with their weapons pointed to the front. The Sumerians also used donkey-drawn carts that eventually paved the way for more efficient horse-drawn chariots. This level of military strategy denotes rigorous training, which in turn implies the use of professional soldiers in ancient Sumer.

Because Sumerian city-states were enclosed within protective walls, most wars between them were resolved by sieges. Sumerians used primitive siege engines to batter down the walls of their opponents' cities, or they attempted to starve the inhabitants by preventing any food or other supplies from getting in. These walls were constructed of mud-brick, which often made them vulnerable to even basic military technology.

Trade and Economy

It is clear that there must have been some far-ranging trade going on around the Persian Gulf during the age of Sumerian prevalence. Lapis lazuli from faraway Egypt and obsidian from Anatolia (modern Turkey) have both been found in lower Mesopotamia, along with various Indus River valley–branded goods dated to the same time period. Many native Sumerian goods also incorporated foreign products such as cedar-oil painted pottery and alabaster jewelry, both of which were inaccessible to Sumerians domestically.

Aside from this, the fact that Sumerians held foreign slaves shows that there were some occurrences of slave trade. In ancient times, the slave trade was one of the most lucrative and expansive trades in all of the Middle East and Africa.

Dwellings and Architecture

The first Sumerian dwellings were primitive but effective. Though these dwellings were originally made with reeds, housing techniques eventually evolved to include mud-brick, which was much more weatherproof and permanent.

Within the cities, houses were usually combined, with at least one wall shared with another dwelling. Upper-class citizens generally lived in larger, U-shaped houses with multiple rooms and a central courtyard. The Sumerians effectively pioneered many architectural techniques still used today. Their religious temples and royal dwellings made use of buttresses and half columns, as well as deep recesses. All of these techniques can be seen in later Greek temples and buildings, as well as more contemporary cathedrals and mosques.

Ziggurats—the hallmark of Mesopotamian architecture—were tall, multilevel stepped temples visually reminiscent of the great pyramids in Egypt and the Mayan temples on the other side of the globe in mesoamerica. Ziggurats were always the focal point of a Sumerian city-state. The Ziggurat at Ur is the best-preserved example of these Sumerian temples. At 210 feet tall and 150 feet wide, this massive tribute to the gods was constructed using millions of mud-bricks. The patron god of Ur, Nanna, was believed to dwell in the Ziggurat at Ur. Each night the bedchamber of the god at the top of the ziggurat was occupied by one woman chosen by the municipal priests to be a companion to the god.

Clothing and Appearance

Sumerian men usually had long hair worn parted in the middle. Most men had full beards, but it was also not uncommon for men to shave. They generally wore wrap-around skirts and robes with a shawl tossed over the left shoulder. It was customary for both Sumerian men and women to leave their right arm exposed. Women usually had long hair worn in a single braid that was piled on top of the head. They wore shawls and long dresses.

—◆—

Until the 19th century, Sumer was a forgotten civilization. Smothered by the crushing power of the Babylonian Empire, the Sumerian way of life faded beneath a long sequence of conquering influences. Perhaps the most lasting and influential contribution Sumerian civilization lent to human history was its writing system, which for the first time made it possible to keep business, legal, and religious records. Furthermore, the development of this writing system required that people learn to use it. As a result, schooling flourished in Mesopotamia for the first time.

Sumer was the world's first organized society, with permanent settlements, structured government, specialized laborers, and a partly urbanized culture. Their housing techniques revolutionized the developing world: Sumerian city-states were some of the first to make it possible for up to 50,000 people to live together in a relatively small area with the use of conjoined mud-brick homes. The Sumerians invented the wheel and the plow, and they led the way for complex astronomical records that were used by the Babylonians and subsequent cultures. Despite ultimately being eclipsed by their conquerors, the Sumerians left many lasting impressions on the whole of Mesopotamian and human history.

FURTHER READING

Linda Armstrong. *Ancient Mesopotamia* (St. Louis, Mo.: Milliken, 2002).

Harriet E. W. Crawford. *Sumer and the Sumerians* (Cambridge, U.K.: Cambridge University Press, 2004).

John Curtis. *Early Mesopotamia and Iran: Contact and Conflict, 3500–1600 BC* (London: British Museum Press, 1993).

Alan P. Dickin. *Pagan Trinity–Holy Trinity: The Legacy of the Sumerians in Western Civilization* (Lanham, Md.: Hamilton Books, 2007).

Amy Rebecca Gansell and Irene Winter. *Treasures from the Royal Tombs of Ur.* Harvard University Art Museums Gallery Series, no. 36. (Cambridge, Mass.: Publications Department, Harvard University Art Museums, 2002).

Jean-Jacques Glassner, Zainab Bahrani, and Marc Van de Mieroop. *The Invention of Cuneiform: Writing in Sumer* (Baltimore, Md.: Johns Hopkins University Press, 2003).

C. Leonard Woolley. *The Sumerians* (New York: Barnes and Noble, 1995).

Suri (Surma)

The Suri inhabit a region that straddles the border between southwestern Ethiopia and Sudan. There are three Suri subgroups: the BALE and the closely related CHAI and TIRMA. The Chai and Tirma live in the lowlands of southwestern Ethiopia on the southern edge of the Ethiopian highlands. The majority of the Bale live across the border in southeastern Sudan. The Suri speak Surmic languages, which belong to the Eastern Sudanic branch of the Nilo-Saharan family of languages.

The majority of the Suri are cattle-raising pastoralists. After experiencing civil conflict in both Sudan and Ethiopia, Suri herders can often be found protecting their herds with automatic rifles, which have become widely available. Guns were easily available from the rebel Sudanese People Liberation Army, and the Suri have now virtually formed a self-governing region of their own. The Chai and Tirma live in a semi-arid region and were badly affected by drought and famine in the mid-1980s, as were many Ethiopians.

Surma *See Suri.*

Susu (Soso)

The Susu are a MANDING people of West Africa. The Susu language is a MANDÉ language, which is part of the Niger-Congo subfamily of African languages. It is the common tongue used by the many ethnic groups living in southern Guinea. The majority of the Susu live in Guinea, where they are very influential. The remainder of the Susu can be found in northwestern Sierra Leone and Guinea-Bissau.

All Manding peoples originated from a mountainous region of the same name that sits astride the border of Mali and Guinea. Before the 13th century, the area was ruled by a Susu leader called Sumanguru. In 1235, however, Sumanguru was defeated by Sundiata—the renowned Malinke leader who founded the great medieval Empire of Mali. For much of the following two centuries the Susu numbered among the many people ruled over by Mali. After the Empire of Mali began to disintegrate in the 15th century, however, the Susu left their traditional homeland and migrated west to the Futa Djallon plateau of Guinea. From there they have continued to spread westward. The majority of the Susu have been Muslims since the 17th century.

Swahili

The Swahili people live in the coastal regions and on the small offshore islands of Kenya and Tanzania. Their name, derived from an Arabic word, means "coast dwellers."

SWAHILI

location:
Kenya and Tanzania

time period:
11th century C.E. to present

ancestry:
Bantu, Cushitic, Arab, Persian

language:
Bantu (Niger-Congo)

ORIGINS

The Swahili people are of mixed black African, Arab, and Persian descent. The coastal black Africans were mainly BANTU and Cushitic groups who had migrated into the area from the northwest, and some Bantu from the south, before 1000 (see CUSHITES). After the Bantu people, came the ARABS and PERSIANS from southwest Asia. Most were attracted by the trade in ivory, skins, and slaves, though some were seeking refuge from political or religious persecution. By the start of the first millennium, there were Arab settlements in Mogadishu, Lamu, Malindi, Zanzibar, and Kilwa. Some of the settlements were ruled by Arabs and others by Africans. Around 1200, Persians from Shiraz established the Shirazi dynasty on the Banadir coast around Mogadishu.

LANGUAGE

The Swahili language, called Swahili (or Kiswahili), belongs to the Bantu group of languages. Swahili contains about 20,000 Arabic words and has borrowed others from English, Persian, Portuguese, Urdu, and Gujarati. Swahili is not confined to the Swahili and is widely spoken by many other people—about 30 million altogether. Swahili is the official language of Tanzania and one of the national languages of Kenya and Uganda. It is spoken by some people in Djibouti, Somalia, Mozambique, and Madagascar, and a dialect is the main language in the Comoros Islands. Those people (about 1 million) who have Swahili as their mother tongue are called Waswahili, but they are not necessarily ethnic Swahili. Pidginized versions of Swahili are spoken in some parts of East Africa. A pidgin language is a grammatically simple one that combines elements of one or more languages. Pidgin Swahili is used as a common language by people of different nationalities, particularly in trade. An attempt was begun in 1925 to standardize Swahili. The Germans, who ruled what is now Tanzania, helped to spread the Swahili language by using it in their administration.

HISTORY

Swahili culture emerged from the intermingling—mainly through marriage and trade—of Arab, African, and Persian groups in East Africa. By the 1100s at the latest, the Swahilis had emerged as a distinct people. They had a number of small kingdoms based on trading cities up and down the coast. One of the most important was Kilwa. Here, gold, gum, ivory, slaves, and lumber from inland were traded for cotton, glass, porcelain, and pottery supplied by Arabian, Chinese, and Indian merchants. Kilwa was just one of about 40 such ports along the East African coast and on the islands of Pemba and Zanzibar, which are now part of Tanzania.

The golden age of Swahili culture came to an abrupt end when Portuguese adventurers arrived on the coast, at first in 1498. By 1509 the Swahili had lost their independence to the Portuguese. In the 17th century, Omani Arab traders began to settle on the East African coast, driving out the Portuguese (see OMANIS). They controlled most of the region by 1699, and between 1822 and 1837 the coast was ruled over as part of the Omani Empire. During this period, the Omani sultan, Seyyid Said, transferred his capital from Muscat in Oman to the island of Zanzibar in order to gain control of the area's trade routes.

Zanzibar dominated East African trade and became an international trading depot during the 19th century. Of particular importance in its prosperity was the slave trade. This was stimulated by the development of Arab plantations of cloves and coconuts on the East African coast and its islands, and French sugar plantations on islands in the Indian Ocean. Caravans began to be sent to the interior of East Africa as far south as present-day Malawi to collect slaves, and many Arab and Swahili traders made their fortunes in this destructive trade. By the 1860s, 70,000 people a year were being sold as slaves at the Zanzibar slave market. Zanzibar declined with the abolition of the slave trade and the advent of German and British colonists. By 1900 Britain and Germany had taken control of Zanzibar and the mainland regions covered by the states of Kenya and Tanzania. Kenya, Tanganyika, and Zanzibar became independent in the 1960s. In 1964, Tanganyika and Zanzibar united to form Tanzania.

CULTURE

The Swahili live in mixed societies alongside other ethnic groups. The coastal area where they mostly live is a narrow strip of fertile land, which gives way inland to a region of dry plains. Dotting the coast are many small islands also occupied by the Swahili.

The Swahili are essentially seen as town dwellers, although this was probably more true in the past than the present. Typically, Swahili houses were built of stone or coral, and their inhabitants had a high standard of living, with plumbing, elaborate furniture, and many imported luxury goods. Town houses are now more likely to be made of wattle-and-daub and thatched with palm leaves. In these houses live various tradesmen, such as carpenters, leatherworkers, and builders. The Swahili no longer dominate trade in East Africa; in fact, retailing and trade are often viewed as an occupation beneath the Swahili.

Outside the towns there are strings of small villages, where inhabitants of farming and fishing communities live in wattle-and-daub or coral houses thatched with palm leaves. Landowning and farming are given a relatively high status by the Swahili. Farmers mostly grow coconuts, millet, rice, sorghum, fruits, and vegetables. Fishing is also an important way of making a living for many. Women fishers wade into shallow water with nets to catch fish, which they carry home in baskets balanced on their heads. Fishermen sail further out to sea to the grounds where fish are plentiful.

The Swahili have a long history of literacy and literature. Although the Roman script is often used today, Swahili has been written for centuries in the Arabic script. There is a long tradition of elaborate poetry and written verse chronicles. The earliest known poem is the *Hamziya,* which survives in a manuscript of 1652. A group of poems in a manuscript of 1728 was probably written a century earlier. Early prose has survived in the form of a letter written in 1772. There are also many historical Swahili chronicles of particular kingdoms, for example, the *Chronicle of Pate* and the *Chronicle of Kilwa.* A Swahili history of Mombasa was translated into Arabic in 1824.

Government and Society

Unlike some African ethnic groups, the Swahili are not a fully distinct people. Having emerged over the years from a mixture of cultures, it can be difficult to determine which people are "true Swahili" and which are marginal. The Swahili themselves give higher status to families who can claim to be true Swahili descended from the earliest settlers. In the past these respected families were distinctive in that they controlled life in the towns, lived in the wealthiest section, were adept at Swahili verse, and dressed in Arab fashions. Clothing today still shows Arab

influence; many women wear black robes, cover their heads, and veil their faces. Although, most women work as hard as the men, wealthier women stay at home and do not work. This is considered to be a symbol of status.

Religion

Swahili culture is based on their religion, which is Islam. Here, the Arab element in Swahili ancestry is paramount. The many mosques, and the ruins of many ancient ones, bear witness to the importance of religion in Swahili life.

See also KENYANS: NATIONALITY; TANZANIANS: NATIONALITY.

FURTHER READING

Mark Horton and John Middleton. *The Swahili: The Social Landscape of a Mercantile Society* (Oxford, U.K.: Blackwell, 2000).

Jan Knappert. *Swahili Culture.* Studies in Swahili Language and Literature, vol. 5a-b (Lewiston, N.Y.: Edwin Mellen Press, 2005).

Alamin M. Mazrui. *Swahili Beyond the Boundaries: Literature, Language, and Identity* (Athens: Ohio University Press, 2007).

John Middleton. *The World of the Swahili: An African Mercantile Civilization* (New Haven, Conn.: Yale University Press, 1992).

Swahili time line

C.E.

first millennium Bantu and Cushitic peoples migrate into East Africa.

900s Arab trading posts established at Mogadishu and Kilwa.

by 1100s A distinct Swahili culture exists.

ca. 1150 Mombasa and Malindi founded.

ca. 1200 Persian Shirazi dynasty founded near Mogadishu.

1200s Mogadishu the preeminent port in East Africa

ca. 1400 Kilwa most important trading center on east coast

ca. 1270 Kilwa starts minting coins.

ca. 1470 Mombasa begins period of growth; Kilwa declines.

1502–09 Portuguese conquer East African coast to control trade.

1699 Omani Arab traders control of much of east coast.

1822–37 East African coast under rule of the sultan of Oman

1832 Zanzibar becomes Omani capital.

1840–80s Height of Swahili-Arab slave trade in East Africa

by 1900 Most Swahili under either German or British rule

1961–63 Kenya, Tanganyika, and Zanzibar win independence.

1964 Tanganyika and Zanzibar unite to form Tanzania.

See also KENYANS: NATIONALITY; TANZANIANS: NATIONALITY

SWAZI

location:
Swaziland, South Africa,
and Mozambique

time period:
15th century C.E. to
present

ancestry:
Bantu

language:
Bantu (Niger-Congo)

Swazi

The Swazi comprise over 90 percent of the population of Swaziland, an independent kingdom located between South Africa and Mozambique. Many more Swazi live in the neighboring areas of South Africa and Mozambique.

ORIGINS

The Swazi are descended from a group of BANTU-speaking peoples called the NGUNI who migrated from present-day eastern Nigeria to what is now Mozambique before the late 15th century. Dlamini I was their leader, and his descendants became the Swazi kings. In about 1750 Ngwane II, the earliest king commemorated in Swazi ritual, led his people into the territory of present-day Swaziland.

LANGUAGE

The Swazi language is Swazi (also known as Swati or siSwazi).

HISTORY

In 1839 Mswati I succeeded to the Ngwane throne at the age of 13, so his mother, Thandile, ruled as regent until he came of age in 1845. Thandile set the foundations for the success of Mswati's reign by centralizing the kingdom and introducing age regiments (groups who could be called upon for work or warfare) and establishing royal villages around the country to control them. The previous king, Sobhuza I (r. ca. 1815–39), and the powerful Mswati I (r. 1839–65) extended their territory and forged Swaziland by fusing local peoples and refugees from the ZULU Mfecane into a nation powerful enough to resist Zulu pressure. *Swazi* means "the people of Mswati," and, since the 19th century, this name has been given to the people and the nation previously known as Ngwane.

The Swazi kings pursued friendly policies toward the BOERS in the later 19th century by granting them concessions; however, the Swazi lost their land, resources, and finally their independence on becoming a British colony, administered by the Boers, in 1894. Swaziland became independent as a constitutional monarchy in 1968. In 1973 Sobhuza II (r. 1921–82) suspended the constitution, banned political parties, and assumed absolute power.

CULTURE

The majority of Swazi are farmers. Over 50 percent of the land in Swaziland is owned by

A Swazi woman wearing a traditional brightly-colored body wrap called an *emahiya*.

the monarchy, managed by local headmen, and granted to small-scale farmers to work. The main food crops are corn, sorghum, sweet potatoes, groundnuts (peanuts), and beans. Cash crops include cotton, rice, tobacco, citrus fruits, vegetables, and sugar. Cattle, goats, sheep, and chickens are kept. Men generally plow fields and sow seeds while women tend and harvest crops. Because many men work as migrant laborers, however, the division of labor is not strict, as the work often has to be done by whoever is available—generally the women.

One third of all adults work for wages in the private sector of the economy. Manufacturing industries employ many people in the processing of agricultural products. Tourism and forestry also provide jobs. Increasingly, men move away temporarily to find paid work elsewhere in the mines of Swaziland or South Africa. The drift of workers to towns and cities and the growth of large-scale commercial farming of citrus fruits, pineapples, and sugarcane are creating new patterns of living.

Government and Society

The basic social unit is the *indlu* (a husband and wife and their children). Several *indlu* make up a *umuti*. Each *umuti* has as its head an *umnumzana,* who is usually male, but with so many men working away from home it is often a woman. The *umnumzana* settles disputes, allocates land, and organizes workers. The members of an *umuti* share agricultural tasks. The clan is the broadest unit.

People belong to the same clan as their father and must marry outside it. Ideally, a man marries a woman from his paternal grandmother's clan. Marriage can be arranged by the parents of the bride and bridegroom, but love matches are just as common. The groom's family gives the bride's family cattle, cash, or both. Some men have more than one wife, but as many Swazi are Christian, so this is not common.

In Swaziland, the king and his mother have supreme legislative, executive, and judicial powers, which are exercised through a framework of local and political officials and organizations. The king inherits the throne from his father, a member of the powerful Nkosi Dlamini clan. If the last king had many sons by different wives, a family council chooses the new king by taking into account factors such as his mother's rank and his own age and character. Until this crown prince's coming of age—marked by his first marriage—his mother acts as queen regent, and she remains influential even after her son is installed as king.

Religion

Over half of the Swazi are Christians, but the Swazi religion is still widely practiced. It involves belief in a creator god, Mkhulumnqande, and in ancestors' spirits who can either help or punish their living relatives and so merit respect and appeasement. Many Swazi seek help from religious practitioners who use herbal cures; from diviners who use bones, cards, or other devices to diagnose the causes of ailments; and from Christian faith healers. Specialist diviners "smell out" witches who are believed to harm people or their possessions. In Swaziland today, most of these practitioners are officially registered and belong to trade organizations, and many also have set fees.

Famous Swazi cultural institutions include *sibhaca* dancing and the annual Umhlanga, or Reed Dance. Sibhaca dancers are teams of men performing vigorous, rhythmic dances in colorful skirts, with their wrists and ankles decorated with cowtails. Dancing also plays a part in the Incwala, or First Fruits Festival, a three-week-long period when king and nation reaffirm their relationship. This festival was introduced by Queen Regent Thandile in the 19th century to unify the kingdom and raise the king's standing.

See also SWAZIS: NATIONALITY.

FURTHER READING

P. L. Bonner. *Kings, Commoners, and Concessionaires: The Evolution and Dissolution of the Nineteenth-Century Swazi State* (Cambridge, U.K.: Cambridge University Press, 2002).

J. S. Malan. *Swazi Culture.* Communications of the Africa Institute, no. 52 (Pretoria, South Africa: Africa Institute of South Africa, 1985).

Margo Russell. *African Village: Living in a Swazi Homestead* (London: Channel 4 Books, 2001).

Swazis: nationality (people of Swaziland)

GEOGRAPHY

The Kingdom of Swaziland is a small landlocked nation in southern Africa. Swaziland has an area of approximately 6,700 square miles and has borders with two other nations; South Africa surrounds Swaziland on the north, west, and south and Mozambique meets the country's eastern border. Swaziland is roughly oval in shape and measures just 110 miles from north to south and 85 miles from west to east.

Swaziland's territory falls steeply in elevation from west to east. The western portion of the country consists of a highland region that is part of the much wider central highland plateau of South Africa. Further east a range of hills marks the transition to the low-lying plains of the eastern third of the country. The extreme east of the country is marked by a narrow range of mountains stretching north to south known as the Lebombo range. Several

SWAZIS: NATIONALITY

nation:
Swaziland; Kingdom of Swaziland

derivation of name:
From the Swazi people

government:
Monarchy

capital:
Mbabane

language:
English is the country's official language. SiSwati (language of the Swazi) is spoken by about 95 percent of the population.

religion:
About 40 percent of the population belongs to Zionist Churches (a form of Christianity unrelated to the Jewish Zionism). Other popular faiths include Roman Catholicism (20 percent) and Islam (10 percent). Anglicans, Methodists, Mormons, Bahai, and Jews are also present.

earlier inhabitants:
Khoikhoi

demographics:
About 95 percent of the population are Swazi, 2 to 3 percent are other southern African peoples, and 2 to 3 percent are Afrikaners or Europeans.

watercourses, including the Maputu and the Pongola Rivers, flow from the western highlands east across the country.

Swaziland's capital, Mbabane, is situated in the western upland region. A quarter to a third of the nation's population live in the capital city and its surroundings.

INCEPTION AS A NATION

According to tradition the ancestors of the modern Swazi migrated from the north into Mozambique before the 16th century C.E. Conflict with peoples living in the area of modern Maputo (Mozambique's capital) forced them to move west to the highlands of the interior. In the early 19th century King Sobhuza I founded the kingdom that was to form the core of modern Swaziland. The emergence of the early Swazi kingdom has parallels with that of the early Kingdom of Lesotho (see BASOTHOS: NATION-ALITY). In both cases the widespread upheavals and migrations of the early 19th century, known collectively as the Mfecane, forced the peoples of the area to withdraw into a defensive upland fastness. Boer settlers began to arrive in the area in the 1830s and the Swazi lost large areas of land to them. Conflict with the BOERS prompted King Mswati II (r. 1840–68) to ask for British protection, beginning an association with Britain that was to last for more than a century. From 1894 to 1902 Swaziland was administered by the South African Republic (a Boer-ruled state, also known as Transvaal Republic) with British approval. The Anglo-Boer War of 1899 to 1902 resulted in the defeat of the South African Republic by the British and the absorption of its territories into the British Empire. From 1902 Swaziland came under direct British control as part of its administration of the Transvaal. In 1906 the Transvaal was granted limited self-rule, but this did not extend to Swaziland, which continued under direct British administration.

Political developments under British administration closely paralleled those in the British administered Kingdom of Lesotho. Under a doctrine known as "indirect rule," Swaziland's kings (and queens) were permitted virtually complete control of internal affairs, although under the veto of a British-appointed commissioner, while Britain retained the right to conduct all foreign affairs. As was the case with Lesotho, Swaziland was not incorporated into the Union of South Africa (the predecessor of the modern Republic of South Africa) because of internal resistance to the idea and

because Britain opposed the apartheid policies of South Africa as they became increasingly stringent after World War II. Political parties with a nationalist agenda began to form in Swaziland's capital in the 1950 but gained little support among the general rural population. In 1964 traditional Swazi leaders, including King Sobhuza II and his inner council, formed the Imbokodvo National Movement (INM)—a political movement that gained widespread support. In elections held in 1964, the INM won all of the available seats in a new legislative council. Having established a popular mandate, the INM began pressing Britain for rapid independence. Swaziland became independent in September 1968 and adopted a constitution that established a constitutional monarchy.

CULTURAL IDENTITY

The early 1970s saw a radical change in the political system that had been adopted by Swaziland at independence. In the country's first postindependence elections, held in 1972, the ruling Imbokodvo National Movement (INM) lost three seats in parliament to an opposition party. King Sobhuza responded by suspending the 1968 constitution and adopting total executive, legislative, and judicial powers—effectively transforming himself into an absolute monarch. In 1977 the parliamentary system was abolished altogether and a system of local rule by hereditary tribal leaders was set up. The following year a new constitution was adopted in which representatives to a restored parliament are elected under a system known as *tinkhundla*. Under this system, traditional local councils select all candidates for parliament, although the king retains the right to appoint a certain proportion of parliamentarians. The *tinkhundla* system guaranteed the power of the monarch by making it virtually impossible for political opponents to be selected as candidates, let alone for them to be elected to parliament. A second body, the Swaziland National Council, made up exclusively of members of the royal family was charged with advising on Swazi tradition, a role that gave it great influence over the local councils.

There have been numerous attempts to bring democratic change to Swaziland since 1972, some of which have called for the complete abolition of the monarchy. The People's United Democratic Movement (Pudemo), an illegal political party founded in 1983, has repeatedly agitated for change through public demonstrations and strike action. Several re-

Swazis: nationality time line

C.E.

1903 Swaziland becomes a British protectorate.

1921 King Sobhuza II ascends the throne.

1962 Formation of the Ngwane National Liberatory Congress (NNLC).

1964 Swaziland's first constitution comes into force; legislative council established. The Imbokodvo National Movement (INM), founded by King Sobhuza II, wins all seats on legislative council.

1967 Bicameral legislature established. The INM wins all seats in the lower house.

1968 Swaziland becomes independent.

1973 King Sobhuza II suspends the constitution and outlaws political parties.

1977 Parliament is dissolved and replaced by a system of local tribal councils.

1978 A new constitution established the local tribal council system, known as *tinkhundla*.

1982 King Sobhuza II dies and is succeeded by Prince Makhosetive under the Queen Mother Dzeliwe as regent.

1983 Queen Ntombi, Prince Makhosetive's mother, becomes regent when Queen Dzeliwe is deposed. Opposition groups form the People's United Democratic Front (Pudemo).

1986 Prince Makhosetive is crowned as King Mswati III.

1991 King Mswati III initiates a constitutional commission, which is rejected by Pudemo.

1995 Swaziland Federation of Trade Unions (SFTU) organizes a general strike in protest at the absence of constitutional change.

1996 Pudemo initiates a campaign of civil disobedience. A new constitutional commission is established.

1997 Second general strike organized by SFTU.

2001 The constitutional commission recommends extending the king's powers and continuing the ban on political parties.

2003 Prodemocracy reformer Obed Dlamini wins a parliamentary seat in elections.

2004 United Nations reports that Swaziland has the highest incidence of HIV infection.

2007 Mass prodemocracy protests in the city of Manzini.

2008 Opposition groups boycott elections.

---

form commissions have delivered their findings, and a new constitution was adopted in 2005, but the power of the monarchy remains largely undiminished. In the first decade of the 21st century, Swaziland is the only nation in the world ruled by an absolute monarch. The influence of this institution has had a distorting effect on Swazi culture. Based on a traditionalist view of Swazi society, the power of the monarchy relies on the continuation of social patterns that have little relevance in the modern world. Lavish pageants and rituals that are presented as celebrations of Swazi culture underpin the regime by indoctrinating the population into the belief that Swaziland stands apart from the rest of the world by virtue of its retention of tradition. At the same time, however, the royal family freely spends the nation's wealth on palaces and private jets, while the average citizen subsists in one of the world's poorest economies. Swazi culture has effectively been redesigned according to a utopian vision of the past, while the general population has had little or no opportunity to develop a modern culture of its own. Examples include the often publicized "reed dance" in which the eligible young women of the kingdom parade in front of the king hoping to be chosen as his new wife. This takes place against the backdrop of one of the world worst AIDS epidemics, which has reduced the average life expectancy to less than 40 years.

Land ownership is a contentious issue in modern Swaziland. Sixty percent of the kingdom's land is held by the crown, while the re-

SYRIANS: NATIONALITY

nation:
Syria; Syrian Arab Republic

derivation of name:
From the ancient Greek name for the geographical region

government:
Republic

capital:
Damascus

language:
Arabic is the country's official language. Kurdish, Armenian, Aramaic, and Circassian are also spoken.

religion:
About 74 percent of the population are Sunni Muslim; other Muslim groups (including Alawis) make up 16 percent, and Christians the remaining 10 percent.

earlier inhabitants:
Amorites; Aramaeans; Canaanites; Eblaites; Phoenicians

demographics:
About 90 percent Arab. Kurds, Armenians, Circassians, and Druze make up the remaining 10 percent.

mainder is under private ownership, often by foreigners. Crown lands are allocated to farmers through chief and elders. Unallocated land is reserved for community use as places for reed harvesting, hunting, or firewood collection. Most Swazis live as subsistence farmers on crown lands. The major crops are sugarcane, cotton, maize, and tobacco. There is little industrial activity in the country. Rich iron ore deposits were depleted in the 1970s, but some foreign companies have set up production facilities. The most important of these are sugar-refining facilities and plants manufacturing soft-drink concentrate. Overgrazing, soil depletion, and frequent droughts have had a major negative impact on the agricultural sector, and the industrial sector has not grown quickly enough to provide jobs for the country's rapidly expanding population, resulting in high unemployment. Many Swazi men find work in South Africa's mining industry and spend many months away from home each year.

The Swazi people are a subgroup of the NGUNI people. The Nguni are one of the most widespread peoples of southern Africa and live in Zimbabwe, Malawi, Zambia, and South Africa. Other Nguni subgroups include the ZULU, the XHOSA, and the NDEBELE. All the Nguni people speak related languages, many of which are mutually intelligible. They are also related by their historical relationship to a breed of cattle known as Nguni cattle. The basic social unit of Nguni culture is the clan—an extended family grouping traced through the male line. The modern Swazi people are a conglomeration of Nguni clans that came together under the leadership of the Dlamini clan early in the 19th century. In the two centuries since the inception of the Kingdom of Swaziland, the Swazi people have attained a high degree of cultural homogeneity, but the individual clans have retained their identity. The Dlamini clan in particular remains distinct from the rest of Swazi society as the clan of the ruling family. Relations between the clans are generally peaceful, and disputes were traditionally settled according to long-established rules.

FURTHER READING

D. Hugh Gillis. *The Kingdom of Swaziland: Studies in Political History*. Contributions in Comparative Colonial Studies, no. 37 (Westport, Conn: Greenwood Press, 1999).

Hilda Kuper. *The Swazi: A South African Kingdom* (Belmont, Calif.: Wadsworth/Thomson Learning, 2002).

Syrians: nationality (people of Syria)

GEOGRAPHY

The Syrian Arab Republic is a Middle Eastern nation situated on the eastern shore of the Mediterranean Sea immediately south of the Anatolian Peninsula. Syria has an area of approximately 72,000 square miles and borders five other nations as well as the Mediterranean Sea. Turkey meets Syria's border in the north, Iraq lies to the east and southeast, Jordon lies to the south and Lebanon and Israel occupy the territory between the southwest quadrant of the country and the sea. Syria's border with Israel has been in dispute since 1967 when Israel captured and occupied part of the Golan Heights. Syria's coastline is about 120 miles long.

Syria may be divided into three broad geographical zones. A narrow, low-lying coastal plain extends along the entire Mediterranean shore from north to south. Rising behind this plain and running parallel to the coast is the Jabal an Nusayriyah mountain range, which has an average elevation of about 4,000 feet. To the east of these mountains is a broad plateau that makes up the majority of the country's area. The mountains' western slopes intercept moisture-laden winds coming off the sea, and these deliver modest but reliable precipitation. Consequently, the coastal plain that lies between the sea and the peaks is the least arid portion of the country and the most densely populated and agriculturally productive region. The eastern plateau is interspersed with several upland regions but is generally flat and arid. There are two areas of very arid desert, the Hamad in the south and the Homs Desert in the north. The Euphrates River, which rises in the mountains of neighboring Turkey, flows diagonally across the country from the north to the southeast between these desert regions and is Syria's most important river, providing much of its water. The narrow corridor of land around the river is also well watered and agriculturally productive.

In the west is a gap in the coastal mountains before they join the Anti-Lebanon Mountains of neighboring Lebanon. Known as the Homs Gap, because the pass is dominated by the city of Homs, this natural corridor between the interior and the coast has been used by traders and conquerors for millennia. Syria's capital, Damascus, lies in the southwest corner of the country in a relatively fertile region at the foot of the eastern slopes of the Anti-Lebanon

The Citadel of Aleppo, Syria. A large fortress built on top of an artificial hill that has been in use since the third millennium B.C.E. as a defensive position. The fortress standing today was built during the 12th and 13th centuries C.E.

Mountains, which form the border between Syria and Lebanon at this point. Other large cities include Aleppo in the north, Hama on the banks of the Orontes River in the west, and Latakia on the Mediterranean coast, which is Syria's main port.

INCEPTION AS A NATION

The heartland of Syria forms part of the area known as the Fertile Crescent, an area stretching from the Nile Valley, along the Mediterranean coast, and down the valleys of the Euphrates and Tigris Rivers to the Persian Gulf that was home to some of the world's earliest civilizations. The earliest known urban civilization in Syria was that of the EBLAITES, which was centered on the city of Ebla about 35 miles southwest of modern Aleppo. In the third millennium B.C.E. the Eblaites built an empire that extended from the Red Sea in the south to Anatolia in the north and east into Mesopotamia. Its wealth was based on controlling trade between the Mesopotamian civilizations of the AKKADIANS and the SUMERIANS in the east and the Mediterranean.

During the second millennium B.C.E. several peoples established themselves in the area

of modern Syria, including the AMORITES, the ARAMAEANS, the CANAANITES, and the PHOENICIANS. Syria was the battleground over which a series of great civilizations battled, including the EGYPTIANS from the south, the HITTITES from the north, and the BABYLONIANS and ASSYRIANS from the east. By the middle of the first millennium B.C.E. the Iranian Achaemenid Empire had established control over the entire Middle East, including Syria. Alexander the Great conquered the area in the fourth century B.C.E., and it was subsequently ruled by the ROMANS and the Byzantines. The seventh century C.E. brought great political change to the entire Middle East when Arab armies carrying the message of Islam spread rapidly across the region from the Arabian Peninsula.

Muslim ARABS captured Damascus in 635, and Syria quickly became an area of central importance to the emerging Muslim caliphate. For more than a century Damascus was the capital chosen by the rulers of the Umayyad dynasty. The city lost some of its prestige after 750 when the Abbasid dynasty established their capital in Baghdad, but it remained a prosperous center of learning and trade.

Syria diminished in importance during the 14th through the 16th century. The Mongol in-

Syrians: nationality time line

C.E.

1918 An Arab army captures Damascus, ending four centuries of rule by the Ottoman Empire.

1920 Syrian National Congress proclaims Faysal bin al-Hussein bin Ali el-Hashemi King Faysal I of Syria.

1920 French forces defeat Syrian troops and dismantle the new kingdom.

1925–26 National uprising against French rule of Syria suppressed militarily.

1936 France agrees to Syrian independence but fails to implement the proposals.

1940 Syria comes under control of the Vichy French government following France's defeat by Germany in World War II; Arab nationalist Baath Party founded in Damascus.

1941 British and Free French forces occupy Syria. French undertake to grant Syrian independence.

1946 Last French forces leave Syria.

1958 Syria and Egypt form the United Arab Republic (UAR).

1961 UAR dissolved after military coup in Syria.

1963 Baath-dominated government established under President Amin al Hafez following another military coup.

1966 Internal Baath Party coup

1967 Arab-Israeli War (also known as the Six-Day War); Golan Heights occupied by Israel.

1970 Hafez al-Assad seizes power.

1973 Arab-Israeli War (also known as the Yom Kippur War); Israel defeats attacks by Syria and Egypt and retains control of the Golan Heights.

1976 Syrian troops intervene in Lebanese civil war.

1980 Muslim Brotherhood insurgency against Assad's government begins.

1982 Tens of thousands killed in Syrian operations against Muslim Brotherhood rebellion in the city of Hama; Israel invades Lebanon and engages Syrian forces.

1990 Syria joins U.S.-led coalition to liberate Kuwait from Iraqi occupation.

1999 Negotiations with Israel over the Golan Heights fail to reach agreement.

2000 President Assad dies; Assad's son, Bashar al-Assad, is installed as president.

2001 Syrian troops leave Beirut but remain in Lebanon.

2003 Syrian denies U.S. accusations that it is harboring Iraqi insurgents and developing "weapons of mass destruction."

2005 Syrian troops withdraw from Lebanon.

2006 Thousands of Lebanese seek refuge in Syria during Israel's military operation against Hezbollah in the south of the country.

2007 Israel bombs a facility in Syria that it claims is being used for a nuclear weapons program.

2008 Islamist militants are blamed for an explosion that kills 17 in Damascus. Syria and Lebanon establish diplomatic relations for the first time.

vasions of the 14th century devastated many of its cities, and during the 16th century sea routes were established between Europe and Africa and India that began to replace the overland routes that had been Syria's source of wealth for millennia (see MONGOLS). Under Ottoman rule between the 16th and early 20th centuries Syria became a cultural and economic backwater cut off from the main streams of commerce and development (see OTTOMANS). Its population fell to levels far below those it had supported during the Roman era a thousand years earlier.

Following the defeat of the Ottoman Empire in World War I, its territory, including

The second century c.e. Roman theater in the ruins of the ancient city of Bosra in present-day southern Syria.

Syria, was partitioned among the victories powers. In 1922 the League of Nations (the predecessor of the United Nations) divided the area traditionally referred to as Syria into two parts and mandated their administration to France and Britain. Britain received the mandate to administer Transjordan and Palestine, and France received the mandate to administer an area that included modern Syria and Lebanon. Damascus had been captured from the Ottomans by an Arab army in 1918 and, in accordance with assurances it had received from the British, expected to establish an independent Arab state. This state was declared in March 1920 under the Hashemite King Faysal but quickly dismantled by the French after they defeated Syrian forces at the Battle of Maysalun in July of the same year. A major rebellion against French rule began in 1925 and was only suppressed after intensive intervention by French forces. From 1920 to 1946 the French established a number of subordinate states within the traditional territory of Syria. These included the State of Aleppo, the State of Damascus, a Jabal Druze state in the south where the concentration of DRUZE people was highest, an Alawite state on the coast, and a Maronite-dominated state known as Greater Lebanon that later became modern Lebanon (*see* MARONITES). An independence agreement was reached in 1936, but France failed to

fully uphold the agreement, and the advent of World War II in 1939 suspended any further negotiation. Following France's defeat by Germany in 1940, Syria came under the control of the French Vichy government until the country was invaded and occupied by Free French and British forces in 1941. Syrian independence was officially recognized in 1944, but the last French troops did not leave the country until 1946.

CULTURAL IDENTITY

The fragmentation of Syria under French rule led to the loss of some territory that had traditionally been regarded as Syrian, most notably the coastal region that became Lebanon and the northwest corner of the country (the Sanjak of Alexandretta), which was ceded to Turkey in 1939. Consequently, Syrian national consciousness tends to be subject to a historical ideal of Syria that extends beyond its current boundaries. Most Syrians have a strong Sunni Muslim Arab identity, which creates a large degree of cohesion within the state, since more than 75 percent of the population conforms to this description, but which also manifests itself in close ties across national borders. The desire to regain control of the part of the Golan Heights lost to Israel in the 1967 Arab-Israeli War (also known as the Six-Day War) is also a strong unifying factor in Syrian society.

There are numerous other ethnic groups within modern Syria, although none of these is large. The ALAWIS, who belong to a Shii Muslim sect, are concentrated in the coastal district around the city of Latakia. Numbering some half a million, they make up the largest of Syria's minorities. The Druze live in remote regions of the Anti-Lebanon Mountains in the southwest and belong to a wider community that extends into neighboring Lebanon. There are also scattered communities of CIRCASSIANS, KURDS, and ARMENIANS. Each of these groups has tended to retain its distinct cultural identity and play a limited part in the mainstream of Syrian political and social life. Since the founding of Israel in 1948, the south of the country has also been home to a large and growing community of displaced PALESTINIANS. Tens of thousands of IRAQIS also migrated into Syria after the start of the U.S.-led occupation of Iraq in 2003.

In the years since independence, Syria has been a significant force in the social and political movements known as Arab nationalism and Pan-Arabism. Arab nationalism is a movement that supports the idea that all Arabic speakers share a common history and cultural heritage regardless of their nationality. Arab nationalists are against what they see as the damaging influence of Western culture on the Arab world and believe that regimes that are too dependent on the West should be overthrown. The Arab Socialist Resurrection Party (more commonly known as the Baath Party), which was one of the earliest and most influential elements of the secular Arab Nationalist movement, was founded in Damascus in 1940. Egypt, under President Gamal Abdel Nasser, was the leading center of Arab nationalism in the postwar period, and in 1958 the Syrian government agreed to unite Syria and Egypt as the United Arab Republic in a move that was hoped to encourage other Arab nations to join a single pan-Arab state. The union was not successful, however, and was dissolved in 1961. A period of political turmoil followed in Syria until 1963, when the Baath Party engineered a military takeover of the government. A similar Baath Party takeover had occurred in neighboring Iraq a month earlier. Negotiations to form a second union between Syria, Egypt, and Iraq foundered when the Baath government in Baghdad was overthrown soon thereafter. Although the Baathists were later restored to power in Iraq, the Baath leadership in Syria and that in Baghdad diverged politically from this point and considerable enmity developed between the two nations.

The Baath Party remained in power in Syria, although there were numerous coups and countercoups within its ranks. In 1970 Hafez al-Assad carried out the last of these coups, installing himself as president at the head of a military government. Assad remained in power for the next 30 years, bringing political stability to the country at the cost of repressive social and political measures. Assad was from an Alawite family and as such was a Shii Muslim governing a predominantly Sunni Muslim nation. He governed according to secular principles, but this, together with his Alawite origins, angered some sections of Syrian society that believed that the government should reflect the faith of the majority of its people. Following the 1979 Islamic Revolution in Iran, a growing trend toward religious fundamentalism made itself felt across the Middle East, and in Syria this took the form of a violent insurgency carried out by the Muslim Brotherhood, an international Sunni Muslim organization that had been founded in Egypt in the 1920s. Against the background of heavy Syrian involvement in Lebanon's civil war, the Muslim Brotherhood in 1980 launched a series of attacks against military and government targets intended to destabilize Assad's regime. These included a nearly successful attempt to assassinate Assad himself. The regime's retaliation was brutal and widespread. Tens of thousands of people are believed to have been killed when the Syrian military shelled the strongholds of radical Sunnis in the city of Hama in 1982. Many more were killed in massacres carried out in Syrian prisons where thousands of suspected militants had been summarily incarcerated.

Syria's response to the Muslim Brotherhood uprisings led to international condemnation, and its repressive regime was regarded with suspicion by Western nations that also disapproved of its long-term involvement in Lebanon. During the 1980s the country became increasingly isolated and internal pressure for reform remained stifled. In 1990 Syria aligned itself with those nations opposing Iraq's invasion of Kuwait and supported the U.S.-led military intervention that followed to liberate the country. This led to a significant thawing in relations between Syria and the West. U.S.-sponsored negotiations between Syria and Israel over the Golan Heights followed, although these failed to reach a satisfactory conclusion. Following President Assad's death in 2000, tension has generally lessened as Syria has withdrawn from Lebanon, but there have also been continuing issues of contention with the United States, particularly over accusations that the Syrian government has harbored Iraqi insurgents and that it is attempting to acquire atomic and biological weapons.

Syrian culture is remarkably rich and embroidered with elements from the dozens of powerful civilizations that have controlled the area over the centuries. Syria is home to some of the most important archaeological remains in the Middle East, and many of its cities are among the oldest continually inhabited places on earth. There is evidence that there were settlement at Damascus in the seventh millennium B.C.E., for example. Successive dynasties have left spectacular buildings and ruins, including the Great Mosque of Damascus (also known as the Umayyad Mosque), one of the oldest and largest mosques in the world, the Citadel of Aleppo, and numerous Roman buildings that demonstrate the great wealth and prestige of the region under Roman rule. The influence of French culture is also evident in the cities, and today Damascus is a large modern city that resembles the metropolitan centers across the world. Islam dominates modern Syrian culture, but decades of secular Baath Party rule and a long tradition of tolerance toward the faiths of minority groups have resulted in more liberal attitudes than those found in Muslim states with essentially religious constitutions, such as Saudi Arabia. In urban areas men and women commonly wear Western-style dress and women are an accepted part of economic life.

FURTHER READING

David Dean Commins. *Historical Dictionary of Syria* (Lanham, Md.: Scarecrow Press, 2004).

Jubin M. Goodarzi. *Syria and Iran: Diplomatic Alliance and Power Politics in the Middle East.* Library of Modern Middle East studies, 55 (London: Tauris Academic Studies, 2006).

Raymond A. Hinnebusch. *Syria: Revolution from Above* (London: Routledge, 2001).

Hannes Möhring. *Saladin, the Sultan and His Times, 1138–1193* (Baltimore, Md.: Johns Hopkins University Press, 2008).

John Morrison and Adam Woog. *Syria* (New York: Chelsea House, 2008).

Robert G. Rabil. *Embattled Neighbors: Syria, Israel, and Lebanon* (Boulder, Col.: Lynne Rienner Publishers, 2003).

James Reston. *Warriors of God: Richard the Lionheart and Saladin in the Third Crusade* (New York: Doubleday, 2001).

Barry M. Rubin. *The Truth About Syria* (New York: Palgrave Macmillan, 2007).

John A. Shoup. *Culture and Customs of Syria* (Westport, Conn: Greenwood Press, 2008).

Jordi Tejel. *Syria's Kurds: History, Politics and Society.* Routledge Advances in Middle East and Islamic Studies, 16 (London: Routledge, 2009).

T

Taita

The Taita are a cluster of BANTU people in East Africa. They live in the Taita Hills of southwest Kenya near the border with Tanzania.

Tajiks (Tadzhik)

The Tajiks, a people of Central Asia, constitute 80 percent of the population of the Republic of Tajikistan; they also live in Uzbekistan, Afghanistan, Iran, and China. The Tajiks originated in the central Iranian plateau and are regarded as the inheritors of a sedentary farming culture that diffused from Iran eastward into the area between the Caspian Sea and the borders of modern China from the prehistoric period. They are one of the largest ethnic groups in Central Asia, numbering up to 30 million, but are the only large Central Asian ethnic group to speak a language related to the Persian language. The term *Tajik* is of Turkic origin and means "non-Turk." It was used by TURKIC PEOPLES to refer generally to the Persian-speaking peoples of Iran and the rest of Central Asia.

Takadi

The Takadi are one of the three main subgroups of the KONSO. The Konso live in southwest Ethiopia.

Talensi

The Talensi are a MOLE-DAGBANE people of northeast Ghana.

Talysh (Talishi)

The Talysh are an Iranian people, most of whom now live in the Republic of Azerbaijan, on the southwestern shore of the Caspian Sea, with smaller numbers in Iran. They speak Talysh (Talishi), an Indo-European language of the Northwest Iranian branch related to Kurdish and Mazandarani, and most are Shii Muslims. Their homeland includes a narrow, fertile coastal strip with rich vegetation and forested mountains inland. The main city is Lankoran (Länkäran). The people came under Arab rule in the early conquests (mid-seventh century) and were ruled by dynasties that succeeded the ARABS in Iran. The area attracted the attention of the Russian tsar Peter the Great, who occupied it in the early 18th century, and after some back-and-forth with Iran, the area became Russian territory in 1813.

Tama

The Tama are a cluster of ethnic groups linked by the Tama language. They are concentrated on and around the border between Sudan and Chad. Tama-speaking peoples include the Tama proper, MARARI, ABU SHARIB, GIMR, and MILERI. Increasingly, however, Tama is being replaced by Arabic. The Tama, along with many other peoples, have been involved in the long-running Sudanese civil war. Although they are considered to belong to the so-called Arab population of Sudan they have been the victims of attacks from the Arab-dominated government.

Tamberma *See* SOMBA.

Tambo

The Tambo are a SADAMA subgroup. The Sadama are an ethnic group living in Ethiopia.

Tanala

The Tanala are a MADAGASCAN PEOPLE living in the southern half of the island inland from the eastern seaboard.

Tandroy *See* ANTANDROY.

Tanzanians: nationality (people of Tanzania)

GEOGRAPHY

The United Republic of Tanzania is a large nation in East Africa. Situated slightly south of the Equator, Tanzania lies in the Great Lakes region of East Africa and has a coastline on the Indian Ocean. Tanzania has an area of approximately 365,000 square miles, of which about 23,000 square miles is inland waters. Eight other nations meet Tanzania's borders: Kenya lies to the northeast, Uganda to the north, Rwanda and Burundi to the northwest, the Democratic Republic of the Congo to the west, Zambia and Malawi to the southwest, and Mozambique to the south. Tanzania's northern border with Uganda bisects Lake Victoria from west to east. Its border with the Democratic Republic of the Congo runs from north to south through the middle of Lake Tanganyika, and its border with Malawi runs along part of the eastern shore of Lake Malawi (also known as Lake Nyasa). Tanzania's coastline extends for 885 miles along the Indian Ocean.

Several islands in the Indian Ocean also form a constituent part of Tanzania's territory. The largest of these islands, Zanzibar (also known as Unguja Island), has an area of about 640 square miles and lies 22 miles off the mainland coast of Tanzania. The second largest island, Pemba, has an area of 380 square miles and lies about 25 miles north of Zanzibar. Other inhabited islands include Chumbe Island and Mafia Island.

Tanzania lies within one of the most geographically spectacular parts of Africa. Lake Victoria, about half of which is within Tanzanian territory, is the largest lake (by area) in Africa and the second largest in the world. Lake Tanganyika is the deepest lake in Africa and the second deepest in the world, and the continent's largest body of fresh water (by volume). Lake Victoria, Tanganyika, and Malawi are part of the Great Rift Valley system—a geological fault that extends from East Africa north to the Middle East. Apart from a narrow coastal plain, much of Tanzania consists of a relatively flat central plateau with an elevation of between 3,000 and 6,000 feet. The northern part of this plateau includes the Serengeti Plains, a grassland habitat covering almost 12,000 square miles that hosts the annual migration of millions of wildebeests, gazelles, zebras, and buffalos following seasonal rains. An upland region in the northeast, close to the border with Kenya, includes the 19,300-foot-high peak of Mount Kilimanjaro, the tallest mountain in Africa, as well as the Ngorongoro Crater, the world's largest unbroken volcanic caldera above water. The Pare and Usambara Mountains are also a feature of Tanzania's northeast quarter. The Kipingere Mountains (also known as the Livingstone Range) are found in the southwest, extending into Malawi at the northern end of Lake Malawi. Numerous rivers flow from west to east, including the Ruaha, the Kagera (which flows along the Tanzania–Rwanda border and the Tanzania–Uganda border), and the Rufiji, which is the country's longest watercourse. Most of Tanzania's rivers dry out periodically.

About 30 percent of Tanzania's population lives in urban areas. The most densely populated regions are close to permanent water sources around the mountains of the northeast, the southern shores of Lake Victoria, and the shores of Lake Tanganyika and Lake Malawi, but the largest city is Dar es Salaam, a port city on the Indian Ocean. Although Dar es Salaam is the economic and cultural center of the nation, it ceased to be Tanzania's capital in 1996 when the seat of government was moved to the city of Dodoma on the central plateau.

INCEPTION AS A NATION

Scientists have discovered the earliest known evidence of human habitation and the earliest known remains of prehuman hominids at sites in present-day Tanzania. Olduvai Gorge in the Serengeti Plains is sometimes referred to as the "Cradle of Mankind" because of the wealth of very early human artifacts and the early human and prehuman remains that have been found there, including stone tools that are more than 2 million years old. Ten thousand years ago hunter-gatherer peoples inhabited Tanzania (possi-

TANZANIANS: NATIONALITY

nation:
Tanzania; United Republic of Tanzania

derivation of name:
A combination of Tanganyika and Zanzibar

government:
Republic

capital:
Dodoma

language:
The country's official language is English. Swahili (or Kiswahili) is the nation's lingua franca. There are more than 100 local indigenous languages, most of them Bantu. Arabic is widely spoken on Zanzibar.

religion:
About 35 percent of the population are Muslim, 30 percent are Christian, and 35 percent follow indigenous faiths. Ninety-nine percent of the population of Zanzibar are Muslim.

earlier inhabitants:
Khoikhoi

demographics:
95 percent of the population are Bantu peoples (between 120 and 130 tribal groups); 4 percent are Cushitic or Nilotic peoples; 1 percent are Arab, European, or of mixed Arab and African ancestry.

Tanzanians: nationality time line

C.E.

ninth century Maritime trade links between Persian Gulf and Tanzania established.

12th century Arab and Persian traders establish settlements on Tanzanian coast and island.

1498 Portuguese explorer Vasco da Gama arrives on Tanzania's coast.

1698 Sultanate of Oman conquers Zanzibar.

1830s Sultanate of Oman moves its capital to Zanzibar.

1850s Sultanate of Zanzibar established independently of sultanate of Oman.

1886 Germany establishes a protectorate over mainland Tanzania.

1890 Britain establishes a protectorate over Zanzibar.

1891 German East Africa established.

1905–06 Maji-Maji Rebellion in German East Africa

1916 British, Belgian, and South African troops occupy German East Africa during World War I.

1920 Britain receives League of Nations mandate to administer former German East Africa territories as Tanganyika.

1929 First indigenous political party, the Tanganyika African Association (TAA), founded.

1946 Tanganyika becomes a United Nations trust territory under British administration.

1954 TAA renamed as Tanganyika African National Union (TANU).

1961 Tanganyika becomes independent, with TANU leader Julius Nyerere as prime minister.

1962 Tanganyika becomes a republic with Nyerere as president.

1964 Zanzibar becomes independent and the sultan is overthrown in a violent republican revolution. Zanzibar and Tanganyika unite to form the United Republic of Tanzania.

1967 Nyerere issues the Arusha Declaration outlining principles of a one-party socialist state.

1977 TANU and Zanzibar's ruling Afro-Shirazi Party unite to form Chama Cha Mapinduzi (CCM), or Party of the Revolution. CMM becomes the only legal political party.

1978–79 War with Uganda; Tanzanian forces depose Uganda's President Idi Amin Dada.

1985 Nyerere retires at the end of his fifth presidential term. Succeeded by former president of Zanzibar Ali Hassan Mwinyi.

1992 Constitutional amendments introduce a multiparty system.

1995 Benjamin Mkapa of CCM elected to the presidency.

2000 Mkapa elected to a second presidential term.

2001 Thirty-one people killed by security forces in Zanzibar during protests over alleged election fraud. Member of the Civic United Front (CUF) arrested over disturbances.

2005 Mkapa retires. Jakaya Kikwete of CCM wins presidential elections. Protests over alleged election fraud on Zanzibar.

2006 Tanzania signs economic agreements with China.

2008 Governor of Tanzania's central bank dismissed after corruption investigation.

---

bly KHOISAN speakers). Between three and five thousand years ago CUSHITES migrated into the area from the north, introducing agriculture. About 2,000 years ago BANTU-speaking peoples moved into Tanzania, bringing knowledge of ironworking.

Maritime trade between the peoples of the Middle East, particularly the Arabian Peninsula, and the Tanzanian coast may have begun early in the first millennium C.E. By the ninth century trade between the Persian Gulf and the Indian Ocean coast of Africa was firmly established, and by the 12th century ARABS and PERSIANS had established trading posts on the Tanzanian coast and its offshore islands. The mingling of Arabs, Persians, and the indigenous peoples of East Africa resulted in the creation of a Swahili-speaking culture that extended along much of Africa's Indian Ocean coast. The island of Zanzibar became one of the most important centers of this culture.

At the end of the 15th century, Portuguese explorers reached the east coast of Africa and soon began to establish trading settlements. By 1525 Portugal controlled Zanzibar and much of the coast of Tanzania, but its control was challenged in the 17th century by the growing power of the sultanate of Oman. The OMANIS took control of Zanzibar and the other islands of the archipelago in 1698. Zanzibar became such an important and wealthy center that the sultan of Oman moved his capital there from Muscat in the 1830s. In the 1850s Majid ibn Said established himself as sultan of Zanzibar, effectively separating the island from the sultanate of Oman. The sultanate of Zanzibar became extremely wealthy by controlling much of East Africa's trade in ivory, gold, and slaves. Its power extended over dozens of Swahili-speaking towns along the coast of Tanzania and over trade routes that stretched inland to the Great Lakes and the Congo River, although its influence was largely commercial and the network never amounted to a unified polity.

European influence in the region came to the fore again in the last decades of the 19th century. In 1885 Germany declared its intention to establish a protectorate over the coastline controlled by the sultanate of Zanzibar and a large area of territory stretching inland to the Great Lakes. Zanzibar protested vigorously to this proposal but was forced to acquiesce when German warships arrived off the island. In 1890 Germany and Britain concluded a treaty in which Britain recognized Germany's self-declared sphere of influence in East Africa in return for German acceptance of British control over Zanzibar and its own sphere of influence further north in Kenya. Britain immediately declared a protectorate over Zanzibar and its associated islands, while Germany set about subduing the mainland. Zanzibar's reluctance to accept British rule was overwhelmed by a short naval bombardment, but Germany faced prolonged resistance to the establishment of German East Africa (which included the modern nations of Rwanda and Burundi) in the form of rebellions by the NYAMWEZI people

of the northwest, the HEHE in the south, and the CHAGGA in the northeast. The most serious opposition to German administration was the Maji-Maji Rebellion of 1905–06, in which the spiritual leader, Kinjikitile Ngwale (also known as Bokero), united several southern Tanzanian peoples to oppose German efforts to force indigenous farmers to grow cotton as a cash crop instead of their traditional millet crop. The rebellion was put down only after a series of brutal military campaigns carried out by the Germans that led to mass starvation among the peoples of the south.

During World War I German forces in German East Africa conducted a long and successful guerrilla war against numerically superior British, Belgian, and South African forces, resulting in great destruction and hardship for the country's indigenous peoples. From 1920 the British administered the former territories of German East Africa as a mandate of the League of Nations. The territory became known as Tanganyika under British administration and remained separate from Britain's Zanzibar protectorate. A Legislative Council for Tanganyika was founded in 1926, and the Tanganyika African Association (TAA), the country's first political party, was founded in 1929. Indigenous Africans were not elected to the council until 1945, however. After World War II Tanganyika became a United Nations trust territory under continued British administration. From 1954 the Tanganyika African National Union (the renamed TAA) began pressing for a timetable for independence, and in 1960 TANU won the majority of seats in the Legislative Council and its leader, Julius Nyerere, became prime minister. Tanganyika became independent in December 1961 and became a republic in 1962, with Nyerere as president.

Zanzibar achieved independence entirely separately from Tanganyika in December 1963 under a system of constitutional monarchy that retained the sultan as head of state. A month later, however, a violent revolution deposed the sultan and established the Republic of Zanzibar and Pemba. In April 1964 the Republic of Tanganyika and the Republic of Zanzibar and Pemba joined to form the United Republic of Tanzania; Nyerere became president of the unified state, although Zanzibar retained its own autonomous government structures.

CULTURAL IDENTITY

Tanzania's postindependence history has been relatively peaceful compared to the litany of interethnic and political conflicts that have afflicted many postcolonial African nations. On Zanzibar the 1964 revolution that ended the rule of the sultans, who had been puppet rulers under British administration, was violent and resulted in the death or expulsion of a large part of the islands' long-established Arab and South Asian population, but on the mainland there have been few upheavals. President Nyerere's regime espoused increasingly socialist principles throughout the 1960s, culminating in the 1967 publication of the Arusha Declaration in which he set out a blueprint for a uniquely African model of development known as African Socialism. Nyerere's model was based around the concept of *ujamma,* a term coined from a Swahili root word meaning "extended family." Nyerere believed that the best way to develop the country's economy for the benefit of its citizens, rather than for the benefit of foreign companies, was to collectivize agriculture and industry, to instigate a nationwide literacy program, and to encourage Tanzanians to believe that they were all part of an extended family. The ideal called for every individual to put the good of the extended family, or *ujamma,* ahead of his own and was supposed to be implemented through traditional family and clan structures in a one-party national state.

African Socialism succeeded in maintaining peace among the nation's multitude of ethnic groups but failed to produce significant economic growth. The chief problems were the sudden rise in oil prices in the early 1970s, corruption in government, and resistance to the idea of collectivization among the rural population. Further damage was inflicted on Tanzania's economy by a war with Uganda. In 1978 Uganda President Idi Amin Dada invaded the northwest Kagera region of Tanzania to strike at antigovernment rebels based there. Tanzania responded by driving the Ugandan army out of Kagera and advancing into Uganda itself accompanied by Ugandan opposition forces. Despite the presence of a heavily armed Libyan force that had been sent to aid Idi Amin's regime, the Tanzanians rapidly advanced on Kampala (Uganda's capital) and captured it, bringing Amin's regime to an end. Although successful, Tanzania's military campaign was costly and added to the country's already serious economic problems.

Nyerere's resignation in 1985 brought a period of economic reform under his successor Ali Hassan Mwinyi in which centralized control of the economy was slowly dismantled. Tanzania's

Chama Cha Mapinduzi (CCM), or Party of the Revolution, party retained absolute control of government, however, and multiparty reforms were slow in coming. The first multiparty local elections were held in 1994 following constitutional changes adopted in 1992. In every election since 1994, however, a CCM candidate has won the presidency and the CCM has retained a majority in parliament. The main opposition to the CCM has come principally from the Civic United Front (CUF), which draws most of its support from Zanzibar, and on several occasions political violence has followed contentious election results.

Between 120 and 130 distinct peoples live in modern Tanzania. The great majority of these are Bantu-speaking peoples, but there are also Nilotic and Cushitic peoples as well as peoples of mixed Arab and African heritage (*see* NILOTES). The historical influence of Arab culture has had both a unifying and a divisive effect on modern Tanzania. The most prominent unifying factor is the Swahili language (also known as Kiswahili), which acts as the lingua franca for the nation and for much of Central and East Africa. Swahili is a Bantu language in structure, but its vocabulary draws heavily on Arabic and English and it evolved over many centuries through interactions between Arab traders and the indigenous peoples of the region. The literacy programs instigated in the 1960s helped to foster a sense of national pride in Swahili and resulted in one of the highest literacy rates found in any African nation. Conversely the cultural divide between mainland Tanzania and Zanzibar has been a source of conflict. In the drive to independence Zanzibar was seen as a symbol of centuries of oppression under foreign masters, particularly for its role in the East African slave trade but also because of the disparity in wealth between the largely rural population of the mainland and the urban traders of the islands. The brutal revolution on Zanzibar that overthrew the sultan in 1964 was the culmination of this resentment, carried out as it was by African nationalists eager to drive what they perceived as foreign influence out of their homeland. Political tension between the mainland and Zanzibar continues to the present day partly as a result of this perception. Although the majority of the inhabitants of the islands today are of African rather than mixed African and Arab heritage, almost all of them are Muslim while the balance between Islam, Christianity, and indigenous faiths on the mainland is much more evenly distributed. In recent years there have been incidents of inter-faith violence on the islands as well as accusations from Muslims that the mainland regime gives preference to Christians in appointments to government posts.

At the beginning of the 21st century Tanzania is one of the poorest countries in the world and the second poorest in Africa. The great majority of Tanzanians live in peace but not prosperity. Few substantial mineral resources are known within Tanzanian territory, and consequently the economy remains predominantly agricultural, with most of its people following patterns of life that have changed little in centuries. The country's abundant and spectacular animal life and the great beauty of its landscape are a major draw for tourists, so the tourist industry is one of the great potential growth areas for the Tanzanian economy. To date, however, this has had little or no impact on the meager earnings of the average citizen. Politically there is a danger of a rift developing between Zanzibar and the mainland that could lead to violence in the future.

FURTHER READING

Colin Darch. *Tanzania* (Santa Barbara, Calif.: Clio, 1996).

Rhonda M. Gonzales. *Societies, Religion, and History: Central East Tanzanians and the World They Created, c. 200 BCE to 1800 CE.* (New York: Columbia University Press, 2009).

William Harold Ingrams. *Zanzibar: Its History and Its People* (London: Stacey International, 2007).

Joe Lugalla. *Crisis, Urbanization, and Urban Poverty in Tanzania: A Study of Urban Poverty and Survival Politics* (Lanham, Md.: University Press of America, 1996).

Gregory Maddox and James L. Giblin. *In Search of a Nation: Histories of Authority & Dissidence in Tanzania.* Eastern African studies (Oxford: James Currey, 2004).

Rodger Yeager. *Tanzania: An African Experiment* 2d ed. (Boulder, Colo.: Westview, 1989).

Taqali

The Taqali are a NUBA people of southern Sudan.

Tayy (Tayyi)

Tayy is an Arab tribe that originated in southern Arabia (modern-day Yemen) and immigrated north to the plateau of Shammar, located in the north-central area of modern-day Saudi Arabia. They are considered a branch of the SHAMMAR. After their migration they became allies of the north Arab tribe of Asad, who occupied the same northern territory. In pre-Islamic times the Tayy were Christian, although some remained pagan after the coming of Christianity. In the early seventh century, as Muhammad began to spread his message of Islam, the Tayy sent representatives to meet with him in Medina, and the tribe accepted Islam. The tribe distinguished themselves as warriors in the early Islamic conquests. Later, during the cultural flowering of the Abbasid period (750–1258), descendents of the Tayy became illustrious poets, among them the celebrated Abu Tammam (d. 845). During this period the tribe also reverted to raiding and plundering caravans along the pilgrim routes to Mecca, as reported in medieval Arabic histories. The Tayy are also associated with legendary generosity, epitomized by the story of a man named Hatim, who, when visited by an unexpected guest, slaughtered his only she-camel, his most prized possession, to honor and feed his guest. The name of Hatim lives on in Arabic expressions such as "as generous as Hatim." The tribe also played a role during the Crusades. The name of the tribe appears in British Foreign Office reports as late as the 1860s, but in more recent times, the tribe has melded into others.

Tchaman *See* BRONG.

Tebou *See* TEBU.

Tebu (Tebou; Tibbu; Toubou)

The Tebu live in the desert and semidesert regions of Niger, Sudan, and northern Chad. The TEDA are a Tebu people.

Teda

The majority of the Teda inhabit the mountainous plateaus of the Tibesti Mountains in northwestern Chad, where Chad's highest point. Emi Koussi (11,237 feet), can be found. Some also live in Niger or in desert oases across the border in southern Libya. The Teda language, Tedaga, is a Nilo-Saharan language.

The majority of Chad's population live in the grasslands of the south; the Teda are one of the several minority groups that do not. The region they live in is arid, since it is part of the Sahara Desert. Unlike their southern neighbors (the SARA, for example), the Teda are mostly nomadic and seminomadic farmers and livestock raisers. The Teda, like other northerners, are Muslims. The religious, economic, and social differences between northerners and southerners have led to tensions and, at times, war between northerners and the state. In Chad, most government posts are filled by southerners.

Teke (Bateke)

The Teke live on a plateau bordering the Congo (Zaire) River in an area that straddles Gabon, the Republic of the Congo, and the Democratic Republic of the Congo; the majority live in the Republic of the Congo. The Teke comprise many smaller groups such as the FUMU and SISI.

ORIGINS

The Teke are a Bantu-speaking people, one of many groups descended from those that settled in the varied habitats of the Congo Basin in the early centuries of the first millennium C.E. By the 15th century, the Teke were established in the middle reaches of the Congo (Zaire) River near its confluence with the Kasai River.

LANGUAGE

The Teke speak various dialects of the Teke language. Some Congolese Teke also speak French.

TEKE

location:
Gabon, the Republic of the Congo, and the Democratic Republic of the Congo

time period:
Third century C.E. to present

ancestry:
Bantu

language:
Bantu (Niger-Congo)

Teke time line

C.E.

ca. 200s Bantu-speaking peoples begin to settle in the Congo Basin.

1400s–1500s Teke, a slave-trading people, at war with neighboring Kongo

1600s Teke kingdom reaches height.

1700s Teke become important traders.

1800s Skirmishes between Teke and neighboring Bobangi

1885 Kingdoms of Teke and Loango become a French colony (Middle Congo). Belgian king's Congo Free State established (in Zaire).

1908 Belgian government takes over Free State as the Belgian Congo.

1960 French and Belgian Congo independence, both as Republic of the Congo. Gabon independent

1967 Omar Bongo, a Teke, becomes president of Gabon. He is accused of favoring his own ethnic group by the opposition

1971 Former Belgian Congo is renamed Zaire.

1997 Elected government in the Republic of the Congo is overthrown; Mobutu is overthrown in Zaire, which is renamed the Democratic Republic of the Congo.

See also CONGOLESE (DEMOCRATIC REPUBLIC OF THE CONGO): NATIONALITY; CONGOLESE (REPUBLIC OF THE CONGO): NATIONALITY

HISTORY

From the 15th century onward, the Teke developed to become a powerful river-trading people. In the 15th and 16th centuries, the Teke waged war with the KONGO to the southwest, and by the mid-15th century, the Teke were trading in slaves and tobacco. The Teke kingdom had, by the early 18th century, grown very large and powerful through trade and military conquest. It extended on both sides of the Congo (Zaire) River from Malebo Pool (formerly Stanley Pool) northward to the area around Bolobo. By the late 18th century, however, the Teke had lost some of this territory to neighboring groups. During the 19th century, there were many skirmishes between the Teke and the Bobangi upriver. The Bobangi set up villages closer and closer to Malebo Pool and began raiding Teke villages for slaves. Following a series of local battles, the Teke agreed to let the Bobangi trade at the pool but did not allow them to found villages.

In 1880 Pierre Savorgnan de Brazza—a French citizen—started a trading station, which later became the town of Brazzaville, near Malebo Pool. De Brazza met the great Teke king, Ilo Makoko, and negotiated with him for the region to become a French colony. In 1882 the Teke kingdom was ceded to the Middle Congo colony (part of French Equatorial Africa), of which de Brazza was the commissioner general. In the late 19th and early 20th centuries, the French operated a harsh, violent, and oppressive regime, and Ilo Makoko's successor tried unsuccessfully to revolt against the colonialists in 1898. Over three quarters of the Teke were killed in reprisals. Independence was finally won in 1960 as part of the Republic of the Congo.

CULTURE

The Teke were originally farmers, hunters, and fishing people of the Congo River. In the late 18th and early 19th centuries, Teke culture underwent fundamental changes: Much of what had been local produce—ironware, raffia cloth and salt—was now replaced by produce imported from the coast such as iron, cloth, pottery, shells, and copper rings; the crafts of smelting iron, carving canoes, and making fine pottery ware were largely lost; and guns replaced the bow and arrow for use in hunting and in warfare. Slaves became the main source of revenue to pay for these items. The Teke received slaves from upriver and passed them on by a variety of routes to points along the coast. The name Teke actually denotes their occupation as traders, as *teke* literally means "to buy." The Teke are unusual among rural African peoples in that they traditionally breed domestic cats and dogs. Teke hunting dogs and cats are well known.

Many Teke now form part of a trained and skilled workforce in industrial centers such as those in and around Brazzaville, the capital of the Republic of the Congo. Subsistence agriculture is still carried out in rural areas, however, and is often supplemented by fishing, hunting, and gathering.

Government and Society

In precolonial times, the Teke's basic political unit was the chiefdom, composed of a scattered group of villages. Any holder of a political office had to be a member of the Teke aristocracy—either father or mother had to be of noble blood. Villages were relatively unstable because ambitious young men would aspire to leave the community and set up their own village a short distance away. Villages are now grouped together under a district chief with a local notable at the head of each village.

Villages were often small, ranging from a nuclear family to up to 40 individuals. Each of the villages was under a chief, who was normally related to all his villagers. The maternal family and its close connections formed the village community. Chieftainship, as with other political offices, was hereditary; son usually succeeded father.

Religion

The Teke religion is based on belief in the existence of an invisible world ruled over by the creator god, Nziam. People who die are believed to be reborn into this world. Various spirits, often representing natural forces, act as mediators between the two worlds. People in the world of the living can communicate with these spirits through prayer or ritual. These prayers can be facilitated by items that are assumed to contain a nature spirit or the spirit of a deceased person. Such items are often kept in a container attached to a wooden statue.

See also CONGOLESE (DEMOCRATIC REPUBLIC OF THE CONGO): NATIONALITY; CONGOLESE (REPUBLIC OF THE CONGO): NATIONALITY.

FURTHER READING

J. Vansina. *The Tio Kingdom of the Middle Congo, 1880–1892* (London: Oxford University Press for the International African Institute, 1973).

Tekna

The Tekna are a BERBER people who live throughout North Africa, especially in southern Morocco but also Algeria and Mali. They are primarily a nomadic people.

Tekrur *See* TUKOLOR.

Tem *See* TEMBA.

Temba (Chaucho; Kotocoli; Tem)

The Temba live largely in Ghana and Togo. They speak the Tem language and are predominantly Muslim.

Temne (Timmannee)

The Temne are the second largest ethnic group in Sierra Leone. They live in a region of the northwest in the coastal hinterland around Port Loko. The MENDE—Sierra Leone's largest ethnic group—live in lands to the south of the Temne. About one third of all Sierra Leoneans are Temne. (*See* SIERRA LEONEANS: NATIONALITY.)

Historically, the Temne were ruled by local chiefs, and they played an important role in the trade with Europeans on the coast at least 500 years ago. In the late 18th century C.E., free blacks and former slaves from Britain and Canada settled on the coast of what is now Sierra Leone, but the Temne were hostile to the colonists and invaded the colony, nearly destroying it. The British then established a colony in the region, large numbers of freed slaves, the ancestors of the modern-day CREOLES, were settled in the region, and expeditions were launched against the Temne.

Tende *See* KURIA.

Tera

The Tera are a KANURI people living in northeastern Nigeria.

Terik

The Terik are one of the several related groups that make up the KALENJIN. The Kalenjin are a large ethnic group in western Kenya.

Teso *See* ITESO.

Tetela

The Tetela are a subgroup of the Mongo of Central Africa. The Tetela live in the south-central region of the Democratic Republic of the Congo.

Tew *See* Tumbuka.

Thembu

The Thembu are a large ethnic group living South Africa. There are several thousand Thembu people, primarily living in the Transkei and Ciskei regions, which lie on southeastern seaboard of South Africa to the east and south of Lesotho.

The Thembu are a Xhosa-speaking people, who originally consisted of the Mpondo, Thembu, and Xhosa proper. These three groups all claim to have originated in a cradleland at the headwaters of the Dedesi River. Their customs and beliefs are similar, as are their languages, which are all dialects of Isixhosa. Today, the Thembu still comprise one of the main Xhosa-speaking groups. By the 18th century c.e., the Thembu were living in large clan-based chieftaincies east of the Kei River.

Nelson Mandela, the first of South Africa's presidents to be brought to power by truly multiracial elections, is a Thembu.

Thlaping

The Thlaping, a southern African ethnic group, are descended from Rolong ancestors. They separated from the main Rolong group in the 18th century.

Thunayyan (Al Thunayyan)

The Thunayyan are a branch of the Saud, the ruling dynasty of Saudi Arabia (*see* Saudi Arabians: nationality). They trace their ancestry to Thunayyan, who was a brother of Muhammad Ibn Saud, the founder of the Saudi rule. Thunayyan, along with his brother, supported the mid-18th-century Muslim reformer Muhammad ibn Abd al-Wahhab, whose teachings continue to form the basis for Saudi society today. Abdallah b. Thunayyan briefly ruled the so-called Second Saudi State, from 1841 to 1843. The Thunayyan are also closely allied with the Sudayr clan. Members of the Thunayyan clan have married into the Saudi ruling family, and many hold high positions in the Saudi government and in business. Princess Effat al-Thu-nayyan, a wife of King Faysal, who ruled Saudi Arabia from 1964 until 1975, founded Saudi Arabia's first private college for women, Effat College, in Jidda, which opened in 1999.

Tibbu *See* Tebu.

Tiddi *See* Meidob.

Tigray *See* Tigre.

Tigre (Tigrinya)

The Tigre, or Tigrinya, are one of the largest ethnic groups in Eritrea, where the population is fairly evenly divided between Tigrinya-speaking Christians and Muslim communities. In Ethiopia, the Tigre are the largest ethnic group in the province of Tigre, which lies in the northernmost part of the country and once housed the capital of the ancient Axumite Kingdom. There are more than 2 million Tigrinya-speakers divided between Eritrea and Ethiopia. Tigrinya is a Semitic language related to Amharic and the ancient Geez language. Although only around 7 percent of the Ethiopian population are Tigre, they have long been an important political force in that country. (*See* Ethiopians: nationality.)

The Tigre share an imperial heritage with the Amhara—members of both groups provided emperors for the throne of the Ethiopian Empire. The last Tigre emperor was Yohannes IV, who reigned in the second half of the 19th century. In more recent decades the Tigre were active in Eritrea's struggle for independence and Ethiopia's fight to establish democracy during the reign of the dictator Mengistu Haile Mariam. The Tigre People's Liberation Front (TPLF), formed in 1975, became a leader among the various Ethiopian and Eritrean liberation movements. With the defeat of Mengistu's government in 1991 the TPLF became the leading element of the Ethiopian People's Revolutionary Democratic Front, which became the ruling party for the next two decades.

Tigrinya *See* Tigre.

Tikar

The Tikar are a Cameroonian people who are part of the Bamileke. They live in the western highlands of the country.

Timmannee *See* TEMNE.

Tirma

The Tirma are one of the three closely related groups that make up the SURI. The Suri live in Ethiopia and Sudan.

Tiv

The Tiv occupy an area that stretches from the foothills of the Adamawa Mountains along the Cameroon–Nigeria border in the southeast to the Jos Plateau, central Nigeria, in the north.

Oral history states that the Tiv originate from the highlands of northern Cameroon. Like many other African societies, the IBIBIO and IGBO, for example, historically the Tiv lived in acephalous (noncentralized) societies. This meant that they had no acknowledged ruler. The basis of Tiv society was lineage (the greater extended family a person belonged to). The Tiv did not live in villages but in family groups, with related groups positioned near to each other. Law and order was maintained largely by discussion and the following of customary mores. To settle a dispute, each side would pick a leader; the two leaders would then argue it out.

Tjekker (Tjakkar)

The Tjekker were a people identified in Ancient Egyptian records as one of the 12th-century B.C.E. SEA PEOPLES, thought to have come from the Aegean Sea. The most important source for the Tjekker is the reliefs and inscriptions recorded on the walls of the temple at Madinat Habu, in Thebes, Upper Egypt, near the Valley of the Kings. Madinat Habu is a mortuary temple, which is a structure built for offerings and worship in honor of a dead pharaoh, in this case, Ramesses III, who conducted a war against the Sea Peoples in the eighth year of his reign, about 1190 B.C.E. Some scholars believe this was not a single event but rather a series of skirmishes on land and sea over a period of time. The temple inscriptions depict the Tjekker, along with a people called the Peleset, also known as the Philistines, as the major forces in this invasion of Egypt, and show the captive Tjekker being led by Ramesses III (*see* EGYPTIANS). The vanquished are depicted praising the pharaoh, saying "Great is thy strength, victorious king, great Sun of Egypt." In the scenes of the land battle, the Sea Peoples are shown in chariots with six-spoked wheels pulled by two horses, similar to the Egyptian chariots. In the sea-battle scenes, they are depicted in ships with sails, but unlike the Egyptian ships, the Sea Peoples' ships had no oars, which suggests they may have developed a different method of steering their ships. They are shown with plumed helmets, very similar to those worn by the ancient GREEKS, carrying short swords, long spears, and circular shields. The details of their clothing suggest a connection with the Greeks, and they may have been displaced by the Trojan War and settled for a time on the Mediterranean island of Cyprus.

Togolese: nationality (people of Togo)

GEOGRAPHY

The Togolese Republic is a small nation in West Africa. It has an area of approximately 22,000 square miles and borders three other nations and the Atlantic Ocean. Ghana meets Togo's western border, Burkina Faso lies to the north, and Benin is to the south. Togo's coastline is in the extreme south of the country and extends for just 35 miles along the Gulf of Guinea, a part of the Atlantic Ocean. Togo territory is a long thin strip of land between Ghana and Benin. It extends 360 miles northward into the interior of the continent but is only 100 miles wide at its broadest point.

The dominant geographical feature of Togo is the Togo Mountain chain, which begins in neighboring Benin and stretches across the middle of the country from the northeast to the southwest before continuing into Ghana. The Togo Mountains have an average elevation of about 2,300 feet, and their highest point, at 3,200 feet, is the peak of Mount Agou, which is situated in the southwest close to the border with Ghana. North of the Togo Mountains the terrain consists of undulating savanna bisected by the wide valley of the Oti River. The Oti River flows from east to west across the northern quarter of Togo before turning south and crossing the border into Ghana, where it joins Lake Volta. South of the Togo Mountains a plateau extends to the gently inclined edge of a coastal plain that backs the shore. Togo's coastline has many inland lagoons and lakes behind wide sandy beaches.

Togo is one of the more densely populated nations in Africa with the highest concentrations living south of the central mountains and close to the coast. The capital city, Lome, is situated on the coast adjacent to the border

TOGOLESE: NATIONALITY

nation:
Togo; Togolese Republic

derivation of name:
From a Ewe word meaning "lake"

government:
Republic

capital:
Lome

language:
The country's official language is French. Ewe and Mina are the two dominant languages of the south; Kabye (the language of the Kabre people) is the most widely spoken in the north. There are more than 30 other local languages.

religion:
About 29 percent of the population are Christian, 20 percent are Muslim, and the remaining 51 percent of the population follow indigenous beliefs.

earlier inhabitants:
Unknown

demographics:
The Ewe constitute about 40 percent of the population and the Kabre another 20 percent. There are between 30 and 35 other ethnic groups. Non-Africans (mainly Europeans) make up less than 1 percent of the population.

Togolese: nationality time line

C.E.

1884 Germany establishes a protectorate over coastal Togo.

1914 French and British forces invade and occupy German Togoland.

1922 The League of Nations mandates control of western Togoland to Britain (as British Togoland) and eastern Togoland to France (as French Togoland).

1956 British Togoland votes to join Gold Coast as it becomes independent Ghana.

1960 French Togoland becomes independent as the Togolese Republic.

1961 Sylvanus Olympio elected as Togo's first president.

1963 Olympio assassinated in a coup that brings Nicolas Grunitzky to power.

1967 Grunitzky deposed by Gnassingbe Eyadema.

1979 President Eyadema establishes one-party rule.

1985 Failed coup attempt

1986 Opposition leader Gilchrist Olympio sentenced to death in absentia for alleged involvement in the 1985 coup attempt.

1991 Eyadema agrees to establishment of a transitional government that includes opposition politicians.

1993 Eyadema dissolves government. Thousands leave Togo following violence between government forces and opposition groups.

1998 Eyadema wins presidential elections.

2002 Eyadema's Rally of the Togolese People (RPT) party wins national elections.

2005 Eyadema dies. His son Faure Gnassingbe wins presidential elections. Hundreds die in protests at election results.

2006 Transitional government that includes opposition leaders established.

2007 RTP wins national elections.

with Ghana. Lome is the country's largest city, its principal port, and its industrial center. The second and third largest cities in Togo, Sokode and Kara respectively, are located in the center of the country.

INCEPTION AS A NATION

Little is known about the history of Togo before the arrival of European explorers in the 15th century. The EWE and Adja peoples are believed to have migrated into the area between the 12th and 18th centuries. The peoples of the central mountains are probably the longest established of Togo's ethnic groups, with archaeological evidence indicating that the Tchamba and Bassar people have been established there since the ninth century C.E. Northern Togo lay within the sphere of influence some of West Africa's great civilizations such as the MOSSI Empire of the 15th century, the Mali Empire, and the SONGHAY Empire. Islam has influenced the culture of the north through contacts with these

powers. The coast of present-day Togo along with the coast of Benin and western Nigerian were known as the Slave Coast from the 17th to the 19th centuries because they were one of the main sources of slaves taken across the Atlantic to the Caribbean and to North and South America. There were no major slave-trading shipment points on the coast of Togo itself, because of the lack of good harbors or suitable offshore islands, but Togo was a source of slaves transported from European settlements in Benin and Ghana.

In the late 19th century Togo became Germany's first colonial possession in Africa. German traders had begun arriving on Togo's coast in the 1850s and in the 1880s started establishing larger trading settlements. In 1884 Germany established a protectorate over a small enclave of coastal territory centered on a village called Togo. Germany swiftly extended its control along the coast and inland over a much wider area, although the territory continued to be known as Togoland. Agreements with Britain and France in 1897 and 1899 respectively established boundaries between German-controlled Togoland and British-controlled Gold Coast (present-day Ghana) to the west and French-controlled Dahomey (present-day Benin) to the east. Togoland became Germany's only economically self-sustaining colony in Africa and received significant investment in infrastructure in the form of roads, railways, and agricultural improvements under German administration.

Shortly after the outbreak of World War I in 1914, British and French forces in Gold Coast and Dahomey invaded Togoland and seized control. After the war Togoland was divided into two administrative zones by the League of Nations (the predecessor of the United Nations). Britain was mandated administrative control of the western half, which became known as British Togoland, and France the eastern half, which became French Togoland. Both of theses territories became United Nations trust territories after World War II, but they continued to be administered by the British and French. The Ewe people, divided between three administrations (Gold Coast, British Togoland, and French Togoland), lobbied the United Nations repeatedly for independence as a single country, but there was resistance from the British and French governments. In 1956 a plebiscite was held in British Togoland in which the majority of voters opted to become part of an independent Gold Coast. When Gold Coast became independent as Ghana in 1957, British Togoland ceased to exist. The following year the Committee for Togolese Union won elections to the Togo Assembly in French Togoland on a manifesto of immediate independence. French Togoland was granted full independence in April 1960 as the Togolese Republic, with Sylvanus Olympio as president.

CULTURAL IDENTITY

Togo's postindependence history has been turbulent and violent. In 1963 President Olympio was assassinated in the first military coup to take place in a postindependence African nation. Four years later the leader of the coup, Nicolas Grunitzky, was also deposed in a coup that brought Gnassingbe Eyadema to power. Eyadema was to remain in power for the next 38 years, first as the head of military regime and then as the victorious candidate in a series of presidential elections that were condemned by international observers as fraudulent.

In 1979 President Eyadema declared a "third republic" and introduced a new constitution providing for an elected National Assembly to serve as a consultative body. Eyadema's hold on power remained firm, however. As the leader of the only legal political party, the Rally of the Togolese People (RPT), his position was unassailable by democratic means. Numerous public demonstrations protesting the absence of a legal opposition took place in the early 1980s, but they were brutally suppressed by the regime's security forces. A coup attempt in 1985 also failed.

The 1990s brought a protracted and bloody struggle for power between Eyadema and opposition groups. A national forum to discuss constitutional reforms was convened in 1991 and almost immediately declared itself the nation's sovereign power. While Eyadema retained the loyalty of the military, however, the self-declared National Conference under its interim prime minister, Joseph Koffigoh, could do little to reduce the president's power. A political stalemate ensued in which the National Conference sought to introduce a new multiparty system while troops loyal to Eyadema carried out intimidation tactics against opposition supporters. Soldiers killed dozens of civilians during street protests in 1993, and opposition leaders were imprisoned or attacked. Almost all opposition parties boycotted the 1993 presidential elections, resulting in a resounding victory for Eyadema, although only about a third of the electorate participated. Elections to the National Assembly in 1994 also resulted in a narrow victory for Eyadema's RPT. Eyadema won another presidential term in 1998 amid widespread allegations of electoral fraud and intimidation of opposition supporters. A national crisis followed in which all opposition parties boycotted the imminent elections to the National Assembly. In an agreement between the RPT and opposition parties in 1999, Eyadema undertook to hold new elections in 2000 under the supervision of an election commission staffed by RPT and opposition representatives. The elections were eventually held two years late in 2002 and were once again boycotted by the main opposition parties, who claimed the RPT has used unfair practices.

Following Eyadema's death in 2005, the army immediately installed his son, Faure Gnassingbe, as president. This was widely condemned by the international community as being tantamount to a coup, and Faure was forced to step down and submit himself to presidential elections. Faure's victory in subsequent elections resulted in widespread violence in which hundreds died. Conciliation talks between the RPT and opposition leaders led to the formation of transitional government in 2006, and international observers judged elections held in 2007 as fair and transparent.

At least 35 distinct ethnic groups live in Togo, many of them representing sections of wider groups divided by modern international boundaries. The Ewe and closely related MINA people constitute the largest single ethnic block and dominate the south of the country. The KA-BRE people, who are predominant in the north, along with other northern groups, speak Sudanic languages. Their languages distinguish them from the peoples of the south, who speak BANTU languages and have a long history of Muslim influence in their cultures. Islam also distinguishes them from the people of the north who were more commonly exposed to Christian influences. Throughout the colonial period the Ewe were the prime agents of first German and then French and British administration. At independence the political elite of the country was dominated by the Ewe, and Ewe culture became the mold from which the new government attempted to form a national Togolese identity. This pattern changed when Eyadema came to power in 1967. Eyadema was a Kabre, and the army that supported him through almost four decades of repressive rule was also dominated by Kabre—the poor economic development of the north made a military career an attractive option. There has been little direct interethnic tension in Togo's history, but there is a generalized tension between the north and the south based on long-standing political allegiance. The most significant opponents to the Eyadema's regime, and the government of his son, have been based in the more populous south.

At the beginning of the 21st century Togo faces an uncertain future. In the political arena, the Rally of the Togolese People (RPT) and its antecedents have held power for more than 40 years, and every election since the introduction of multiparty politics in the 1990s has brought violence. Economically, Togo has suffered from decades of poor management, corruption, and political instability, with the result that it is one of the poorer states of West Africa. The emergence of a unified Togolese culture has been hampered by a north–south political divide, but there is no history of severe interethnic conflict, and the country's many peoples intermarry and conduct business freely.

FURTHER READING

Samuel Decalo. *Historical Dictionary of Togo* (N.J.: Scarecrow Press, 1976).

Arthur J. Knoll. *Togo Under Imperial Germany, 1884–1914: A Case Study in Colonial Rule.* Hoover colonial studies (Stanford, Calif: Hoover Institution Press, 1978).

Benjamin N. Lawrance. *A Handbook of Eweland: The Ewe of Togo and Benin* (Accra, Ghana: Woeli Publishing Services, 2005).

Benjamin N. Lawrance. *Locality, Mobility, and "Nation": Periurban Colonialism in Togo's Eweland, 1900–1960.* Rochester studies in African history and the diaspora, v. 31 (Rochester, NY: University of Rochester Press, 2007).

Paul Nugent. *Smugglers, Secessionists & Loyal Citizens on the Ghana-Toga Frontier: The Life of the Borderlands Since 1914.* Western African studies (Athens: Ohio University Press, 2002).

Toka

The Toka are a TONGA subgroup living in southern Zambia.

Toma   *See* LOMA.

Tonga

The Tonga live in a region called Butonga, which spreads from the Southern Province of Zambia southeastward across the border to the middle of the Zambezi plain in northern Zimbabwe. There are about 1 million Tonga, the majority of whom live in Zambia, where they form roughly 10 percent of the population.

ORIGINS

Archaeologists have discovered remains that suggest the Tonga have been in their present location for about a thousand years. The early Tonga were farmers and fishermen who raised cattle and goats. Bones found in waste dumps show that they also hunted antelopes.

LANGUAGE

The main language of the Tonga is Tonga (or Citonga), of which there are several dialects. The dialect used by the Plateau Tonga is the one most often used in schools. Tonga literature is usually written in English.

HISTORY

The British explorer David Livingstone visited Butonga in the 1850s and found the Tonga living in small, scattered settlements. In the ear-

TONGA

location:
Zambia and Zimbabwe

time period:
11th century C.E. to present

ancestry:
Bantu

language:
Bantu (Niger-Congo)

lier 1800s they had been subjected to raids from other groups, including the Lozi, Kololo, and Ndebele, who had taken many of their cattle. The Tonga were not a warlike people, although they had weapons such as spears and clubs. They had a simple system for dealing with raids: They hid grain in their long hair, so that if they had to flee to fresh territory they had the means of planting fresh crops and beginning again.

In the 1890s Cecil Rhodes's British South Africa Company (BSA) occupied Southern Rhodesia (present-day Zimbabwe) and Northern Rhodesia (present-day Zambia). White settlers consequently took over much of Butonga. In the 1920s the company handed its Rhodesian lands over to British government rule. Under colonial rule, the Tonga were grouped into three small native reserves, leaving the better land for the white settlers. The first group was the Plateau Tonga in Northern Rhodesia. The Toka Tonga of Kalomo and Livingstone districts were allocated land with poor soils, while the Gwembe Tonga were in the more isolated locality of the Zambezi Valley. Unable to survive solely by farming in the inadequate reserves, the Toka and the Gwembe Tonga were forced to work mainly as migrant laborers for the whites—in particular, in the copper mines of the Copperbelt in north-central Zambia.

In the late 1950s, the building of the Kariba Dam on the Zambezi River displaced over 50,000 Gwembe Tonga. They were forcibly evicted to new homes in the hills above Lake Kariba or to the more arid lands below the dam where rainfall is irregular. Conditions changed for the Tonga after Zambia, in 1964, and Zimbabwe, in 1980, finally became independent, as they were no longer restricted to these artificial native reserves.

CULTURE

Butonga is plateau country, intersected by the Zambezi River and Lake Kariba and the Kariba Dam. The rainy season lasts from November through March, while from April to early August the weather is cold and dry. Hot weather starts in late August. Rainfall is unreliable and droughts are common. In this environment, many Tonga are subsistence farmers, working on their own plots of land and growing food for their own needs. The main crop is maize; other crops include groundnuts (peanuts), millet, sorghum, and vegetables. The chief cash crop is cotton. Plateau farmers include many who have substantial holdings and large herds of cattle. Others, including small-scale farmers, work on

Tonga time line
C.E.
1000s Tonga settled in present location.
1850s Tonga visited by British explorer David Livingstone.
1890s Tonga come under control of British South Africa (BSA) Company as part of Northern and Southern Rhodesia.
1923–24 BSA hands over Northern and Southern Rhodesia to British government. White settlers take much of Tonga land. Tonga divided into three inadequate native reserves.
1940s Tonga begin to migrate to urban areas in search of employment.
1950s Many Tonga displaced by building of the Kariba Dam on the Zambezi River.
1953 White-minority ruled Central African Federation (CAF) formed including Rhodesia colonies.
1963 CAF dissolved.
1964 Northern Rhodesia independent as Zambia
1965 White-minority declare illegal independence of Southern Rhodesia as Rhodesia.
1980 Rhodesia independent with majority rule as Zimbabwe

See also Zambians: nationality; Zimbabweans: nationality

the land of rich farmers. As the Zambian government allocates areas of land to multinational businesses, a landless rural class is developing.

Since the 1940s, many Tonga in Zambia have migrated to urban areas in search of employment. Although the Tonga are predominantly rural, around 40 percent live in urban areas where they are mostly engaged in commercial and service industries. Traditional crafts such as blacksmithing, carpentry, pottery, and basket weaving have been revived in the last few decades. The high cost of transportation and the rising costs of imports have reversed the trend for factory-made foreign goods.

Men are usually responsible for building houses, herding cattle, and hunting. Women do most of the other farm work, make pots and baskets, and are largely responsible for child care. Women also dominate trading at local markets. Increasingly they do paid work as domestic servants or shop assistants, and many hold professional jobs. Both men and women work in various trades and craft professions, which include car repairs, brick making, tailoring, and needlework.

Government and Society

The Tonga are divided into clans. The family, headed by the husband, is the core of the social structure, but descent is traced through the female line. Increasing numbers of families are headed by single mothers. This may be because under customary law a divorced wife does not receive an equal share of the assets (those built up jointly by both husband and wife usually go to the man), and if the wife is widowed she does not inherit anything (the husband's maternal family does). Civil courts, however, often try to ensure that women and their children are treated fairly.

Religion

Large numbers of Tonga are Christians, and many combine this with features of the Tonga religion. The Tonga religion involves belief in a creator god called Leza, who is now often identified as the Christian God. The Tonga have a great veneration for the spirits of the dead and make offerings to their ancestors, or *mizimo*. *Basango* are spirits who have a wider influence than *mizimo* and are thought to affect whole neighborhoods, not just families. *Mizimo* and *basango* are consulted on family and communal matters by mediums. *Masabe* are invasive spirits who are thought to attack people. Both men and women can be possessed by *masabe,* and after recovery, they may go on to help others similarly afflicted. New *masabe* have emerged to represent the particular ills of the 20th century.

See also; ZAMBIANS: NATIONALITY; ZIMBABWEANS: NATIONALITY

FURTHER READING

Elizabeth Colson. *Tonga Religious Life in the Twentieth Century* (Lusaka, Zambia: Bookworld Publishers, 2006).

Chet S. Lancaster, Kenneth Powers Vickery, and Elizabeth Colson. *The Tonga-Speaking Peoples of Zambia and Zimbabwe: Essays in Honor of Elizabeth Colson* (Lanham, MD: University Press of America, 2007).

Santosh C. Saha. *History of the Tonga Chiefs and Their People in the Monze District of Zambia* (New York: P. Lang, 1994).

Elisabeth Thomson and Olivia Bennett. *Our gods never helped us again: the Tonga people describe resettlement and its aftermath* (Lusaka, Zambia: Panos Southern Africa, 2005).

Toposa

The Toposa are a Nilotic people of southern Sudan and parts of Ethiopia (*see* NILOTES). There are more than 90,000 Toposa in Sudan and about 10,000 in Ethiopia.

Toro

The Toro are a BANTU people of western Uganda. They share a common origin with the NYORO people of the lakes region of western Uganda. The region they inhabit lies south of Lake Albert along Uganda's western border with the Democratic Republic of the Congo. The majority of the Toro are Christians, though many also follow the Toro religion. A very small minority are Muslim.

The Nyoro people had established a powerful kingdom—Bunyoro-Kitara—in the region by the 14th century. Bunyoro was a federation of provinces called a *saza*. In the first half of the 19th century, the Toro *saza* became an independent kingdom under the rule of the first Toro *omukama* (king), Kaboya, who was the rebellious son of the Bunyoro *omukama*. After Kaboyo's death in the 1850s, however, Toro nearly lost its newfound independence. When British forces overthrew the Bunyoro *omukama,* however, Toro independence was restored. In 1966 all the Ugandan kingdoms, including Toro, were abolished by the Ugandan government, and it was not until 1993 that the Toro kingdom was restored. It functions largely as a cultural institution, however, and the *omukama* has limited political powers.

Torodo   *See* TUKOLOR.

Toubou   *See* TEBU.

Toucouleur   *See* TUKOLOR.

Trojans

Trojans were the inhabitants of the ancient city of Troy, located on the Aegean coast of modern-day Turkey, about four miles inland, at the city of Hisarlık. The ruins of Troy, also known as Troia, Ilios, Ilion, or Ilium, are just south of the mouth of the Hellespont, or the Dardanelles, an important waterway that links the Aegean to the Black Sea. While it has never been incontrovertibly proven, most scholars believe that this is indeed the site of ancient Troy, the city immortalized by the Greek bard Homer in the epics the *Iliad* and the *Odyssey* and by the Roman poet Virgil in the *Aeneid*. These poems all relate the story of the Trojan War, which, according to legend, began when the Mycenaean GREEKS set out for Troy to bring back Helen, the beautiful wife of Menelaus, the king of Sparta, who had been carried off to Troy by the Trojan prince Paris. The Greeks besiege the city for 10 years but are unable to defeat the Trojans. But then, with the help of the goddess Athena, they build the Trojan horse, in which Greek warriors hide, and they present it to the Trojans as an offering to Athena. Once the horse is inside the city, the Greek warriors climb out of the horse and throw open the gates to the rest of the Greek army. The war ends with the sack of Troy and the burning of the city. The *Odyssey* relates the 10-year journey of the Greek warrior Odysseus as he makes his way back home after the war. The *Aeneid* tell the story of the Trojan Aeneas, who escapes the burning city, carrying his aged father on his shoulders, and then wanders westward across the Mediterranean, eventually founding the city of Rome.

The site at Hisarlık is believed to have been settled since the early Bronze Age, about 3000 B.C.E. Archaeologists have excavated many layers attesting to different eras of settlement, and it is generally assumed that the layers known as Troy VI, VIIa, or VIIb are the most likely remains of the city destroyed by the Mycenaeans in the Trojan War, as told in Homer's epics. This assumption is based on the fact that the dating of these ruins places them at a time when both Mycenaea and Troy were at the height of their power. The ruins of Troy VI show monumental buildings and large houses, in keeping with the grandeur of the city depicted in the epics. Troy VI was destroyed in about 1300 B.C.E., probably by an earthquake, as suggested by traces of fire and fallen buildings. Troy VIIa was destroyed about 1250 B.C.E., and archaeological evidence points to it as the most likely city of legend. The houses built close together with unusual food-storage vessels suggest a city built to withstand a siege, and the evidence of fire, along with human bones found in the houses and in the streets, are in keeping with the descriptions of the sack of Troy. Troy VIIb vanished in about 1100 B.C.E. Greek colonists resettled the area, then known as Illium, around 700 B.C.E. Hellenistic, then Roman settlements followed. An important temple of Athena was built there, and Roman emperors took a special interest in the city because of the legend of the Trojan Aeneas as the ancestor of the ROMANS. The site was occupied until about 1200 C.E. It was not until the 19th century that archaeologists began to think that Troy was a real place, not simply a legend, and that this was its location. The German archaeologist Heinrich Schliemann, who led major excavations at the site from 1870 to 1890, is primarily responsible for identifying the ruins at Hisarlık with the city of the Trojans.

Tshidi

The Tshidi are one of the four main subgroups of the ROLONG. The Rolong are a TSWANA people of Southern Africa.

Tsimihety

The Tsimihety are one of the more numerous MADAGASCAN PEOPLES. They live in an inland region in the northern end of the island. The Tsimihety claim to be descended from the SIHANAKA.

Tsonga

The Tsonga are one of the largest ethnic groups in Mozambique, but at least 1 million live in the northern Transvaal region of Southern Africa. The Tsonga have been living in this region for several hundred years and were settled there before the 16th century. The NGUNI peoples of Southern Africa are probably descended from the Tsonga of Mozambique.

In southern Mozambique around what is now Maputo Bay, the Tsonga established kingdoms whose wealth was based on agriculture and trade. After the Portuguese introduced corn into the region in the 16th or 17th century, food production and population expanded. Europeans visiting the coast also provided opportunities for trade in ivory and copper. Other Africans captured by the Tsonga in battle were sold as slaves to the Europeans. Such trade played a part in the emergence of three powerful Tsonga kingdoms: Nyaka, Tembe, and Maputo, which successively dominated the region from the 1500s to the 1700s. In the 1800s, however, NGONI refugees fleeing a turbulent era of southern Africa's history came to dominate the region. As a result, the Tsonga came under a ZULU cultural influence, adopting cattle as a central aspect of their economy as well as the Zulu language.

Tswana (Batswana; Western Sotho)

The Tswana are one of the principal BANTU-speaking peoples of southern Africa. The Tswana number about 3 million and live in a region stretching southeast from the Okavango Swamps to the Limpopo River, and southwest from there to the Kuruman River area. This region includes eastern and northwestern Bo-

TSWANA

location:
Southern Africa

time period:
Fourth century C.E. to present

ancestry:
Bantu

language:
Bantu (Niger-Congo)

Tswana time line

C.E.

200s Bantu-speaking peoples begin to arrive in Southern Africa.

300s–400s Bantu-speakers reach present-day Transvaal (South Africa).

650–1300 "Toutswe tradition" in Botswana: large, cattle-owning communities

by 1400 Tswana emerge from Sotho.

1801 First contact with Europeans

1816 First Christian mission

1819–39 Mfecane: period of mass migrations and wars

1836–48 Great Trek brings Boers into conflict with people inland.

1884–85 Bechuanaland, British colony, established over Tswana.

1910 Boers and British form white-ruled Union of South Africa.

1913 Tswana in South Africa restricted to native reserves.

1966 Bechuanaland independent as Botswana; Tswana leader Seretse Khama is president.

1970 Bophuthatswana, Tswana homeland, created by South African government; many Tswana forcibly relocated to this homeland in following years.

1994 First nonracial elections are held in South Africa.

1996 South Africa adopts new constitution.

See also BOTSWANANS: NATIONALITY; SOUTH AFRICANS: NATIONALITY

tswana, and the former Tswana homeland of Bophuthatswana, which consisted of a number of separate blocks of territory in South Africa.

ORIGINS

The Tswana are descended from Bantu-speaking peoples who migrated southward from present-day eastern Nigeria. They reached the eastern part of their present lands sometime between 300 and 400. From there, groups spread slowly westward over the following two centuries and set up new territories and settlements.

LANGUAGE

The Tswana language is called Setswana, which is a Bantu language.

HISTORY

The Tswana originally emerged as a separate group from within the SOTHO group of people sometime before the 1400s. Over many years, groups of Sotho clans came together to form the three major divisions of the Sotho people: the Northern Sotho, the Southern Sotho, and the Tswana (or Western Sotho)—who are now often viewed as a separate group.

The first half of the 19th century was a period of turmoil for the Tswana. They had to endure a series of civil wars followed by the Mfecane—a period of devastating invasions by neighboring peoples fleeing the Zulu expansion. The Tswana's first contact with Europeans came in 1801, when a small group of explorers reached the southernmost Tswana settlements. These events were followed by occupation and rule by the AFRIKANERS, or BOERS, and the British under whom Tswana lands were divided between South Africa and the British protectorate of Bechuanaland, which became independent in 1966 as Botswana.

In South Africa, the Tswana were reduced to third-class status by the government's policy of apartheid and were required to live in the Bophuthatswana homeland, but they were allowed to work as migrant laborers elsewhere in South Africa. The Tswana in South Africa have benefited from the abolition of the apartheid laws in the early 1990s, which has given all South Africans equal rights.

CULTURE

Tswana villages can be very large with populations of up to 25,000 people. A typical Tswana compound is built in a large yard, usually enclosed by a fence or hedge and containing a garden area plus one or more large trees for shade. Within the yard, two or more houses providing dwelling and storage space for the family stand in or next to the *lolwapa*, a low-walled courtyard that is the heart of the compound.

As well as its compound, each Tswana family has houses on its farming and cattle-grazing lands, which may be some distance from the village. During the farming season, from November to June, most people in the villages leave for these outlying areas to plow their land, plant and harvest crops, and tend their cattle, goats, and sheep. In Botswana, cattle make up 85 percent of total agricultural output, and meat products are a major export.

Away from the land, many Tswana men have found work in the mines and industries of South Africa, or in the rapidly expanding mining industries of Botswana and Zimbabwe.

The farming work and other tasks are divided between men, women, and children. The men herd and milk the livestock, do the heavier building work, and hunt wild game. They also help with the plowing, but that is often left to the women. The women also tend and harvest the crops—which include sorghum, corn, millet, vegetables, and fruit—and do the cooking and other household jobs. With many men working away from home as migrant laborers, however, it increasingly falls to the women to perform most agricultural work. The children usually help by collecting water and firewood.

Government and Society

In the past, everyone joined an age regiment after initiation into adulthood. These provided a pool of labor for large-scale activities such as rounding up cattle or building compounds, and in the case of the men, they also comprised the army when needed. During the colonial era, many male age regiments fought for the British army abroad, while others were forced to provide labor for tasks such as building roads. In the modern era, the tasks that an age regiment can be called on to perform are defined in law. Also, every Tswana is no longer a member of an age regiment. The role of these institutions has largely been replaced by the existence of social clubs, voluntary associations, churches, and other groups that cross divisions based on ethnicity, age, and class.

Although marriages between cousins are encouraged in Tswana society—as they help to keep wealth and property within family groups and strengthen the bonds of kinship between them—most marriages are between people from different family groups. A man may have more than one wife, and marriages are usually arranged by the family group or relatives of the bride and groom.

Religion

The first Christian missionaries arrived in Tswana lands in 1816. Most Tswana are now Christians, yet their own religion, based on ancestor reverence, still survives and is widely followed. Like Christianity, it is based on the belief that people have immortal souls and that the world was created by a supreme being, called Molimo. The Tswana believe that the souls of the dead have the power to influence the lives of the living and make offerings to them to thank them for their help or to ask them for assistance. They also have an enduring belief in the power of magic and its practitioners. The Tswana used to perform rainmaking ceremonies at the beginning of the farming season. Although these ceremonies have fallen into disuse, many Christian churches now hold prayer days for rain.

See also BOTSWANANS: NATIONALITY; SOUTH AFRICANS: NATIONALITY.

FURTHER READING

Paul Rantao. *Setswana Culture and Tradition* (Gaborone, Botswana: Pentagon Publishers, 2006).
The Setswana-Speaking People. A Cultural Image of South Africa, 7 (Alberton, South Africa: Lectio Publishers, 2006).

Tuareg (Kel Tagelmust; Kel Tamacheq)

The Tuareg are Berber in origin. Most live in and around the Sahara Desert from Algeria and Libya in the north to northern Nigeria and Mali in the south. This area covers a variety of terrains including desert and semidesert, mountainous regions in southern Algeria, and savanna (grasslands with scattered tress and shrubs). The southern part of Tuareg territory is in the Sahel—a strip of semi-desert south of the Sahara—and in the savannas to its south. The majority of the Tuareg inhabit the Sahel.

ORIGINS

About 5,000 years ago, the Berber ancestors of the Tuareg lived along the North African coast of the Mediterranean, probably in present-day Libya (*see* BERBERS).

LANGUAGE

The Tuareg speak a Berber language called Tamacheq. It has four main dialects, which are largely mutually intelligible. The Tuareg often call themselves "Kel Tamacheq," meaning "People of the Tamacheq Language." Many Tuareg also speak SONGHAY, HAUSA, or French. Tamacheq is written in a script called Tifnagh.

HISTORY

Since the seventh-century C.E. Arab invasion of North Africa, the Tuareg have traveled southward in a series of migrations. A proud and independent people, they fought with Arab, Turkish, and European invaders over the years. ARABS had conquered all of North Africa by 711, however, and the Tuareg were driven south into the desert.

In the 15th century, the Sultanate of Aïr emerged as a centralized Tuareg state with its capital at Agades (modern Agadez) in present-day Niger. Aïr's wealth was based on control of the trans-Saharan trade routes. Great Tuareg trading caravans crossed the Sahara bringing gold, ivory, ostrich feathers, and slaves from West Africa to the Mediterranean coast. Southbound caravans carried salt and Arab and European goods to West Africa. Agades was part

---

TUAREG

location:
North Africa

time period:
17th century C.E. to present

ancestry:
Nilotic

language:
Nilo-Saharan

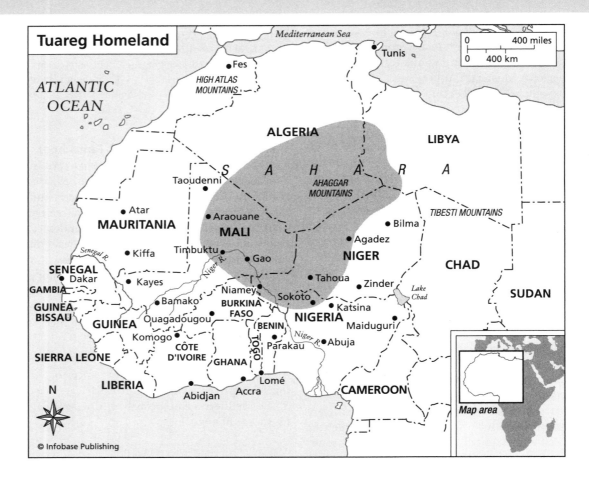

Tuareg Homeland

of the Songhay Empire from 1501–32 and was tributary to the Kanem-Borno Empire from 1532 until the 1600s. After attacking Borno, Aïr greatly expanded its territory at the expense of neighboring states during the 17th and 18th centuries. In the 1800s the Sultanate of Aïr reached its greatest extent and Agades became an important political center in the region. By 1870, however, Agades had ceased to be of political importance, and by 1900 Aïr had become part of the French West Africa colony.

In 1917 a Tuareg rebellion against French rule was harshly suppressed. Many were killed and tens of thousands of others fled to northern Nigeria. By the 1960s, North and West Africa were independent from colonial rule, but the Tuareg found themselves divided up between various different nations that had no relevance to their history, lifestyle, or social and political structures.

Sahelian droughts have been increasingly frequent since the 1960s. They have forced many Tuareg to migrate northward to Algeria and Libya. Returning Tuareg refugees have come into conflict with the Malian and Niger governments in particular. In the early 1990s

decades of frustration at what the Tuareg regarded as the failure of national governments to address their needs erupted into a widespread rebellion by Tuareg groups in Niger and Mali. Conflict between Tuareg rebels and government forces in Mali between 1990 and 1991 led to an agreement that established the semi-autonomous Kidal region in the east of the country. Intense fighting between Tuareg and government forces broke out again in 1994 propelling Mali into a state of civil war that was ended by peace accords in 1995. Between 1990 and 1995 Tuareg rebels in Niger conducted a long-running campaign against government forces in the Air Mountains in the north of the country and around the cities of Agadez and Arlit, the latter being the center of Niger's uranium mining industry. This conflict ended in an uneasy peace with some Tuareg groups continuing sporadic attacks into the late 1990s. From 2007 new conflicts began in Niger and Mali as Tuareg groups once again began anti-government campaigns. In Niger the Tuareg group Niger Movement for Justice (MNJ) carried out attacks on government installations and facilities belonging to foreign companies.

In Mali Tuareg groups have also restarted insurgency campaigns. Attempts to reach peace settlements in Mali and Niger have met with limited success as of the end of 2008.

CULTURE

Precolonial Tuareg were largely nomadic pastoralists who kept and maintained large herds of cattle, camels, sheep, and goats. The Tuareg would migrate with their herds of animals, moving from one water hole or pasture to another. Oases provided resting places and water. Surplus produce could be exchanged at oases for products such as dates and millet grown by the resident cultivators.

Many Tuareg are still nomadic, but colonial and government policies, drought, and pressure on the land from an increasing population have changed the way of life of many. Colonial governments limited each group of nomads to specific areas, and the new national boundaries that were imposed further restricted nomadic activities. Since the colonial era, the improvement of existing wells and the provision of new ones has had side effects. Combined with improved veterinary care, permanent water holes have allowed herds to increase dramatically in size, and overgrazing has seriously damaged pasturelands. Attempting to control the Tuareg, governments have often pursued policies that encourage them to settle and practice farming. Until recently, the Algerian government even had a policy of forced sedentarization, which grouped the Tuareg into settled agricultural cooperatives.

A severe drought struck the Sahelian lands in 1968–74 and again in 1984–85, permanently changing the Tuareg lifestyle. Thousands of people and whole herds of cattle died, while others were forced to sell their herds and thousands more moved south to Niger and Nigeria. Although many returned to nomadic pastoralism—with greatly depleted herds—others did not. As a result, many Tuareg are now settled farmers or seasonal laborers in the ports and docks of North and West Africa.

Most Tuareg engaged in trading across the Sahara as well as nomadic pastoralism in the precolonial era. Trade was deeply affected by the arrival of the French, however. Trans-Saharan trading was largely curtailed by the imposition of customs duties and competition from new coastal trading centers. Only the salt trade remained active. International trade has partly replaced the trans-Saharan trade, but it is not as lucrative. Using their camels to travel cross-country in long caravans, the Tuareg take advantage of price differences between countries to make a profit. Potash, which is used in fertilizers and soaps, is taken from Bilma in Niger to Katsina in northern Nigeria, for example.

Although trucks now cross the Sahara, most Tuareg still rely on camels for transportation, as they can go places where no wheeled vehicle can. The camel has large eyes, protected by long eyelashes and heavy eyebrows. Its long legs end in cushionlike feet that act on the loose sand like snowshoes on snow. Camels can travel for days with little food and for weeks without water. A camel can eat almost any kind of plant, no matter how thorny. The camel's strength and endurance have earned it the name "ship of the desert." The Tuareg take great care of their camels, making sure that they get enough rest and are unloaded when they stop. Typically, the animal's burden includes trade goods, tents, blankets, provisions, and pots and pans.

Tuareg time line

B.C.E.

3000 Berber ancestors of Tuareg settled on the Mediterranean coast of North Africa.

C.E.

ca. 100 Camels are introduced to North Africa.

640 Arab invasion and conquest of North Africa begins.

711 Arabs control North Africa.

1400s Sultanate of Aïr established.

1500s Aïr loses its independence to Songhay Empire, then to Kanem-Borno Empire.

1600s Aïr independent again

1800 Aïr reaches greatest extent.

1899 First French military expedition against the Tuareg

1900 Aïr part of French West Africa

1917 Tuareg rebel against French.

1954 Algerian war of independence

1960 Niger and Mali independent

1962 Algerian independence

1990–95 Tuareg rebellion in Niger and Mali; Tuareg elements attempt to establish an independent state. Peace agreements are reached with most rebel groups.

2007 Second Tuareg rebellion in Niger and Mali; Niger Movement for Justice (MNJ) attacks government forces.

2008 United Nations special envoy Robert Fowler goes missing in Niger; Nigerien government accuses Tuareg rebels of kidnapping Fowler.

A Tuareg man preparing his camel for travel

The Tuareg are sometimes known as the "People of the Black Veil" because the men shield their faces with a *tagelmust* (a long strip of cloth). The *tagelmust* can be as much as 20 feet long. The cloth is, in fact, not black but dark blue. In the past, the veil was made from strips of Sudanese indigo cotton, but today this material is expensive and cheaper imported fabrics are used instead. Sudanese cotton is still used for special garments though. Some of the blue dye of this fabric comes off on the faces of the wearers, giving the Tuareg their other nickname of "Blue Men." Women usually go unveiled but often wear a headcloth.

Government and Society

In the past, the Tuareg were divided into seven main groupings or confederations: the Kel Ahaggar, Kel Ajjer, Kel Adrar, Kel Aïr, Kel Geres, Aullemmeden Kel Dennek, and the Aullemmeden Kel Ataram. The Kel Ahaggar and the Kel Ajjer of southern Algeria are known as the Northern Tuareg. The other groups, who live mostly in the Sahel, are known as the Southern Tuareg. Each confederation was led by an *amenokal* (king). These confederations have been disempowered since the colonial era;

each *amenokal* now provides a link with the relevant central government.

There are three main Tuareg social classes. At the top are the *imajeghen* (nobles), one of whom is elected as the *amenokal* of each confederation. The *imajeghen* were decimated by French reprisals after the rebellion of 1917 and today form less than 1 percent of the total Tuareg population. After the nobles come the *imghad*—the ordinary people. The third main group is the *iklan,* descendants of black Africans who were once Tuareg slaves. Postcolonial governments have largely eradicated slavery, however, and many *iklan* are now farmers, herders, artisans, blacksmiths, or laborers.

Women and men have equal status, and husbands and wives may both own property. Women join in the decision-making processes of the group, and both men and women tend to be equally well educated. Usually, the men tend the animals, while the women look after the children, prepare food, and milk the animals.

Religion

The vast majority of Tuareg are Muslims—Islam was introduced to North Africa by Muslim Arabs in the seventh century. Most Tuareg groups have *ineslemen* or *marabouts* (a religious class that was introduced after the adoption of Islam). *Ineslemen* act as teachers, counselors, and mediators in local disputes.

See also ALGERIANS: NATIONALITY; MALIANS: NATIONALITY; NIGERIANS: NATIONALITY.

FURTHER READING

Jeremy Keenan. *The Lesser Gods of the Sahara: Social Change and Contested Terrain Amongst the Tuareg of Algeria.* Cass series (London [u.a.]: Cass, 2004).

Tugen

The Tugen are a subgroup of the KALENJIN of Kenya. They live in the hills above the Kerio River.

Tukolor (Tekrurs; Torodos; Toucouleurs)

There are around 1 million Tukolor people spread throughout West Africa but are particularly concentrated in the north of Senegal near the border with Mauritania, and several thousand others live in Guinea. Originally a FULANI people, modern-day Tukolors are descended from Fulani, MOORS, SONINKE, and other ancestors.

Although most Fulani groups are nomadic, the Tukolor have long been settled farmers. The Tukolor Fulani people founded the state of Tekrur in what is now Senegal several hundred years ago. The Tukolor are said to have been the first large group of West Africans to adopt Islam as their religion. The Tukolor were very active in the Islamicization of West Africa, through both jihad (holy war) and their widespread trade contacts with other peoples. The best-known Tukolor in the spread of Islam was Al Hajj Umar Tall, who established the powerful, though short-lived, Tukolor Empire across present-day Guinea, Senegal, and Mali in the 19th century.

Tukulor *See* TUKOLOR.

Tulama

The Tulama are one of the nine main subgroups of the OROMO. They live in Ethiopia.

Tumbuka (Tew; Tombuca)

The Tumbuka are related to the TONGA. They live primarily in northern Malawi and northeastern Zambia.

Tunisians: nationality (people of Tunisia)

GEOGRAPHY

Although it is the smallest of all North African countries at 63,170 square miles, Tunisia's unique geography affords the country a historical and economic importance far greater than its size. Tunisia is surrounded by Algeria on the west, Libya to the southeast, and the Mediterranean Sea to the north and northeast. The island of Sicily is located just to the north of Tunisia. Indeed, the relative ease of access between Europe, Sicily, and Tunisia has allowed extensive opportunities for trade, exchange, and conquest for centuries.

Once known as the "breadbasket of Rome," the climate of Tunisia has become dryer over recent centuries. Still, there is significant rainfall in the north, especially on the northwestern Khroumiria Mountains. Levels of rainfall drop off gradually further south according to latitude. The southern tip of Tunisia, squarely in the Sahara Desert, experiences virtually no rain, while the northernmost parts are exposed to Mediterranean storms. There are important mountainous regions in the center of the country, such as el-Kef, and in the north and northwest, which see occasionally high precipitation that sustains cork tree forests.

Tunisia is not a country rich in rivers. The only significant river, the Majerda, flows from

A typical *souk* (market place) in a present-day Tunisian town

TUNISIANS: NATIONALITY

nation:
Tunisia; Tunisian Republic

derivation of name:
From the capital city, Tunis

government:
Republic

capital:
Tunis

language:
The country's official language is Arabic, but French is also widely spoken.

religion:
98 percent of the population are Muslim. Jews and Christians make up the remaining 2 percent.

earlier inhabitants:
Berbers

demographics:
Arabs make up 98 percent of the population. Europeans and other North Africans make up the remaining 2 percent.

A pavilion situated on the approach to the mausoleum of Tunisian president Habib Bourguiba (in office 1957–87). The pavilion has an octagonal shape reminiscent of the Dome of the Rock in Jerusalem.

west to east through central Tunisia. Although it is low and muddy in the summer months, the Majerda and its tributaries do allow for agricultural production of grain, citrus fruits, and cattle. The semi-arid mountainous and hill regions that make up most of northern Tunisia are dedicated to the production of olives. Dates are produced from a few oases in the desert south. Large brackish salt lakes, or *chotts,* exist across the middle of the country bordering the southern, Saharan region.

Despite some opportunities for agricultural production in the northwest and center, the great majority of Tunisia's population is located on the eastern coastline. With several natural ports and opportunities for commerce across the Mediterranean, port cities on the eastern coastline have allowed Tunisia to become of vibrant center of trade. The largest and most significant city, Tunis, is located near the ancient city of Carthage to the northeast. Other major towns and cities on the eastern shore include Sousse, Sfax, and Mahdiyya. The unique island of Jerba, a haven for Jews and unorthodox Muslims, lies north of where the Tunisian border meets Libya on the coast.

INCEPTION AS A NATION

From the earliest period the geography of the region of Tunisia has allowed its population to enjoy a separate identity, despite periods of domination by outside powers. Tunisia's eastern coastline has attracted settlers and traders since ancient times. While Berber nomadic and seminomadic tribes inhabited the interior of Tunisia, the coastline was populated by Phoenician traders, who founded Carthage in 814 B.C.E. (*see* BERBERS; PHOENICIANS). By the sixth century B.C.E. Carthage was wealthy enough to control most of the trading routes of the western Mediterranean. Carthage met its match, however, in Rome. After centuries of warfare and the near conquest of Rome by the famed Carthaginian warrior Hannibal, Carthage was finally destroyed by the ROMANS in 146 B.C.E.

Tunisia was an important agricultural province of Rome in the imperial period and remained prosperous and wealthy, even after the Vandal invasions of Roman North Africa in 429 C.E. Throughout the Roman period the Tunisians maintained Phoenician gods and culture by adapting their deities to the Roman pantheon. The Byzantines regained control of Tunisia from the Vandals but were themselves routed by the ARABS who invaded Tunisia in 647 and took control of Carthage in 698.

The Arabs faced sustained resistance from the Berber tribes who were led by the charismatic Berber princess. The founding of the great Islamic city of Qayrawan in the center of the country, however, spelled the beginning of the end of Berber independence. A series of Arab governors were sent to Qayrawan from

Tunisians: nationality time line

B.C.E.

814   Carthage founded by Phoenicians on the Tunisian coast.

sixth century   Carthage become a dominant power in the Mediterranean.

146   Carthage defeated by Rome after centuries of warfare.

C.E.

429   The Vandals invade North Africa and end Roman rule.

seventh century   Tunisia is invaded by Muslim Arab armies, who face fierce resistance from local Berber tribes.

909   The Fatimids overthrow the Aghlabids.

1159   The Almohads, invading from the Atlas Mountains of Morocco, conquer Tunisia and make it an Almohad province.

1230–ca. 1547   The Hafsids rule Tunisia.

16th century   Spain conquers several coastal cities but is driven out by the Ottomans.

1705   The Beys (Ottoman governors of Tunisia) establish an independent dynasty that lasts until 1957.

1881   The French take control of Tunisia.

1934   The Neo-Destour party, led by Habib Bourguiba and a group of young radicals, calls for independence from France.

1957   Bourguiba becomes the ruler of Tunisia as the institution of the hereditary bey is abolished.

1987   Bourguiba is deposed in a bloodless coup.

1989   Ben Ali wins presidential elections.

1999   Ben Ali wins a third presidential term in Tunisia's first multiparty presidential elections.

2004   Ben Ali wins a fourth presidential term.

2006   The main opposition party the Progressive Democratic Party elects a female leader. May Eljeribi is the first woman to lead a major Tunisian political party.

2007   Islamic militants and security forces are involved in street battles in Tunis.

---

the caliphal capital Baghdad to pacify and convert the Berbers. With crises in Baghdad, however, these governors were soon able to become almost completely independent from the caliph in the east. Al-Aghlab bin Salim al-Tamimi set up his own dynasty and independent kingdom. He and his descendants modeled Qayrawan after the glories of Baghdad, creating a house of wisdom, hospitals, and a magnificent mosque that still stands today as one of the largest, most ancient, and best preserved in the world.

Despite the power of the Aghlabid Arab governors in cities such as Qayrawan, the Berbers in the countryside were openly rebellious. One Berber confederation, the Kutama, was convinced by Ubayd Allah, a descendant of the prophet Muhammad, that he was the Mahdi, the expected Muslim messiah. Led by their Mahdi, the Kutama rose up and defeated the Aghlabids, establishing the Fatimid dynasty in 909. After the Fatimids conquered Egypt, however, they lost interest in Tunisia, allowing it to be ruled by independent governors. One dynasty of governors, the Zirids, rose up against the Fatimids. In response, the Fatimids invited an Arab tribe, the BANI HILAL, a group of warrior nomads, into Tunisia and North Africa. The Bani Hilal allegedly wreaked havoc on the cities of Tunisia.

An age dominated by tribal chiefs began. Tunisia was so vulnerable at this point that the Christian Normans were able to attack, and briefly conquer, important Tunisian cities such as Mahdiyya. By the middle of the 12th century, however, the Almohads, a religiously inspired group of Berbers from Morocco, declared holy war against the Normans and attacked the tribal states of the Bani Hilal. Tunisia was again united under a virtually independent governor of a distant empire. The Almohad territory of Tunisia, known as Ifiriqiyya before modern times, was independently governed by the Hafsids, descendants of an important Almohad tribal chief. After the fall of the Almohad Empire in the 13th century, the Hafsids remained in power in Tunisia and presided over a period of relative prosperity despite failed attempts by Crusaders such as the French King Louis IX (d. 1270 in Tunis) to conquer Tunisian territory.

The Hafsids ended their long reign only with the arrival of the OTTOMANS in 1574. Tunisia went from being an independent state to an Ottoman province ruled from Istanbul. Soon, however, Tunisia would, as it had under empires in the past, return to a situation of virtual autonomy ruled by a pasha (governor). Various revolts lead to the rise of the corsairs, or pirates, who controlled Tunisia as a center for trade and contraband.

The Moriscos, Muslim expelled from Spain, entered Tunisia in the 17th century, bringing a distinctive Andalusian flavor to Tunisian culture. By the 19th century several beys (governors) achieved a certain level of power, but none were able to reverse the rise of European influence in the region, especially from France. One ruler, Ahmad Bey (1837–55), attempted several internal reforms that planted the seeds of a sense of Tunisian identity. In 1881, however, the bey of Tunisia was forced to sign a treaty of protection with France, and from that time the bey became a largely symbolic figure.

Colonization did lead to some economic developments and reforms, and ideals of self-determination brought from Europe were translated into a nationalist movement. The Young Tunisians, an elite group of French-educated nationalists who demanded the same rights as French settlers, set the stage for the eventual rise of the Neo-Constitutional movement and eventual independence from France in 1956. Although many dreamed of democracy, Tunisia came to be dominated by the strong hand of the dictatorial president Habib Bourguiba, who instituted an ambitious set of highly-centralized reforms of religious, economic, and daily life that would have a profound impact on Tunisians and Tunisian identity. Bourguiba made education a central objective and mandated the equal treatment of women. Bourguiba remained in power until he was toppled in an internal coup led by his successor, Ben Ali, in 1987. Ben Ali has continued Bourguiba's legacy of centralized control.

CULTURAL IDENTITY

Although Tunisia began as a Berber territory ruled by successive powers, from Rome, to the Fatimids, to the Hafsids, the influx of ARABS from the east and the migration of Berbers further west has meant the virtual disappearance of the original inhabitants of the region. It is estimated that only about 1 percent of Tunisia's current population still speaks Berber. Being closer to the Middle East and more accessible to influences from the Arab and Ottoman East, especially under Ottoman domination, Tunisians have an identity that is both Middle Eastern and North African.

From the establishment of Franciscan monasteries in Tunisia in the 13th century, to the influences from Sicily and the rise of French colonialism, Tunisia and especially Tunisia's coastal cities have been exposed to influences from European powers. This is particularly true today. Many Tunisians speak French, not Arabic, as their first language. The Tunisian elite see France, and the ideals of their former colonizer, as their cultural, political, and economic inspiration. Islam, in particular, has taken a backseat to economic modernization. Although many Tunisians have maintained their strong religious identity, the focus of Tunisian life is more concentrated on the beach resorts catering to large numbers of European tourists than on the mosque. Thus, modernization, represented by Europe and advocated by the absolutist regime, and tradition, represented by Islam, are in constant tension, not only in Tunisia as a state but also in the minds of Tunisians.

FURTHER READING

B. D. Hoyos. *Hannibal: Rome's Greatest Enemy* (Exeter, U.K.: Bristol Phoenix, 2008).

Kenneth J. Perkins. *A History of Modern Tunisia* (New York: Cambridge University Press, 2004).

Kenneth J. Perkins. *Historical Dictionary of Tunisia* (Metuchen, N.J.: Scarecrow Press, 1989).

Tunjur

The Tunjur are a relatively small ethnic group today, but they had established a powerful kingdom by the 16th century in what is now Sudan. The present-day Tunjur live in Darfur, western Sudan, and across the border in Chad.

Tupur

The majority of the Tupur live in northern Cameroon, but significant numbers also live in southwestern Chad and southeastern Nigeria.

Turka

The Turka are a subgroup of the Senufo. The Turka live in northern Ivory Coast, southern Mali, and southwestern Burkina Faso.

Turkana

The Turkana inhabit the semidesert regions of northwestern Kenya. The region they occupy is bordered to the east by the western shores of Lake Turkana and to the west by the Rift Valley. Turkana District is now an official administrative region of Kenya. The Ngimonia and the Ngichoro are the two main divisions of the Turkana people.

The Turkana are sometimes considered to be part of the Karamojong cluster of peoples. The Karamojong live across the border in northeastern Uganda, and the Turkana and Karamojong speak closely related Nilotic languages. They also share a common ancestry, descending from Nilotes who originated several millennia ago on the southwestern fringe of the Ethiopian highlands. The Turkana are Plains Nilotes, who emerged as a new and powerful force in East Africa during the second millennium c.e.

Like many other Nilotic peoples, the Turkana have a history of pastoralism and many are still herders today. The Turkana adapted to their arid environment and variable climate by herding a variety of animals and by moving frequently to find new pastures and water.

Turkic Peoples

The Turkic peoples may be defined as those peoples originating in areas from Siberia and western China to eastern Europe and the Mediterranean who speak languages that are part of the Turkic language family. This linguistic family is comprised of some 30 tongues that are sometimes described as belonging to the larger Altaic language family. Today some 180 million people speak these as a first language. Nearly half of these 180 million speak Anatolian Turkish, the language of the modern Turkish Republic (*see also* Turks: nationality).

Outside of Turkey, Turkic speakers make up important minorities in other countries of the Middle East and elsewhere. In the Middle East the largest of these minorities is located in Iran, where 24 percent of the population speak Azeri, one of the Turkic languages.

The name "Turk" derives from the term *tujue*, meaning "strong" or "powerful," used in sixth-century c.e. Chinese sources to refer to the Göktürks (the "blue" or "celestial" Turks). These were the first of the Altaic peoples to use the term *Turk* in reference to themselves and the first to use a runic script for their language. In the sixth century c.e. the Göktürks united and assumed leadership of the Inner Asian Turkic peoples, including, for example, Uighur, Khitan, and Kyrgyz elements. By the seventh century they had created an empire that stretched from the Sea of Japan in the east to the Crimea in the west. This expansion was the first of a series of migrations of Turkic peoples from their ancestral homeland, an area comprising lands from Central Asia to Siberia along the Yenisei river system westward. These migrations continued until the 11th century.

ORIGINS

The Göktürks lived in the Xinjiang region of modern China. Xinjiang is bordered by Tibet to the south, Mongolia to the east, Russia to the north, and Afghanistan, Tajikistan, and Kashmir to the west. Their expansion westward from the sixth century c.e., at the head of a grand tribal confederation, was the first of several waves of Turkic migrations into the West. The Uighurs, Kyrgyz, Oghuz, and Turkmen were among the other Turkic elements that later also founded empires in the region from Mongolia to Transoxiana. The Uighurs and Kyrgyz remained mainly in eastern Asia and China.

In the Middle East, branches of the Oghuz, who had been migrating westward from the fifth century, moved into Anatolia and founded the Seljuk Empire (1037–1194) and the Ottoman Empire (1299–1922) (see Seljuks; Ottomans). The Mongols, who conquered Beijing in 1215 under Chenggis Khan (d. 1227) and then swept westward through Iran and captured the Abbasid capital of Baghdad in 1258, were not a single people but a large tribal confederation that included many Turkic clans. Their immediate successors were the Ilkhanids. The Timurids, who swept westward in the 14th century under their famous leader Timur, were also a large confederation whose numbers included Turkic elements. The Timurid Empire and its Turkic successors dominated the Iranian plateau until the early 16th century. The Safavid and Qajar dynasties, rulers in Iran from 1501 to 1722 and from 1795 to 1925 respectively, were Turkic in origin (see Qajars; Iranians: nationality). Early Safavid leaders, for example, probably spoke Chagatay, the literary language of Cen-

TURKIC PEOPLES

location:
Eastern Asia, Central Asia, West Asia, Eastern Europe

time period:
Sixth century to present

ancestry:
Turkic

language:
Turkic

A 13th-century stone relief depicting Seljuk soldiers. Troops such as these were involved in fighting European Crusaders in this period.

tral Asia in the Middle Ages related to the modern Uzbek and Uighur languages.

Some experts maintain that the Huns, the ancestors of the Mongols, were one of the earliest known Turkic peoples. The Huns moved into Europe in the fourth and fifth centuries under their leader Atilla the Hun (d. 453). Others believe the Huns, in common with groups such as the Scythians and the later Mongols, were, in fact, confederations of ethnic groups that included Turkic speakers.

LANGUAGE

Classifying and describing the development of the languages spoken by Turkic peoples over time is extremely difficult and complex. During the course of many migrations across many centuries, Turkic-speaking peoples intermingled with a host of other peoples, and their languages were influenced by these interactions as well as influencing the languages of the peoples they came into contact with. Recent attempts at classification suggest there are six branches of the Turkic languages: Southwestern, or Oghuz Turkic; Northwestern, or Kypchak Turkic; Southeastern, or Uighur Turkic; Northeastern, or Siberian Turkic; Oghur Turkic; and Arghu Turkic.

Oghuz Turkic is associated with the Oghuz peoples. Today some 110 million people from China to the Balkans speak one of the Oghuz languages. They are at least three subgroups of Oghuz Turkic in the Middle East. The Western subgroup includes Turkish, a classification that itself includes modern Turkish, Ottoman Turkish, and Azerbaijani. The latter comprises QASHQAI and AFSHAR and the languages of the Iraqi Turkmen. An eastern subgroup includes the Turkmen language and a dialect of Uzbek (see UZBEKS). The Southern subgroup includes some other Turkic dialects spoken in Iran and Afghanistan.

Another branch of Oghur Turkic is Khazar, which is spoken by those peoples who dominated the Northern Caucasus, along the Caspian Sea, from the seventh to the 10th centuries C.E. (see Khazars). Khalaj, a branch of Arghu Turkic, is heavily influenced by modern Persian, and is spoken by a small number of people in modern-day central northwestern Iran and Afghanistan. Oghuz and Khalaj both have no initial h sound, nor do they feature an instrumental case for the noun.

Some scholars have suggested that Mongolian and the various Turkic languages are affiliated by virtue of their being of the larger Altaic family of languages, but this is not a universally accepted theory.

HISTORY

The Oghuz Turks were the Turkic grouping whose migrations from Central Asia most affected the Middle East. The term "Oghuz" is less an ethnic marker than a term that refers generally to those Turkic peoples who, following the collapse of the Göktürk Empire, migrated west beginning in the eighth century. The same group is also sometimes referred to as the "Western Turks."

The original homeland of the Oghuz was the region called Turan, a Persian-language term denoting Central Asia generally and the Ural-Altay area in particular. Some historians maintain that the word Oghuz is a reference to the Hun Empire whose founder was supposedly given the title "Oghuz" in the second century B.C.E. Prior to the rise of the Göktürk confederation, there are also references to an Oghuz confederation that united eight or nine Turkic groups. During the period of the Göktürk Empire itself, Oghuz elements are said to have been based in the Altay Mountains as well as Mongolia. Arab sources date their presence in Transoxiana, the area comprising modern-day Uzbekistan, Tajikistan, and parts of Kazakhstan, from the late eighth century C.E., and the area between the Caspian and Aral Seas came to be known as the Oghuz Steppe. From this base the Oghuz established contacts with the Muslim Abbasid caliphate (750–1258) to the south and eventually abandoned their shamanist spiritual beliefs for Islam.

The Seljuks

The first of the great Oghuz empires of the Middle East was the Seljuk Empire, the putative founder of which—named Seljuk—was the commander of the Khazar army. In the mid-10th century Seljuk led Khazar forces into

Turkic Peoples time line	
C.E.	
fifth century	Branches of the Oghuz Turks begin to move West from Central Asia.
522–745	Göktürk Empire in Asia
1037–1194	Seljuk Empire
1055	Seljuks capture Abbasid capital of Baghdad.
1071	Seljuks defeat Byzantines at Manzikert.
1077–1307	Seljuks of Rum
1092	Death of the administrative reformer Nizam al-Mulk
1194	Death of last of the Great Seljuks
1243	Seljuks become vassals of the Mongols.
1258	Mongols under Chenggis Khan capture the Abbasid capital Baghdad.
1265	Death of Hulegu, grandson of Chenggis Khan and founder of Ilkhanid dynasty
1402	Timur defeats Ottomans at Ankara.
1405	Death of Timur
1447–51	Wars between the Black Sheep and White Sheep tribal confederations
1453	Ottomans capture Constantinople.
1501–1722	Safavid dynasty rules Iran. Establishment of Twelver Shia as the state's official faith.
1795–1925	Qajar dynasty in Iran
1923	End of Ottoman dynasty in Turkey

See also Turks: nationality

Khwarezm, the area south and southwest of the Aral Sea. During this time Seljuk elements hired themselves out as mercenaries both to the Persian Samanid dynasty (819–999), whose chief cities were Bukhara, Samarkand, and Heraart, and to other polities in the area.

Seljuk's grandson Tughril (d. 1063) led an army that was defeated by the Ghaznavid Empire (975–1187), itself Turkish in origin. However, Seljuk forces continued raids into Khurasan and into northern Iran after this defeat, their lighter, quicker forces often defeating the more ponderous Ghaznavid troops. Tughril captured Merv and Nishapur in eastern Iran in 1028–29 and, in 1037, took the capital of Ghazni, which was located in modern central Afghanistan. In 1040, following the Battle of Dandanaqan, the last Ghaznavid ruler fled to India. Tughril then pushed westward into the Iranian plateau in the early 1040s. His forces challenged the Byzantines for Anatolia, and in 1055 Tughril entered

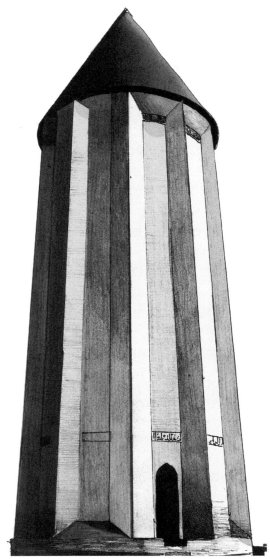

An early 11th-century brick-built tomb in the northern Iranian city of Gonbad-e Qabus.

constituted the high point of Seljuk rule, with Iran and Iraq enjoying great economic prosperity. Alp Arslan added Armenia and Georgia to the Seljuk domains in 1064 and from 1068 maintained constant pressure on the Byzantines. The decisive Seljuk defeat of Byzantine forces at Manzikert in 1071 paved the way for Turkish settlement of Anatolia, and by 1081 Seljuk forces were raiding as far west as the Sea of Marmara. Under Malikshah the empire also expanded east as far as China.

Initially the empire was strong enough to withstand the infighting that marked the years after Malik Shah's death. The appearance of Crusaders in Syria and the upper Euphrates in 1098 was not seen as a threat. Gradually, however, the empire fragmented into small provincial entities. A decisive defeat of Seljuk forces in 1141 by Qara Khitan elements invading from China resulted in the loss of Seljuk territory in the Transoxus region.

In western Iran and Iraq internal feuding and local politics quickly came to limit Seljuk central authority, while external challengers, such as the Christian GEORGIANS, made small gains at the borders of Seljuk territory. Even the Abbasid caliphs moved to reestablish some of their authority in the midst of the struggles of rival contenders for the Seljuk sultanate. Some of these contenders or their associates achieved some measure of authority over smaller parts of Seljuk territory, such as Azerbaijan, Fars, and the region around Mosul. Various Turkish military commanders came to enjoy considerable power in this period. In the Kirman region of the Iranian plateau, the Seljuk line of succession continued until late in the same century. The area remained prosperous, and its rulers were generally content to maintain their borders rather than trying to extend them. Gradually military commanders assumed increasing authority here also.

Perhaps the most important of the Seljuk subdivisions was the sultanate of Rum, which ruled in Anatolia (modern Turkey) from 1077 to 1307. The word Rum referred to the Arabic term for lands in that area that had once belonged to the Roman Empire and which had subsequently been captured by Muslim armies. By the late 12th century, despite the arrival in the area of forces participating in the First Crusade (1095–99) and the Second Crusade (1145–49), the sultanate of Rum controlled nearly all of central Anatolia. In the late 12th and early 13th centuries the sultanate also captured key seaports on the Mediterranean and Black Sea

the Abbasid capital of Baghdad and deposed the last of the BUYIDS who had been the power behind the Abbasid throne since the 940s. In 1058 he entered the capital officially and was granted various honorific titles and a robe of honor from the caliph, and he was styled "sultan." From this time the division of authority in Islam between the Seljuk sultan, a secular political figure, and the Abbasid caliph, the spiritual and moral head of the Muslim community, was solidified.

From their base in Merv other Seljuk leaders extended their own territory into Kirman and held sway over nearby Sistan as well. Tughril died without an heir and was succeeded by Alp Arslan (r. 1063–73). The reign of Alp Arslan and that of his son Malikshah (1073–92) coasts from the Byzantines. With the death in 1194 of the last of the Great Seljuks, the Rum Seljuks became the sole remaining branch of the dynasty. In the early 1200s the Rum Seljuks recaptured Konya from German Crusaders.

The Seljuk sultans of Rum withstood the Crusaders for the most part, but Mongol invasions put an end to the independence of their sultanate. The Seljuks became vassals of the Mongols in 1243. Thereafter the Seljuk state split into small entities called beyliks. One of these beyliks was ruled by the Ottomans, who went on to establish their own dynasty.

The Black Sheep and White Sheep Tribal Confederations

Among the later states in the region whose origins may also be traced to the Oghuz are the White Sheep and Black Sheep Turkish tribal confederations.

The latter, called the QARA-QOYUNLU (or Kara-koyunlu) in Turkish, were powerful in areas of modern-day Armenia, Azerbaijan, the southern Caucasus, Iraq, and Iran from the late 14th to the late 15th century. Their leader Qara Yusuf (d. 1420) established the confederation's independence from the Baghdad and Tabriz-based Iranian Jalayirid dynasty. After Timur's death in 1405, Qara Yusuf captured Tabriz in 1406 and took Baghdad in 1408. Later Black Sheep rulers established independence from the Timurids and extended their control over Iraq, parts of Georgia, and central Iran.

From 1447, the dynasty became embroiled in conflict with the White Sheep confederation, called the AQ-QOYUNLU (or Ak-koyunlu) in Turkish. These seem to be have been present in eastern Anatolia from the early 14th century. Wars between the two tribal confederations lasted until 1451. In 1467 Black Sheep forces suffered a devastating defeat at the hands of the White Sheep led by Uzun Hasan (d. 1478). The latter rapidly expanded White Sheep lands, and by the end of his reign the White Sheep held sway over modern-day Armenia, Azerbaijan, eastern Turkey, Iraq, and western Iran down to the shores of the Persian Gulf and northward into Khurasan. In 1473 the Ottomans defeated Uzun Hasan. Uzun Hasan's son Yaqub held the empire together, but at his death in 1490 the White Sheep confederation broke up. Some White Sheep elements defected to the Safavids. The Safavid line itself may have been at least partly Oghuz in origin, although it also had Kurdish roots (see KURDS). Ismail I (1487–1524), the founder of the Safavid dynasty who captured Tabriz in 1501 and declared Twelver Shia as his empire's official faith, was the grandson of Uzun Hasan and a Byzantine princess (see TWELVERS).

The Ottomans

Another group of Turks of Oghuz origins were the Ottomans, who took their name from Osman I (r. 1299–1326), the founder of the dynasty who declared his independence from the Seljuk Turks in 1299 and conquered nearby tribes. Osman's grandson Murad I (r. 1359–89) named the dynasty and assumed the title sultan. In 1453 the Ottomans captured Constantinople from the Byzantines. At its height in the 16th and 17th centuries, the Ottoman Empire encompassed territory spanning three continents—from southeast Europe through the Middle East into North Africa and stretching from the Atlantic coast of modern-day Morocco in the west to the Caspian Sea and the Persian Gulf in the east, and from modern-day Austria and the Ukraine in the north to Sudan, Somalia, and Yemen in the south. For 600 years the Ottoman Empire was the center of and mediator of interactions between East and West. The Ottoman Empire came to end with the declaration of the Republic of Turkey in 1923.

The Safavids

The Safavids were a dynasty who ruled Iran from 1501 to 1722 and who established Twelver Shia as their empire's state religion. The Safavid family were of mixed Kurdish, Greek, and Azerbaijani Turkish descent, the latter being Oghuz in origin. The dynasty's spiritual discourse combined a new messianic militarism that appealed to the tribes' millenarian tendencies, which had engulfed the region's mainly Turkic tribes in the years following the death of Timur in 1405. The dynasty had its origins in Ardabil, in modern northwestern Iran, and went on to establish control over an area whose borders approximate those of modern-day Iran.

Non–Oghuz Turks and the Middle East

Many Mongol clans were of Turkic origin. The Mongol invasions into the Middle East began in the mid-13th century, and Mongol forces defeated the Seljuks of Rum in 1243. Under Hulegu Khan (d. 1265)—the grandson of Chenggis Khan—the Mongols sacked the Abbasid capital of Baghdad in 1258, thereby ending the Abbasid caliphate, and moved into Syria in 1259. The Mongol defeat in 1260 at Ayn Jalut, in the present-day West Bank, at the hands of Egypt's

Timur: The Turkic Conqueror ☞

Timur was a renowned military leader and champion of Persian culture who founded the Timurid dynasty in the 14th century C.E. The Timurids ruled much of western and central Asia from the end of the 14th to the end of the 15th century.

Timur was born in the city of Kesh, known today as Shahrisabz, in Uzbekistan in 1336. At that time Kesh was a city in a region known as Transoxiana, which was part of the Chagatai Khanate ruled by the successors of Chagatai Khan, the second son of the Mongol conqueror Chinggis Khan (ca. 1162– 1227). His family was an aristocratic clan of the Barlas tribal confederation of Turkic and Mongolian descent. Timur was a devout Muslim, though there is some uncertainty as to whether he belonged to the Sunni or Shii branch of the faith. Historically Timur was known as Timur the Lame, or Tamerlane in Western culture. According to some sources Timur suffered from a limp as a result of a wound to his leg and this was the source of his unusual nickname.

Timur spent almost his entire life engaged in military campaigns, and his conquests stretched from Smyrna at the western end of Anatolia (present-day Turkey) to Dehli in India. He rose to prominence in Transoxiana through a series of campaigns against neighboring powers on behalf of the Chagatai khans, though these were little more than puppet rulers. In 1369 Timur declared himself emir at his capital, Samarkand, a title he retained for the rest of his life. Despite his de facto absolute power over a vast empire, Timur never claimed the greater title of khan for himself, preferring to retain a figurehead Chagatai khan.

For the next 35 years Timur waged endless campaigns, conquering the Caucasus, most of Iran, much of Iraq, and large areas of southern Russia. In 1398 he launched a major campaign into India, which resulted in his capture of Delhi. At the end of the 14th century Timur became embroiled in a conflict with the Ottoman Empire, which was then establishing itself as a major power in Anatolia. Timur decisively defeated the Ottomans at the battle of Ankara in 1402, initiating a 12-year period of chaos and occupation known as the Ottoman interregnum. At the time of Timur's death in 1405 he was preparing to invade China.

In the West Timur has had a reputation as a brutal and uncivilized conqueror. Historical accounts of his campaigns are full of references to the massacre or enslavement of entire populations, particularly of non-Muslims. It is likely that many of these accounts are exaggerations or fabrications, some perhaps originating from Timur himself. Timur was a master of all aspects of war, including propaganda and espionage. It is known that before a campaign began, Timur would send agents into enemy cities to bribe captains and officials to betray their rulers and to spread tales of the brutality and might of Timur's armies intended to undermine morale. There is, however, evidence that cities such as Delhi, Baghdad, and Damascus were in fact extensively depleted and damaged during Timur's conquests.

Central Asia experienced a cultural and economic renaissance under Timur and his successors. Timur's capital, Samarkand, was an ancient center of trade and culture even 700 years ago, and Timur spent a great deal of his wealth building a new city that became the cultural heart of his empire. Artists and craftsmen from all the territories Timur campaigned in were sent to Samarkand to work under his patronage. The Bibi-Khanym Mosque, built with the treasure captured by Timur in India, was perhaps the most remarkable of these achievements. Timur and his successors were strongly influenced by Persian culture and Persian literature, arts, and sciences blossomed under Timurid rule.

Mamluk Empire, checked further Mongol western expansion.

The Ilkhan dynasty (its name means "subordinate khan") was one of four dynastic successors (khanates) to the Mongol dynasty in the 13th and 14th centuries, in this case established by descendants of Hulegu Khan (see ILKHANS). They ruled Iran for more than a century: In Iran the prominent local dynasties included the Jalayirids, who ruled Iraq and Azerbaijan, the Muzaffarids in Fars, Kirman, and Esfahan, and the Kart dynasty in Khurasan.

The rulers of the Timurid dynasty were said to be descendants of Chenggis Khan through Barlas Turkic elements. They were led by Timur (d. 1405), who was born near Samarkand. Timur captured Samarkand in 1369 and declared that city his capital. He began the conquest of Iran in 1383 and had captured Herat and all of eastern Iran by 1385. He then turned his attention to the Indian subcontinent and, in 1398, captured Delhi. The next year, 1399, he resumed his westward conquests. He moved through Iran reaching Baghdad in 1401 and defeated the Ottomans at Ankara in 1402. In the aftermath of the fighting that broke out in western Iran after Timur's death, and the conflict between the Black and White Sheep confederations, Timur's great-great-grandson, Sultan Husayn Baiqara (d. 1506), and his minister, Mir Ali Shir, succeeded in carving out a small, quiet kingdom centered in Herat between 1469 and 1506, which, though both were Turkish, became a great center of Persian culture.

The Mamluk dynasty, which stopped the advance of the Mongols, were themselves descendants of Kipchak and Yoruk Turks as well as other elements recruited by the Abbasids into their army. After their conversion to Islam the Mamluk forces were kept under the direct command of the ruling caliph. Mamluk forces based in Egypt founded a state that lasted from 1250 until 1517.

CULTURE

Government, Society, and Economy

Traditionally, the Oghuz were nomadic pastoralists and, as such, their natural mobility facilitated the swift and decisive movements necessary for rapid military conquest. The Oghuz and Oghuz territory grew both by natural expansion but also by alliances with other extended family and tribal groupings, mainly through marriage. Ceremonies marking births, deaths, and marriages brought together affiliated elements that were otherwise dispersed geographically. Men and women were active participants in Oghuz political, military, and social activities. Tribal elders played a key role in enforcing local customs and behavior.

As the various waves of Oghuz elements expanded into the Middle East, however, each gradually adopted the traditions held by the peoples into whose regions they had moved. Early Seljuk methods of governance, for example, may be regarded as most closely approximating preconquest nomadic tribal governance in that the rule of territory was spread among different family members who were assigned parts of the empire. Often possessing considerable autonomy from each other and from any nominal central state organization, these local rulers often fell to fighting among themselves to maintain or expand their holdings at the death of the nominal ruler of the empire or that of a nearby relative.

In all aspects of life the successive waves of Turkic immigrants who settled in the Middle East initially maintained their own cultural and other traditions of organization and activity. Gradually, however, more centrally organized and bureaucratic political structures traceable to pre-Islamic and, especially, Iranian settled society were adopted. Successive generations gradually adapted these to existing indigenous patterns. Inasmuch as these waves moved from east to west, the latter encompassed, in the main, Persian cultural references and Islam as the spiritual basis of their existence. Iran's role as a crossroads for the influx of Turks into the Middle East both contributed to, and was further encouraged by, the traditional Persian tolerance of cultural, religious, and language differences (see PERSIANS).

The Seljuks, for example, adopted Persian as their court language and were enamored of Persian culture; their patronage was key to the development of the Turko-Persian tradition throughout the subsequent history of the region. During the Seljuk period the Iranian-born Nizam al-Mulk, vizier from 1063 to his death in 1092, was influential in further centralizing the Seljuk administration along traditional Persian lines. Under the Mongol Ilkhans, the Persian Shams al-Din Juvayni (d. 1285) and his brother Ata al-Mulk (d. 1283), members of a Persian family that had long provided administrative officials to the political authorities, held positions of great influence. The latter was appointed governor of Baghdad and authored *The History of the World Conqueror,* a chronicle of the Mongol and Ilkhanid conquest of Iran. The Safavids became increasingly Persianized and, indeed, contributed to the spread of the Persian language and culture throughout Iran.

Timur himself was well acquainted with Persian culture. As a result, although Turkish became a state and literary language and some important contributions to Turkic literature were made during the Timurid era, Persian was the language of administration and literary culture. In fact, the Timurid Empire witnessed the consolidation of a Turko-Persian cultural synthesis in Transoxiana, and a form of Chaghatay Turkish was used alongside Persian as both a cultural and official language. Chaghatay remained important in the region until well into the Safavid period.

Art

Under the Seljuks, Persian art became established in an important position within Islamic art as a whole from Syria to northern India. The Seljuks were especially avid patrons of the visual arts, with figures of animals and images of hunting, zodiacal themes, banqueting, and music making featuring in the decoration of scenes from the traditional Persian historical epic, *Shah-name,* by Firdawsi (d. 1020). The traditional Iranian art of book illustration was given new impetus in this period. Sculpture in ceramic, metal, and stucco also featured prominently during this period. On the whole, Seljuk productivity in all these areas has been held to have exceeded that of previous centuries, even if Seljuk cultural output had its roots firmly in established, especially Persian, artistic traditions. To be sure, however, in Anatolia, where Turks made up a larger proportion of the population, references to distinctly Turkish pagan beliefs and customs are found.

Especially under the Ilkhans, the successors to the Mongols, manuscript illustration was given new life. Indeed, it is often held that Iranian miniature painting began only in the aftermath of the Mongol invasions. The vizier Rashid al-Din is known to have established a school in Tabriz, the Ilkhanid capital. The school became an important center for gathering in new styles and for the production of a number of well-known illustrated texts. The penchant for sponsorship of manuscript illustration was also manifest at various provincial centers throughout the region, including, for example, Shiraz. By approximately 1370 a new Iranian art of painting, under the sponsorship of the Ilkhanid rulers, was clearly discernible.

An example of the manner in which Ilkhanid painting differed can be seen in the increased use of images in illustrated manuscripts of importance to Iran's legendary history. The establishment of centers for such illustration being extremely expensive, it follows that central and provincial court patronage was a key factor in the appearance of this form of art. More particularly, it is clear that the Mongol rulers, newly arrived in the region, were eager to have their own deeds and traditions recorded for posterity by means of this art form. Indeed, a marked fascination with history generally is characteristic of the Ilkhanid period. The best example of manuscript illustration from this period is the 14th-century *Shah-name* (*The Book of Kings*), an illustrated version of Firdawsi's early 11th century history of Iran from the beginning of the world to the arrival of Islam in Iran in the seventh century. Manuscript copies of Rashid al-Din's famous *Jami al-Tawarikh*, (*The Collection of Chronicles*), a history of the world in three parts, were also lavishly illustrated. What is especially notable is that, while the illustrations of such texts featured various events and figures of historical import, the images used in their illustration were historically correct: Westerners were illustrated using western-style figures, for example. Nevertheless, a strong Chinese influence was also at work in the illustration—mountains depicted in the Chinese style, for example, feature prominently, and "Chinese" facial patterns and clothes are also clearly visible.

Art and Architecture

The *yurt,* a portable felt-covered wood-framed structure, was the traditional "home" of Oghuz and other Turkic tribal peoples. Once established in settled societies, however, the art and architecture of the various Turkic empires became a fusion of traditional Turkic forms with those of the established, settled societies that they ruled.

Timurid painting of the 15th century especially utilized smaller figures and static compositions. The period is also famous for the greater integration of Chinese influences into the art of the Middle East and a greater sense of space. Marginal decoration and double-page compositions were also features of Timurid manuscript illustration. Shah Rukh was an especially prominent patron of the "arts of the book," his greatest lasting monument being a 1436 copy of the famous *Miraj nama* (*Ascension of the Prophet Muhammad*). Other manuscript illustrations on this tradition are notable for their skilled and varied compositions and their brilliant coloring. Bihzad (d. 1535) was an important painter of miniatures and manuscript illustrator in Herat in the late Timurid period. Supported by both Sultan Huysan Baiqara and his minister Mir Ali Shir, Bihzad introduced a greater naturalism to Persian painting, especially in his painting of individuals, whom he endowed with greater freedom of movement. He also used Sufi mystical symbols. Both features are visible in an illustrated manuscript copy of Nizami's *Khamse* dated to this period. The Herati style of illustration was also visible in those illustrations commissioned for manuscripts by the rulers of the Black and White Sheep confederations. Overall, a harmony of man and nature was the dominant feature of miniature painting in this period.

The Seljuk contribution to Islamic architecture consisted mainly in the ability of its finest architects to draw from and extend the variety of classical forms of Persian architecture. Thus, for example, the "Iranian plan" of mosque building became an influential model throughout the region in the Seljuk period. Iranian plan mosques featured a large central court with a large portal that lead into the domed hall in the side of the building facing Mecca. Inside the domed hall was the *mihrab,* a niche in the wall of a mosque that indicates the direction of Mecca. The other three sides of the courtyard were lined with arcades and had a smaller *ivan* (portal) in the center of each.

The Ilkhanid successors to the Mongols also had their own distinctive architectural style. The Muzaffarid rulers in Fars, Kirman, and Esfahan are perhaps best known in this regard, since little remains of the contributions of the other Ilkhanid states, mainly owing, it is usually suggested, to the destruction wrought as Timur swept into the region. The Great Mosque at Yazd and that of Kirman are two religious buildings that illustrate the continuity with and development from earlier styles, visible, for example, in the Great Mosque at Varamin (built from 1322 to 1326). The Kirman mosque features portals linked by single-story arcades. Colored faience, for example, became the accepted mode of surface decoration. The architects of Shiraz and Esfahan played a key role in later Timurid architecture in Khurasan and Transoxiana. As well as the putative destruction blamed on Timur, it may well have been that the migration of these individuals to Timur's court that was a contributing factor in the relative paucity of buildings in the late Ilkhanid period.

Although they were but recently arrived in the region, the Timurids' architecture employed distinctly Persian traditional forms but with important new variations. Thus, for example, mosque decoration used faience carved in relief, a technique not previously used in the region but that was prevalent in Central Asia in the previous century. On the other hand, mosaic tile work in Samarkand and Balkh was most likely introduced by itinerant tile workers from Iran who had made their way to Timur's court in the late 1300s. Some of these embellishments were also seen in such secular buildings as palaces. The scale of the buildings erected in the early Timurid period also dwarfed that of earlier structures.

There were innovations as well. The first cruciform mosque to appear in Khurasan was that built in 1418–19 under the patronage of Gawhar Shad (d. 1457), the wife of Timur's son and successor Shah Rukh (d. 1447), at the shrine of the eighth Shii Imam Ali al-Rida (d. 818) in Mashhad. The same architect also built the religious school at a vast mosque-and-school complex for Gawhar Shad, just north of Herat. The interior intersecting vaulting system used in the school, described as a masterpiece of engineering skill, had in fact been used in Samarkand and was used to add further strength against the earthquakes that afflict the region.

The White Sheep and Black Sheep Turkish dynasties that succeeded the Ilkhanids in the west also pursued building activity. In 1435 Tabriz became the capital of the Black Sheep, and in 1452 their ruler Jahan Shah (d. 1467) occupied Esfahan in central Iran. The "Blue Mosque" that Jahan Shah's daughter built in Tabriz is a rare example of a covered mosque.

The Timurids were also great patrons of the Persian "art of the book," and their religious architecture employed traditional Persian forms. The congregational mosque of Gawhar Shad, wife of Timur's fourth son, Shah Rukh (d. 1447), in Mashhad is typical in this regard.

To the west, also, incoming cultural heritage intermingled with the extant tradition. Thus the fusion of Ottoman Turkic tradition with existing Byzantine forms shaped Ottoman architecture. Hagia Sophia in Istanbul is a good example of this process. Built by the Byzantines in the sixth century as a Christian church, it was converted into a mosque by the Ottomans following their conquest of Constantinople (as Istanbul was then called) in the 15th

A 12th-century Iranian bronze incense burner

century. Together with Ilkhanid and Seljuk of Rum forms, these elements formed the pool of architectural traditional from which Ottoman architecture drew its inspiration. Sinan (d. 1588) was perhaps the most famous of Ottoman architects. His designs of such well-known structures as the Sultan Selim Mosques in Istanbul and that in Edirne incorporated aspects from all these traditions. A student of Sinan later built Istanbul's famous Blue Mosque, also called the Sultan Ahmad Mosque, between 1609 and 1616. This building also featured a mixture of Byzantine church styles and the forms used in the building of Ottoman mosques.

Literature

The *Book of Dede Korkut* is believed to have been the ultimate repository of the history and customs of the Oghuz Turks. The book's narrative begins in Central Asia and continues into Iran and then the Caucasus and is understood to celebrate the Oghuz struggle for freedom against other Turkic peoples. The book is made up of 12 stories and is believed to have been compiled from existing oral traditions in the ninth century. This date is after the Turks' conversion to Islam, and the tales contain references to Muslim and non-Muslim Turks but also to pre-Islamic Turkic traditions and practices involving shamanism and magic. This indicates that the origins of the stories may date to well before the Turks' mass conversions to Islam. As one story in the volume involves a creature similar to the Cyclops in the *Odyssey* of Homer, there may be ties between this story and some older metanarrative. Dede Korkut ("grandfather" Korkut), the central figure of the book, is portrayed as a bard or poet who is able to solve dilemmas brought him by tribal members.

Turkic involvement with literature, like that in art and architecture, became increasingly Persianized over time. The Seljuks, the Middle East's first major Turkic dynasty, were important patrons of Persian literature, especially panegyric poetry in of the new *qasida* format as well as narrative and didactic poetry and literary prose. The *qasida* style of poem in fact reached its heights in this period as the older forms of poetical expression were dying and new forms of expression were being sought. It underwent a reinvigoration owing to the combination of erudition and refined rhetoric that marked the poetry of the period.

Later in the period, however, the *qasida* became overshadowed by the rise of the *ghazal*—consisting of rhyming couplets and a refrain—and quatrain forms of poetry; by the late 12th century the *ghazal*, whose origins date to pre-Islamic Arabia, won pride of place. The Sufis were enamored of the *ghazal* and played an important role in its rise to prominence and its spread into the India and beyond.

Romantic epic poetry, whose origins lies well before this period, achieved a new prominence during the Seljuk period. Perhaps its greatest practitioner was the poet Nizami (d. 1209), whose work became the model for later Iranian poets. The epics of Nizami, an Azerbaijani by birth, consist of five independent poems, each with its own meter, which were later grouped into a collection known as the *khamseh* (the five). One in particular contains Sufi allusions as well as ethical and philosophical references. His works are also known for their occasional criticism of political figures and for the defense of the common person and common rights. Another of these is notable for revealing the distinctly Persian understanding of Arabia and Arabs. Nizami did much to introduce common language and patterns of speech into poetry, thus contributing to the decline of the elite ancient forms of epic poetry. If in these ways Nizami's contribution was revolutionary, he was no innovator when it came to form; his poems made use of traditional forms, including the *mathnavi*, a form consisting of an indefinite number of couplets, the best-known example of which is in the work of the 13th-century Sufi poet Jalal al-Din Rumi. The great Persian mystic poet Attar (d. ca. 1221), born in Nishapur, utilized both the *qasida* and the *ghazal*, although he seldom used the former for panegyric purposes, as he was not at all enamored of those who held power; his poetry is marked by mystical symbolism and ecstatic fervor.

Although both died after the Mongol invasion, the poets Jalal al-Din Rumi (d. 1273) and Saadi (d. 1292) may both be said to have been products of the Seljuk age. Rumi, sometimes referred to as Mawlana (or in Turkish as Mevlana) was born in Balkh, traveled to the Hijaz for the pilgrimage, and then made his way through Damascus to settle in Konya in the central Anatolian plateau in about 1221. At that time Konya was a major city and capital of the Seljuks of Rum. The city was captured by the Mongols in 1243, but thereafter retained its status as a capital but in vassal relation to the Mongol overlords.

In the 1240s Rumi met Shams Tabrizi, who became Rumi's *pir* (mystical teacher). Rumi developed a great affection for Tabrizi and created a collection of his sayings and poetry. Rumi's poetry in particular is imbued with the notion of the mystical merging of subject and object. Rumi's *Mathnavi* is considered to be his most important work and one of the most important works of Persian literature. The six volumes of *Mathnavi* include more than 400 tales, many of them with a moral message.

Saadi Shirazi (d. ca. 1283–91) was another author whose career spanned the Seljuk and later periods. Born in Shiraz in the Fars region of Iran, he spent time elsewhere in Iran but also in Iraq, Syria, and Arabia. He was famous for his works of lyric poetry and didactic epics as well as the elegance of his prose. His two epic didactic works, in which he raised moralizing verse to the level of true poetry, were *Bustan* (*The Orchard*) and *Gulistan* (*The Rose Garden*). They were completed in 1257 and 1258, respectively, the latter being the year the Mongols captured Baghdad. *The Orchard* reveals Saadi's clear interest in Sufism, but both works contain numerous parables on ethical issues, often presented with a hint of irony.

The Ilkhanid period was marked by the reappearance of panegyric poetry, especially at the various courts around the region. Among the best-known poets of the period was Hafez, born in Shiraz between 1310 and 1337, who used the *ghazal* to great effect in highlighting mystical themes. Hafez's *diwan*, or collection of poems, was assembled by later scholars.

Many Timurid princes were also accomplished in the literary arts. The most important literary center of the 15th century was at Herat in the west of present-day Afghanistan. The ruler, Sultan Husayn Baiqara (d. 1506) and his minister Mir Ali Shir were both accomplished poets in both Turkish and Persian. Mysticism was an especially favored subject in their poetry. The *ghazal* was the favored medium of expression and the simplicity of their style is noticeable as was the tendency of the period's language to approximate colloquial speech more closely than had been the case previously. This tendency toward simplicity and use of the colloquial was also a feature of prose writing over the period. Histories continued to be popular, as did biographies. The great mystical poet Jami (d. 1492) was another important literary figure based at Sultan Husayn's court, and he composed a biography of some 614 prominent Sufi figures. The *qasida* also remained much used in the period for panegyric poems, many of which were composed for local princes or in praise of the various Shii imams.

Science

Turkic rulers acted as patrons for various forms of scientific inquiry. Observational astronomy enjoyed the favor of the Seljuks in particular. The astronomer, mathematician, and poet Omar Khayyam (d. 1131) was among those who enjoyed Seljuk patronage and was invited by Malikshah to direct the sultan's observatory in Esfahan, in Iran.

The Mongols and Ilkhanids were also well known for their patronage of Islamic science. The astronomer and mathematician Nasir al-Din Tusi (d. 1274), previously associated with the ASSASSINS, was freed at the capture of the latter's fortress in Alamut by Hulegu. After the capture of Baghdad in 1258, Hulegu built a large observatory at Maragheh in northwest Iran at Tusi's urging. This was the world's first astronomical observatory. Tusi made important contributions to astronomy and algebra under Hulagu's patronage. Tusi produced the *Zij-e Ilkhani,* a book of astronomical tables based on 12 years of observations from the Maragheh observatory, which was designed to facilitate the calculation of planetary movements. His interest in algebra derived its impetus from his interest in astronomy and the celestial bodies. These contributions were further consolidated during later years, and the high point of Islamic computational science was, in fact, reached in the Timurid period. Students at Maragheh are known to have made important contributions to the understanding of rainbows and their formation and to optics more generally. Copernicus (d. 1543), the discoverer of heliocentric cosmology, may have been influenced by later translations of Tusi's work in developing his theory of planetary motion.

During the Ilkhanid period, the physician Rashid al-Din (d. 1318) completed his monumental *Jami al-Tawarikh* (*The Collection of Chronicles*), a history of the world in three parts composed in Persian. As befits a work dedicated to his Mongol patrons, the author devoted considerable attention to Mongol and Ilkhan history.

Under the Timurids this interest in science continued apace. During the late Timurid period, the astronomer and mathematician al-Kashi (d. 1429) enjoyed court patronage at Samarkand, and a year later, in 1430, the Timurid prince Ulugh Bey, himself an astronomer, established an observatory at Samarkand.

The Timurid period also witnessed important contributions to medicine. Among the best-known ancient medical illustrations in the Islamic world are a set of full-page anatomical drawings, with Persian and Arabic labeling, which illustrate the arteries, veins, nerves, bones, muscles, and organs of a pregnant figure. Though the origin of these illustrations is unclear, many of them are found with copies of *Tashrih-e Mansuri* (*Anatomy by Mansur*), a

Persian-language treatise on human anatomy composed in 1386 by Mansur ibn Muhammad ibn Ilyas for the Timurid ruler of Shiraz. The same Ibn Ilyas had earlier composed another, more general, Persian-language medical work for the Mazaffarid ruler of Fars, the last Ilkhanid ruler before the arrival of the Timurids. Ibn Ilyas's composition of a second, more specific, work on medicine for the Timurids attests to the interests of these later rulers. Although he is not otherwise well known in the field, Ibn Ilyas's works demonstrate his strong acquaintance with a variety of earlier works on the subject, including texts from the Greek medical tradition, most of which were available only in Arabic by this time.

During the late Timurid period, the astronomer and mathematician al-Kashi (d. 1429) enjoyed court patronage at Samarkand.

Religion

As in other activities and commitments, successive wave of Turkic immigrants into the Middle East initially retained their traditional affiliations but gradually become more interested in and committed to Islam. Traditionally these groups' religious beliefs were shamanistic. Shamanism, generally speaking, maintains that spirits play roles in human activity and that the *shaman* can understand and influence these for the benefit of individuals and the community.

The Seljuks had inhabited the eastern marches of the Abbasid Empire for many years before their 10th-century migration into Khurasan in the Persian northwest, where they became acquainted with Persian culture and Islam. Iran in this time frame was mainly Sunni Muslim, with pockets of Shia in such cities as Kashan and Qum and in Mazanderan, the area along the Caspian Sea. By the time the Seljuks y reached Baghdad in 1055, they were themselves committed Sunni Muslims. They purged the capital of Shii influences, which the Buyids had encouraged, and they generally remained intolerant of extremist Shia over the succeeding generations. The Iranian vizier Nizam al-Mulk was noted for his hostility to Shia, especially the extremist variant practiced by some Ismaili Shia (see ISMAILIS). Nizam al-Mulk's famous *Siyasat-name* (*The Book of Government*) is perhaps the best-known Persian prose writing of the period. Although ostensibly composed as advice to Sultan Malikshah on good government, those sections detailing dangers to the empire are full of anti-Shia invective, generalizing the many different Shii sects extant at the time into one undifferentiated group. There are reports that a member of the extremist Ismaili Assassins sect eventually assassinated him.

Nevertheless, non-Ismaili Shii groups were active in the region, especially in Iran, over the period. In these centers the Shia had mosques, schools, and libraries. Indeed, however, several important scholars of the Twelver Shii faith, the branch of Shia that became the established faith in Iran in the 16th century, did achieve positions at the Seljuk court. Many others are known to have occupied lesser posts at court and in the administration, as scribes, for example. In the period after the death of Nizam al-Mulk, some Shii scholars and writers of the day are known to have praised "the Turks" for their tolerance and protection of members of the faith.

The Seljuks were especially noted for establishing institutions for the teaching of Islam, although relative newcomers to the faith themselves. The vizier Nizam al-Mulk was especially active in this area, establishing "colleges" called *nizamiyya* with scholarships for students, good salaries for the teaching staff, and well-organized courses of study. Almost all the larger towns had such centers, but the best known were the center in Baghdad itself, built from 1065 to 1067, and that in Nishapur in northeastern Iran. The teachers in both were directly appointed by Nizam al-Mulk or his heirs. Other such colleges founded in later years were all modeled after the *nizamiyya* schools. The curriculum consisted of law, the traditions (*hadith*) of the prophet, and exegesis of the Quran as well as literary theory, mathematics, and medicine. Each student has his own room and a regular stipend. Each college also had a well-stocked library.

The Seljuks are known to have patronized Sunni propagandists but were also tolerant of those who venerated and publicly praised the different Shii imams among the scholarly elite and among popular preachers as well. The Seljuks are even known to have tolerated performances of the traditional Shii "passion play" commemorating the death of the third Shii imam, Ali's son al Husayn, at Karbala in 680.

The Seljuk period was also an important one in the history of Islamic mysticism, or Sufism. It is the period in which Sufism, especially under such figures as Ghazali (d. 1111), achieved a measure of tolerance from orthodox Sunni clerics; Ghazali himself was just such a scholar who turned to mysticism. Some of the greatest Sufi orders date to the 11th and 12th centuries. The regions of Transoxiana and Khurasan, as well as parts of Iraq, had a number of Sufi centers and cloisters (*khanqah*) in which Sufi "saints" lived, worshipped, and taught students. In this period, in fact, Shii scholars were often more hostile to Sufism than Sunni scholars and Sufis often enjoyed the protections of princes and courts throughout the region.

The Mongols, their Ilkhanid successors, and the Timurids were all noted for their religious tolerance. The early Ilkhans were inclined to Buddhism, for example, but they were also tolerant of Nestorian Christianity (see NESTORIANS). Nasir al-Din Tusi was a Shii, and the physician and historian Rashid al-Din, a Jew, served as vizier to several Ilkhanid rulers. One of these, Oljaitu (r. 1304–16), is said to have been baptized a Christian, then converted to Buddhism and later to Sunni Islam. Upon his succession as Ilkhan, he is reputed to have converted again to Twelver Shia.

In the aftermath of both the Mongol conquests of the 13th century and those of Timur, both sets of Turkish rulers adopted Islam as the dominant spiritual discourse and sponsored various projects that attested to their regard for the faith. Cognizant of the region's historical and religious diversity, they also patronized discussions between spokesmen for the various indigenous religious traditions, thereby acknowledging the legitimacy of each and their own authority over all of their adherents. These rulers also employed skilled members of the Tajik (native Persian) class to administer their empire and adopted, and patronized, the latter's distinctive cultural discourse, especially the traditional Tajik literary arts and crafts (see TAJIKS).

The Qara-qoyunlu and Aq-qoyunlu tribal confederations that succeeded the Timurids pursued a similarly inclusive agenda. Islam was their religion, their tribal military levies were Turks, their administrators were Tajiks, and their cultural discourse was Persian. Such inclusiveness was especially a feature of the reign of Uzun Hasan, the ruler of the White Sheep tribal confederation who, in the face of opposition from the Ottomans, Mamluks, and the Black Sheep Turkish tribal confederacy, held sway over a territory stretching from the Euphrates in the west to Kirman in the east and from Transcaucasia in the north to the Persian Gulf in the south. In the tradition of both Timur and the Qara-qoyunlu ruler Jahan Shah, during whose 30-year reign the Qara-qoyunlu had amassed considerable territory, Uzun Hasan's spiritual discourse paid homage to urban and rural, and especially tribal, spiritual discourse, even while it underlined his own claims to universal leadership over them all. Uzun Hasan patronized religious structures and encouraged religious endowments and students, including Tajik sayyids, as well as patronizing the arts and sciences. He also claimed his victories were foretold in the Quran and was hailed by the theologian and philosopher Jalal al-Din Dawani (d. 1503) as "the envoy of the ninth century" (according to the Muslim calendar) in reference to the prophet's statement that in every century Allah would send someone to 'renew' the faith. The Persian mystical poet Jami, evoking an earlier religio-political legitimacy associated with holy war, described Uzun Hasan as "Sultan of the warriors." In some mosque inscriptions Uzun Hasan was also described as "the just sultan" and "the just Imam," terms that in Twelver Shii discourse could be construed as identifying Uzun Hasan as the prophesized Twelfth Imam himself.

In his struggle for the "hearts and minds" of Turk and Tajik, Uzun Hasan undertook to identify himself with such discourse as was espoused by various of these Sufi mystical orders. Among these the Safavids, based at Ardabil, were deemed of sufficient importance to merit two marriage alliances. Between 1456 and 1459, Uzun Hasan married his sister to the order's leader, Junayd (d. 1460), a direct descendant of its founder, Shaykh Safi al-Din. He also supported Junayd's claim to rule the order over that of an uncle who had enjoyed Qara-qoyunlu support. In 1471 or 1472, Uzun Hasan married his daughter, herself the daughter of the last Christian emperor of Trabzond and thus of noble Greek descent, to Junayd's young son, and leader of the order, Haydar (d. 1488). Haydar's three sons from this marriage included his third son, Ismail, born in 1487.

In 1501, a century after the death of Timur, Ismail entered Tabriz, the capital of the Ilkhanids, Jahan Shah Qara-qoyunlu and his own grandfather the Aq-qoyunlu Uzun Hasan. In 1503 Ismail defeated another Aq-qoyunlu force near Hamadan and secured control over central and southern Iran. Diyar Bakr, Uzun Hasan's homeland where his son-in-law and Ismail's father, Haydar, had spent his formative years, was also taken. Baghdad fell in 1508. Shirvan and Khurasan fell, the latter after a decisive battle at Marv in 1510 with the Uzbeks, who had taken the area in 1507. Several days later Ismail entered Herat and soon thereafter the rest of Khurasan also came under Safavid control.

In the tradition of their Turkish ancestors in Iran the Safavids and, later, the Qajars similarly were generally more tolerant of the different faiths of their subjects (Sunni, Jewish, and Christian) than were most European states in the same period.

———◆———

The story of the Turks in Safavid, Qajar, and modern Iran is the story of the further intermingling of Tajik and Turkic peoples with those of Arabs, Kurds, and other ethnic tribal and nontribal groups whose presence in Iran dates back centuries. In fact, this was the pattern of integration of Turks into the Middle East from the earliest times. The Turks brought with them their own beliefs and customs and retained these during the first years of their settlement in these regions. Gradually, however, these were incorporated into and further enhanced indigenous patterns of life. Persian Iran was the first of the settled societies with which the successive waves of Turkish immigrants interacted, and Islam was the main religious discourse. The traditional Persian tolerance of cultural, religious, and language differences further enhanced this mutual exchange between settled and incoming communities.

See also TURKS: NATIONALITY.

FURTHER READING

J. A. Boyle, ed. *The Cambridge History of Iran*, vol. 5, *The Saljuq and Mongol Periods* (Cambridge, U.K.: Cambridge University Press, 1968).

C. V. Findley. *The Turks in World History* (Oxford, U.K.: Oxford University Press, 2005).

L. Golombek and D. Wilber. *The Timurid Architecture of Iran and Turan* (Princeton, N.J.: Princeton University Press, 1988).

C. Hillenbrand. *Turkish Myth and Muslim Symbol: The Battle of Manzikert* (Edinburgh: Edinburgh University Press, 2007).

R. Hillenbrand. *Islamic Art and Architecture* (London: Thames and Hudson, 1999).

P. Jackson. and L. Lockhart, eds. *The Cambridge History of Iran*, vol. 6, *The Timurid and Safavid Periods* (Cambridge, U.K.: Cambridge University Press, 1986).

L. Johanson and É. Csató, eds. *The Turkic Languages* (London: Routledge, 1998).

C. L. Klausner. *The Seljuk Vezirate: A Study of Civil Administration, 1055–1194* (Cambridge, Mass.: Harvard University Center for Middle Eastern Studies, 1973).

J. Kolbas. *The Mongols in Iran: Chingiz Khan to Uljaytu, 1220–1309* (London: Routledge, 2006).

M. F. Köprülü. *The Seljuks of Anatolia: Their History and Culture According to Local Muslim Sources*, trans. and ed. by G. Leiser (Salt Lake City: University of Utah Press, 1992).

T. Lentz and G. D. Lowry. *Timur and the Princely Vision: Persian Art and Culture in the Fifteenth Century* (Los Angeles: L.A. County Museum of Art, 1989).

F. Lewis. *Rumi Past and Present, East and West* (Oxford, U.K.: Oneworld Publications, 2000).

G. Lewis, ed. *The Book of Dede Korkut* (Harmondsworth, U.K.: Penguin, 1974).

Karl H. Menges. *The Turkic Languages and Peoples* (Wiesbaden, Germany: Harrassowitz, 1968, 1995).

A. J. Newman. *The Safavids: Rebirth of a Persian Empire* (London and New York: I. B. Tauris, 2006).

Peter E. Pormann and E. Savage-Smith. *Medieval Islamic Medicine* (Edinburgh: Edinburgh University Press, 2007).

B. O'Kane. *Timurid Architecture in Khurasan.* (Costa Mesa, Calif.: Mazda, 1987).

J. Woods. *The Aqquyunlu: Clan, Confederation, Empire*, rev. ed. (Salt Lake City: University of Utah Press, 1999).

Turks: nationality (people of Turkey)

GEOGRAPHY

The Republic of Turkey is a large nation that extends across the Anatolian Peninsula (also known as Asia Minor), which is geographically part of Asia, and into the Balkan region of southeast Europe. The Anatolian Peninsula is situated at the eastern end of the Mediterranean Sea and also forms the southern shore of the Black Sea. Turkey has an area of approximately 300,000 square miles and 4,500 miles of coastline. The geographically Asian portion of Turkey, which makes up about 97 percent of the country, is separated from the much smaller European portion by the Sea of Marmara and the narrow Bosporus and Dardanelles Straits, which link the Sea of Marmara to the Black Sea and the Mediterranean Sea respectively. The Bosporus Strait is less than half a mile wide at its narrowest point and bisects the Turkish city of Istanbul.

Turkey has borders with eight other nations. The European portion of Turkey has borders with Bulgaria and Greece and coastlines on the Mediterranean and the Black Sea. The Asian portion has borders with Georgia in the northeast; Armenia, Azerbaijan, and Iran in the east; and Iraq and Syria in the south. The Black Sea extends along the entire length of the north of the country, and the Mediterranean Sea extends along its western edge and much of its southern edge. Most of the large islands that lie just off Turkey's western coast are part

TURKS: NATIONALITY

nation:
Turkey; Republic of Turkey

derivation of name:
From the Turkish name "Türkiye"

government:
Republic

capital:
Ankara

language:
Turkish is the country's official language and is spoken by the overwhelming majority of the population. Kurdish, Azer, and Kabardian are spoken by small minorities.

religion:
About 99 percent of the population are Muslim (overwhelmingly Sunni). Christians and Jews make up less than 0.5 percent of the population.

earlier inhabitants:
Hittites; Lydians; Turkic Peoples

demographics:
Turks make up about 80 percent of the population; Kurds are the majority of the remaining 20 percent. There are also very small Azeri and Kabard minorities.

of Greece. Since 1974 Turkey has exercised nominal control over the Turkish Republic of Northern Cyprus, but this is not part of Turkish territory and the Turkish Republic of Northern Cyprus is not internationally recognized.

Turkey has a diverse geography with several different climatic zones. The Black Sea coast is isolated from the interior of the country by the Pontic Mountains, a range of high peaks (up to 13,000 feet) covered in thick conifer forests that is only penetrated in a few places by steep-sided valleys. The coastline is rocky, but the climate is good for agriculture and the narrow coastal plain and some valleys are intensively farmed. The Marmara region, that part of Turkey that straddles the Asian–European divide, is generally low lying and is the country's most densely populated region. Istanbul, Turkey's largest city and, with a population of about 11 million, one of the world's largest cities, is situated here along with several other urban centers. The Aegean coast, along Turkey's western fringe, is low lying and has a typical Mediterranean climate. It is also one of the most highly agriculturally productive areas of the country. Izmir, Turkey's third largest city and its second largest port (after Istanbul), is situated on the Aegean coast.

Turkey's southern Mediterranean coast is also separated from the interior by a range of mountains. The Taurus Mountains run roughly parallel to the southern coast and include many peaks above 12,000 feet. To the south of the mountains the Mediterranean shore is generally rocky and punctuated by many natural harbors. Much of the interior of the Anatolian Peninsula is dominated by a wide plateau that rises from the Aegean shore in a series of uplands and extends east to west through the middle of the country. The climate of the plateau is generally arid, with hot summers and cold winters. Isolated drainage basins produced by limestone erosion dot the landscape, but the lakes that form in these basins are often highly saline. Turkey's capital city, Ankara, is situated on the Anatolian plateau. The Taurus and Pontic Mountain ranges, which mark the southern and northern edges of the central plateau respectively, converge in the east and southeast to produce the rugged terrain known as the Anti-Taurus. Turkey's highest mountain, the 16,800-foot-high Mount Ararat, is one of the peaks of the Anti-Taurus. The region also contains Turkey's largest body of fresh water, Lake Van, and the headwaters of the Tigris and Euphrates Rivers, which both flow southward to Iraq and the Persian Gulf.

Kemal Mustafa Atatürk, (1881–1938) founder of the modern state of Turkey and its first president (1923–38).

INCEPTION AS A NATION

Archaeologist have discovered some of the oldest known human structures, a series of ritual or temple sites, in southern Anatolia. Dating from 9000 or 8000 B.C.E., structures at Gobekli Tepe and other places are believed to have been built by preagricultural cultures and include some of the earliest representations of human and animal figures ever discovered. Bronze Age technology also came to Anatolia early, and the peninsula was one of the centers of early civilization from the fourth millennium B.C.E. In the third millennium B.C.E. Anatolia was part of the Akkadian Empire, the world's earliest known empire, and seems to have been an important source of metals for its Mesopotamian overlords (*see* AKKADIANS).

The greatest indigenous civilization to arise in Anatolia was that of the HITTITES, which thrived from the 17th to the 14th centuries B.C.E. and enjoyed a revival between about 1200 and 700 B.C.E. This was supplanted by the Lydian Kingdom (*see* LYDIANS), which was then conquered by the Iranian Achaemenid Empire in the sixth century B.C.E. (*see* ACHAEMENIDS; PERSIANS). Conquest by Alexander the Great in

Turks: nationality time line

C.E.

1923 The Republic of Turkey is declared with Mustafa Kemal as its first president. This marks the end of centuries of rule by the Ottoman dynasty.

1925 Turkey adopts the Western Gregorian calendar.

1928 Turkey becomes a secular state.

1934 Mustafa Kemal is awarded the title "Atatürk" ("Father of the Turks") by parliament.

1938 Death of Mustafa Kemal Atatürk. He is succeeded by Ismet Inonu.

1945 After remaining neutral for most of World War II, Turkey symbolically declares war on Germany and Japan in the closing months.

1952 Turkey joins NATO.

1960 Military coup overthrows the government.

1961 New constitution providing for a dual-chamber parliament is adopted.

1965 Suleyman Demirel becomes prime minister. He will hold the office six more times in the coming decades.

1971 Second military coup overthrows Demirel's government.

1974 Turkey invades northern Cyprus following a period of political violence between Turkish and Greek inhabitants of the island.

1980 Third military coup and the imposition of martial law

1982 New constitution providing for a seven-year presidential term and a single-chamber parliament is adopted.

1984 Kurdish Workers Party (PKK) begins a secessionist campaign in southeast Turkey.

1990 Turkey permits the United States to launch air strikes against Iraq from Turkish airfields.

1993 Tansu Ciller becomes Turkey's first female prime minister.

1995 Turkish military launches a major offensive against Kurdish separatists.

1996 The pro-Islamic Welfare Party forms a government.

1997 Welfare Party government is brought down in a military-led political campaign.

1998 Welfare Party banned despite it being the largest party in parliament.

1999 PKK leader Abdullah Ocalan is captured, leading to major reduction in separatist activities.

2001 Pro-Islamic Virtue Party banned.

2002 Pro-Islamic Justice and Development Party (AK) wins national elections.

2004 Death penalty outlawed; state television broadcasts the first Kurdish-language programs.

2005 Turkey enters membership negotiations with the European Union.

2006 An attack on a Turkish courtroom provokes protests among those who believe it is an act of Islamic fundamentalist terror. A new group, the Kurdistan Freedom Falcons (TAC), claims responsibility for bomb attacks in Istanbul.

2007 Justice and Development Party win national elections for a second time.

2008 Turkey's Constitutional Court agrees to consider an indictment against the ruling Justice and Development Party alleging that it is seeking to create an Islamic state.

the fourth century B.C.E. was followed by rule under the Seleucids (*see* GREEKS) and eventual incorporation into Roman territory (*see* ROMANS) in the second century B.C.E. Parts of Anatolia were ruled by the Romans and their successors, the Byzantines, for over a thousand years until the 15th century C.E. Other parts of Anatolia, especially in the south and east, were ruled by a succession of colorful and powerful kingdoms including the ARMENIANS, the Seljuk sultans of Rum (*see* SELJUKS; TURKIC PEOPLES), and the ILKHANS.

The movement of Turkic peoples into Anatolia began in the 11th century C.E. following the defeat of Byzantine forces by the Seljuks at Manzikert in 1071. The Seljuks rapidly engulfed Anatolia and were raiding Byzantine sites on the Sea of Marmara within a decade. From the late 12th century Anatolia became the last refuge of the Seljuks, in the form of the Seljuk sultans of Rum, who ruled most of the peninsula until their subjugation by the MONGOLS in 1243. The predecessors of the OTTOMANS ruled one of the small Turkic kingdoms that arose in Anatolia after the Mongol conquest.

The Ottomans were a Turkic people who went on to build one of the greatest empires of the Middle East, with Anatolia at its heart. Osman I founded the Ottoman dynasty in 1299 when he declared independence from the Seljuks, who were themselves vassals of the Mongols and their successors by this time. Osman's grandson, Murad I (r. 1359–89) began the process of expansion that would eventually see the Ottomans establish themselves as the rulers of an empire than extended from southeast Europe through the Middle East into North Africa and that stretched from the Atlantic coast of modern-day Morocco in the west to the Caspian Sea and the Persian Gulf in the east, and from modern-day Austria and the Ukraine in the north to Sudan, Somalia, and Yemen in the south. For 600 hundred years the Ottoman Empire was the center of and mediator of interactions between East and West.

The 19th century saw the gradual dissolution of the Ottoman Empire as territories such as Greece and Cyprus gained independence and the Ottoman sultans were forced to reach accommodations with France and Britain in return for alliances against the growing imperial ambitions of Russia to the north. In 1908 the Young Turk Revolution forced a tide of change that included greater secularization, the establishment of a system of constitutional monarchy, including a parliament, and reforms to the system of centralized rule that promised greater autonomy for the territories of the empire beyond Anatolia. A coup in 1913 ushered in a government known as the Rule of the Three Pashas under which an alliance was made with Germany, resulting in the Ottoman Empire aligning with the Axis powers in World War I.

The combination of the British-assisted "Arab revolt" (1916–18) and World War I led to the empire's defeat. Immediately after the war

---

Mustafa Kemal Atatürk: The Father of Modern Turkey

Mustafa Kemal Atatürk was a revolutionary leader in the struggle for Turkish independence and the first president of the Republic of Turkey. He was a highly popular leader during his life and was given the name Atatürk, meaning "father of the Turks," by the Turkish parliament in recognition of his central role in the formation of modern Turkey. Atatürk, as he is commonly referred to in present-day Turkey, remains a highly respected figure in Turkish culture.

Born in 1880 or 1881, he was given the name Mustafa by his family and later the name Kemal by one of his teachers. Mustafa Kemal was born in the city of Salonika (present-day Thessaloniki) in the Macedonian region of the present-day Republic of Greece, which was then part of the Ottoman Empire. His father was a customs official, who died when Mustafa Kemal was six or seven, and his mother has been described as a highly devout woman who favored educating their son in an Islamic school.

Though he studied in a religious school for a short time, Mustafa Kemal decided to enter the military and eventually graduated as an officer in Istanbul in 1905. Posted to Damascus, Syria, he became involved in the Young Turk movement and participated in the Young Turk Revolution of 1908, which restored the Ottoman parliament suspended since 1878. He served against the Italians in Libya in 1911 and in the Balkan Wars of 1912–13. During World War I he acquired a formidable military reputation for his part in repelling the Allied invasion of the Dardanelles in 1915.

Despite the Ottomans' success in the Dardanelles campaign, the empire was defeated by the Allies and their former territories were partitioned to be administered by the victors. The Allied occupation of Istanbul and Izmir and the Greek invasion of Anatolia, however, provoked a Turkish nationalist uprising in 1919 in which Mustafa Kemal was to play a central role. In the midst of this war he established the Grand National Assembly of Turkey, which remains the sole legislative body in Turkey to the present day. By 1923 the Ottoman Empire had been formally dissolved and foreign troops in Anatolia had been defeated by the National Army commanded by Mustafa Kemal or forced to reach peace settlements with the provisional Turkish government. The Republic of Turkey was declared in October 1923 with Mustafa Kemal as its first president.

As president Mustafa Kemal embarked on a radical and far-reaching program of social, political, and economic reform intended to modernize Turkey. These reforms included the emancipation of women, the abolition of Islamic institutions, and the establishment of a strictly secular and democratic form of government. He also introduced Western legal codes, dress, calendar, and alphabet and embarked on a program of modernizing Turkey's industrial base. The underlying ideology of these reforms became known as Kemalist ideology, and they continue to form the foundation of the Turkish state today. Mustafa Kemal was given the surname Atatürk in 1934 when parliament introduced a surname law.

Mustafa Kemal married his wife Latife in 1923. They couple did not have children, but Mustafa Kemal adopted seven girls and one boy during his life. One of these girls, Sabiha Gökçen, became a Turkish aviation pioneer. Latife was a leading figure in the women's emancipation movement in Turkey. Mustafa Kemal Atatürk died in Istanbul in 1938 while still holding the office of the presidency.

---

the empire was partitioned. Britain gained a mandate over Iraq, Palestine, and Transjordan, and the French gained control over Syria and Lebanon. Turkish nationalist elements meeting in Ankara in 1920 rejected both the partitioning and the surviving Ottoman government in Istanbul. Two years later, these forces reclaimed Istanbul and abolished the Ottoman sultanate, officially ended the Ottoman Empire. The Republic of Turkey was declared in October 1923, with Mustafa Kemal (later known as "Atatürk," or "father of the Turks") as its first president.

CULTURAL IDENTITY

The reconstitution of the heart of the old Ottoman Empire as the modern nation-state of Turkey was a very deliberate program carried out under the rule of Mustafa Kemal Atatürk. The goal was to create a Western-style secular nation, and to that end the government disestablished Islam as the state religion, adopted legal codes based on those of Western nations, and established a universal system of secular education. Part of this program was the reengineering of the Turkish language using a Western-style alphabet and the suppression of minority languages. The prime goal of this system of education was to indoctrinate the citizens of the new republic into a vision of a unified Turkish ethnicity that was imposed on the reality of a very varied ethnic mix inherited from centuries of imperial power. It was a social engineering program of ambitious proportions and achieved a great deal of success. Most citizens of modern Turkey identify with a Turkish ethnicity and nationality that has been selectively constructed from the labyrinthine cultural history of Ottoman and pre-Ottoman Anatolia.

The constitution of the Republic of Turkey defines a "Turk" as any citizen of Turkey, thereby creating a distinction from the historical ethnicity of the Turkic people, which includes peoples across western and central Asia. The only distinct ethnic groups that were recognized at the foundation of the republic were the very small enclaves of JEWS, Christian Armenians, and Orthodox Christian Greeks. The large groups of KURDS, CIRCASSIANS, ARABS, GEORGIANS, and other ethnicities living within Turkey were to be subsumed in the new Turkish identity. This policy has been very successful at eliminating the potential for interethnic conflict and at establishing a strong national identity. Perhaps the only failure has been in the experience of the Kurdish minority.

The Kurdish region of modern Turkey is centered in the mountainous southeast, a part of the historical homeland of the Kurdish people. It is estimated that Kurds make up about 20 percent of the population of Turkey, but official figures do not exist because the government discourages the collection of information on ethnic identity. This is in line with the long-established policy of promoting a single Turkish identity. About half of Turkey's Kurds live in the southeast; the rest have been more or less assimilated into the general population and do not generally self-identify as Kurds. The poverty of the southeast region, far from the densely populated northwest of the country, is due in part to its extreme remoteness and in part to a lack of investment from a central government that concentrated on improving the economic fortunes of the more populated areas in the decades after the establishment of the republic. During the 1970s there was a revival in Kurdish identity based in part on a revival of the Kurdish language, which took place among Kurdish immigrants to Europe. This revival prompted renewed ambitions for an independent Kurdish homeland, a thread that has emerged time and time again over the centuries. From the early 1980s an armed secessionist movement led by the Kurdish Workers Party (PKK) fought government troops and carried out terrorist attacks in a campaign that had claimed 30,000 lives by 2000. As part of their operations in the southeast, the Turkish army forcibly relocated a million people and destroyed thousands of Kurdish villages. The arrest and imprisonment of the PKK's leader, Abdullah Ocalan, in 2000 led to a cease-fire, but the establishment of a virtual Kurdish state in the north of Iraq following the Second Gulf War has raised tensions once again.

Turkey is an overwhelmingly Muslim country, but from its foundation the Republic of Turkey has been firmly committed to secular government. This very deliberate policy had two aims: first, to disassociate the government of the republic from the Ottoman sultans, who were tightly bound to the Islamic faith; and second, to discourage religious tensions and encourage a sense of nationhood. Religious symbols are not allowed to be displayed on public or government buildings, religious headdress may not be worn in public, and the official census does not record religious affiliations. The imposition of secularism has been less successful than the construction of a sense of national identity, however. In particular it has proved difficult to export the cosmopolitan lassaiz-faire ideals of the big cities to the rural heartland of central Anatolia and the isolated communities of the south and east. A degree of compromise and accommodation has resulted

A bridge over the Tigris River near the town of Cizre in southeast Turkey close to the border with Syria. It was built in the first half of the 12th century by the Zangid rulers of Mosul.

in a broad spectrum of social conditions in modern Turkey, ranging from Western-style liberalism in parts of Istanbul to stolidly traditional patterns in some rural areas. For example, although women have technically had full and equal rights under the law from the inception of the republic, it was necessary to pass a law in 2002 that ended the practice of regarding males as the head of households. Planned marriages to which the bride or groom had not consented were also illegal from the 1920s, but a poll in the 1960s found that up to 15 percent of married women had not consented to their match and up to 65 percent of marriages had been planned with consent.

Since the 1980s social attitudes have become more liberal across much of Turkey, but the start of the 21st century has also brought a religious conservatism to the political arena. Some Turks fear this movement may threaten the country's secular norms, while others have supported it as an antidote to the erosion of traditional values. In 2001 Turkey's Constitutional Court banned the pro-Islamic Virtue Party on the grounds that it had become the focus for growing antisecular activities, but in 2002 the strongly Islamic and conservative Justice and Development party won a landslide victory in national elections. Since 2002 there has been growing tension between secularists and Islamic conservatives.

The politics of the Republic of Turkey have often been turbulent. Turkey's military, which regards itself as the protector of Mustafa Ke-

mal Atatürk's legacy and secularism, has often intervened in the country's politics. The first military coup took place in 1960 when the ruling Democratic Party was ousted and a new bicameral parliament was set up. A second military coup took place in 1971 following widespread political violence, and a third in 1980 ushered in a period of martial law. Martial law ended with the adoption of a new constitution in 1982 that created a seven-year presidency and amalgamated parliament into a single chamber. In 1997 the military headed a campaign that brought down a government headed by the pro-Islamic Welfare Party. Turkey's military retains an influential role through its permanent position on the National Security Council, which is composed of the prime minister, the chief of the general staff, and several key ministers as well as the heads of the armed forces and the police.

The 1980s brought a liberalization of Turkey's economy, but international debt continued to rise in the last two decades of the 20th century until the country faced near bankruptcy. Since the implementation of an International Monetary Fund program in 2002, Turkey has made significant economic progress, although foreign debt remains a serious problem. Since its inception the Republic of Turkey has sought close links with Europe and the United States, regarding these as vital to its economic growth. In 1963 Turkey signed an association agreement with the European Economic Community (the predecessor to the European Union) and applied for full membership in 1987. Concerns about human rights abuses and Turkey's underperforming economy tended to make the EEC and the EU reluctant to accept the republic's overtures, however. Since 2000 negotiations between the Turkish government and the EU have resulted in several reforms that have brought the country closer to the political and social norms of the existing EU nations. These have included a lifting of restrictions on the use of the Kurdish language and other minority languages, the abolition of the death penalty, the loosening of broadcasting restrictions, an overhaul of the penal system in general, and economic reforms.

Today the Republic of Turkey faces the challenge of further integrating itself with Europe, a move that it sees as economically and strategically vital, while at the same time maintaining those substantial parts of its traditional identity that are firmly based in Asia and the Muslim world. Turkey also faces a continuing internal conflict between religious and secular elements within society.

FURTHER READING

Feroz Ahmad. *Turkey: The Quest for Identity* (Oxford, U.K.: Oneworld, 2003).

Taner Akçam. *From Empire to Republic: Turkish Nationalism and the Armenian Genocide* (London: Zed Books, 2004).

Sina Akşin. *Turkey from Empire to Revolutionary Republic: The Emergence of the Turkish Nation from 1789 to the Present* (Washington Square: New York University Press, 2007).

Reşat Kasaba. *Turkey in the Modern World. The Cambridge History of Turkey*, vol. 4 (Cambridge, U.K.: Cambridge University Press, 2008).

Hans-Lukas Kieser. *Turkey Beyond Nationalism: Towards Post-Nationalist Identities* (London: I.B. Tauris, 2006).

Bernard Lewis. *The Emergence of Modern Turkey* (New York: Oxford University Press, 2002).

Andrew Mango. *The Turks Today* (London: John Murray, 2004).

Nicole Pope and Hugh Pope. *Turkey Unveiled* (London: Duckworth, 2005).

Heather Lehr Wagner. *Turkey* (Philadelphia: Chelsea House, 2003).

Erik Jan Zürcher. *Turkey: A Modern History* (London: I.B. Tauris, 2004).

Turo

The Turo are one of the three main subgroups of the KONSO. The Konso people live in southern Ethiopia.

Turu

The Turu are a BANTU people of central Tanzania.

Tutsi *See* HUTU AND TUTSI.

Twa *See* MBUTI, TWA, AND MBENGA.

Twelvers (Imami Shia, Ithna Ashariyya)

Twelvers are a subsect of Shii Muslims, distinguished by their belief that religious and political authority were passed down from the prophet Muhammad through a line of Twelve Imams, or religious leaders. Twelvers account for the majority of the world's Shia today and make up the majority of the population of Iran and Iraq. They also account for important minorities in Lebanon, eastern Saudi Arabia, Bahrain and other Gulf States, and Afghanistan. In Twelver belief, the first of these Twelve Imams is Ali, the cousin of Muhammad and husband of his daughter Fatima, and the 11 Imams who followed Ali were all his descendants. These Twelve Imams, along with Muhammad and his daughter Fatima, are the "Fourteen Immaculate Ones," that is, without sin. The Twelfth Imam, Muhammad al-Mahdi, "Muhammad the Guided One," or "Muhammad the Messiah," is believed to have been taken into miraculous hiding, or occultation, in 873, when he was still a child. Known as the Hidden Imam, he continued to communicate through his deputies on earth until 940, when the last of his deputies died and he went into major occultation. He remains hidden, and his return to earth on the Day of Judgment will usher in a new era of divine justice, according to Twelver belief. In Twelver society, religious scholars, or *ulama*, have played an important political role and are often at the forefront of political movements. Recent examples are the Ayatollah Khomeini, a central figure in the Iranian Revolution of 1979, and Muqtada al-Sadr, an Iraqi cleric whose militia, the Mahdi (also spelled Mehdi) Army, at times mounted violent opposition to the foreign forces that occupied Iraq after the U.S.-led invasion and subsequent overthrow of Saddam Hussein in 2003.

Twi

Twi is used to refer to the AKAN language. The ASANTE and FANTE speak Twi languages.

U

Udok *See* UDUK.

Uduk (Udok)

The Uduk live mostly in eastern Sudan but also across the border in western Ethiopia.

Ugandans: nationality (people of Uganda)

GEOGRAPHY

The Republic of Uganda is a landlocked country in East Africa. It has an area of approximately 91,000 square miles, 14,000 square miles of which are inland waters, and is bordered by five other nations. Sudan meets Uganda's border in the north, the Democratic Republic of the Congo in the west, Rwanda in the southwest, Tanzania in the south, and Kenya in the east. Uganda is situated in the Great Lakes region of East Africa. Its western border with the Democratic Republic of the Congo bisects Lake Albert and Lake Edward, and its southern border with Tanzania runs from east to west through the middle of Lake Victoria, the largest lake (by area) in Africa. Lake George lies entirely within Uganda's territory in the southwest corner of the country close to Lake Edward. Lake Kyoga and Lake Kwania are situated in central Uganda, although these are not classified as Great Lakes. Uganda has several rivers, the most significant of which is the watercourse that begins as the Victoria Nile, which flows northward from

the northern shore of Lake Victoria into Lake Kyoga and then continuing into Lake Albert. The Albert Nile, which flows north from Lake Albert, is known as also known as the White Nile, one of the two principal tributaries of the Nile River.

Uganda's territory consists of a high plateau surrounded by a rim of highlands in the east, west, and south. The central plateau has an altitude of 2,600 to 6,600 feet, with the highest elevations in the south and the lowest in the north where Uganda meets Sudan. The Rwenzori Mountains on Uganda's western border with the Democratic Republic of the Congo stretching between Lake Albert and Lake Edward include Uganda's highest point—the 16,761-foot-high peak of Mount Margherita. In the east Mount Elgon is part of a highland chain that divides Uganda from Kenya. The Great Rift Valley runs from north to south through the western portion of the country.

The area to the north of Lake Victoria is the most densely populated part of the country. The eastern and western highlands are less densely populated, and the most sparsely populated is the northern region, where Uganda's generally verdant and agriculturally productive interior begins to give way to the arid plains that extend into Sudan. The capital city, Kampala, is situated close to the northern shore of Lake Victoria and is Uganda's economic center. Other important cities include Jinja, also just north of Lake Victoria; Masaka, which is west of Lake Victoria; and Mbale in the southeast corner of

UGANDANS: NATIONALITY

nation:
Uganda; Republic of Uganda

derivation of name:
From the Swahili word for the Kingdom of Buganda

government:
Republic

capital:
Kampala

language:
The country's official language is English. Ganda (or Luganda), the language of the Baganda, is the most widely spoken of the Bantu languages of the south. Nilotic languages are spoken in the north.

religion:
About 42 percent of the population are Catholic, 42 percent are Protestant, 12 percent are Muslim, and 4 percent follow indigenous faiths.

(continued)

(continues)

earlier inhabitants:
Unknown

demographics:
The largest ethnic groups are the Baganda (17 percent), Banyakole (10 percent), Basoga (9 percent), Bakiga (7 percent), Iteso (6 percent), Langi (6 percent), Acholi (5 percent), Bagisu (5 percent), Lugbara (4 percent), and Bunyoro (3 percent). The remaining 28 percent are made up of dozens of smaller ethnic groups.

the country. Approximately 15 percent of the population lives in urban areas.

INCEPTION AS A NATION

According to tradition the Empire of Kitara ruled much of Uganda, northern Tanzania, the eastern part of the Democratic Republic of the Congo, and Rwanda and Burundi between the 14th and 16th centuries C.E. (*see* CONGO-LESE [DEMOCRATIC REPUBLIC OF THE CONGO]; RWANDANS; BURUNDIANS: NATIONALITY). Although there is little evidence remaining of the Kitara, many of the later kingdoms established in Uganda claim historical associations with this great power. The earliest of these successor kingdoms was the Kingdom of Bunyoro (or Bunyoro-Kitara), which developed on the eastern shore of Lake Albert following the collapse of the Empire of Kitara. At its height in the 18th century the Kingdom of Bunyoro controlled all the territory between Lake Albert, Lake Victoria, and Lake Edward. With the decline of the Bunyoro in the late 18th century, the Buganda Kingdom rose to prominence. Centered on the northern shore of Lake Victoria, the Kingdom of Buganda became the dominant power in the region by the middle of the 19th century. The TORO Kingdom, situated in the area between Lake Albert and Lake Edward, asserted its independence from Kitara in the 1830s, and the Busoga Kingdom, in the southeast corner of the country, was also an established independent polity by the mid-19th century. The Kingdom of Ankole (also known as Nkole) dominated the southwest corner of the country close to the present-day border with Tanzania.

When European explorers reached the Great Lakes region in the 1860s, they found the four sophisticated and militarily powerful kingdoms of Buganda, Toro, Busoga, and Ankole at the height of their power. Christian missionaries followed the first European explorers into the region in the 1870s and were welcomed by King Mutesa I of Buganda (d. 1884), who was eager to establish links with the British and secure their aid in fighting incursions by Egypt from the north. Arab merchants had established links with the area from their settlements on the Indian Ocean coast during the 18th century, and Egyptian traders from the north had also brought a Muslim influence to the region in the decade before European involvement. Following a period of internal conflict in the Buganda Kingdom between Christian and Muslim converts, Mutesa's successor, Mwanga, accepted the establishment of a British protec-

torate in 1894. The protectorate was extended to include much of the rest of the territory of modern Uganda in 1896. A rebellion led by Mwanga in 1897 was quickly extinguished, and the king was deposed and replaced by his infant son. From 1900 Britain gained control of Buganda under a system of indirect rule that left the ruling family in place. From this time the Baganda (the people of Buganda) became the prime agents by which Britain extended its control to the rest of the country.

Uganda achieved independence relatively peacefully. A legislative council was set up by the British in 1921, although its first African delegate was not appointed until 1945, and internal autonomy was granted in 1958. The principal challenge faced at constitutional conferences held in London in 1961 and 1962 was the status of the four traditional kingdoms of Uganda in a postindependence state. Eventually a federal system was adopted in which the four kingdoms retained a degree of autonomy. Uganda became independent in October 1962. In 1963 Uganda became a republic with Kabaka Mutesa II (the reigning king of Buganda) as its first president.

CULTURAL IDENTITY

In the decade following independence the federal structure of Uganda broke down rapidly. The Kingdom of Buganda continued to dominate the new nation thanks to its superior economic status and the tradition of Bugandan administration that had grown up under British rule. Resentment at Buganda's power was widespread, especially in the north. In 1966 Prime Minister Milton Obote, who was from the north but had formed a political alliance with Buganda's royalist Kabaka Yekka party in the run-up to independence, suspended the 1962 constitution and adopted emergency powers. A new constitution was rapidly promulgated, and Obote became president the same day. During riots protesting Obote's seizure of power, the king's palace was occupied by Ugandan federal troops and King Mutesa II was forced to flee the country. In 1967 Obote abolished Uganda's federal structure, establishing a unitary state.

In 1971 a military coup deposed Obote and brought Idi Amin Dada to power. Amin's eight-year regime was characterized by serious human rights abuses, rampant corruption, and the almost total collapse of the country's economy. Historians estimate that 100,000 to 300,000 people were killed by Amin's regime, often as the result of "purges" carried out by the security forces among ethnic groups that were not considered to be loyal to the government. In 1972 Amin required all Asians to leave the country as part of a campaign referred to as an "economic war." Uganda's 80,000 Asians owned many of the country's businesses, and their sudden departure brought economic chaos. Businesses with British and other foreign owners were also nationalized, adding to the disruption. Amin's 1978 attempt to seize part of neighboring Tanzania, where rebels loyal to the former-president Obote were based, led to his downfall. Tanzania responded to the attack by invading Uganda and advancing rapidly on the capital. Amin fled the country in 1979, and Obote returned from exile in Tanzania to retake the presidency of Uganda in elections held in 1980. (*See also* TANZANIANS: NATIONALITY)

Obote's second term as president, although initially welcomed by Ugandans who had lived through almost a decade of state terror, soon rivaled Amin's in brutality and corruption. Intense fighting continued between the new government and rebel forces who were dissatisfied with Obote's reelection. Poorly disciplined troops on both sides committed massacres, and an estimated 100,000 Ugandans died as a result of violence or starvation in the five years of Obote's second term. Obote's chief opposition came from the National Resistance Movement (NRM) in the form of its military wing, the National Resistance Army (NRA). The NRA's eventual victory over Obote's successor, Tito Okello, brought the NRM to power in Kampala in 1986. Violence continued as the Karamojong region of northeast Uganda attempted to secede and a fundamentalist Christian militia known as the Holy Spirit Movement fought government troops in the north. Violence has continued in the northern Acholiland region, the homeland of the ACHOLI people, to the present day. President Okello, who was deposed by the NRM in 1986, was an Acholi. Following his defeat by the NRA, a rebel group known as the Ugandan People's Democratic Army (UPDA) began an armed resistance movement against the new government in Acholiland. The UPDA achieved little, but the harsh response of the NRA to their activities strengthened antigovernment feeling in the region. Many UPDA members joined the Holy Spirit Movement or another fundamentalist Christian group known as the Lord's Resistance Army, which continued fighting the Ugandan government. The Lord's Resistance Army (LRA) has the stated aim of establishing a theocratic state in

Kabaka Mutesa II, the first president of the Republic of Uganda and the ruler of Buganda from 1939 to 1967

northern Uganda based on its interpretation of the Christian faith and traditional Acholi beliefs. For more than 20 years the LRA has engaged in massacres, mutilations, sexual slavery, and the forced recruitment of children, bringing chaos to northern Uganda.

The development of a national identity among Ugandans has been seriously hampered by long-standing interethnic enmities and the two decades of divisive government that followed independence. The stark contrast between the relative wealth of the Kingdom of Buganda in the south and center of the country and the poverty of the north was a serious problem from the moment independence was achieved, but the despotic and avaricious regimes of Obote and Amin not only failed to address this issue but also exacerbated the problem by

Ugandans: nationality time line

C.E.

1830s Muslim traders from the Indian Ocean coast establish trade links with the Kingdom of Buganda.

1862 British explorer John Speke is the first European to make contact with Buganda.

1870s European Christian missionaries enter Buganda.

1890 Britain and Germany sign an agreement dividing East Africa into spheres of influence.

1894 Kingdom of Buganda becomes a British protectorate.

1896 British protectorate extended over much of the territory of modern Uganda.

1900 Buganda receives internal autonomy under indirect British rule.

1921 Britain sets up a legislative council in Uganda.

1958 Uganda granted internal self-government by Britain.

1962 Uganda becomes independent. A federal structure gives considerable autonomy to Buganda and the other kingdoms.

1963 Uganda becomes a republic, with Buganda's King Mutesa II as president and Milton Obote as prime minister.

1967 Obote becomes president and dismantles Uganda's federal structure.

1971 Obote deposed in a military coup. Idi Amin Dada becomes president.

1972 Sixty thousand Asian Ugandans are deported.

1976 Idi Amin declares himself president for life.

1978–79 War with Tanzania ends with Tanzanian forces deposing Idi Amin.

1980 Milton Obote reinstated as president.

1985 Obote deposed in a military coup. Tito Okello becomes president.

1986 National Resistance Army (NRA) captures Kampala and deposes Okello. Yoweri Museveni installed as president.

1993 Four traditional kingdoms of Uganda restored, but without executive power.

1996 Museveni elected to a second presidential term in Uganda's first direct elections.

1997–98 Ugandan troops intervene in civil war in the Democratic Republic of the Congo.

2001 Museveni elected to a third presidential term.

2003 Ugandan troops leave the Democratic Republic of the Congo.

2004 Ugandan government and Lord's Resistance Army (LRA) conduct inconclusive peace talks.

2007 Ugandan troops deployed in Somalia as part of a peacekeeping force.

2008 Cease-fire agreed between Ugandan government and LRA.

sanctioning ethnic violence. The carrying over of colonial administrative boundaries into the formation of a nation-state also contributed to Uganda's contentious history, since the Nilotic peoples of the north had a fundamentally different culture to the BANTU people of the south, where centralized rule by militaristic kings had been the norm for centuries (*see* NILOTES).

Since 1986 slow but steady progress has been made toward an open and democratic political system despite the continuing violence in the north and numerous smaller rebellions in other marginal regions. Uganda's economy remains underdeveloped and primarily agricultural, its people among the poorest in the world and subject to variation in the international market price of coffee—the nation's primary export. In 1993 the four traditional kingdoms of southern Uganda (Buganda, Toro, Busoga, and Ankole) were restored and permitted to reinstate hereditary rulers, although these kings have no executive power at the national level.

FURTHER READING

Donald H. Dunson. *Child, Victim, Soldier: The Loss of Innocence in Uganda* (Maryknoll, N.Y.: Orbis Books, 2008).

Peter H. Eichstaedt. *First Kill Your Family: Child Soldiers of Uganda and the Lord's Resistance Army* (Chicago: Lawrence Hill Books, 2009).

Ben Jones. *Beyond the State: Development in Rural Uganda* (Edinburgh: Edinburgh University Press, 2008).

Bob Measures and Tony Walker. *Amin's Uganda* (London: Minerva Press, 1998).

Kefa M. Otiso. *Culture and Customs of Uganda* (Westport, Conn: Greenwood Press, 2006).

Andrew Rice. *The Teeth May Smile but the Heart Does Not Forget: Murder and Memory in Uganda* (New York: Metropolitan Books, Henry Holt, 2009).

Umbundu   *See* OVIMBUNDU.

Unga

The Unga are a subgroup of the BEMBA of Zambia. The Unga live near Lake Bangweulu in the northeast of Zambia.

Upila

The Upila are a subgroup of the EDO. They live in south-central Nigeria north of Benin City.

Urartians

The Urartians are an ancient people of the mountainous regions of eastern Anatolia and northwestern Iran. They rose to considerable power in the ninth and eighth centuries B.C.E., vying with the ASSYRIANS for dominance in the region. Their kingdom is known as Urartu; in Hebrew, Ararat. The Urartians spoke a language belonging to the Caucasian group, languages from the region of the Caucasus that appear to be unrelated to other language families (*see* CAUCASIANS). Urartian civilization is known largely from the monumental cuneiform inscriptions it left, dating from about 830 to 640 B.C.E., and from Assyrian sources, which mention the Urartians as early as the 13th century B.C.E., recording a history of hostile relations between the two peoples spanning many centuries. The Assyrians were the Urartians' main rivals but also an important cultural influence. Even the name "Urartu" is an Assyrian name; the Urartians themselves called their country "Biainili." While the Urartians eventually came to create their own unique culture, it was founded on a base of cultural borrowings from the Assyrians, which included the Assyrian alphabet, literary forms, military and diplomatic practices, and artistic motifs. The capital of Urartu was on the southeast shore of Lake Van, in eastern Turkey, preserved in an important archaeological site near the modern city of Van. Inscriptions from the eighth century B.C.E. chronicle the expansion campaigns of Urartu kings, reaching southwest to the Euphrates River and almost as far as the modern-day city of Aleppo in northern Syria. They were also able to conquer and exploit the Aras River valley, which runs east–west, between Lake Van and the Black Sea, associated with the legendary Garden of Eden. Prisoners taken in military campaigns provided the slave labor to cultivate these lands. The Urartians were skillful engineers, and one of their irrigation canals, built to carry fresh water over a distance of about 46 miles, is still in use. Many of the extant cuneiform inscriptions deal with religious subjects and indicate a hierarchy of many gods and the sacrifices to be offered to them.

Toward the end of the eighth century B.C.E., the Urartians were under serious threat on several fronts. The Assyrians were making steady inroads into Urartian territory, partly by their own incursions and partly by encouraging Urartian enemies. Around 717, the Cimmerians, a nomadic people from the Caucasus who were to go on to conquer Phrygia farther west, invaded from the north. Meanwhile the Assyrian king Sargon II (r. 721–705 B.C.E.) took advantage of the situation and attacked from the south. This series of attacks was to prove to be the final blow to Urartian expansionist ambitions. Nevertheless, the civilization flourished for nearly 100 years more until at the end of the seventh century B.C.E. the ARMENIANS invaded, bringing Urartian civilization to an end.

Urhobo

The Urhobo are closely related to the EDO. Most of the Urhobo live in southeastern Nigeria.

Usilele   *See* LELE.

Uzbeks   (Ozbeks)

The Uzbeks in a national sense are the people of Uzbekistan, a mostly desert nation that lies between central Asia's two largest rivers, the Amu Darya and the Syr Darya. Uzbekistan borders the Aral Sea to the north and the Tian Shan and Pamir mountain ranges in the east. In this

---

UZBEKS

location:
West-central Asia south of the Aral Sea and between the Amu Darya and Syr Darya rivers; the Uzbek Empire extended from the Black Sea and Turkey to India.

time period:
14th century C.E. to present

ancestry:
Turkic; Mongol; Persian

language:
Turkic

sense the Uzbeks can be seen as a people shaped by the federal institutions of the Soviet Union in the 20th century, of which it was a part.

In an ethnic sense the Uzbeks are descended from the Mongol peoples who mingled with Turkic and Iranian nomadic ethnic groups and who were lead by Ozbeg (or Uzbek) Khan from 1312 to 1342. In this sense the Uzbeks are a people of complex cultural heritage who still live in groups throughout Asia and the Middle East.

ORIGINS

The geographical area of modern Uzbekistan has been settled and conquered by many different peoples throughout history. These people include the Huns, PERSIANS, MACEDONIANS, Uighurs, ARABS, TURKS, and MONGOLS. In the 14th century C.E. the Uzbek Empire formed, lead by Emir Timur (commonly known as Timur). At its height between 1381 and 1404 C.E., this empire extended from the Black Sea in the west to India in the east. Timur died in 1405, and without him his empire began to break up in 1447.

Uzbekistan's important location between Asia and India in the east and Europe and the Middle East in the west has made it vulnerable to invasion throughout history. The city of Samarkand was one of the major stopping points along the Silk Road, the major trade route linking the Far East with Europe and the Mediterranean that has been in use since at least 3000 B.C.E. Because of the constant shifting of power and people in the region, the Uzbeks' heritage is extremely diverse, and their ancestry includes to some extent elements of almost all other ethnic groups in the region.

LANGUAGE

Uzbek is of the Turkic language family. At least 12 dialects are referred to as "Uzbek" and are still spoken by some 15 million people around the world. Like the Mongols, from whom they are partially descended, there was originally no written language. In the 1430s the Uzbek Khans began to utilize emigrant Persian scholars who transcribed the Uzbek language using the Arabic alphabet. These scribes also wrote much of Uzbek history in their native Farsi. This created a unique historical perspective for the Uzbeks, as much of their early local history was written by non-Uzbeks.

The Arabic alphabet was changed to the Latin by the Soviets in the 1924, and changed again by the Soviets to the Cyrillic alphabet in the 1930s. In the 1996–97 school year in Uzbekistan, the Latin alphabet was once again set as the standard to be taught to children, though the Cyrillic is still widely used in daily life.

HISTORY

Early History

The early ancestors of the Uzbeks inhabited the valleys of west-central Asia for thousands of years. As nomads, they descended from the inhabitants of many of the surrounding lands, including Tajik and Turkic peoples who migrated from the north as early as 5000 B.C.E. (*see* TAJIKS; TURKIC PEOPLES) By 500 B.C.E. three major kingdoms had developed: Khorezem, Transoxiana, and Saka. Although the culture was nomadic, the area is also home to a great city, Samarkand, built by the Persians in about 700 B.C.E. The city was conquered in 329 B.C.E. by the armies of Alexander the Great. At the end of the 12th century C.E. the Mongols lead by Chenggis Khan moved west and the Uzbeks fell under the sway of the Mongol Empire.

Ozbeg Khan and Islam

In the years after Chenggis Khan's death, the Mongol Empire began to crumble, and from 1342 to 1357, the Golden Horde, as the western half of the Mongol Empire had become known, came under the rule of Ozbeg Khan, also known as Uzbek Khan. During his reign the Golden Horde became a full-fledged Islamic state and the culturally diverse people of the region became known as the Uzbeks.

Timur

As a people the Uzbeks are named after Ozbeg Khan, but true Uzbek history is usually said to begin later with the conquests of Timur. Born to a Turkic emir and devout Muslim named Taraghai in 1336, he grew up to be, like his father, well liked and respected among the ruling clans of the time. Throughout the 1360s he was able to establish a large military following and a strong position among the emirs and chieftains of the ruling Turkish-Mongol CHAGATAI Ulus, who had dominated the region since the Mongol conquests of half a century earlier. Timur gained a reputation as both a fierce warrior and a leader who encouraged science and the arts. In 1370 he seized the city of Balkh, where he repaired the destruction caused by the Mongols, and from 1370 to 1395 he also rebuilt Samarkand, also destroyed in the Mongol invasion, and made it his capital. In 1395 he defeated the weakened Mongol-Uzbek Khanate, further strengthening his hold on Central Asia and a large part of Russia.

Like Chenggis Khan before him, Timur united the nomads of the region, this time under Islam. From 1381 to 1404 he expanded the Uzbek Empire into Iran, Azerbaijan, Iraq, Syria, India, Siberia, and parts of China. Timur died in 1405, and by 1447 his huge empire had begun to break up into independent khanates.

Russian Conquest

In the mid-19th century Russia began imperial expansion south. In 1865 the Uzbek city of Tashkent fell and the region was absorbed into the Russian Empire. By the late 19th century it was fought over again, this time by Russia and the Britian. The conflict was largely fought with spies and puppet regimes led by khans controlled by one side or the other. The conflict became known in Britain as the "Great Game," while in Russia it was referred to as the "Tournament of Shadows." It was arguably won by Russia, which took complete control of the region, and in the 20th century the area became the Soviet Socialist Republic of Uzbekistan until it declared its independence in 1991 after the disintegration of the Soviet Union.

CULTURE

Government and Society

The Uzbeks have had a variety of governments throughout their long history, from the small nomadic groups lead by minor khans who originally lived in the area to the Mongol and Uzbek Empires, to a communist republic as part of the USSR, and today an independent national government.

Before Conquests

Until the region of Central Asia rose in importance because of trade and the Silk Road, the Uzbeks were split into many nomadic groups, each headed by a khan (chieftain). Eventually they formed three kingdoms: Khorezem, Transoxiana, and Saka. All three of these kingdoms traded and had regular contact with the Roman Empire. These groups alternately warred and traded with each other until they were absorbed into the empire of Alexander the Great, and later the Iranian and the Mongol Empires.

The Uzbek Empire

The Uzbek Empire rose and fell between 1381 and 1447 C.E. Despite its brevity, it exerted a

Uzbeks time line
B.C.E.
ca. 5000 Turkic ethnic groups move into the region from the north.
ca. 500 The nomadic peoples of the area organize into three kingdoms: Khorezem, Transoxiana, and Saka.
329 Alexander the Great conquers the three kingdoms.
C.E.
seventh and eighth centuries The area falls under repeated invasions from the Arabs. By the end of the eighth century the various nomadic religions begin to be replaced by Islam.
14th century Ozbeg (Uzbek) Khan officially converts the western Mongol Empire (the Golden Horde) to an Islamic state. Thereafter it becomes known as the Uzbek Khanate.
1336 Timur is born to Taraghai, a minor but popular Turkish emir.
1360s Timur gains a large military following and begins his campaign to conquer central Asia and the Middle East.
1395 Timur defeats the already weakened Uzbek Khanate, thereby gaining control over a large part of Russia.
1381–1404 Timur conquers Iran, Iraq, Syria, India, and parts of the Ottoman Empire, enlarging the new Uzbek Empire to a scale comparative to that of the Mongols of the previous century.
1405 Timur dies.
1447 The Uzbek Empire begins to break up.
16th century Uzbek Empire dissolves into several independent Khanates.
19th century Russia begins expansion into Central Asia, as does Britain.
1924 The Bolshevik Revolution succeeds in Russia and Uzbekistan becomes the Soviet Socialist Republic of Uzbekistan.
1991 The Soviet Union collapses and Uzbekistan declares its independence.

great deal of influence throughout Central Asia and the Middle East, and today its founder, Timur, is still considered by many Uzbeks to be a historical hero. Although he himself was illiterate, under his rule the Uzbek language became a written language for the first time and Samarkand became a capital city known from Rome to Beijing. Despite its strengths both militarily and economically, the Uzbek Empire, like the Mongol Empire before it, could not hold together without its leader. It was, however, the first of several large migrations of the Uzbeks who spread throughout Asia and the Middle East.

Economy

The first people who would eventually become known as Uzbeks were, like many of the peoples of the steppes of Central Asia, nomadic herders of sheep, goats, and horses and traded with each other and neighboring peoples for thousands of years. As civilizations in both the East and West expanded, the Silk Road became the basis of the region's economy from the first century C.E. until the 1500s, when European explorers began to find alternate routes to the Far East and trade through the area began to decline.

The Silk Road

The city of Samarkand lay at the center of the Silk Road and became a crossing of cultures and ideas from the Roman Empire, Persia, China, and India. Traders passed goods, ideas, and even religions between each on their journeys. Although there is some evidence of the gemstone lapis lazuli from northern India being traded in Egypt as far back as 4000 B.C.E., the Silk Road became a major route of commerce in the first century C.E. as trade grew between the Byzantine and Sassanid Empires in the west and the Three Kingdoms and eventually the Yuan dynasty in what is now China in the east (*see* SASSANIANS).

The Silk Road was not so much one long trade route across Asia as it was many interconnected shorter routes. Caravans would travel an average of only 20 miles along designated routes before meeting other caravans that would trade merchandise and news before turning around and heading back again. Only a few people traveled the entire length of the road.

This major trade route put the nomads of Central Asia, particularly around the wealthy city of Samarkand, in a unique position to easily acquire wealth and power without great change to their nomadic ways. They were already skilled horse riders and bowmen, and it was not a large step to becoming great warriors who amassed great wealth and power through both trade and war. The decline of the Silk Road was directly related to the decline of the region, a decline that would continue until the 19th century when cotton, grown for centuries in the Aral Sea basin, would aid the area's economic strength.

Religion

Before the Arab conquests in the seventh and eighth centuries C.E. the nomadic groups of the area practiced a variety of different religions, including Buddhism, Shamanism, and Zoroastrianism, as well as Judaism and Nestorian Christianity (*see* NESTORIANS). After the Arab conquests Sunni Islam became the dominant religion of the region and was even embraced by invading peoples such as the Mongols and the Karakhandis.

Architecture

The structures and homes of the Uzbeks are as varied as their history. The nomadic peoples lived in tents of black goat hair and would migrate with their homes several times a year or more, usually along annual routes, in search of fresh pasture for their herds. The cities of the region, on the other hand, were decorated with ceramic tiles and domes of different colors, most notably after Timur formed the Uzbek Empire. Each city could be recognized by the colors of its domes: Samarkand was blue, Khorezm was green, and Bukhara was gold.

———◆———

The modern descendents of the Uzbek ethnic group now also live in Afghanistan, Tajikistan, and Kyrgyzstan, with smaller populations in China and Turkmenistan. They are disseminated throughout the lands of the various empires that rose and fell throughout their history. Most are still Sunni Muslims and most, but not all, speak Uzbek as well as the native language of whatever nation they reside in.

The government and politics of Uzbekistan is much the same as it was under Soviet rule, except that Uzbek has replaced Russian as the national language and the Sunni branch of Islam has once again become the state religion, though other religions are tolerated.

FURTHER READING

Edward A. Allworth. *The Modern Uzbeks* (Stanford, Calif.: Hoover Press, 1990).
Rob Ferguson. *The Devil and the Disappearing Sea* (Vancouver, B.C.: Raincoast Books, 2003).
Hilda Hookam. *Tamburlaine the Conqueror* (London: Hodder and Stoughton, 1962).
Aisha Khan. *A Historical Atlas of Uzbekistan* (New York: Rosen Publishing Group, 2003).
MaryLee Knowlton. *Uzbekistan: Cultures of the World* (New York: Marshal Cavendish Benchmark, 2006).
Harold Lamb. *Tamerlane, the Earth Shaker* (Garden City, N.Y.: Garden City Publishing Co., 1928).
Robert Rand. *Tamerlane's Children* (Oxford, U.K.: Oneworld Publications, 2006).
John Ure. *The Trail of Tamerlane* (London: Constable and Company, 1980).
Resul Yalcin. *The Rebirth of Uzbekistan* (London: Garnet Publishing Limited, 2002).

Vai (Gallina; Vei; Vey)

The Vai are of MANDING origin and are closely related to the KONO. They live in Liberia, Guinea, and Sierra Leone.

Vandau *See* NDAU.

Vei *See* VAI.

Venda (Vhavenda)

The Venda (also known as the Vhavenda or "the People of Venda") live in the province of Transvaal in northeastern South Africa just south of the border with Zimbabwe. Their region is also known as Venda. The Venda comprise several subgroups, including the VHASENZI, VHALEMBA, VHATAVHATSINDI, and VHANGONA. Each subgroup has its own customs and further subdivisions, yet most share the same language and culture that distinguishes them from southern Africa's other BANTU-speaking peoples.

ORIGINS

The Venda migrated from East Africa's great lakes region to the north of their present home in several waves. The first arrivals, the Vhangona, reached the Limpopo River by the 1100s. A Venda group led by Thoho ya Ndou was the first to cross the Limpopo and enter the northern region of present-day Transvaal, most likely in the 1600s. Large, powerful bows probably gave the Venda a military edge over the previous inhabitants, and for a time they controlled much of southeast Africa. Rivalries between Thoho ya Ndou's descendants lost the Venda their supremacy, however, and kept them divided into a number of chiefdoms. During a SWAZI invasion in 1839, the decentralized structure of the state and its mountain refuges helped save the Venda from being wiped out. Later that century, though, they suffered from famines and wars of succession.

LANGUAGE

The Venda language is Luvenda (also known as Tshivenda).

HISTORY

In the 1840s, AFRIKANERS established the Soutpansberg republic in Venda. At first it was essentially a hunting settlement, employing Venda men to hunt for ivory, but the BOERS (Afrikaner farmers) established a large army to carry out slave raids on Venda villages. The Venda rose in rebellion and by 1867 had ousted all the white settlers from their land. Gradually, however, Boer commandos isolated and defeated the Venda chiefdoms one by one. An onslaught in 1898 finally drove the remaining Venda north of the Limpopo River and the Venda lands were incorporated into the Boers' South African Republic (later, Transvaal).

In 1910 the British colonies and the Boer republics were united as the white-minority-ruled

VENDA

location:
South Africa

time period:
17th century C.E. to present

ancestry:
Nilotic

language:
Nilo-Saharan

Venda time line

C.E.

by 1100s First Venda group, Vhangona, reach north of Limpopo River after migrating from Great Lakes region of East Africa.

1600s Venda led by Thoho ya Ndou cross Limpopo River and settle in present-day Transvaal.

1819–39 Mfecane period of mass migrations and wars

1836–48 Great Trek brings Boers into conflict with people inland.

1840s Boer republic of Soutpansberg established on Venda lands.

1858–64 Soutpansberg incorporated into Boer's Transvaal republic.

1860–67 Venda drive Boers out of their lands north of Olifants River.

1898 Venda conquered by Transvaal.

1910 British Natal and Cape colonies and Boer's Orange Free State and Transvaal republics unite to form the white-minority ruled Union of South Africa.

1913 Venda restricted to inadequate native reserves.

1973 Venda homeland created from native reserves.

1979 Venda homeland given artificial "independence," which is not recognized outside of South Africa.

1991 Apartheid legislation repealed

1994 Venda homeland is re-absorbed into South Africa.

See also SOUTH AFRICANS: NATIONALITY

Union of South Africa. Racist policies increasingly began to be used to oppress the Venda, along with all other black South Africans, and the Venda were restricted to three small "native reserves." After the 1948 election, apartheid (the racist doctrine of "separate development") came into being. In 1973 the government turned the reserves into a self-governing homeland, which was given independence in 1979. This independence was fictional, however, and never recognized outside of South Africa. After the end of white-minority rule in 1994, South Africa reabsorbed the homelands.

CULTURE

Most Venda inhabit the well-watered land between the Soutpansberg Mountains and the Letaba River to the southeast. A large tract north of the mountains is drier, more subject to drought, less fertile, and more sparsely peopled. The majority of the Venda live in sizable farming villages of stone or thatched homes surrounded by fences or walls and sited on hillsides. The region allocated to the Venda by the apartheid system was insufficient for the population and never received adequate investment.

Consequently, cropland is in short supply and is shrinking further as the population rises, and soil erosion is a problem. The Venda chiefly grow crops to eat, yet most of their food has to be imported from other parts of South Africa. Dry-land food crops include corn, millet, sorghum, and peanuts. On the region's much smaller area of irrigated land, people grow corn, wheat, sweet potatoes, beans, peas, vegetables, and citrus fruits. Cash crops include sisal (a fiber crop), tea, coffee, sugarcane, tobacco, and cotton. Nearly nine tenths of the land is suitable only for grazing. The Venda raise a few cattle and also sheep, goats, and chickens.

Lack of investment in Venda during the apartheid years has meant that the region has poor infrastructure and therefore few large industries. Also, businesses were previously encouraged to set up on the edge of homelands in order to take advantage of the cheap labor force, but not inside. As a result, more than 10 percent of the population commutes to work in mines and factories outside Venda. Nevertheless, there is some forestry and freshwater fish farming within Venda. Mines yield some copper and graphite, and quarries produce sandstone. Various small-scale industries include ceramics, woodcrafts, and sawmilling.

The basic social unit consists of a husband (generally the head of the family), his wife or wives, and their children. Each extended family involves two sets of relationships, based on male and female lines of descent. The male line includes a father, his brothers and sisters, and his and his brothers' children. The female line includes a wife, her brothers and sisters, and her and her sisters' children. This female line is especially important on religious occasions. Lineages that share a common ancestor or ancestors are grouped into clans, whose members generally do not intermarry.

Government and Society

Historically, large Venda chiefdoms ruled over, or strongly influenced, smaller ones. Within his area, each chief had the role of lawmaking and other powers, but certain officials and relatives played important roles too. A council advised him on royal village affairs such as ceremonies and public works. A private council of influential men advised him on local affairs, including items he planned to bring up at the next meeting of the council—a body that could freely criticize any of the chief's decisions.

Apartheid established a framework of so-called traditional chiefs to administer the Venda homeland. These chiefs were at first appointed by the government, but provisions were later made for limited voting rights within the Venda homeland. This established a falsely traditional political structure because it was dependent not on Venda culture but the approval of the white-minority South African regime, even after the Venda were given their independence in 1979. Since the dismantlement of apartheid, the Venda can vote for representatives to the national government and the homeland government has been abolished.

Religion

The majority of Venda are Christians, yet traces of the Venda religion linger in everyday beliefs and superstitions. Many Venda believe witches are women who are unaware of their malign influence, and they try to remove this by "good" magic or by detecting witches and driving them out. The Venda also consult diviners who try to foretell the future from the patterns produced by seeds and other ingredients placed in a bowl.

At puberty, girls enter a large building and undergo the six-day *vhusha* initiation process. This includes learning the evils of premarital sex and adultery. Later, they attend a school known as the *domba* to learn the duties expected of wives and mothers. The process can last from three months to a year. Its special features include the python dance, which is performed by a chain of chanting girls, each holding the forearms of the girl in front. For boys entering adulthood, *murundu* (a circumcision ceremony), has largely replaced older initiation rituals.

See also SOUTH AFRICANS: NATIONALITY.

FURTHER READING

Edward Lahiff. *An Apartheid Oasis?: Agriculture and Rural Livelihoods in Venda* (Portland, Ore.: Frank Cass, 2000).

A. de V. Minnaar, D. Offringa, and C. Payze. *To Live in Fear: Witchburning and Medicine Murder in Venda* (Pretoria: Human Sciences Research Council, 1992).

Louise Olivier. *The Needs and Problems of the People of Venda* (Pretoria, South Africa: Human Sciences Research Council, 1989).

Vey *See* VAI.

Vhalemba

The Vhalemba are one of the many subgroups of the VENDA. The Venda live in the province of Transvaal in northeastern South Africa.

Vhangona

The Vhangona are one of the many subgroups of the VENDA. The Venda live in the province of Transvaal in northeastern South Africa.

Vhasenzi

The Vhasenzi are one of the many subgroups of the VENDA. The Venda live in the province of Transvaal in northeastern South Africa.

Vhatavhatsindi

The Vhatavhatsindi are one of the many subgroups of the VENDA. The Venda live in the province of Transvaal in South Africa.

Vhavenda *See* VENDA.

Vidunda

The Vidunda are part of the ZARAMO. They are a BANTU people living in the mountainous highlands of coastal Tanzania.

Vili

The Vili are a subgroup of the KONGO. The majority live in southwestern Gabon and neighboring parts the Republic of the Congo.

Voltaic *See* MOLE-DAGBANE.

Voutere *See* BAFOU.

Vute (Mbute)

The Vute are closely related to the BAYA and MBUN peoples. The majority of the Vute live in Cameroon.

Wagadugu *See* OUAGADOUGOU.

Wagga *See* WAJA.

Waja **(Wagga; Wuya)**
The Waja live in northeastern Nigeria, Niger, and northern Benin. The Waja people are re-knowned sculptors in Nigeria and their language is known as Vemngo.

Wajunga
The Wajunga are a subgroup of the DAZAGA. They live to the east of the Tibesti Mountains in northwestern Chad.

Wala
The Wala are a MOLE-DAGBANE people. They live largely in northern Ghana and Togo.

Walega
The Walega are one of the nine main subgroups of the OROMO. They live in Ethiopia.

Walia *See* MASSA.

Wambulu *See* IRAQW.

Wangara *See* DYULA.

Wanjare
The Wanjare are one of the main subdivisions of the GUSII. The Gusii are a large ethnic group of western Kenya.

Wanyamwezi *See* NYAMWEZI.

Wara-wara **(Ouara)**
The Wara-wara are part of the SENUFO. They are a small ethnic group living in southwestern Burkina Faso.

Warsha *See* WASSA.

Wassa **(Warsha)**
The Wassa are an AKAN people. They live in western Ghana and eastern Ivory Coast.

Wassalunka *See* OUASSOULOUNKE.

Watyi
The Watyi are one of the main subdivisions of the EWE. They live in the southeast of Togo.

Wee *See* GUERE.

Welamo
The Welamo are an Ethiopian OMOTIC people.

Western Saharans *See* SAHARAWIS.

Western Sotho *See* TSWANA.

Westerners *See* ANGLOPHONES OF CAMEROON.

Widekum

The Widekum are a BAMILEKE people. They live in the western highlands of Cameroon.

Wodaabe (Bororo)

The Wodaabe are a FULANI people of West Africa. Sometimes referred to as the cattle Fulani (as opposed to the settled groups such as the TUKOLOR), the Wodaabe are a largely nomadic people who travel in the semidesert Sahel regions on the southern border of the Sahara Desert. Nomads travel with their herds of animals in search of water and fresh pasture. The Wodaabe range over broad stretches of northern Nigeria and southern Niger. Their nomadic activities have been greatly restricted in recent years, however, by drought and government intervention. Large numbers of cattle died, and many people were forced to sell their animals and migrate to urban areas or refugee camps to avoid starvation.

The Wodaabe men are famous for their concern with personal appearance. At certain festivals they paint their faces to accentuate their good features and wear elaborately embroidered clothing. Each woman then chooses the man she finds most attractive.

Wollo

The Wollo are one of the nine main subgroups of the OROMO. They live in Ethiopia.

Wolof (Djollof; Jalof; Yolof)

The Wolof figure among the largest ethnic groups in two West African countries, Senegal and Gambia, where they are concentrated in the northwest of the Senegambia region between the Senegal and Gambia Rivers. There are well over 2 million Wolof, and their language (also called Wolof) is the lingua franca of Gambia and Senegal. The Wolof language is related to SERER and Fulfulde, which is spoken by the FULANI.

Positioned with the Sahara Desert to the north and the Atlantic to the west, the Wolof became powerful from involvement in both the Atlantic and Saharan trades. By the end of the 15th century C.E., the Wolof Kingdom had become an empire with much of modern-day Senegal under its control. The empire was divided into five kingdoms: Djollof, which was inland, and Walo, Cayior, Baol, Sine, and Saloum on the coast. Each *burba*, or king, was elected, and 16th-century Portuguese travelers recorded that the Burba Djollof had a more than 100,000-strong army. The Wolof empire declined in the mid 16th century as vassal states that had themselves become wealthy through trade began to assert their independence.

Wute *See* BAFOU.

Wuya *See* WAJA.

Xesibe

The Xesibe are a subgroup of the XHOSA. They live in the northeastern corner of Transkei, which is on the eastern coast of South Africa.

Xhosa

The Xhosa live mostly in rural areas of southeastern South Africa. The overwhelming majority of the black population of Cape Town, Port Elizabeth, and East London are Xhosa, and there are also very large Xhosa populations in the Johannesburg area. They belong to a diversity of groups, the main ones being the MPONDO, THEMBU, HLUBI, NGQIKA, and GCALEKA. Together, they are sometimes referred to as southern NGUNI peoples.

ORIGINS

The Xhosa are descended from BANTU-speaking peoples from present-day eastern Nigeria who arrived in Southern Africa around the 200s. The Xhosa are one of many ethnic groups who emerged from the Nguni Bantu-speaking peoples. They originally consisted of three main groups: the Mpondo, the Thembu, and the Xhosa. These groups share the same language and hold the belief that their cultures originate from the same source.

LANGUAGE

The Xhosa language is Xhosa (also known as isiXhosa), which is one of the Bantu languages.

Along with ZULU, it is one of the most widely spoken South African languages.

HISTORY

Over the course of many centuries, internal friction, migration, and contact with the KHOISAN-speaking peoples created subdivisions within the original Xhosa groups, which fragmented into numerous clans. Sons of chiefs established new chiefdoms of their own, and this was the main way in which the Xhosa gradually expanded their territory. Eventually, they occupied an area along the eastern coast that reached roughly from the Groot-Vis River to present-day KwaZulu-Natal and spread inland to the Drakensberg Mountains. The various Xhosa groups remained linked through marriage and political and military alliances.

Between 1779 and 1878 there was a series of nine frontier wars—the Cape–Xhosa Wars between the Xhosa and the BOERS (AFRIKANERS) and British of the Cape Colony. In addition, in the early 1800s many Xhosa fled from the northeast of their territory (in what is now KwaZulu-Natal) to escape the armies of the great Zulu leader Shaka. The Xhosa suffered their most traumatic blow in the "cattle-killings" of 1856–57. A young girl called Nongqawuse—said to be possessed by the spirits of the ancestors—had a vision that the white invaders would be swept into the sea, great Xhosa chiefs would return from the dead, and the land would be filled with cattle and crops. For this to happen, Nongqawuse said, all existing cattle and food supplies must first be destroyed. Coming at a time of great conflict for the Xhosa, many people saw this as a way out of the turmoil. Despite the slaughter of 200,000 cattle, however, the prophecy was not fulfilled and only hunger, death, and poverty resulted. Survivors of this desperate act of resistance were compelled to seek work on the invaders' farms, and the Xhosa were finally defeated in 1878.

Under apartheid, the South African government created homelands for the country's black population. The Xhosa homelands of Ciskei and Transkei were later declared "independent" by the government, which then withdrew South African citizenship from all Xhosa. After South Africa's first nonracial elections in 1994, Ciskei and Transkei were reabsorbed into South Africa.

CULTURE

Until most of their land was taken by Europeans, the Xhosa were a cattle-raising people whose herds represented wealth and social stability. Although cattle continue to be important in rural areas, few Xhosa survive purely from the land (which tends to be of poor quality). Instead, most rural Xhosa rely on family members working in the cities to send money home.

Under apartheid, black Africans were unable to live within city boundaries and instead were confined to government-built townships, usually located considerable distances from places of work and with residency dependent on continuous employment. With the end of apartheid, there are no longer restrictions on where people may live, but living conditions remain fundamentally unchanged. In common with the black urban population as a whole, most Xhosa are employed in manufacturing industries, mining, and domestic service.

The Xhosa have a long history of literature. Earlier forms are mostly oral and include praise poems, folk tales, and prophecies, many of which have now been written down. This tradition has continued into the present, and there are several important Xhosa writers, such as the novelist and playwright John Knox Bokwe and the novelist Sinxo.

Government and Society

Historically, the Xhosa's allegiance was to their clan, led by an *inkosi* (chief) whose status was gained through his mother. *Inkosi* were obliged to be hospitable and generous—INKOSI actually means "thank-you"—and their powers were

Xhosa time line
C.E.
200s Bantu-speaking peoples begin to arrive in Southern Africa.
300s–400s Bantu-speakers reach present-day KwaZulu-Natal.
1799–1803 Cape–Xhosa Wars I, II, and III: Xhosa–Boer frontier wars
1811–12 Cape–Xhosa War IV: British drive many Xhosa east of Groot-Vis River.
1818–19 Cape–Xhosa War V: British drive remaining Xhosa east of Groot-Vis River.
1819–39 Mfecane: period of mass migrations and wars
1834–35 Cape–Xhosa War VI: British annex Xhosa lands.
1836 British return Xhosa lands.
1846–47 Cape–Xhosa War VII: British annex Xhosa lands as far east as Great Kei River.
1850–53 Cape–Xhosa War VIII: Xhosa rebel against British.
1856–57 Xhosa sacrifice 200,000 cattle in accordance with prophecy.
1877–78 Cape–Xhosa War IX: final defeat of Xhosa by British
1910 British and Boers form white-ruled Union of South Africa.
1913 Xhosa restricted to inadequate native reserves.
1959 Transkei and Ciskei Xhosa homelands created.
1976 Transkei "independent"
1981 Ciskei "independent"
1991 Apartheid legislation repealed.
1994 Transkei and Ciskei homelands re-absorbed into South Africa.

See also SOUTH AFRICANS: NATIONALITY

limited by public opinion and counselors. Within the homelands, so-called traditional forms of government were encouraged by the South African government. In fact, these traditional forms of government were not like the Xhosa's own system of government, since they had none of the power balances the Xhosa's own system incorporated. The use of ethnicity and tradition in this way during apartheid has led many to regard them as inappropriate. After the homelands were reincorporated into South Africa in 1994, their governments were abolished and replaced by national government structures.

During the early 20th century, an urban elite developed that became increasingly distanced socially and culturally from the rural Xhosa. The urban Xhosa were commonly called "School" Xhosa and the rural "Red" Xhosa—named for the fashion of using red ocher (a yellow or reddish-brown clay) as a body decoration. The conservative Red Xhosa kept Xhosa beliefs and traditions while the School Xhosa adopted new customs and Christianity. Despite changes in rural areas in recent decades and rural-urban migration, these divisions remain.

Although the majority of Xhosa are Christians, many still retain traditional marriage customs. *Lobola* (or bridewealth—gifts given by the groom's family to the bride's family) is still given even by Christians. The function of *lobola* is to legitimize the marriage and any children born to the couple.

Religion

The sufferings that followed the cattle-killings of the mid-19th century caused many Xhosa to lose faith in the power of their own beliefs and turn to Christianity, which is now the Xhosa's main religion.

See also SOUTH AFRICANS: NATIONALITY.

FURTHER READING

Elisabeth Anderson. *A History of the Xhosa of the Northern Cape, 1795–1879* (Rondebosch, South Africa: University of Cape Town, 1987).

Beverley Kirsch, Silvia Skorge, and Sindiwe Magona. *Xhosa* (Lincolnwood, Ill.: NTC Publishing Group, 1999).

Noël Mostert. *Frontiers: The Epic of South Africa's Creation and the Tragedy of the Xhosa People* (New York: Knopf, 1992).

J. B. Peires. *The Dead Will Arise: Nongqawuse and the Great Xhosa Cattle-Killing Movement of 1856–7* (Johannesburg, South Africa: Ravan Press, 1989).

Richard Price. *Empire and Its Encounters: Colonial Encounters and the Creation of Imperial Rule in 19th-Century Africa* (Cambridge, U.K.: Cambridge University Press, 2008).

Xhu   *See* KUNG.

Y

Yacouba *See* Dan.

Yaka of Minikongo *See* Suku.

Yakö *See* Yakurr.

Yakurr (Yakö)

The Yakurr live in the so-called Cross River region of southeastern Nigeria, northeast of the Niger Delta. Yakurr territory lies roughly 60 miles inland from the town of Calabar on the coast. The biggest town in the region is Obubra, which lies on the Cross River. The land they inhabit was once densely forested, and although much of this forest remains, large areas have been cut down to provide land for farming and firewood. The Yakurr speak a language called Kö, which is a Bantu language.

Yakurr oral history states that fairly recently, perhaps as late as the early 19th century, they migrated north into their present lands from the Oban Hills to the southeast, just north of Calabar. They established five main towns in the region of considerable size. The Yakurr are not truly urbanized, however, as the majority are farmers.

Yalunka

The Yalunka are a Manding people. They live in northeastern Sierra Leone and across the border in Guinea.

Yamarico

The Yamarico are one of the two main Sadama subgroups. The Sadama live in Ethiopia.

Yao

The Yao are a large ethnic group of East and Central Africa and can be found in Malawi, Tanzania, and Mozambique. They are not to be confused with another group also called Yao (or Pila-Pila) who live in Benin, West Africa. The Makua-Lomwe of Tanzania and Mozambique are closely related to the Yao, with whom they are sometimes grouped as part of the larger Yao cluster of peoples.

The Yao are a Bantu people, whose ancestors originated from the Niger-Congo region of West-Central Africa more than 2,000 years ago. The Malawian Yao population dates from the 1850s, when groups of Yao people from the north of present-day Mozambique began migrating into the region. One group, the Amchinga, settled at the southeastern corner of Lake Malawi in the 1860s. During the 1870s, Makanjila founded a powerful Yao kingdom in the area. Other, smaller kingdoms (or chiefdoms) were established by other Yao leaders. The Yao states were important in East African trade between the coast and interior, dominating the trade in slaves and ivory around the Lake Malawi region. During this era the Yao came under the cultural influence of the Swahili people, adopting the Muslim religion, learning Arabic, and wearing Arabic clothes.

Yarse

The Yarse are one of the many separate ethnic groups that make up the MOSSI. The Mossi live in Burkina Faso.

Yatenga

The Yatenga are a MOLE-DAGBANE people. They live in northwestern Burkina Faso and neighboring parts of Mali.

Yazidis

The Yazidis are a Kurdish-speaking group, most of whom live in northern Iraq and the autonomous province of Kurdistan (see KURDS). Small numbers live in the Caucasus republics of Armenia and Georgia and in northern Syria and southeast Turkey. An immigrant community of perhaps 20,000 lives in Europe, mainly Germany. Estimates of the total Yazidi population vary, but it is thought to number about 500,000. The name Yazidi is thought by many to derive from an Old Iranian word meaning "divine being," but Western scholars generally connect the name to the Umayyad caliph Yazid ibn Muawiya, who ruled the Muslim empire from 680 to 683 C.E. and with whom Yazidis identify. The group is distinguished by its religion, which incorporates elements of ancient faiths along with elements of Christianity and Islam, even though most modern adherents reject any connection with Islam. Yazidis believe in one God, the Creator, and they accept the prophets of Christianity and Islam. Distinctive in Yazidi worship is the central figure, an archangel, often represented as a peacock. A major religious ritual is the seven-day Jamaa feast, the "feast of the assembly," celebrated in the village of Shaykhan in the mountains of northern Iraq, northeast of Mosul, where the Lalish temple is located. Lalish means "source of light and brightness," and Yazidis are supposed to make the pilgrimage to the this temple at least once in their lives. Each pilgrim walks barefoot down narrow alleys to the temple, within which are seven columns representing seven archangels, the "Seven Mysteries," the leader of whom is the Peacock Angel. Each column in the temple is wrapped with colorful fabric that can be tied into knots. Pilgrims untie one knot, representing the wish of someone who has come before them, and they tie another, which will, in turn, be untied by a future pilgrim.

Under the rule of Saddam Hussein in Iraq, Yazidis were a protected minority. However, since the overthrow of Saddam in 2003, Yazidis have been persecuted and many have fled the country.

Yedina See BUDUMA.

Yemenis: nationality (people of Yemen)

GEOGRAPHY

The Republic of Yemen is a coastal nation at the southern tip of the Arabian Peninsula. It has an area of approximately 204,000 square miles and borders two other countries; Saudi Arabia meets its northern border and the Republic of Oman lies to the east. Yemen's 1,200-mile-long coastline extends along the Arabian Sea and the Gulf of Aden in the south and the Red Sea in the west. At the mouth of the Red Sea mainland, Yemen is only 20 miles from the coast of the Republic of Djibouti across the Bab-el-Mandeb Strait (also known as the Mandeb Strait). The Bab-el-Mandeb Strait is one of the busiest and most strategically important shipping lanes in the world because all shipping from the Mediterranean to the Arabian Sea via the Suez Canal must pass through it. The Yemeni island of Perim lies in the middle of the strait, dividing it into two narrow channels. Yemeni territory also includes the large island of Socotra in the Arabian Sea and the Hanish Islands in the Red Sea.

Yemen can be divided into four main geographical regions. A narrow coastal plain extends along the Red Sea coast in the west. The plain receives little rainfall but has many lagoons and is well watered by streams flowing toward the sea from the western highlands. These highlands rise sharply from the eastern limit of the coastal plain and constitute the most hospitable and agriculturally productive region of the country. The western highlands receive regular seasonal rainfall, and its slopes are extensively terraced for agriculture. Most of the country's urban centers, including the capital city, Sanaa, are situated in the western highlands. The eastern highlands become increasingly arid as they gradually merge into the inhospitable desert of the interior of the Arabian Peninsula. Known as the Rub al Khali (or the Empty Quarter), this desert dominates the southern third of the peninsula and extends across parts of neighboring Oman and Saudi Arabia. Agriculture is impossible here, and

Yemenis: nationality time line

C.E.

1918 North Yemen becomes independent as the Mutawakkilite Kingdom of Yemen following the collapse of the Ottoman Empire.

1962 The royal family of North Yemen is overthrown in a military coup and the country is renamed the Yemen Arab Republic.

1967 South Yemen gains independence from British rule as the People's Republic of South Yemen.

1970 South Yemen is renamed the People's Democratic Republic of South Yemen.

1972 Armed conflict between North and South Yemen over border disputes

1979 Renewed conflict between North and South Yemen amid attempts to unite the two countries

1990 North and South Yemen unified as the Republic of Yemen. Ali Abdallah Saleh, former president of North Yemen, become president of the new republic.

1993 Coalition government made up of ruling parties of former North and South Yemen formed.

1994 South Yemeni members of government expelled; sporadic fighting between North and South Yemeni armies, which have remained separate. South Yemen declares independence, but Northern forces take Aden and stall secessionist moves.

2000 U.S. naval vessel USS *Cole* damaged in suicide attack in Aden. Bomb attack on British embassy. Both attacks blamed on Muslim extremists.

2004–05 Government forces fight supporters of Husayn Badreddin al-Houthi in northwest Yemen.

2007 Renewed fighting in northwest Yemen

2008 Series of bomb attacks against government, tourist, and foreign company targets

even the nomadic peoples of the region confine themselves to its margins. Yemen's Arabian Sea coast is rugged and arid, but there are a series of fishing ports along its length.

INCEPTION AS A NATION

Human habitation in the area of modern Yemen is extremely ancient. According to some theories concerning the original dispersal of humans from Africa, the Bab-el-Mandeb Strait may once have constituted the land bridge that allowed humans to cross from East Africa into Asia for the first time during an era when sea levels were lower than today. Recorded history in Yemen begins in the first millennium B.C.E. when trade contacts between the people of the southern Arabian Peninsula and the PHOENI-CIANS introduced the Phoenician script. By this time the Semitic peoples of the southern Arabian Peninsula (*see* SEMITES) had a long-established civilization that had grown wealthy from its position on ancient trade routes from East Africa to Mesopotamia, the Mediterranean, and India. Even today Yemen receives the highest rainfall of anywhere on the Arabian Peninsula, and thousands of years ago local conditions are believed to have been even more conducive to agricultural production. Archaeological evi-

dence suggests that East Africa and the Arabian Peninsula have become significantly more arid in the last two thousand years. The first-century C.E. geographer Ptolemy referred to the area as "fortunate Arabia" because of its hospitable climate and the great wealth of its cities.

From the eighth century B.C.E. to the third century C.E. the SABAEANS dominated the southwest corner of what is now Yemen. The Sabaeans were a great trading people who controlled the southern half of the Red Sea. They either founded or were influential in the development of the D'mt civilization in Ethiopia and Eritrea, which was the precursor of the Axumite Kingdom, one of the great ancient civilizations of East Africa. The legendary land of Sheba, referred to in the Hebrew Bible, the Quran, and ancient Ethiopian texts, is believed to be synonymous with the country of the Sabaeans. The Sabaeans were well known for their sophisticated use of irrigation techniques and for the construction of the Marib Dam, one of the technological wonders of the ancient world. The Marib Dam stored water from the seasonal rains, allowing the Sabaeans to water large areas of agricultural land during the dry season. First constructed in the eighth century B.C.E., the dam stood until the sixth century C.E., when it was breached and left unrepaired. Other kingdoms in the region included those of the Minaeans and the Himyarites, which also rose to prominence as Sabaean influence diminished. These kingdoms flourished until the sixth century C.E. when the Iranian Sassanid Empire conquered much of the Arabian Peninsula (see SASSANIANS). Iranian rule continued until the mid-seventh century when Arab armies drove them out of the peninsula and brought Islam to the south. The rulers of Yemen were among the first to adopt the Muslim faith, and from this period Yemen was ruled by a series of imams to a greater or lesser under the overarching authority of successive Muslim empires.

The OTTOMANS seized control of coastal areas of Yemen in the 16th century and were able to extend their power inland during the 19th century as the power of local dynasties diminished. The 19th century also brought the first British influence to the area. In an attempt to stop raids on British merchant shipping between Europe and India, Britain conducted military raids and concluded protection agreements with numerous territories around the Red Sea and the Persian Gulf. In 1839 the city of Aden, a natural harbor a short distance from the entrance to the Red Sea, was designated as a British protectorate in an agreement with the ruler of the sultanate of Lahej. During the course of the 19th century Britain extended its influence over neighboring territories until, by the beginning of the 20th century, it had control of most of the southern half of present-day Yemen. The city of Aden was designated a British colony and became a provisioning port on the sea route to India after the opening of the Suez Canal in 1869. While Britain built its power in the south of Yemen, the north came fully under the control of the Ottoman Empire.

Following the defeat of the Ottoman Empire during World War I, the northern part of Yemen became independent in 1918 as the Mutawakkilite Kingdom of Yemen (or North Yemen). British rule of the Aden Protectorate in the south evolved through several stages. In 1959 the Federation of Arab Emirates of the South was formed as an amalgamation of British protectorates in the western half of British-controlled Yemen. Protectorates in the sparsely inhabited eastern half were united as the Protectorate of South Arabia. The Federation of Arab Emirates of the South was extended in 1962 and renamed the Federation of South Arabia, and the Aden Colony was integrated into this extended federation in 1963. From that year an armed separatist movement began to campaign for independence from Britain, and in November 1967, the Federation of South Arabia and the Protectorate of South Arabia were united as the independent nation of the People's Republic of South Yemen (known as the People's Democratic Republic of South Yemen from December 1970). In 1962 a revolution in the Mutawakkilite Kingdom of Yemen had deposed the monarchy and renamed the country the Yemen Arab Republic. The two states, commonly referred to as North Yemen (the Yemen Arab Republic) and South Yemen (the People's Democratic Republic of South Yemen), remained separate until May 1990. The unification of North and South Yemen to form the present-day Republic of Yemen came about partly as the result of long-held ambitions in both states to achieve unification and partly as a means of resolving disputes about the future distribution of revenue from oil reserves discovered along their common border.

CULTURAL IDENTITY

Yemen has been a unified nation for only a few decades and consequently has had little time to develop an inclusive and unifying national identity. The unification of Yemen was not an immediate success. Six months after unification the first Gulf War began. The Yemeni government did not support the stance of its powerful neighbor, Saudi Arabia, which invited the United States and other nations to deploy troops on its territory in preparation for the liberation of Kuwait from Iraqi occupation. In retaliation the Saudi government deported up to 800,000 Yemeni workers dealing a severe blow to the Yemeni economy. In 1994 a civil war broke out when political leaders in the south attempted to secede from the newly formed state and declared an independent Democratic Republic of Yemen. This entity was not internationally recognized, and the secessionists were defeated within a few months. Tensions between south and north continue into the present. South Yemenis often believe that the north receives more than its fair share of economic development, and there are ingrained cultural differences between the north and the south based on the political histories of the two formerly separate states. South Yemen was governed according to secular communist principles from the 1970s until the early 1990s, while North Yemen retained a more traditional social structure following its independence from Ottoman rule.

A second internal conflict began in 2004 when followers of Husayn Badreddin al-Houthi, a cleric belonging to the Zaydi sect (a branch of Shii Islam), began a separatist insurgency movement against the Yemeni government (*see* ZAYDIS). Centered on the Sadah district of northwest Yemen, which borders Saudi Arabia, the insurgency has cost hundreds of lives and involved attacks on military and civilian targets. The Yemeni government accuses the rebels of attempting to overthrow the government and establish a Shii Islamic state in its place and also claims that Iran has directed and financed the uprising. The rebels claim they are defending their heritage against institutionalized oppression from a Sunni-dominated state.

Yemen is one of the world's poorest nations and the poorest nation in the Middle East. Yemeni society remains highly traditional, with clearly delineated social strata. The top strata consists of families who are accepted as tracing their lineage from the family of the prophet Muhammad. Traditionally, the males of these families have competed to become the most important religious leaders in the country (and therefore the most politically powerful, since there is little distinction between religious and political status). Below these is a class of less prestigious families (nevertheless of ancient Arabian lineage), the males of which tend to hold positions as religious judges and the heads of tribes or clans. Beneath this is a much larger group made up of farmers and traders. These people are part of the tribal structure, in that they have an established lineage, but are not members of the tribal elite. They own land, which they usually cultivate themselves rather than leasing to others, and traditionally they have been permitted to own weapons. At the bottom of the social structure are all those people of obscure or unknown lineage and foreigners. These people traditionally work at low-status occupations, such as metalworking, carpentry, and weaving and dying, which are often hereditary. In the past the majority of Yemen's Jewish population were part of this skilled underclass, but since an Israeli-sponsored migration in 1949 and 1950 that saw 50,000 Yemeni Jews relocated to Israel, there are only a few hundred Jewish people remaining in the country (*see* ISRAELIS: NATIONALITY; JEWS). The repatriation of hundreds of thousands of Yemenis from Saudi Arabia and other Arab countries in the early 1990s have created some social tension in the country because some of these people have non-Yemeni wives and children of mixed ancestry who do not fit into the traditional social pattern. Traditional

A modern Yemeni woman wearing a *niqab*.

social patterns are stronger in former North Yemen and in the rural areas of former South Yemen. The urban areas of former South Yemen were subject to the egalitarian principles of communism under the period of communist rule, which discouraged these traditions.

Although modern Yemen has an established set of democratically elected government institutions, including a bicameral legislature and prime ministerial and presidential offices, these are somewhat tenuously connected to the real exercise of political power, which takes place at the level of personal relationships through family, social, and regional links. A series of reforms have attempted to make government more genuinely transparent, and especially to encourage citizens to use the state legal system rather than the traditional system of tribal arbitration. Women are guaranteed equal legal rights in the country's constitution, but in reality there continues to be a great disparity between the status of men and women, and this disparity is reinforced and maintained by religious leaders.

Distinctive elements of Yemeni culture include the widespread use of khat, a plant with mild stimulant properties chewed by many

Yemenis; the *jambiya,* a dagger with a short curved blade traditionally worn as a symbol of male status; and the remarkable high-rise architecture of the old city of Sanaa. Khat is a controlled or illegal substance in many countries, and its use is banned in most other Muslim countries, but it is legal and extremely popular in Yemen. The leaves of the plant are chewed at many social gatherings, and its cultivation is an important source of income in many rural areas. The *jambiya* is not specifically Yemeni in origin (the word means "dagger" in Arabic, and similar weapons are found across the Arabian Peninsula), but it has come to be associated with Yemen because it has remained a popular cultural symbol into the modern era. It is worn in a sheath, which is held in front of the body by a cloth or leather belt. The handle of a *jambiya* often indicates the wealth and status of its owner; the most expensive and prestigious examples are made from ivory or rhinoceros horn.

The old city of Sanaa is a United Nations–designated World Heritage Site and has been inhabited since at least the period of the Sabaeans in the sixth century B.C.E. The city is surrounded by a clay-brick wall that is up to 30 feet high in places. Many of the ancient houses that make up the city are seven or eight stories high and decorated with intricate friezes and wooden lattices.

FURTHER READING

Sheila Carapico. *Civil Society in Yemen: A Political Economy of Activism in Modern Arabia* (Cambridge, U.K.:Cambridge University Press, 1998).

Paul Dresch. *A History of Modern Yemen* (Cambridge, U.K.: Cambridge University Press, 2000).

Peter Hinchcliffe, John T. Ducker, and Maria Holt. *Without Glory in Arabia: The British Retreat from Aden* (London: I.B. Tauris, 2006).

Naomi Lucks. *Queen of Sheba* (New York: Chelsea House, 2008).

Kamil A. Mahdi, Anna Würth, and Helen Lackner. *Yemen into the Twenty-First Century: Continuity and Change* (Reading, U.K.: Ithaca Press, 2007).

Spencer Mawby. *British Policy in Aden and the Protectorates 1955–67: Last Outpost of a Middle East Empire* (London: Routledge, 2005).

Jillian Schwedler. *Faith in Moderation: Islamist Parties in Jordan and Yemen* (Cambridge, U.K.: Cambridge University Press, 2006).

Shelagh Weir. *A Tribal Order: Politics and Law in the Mountains of Yemen* (Austin: University of Texas Press, 2007).

Yergam See YERGAN.

Yergan (Yergam)

The Yergan are a BANTU people who live in central Nigeria's Plateau State.

Yerwa See KANURI.

Yimbe See LIMBA.

Yolof See WOLOF.

Yombe

The Yombe are a subgroup of the KONGO. Their homelands are the Yombe Mountain region of the Republic of the Congo.

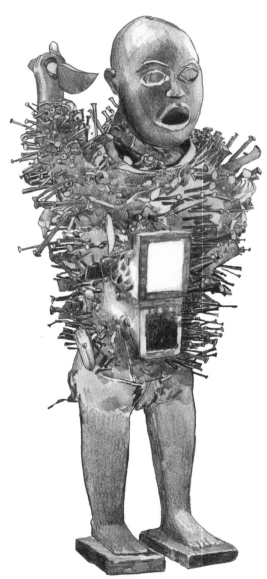

A Yombe *nkisi nkondi,* or "power figure" sculpture embedded with nails and a mirror

Yoruba

The Yoruba mainly live in the southwest of Nigeria, in eastern Benin, and in parts of Togo.

ORIGINS

Through their myths, the Yoruba believe that they have lived in their present homeland for thousands of years. The kingdom of Ife is accepted as the birthplace of the Yoruba as a separate people. The town of Ife is considered to be the Yoruba spiritual capital, perhaps having emerged in the seventh or eighth century. The Yoruba's traditional ruling families are able to trace their ancestors back to the 12th century.

LANGUAGE

In the past, the Yoruba spoke a number of dialects of Kwa, a branch of the Niger-Congo family of languages. Over the past hundred years, however, a common version of their language has developed called Yoruba. There is a rich heritage of literature and poetry written in Yoruba; the playwright Duro Lapido is one example of a well-known writer in the Yoruba language.

HISTORY

From Ife, new Yoruba kingdoms were later established, the most powerful being Oyo in the grasslands to the north. Oyo grew into a great empire, controlling the trade routes linking the sea with the north. In the 18th century, the Oyo Empire was torn apart by civil war, collapsing completely in the 1830s. After the demise of Oyo, Ibadan became the most powerful Yoruba town, eventually controlling a large empire. European slave traders benefited from Yoruba divisions, with rival kings capturing and selling large numbers of their enemies into slavery for transportation to the Americas. Even today clear elements of Yoruba culture survive in the Americas, in particular in Brazil.

As the 19th century progressed, more and more British traders, missionaries, soldiers, and government officials entered Yoruba territory, making agreements with local kings or forcefully stripping power from those who resisted, often destroying and looting their towns. By 1897, the British had established control over the Yoruba and the region was incorporated into the protectorate of Southern Nigeria in 1900. The Yoruba played an important role in Nigeria's gaining independence in 1960; since then they have continued to be of major importance in political life. (*See also* NIGERIANS: NATIONALITY.)

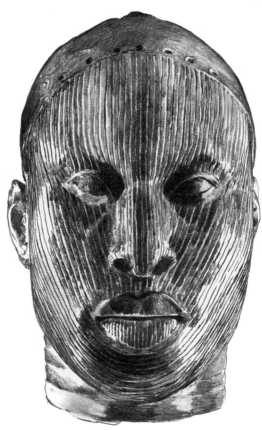

A bronze head created by a Yoruba sculptor in the 13th or 14th century

YORUBA

location:
Nigeria, Benin, and Togo

time period:
Seventh century C.E. to present

ancestry:
Bantu

language:
Bantu (Niger-Congo)

CULTURE

Although an agricultural people, the Yoruba have always lived in towns—Ibadan was the largest city south of the Sahara in precolonial Africa. In a typical Yoruba town the majority are farmers but a few are artisans or traders. Farms can be up to 20 miles from town and produce a wide range of crops including yams, cassava, and cocoa.

Historically, Yoruba towns were enclosed by a high wall with the palace of the *oba* (king) marking the central point. In front of the palace was the central market, and around the palace were grouped the interconnecting courtyards, houses, and rooms that formed the compounds where other families lived. The compounds could be huge, often housing more than a thousand people. In modern times, compounds have largely been replaced by two-story houses, and many *oba* have built luxurious palaces.

Government and Society

The position of *oba* is held by a descendant of the town's founder, passing in turn to princes from several ruling houses. Decision-mak-

Yoruba time line

C.E.

600s Emergence of Ife Kingdom

1300s Bronze and terra-cotta sculpture produced in Ife. Oyo state founded.

1510 Start of Atlantic slave trade

1789 Oyo Empire reaches greatest extent.

1836 Oyo dominated by Sokoto Caliphate: Oyo dissolves.

1862 Ibadan Empire established in Nigeria and becomes most powerful in region.

1897 British conquest of Yorubaland completed.

1950s Discovery of petroleum deposits in Nigeria

1960 Nigeria wins independence.

1967–70 Biafran (Nigerian Civil) War between Yoruba and northern Nigerians against eastern (mainly Igbo) secessionists.

1993 Yoruba politician Moshood Abiola wins presidential election but is subsequently jailed by the military government and dies in prison.

1997 Oodua Peoples Congress (OPC) formed; a Yoruba group attempting to establish an independent Yoruba nation.

1999 Oodua Liberation Movement (OLM), a radical wing of the OPC, is formed.

2000–09 Ethnic violence between Yoruba and Hausa in Nigerian cities.

See also NIGERIANS: NATIONALITY

ing powers, however, were held by a council of chiefs made up of representatives of the town's families. Chiefs would meet every day in a palace courtyard, sending their decisions to the *oba* for formal approval. This form of government made it possible to unite the people of each town. This system, however, meant that it was extremely difficult to unite with neighboring towns, making resistance to colonial rule more difficult.

Religion

Today, over half of the Yoruba are Muslim or Christian. Even so, the Yoruba religion remains important to Yoruba life and culture, although some of the purest forms are found not in Nigeria but among the descendants of former Yoruba slaves living in Brazil. Yoruba religion centers on a supreme god, Olodumare (the owner of Heaven), but few temples or shrines are erected in his honor. This is because he is considered detached from everyday life, so lesser deities are more likely to be approached to deal with specific situations. These deities or spirits can act as intermediaries between Olodumare and his followers; called *orisa*, they concern themselves with the affairs of the earth. Each *orisa* has its own cult, priests, temples, and shrines. *Orisa* have two roles, to protect and provide for the individual cult member and to provide a particular service to all members of the community.

There are hundreds of *orisa*, some considered more important than others. Obatala, as the chief representative of Olodumare on earth, is the most important of the *orisa*. Obatala was taught to create the human form into which Olodumare then put life. Esu is the messenger of good and evil and the main link between heaven and earth. Esu, often described as the "trickster god," tells Olodumare of the activities of the other *orisa* and of people. Sango is associated with thunderstorms and the anger of Olodumare. Yemoja is a female *orisa*, associated with water, rivers, lakes, and streams. Olokun is an *orisa* who lives in the sea, controlling its anger and sharing its riches. Over time, *orisas* can acquire new associations. For example, Ogun, the god associated with iron and other metals and metalwork, is often shown respect by taxi drivers, who have singled him out for to provide protection while they drive their vehicles—as cars are made from metal.

Respect for ancestors forms a major part of the Yoruba religion. Dances and dramas are performed to praise the dead and promote the wellbeing of the community.

FURTHER READING

Toyin Falola and Ann Genova. *The Yoruba in Transition: History, Values, and Modernity* (Durham, N.C.: Carolina Academic Press, 2006).

Toyin Falola and Ann Genova. *Yorubá Identity and Power Politics* (Rochester, N.Y.: University of Rochester Press, 2006).

Nike Lawal, Matthew N. O. Sadiku, and Ade Dopamu. *Understanding Yoruba Life and Culture* (Trenton, N.J.: Africa World Press, 2004).

Kola Abimbola. *Yoruba Culture: A Philosophical Account* (Birmingham, U.K.: Iroko Academic Publishers, 2006).

Zaghawa

The Zaghawa are the largest subgroup of the Beri. They live in Chad and Sudan.

Zambians: nationality (people of Zambia)

GEOGRAPHY

The Republic of Zambia is a landlocked country in south-central Africa. It has an area of approximately 290,600 square miles and is bordered by nine other nations: The Democratic Republic of the Congo lies to the north; Angola to the west; Namibia, Botswana, and Zimbabwe to the south; Mozambique and Malawi to the east; and Tanzania to the northeast. There are five large lakes within Zambia or on its borders. Zambia's borders with Tanzania and the Democratic Republic of the Congo cross the southern portion of Lake Tanganyika in the northeast corner of the country, and the border with the Democratic Republic of the Congo also bisects Lake Mweru. In the south, Zambia's border with Zimbabwe passes through Lake Kariba, one of the world's largest artificial lakes. The two lakes entirely within Zambia's territory are Lake Bangwelu in the north central region and Lake Mweru Wantipa, which lies very close to Lake Mweru in the north.

The southern portion of Zambia lies within the drainage basin of the Zambezi River. The source of the Zambezi, Africa's fourth longest river, is located in the northern highlands of Zambia. From there the river flows south and then turns east toward the Indian Ocean, forming the boundary between Zambia and Namibia and Zambia and Zimbabwe before continuing into Mozambique. Before reaching Lake Kariba, the Zambezi drops into a series of slotlike gorges, forming the Victoria Falls (also known as Mosi oa Tunya), Africa's greatest waterfall. The north of Zambia lies within the drainage basin of the Congo River. The two primary tributaries of the Congo, the Lualaba River and the Chambeshi River, both rise in Zambia.

Topographically the bulk of Zambian territory consists of an elevated plateau with an altitude of 3,000 to 4,500 feet. Highlands are found in the northeast and northwest of the country, the latter forming part of the Muchinga Mountains with elevations in excess of 5,900 feet.

There are two centers of population concentration in Zambia. The capital and largest city, Lusaka, is situated on the southern part of the central plateau close to the border with Zimbabwe. Lusaka is one of Africa's fastest growing cities and was formerly the seat of the British colonial administration of Northern Rhodesia. The second concentration is in the Copperbelt Province of north central Zimbabwe, so called because of the area's rich deposits of copper ore and the mining and smelting industries that grew up around them. The largest cities in the copper belt are Ndole, Kitwe, and Chingola. Up to 45 percent of the population of Zambia live in urban areas, making it one of Africa's most urbanized countries.

ZAMBIANS: NATIONALITY

nation:
Zambia; Republic of Zambia

derivation of name:
From the Zambezi River

government:
Republic

capital:
Lusaka

language:
The country's official language is English. There are about 75 indigenous languages, the most widely spoken of which are Bemba, Kaonda, Lozi, Lunda, Luvale, Nyanja, and Tonga.

religion:
Between 50 and 75 percent of the population are Christian; between 25 and 50 percent are Muslim or Hindu.

earlier inhabitants:
San peoples

(continued)

(continues)

demographics:
The Bemba people make up 37 of the population. Other large groups include the Tonga (19 percent), Lunda (12 percent), Nyanja (11 percent), Mambwe (8 percent), and Lozi (7 percent). There are about 70 other smaller ethnic groups.

INCEPTION AS A NATION

BANTU peoples are believed to have migrated into the area of present-day Zambia in the fourth of fifth century C.E. They brought knowledge of metalworking and agriculture and gradually marginalized the earlier SAN peoples who had inhabited the region. By the beginning of the 19th century three kingdoms had emerged. The BEMBA people controlled the highlands of northeastern Zambia, the LUNDA Kingdom extended from the Congo Basin (in the present-day Democratic Republic of the Congo) into northwest Zambia, and the LOZI people were dominant in the southwest. In the mid-19th century the NGONI people, displaced by the widespread wars and migrations in southern Africa known as the *Mfecane,* moved north across the Zambezi River into present-day southern Zambia. Resistance from the established Lunda Kingdom stemmed their continued northward migration, however. In the same era more northerly peoples who were involved in the long-distance overland trade routes that terminated in the Arab settlements on the Indian Ocean coast also began to penetrate this remote and isolated part of the continent.

European explorers seeking the sources of Africa's great rivers also arrived in present-day Zambia in the mid-19th century. The British explorer David Livingston is the first European known to have visited the great waterfalls on the Zambezi River, one of which he named Victorian Falls. The city of Livingstone near the falls is named for him. Christian missionaries, primarily from Britain and France, followed soon after the first explorers. In the 1890s the British South Africa Company (BSAC), which had been granted a charter by the British government to develop British trade interests in south-central Africa, unilaterally extended its remit north of the Zambezi River to take in the territory of modern-day Zambia. The BSAC, although technically a commercial organization, established itself as the de facto government of the territories in which it operated. It employed a police force and routinely resorted to armed violence when indigenous peoples attempted to resist its seizure of lands.

In 1923 the British government took direct control of BSAC territories, administering the area north of the Zambezi as the protectorate of Northern Rhodesia (Southern Rhodesia to the south of the Zambezi later became the modern nation of Zimbabwe). Large deposits of copper ore were discovered in the north central part of Northern Rhodesia in the 1930s, and the pro-

tectorate quickly attracted significant investment in industry and infrastructure as a result. European settlement in the area also increased dramatically. Self-government was granted in the 1920s in the form of an elected Legislative Assembly, but white settlers were the only section of society entitled to stand for election or to vote.

Plans to unite the two Rhodesias had been made in the late 1930s but they were interrupted by World War II. They came to fruition in 1953 when Northern Rhodesia (present-day Zambia), Southern Rhodesian (present-day Zimbabwe), and Nyasaland (present-day Malawi) were united to form the Central African Federation (also known as the Federation of Rhodesia and Nyasaland). The unification was strongly opposed by the indigenous inhabitants of all three territories and was one of the chief motivating factors for the independence movement that grew rapidly across the region in the early 1950s. The Central African Federation was dominated by Southern Rhodesia, which had the largest and most established white population of the three territories. There were strong objections in Northern Rhodesia both to the dominance of a white-minority government and to the extent that the wealth generated by Northern Rhodesia's mining industry was being used disproportionately to develop Southern Rhodesia.

In 1962 the adoption of a new constitution for Northern Rhodesia was followed by elections that brought a black African majority to the Legislative Council for the first time. The Central African Federation was dissolved at the end of 1963, and in October of 1964 Northern Rhodesia became independent as Zambia. Kenneth Kaunda, the leader of the United National Independence Party (UNIP), was the country's first president.

CULTURAL IDENTITY

The dissolution of the Central African Federation marked the end of Southern Rhodesia's virtual hegemony over Zambia, but it did not end the contentious relationship between the two newly separated countries. Kaunda's government actively supported rebel groups in Rhodesia that were fighting to overthrow the white majority government there. The border between Zambia and Rhodesia was closed from 1973 until 1978 in retaliation for Rhodesian raids into Zambian territory that sought to target rebel bases. Kuanda also supported groups opposing colonial rule in neighboring Angola and Namibia and gave sanctuary to anti-apartheid activists from South Africa.

Kuanda held power in Zambia for 27 years, winning presidential elections in 1969, 1973, 1978, and 1983. His election in 1969 was unopposed, but shortly thereafter a one-party system was introduced with all political parties other than the United National Independence Party (UNIP) being outlawed in 1972. Kuanda's regime pursued socialist policies similar to those adopted in other postindependence African nations, notably in Tanzania under President Nyerere (see TANZANIANS: NATIONALITY). Collectively, these similar socialist systems are known as African Socialism because they took a form unique to the African continent and were closely connected to an ideology of erasing the economic and social conditions imposed under colonialism. In the 1960s and 1970s many of Zambia's industries were nationalized, including its critically important mining industry. Private land was also nationalized as part of a centrally planned agricultural improvement program that had mixed results. In the 1980s a dramatic fall in the world market price for copper had a devastating impact on Zambia's economy. A country that had been one of the richest in Africa at independence swiftly became one of the poorest. Government mismanagement, corruption, and the general failure of the agricultural improvement program contributed to the worsening situation. Strong political opposition to Kuanda began to develop as miners lost their jobs and food prices soared.

There were a series of coup attempts against Kuanda in the early 1980s, and in 1986 mass public protests broke out over the removal of subsidies on staple foods. The economic situation worsened as the 1980s progressed, and by 1990 opposition groups had come together to form the Movement for Multiparty Democracy (MMD). Food riots in Lusaka and another coup attempt finally persuaded Kuanda to open negotiations with the MMD the same year. A new constitution allowing for multiparty elections was adopted in 1991, and in the first openly contested presidential elections Kuanda was defeated by the MMD leader Frederick Chiluba.

Chiluba's attempts to revitalize the economy in accordance with International Monetary Fund guidelines were unpopular, particularly his plans to privatize the mining industry, which drew opposition from the country's powerful trade unions. His regime also became corrupt and autocratic. International observers cited serious irregularities in the 1996 elections that returned Chiluba to power, and although his attempt to amend the constitution to allow him to run for a third term were defeated in parliament, the MMD hung on to power when Chiluba's nominated successor, Levy Mwanawasa, was elected in a 2001 poll that was also widely denounced as fraudulent. Since 2001 Zambia's political arena has remained turbulent. Corruption charges have been brought against former president Chiluba and other high-ranking officials, but economic reforms are slowly improving the state of Zambia's industries.

The more than 70 ethnic groups that make up Zambia's population have a history of relatively harmonious coexistence, and there have been no significant instances of interethnic conflict since independence. Although most

---

Zambians: nationality time line

C.E.

1851 British explorer David Livingstone visits the Zambezi River.

1890s British South Africa Company (BSAC) establishes control over Northern Rhodesia (modern Zambia).

1923 British government annexes BSAC territory of Northern Rhodesia.

1953 Northern Rhodesia (present-day Zambia), Southern Rhodesian (present-day Zimbabwe), and Nyasaland (present-day Malawi) are united to form the Central African Federation.

1960 United National Independence Party (UNIP) founded by Kenneth Kaunda.

1963 Central African Federation dissolved.

1964 Northern Rhodesia becomes independent as the Republic of Zambia with Kaunda as president.

1972 UNIP becomes the only legal party.

1975 Tan-Zam railway opened linking Zambia's copper belt with the Tanzanian port of Dar es Salaam.

1991 Zambia adopts a new constitution allowing for multiparty elections. The Movement for Multiparty Democracy (MMD) wins elections and Frederick Chiluba becomes president.

1996 Chiluba wins a second presidential term.

1997 Unsuccessful coup attempt

2000 Up to 60,000 displaced persons cross the border into Zambia fleeing fighting in the Democratic Republic of the Congo.

2002 Levy Mwanawasa of the MMD elected president.

2003 Former president Chiluba charged with corruption.

2006 Mwanawasa elected to a second presidential term.

2007 China makes large investments in Zambia's copper belt.

Zambians identify with their ethnic group first and their nation second, there is a relatively strongly developed sense of Zambian identity. This can be attributed to several factors. Zambian independence came about as a result of opposition to the British-imposed federation of Northern Rhodesia (Zambia) and Southern Rhodesia (Zimbabwe). This gave Zambians a strong sense of unity, and the subsequent struggle against the white minority government of Zimbabwe enhanced this feeling of unity. A second factor is Zambia's mineral wealth and the mining industry that has grown up around it. Since the 1930s Zambia has been one of the world's largest producers of copper, and Zambians are proud of the status this gives their country in international markets. Although the profitability of the copper industry dipped in the 1980s, it has seen strong growth since the 1990s. Miners and miners' trade unions have played a central part in the country's politics. Significant urbanization, a factor related to the mining industry, has also helped to form a cohesive Zambian identity. In urban areas members of different groups tend to socialize and intermarry, strengthening common feeling.

FURTHER READING

Jan-Bart Gewald, Marja Hinfelaar, and Giacomo Macola. *One Zambia, Many Histories: Towards a History of Post-Colonial Zambia* Afrika-Studiecentrum series, v. 12 (Leiden: Brill, 2008).

William Grant. *Zambia: Then and Now* (London: Kegan Paul, 2008).

Chet S. Lancaster, Kenneth Powers Vickery, and Elizabeth Colson. *The Tonga-Speaking Peoples of Zambia and Zimbabwe: Essays in Honor of Elizabeth Colson* (Lanham, MD: University Press of America, 2007).

David John Simon, Jim Pletcher, Brian V. Siegel, and John J. Grotpeter. *Historical Dictionary of Zambia* (Lanham, Md: Scarecrow Press, 2008).

Arun Kumar Talwar. *Population Settlement and Development* (New Delhi: Commonwealth Publishers, 2008).

Zande See AZANDE.

Zaramo

The Zaramo occupy a 100-mile-wide strip of the Tanzanian coastline centered on Tanzania's biggest city, Dar es Salaam. This strip extends from Kisiju, roughly 50 miles south of Dar es Salaam, to Bagamoyo, roughly 50 miles north of Dar es Salaam. The Zaramo language is called Kizaramo, but most also speak SWAHILI, East Africa's common language.

More than 200 years ago, the Zaramo migrated into their present lands. They share a common ancestry with the LUGURU of the Uluguru Mountains about 125 miles west of Dar es Salaam. The name Luguru simply means "people of the mountains," and when these people migrated eastward, they developed into new ethnic groups. Kizarama and the Luguru language have only slight differences.

Today, the majority of Zaramo are Muslims, but as recently as 100 years ago they were worshipping a god called Kolelo. The Zaramo traveled west to pray to Kolelo at a cave in the Uluguru Mountains.

Zarma See ZERMA.

Zaydis (Fivers; Zaidis; Zaidiya; Zaydiyya)

Zaydis are a branch of Shii Muslims who take their name from Zayd, whom they consider the Fourth Imam, or spiritual leader. They are represented most notably in modern-day Yemen, where they established themselves in the 10th century C.E. (*see* YEMENIS: NATIONALITY). While Sunnis make up the majority of the population of Yemen (about 58 percent in 2005), the rest of the population of more than 22 million are Shia, most of them Zaydis. The town of Saada, about 150 miles north of Yemen's capital, Sanaa, is the spiritual center of the Zaydis. Another Zaydi community took root at about the same time in the Caspian Sea area, but it survived only until about the 16th century, when those remaining Zaydis converted to Twelver, or Imami, Shia (*see* TWELVERS).

Zaydis trace their history back to an unsuccessful revolt that took place in the city of Kufa, in modern-day Iraq, in 740 C.E. The Shia, whose name comes from the Arabic phrase Shiat Ali, "the party of Ali," believed that Ali, the cousin and son-in-law of the prophet Muhammad, should have succeeded Muhammad as spiritual and political leader of the Muslims. Instead, though, other Muslim leaders were chosen, and Ali was named caliph, or "successor," only after three others, all of whom were close associates of the prophet, had preceded him. When Ali became caliph, war broke out, and in 661 Ali was killed. The Umayyad dynasty was established, but the partisans of Ali pressed the claim of Ali's son Husayn to the caliphate. But he and his family were slaughtered by Umayyad forces in 680 at Karbala, Iraq.

The Shia did not abandon their claim that Ali's descendants were the proper heirs to the caliphate, and in 740 Zayd ibn Ali ibn al-Husayn (Ali's great-grandson), from whom the Zaydis take their name, prepared to lead a revolt against the Umayyads. But he was not radical enough for some Shia, who withdrew their support from him because he refused to condemn the caliphs who had preceded Ali. Those who withdrew became the Imami Shia, or Twelvers, while those who remained with Zayd became the Zaydis. Zayd was killed in battle. This schism is seen as separating the Shia into the more radical Imamis and the more moderate Zaydis, who are closer in their beliefs to Sunnis, and this distinction persists today. The Zaydis, then, believe that the line of Imams is Ali, his two sons, Hasan and Husayn, Sajjad (the son of Husayn, who survived the massacre at Karbala), and Zayd, the Fifth Imam. Zaydis, in contrast to Twelvers, believe that after the Five Imams, the imam can be any pious, learned adult male and that the imamate is not hereditary. They reject the Twelver belief in the Hidden Imam who will return at the end of time to initiate a reign of divine justice.

Zemarites

The Zemarites were an ancient Hamite tribe who claimed descent from the patriarch Canaan, and lived in the area of modern-day Lebanon and Syria (see CANAANITES). They are mentioned in the Old Testament of the Bible, in Genesis 10:18 and I Chronicles 1:16. The city of Zemar, or Zumur, was also mentioned in the Amarna tablets, chronicles found in Egypt dating from about 1350 B.C.E. In that record, Zemar is named as one of the most important Phoenician cities (see PHOENICIANS). After that time, though, the city seems to have disappeared from the historical record. It is, however, identified with the modern-day town of Sumra, on the coast of Lebanon, north of the city of Tripoli.

Zerma (Djerma; Zarma)

After the HAUSA, the Zerma are the largest ethnic group in Niger. They are closely related to the SONGHAY people of Niger and Mali, and the two groups speak different dialects of the Songhay language. Although Songhay has been classified as a Nilo-Saharan language, it is not obviously related to any other known language. Together the Zerma and Songhay account for around 20 percent of Niger's population.

The Zerma are spread across a region in western Niger that is bordered by the Niger River in the east and extends west to a seasonally dry river, the Dallol Maouri, in the east. Many Zerma can be found living in the large towns of western Niger such as the capital, Niamey. The Zerma are thought to have originated from the swampy inland delta of the Niger River, near Lake Debo in modern-day Mali. They were part of western Songhay—the medieval empire founded by the Songhay people in about 750 C.E. on the Niger River, an important trade route. The Zerma began migrating southward in the 15th century, reaching their present lands in the 17th and 18th centuries.

Zezuru

The Zezuru are a SHONA subgroup. They make up a quarter of the Shona population in Zimbabwe. The Zezuru speak the Zezuru, Karanga, Manyika, Ndau, or Korekore dialects of the Shona language.

Zhu *See* KUNG.

Zhutwasi *See* KUNG.

Ziba *See* HAYA.

Zigalu

The Zigalu are part of the ZARAMO. They are a BANTU people living principally in Tanzania's coastal lowlands.

Zimbabweans: nationality (people of Zimbabwe)

GEOGRAPHY

The Republic of Zimbabwe is a landlocked country in south-central Africa. It has an area of approximately 150,800 square miles and is bordered by four other nations: Zambia lies to the northwest, Botswana to the southwest, South Africa to the south, and Mozambique to the east and northeast. Zimbabwe's border with Zambia in the northwest follows the course of the Zambezi River and bisects Lake Kariba, one of the largest artificial lakes in the world. The Victorian Falls (also known as Mosi-oa-Tunya),

---

ZIMBABWEANS: NATIONALITY

nation:
Zimbabwe; Republic of Zimbabwe

derivation of name:
From the ancient city of Zimbabwe

government:
Parliamentary democracy

capital:
Harare

language:
The country's official language is English, but English is the first language of only about 2 percent of the population. Shona and Sindbele (the languages of the Shona and Ndebele people respectively) are widely spoken.

religion:
About 50 percent of the population follows a syncretic faith combining elements of Christianity and indigenous beliefs. About 25 percent are Christian, 24 percent follow indigenous faiths, and the remaining 1 percent are Muslim.

earlier inhabitants:
San peoples

demographics:
The Shona peoples make up 82 percent of the population; the Ndebele 14 percent; other African peoples about 2 percent; and people of European, Asian, or mixed European and African or European and Asian ancestry the remaining 2 percent.

Zimbabweans: nationality time line

C.E.

third–fourth centuries Bantu-speaking peoples migrate into present-day Zimbabwe.

11th–15th centuries Height of the Monomotapa Kingdom associated with the city of Zimbabwe

1830s Ndebele people migrate northward and settle in present-day Matebeleland, displacing Shona peoples northward.

1850s British explorer David Livingstone travels along the Zambezi River.

1889 The British South Africa Company (BSAC) receives permission from the British government to colonize Zimbabwe.

1890 White settlers establish city of Salisbury (present-day Harare).

1893 Ndebele uprising defeated by BSAC troops.

1923 British government takes control of all BSAC territories.

1930 Land Apportionment Act gives white settlers control of the majority of Southern Rhodesia's (present-day Zimbabwe) arable land.

1953 Northern Rhodesia (present-day Zambia), Southern Rhodesian (present-day Zimbabwe), and Nyasaland (present-day Malawi) are united to form the Central African Federation.

1963 Central African Federation dissolved.

1964 Northern Rhodesia becomes independent as the Republic of Zambia. Ian Smith of the Rhodesian Front becomes prime minister of Southern Rhodesia.

1965 Smith unilaterally declares independence from Britain under a white minority government. Rhodesian independence and Smith's government are not internationally recognized.

1970s African nationalist groups, the Zimbabwe African People's Union (ZAPU) and the Zimbabwe African National Union (ZANU), conduct a guerrilla war against Smith's government.

1978 Transitional government led by Bishop Abel Muzorewa established. Country renamed Zimbabwe Rhodesia but not internationally recognized.

1979 Government and opposition groups agree to a new constitution and a cease-fire.

1980 Zimbabwe becomes independent. Canaan Banana is the country's first president. ZANU party wins the country's first elections and its leader, Robert Mugabe, becomes prime minister.

1982 ZAPU leader Joshua Nkome is expelled from Mugabe's cabinet.

1983–84 Government forces massacre ZAPU supporters following rebellions in Matebeleland.

1987 ZAPU and ZANU merge to form the ZANU Patriotic Front (ZANU-PF).

1998–2002 Zimbabwean troops involved in civil war in the Democratic Republic of the Congo.

1999 Movement for Democratic Change (MDC) opposition alliance formed.

2000 MDC makes significant gains in parliamentary elections. "War veterans" begin occupying white-owned farms.

2002 Mugabe reelected in presidential elections described as flawed by international observers.

2003 General strike followed by mass arrests of opposition supporters

2005 Government begins clearance of shantytowns. Up to 700,000 people are made homeless.

2008 Mugabe wins a sixth presidential term after opposition leader Morgan Tsvangirai withdraws.

2009 Morgan Tsvangirai becomes prime minister as part of a power sharing agreement.

Africa's greatest waterfall, are on the Zambezi River and lie partly within Zimbabwean territory and partly within the territory of neighboring Zambia. Zimbabwe's southern border with South Africa is defined by the course of the Limpopo River.

Topographically Zimbabwe consists of an elevated central plateau with low-lying regions in the north and the southeast. A central highland spine crosses the central plateau from the northeast corner to the southwest corner. Rivers north of this central spine, including the Shangani River, the Sanyati River, and the Hunyani River, flow generally northwest. Rivers to the south of the central highlands, including the Save River, the Lundi River, and the Mwenezi River, flow generally southeast toward Mozambique and the Indian Ocean. The Eastern Highlands (also known as the East African Highlands) run from north to south along the eastern margin of Zimbabwe, defining much of the country's border with Mozambique. Zimbabwe's highest point, the 8,500-foot peak of Mount Nyangani, is situated in the Eastern Highlands.

A relatively high proportion of Zimbabwe's population, about 40 percent, lives in towns and cities. The largest city, Harare (formerly known as Salisbury), is also the capital and the country's industrial center. It is situated in the north-central part of the country. Other large cities include Bulawayo in the southwest; Chitungwiza, a densely populated dormitory town close to Harare; and Gweru in the geographical center of the county.

INCEPTION AS A NATION

BANTU-speaking peoples are believed to have migrated into the territory of present-day Zimbabwe in the third or fourth century C.E., displacing or assimilating the KHOISAN peoples who had previously lived there. Among these immigrants were the ancestors of the modern SHONA people, who make up about 80 percent of the present-day population of Zimbabwe. From the 11th to the 15th centuries a powerful and wealthy civilization with its capital at a great stone city known as Zimbabwe became established. The modern nation of Zimbabwe takes its name from this ancient city, which was abandoned and ruined when Portuguese explorers first visited the site early in the 16th century. Archaeological evidence shows that the inhabitants of this city participated in trade routes that stretched as far as the Arabian Peninsula and China, probably through Arab traders who had settled on the Indian Ocean coast.

In the late 1830s the dominance of the Shona people was challenged by the arrival of the NDEBELE, who began to migrate into present-day Zimbabwe from south of the Limpopo River. The Ndebele established themselves in the west and southwest, forcing the Shona to concentrate in the north. The British began arriving in Zimbabwe in the 1860s following the explorations carried out by David Livingstone along the Zambezi River in the 1850s. Christian missionaries were soon followed by those with commercial interests as reports of the mineral wealth of the region became known. The area attracted the attention of Cecil Rhodes, who had previously become wealthy from diamond mining in South Africa, and who wanted to open the region to commercial exploitation by Britain. In 1888 the king of the Ndebele agreed to a treaty with Britain and granted exclusive mineral rights in his kingdom to an agent of Rhodes. The area that the Ndebele inhabited became known to the British as Matabeleland. In 1889 Rhodes's British South Africa Company (BSAC) obtained a charter from the British government to secure mineral rights in Mashonaland (the area inhabited by the Shona) as well. From 1893 to 1897 the heavily armed "police" of the BSAC stifled opposition from the Ndebele and the Shona and established themselves as the de facto government of the area. Tens of thousands of Shona and Ndebele were killed in these actions. From 1895 the area controlled by the BSAC was commonly referred to as Rhodesia in honor of Cecil Rhodes. Lands to the north of the Zambezi were known as Northern Rhodesia (present-day Zambia) and lands to the south as Southern Rhodesia (present-day Zimbabwe).

As well as mineral wealth, Southern Rhodesia offered excellent farmland, and British settlement was rapid and extensive under the BSAC. Disputes between settlers and the BSAC, however, eventually led to the British government assuming direct control of all BSAC territory in 1923. Southern Rhodesia was granted limited self-rule soon after its annexation by the British crown, although only white settlers were permitted to vote for representatives in the Legislative Assembly. In 1930 Southern Rhodesia adopted a land apportionment act that was accepted by the British government. Under this measure, about half of the country's land, including all the mining and industrial regions and all the areas served by railroads or roads, was reserved for Europeans. Most of the rest was designated as Tribal Trust Land, native purchase land, or unassigned land. Later acts firmly entrenched the policy of dividing land on a racial basis. This act was to prove a source of great political turmoil in the decades to come.

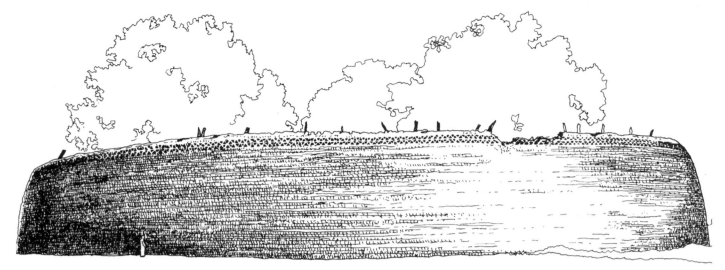

Part of the stone walls of Great Zimbabwe

In 1953 Northern Rhodesian, Southern Rhodesian, and Nyasaland (present-day Malawi) were united to form the Central African Federation (also known as the Federation of Rhodesia and Nyasaland). Although each territory retained its own constitution, the inhabitants of Northern Rhodesia and Nyasaland strongly opposed the federation because it inevitably resulted in political and economic dominance from the white-minority government in Harare. The Central African Federation was dissolved in 1963, and Northern Rhodesia and Nyasaland quickly became independent thereafter. The government of Southern Rhodesia, made up of white settlers, also demanded independence, and African nationalists groups demanded independence but with the condition that the constitution be amended to facilitate African majority rule. In November 1965 Rhodesia's prime minster Ian Smith declared unilateral independence from the United Kingdom.

Britain did not recognize Rhodesia's declaration of independence but took no action to reassert its control. The country's predominantly white electorate voted to establish Rhodesia as a republic in 1969, a decision that prompted the United Nations Security Council to call on its members to refuse to recognize any acts by the regime. Following a decade of conflict between the white majority government and black African groups demanding the establishment of true democracy, Rhodesia's period of racial segregation came to an end in 1980 with the country's first multiparty elections under full adult suffrage. A new constitution was adopted, and Rhodesia became the internationally recognized independent state of Zimbabwe in April 1980.

CULTURAL IDENTITY

The 15-year period between Rhodesia's unilateral declaration of independence under a white minority government in 1965 and the establishment of the modern state of Zimbabwe in 1980 constituted an interregnum during which the country's cultural development was arrested in a climate of political instability. During this period the principal opposition groups were the African National Congress (ANC), which was also active in white-ruled South Africa, the Zimbabwe African People's Union (ZAPU), and the Zimbabwe African National Union (ZANU). By the late 1970s ZAPU and ZANU formed an alliance known as the Patriotic Front. ZANU, led by Robert Mugabe, drew its support from the Shona majority, while ZAPU, led by Joshua Nkome, had its roots in the Ndebele community. Zimbabwe's first democratically elected government in 1980 was a coalition led by Mugabe as prime minister and included Nkome. Conflict between the political representatives of the country's two major ethnic groups soon emerged. In 1982 Mugabe ejected Nkome from the cabinet, citing evidence of an alleged coup attempt by ZAPU, and ZAPU supporters began carrying out guerrilla attacks against government forces in Matebeleland (the Ndebele homeland) from this date. The government's military response to these activities was brutal and resulted in a series of massacres in Matabeleland. Food supplies to the region were also severely curtailed, resulting in widespread famine. Sporadic fighting continued until 1987, when an effectively defeated ZAPU agreed to merge with ZANU to form a single political party, the ZANU Patriotic Front (known as ZANU-PF). Zimbabwe effectively became a one-party state from this time. In the same year Mugabe altered the country's constitution, making himself president.

Since the land apportionment laws of the 1930s, land redistribution has been a major political issue first in Rhodesia and then in Zimbabwe. Under these laws, white settlers received almost total control over the best agricultural land. In 1979 the white minority government of Rhodesia and the leading opposition parties met in London to agree to terms for the transition to a new constitution, and land reform was the issue that caused the greatest disagreement. ZANU and ZAPU wanted an immediate redistribution of white-owned land among the landless black population, while the former government argued that farmers should not be forced to give up their lands and livelihoods irrespective of whether they were white or black. The two parties reached a compromise in the 1979 Lancaster House Agreement, which established the principle that the new government of Zimbabwe would be entitled to buy land from farmers who were willing to sell but could not seize land from those who were unwilling. This became known as the "willing buyer, willing seller" principle, and the British and U.S. governments agreed to provide funds to Zimbabwe for a decade to help carry it out. When Mugabe's ZANU party came to power, about 70 percent of the nation's arable land was owned by less than 1 percent of the population. Not many of these white farmers were inclined to abandon their homes, so the process of redistribution was slow and also became increasingly corrupt as the years of one-party rule passed. In the decade between 1980 and 1990, only about 70,000 families were resettled.

In 1992 the Zimbabwean government abandoned the "willing buyer, willing seller" principle and adopted powers to compulsorily purchase land for redistribution. Opposition from commercial farmers, both black and white, was intense, but many white farmers also abandoned their land and left the country. Corruption had become endemic by this time, however, and much of the newly available land was gifted to cabinet ministers or government supporters rather than being redistributed to the landless. Even when formerly landless families were given land, they lacked the resources to continue the technologically advanced intensive farming techniques that had been used by the former occupants, so productivity dropped dramatically as a consequence. In 1999 the government drafted a new constitution that included provisions for the seizure of land without compensation. The new constitution also included measures that would have further cemented Mugabe's political power and as such was opposed by the newly formed Movement for Democratic Change (MDC) opposition alliance. When the new constitution was voted down in a 2000 referendum, there was a widespread expectation within Zimbabwe and internationally that this defeat would mark the end of Mugabe's power. Instead Mugabe seized on the land issue as a means of summoning popular support. In the aftermath of the referendum defeat, ZANU-PF organized groups of activists, who were described as veterans of the independence war of the 1970s, although many were too young to have taken part in that conflict, to march onto white-owned farms and occupy the land. Although these seizures began peacefully, incidents of violence against farmers and their families became increasingly common as the movement gathered pace and became uncontrollable. In the parliamentary elections that took place against the backdrop of this turmoil, the MDC made significant gains but ZANU-PF retained its majority. In 2002 Mugabe defeated a challenge for the presidency from MDC leader Morgan Tsvangarai following a campaign in which the so-called "war veterans" were accused of intimidation and violence against opposition supporters.

The negative economic effects of chaotic land redistribution were compounded by Zimbabwe's involvement in the Democratic Republic of the Congo's civil war between 1998 and 2002, which cost the government millions of dollars. The government's failure to address accusations of human rights abuses or to hold free and fair elections led international donors to withdraw their financial support in the early 2000s, worsening the economic situation. The results have been hyperinflation, mass unemployment, mass economic migration into Botswana and South Africa, and a dramatic fall in average life expectancy. In 1998 Zimbabwe's official rate of inflation stood at 32 percent; in 2007 the official figure was 26,000 percent, with unofficial estimates suggesting a true figure of over 100,000 percent. Average life expectancy dropped from over 60 years in the mid-1990s to 37 years for men and 34 years for women in 2006, then the lowest in the world. More than 3 million Zimbabweans, a quarter of the population, were believed to have left the country by mid-2007, most traveling to South Africa in search of better economic conditions. Up to three quarters of a million people are believed to have been internally displaced.

Despite their nation's many economic and political problems, at the beginning of the 21st century Zimbabweans retain a strong sense of national identity. This can be attributed both to the predominance of a single ethnic group, the Shona, who make up about 80 percent of the population, and to the unifying effect of the long struggle to overthrow the white minority government that took place between 1965 and 1980. Zimbabweans are particularly proud of the ancient city of Zimbabwe and its associated settlements, regarding them as evidence of a long history of technologically advanced urban civilization that predates colonial rule. The city itself is a sacred site in the Shona religion, and symbols from the period of its greatest flourishing, such as soapstone statues of the African fish eagle (known as the Zimbabwe bird), are common in Zimbabwean culture. The Zimbabwe bird, for example, features on the Zimbabwean flag.

FURTHER READING

Alexander Charles Laurie. *Every Man Has His Price: The Story of Collusion and Corruption in the Scramble for Rhodesia* (Lanham, Md.: University Press of America, 2008).

Martin Meredith. *Our Votes, Our Guns: Robert Mugabe and the Tragedy of Zimbabwe* (New York: PublicAffairs, 2002).

Oyekan Owomoyela. *Culture and Customs of Zimbabwe* (Westport, Conn: Greenwood Press, 2002).

Michael O. West. *The Rise of an African Middle Class: Colonial Zimbabwe, 1898–1965* (Bloomington: Indiana University Press, 2002).

Zombo

The Zombo are a subgroup of the KONGO. They live in Angola and the Democratic Republic of the Congo.

Zulu

There are about 7 million Zulu, most of whom live in the province of KwaZulu-Natal on the east coast of South Africa. The Zulu emerged from the NGUNI group of BANTU-speaking peoples and have close cultural and linguistic links with other Nguni peoples such as the XHOSA and the SWAZI. The term "Zulu" originally referred to the people descended from a man of the same name, but it came to refer to a much broader population after the Mfecane period of the early 19th century.

ORIGINS

Before 1816 the Zulu chiefdoms belonged to the Mthethwa kingdom, which was ruled by Dingiswayo. When Dingiswayo died, his Zulu general Shaka took over. With military skill and ruthlessness, Shaka founded the Zulu kingdom, precipitating the Mfecane—a series of wars and migrations triggered by the rapid expansion of the Zulu nation. This wave of conflict, which lasted from 1819 to 1839, left an estimated 5 million people dead and made the region vulnerable to takeover by white settlers.

LANGUAGE

The Zulu language is also called Zulu (or isiZulu). Zulu has some 19,000 words and one of the most complex grammars in the world. Many Dutch and English words have been incorporated into Zulu.

HISTORY

After 1836 the Zulu came into conflict with the growing number of white settlers, first the AFRIKANERS, or BOERS, and later the British. In 1879 at Isandhlwana, a massive onslaught of Zulu warriors defeated the British, who retaliated later that year and defeated the 40,000-strong Zulu army led by Cetshwayo at Ulundi.

In the 20th century, the Zulus' lives were dominated by the South African policy of apartheid (the racist doctrine of "separate development"), which discriminated against black people in every area of life. A homeland, consisting of only a portion of the original Zululand, was set up for the Zulu in the 1970s. This homeland, called KwaZulu, was in the region of the modern KwaZulu-Natal province of South Africa. Following the end of apartheid in the early 1990s, the Zulu have become a significant political force through the Inkatha Freedom Party (IFP).

CULTURE

Although many men have left Zululand to work as laborers in South Africa's mines and industries, farming is still the backbone of the Zulu economy. The soil is generally poor and suffers from increasing erosion, but in spite

ZULU

location:
South Africa

time period:
19th century C.E. to present

ancestry:
Bantu

language:
Bantu (Niger-Congo)

of this the Zulu are able to grow crops such as millet, corn, sweet potatoes, and vegetables and to raise cattle, sheep, and goats. Like many other peoples of southern Africa, the Zulu have a long tradition of metalworking and use their skills to manufacture axes, hoes, spears, and other tools and weapons. Their ceramics are all well made, simple, and practical and have few decorative additions. Many Zulu are skilled woodworkers and makers of baskets and beadwork artifacts.

Government and Society

The Zulu have a complex social organization that has survived the pressures of modern life relatively intact. It is based on the *imzi,* or homestead, a group of circular thatched houses (or, increasingly, brick-built houses) enclosed by a fence. A number of *imzi,* spaced at intervals of half a mile to a mile apart, make up a ward, or village. Each *imzi* is occupied by an elder or *imzi* head and his extended family, and the other *imzi* in the ward are usually occupied by related families.

From ward level, the social structure extends upward through district head and clan chief levels to the ultimate head of the Zulu nation, the king. The position of the king is one of solely cultural and social importance, however, as the Zulu are governed by the Republic of South Africa.

A man may have more than one wife, but no marriage is considered legitimate until the husband has given *lobola* (or bride-wealth), usually a gift of cattle, to the bride's family to compensate them for their loss. Marriage between members of the same clan is discouraged.

Religion

Christianity is widespread among the Zulu. There are many independent churches with Zulu clergy as well as Anglican and Catholic churches. Zionist Spirit churches that stress faith healing are also popular. During the apartheid era, people were denied a political voice, and this, in part, explains the vibrancy of many churches as they often provided the only forum for people to air their complaints. Christianity coexists with the Zulu religion, which is still widely followed. The Zulu religion is mostly concerned with the reverence of ancestors. Ancestors are believed to directly influence their living descendants so respect must be shown to them. Healing methods as practiced by religious practitioners of the Zulu religion (diviners, or *sangomas,* for example) also survive, alongside modern clinics and hospitals, and are used to alleviate diseases thought to arise from defective personal relationships or from supernatural causes. Many of these healers work within the official health-care system at the local level.

See also SOUTH AFRICANS: NATIONALITY.

Zulu time line

C.E.

200s Bantu-speaking peoples begin to arrive in Southern Africa.

300s–400s Bantu-speakers reach present-day KwaZulu-Natal.

1787 Birth of Shaka

1816 Shaka becomes Zulu leader.

1818–19 Zulu–Ndwandwe War establishes Zulu supremacy.

1819–39 Mfecane: period of mass migrations and wars

1828 Shaka assassinated; Dingane succeeds him as Zulu leader.

1838 Zulu defeated by Boers at the Battle of Blood River.

1840 After defeating Dingane, Mpande becomes Zulu leader.

1872 Cetshwayo becomes Zulu king.

1879 British conquer Zulu.

1883–84 Zulu Civil War after British partition Zululand.

1885–87 Zululand divided between British Zululand and Transvaal.

1910 White-minority-ruled Union of South Africa created.

1913 Zulu restricted to inadequate native reserves.

1920 Zululand joined to South Africa.

1928 Inkatha, Zulu nationalist movement, founded.

1970s KwaZulu homeland created.

1975 Inkatha reconvened.

1980s–90s Fighting between Inkatha and African National Congress (ANC) supporters.

1991 Apartheid legislation repealed.

1999 ANC wins large majority in South African elections; the Inkatha Freedom Party (IFP) comes in third with 8 percent of the vote.

2004 IFP ends its alliance with ANC and joins the Democratic Alliance, the main opposition party.

FURTHER READING

Benedict Carton, John Laband, and Jabulani Sithole. *Zulu Identities: Being Zulu, Past and Present* (Scottsville, South Africa: University of KwaZulu-Natal Press, 2008).

Jeff Guy. *Remembering the Rebellion: The Zulu Uprising of 1906* (Scottsville, South Africa: University of KwaZulu-Natal Press, 2006).

Dan Wylie. *Myth of Iron: Shaka in History* (Scottsville, South Africa: University of KwaZulu-Natal Press, 2006).

APPENDIX I
LIST OF INDIVIDUALS FEATURED IN BIOGRAPHICAL SIDEBARS, ORGANIZED ALPHABETICALLY

Abdullah ibn al Hussein—Hashemites
Yasir Arafat—Palestinians
Alp Arslan—Seljuks
Mustafa Kemal Atatürk—Turks: nationality
Sultan Barquq—Circassians
David Ben-Gurion—Israelis: nationality
Muammar al-Qaddafi—Libyans: nationality
Haile Selassie—Ethiopians: nationality
Saddam Hussein—Iraqis: nationality
King Hussein I—Jordanians: nationality
Abd al-Aziz Ibn Saud—Saudi Arabians: nationality

Ayatollah Khomeini—Iranians: nationality
Khosrau I—Sassanians
Nelson Mandela—South Africans: nationality
Gamal Abdel Nasser—Egyptians: nationality
Ramasses III—Sea Peoples
Edward Said—Palestinians
Saladin—Kurds
Léopold Sédar Senghor— Senegalese: nationality
Suleyman I—Ottomans
Timur—Turkic Peoples

APPENDIX II
THE GEOGRAPHY OF AFRICA

THE NAME

There are several theories concerning the etymology of the name Africa. The most widely accepted current theory points to the Latin name Afri for an ancient people who lived on the Mediterranean coast in present-day Tunisia who are first recorded in Roman writings from the time of the Punic Wars (264–146 B.C.E.). The Romans referred to the region in which the Afri lived as *Africa terra,* meaning "land of the Afri." Following the Roman victory over the Carthaginians in the Third Punic War (149–46 B.C.E.) they established a colony in the region known as *Africa Proconsularis* (province of Africa). The etymology of the name Afri is unclear.

GEOGRAPHICAL LIMITS

Africa is the Earth's second largest continent, after Asia, with an area of approximately 11.7 million square miles. The limits of the great majority of the continent are clearly delineated by its coastline; it is bounded in the north by the Mediterranean Sea, in the west by the Atlantic Ocean, in the south by the Southern (or Arctic) Ocean, and in the east by the Indian Ocean. Africa's only point of contact with another continent is in the extreme northeast where the Sinai Peninsula forms a land bridge to Asia. Geographers usually include the Sinai Peninsula as part of Africa rather than Asia.

Africa's northernmost point is at Ras ben Sakka, a promontory on the coast of Tunisia, and its southernmost point is Cape Agulhas (or the Cape of Needles) in South Africa; a distance of about 5,000 miles separates these two points. The continent's westernmost point is Cape Verde (or Cap-Vert) on the Senegalese coast, and its easternmost point is Ras Hafun in Somalia; a distance of about 4,600 miles separates these two points. Africa's coastline is approximately 16,100 miles long and is notable for its lack of indentations and promontories compared to the coastlines of other continents.

NATIONS AND AREAS

Africa is the world's second most populous continent, after Asia, with approximately 14 percent of the global population. There are 53 nations on the continent (including island nations such as Madagascar). Geopolitically Africa is commonly considered in five sections: Northern, Western, Central, Eastern, and Southern.

Northern Africa is broadly separated from the rest of the continent by the Sahara Desert and the Atlas Mountains and borders the Mediterranean Sea to the north. The United Nations defines Northern Africa as the territories of Algeria, Egypt, Libya, Morocco, Sudan, Tunisia, and Western Sahara (a disputed territory occupied by Morocco). Historically the western half of Northern Africa (Morocco, Algeria, and Tunisia) has been referred to as the Maghreb, and this term also used today by some historians and geographers.

Western Africa is that part of the continent that forms a large promontory protecting into the Atlantic Ocean north of the Gulf of Guinea. The United Nations defines Western Africa as including the territories of Benin, Burkina Faso, Cape Verde, The Gambia, Ghana, Guinea, Guinea-Bissau, Ivory Coast, Liberia, Mali, Mauritania, Niger, Nigeria, Senegal, Sierra Leone, and Togo.

Central Africa is roughly the area between the Gulf of Guinea in the west and the Great Rift Valley in the east. It is dominated by the drainage basin of the Congo (or Zaire) River, Africa's second greatest river. The United Nations defines Central (or Middle) Africa as including the territories of Angola, Cameroon, Central African Republic, Chad, Democratic Republic of the Congo, Republic of the Congo, Equatorial Guinea, Gabon, and São Tomé and Principe.

Eastern Africa is approximately that area of the continent that lies between the Great Rift Valley in the west and the Indian Ocean in the east. The United Nations includes the territories of 17 nations in its definition of Southern Africa: Burundi, Comoros, Djibouti, Eritrea, Ethiopia, Kenya, Madagascar, Malawi, Mauritius, Mozambique, Rwanda, Seychelles, Somalia, Tanzania, Uganda, Zambia, Zimbabwe (plus the French overseas territories of Réunion and Mayotte). Other authorities exclude Madagascar, Malawi, Mozambique, Zambia, and Zimbabwe, regarding them as part of Southern Africa. The territories of Djibouti, Eritrea, Ethiopia, and Somalia are often referred to collectively as the Horn of Africa.

Southern Africa is often defined as the territory south of the Zambezi River, although the United Nations includes a less extensive area, restricting its definition of Southern Africa to the territories of Botswana, Lesotho, Namibia, South Africa, and Swaziland.

ISLANDS

With the notable exception of Madagascar, the islands that lie close to the African continent are generally small and sparsely inhabited. Madagascar is the world's fourth largest island and lies about 250 miles off the southeast coast of mainland Africa. The Mozambique Channel, which separates Madagascar from the mainland, is the location of the Comoro Islands. The islands that make up the Republic of the Seychelles lie north of Madagascar, and the islands of the Republic of Mauritius lie to the east of Madagascar. Other notable island groups are the Canary Islands and the Cape Verde islands, both of which lie off the continent's northwest coast, and a chain of islands in the Gulf of Guinea that includes São Tomé and Principe.

HIGHLANDS AND LOWLANDS

The African continent is unusual in that it has relatively little very high ground or very low-lying ground compared to the other continents; much of the land area of Africa lies close to the continental average elevation of about 2,000 feet above sea level. Maximum elevations in all areas of Africa are consistently less than maximum elevations in Asia and North and South America. The little land area above 10,000 feet consists almost entirely of a small number of isolated peaks. Aside from the relatively small Atlas and Drakensberg ranges, there are none of the young massively folded regions that constitute the extensive high mountain ranges, such as the Andes, the Rockies, and the Himalayas, on other continents. Most of Africa's highest peaks are volcanic in origin. The continent's highlands are typically composed of elevated plateaus with relatively homogeneous elevations rather than dramatic peaks and valleys.

A major plateau dominates much of the interior of the continent south of Congo Basin. This plateau, which has a mean elevation of about 3,500 feet, is bounded by mountain ranges on its western, southern, and eastern side that form an abrupt drop to the low-lying coastal strip that surrounds it. In the north the land falls away more gradually into the low-lying Congo Basin. Another highland area, known as the East African Plateau or the East African Highlands, extends northward from the northeast corner of the southern plateau. This feature is notable for two great depressions on a north–south axis, which contain some of the continent's largest lakes. The Great Rift Valley extends northward from this highland region toward the Red Sea.

The Great Rift Valley is perhaps the most striking topographical feature of Africa and one of the most striking geological features in the world. Running for approximately 3,700 miles from Syria in the Middle East to Mozambique in East Africa, the Great Rift Valley is a deep but narrow depression in the Earth's crust associated with a string of mountainous

peaks along its edges. The Great Rift Valley splits into two distinct branches in East Africa: the Western Rift Valley and the Eastern Rift Valley. The peaks that lie along the edge of the Western Rift Valley are some of the highest in Africa and include the Virunga, Mitumba, and Ruwenzori ranges. The low-lying floors of the valleys contain some of the world's largest and deepest lakes.

At the northern end of the Great Rift Valley there is a third major upland region known as the Ethiopian Highlands. The Ethiopian Highlands represent the single largest area of upland with altitudes in excess of 5,000 feet on the entire continent. The Atlas Mountains, which extend through Morocco, Algeria, and Tunisia, are isolated from the main upland features of eastern and southern Africa by the low-lying Sahara Desert and the great plains of central Africa.

The three highest peaks on the continent are Mount Kilimanjaro (19,340 feet) in Tanzania, Mount Kenya (17,058 feet) in Kenya, and Mount Stanley (16,763 feet) in the Democratic Republic of the Congo.

A vast low-lying plain, divided into a series of drainage basins, dominates the area between the Eastern Highlands and the Atlas Mountains. There are isolated mountainous outcrops within this plain, notably in the Sahara Desert, but these are few and rarely reach more than 8,000 feet.

RIVERS AND LAKES

A large number of rivers flow the relatively short distance from the mountainous fringes of the southern and eastern plateaus to the sea, but the continent's greatest rivers drain the vast low-lying basins of the central and western plains. The Nile, the longest river in Africa, and the Congo, the second-longest river in Africa, both rise in the mountains of East Africa. The Nile flows north to the Mediterranean while the Congo flows west to the Atlantic. The Niger River, the third-longest river on the continent, follows a highly eccentric course. Rising in the Guinea Highlands, a short distance inland from the Atlantic coast, it flows toward the center of the continent before turning sharply south at the southern margin of the Sahara Desert and continuing to the Gulf of Guinea. Other notable watercourses include the Orange River in Southern Africa and the Zambezi River, which is the fourth-longest river on the continent and the only major African river that empties into the Indian Ocean.

Most of Africa's largest lakes are found in the Great Lakes region of East Africa. These bodies of water are associated with the Great Rift Valley system, many of them having formed in the deep, steep-sided rift valleys. Lake Victoria, Lake Tanganyika, Lake Nyasa, Lake Turkana, Lake Albert, and Lake Kivu are generally included in lists of the Great Lakes. Lake Victoria is Africa's largest lake in terms of area and the second largest lake in the world according to the same criterion. Unlike the other Great Lakes, Lake Victoria is relatively shallow, having a mean depth of about 130 feet, and fills a wide basin located between the Western and Eastern Rift Valleys rather than being located in the valleys themselves. Lake Tanganyika is the second largest lake in the world by volume and the second deepest, having a maximum depth of about 4,800 feet. It is situated in the steep-sided Western Rift Valley. Lake Nyasa, also known as Lake Malawi, is the continent's third largest lake. It is situated in the Eastern Rift Valley and is the most southerly of the Great Lakes of Africa.

Lake Chad is another notable body of water entirely unconnected with the Great Lakes region. Located in West Africa on the borders of Nigeria, Niger, and Chad, Lake Chad was one of the largest lakes in the world when it was first visited and recorded by European explorers in the 19th century. Today, however, it has decreased in size dramatically as a result of desertification and increasing demand for water from the human population living around its shores. Lake Chad is very shallow considering its size, having a maximum depth of just 34 feet.

Hydroelectricity programs have created numerous artificial reservoirs across Africa. Lake Volta, the world's largest reservoir, is situated in Ghana and was formed as a result of building the dam of the Akosombo Hydroelectric Project on the Volta River. Other large reservoirs include Lake Kariba on the Zambezi River bordering Zambia and Zimbabwe, and Lake Nasser on the Nile River in Egypt and Sudan.

CLIMATE

Africa straddles the equator, and the majority of its area lies within the tropics. The land area to the north of the equator is roughly equal to the land area south of the equator, and to a large degree the climatic conditions in the north are mirrored in the south. The extreme north and south of the continent both experience a warm temperate climate. Moving toward the equator from these coastal zones, the interiors of both the northern and southern halves of the continent feature large desert zones, the Sahara Desert in the north and the Kalahari Desert in the south. These desert zones are created by a combination of high solar heating and low rainfall. The Sahara is the larger and more arid of the two because the north of the continent is much wider than the south, so the interior is further from the moisture of the surrounding oceans. Maximum temperatures are generally higher in the northern half of the continent than the south both because of the greater distance from the interior to the cooling ocean in the north and because the principal highlands areas, where temperatures tend to be lower, are located in the south.

The annual movement of the tropical rain belt dominates the climate across the central tropical band of the continent. The tropical rain belt, a constantly shifting east–west band of high rainfall, moves through the tropical latitudes, completing one journey between the Tropic of Cancer and the Tropic of Capricorn every 12 months. Tropical latitudes south of the equator experience a wet season between October and March while tropical latitudes north of the equator experience a corresponding dry season during the same period. Between April and September the tropical rain belt is north of the equator, and tropical latitudes south of the equator experience a dry season. On the equator there are two wet seasons every year as the tropical rain belt passes overhead twice, once moving south and once moving north. Latitudes close to the equator typically experience one long and one short wet season each year. This general picture typical of the tropical zones around the globe applies well to tropical Africa, although local geography can disrupt this overall pattern. East Africa, for example, is much drier throughout the year than its tropical latitude would suggest. This can be attributed to the disrupting effects of the East African Highlands on weather patterns. The southwest coast is also drier than might be expected. The area with the highest annual rainfall lies along the coast of the Gulf of Guinea.

Almost every climate type can be found in Africa, ranging from subarctic conditions near the peaks of the continent's highest mountains to tropical conditions in the low-lying basins of the central interior. These low-lying tropical zones of Central and West Africa are dominated by dense tropical rainforest and tropical savanna (grasslands). The transition zones between the arid deserts in the north and the south and the well-watered central tropical band are typified by tropical or subtropical savanna. These areas experience one short but intense wet season every year and very little precipitation for the rest of the year. In the northern half of the continent this transitional zone between the desert and the tropical areas can be divided into two zones: the Sahel and the Sudanian Savanna.

The Sahel is the more northerly of these transition zones, bordering the Sahara Desert. Rainfall in the Sahel is unpredictable. In the 20th century rainfall patterns oscillated dramatically over the course of several decades. There was a severe drought between approximately 1910 and 1919, peaking in 1914, when annual rainfall was significantly lower than average. The period from 1950 to 1970 saw unusually high annual rainfall but between 1970 and 1990 there was a prolonged period of very low annual rainfall that caused devastating famines across the region. Evidence of large-scale migrations in the past and firsthand accounts from visitors to the region during the 17th, 18th, and 19th centuries indicate that this irregular pattern of wet decades and drought decades has been occurring for centuries.

To the south of the Sahel is the Sudanian Savanna, a belt of tropical savanna where rainfall is still restricted to a single annual wet season but is greater in volume and more consistent. At its southern limit the Sudanian Savanna breaks up into a patchwork of savanna and tropical forest that gradually gives way to tropical rainforest.

ANIMAL LIFE

Much of the animal life characteristic of Africa is found south of the Sahara Desert. The central tropical region is one of the world's most species-rich environments, and Africa's equatorial rainforests are home to about 50 percent of the continent's animal species. Madagascar is also a biodiversity hotspot of global importance. Its long geographical isolation from mainland Africa has allowed many unique species to evolve there.

The arid north is home to a few large Afrotropical mammals, such as the African wild sss and the Nubian ibex, but the majority of smaller mammals, birds, and reptiles are found across the Mediterranean region. The desert regions of the south have a number of rare African mammal species including the aardwolf, the meerkat, and the black-footed cat.

Africa's extensive savannas are home to some of its most characteristic species such as the lion, the African elephant, the black rhinoceros, the leopard, the cheetah, the african wild dog, the hyena, the zebra, the gazelle, the wildebeest, and the giraffe. Many of the savanna's grazing animals undertake annual migrations that follow the seasonal rains. There is evidence that the Sahel region was formerly more densely populated with some of these animals, but human activities and an historical trend toward greater aridity have greatly reduced their numbers in the present day.

The tropical rainforest of Central and West Africa are home to four of the world's species of Great Ape: the western gorilla and the eastern gorilla, and the common chimpanzee and the bonobo. There are also numerous other mammal species endemic to Africa such as the okapi, the potto, and the bongo. The forested regions of Madagascar are home to a large number of mammal species that are found nowhere else in the world, including lemurs, tenrecs, the fossa, and the aye-aye. Of the 64 species of primate living in Africa most live in forested regions.

The Great Lakes Region of East Africa is a biodiversity hotspot for many freshwater fishes, and the rivers and mangrove forests of tropical West Africa are also home to a large percentage of the continent's fish species. Overall Africa has the largest number of freshwater fish species of any continent. The lakes of East Africa are also a biodiversity center for invertebrates, particularly mollusks. It is estimated that between 10 and 20 percent of the world's insect species are endemic to Africa, with more than 100,000 species described to date. There are 1,600 known species of bees, more than 1,000 known termite species, 2,000 species of ants, and more than 3,600 species of butterfly. Many of the 2,600 bird species found in Africa are migratory, spending only part of the year on the continent, but there are endemic species and families as well such as the ostrich, the secretary bird, sunbirds, guinea fowl, mousebird, and mesites, which are endemic to Madagascar. Reptiles are well represented in Africa, but almost all belong to families that are widespread around the globe. Chameleons are an exception in that the great majority of chameleon species are found only in Africa and Madagascar.

APPENDIX III
THE GEOGRAPHY OF THE MIDDLE EAST

THE NAME

The term Middle East was first used in the 19th century in the United Kingdom, and at that time was used to refer an undefined area surrounding the Persian Gulf. The first known use of the term comes from a British current-affairs journal published in 1902. In the early decades of the 20th century British and U.S. sources commonly referred to the eastern shore of the Mediterranean as the Near East, the area between Persian Gulf and western India as the Middle East, and the part of Asia centered on China as the Far East. Today the term is widely used in the English-speaking world to refer to the Arab nations (which include nations in North Africa) but also to refer to the Arab nations and Iran.

Alternative terms for parts of the area commonly described as the Middle East include the European term Levant and the Arabic term Mashriq. The Levant is a historical geographical designation for the area bounded in the north by the Taurus Mountains of southern Turkey, in the west by the Mediterranean, and in the south by the Arabian Desert. The eastern limit of the Levant is often described as northern Mesopotamia, but some sources include almost the whole of Mesopotamia to the shore of the Persian Gulf. Mashriq is a general term that includes the Arabic-speaking countries north of the Arabian Peninsula.

Numerous authorities have criticized the usage of the term Middle East on the grounds that it is Eurocentric, since the area of the world it refers to is only in the east from a European perspective. Nevertheless, the term remains in common usage and is widely understood to refer to a group of nations or territories with closely interrelated histories and cultures. The United Nations designates the area as Western Asia.

GEOGRAPHICAL LIMITS

There are no clear physical boundaries to the Middle East, a fact reflected in the vagueness of the term itself. Some authorities cite a narrow definition that is restricted to the territory of the nations surrounding the Persian Gulf, others include parts of North Africa and the Levant. More recently the term Middle East has been used to refer to an extended area including all of North Africa, Turkey, the Caucasus, Iran, and parts of Central Asia such as Afghanistan. This work is based on the broader rather than the narrower definition of the term with the exception that North Africa is described in the Geography of Africa appendix.

NATIONS AND AREA

For the purposes of this work the nations and territories of the Middle East are taken to include Bahrain, Iran, Iraq, Israel, Jordan, Kuwait, Lebanon, Oman, the Palestinian territories, Qatar, Saudi Arabia, Syria, Turkey, the United Arab Emirates, and Yemen. Together these nations and territories have an area of about 2.4 million square miles and have coastlines on the Black Sea, the Mediterranean Sea, the Red Sea, the Arabian Sea, the Persian Gulf, and the Caspian Sea.

ISLANDS

There are no large islands within the area defined as the Middle East in this work, although the Kingdom of Bahrain is an island nation situated in the Persian Gulf. The largest island included in the territory of any of the nations of the Middle East is Socotra in the Arabian Sea, which is part of the Republic of Yemen. Other strategically important islands include the Hanish Islands, Kamaran Island, and Perim Island in the Red Sea; and Abu Musa, the Greater and Lesser Tunb islands, Farsi Island, Hormuz Island, Larak Island, and Qeshm Island in the Persian Gulf. There are numerous other small islands lying just off Iran's Persian Gulf coast and numerous islands off the Aegean coast of Turkey.

HIGHLANDS AND LOWLANDS

Broadly speaking there are two separate highland areas in the Middle East. The first stretches from central Anatolia (modern Turkey) east through the Caucasus and then south and east through western and northern Iran. The second area extends south from Lebanon through western Jordan and along the Red Sea coast of the Arabian Peninsula.

The Anatolian plateau dominates central Turkey, rising from an average elevation of about 2,000 feet above sea level in the west to 4,000 feet in the east. The plateau is bounded in the north by the Pontic Mountains, rising to 12,000 feet, and in the south by the Taurus Mountain range, which also has peaks above 12,000 feet. In the east of Turkey, where the Pontic and Tauris mountains converge, the land is rugged and mountainous with an average altitude above 9,000 feet and a maximum of almost 17,000 feet at the peak of Mount Ararat. The northeast corner of Iran, which borders the east of Turkey, is also a prominent highland area, being the region where the Zagros Mountains of western Iran and the Alborz Mountains of northern Iran converge. Iran is one of the world's most mountainous nations. The Iranian plateau, which extends eastward beyond the borders of Iran into Afghanistan and Pakistan, is made up of a series of mountainous spines surrounding lower lying basins. The Zagros Mountains, which extend along the western edge of the plateau all the way to the Straits of Hormuz at the mouth of the Persian Gulf, are one of Asia's great mountain ranges, and the Alborz Mountains, which separate the Iranian plateau from the coastal plain of the Caspian Sea, include many peaks over 11,000 feet and the peak of Mount Damavand—the highest mountain in Iran at more than 15,300 feet.

The highland area extending south from Lebanon through Jordan and along the western edge of the Arabian Peninsula has a much lesser average elevation than the highlands of eastern Turkey and Iran. Much of Lebanon is mountainous, being dominated by the parallel north–south ranges of Mount Lebanon and the Anti-Lebanon Mountains. To the south of Lebanon the highland area of southwest Syria is a continuation of this highland band. The western edge of Jordan is also a highland area. South of Jordan the area of high ground continues in the form of a high escarpment that runs parallel to the coast of the Red Sea through western Saudi Arabia. This escarpment gradually becomes progressively higher moving south, apart from a significant low-lying gap around the city of Mecca.

The lowland areas of the Middle East are typically coastal. The narrow coastal plain that extends along Iran's Caspian Sea coast is no more than 100 feet above sea level at its highest point, and much of the western shore of the Red Sea is very low lying. The area to the west of the Zagros Mountains, historically referred to a lower Mesopotamia, is also a lowland area. In the Levant the most striking lowland area is the Jordan Valley—a narrow depression divided from north to south by the border between Jordan and Israel. The Jordan Valley is associated with the Great Rift Valley features that extend as far south as East Africa. The shore of the Dead Sea, which lies in the Jordan Valley, is the lowest point above water on the Earth's surface, lying at approximately 1,300 feet below sea level.

RIVERS AND LAKES

The three major rivers of the Middle East rise in the highland area of eastern Turkey. Of these the two longest are the Euphrates and the Tigris, both of which flow southeast into the lowlands of southern Iraq before emptying into the Persian Gulf. These two great rivers follow parallel courses before mingling in a great marshland and then joining to form the Shatt al-Arab about 100 miles before reaching the sea. The third of these rivers, the Aras, flows east through Armenia, Iran, and Azerbaijan before emptying into the Caspian Sea.

The Jordan River is the major watercourse of the Levant, although at just 150 miles in length it is not a major river from a global perspective. The Jordan River rises in the Anti-Lebanon Mountains of Lebanon and flows south through the Jordan Valley. Along its course the Jordan River feeds a series of increasingly low-lying lakes that are also located in the valley. From north to south these lakes are Lake Hula, the Sea of Galilee (also known as Lake Tiberias), and the Dead Sea. The Dead Sea has no outlet, and to its south the Jordan Valley is arid.

The largest lakes of the Middle East are in Turkey and Iran. Lake Van, with an area of 1,450 square miles, is the largest lake in Turkey and is situated in the mountainous east of the country. Lake Urmia, with an area of approximately 2,000 square miles, is the largest lake in Iran and is situated in the northwest of the country. Lake Urmia and several permanent lakes in Turkey are highly saline. The Dead Sea, situated on the border between Jordan and the West Bank, is also highly saline.

CLIMATE

The Middle East represents only a small proportion of the world's total land area but it features a great range of climatic conditions. The coastal regions of Turkey, the Levant, and the extreme north of Iran have a Mediterranean climate featuring hot dry summers and cool wet winters. The interior of the Anatolian Peninsula, northern Iraq, and northern Iran are all highland areas with relatively low precipitation and low temperatures during winter. South of the mountainous belt that extends across Turkey, northern Iraq, and into Iran, much of the Middle East is arid or semi-arid with high summer temperatures, and this is increasingly true moving south. The interior of the Arabian Peninsula is dominated by desert, and the southern portion of Iraq is also arid. Despite the prevailing arid climate there are numerous pockets of fertile land across the region. The area between the Euphrates and Tigris Rivers in southern Iran has been a center of agriculture for thousands of years, as has the Jordan Valley.

ANIMAL LIFE

The majority of the Middle East lies within the Palearctic ecozone (an area with broadly related plant and animal types), which extends across the entire Asian continent north of the Himalayas, the whole of Europe, and into North Africa. Only the southern half of the Arabian Peninsula is considered to be part of the Afrotropic ecozone. Consequently much of the plant and animal life found in the Middle East is also found across a much wider area of Asia and North Africa.

APPENDIX IV
THE EARLIEST HUMANS

Around 6 million years ago the earliest identifiable human ancestors emerged in the African continent. A considerable body of evidence supports this claim, ranging from fossils to DNA analysis, with scholars from a number of disciplines contributing to the history thus far reconstructed. Africa has been shown to be the cradle of human evolution, and it is here that the fascinating story of our earliest human ancestors begins.

HOMINIDS

The term *hominid* refers to any creature—extinct or extant—of the family Hominidae (of the order Primates), which is made up of erect bipedal (i.e., walking on two feet) primate mammals. Of this family, the only species that exists today is *Homo sapiens,* literally, "knowing man," that is, humans. Extinct members of this family, the earliest humans, are attested through fossil remains. The earliest hominids are represented by the genus *Australopithecus,* followed by later species of the genus *Homo* ("man"), among them *Homo habilis* ("handy man"), *Homo ergaster* ("working man"), *Homo erectus* ("standing man"), and most recently, *Homo sapiens.*

The study of human prehistory involves a number of disciplines, including paleontology, the study of fossils; anthropology, the study of human societies and cultures; physical anthropology, which focuses on human zoology and evolution; paleoanthropology, the branch of anthropology concerned with fossil hominids; and archaeology, the study of the physical remains of human life.

THE DIVERGENCE OF HUMAN ANCESTORS FROM APES

Humans and apes descend from a common ancestor, and when the human ancestral species began to diverge and differentiate from this common ancestor, this process marked the appearance of the hominids. This divergence of species, or speciation, took place during a period of climate change, when the warm and moist tropical to subtropical climate prevailing in Africa was interrupted for periods of several million years at a stretch by cooler, drier weather. Against this backdrop, the earliest human species began to differentiate from the apes. While fossil evidence uncovered from the 19th century on has supported the postulation of human ancestors dating back to eras too distant in the past to imagine, it was not until the late 20th century that those dates could be better approximated. In the 1990s, DNA studies comparing genetic material from modern-day humans to that of chimpanzees allowed for the extrapolation back to a common ancestor and for the rough dating of that ancestor to sometime between 6 million and 4.5 million years ago. This dating would put the divergence of species as coinciding with climate shifts in Africa. Fossil evidence to support this claim, though, was unknown until, in 1994, an announcement was made of the discovery of fossil bone fragments much older than anything previously known. These fragments, found at Aramis, in north-central Ethiopia, were dated to 4.4 million years ago and provided the oldest fossil evidence for a hominid with an upright stance and bipedal gait rather than the knuckle walking of chimpanzees. This hominid, originally classified as an *Australopithecus,* was reclassified under a new genus and is now known as the *Ardipthecus ramidus.*

Additional early fossil finds include *Australopithecus anamensis,* dated to between 3.9 million and 4.2 million years ago. Remains of this hominid were found in Kenya by the anthropologist and archaeologist Mary Leakey (d. 1996). Mary Leakey and her husband, Louis Leakey (d. 1972), were the pioneers of the study of human evolution. They spent much of their lives working in Kenya and are credited with demonstrating that human ancestors go back much farther in history than had been previously believed and that human evolution centered in Africa, not Asia, as had been assumed from earlier discoveries. The Leakeys and their co-workers made many of the discoveries that have shaped our understanding of human evolution. Their work has also provided evidence for a common ancestor of apes and humans, a species called *Proconsul africanus,* which lived about 25 million years ago, discovered in 1948 at Rusinga, an island in Lake Victoria, Kenya. In 1962, Louis Leakey's team discovered fossils of another species, *Kenyapithecus,* dating to about 14 million years ago, the era before the divergence of apes and hominids, thus making this, too, a common ancestor of apes and humans.

Climate change played an essential role in the emergence of early humans. The shift to a cooler and drier climate transformed the dense tropical forest in ways that supported the divergence of species. The tropical forest opened into zones of forest and of open savanna, or grasslands, providing a habitat well suited to the australopithecines, who could walk upright in search of food, then if necessary retreat quickly to the shelter of the forest, carrying with them the food they had gathered.

The next wave of speciation took place around 3 to 2 million years ago, a period when the climate was again cooler and drier. This wave, too, has left fossils of hominids and many other species. The fossils suggest that many forest-dwelling species of bovids, members of the cattle family such as antelopes, became extinct during this period, while others more suited to open habitats evolved. At the same time, the forest-dwelling hominid genus *Australopithecus* diverged into species of the genus *Paranthropus* (although not all paleontologists accept this notion). Up until this point, all the hominids, along with their ancestors the apes, were forest-dwelling herbivores. The genus *Homo*, though, as aggressive, omnivorous scavengers and possibly hunters, was able to exploit the new habitats. The bovids ranged across wide areas, an adaptation probably necessitated by the lower density of nutrients in grasslands as compared with the denser nutrients of the forest. Members of the genus *Homo*, distinguished by their larger size, longer legs, and a pelvic structure that allowed a bipedal gait, were well adapted to follow the bovid herds and perhaps dispersed with them.

GENUS *AUSTRALOPITHECUS*

The *Australopithecus,* a name that means "southern ape," is a genus of extinct hominids that lived in Africa from about 5.3 million years ago to about 1.6 million years ago. Most scientists believe this genus is an ancestor of modern humans. Members of this family differed from early apes in their upright posture and bipedal gait, as attested by the development of the arm and leg bones preserved in the fossils of this genus that have been found. Their brains were relatively small, like those of apes today, but their teeth were similar to those of modern humans.

The identification of this genus dates from the discovery by the Australian-born paleontologist Raymond Dart in 1924 of a skull found at Taung, South Africa, near the Kalahari Desert. The fossil was determined to be the remains of a juvenile, nicknamed the "Taung baby." The position of this specimen's foramen magnum, the opening in the base of the skull through which the spinal cord attaches to the brain, would have allowed it to walk upright. Over the next 30 years many other fossils were found in other South African sites, and all of these were eventually given the species designation *Australopithecus africanus.* The species is dated to about 3 to 2 million years ago. This hominid had a relatively small cranium; it stood about five feet tall and weighed between 75 and 130 pounds. The brain size in relation to the size of the body falls between that of modern apes and modern humans. Few upper-limb bone fossils have been found, and from those that do survive, nothing can be determined about the manipulative abilities of these hominids, although the shoulder bones suggest that they were well adapted for climbing. Their teeth are not arranged in the usual U-shape of the apes but instead follow a more rounded line. Other aspects of the teeth set them apart from the apes, as, for example, the fact that the canine teeth are small and do not project above the other teeth, as they always do in apes. On the other hand, the order in which the teeth appeared and their rate of maturation are more similar to that of apes than that of modern humans. The pelvic cavity is wider than that of apes, allowing for the birth of babies with larger heads, providing additional evidence for a larger brain size.

Another species, the *Australopithecus afarensis,* was postulated, based on two major finds: In 1978 Mary Leakey discovered three trails of footprints in volcanic ash at a site in Tanzania, dating from about 3.5 million years ago and providing striking affirmation of the bipedal gait of the individuals who left the footprints. Between 1972 and 1977 excavations carried out by a team led by Donald Johanson, Maurice Taieb, and Yves Coppens, in Hadar, Ethiopia, uncovered a remarkable female skeleton, nicknamed "Lucy," of which nearly half survived intact, and another set of fossils, nicknamed "the First Family," which includes the remains of at least 13 individuals. Features from both these finds were taken as evidence for a new species, A. *afarensis,* distinguished from A. *africanus* by a more projecting face, the shape of the teeth and their placement in the jaw, and differences in the cranium.

A number of other species of the genus *Australopithecus* have been identified and grouped into two broad categories according to body type: gracile (of slender build) and robust. The gracile group, which includes A. *africanus,* have lighter bones, especially in the face, than robust species, such as A. *boisei,* which are characterized by powerful jaws and teeth adapted to crushing tough foodstuffs, probably mostly plant foods, and a ridge running from front to back on the top of the skull that served to anchor powerful jaw muscles. The average brain size of the robust australopithecines is a little larger than that of the gracile group, but because the robust group is 10 to 25 percent larger in body size, the brain-to-body ratio is roughly the same as that of the gracile group. Robust species are classified alternately as belonging to the genus *Paranthropus,* a name meaning "next to man," or as belonging to *Australopithecus.* The fossil record of early hominids is still so sparse as to make it impossible to ascertain with authority relationships between lineages. Accordingly, it is still uncertain which lineage of *Australopithecus* is the direct ancestor of the genus *Homo.*

GENUS *HOMO*

The earliest known members of the genus *Homo* are *Homo habilis* (handy man) and *Homo rudolfensis,* named for Lake

Rudolph, now Lake Turkana, in Kenya, where the fossil that provided the first evidence for this species was found. These two species are thought to have been contemporaries, living about 2.4 to about 1.6 million years ago. *Australopithecus africanus* and other australopithecines were also living at that time. *H. rudolfensis,* first identified from fossils found in 1972 by a team led by Richard Leakey, son of Mary and Louis Leakey, differs from other *Homo* specimens in that it has a larger brain and larger teeth, but it is not known whether these traits simply reflect the likelihood that the entire body was larger. The most striking ways in which *H. rudolfensis* differs from *H. habilis* is in terms of facial features—the former has a much longer face, with the upper part narrower than the middle—and the placement and type of teeth. There is continuing controversy as to whether *H. rudolfensis* should, in fact, be seen as a separate species or not. Some palaeoanthropologists have suggested that *rudolfensis* is the male and *habilis* the female of the same species. Others have theorized that *rudolfensis* is the ancestor of *habilis,* while others see the two as on completely different evolutionary lines. Again, with the paucity of specimens, it is impossible at this point to know for certain.

Fossils categorized as remains of *H. habilis* were first reported in the early 1960s, discovered by Louis Leakey and his colleagues at Olduvai Gorge in Tanzania. Though the species had a brain size considerably smaller than that of modern humans, it was postulated that it was indeed human, based on the fact that numerous stone tools were found in the same geologic horizon (layer) as the jaw and cranial specimens. Leakey saw *H. habilis* as a direct ancestor of *H. sapiens,* and while that claim was initially disputed, the notion is now widely accepted that *H. habilis* is the direct evolutionary link between the australopithecines, who eventually became extinct, and *H. erectus,* the direct ancestor of modern man.

The next step in human evolution, emerging in Africa about 1.9 million years ago, is *Homo ergaster.* This species was originally seen as part of the species *H. erectus,* which is attested across Africa, Europe, and Asia. More recently scientists have categorized the two as distinct species: *H. ergaster* as the African specimen, with the designation *H. erectus* reserved for later, mainly Asian populations. Features that distinguish *H. ergaster* include a rounded cranium, a prominent ridge that runs over the eyes, called a supraorbital torus, and teeth much smaller than those of australopithecines. *H. ergaster* had a dramatically larger brain and engaged in recognizably human behavior, such as utilizing fire and hunting. Members of this species were tall and thin, a body type that most likely reflects an adaptation to hot weather, and they had hips that were narrow in relation to adult brain size, suggesting that their young were born small and helpless. Apes give birth to infants whose brains weigh 50 percent of the weight of an adult brain, whereas modern human babies are born with a brain only 25 percent of the adult size. The body structure of *H. ergaster* would not have allowed members of this species to give birth to infants with a brain larger than 30 percent of adult size. The long childhood of humans provides the advantages of fostering intelligence, learning, and socialization. An advance in stone tool technology, known as the Achulean (also spelled Acheulean or Acheulian) stone tool industry, dating from about 1.6 million years ago is associated with this species, and included the development of large tools such as axes and cleavers.

Among the fossils classified as *H. ergaster* is a 90 percent complete adolescent skeleton known as Turkana Boy or Nariokotome Boy, dating from about 1.6 million years ago, found in 1984 in Kenya by Kamoya Kimeu. Possibly one of the most important finds in paleoanthropology, the skeleton provides a wealth of information on the anatomy of this species. It shows a clear departure from apelike features and striking similarity to modern humans. This male, thought to have been somewhere between 9 and 12 years of age at the time of his death, based on analysis of his teeth and bone growth, had already reached a height of more than five feet. The hips were narrow and adapted to walking and running over long distances. The proportions of the arm bones to the leg bones mirror that of modern humans. He had a large cranial capacity and his body was long and slender.

OUT OF AFRICA

Fossil finds that have been reliably dated to at least 1.6 million years ago attest to the presence of hominids outside Africa. Included in this evidence is the so-called Java Man, found in 1891 by the Dutch anatomist and geologist Eugene Dubois near the Solo River in Java. With continuing excavations, remains of about 40 individuals have been recovered in Java. In the 1950s, Java Man was connected with fossils from caves near Zhoukoudian (Choukoutien), China, discovered in the 1930s, known as Peking Man. The two sets of fossils were classified as *H. erectus.* While some palaeoanthropologists have argued for dates as far back as 1.8 and 1.9 million years ago, this claim is not widely accepted. A find that has been reliably dated is the 1999 discovery of two skulls in Dmanisi, in the Republic of Georgia, dated to 1.7 million years ago, considered reliable because the dating is based on the age of volcanic sediments contemporary with the fossils. These skulls are more closely related to *H. ergaster* than to *H. erectus.* Of great significance is the fact that more than a thousand stone tools were found with these skulls. These tools, though, were made in the Olduwan style (named for the Olduvai Gorge, where the Leakeys found many tools of this tradition) used by *H. habilis* in Africa, more primitive than the Achulean-style tools. The fact that these tools were not so highly developed demonstrates that the advances of the Achulean stone tool industry were not a necessary component of the hominid migration from Africa, and that, in fact, the migration out of Africa predated the Achulean advances.

The features that define *H. erectus* include an elongated skull with thick cranial walls. The back of the skull shows a protuberance known as a transverse torus, and like *ergaster, erectus* also has the supraorbital torus. The brain size is far larger than that of earlier australopithcines and other early *Homo* species, and the teeth are nearly identical to modern human teeth, although somewhat larger, with a larger jawbone. The species *H. erectus* is thought to have diverged from *H. ergaster* about 1.6 million years ago and subsequently migrated to Asia.

Recent studies have challenged the theory that *H. erectus* disappeared about 400,000 years ago, as other species continued to evolve. Modern stratigraphic analysis of the complicated layers at the Java sites has shown Java Man and other Solo River fossils to be only 50,000 years old, making this population of *H. erectus* contemporary with *H. sapiens,* that is, modern humans.

Among the questions that remain are how and where populations of *H. erectus* evolved into early *H. sapiens,* whether dispersed populations evolved independently, or whether a population in a particular geographic area evolved rapidly and then migrated into other areas. The study of human evolution is still a young field, and because relatively few specimens have been recovered, a single find or newly developed methods of analysis can result in the dramatic realignment of the human family tree. In 2006 such a redefining find was made when a skull was uncovered in Gawis, Ethiopia, northeast of the capital, Addis Ababa. Some scientists believe that this may prove to be the missing link between *H. erectus* and *H. sapiens.* This specimen is thought to be between 500,000 and 200,000 years old and comes from an area rich in paleoanthropological finds. In this area of Ethiopia, the oldest known stone tools, dated from about 2.6 million years ago, were found, as was the skeleton known as Lucy, and in 2005, specimens of the *Ardipithecus ramidus* hominids, dated to between 4.5 and 4.3 million years ago.

HOMO SAPIENS

Fossil remains of early *H. sapiens* are known not only from sites in Africa, but also from sites in the Middle East and Europe, dating from the Paleolithic Period—the Old Stone Age—from about 200,000 to about 15,000 years ago. With *sapiens,* the genus *Homo* takes on characteristics much more recognizable as "human" and distinct from their more apelike forebears. This is particularly evident in the many features that distinguish the *sapiens* skull from that of *erectus.* The overall direction of this evolution shows an increase in cranial capacity (and thus brain size), the rounding of the cranial vault (the top of the head), and the gradual reduction in the masticatory, or chewing, complex of features, including the jaws and the teeth. Accordingly, the *sapiens* skull is marked by a well-developed and vertical brow that lacks the prominent supraorbital torus of earlier species. The jaws and teeth are smaller, and thus the muscles required to support them would not have been as heavy. The lighter, more delicate face could have been supported by a smaller neck and reduced neck muscles. With the smaller teeth, the chin becomes a more prominent feature and the "muzzle" aspect of earlier species recedes. The arrangement of teeth, called

dentition, observed in *sapiens* shows smaller teeth crowded into the jaw, with a markedly smaller third molar. Interestingly, in modern humans, too, the third molars—commonly referred to as wisdom teeth—are genetically unstable and are often missing or impacted.

The skeleton of *H. sapiens* supports a fully upright posture and an efficient bipedal gait, with a spinal column curved only at the neck and the small of the back, evenly dispersing weight along the line of gravity and allowing the pelvis to tilt back, which in turn allows the legs to swing freely over the ground. The structure of the leg bones and the feet add further efficiency to the stride. The evolving capacity and refinement of grip mechanisms and the continued evolution of the hand, along with increased brain capacity, allowed for greater and greater manipulative skills, essential to the development of more advanced tools and other skills.

The earliest human found in Europe is *H. neanderthalensis,* the Neanderthal, named after the Neander River valley in Germany, where the first specimen—a skullcap—was found in 1856, dated to about 200,000 years ago. These hominids, while more like modern humans than any other hominid found, are also very unlike humans in their massive physique and extremely heavy bones. The question remains as to whether the Neanderthals represent a species distinct from *H. sapiens* or are a subspecies of *H. sapiens.* In any case, the Neanderthals are thought to be the immediate predecessors of early modern man. Neanderthal populations lived in an area that extended from Europe to Central Asia, to the eastern Mediterranean region. Excavated sites include not only those in the Neander Valley and other parts of Europe but also sites in the Middle East: Shanidar (in Iraq), Tabun (Mount Carmel, in the West Bank and Israel), and Amud and Kebara (in Israel).

Other early human populations roughly contemporaneous with but different from the Neanderthals have been identified across Africa and the Middle East. East African remains include fossils found in southern Ethiopia by an expedition led by Richard Leakey and dating from about 200,000 to about 70,000 years ago, known as Omo I and Omo II. Remains found in the Border Cave site, between South Africa and Swaziland, have been dated to between 110,000 and 90,000 years ago and are undoubtedly *H. sapiens.* Another cave site, this one near the city of Nazareth, in Israel, called Jebel Qafzeh, yielded remains of about a dozen individuals, stone tools, and a variety of animal remains, including those of horses, rhinoceroses, deer, oxen, and gazelles. Skeletons from this site have been dated to about 115,000 to 90,000 years ago. The human skulls and bones from limbs found there are not those of Neanderthals or of *H. erectus* but are clearly related to *H. sapiens.*

Generally speaking, the early *H. sapiens* sites are still few and widely scattered, making it impossible to outline with certainty patterns of migration. Nevertheless, evidence now points to the emergence of modern humans from sub-Saharan Africa sometime before 50,000 years ago. This is the widely held "Out of Africa" theory of human origins. The

Omo finds of Ethiopia, as well as those from sites in Kenya, Tanzania, and South Africa, are considered to be the precursors of these modern humans. From these sites in Africa this species spread northward, absorbing and sometimes displacing other populations, including the Neanderthals. It had been thought that the Neanderthals and other extinct species died out, but research published in 2002, conducted by Alan R. Templeton, a population biologist at Washington University in St. Louis, found two evolutionary links to Africa imprinted in the genes of modern populations, suggesting there were at least two migrations out of Africa of *H. sapiens*, one dating from about half a million years ago and the other beginning no more than 100,000 years ago. The findings of this study also suggest that *H. sapiens* interbred with the Neanderthals, and thus traces of Neanderthal genes live on in modern-day European populations.

A number of sites in Morocco have also provided fossils, but these have not yet been definitively placed in the evolutionary sequence. These early modern humans are thought to date from between 70,000 to 40,000 years ago.

LANGUAGE

While skeletons and skulls attest to the evolution of the human body and archaeological artifacts help us reconstruct the development of material culture, we have no such evidence to draw upon for the history of human language. Anthropologists and linguists have drawn some conclusions from the shape of the cranium—whether certain physiological developments at least would have allowed for vocalization and the development of speech—but the leap from vocalization to the complex symbolic system that characterizes language is enormous. Language also requires a highly developed brain, capable of processing and storing complex symbols.

Because fossils reveal next to nothing about the development of language in humans, experiments have been conducted on one of humankind's closet relatives, the chimpanzee, to explore the development of this most human of behaviors. Since chimpanzees do not have a larynx that would allow them to make the sounds necessary for human speech, these experiments have focused on teaching them sign language for the deaf, which, like other forms of human language, is a rich symbolic system that allows for the creation of an infinite number of new "utterances." Washoe, the female chimpanzee raised and observed at the University of Nevada, Reno, and Central Washington University, reportedly learned to make signs for more than 100 words and could understand more than 300 signs. She was able to construct simple sentences, usually asking for food, but never used signs in a spontaneous way to communicate ideas, an essential feature of human use of language. Washoe died in 2007. While this and other research on chimpanzees has undoubtedly shed light on the workings of primate cognition, most linguists and cognitive scientists agree that Washoe's use of language fell far short of qualifying as human language.

THE BEGINNINGS OF AGRICULTURE

It was only rather recently that humans made the leap from hunting and gathering—an activity that rests on a somewhat passive relationship with the environment—to taking control of the food supply through agriculture. This leap was made about 11,400 years ago, as evidenced by nine small figs uncovered in the ruins of a prehistoric village near Jericho, in the Palestinian territory of the West Bank. This is the earliest evidence for a cultivated food crop so far discovered anywhere in the world. The find was announced in 2006 by archaeobotanists Mordechai Kislev and Anat Hartmann of Bar-Ilan University in Israel, and Ofer Bar-Yosef, an archaeologist at the Peabody Museum of Harvard University.

The dawn of agriculture was a major event in human history. In Dr. Bar-Yosef's words, "People decided to intervene in nature and supply their own food rather than relying on what was provided by the gods. This shift to a sedentary lifestyle grounded in the growing of wild crops such as barley and wheat marked a dramatic change from 2.5 million years of humans as mobile hunter-gatherers."

These cultivated figs have been shown to predate by about 1,000 years the staple crops of wheat, barely, and chickpeas, which were cultivated across wide areas of the Middle East. Before the discovery of these figs, the staple grains and legumes had been assumed to be the earliest cultivated crops. The figs were discovered in the remains of a building that had burned, charring the figs but preserving them well for detailed analysis. The age of the figs was established by dating the detritus left by the fire. The carbonized figs had retained their shape, suggesting they may have been dried for human consumption. It is thought that figs came to be cultivated before other fruits because they can be propagated by the simplest of techniques: one can take a shoot from a fig tree, plant it in the ground, and it will take root and grow into a tree. This ease of cultivation may explain why figs were cultivated much earlier than grapes, olives, and other plants normally grown from seed.

As for where grains were first cultivated, researchers have differing views. Some think they were introduced in what is now Israel and the upper Euphrates River valley, while others contend that southern Turkey is the likely site.

PREHISTORIC SOCIETY

Ideas about the complexity and organization of human society in the period between the dawn of agriculture—about 11,000 years ago—and the time when humans began to write things down—about 6,000 years ago—have changed dramatically over recent decades as new evidence has come to light. Until recently, most anthropologists believed that humans lived in simple, self-sufficient farming villages from the dawn of agriculture right up until the great leap in human history known as the Urban Transformation, which took place around 6,000 to 5,500 years ago, defined by the rise of cities in the Middle East and the concurrent beginnings of metal making and the invention of writing. In light of finds of the last few decades and reassessment of earlier ones, this view has been reformulated to posit a much more complex and sophisticated village life that developed 3,000 to 1,000 years before the rise of cities.

One of the sites that has played a central role in this new understanding of early society is Cayonu, in eastern Turkey, currently under excavation. The site contains the remains of a village of about 100 to 200 people, dating from about 9,000 to 8,000 years ago—that is, from the Neolithic (New Stone) Age. The people of Cayonu are thought to have been the first farmers of Anatolia, cultivating wheat and barley and possibly other plants. The settlement includes a number of storage facilities probably used for grain. Evidence points to the dog as the first animal domesticated in this village, followed by the pig, and then sheep and goats. A figurine of a female deity was found, one of the earliest relics of a cult known as that of the Mother Goddess of Anatolia. The dead were buried under the floors of the dwellings, and decorative items such as buckles and beads have been found in some of these burials. Metal objects, though, have provided some of the biggest surprises of this site. Copper items in various shapes were uncovered—sheets that had been hammered flat and various sorts of tools, such as awls, pins, and hooks. Careful analysis of these pieces has shown that the copper was heated before it was shaped. This discovery puts the date at which early villagers were heating metals in order to work them 3,000 years earlier than had been previously thought. Another site in Turkey, Gritille, southwest of Cayonu, produced lumps of iron that had been heated.

Other villages contemporaneous with Cayonu show a degree of social organization and division of labor that was not thought to have existed so early. At Beidha, in Jordan, one house was apparently used for bead making, another for butchering, and another for making flints. Umm Dabaghiya, a site between the Tigris and the Euphrates Rivers in northern Iraq, includes a storage facility with hundreds of separate chambers, pellets that could be shot from slings, and flint tools for scraping. Archaeologists believe this village specialized in tanning animal hides and that it supplied a wide area with leather. Evidence of specialized industry has also been found in other areas. Yarim Tepe and Tell-es-Suwwan, also in Iraq, have sophisticated pottery kilns that would have been suited for mass production, suggesting that the surplus would have been traded.

Trade took place across great distances. Obsidian, the volcanic glass prized for its sharpness, was an essential tool of Neolithic culture and has been traced across the Middle East to areas to which it had to have been carried by traders. Similarly, pottery has been analyzed to identify trace elements in the clay, allowing a particular pottery sample to be traced to a specific locale, providing additional proof for wide-ranging trade routes.

One of the most astonishing Neolithic sites is the settlement of 6,000 to perhaps 10,000 inhabitants called Catal Huyuk (Çatalhöyük), near Konya, in south-central Turkey, first excavated in the 1960s, with new excavations begun in 1993 and still under way. The town is believed to have been a trading center, and artifacts uncovered there include fabrics, cosmetics, sticks for applying eye makeup, mirrors made of obsidian, wooden vessels, and other items. The dwellings, built close together, were rectangular mudbrick houses probably entered through the roof by means of a wooden ladder. Each house had a hearth, an oven, and platforms where one could sleep or work. The dead were buried under these platforms. Grains, oil-producing seeds, and nuts were cultivated and animal husbandry practiced.

THE HUMAN FAMILY: OUT OF AFRICA REVISITED

Who we are and where we came from are questions that humans have pondered using many different approaches and the tools of many disciplines. Since the 1980s, molecular biologists have produced strong DNA evidence supporting the claim that humans of today of all races and inhabiting all corners of the earth share a common genetic ancestry that can be traced back to Africa about 150,000 years ago. That research is the basis for the "Out of Africa" theory held by most anthropologists, which posits a relatively recent migration of human ancestors leaving Africa in several waves, crossing into Asia and Europe, and establishing populations there and eventually across the globe.

In early 2008 results were announced of a large-scale study of genetic markers gathered from nearly a thousand individuals from 51 populations around the world. This study, coauthored by Marcus Feldman, an evolutionary biologist, and Richard Myers, a geneticist, both of Stanford University provides surprising insights into human evolution and into the migrations that populated the earth. This research examined 650,000 genetic locations in the DNA of members of this wide variety of populations. The result is the highest resolution map of human genetic diversity to date. The map brings into focus in astonishing detail human genetic history, substantiating theories of migration and population variation. A sequence of genes identified in the Yakut people in northeastern Siberia, for instance, was shown to be shared by Native Americans. The shared sequence, then, confirms that the two populations now widely separated on the face of the earth are, in fact, closely related. The shared genetic marker serves to confirm the archaeological evidence that a migration took place tens of thousands of years ago from Siberia across the Bering Strait and into the Americas.

The study of these genetic markers bolsters the Out of Africa model. This conclusion is drawn from the finding that the greatest genetic variation occurs among African populations, and variation becomes less and less with populations farther from this source. If the first humans migrated out of Africa each group that broke away would have carried only a sampling of the parent population's genetic diversity. Thus, with each breaking away, the genetic variation in the population would diminish, and that's exactly what this study shows.

APPENDIX V
CHRONOLOGY OF AFRICAN AND MIDDLE EASTERN PREHISTORY AND HISTORY ❧

The following chronology is intended to provide the reader with an overview of the entire span of human history in the Middle East and Africa. This chronology concentrates on broad cultural trends and the rise and fall of cultures, peoples, and empires. More detailed chronologies can be found accompanying each of the major entries in the main body of these volumes.

Our sources of knowledge about the past depend on the time period in question. Information about the very earliest human history is derived primarily from archaeological evidence, and this evidence generally becomes more sparse the more ancient the period. With the adoption of writing the history of a culture can become much more detailed and accessible. The first part of this chronology, the prehistoric period, is concerned with the period before writing systems were adopted while the second part, the historic period, is concerned with the period after their adoption. Periods of cultural or technological development in the prehistoric section often overlap both because there is conflicting archaeological evidence for their inception and decline and because different technologies (or industries) were in use in different parts of the Middle East and Africa during the same time periods. The transition to written history occurs comparatively early in the history of the Middle East but much later in sub-Saharan Africa producing a much greater emphasis on Middle Eastern rather than African history in the corresponding period. The great concentration of archaeological research in the Middle East and Egypt has also provided historians with a much greater range of information on these areas than is the case with sub-Saharan Africa.

PART ONE: PREHISTORIC PERIOD

Paleolithic (Old Stone Age): ca. 2.6 million years before present (B.P.)–10,000 B.P.

This period includes the great majority of human history beginning with the earliest production of stone tools and ending just before the emergence of agriculture. In cultural terms it can usefully be subdivided into periods in which pre-humans and humans made advances in tool-production methods and other significant steps such as the controlled use of fire. These sub periods are usually referred to as the Lower, Middle, and Upper Paleolithic.

Lower Paleolithic: ca. 2.6 million B.P.–100,000 B.P.

The emergence of the first species of the genus *Homo*; the genus to which modern humans and their closest ancestors belong. *Homo habilis*, *Homo ergaster*, and *Homo erectus* emerge in East Africa and begin to migrate across the continent and into West Asia (the Middle East) and southern Europe. The ancestral relationships between these species is unclear but it is generally accepted that *Homo habilis* was the earliest and *Homo erectus* was the latest, and that *Homo habilis* was less adept at tool making than its successors.

ca. 2.6–1.7 million B.P.

Oldowan industry: The period of the earliest known tool-making industry. "Industry" in this sense refers to a common method of producing tools. These tools consist of roughly spherical quartz, quartzite, basalt, obsidian, flint, or chert stones with a segment struck away to create a cutting edge. The earliest known Oldowan artifacts are created by pre-human hominids in the Olduvai Gorge in present-day Tanzania.

ca. 1.7 million B.P.–100,000 B.P.

Acheulean industry: Roughly corresponding with the emergence of *Homo erectus* a new method of tool production comes into use. The stone tools produced in this period are more extensively and precisely worked and there is increasing sophistication over time. During this period *Homo erectus* groups are believed to have migrated from Africa into West Asia and Europe taking their tool-producing methods with them. The earliest known evidence of the controlled use of fire occurs at sites in East Africa dating from ca. 1.4–1.5 million B.P.

Middle Paleolithic (Middle Stone Age): ca. 300,000–50,000 B.P.

The emergence of anatomically modern humans (*Homo sapiens*) in East Africa. *Homo sapiens* begin migrating across Africa and into West Asia replacing earlier hominin species. Some features of behavioral modernity begin to emerge such as ritual, art, and the production of increasingly sophisticated bone and stone tools. Many historians argue that sophisticated language probably emerged during this period.

ca. 300,000–30,000 B.P.

Mousterian industry: Roughly corresponding with the emergence of *Homo sapiens* (anatomically modern humans) in East Africa and *Homo neanderthalensis* (Neanderthals) in Europe and West Asia a more sophisticated method of tool production comes into use. Mousterian industry tools are primarily made from flint and are produced in North Africa and the Middle East as well as across unglaciated regions of Europe.

Upper Paleolithic (Middle Stone Age): ca. 50,000–10,000 B.P.

The last sub period of the Paleolithic is characterized by the full emergence of human behavioral modernity. Fully modern humans (*Homo sapiens sapiens*) become the dominant species replacing all other earlier *Homo* species. Humans begin to establish semi-permanent settlements and to develop stone tools to work bone, antler, and hides. There is an apparent explosion of invention including fishhooks, eyed needles, rope, oil lamps, and advanced projectile weapons such as harpoons and the bow and arrow. The production of artworks such as cave painting and figurative sculpture becomes widespread, suggesting an increasingly sophisticated form of ritual and culture. Evidence of long distance trade in rare raw materials also emerges. In North Africa the region of the present-day Sahara Desert is a well-watered patchwork of grassland and woodland supporting numerous herbivores and predators.

Epipaleolithic: ca. 20,000–10,000 B.P.

Unlike in Europe, where there is a distinct period of cultural change associated with the dramatic climatic changes at the end of last glacial period (usually known as the Mesolithic or Middle Stone Age), climatic change in the Middle East and most of Africa was less dramatic and the transition from a hunter-gatherer lifestyle to settled agriculture (the mark of the later Neolithic period) was more gradual and less clearly defined. A group of transitional cultures exist, primarily in the Middle East, during this period.

ca. 18,000–14,000 B.P.

Kebaran culture: A nomadic culture of hunter-gatherers making use of microliths (small stone tools probably used as arrowheads or barbs) is in existence across much of western Asia.

ca. 14,500–11,500 B.P.

Natufian culture: In the eastern Mediterranean the earliest known settled communities emerge. This culture builds permanent dwellings, partially of stone, but continues to live a hunter-gatherer lifestyle. This unusual combination of settled habitation and hunting and gathering is thought to have been made possible by an abundance of game and wild cereals produced by a favorable climate. The Natufians make use of microliths (small stone tools probably used as arrowheads or barbs), bows and arrows, numerous stone and bone tools including sickles, and create sculpture. The presence of canine remains in human burials indicates that the domestication of the dog occurs in this period.

ca. 13,000–9,000 B.P.

Qadan culture: This culture in Upper Egypt (present-day southern Egypt) appears to be the first in the region to develop the systematic harvesting of wild cereal crops—a stage immediately preceding the development of true agriculture. Stone blades that may have been used to harvest cereals and associated grinding stones are in use. The people of the Qadan culture also practice ritual burial in cemeteries. Up to 40 percent of the individuals buried at the Jebel Sahaba cemetery show evidence of having died from wounds received from projectiles, suggesting a period of invasion or intense inter-tribal conflict.

Younger Dryas: ca. 12,900–11,500 B.P.

A brief period, in geological terms, in which glacial conditions return to northern latitudes and abruptly alter the climate of North Africa and the Middle East. The resulting drought in North Africa and the Middle East may have been a motivating factor for the development of settled agriculture by cultures in these regions.

ca. 11,000–8,000 B.P.

At Gobekli Tepe in present-day southeastern Turkey the earliest known shrine or temple complex is built by a hunter-gatherer culture. The builders of Gobekli Tepe may have been the first to develop settled agriculture as climate change forced them to abandon hunting and gathering as their primary means of subsistence.

Neolithic (New Stone Age): ca. 10,000–6,000 B.P. *(ca. 8,000–4,000* B.C.E.*)*

Cultures in the Middle East and North Africa continue to use stone tools but settled agriculture emerges as the most successful and widespread way of life. The earliest farmers raise einkorn wheat, millet, and spelt and keep dogs, sheep, and goats. In the Middle East and North Africa the advent of settled agriculture precedes the use of pottery, which does not become common until ca. 7,500 B.P. Across much of the rest of Africa a hunter-gatherer lifestyle continues to be viable.

ca. 8,000–7,300 B.P. *(ca. 6,000–5,300* B.C.E.*)*

Halafian culture: In northern Mesopotamia and present-day Turkey and Syria an agricultural society characterized by the production of glazed pottery decorated with animal designs and geometric patterns emerges. They build houses and temples from mud brick and produce ceramic female figurines.

Chalcolithic (Copper Age): ca. 7,500–6,000 B.P. *(ca. 5,500–4,000* B.C.E.*)*

Cultures in the Middle East begin to use copper tools alongside stone tools and to manufacture copper ornaments. The Chalcolithic is relatively brief in the Middle East where experimentation with alloying copper and tin to produce bronze (the characteristic technology of the succeeding Bronze Age) occurs soon after copper itself begins to be exploited.

ca. 7,300–6,100 B.P. *(ca. 5,300–4,100* B.C.E.*)*

Ubaid culture: This culture, centered on southern Mesopotamia, represents the first known permanent settlement of the area. The Ubaid culture develops through three stages: Early, Middle, and Late (or Classical). Early Ubaid culture is characterized by the development of new techniques for growing crops in a comparatively arid area. Middle Ubaid culture is characterized by the development of systematic irrigation by means of an extensive network of canals. Late Ubaid culture sees the beginnings and rapid northward spread of urbanization as well as the development of trade routes stretching from the Mediterranean to the southern tip of the Arabian peninsula. The wheel is invented, originally in the form of the potter's wheel.

ca. 6,000 to 5,000 B.P. (ca. 4,000 to 3,000 B.C.E.)

Uruk culture: This culture, which stretches across Mesopotamia, develops from the earlier Ubaid culture. Urbanization becomes the standard model of settlement across the region. Government and strong social stratification begin to develop in the new urban centers. Late in this culture the Early Dynastic Period of the Sumerian and Egyptian civilizations begin to emerge. Towards the end of this period some urban centers have populations of up to 20,000 people.

Bronze Age: ca. 5,300–3,200 B.P. (ca. 3,300–1,200 B.C.E.)

Cultures in the Middle East and North Africa develop the techniques to produce high quality bronze artifacts. The first systematic production of bronze artifacts begins in Mesopotamia and the technology subsequently spreads rapidly to Egypt, the Levant, and Anatolia (present-day Turkey). The early Bronze Age in the Middle East and North Africa coincides with the first writing systems and the beginnings of recorded history in those regions. In Mesopotamia the late period of the Uruk culture, the early period of Sumerian history, the Akkadian Empire, the Old Babylonian and Old Assyrian periods, and the period of the Kassite kings of Babylonia all occur in the Bronze Age. Egyptian history from the Early Dynastic Period to the New Kingdom Period takes place during the Bronze Age. In much of sub-Saharan Africa Bronze Age technology never becomes established and stone tools continue to be used until the introduction of iron smelting in West Africa in ca. 1200 B.C.E.

PART TWO: HISTORIC PERIOD

ca. 3200 B.C.E.

The earliest known Sumerian cuneiform tablets are produced.

The earliest known Egyptian hieroglyphics are produced.

ca. 3100–2686 B.C.E.

The Early (or Archaic) Dynastic Period in Egypt.

ca. 2900–2270 B.C.E.

The Early Dynastic Period of Sumerian culture.

ca. 2700 B.C.E.

The beginning of the Old Elamite Period and the reign of the first recorded Elamite king. The Elamite civilization was centered on an area east of Mesopotamia roughly corresponding to the Khuzestan province in the west of present-day Iran.

ca. 2686–2134 B.C.E.

The Old Kingdom Period in Egypt.

ca. 2500–2400 B.C.E.

In Egypt the pyramids of the Giza Necropolis are constructed.

ca. 2457 B.C.E.

King Eannatum of Lagash conquers all of Sumer (southern Mesopotamia) establishing the first known empire in the world.

ca. 2350 B.C.E.

King Lugal-zage-si of Uruk begins the expansion of Akkadian power across Sumer.

ca. 2300–2200 B.C.E.

Akkadian culture spreads as far west as Anatolia and the Mediterranean Sea and east to Elam in present-day Iran and the Akkadian language becomes the lingua franca of the Middle East.

ca. 2270–2083 B.C.E.

The period of the Akkadian Empire. Centered on the city of Akkad in present-day Iraq the Akkadian Empire supersedes Sumer as the predominant culture of Mesopotamia.

ca. 2270–2215 B.C.E.

Sargon rules the Akkadian Empire.

ca. 2150–2050 B.C.E.

The Gutian dynasty rules the Akkadian Empire.

ca. 2100–2000 B.C.E.

The collapse of Mesopotamian agriculture precipitates the downfall of the Akkadian Empire.

ca. 2040–1640 B.C.E.

The Middle Kingdom period in Egypt.

ca. 2000–1600 B.C.E.

The Old Period of Assyrian history. The first Assyrian Empire is established in northern Mesopotamia.

ca. 1900 B.C.E.

The southern Mesopotamian city of Babylon begins to grow in power; within 200 years it is the largest city in the world.

ca. 1792–50 B.C.E.

Reign of Hammurabi, the sixth Amorite king of Babylon. Hammurabi founds the Old Babylonian Empire.

ca. 1670 B.C.E.

Labarna, the first recorded Hittite ruler, extends his realm from an ancestral power base in Anatolia.

ca. 1650 B.C.E.

King Hattusili founds the Hittite capital of Hattusa (central Anatolia) and makes conquests throughout eastern Anatolia.

ca. 1648–1540 B.C.E.

The non-Egyptian Hyksos kings rule Egypt.

ca. 1600–1000 B.C.E.

The Middle Period of Assyrian history. Assyria emerges as a leading power in Mesopotamia. Conflicts with the Sea Peoples, the Arameans, and the Hittites eventually lead to a decline in Assyrian fortunes.

ca. 1595 B.C.E.

Samsuditana, the last king of the Old Babylonian Empire, is overthrown by Hittite invaders.

ca. 1540–1070 B.C.E.

The New Kingdom period in Egypt.

ca. 1500–1100 B.C.E.

The Kassite kings rule Babylon. Babylonia emerges as a unified state in southern Mesopotamia.

ca. 1500 B.C.E.

The beginning of the Middle Elamite Period.

ca. 1479–1425 B.C.E.

Thutmose III, sixth Pharaoh of the Eighteenth Dynasty, rules Egypt, first as coregent with his stepmother Hatshepsut and later as pharaoh. In a series of military campaigns Thutmose extends Egypt's empire to its greatest ever extent.

1440 B.C.E.

The traditional date of the exodus of the Jewish people from Egypt.

ca. 1400 B.C.E.

The ascendancy of King Tudhaliya marks the beginning of the Hittite New Kingdom.

ca. 1353–1336 B.C.E.

The reign of Pharaoh Akhenaten over Egypt, who attempts to impose a monotheistic faith on the entire kingdom—the worship of the sun god Aten.

ca. 1350–1322 B.C.E.

The height of Hittite power under Suppiluliuma I; his empire stretches from western Anatolia to present-day Lebanon.

ca. 1279–1213 B.C.E.

The reign of Pharaoh Ramesses II, also known as Ramesses the Great, over Egypt.

1274 B.C.E.

The Hittite and Egyptian empires clash at the Battle of Kadesh, in modern-day Syria. Both sides claim victory.

ca. 1274–1245 B.C.E.

The reign of Shalmaneser in Assyria. The First Assyrian Empire reaches its zenith under his rule and that of his son, Tukulti-Ninurta I.

1205 B.C.E.

The last recorded ruler of the Hittite New Kingdom dynasty, Suppiluliuma II, comes to the throne in Hattusa. Following the end of his reign at some time in the 1270s Hattusa was destroyed by fire, possibly by Sea Peoples.

ca. 1100 B.C.E.

The Beginning of the Neo-Elamite Period. The Elamites and the Babylonians ally against the rising power of the Neo-Assyrian Empire and Elamite kings rule in Babylon for a time.

ca. 1000–612 B.C.E.

The period of the Neo-Assyrian Empire.

ca. 813 B.C.E.

The Phoenician colony at Carthage in present-day Tunisia is founded.

ca. 700 B.C.E.

After a century of struggle, the Neo-Hittite city-states finally fall into the hands of the Assyrians. All semblance of Hittite identity seems to be lost at this time.

ca. 689 B.C.E.

Sennacherib, the ruler of Assyria, sacks the city of Babylon.

ca. 669–627 B.C.E.

The reign of Ashurbanipal II, the last of the great king of the Neo-Assyrian Empire.

ca. 646 B.C.E.

Ashurbanipal II defeats the Elamites and destroys their capital Susa.

ca. 627–605 B.C.E.

The reign of Nabopolassar, the first Chaldean king of Babylon and founder of the Neo-Babylonian Empire.

612 B.C.E.

The combined forces of the Medes and the Babylonians conquer the Assyrian capital Nineveh, and the Babylonian leader Nebuchadrezzar II seizes the territory of the Neo-Assyrian Empire.

ca. 600 B.C.E.

The Kingdom of Armenia is established under the Orontonid dynasty.

586 B.C.E.

The destruction of the Jewish First Temple (or Solomon's Temple) as the Babylonians capture Jerusalem and end the Kingdom of Judah. The Jewish elite are exiled to Babylon.

ca. 558–529 B.C.E.

The reign of Cyrus the Great, founder of the Achaemenid dynasty in Iran.

550–539 B.C.E.

Anatolia and Babylon are added to the Iranian Achaemenid Empire.

547 B.C.E.

The Kingdom of Lydia is conquered by the Achaemenids.

ca. 538 B.C.E.

Some Jews return to Jerusalem from Babylon.

539 B.C.E.

The Elamites are conquered by Cyrus the Great effectively ending the Elamite state.

Cyrus the Great conquers Babylonia ending the Neo-Babylonian Empire.

525–404 B.C.E.

Egypt is conquered by the Achaemenids.

522 B.C.E.

Darius I becomes ruler of the Achaemenid Empire after the death of Cambyses II.

515 B.C.E.

The Jewish Second Temple is built in Jerusalem.

490 B.C.E.

The Achaemenid ruler Darius I is defeated at the Battle of Marathon by Greek forces.

336–323 B.C.E.

The reign of Alexander the Great (also known as Alexander III of Macedon) over Macedon. During his rule Alexander defeats and conquers the territory of the Achaemenid Empire and Egypt and extends his empire into India.

332 B.C.E.

Alexander the Great conquers Egypt.

330 B.C.E.

Darius III, the last ruler of the Achaemenid dynasty, is defeated by Alexander the Great.

323 B.C.E.

Ptolemy is appointed satrap (governor) of Egypt after Alexander the Great's death.

312 B.C.E.

The Seleucid Empire is founded by Seleucus I.

305 B.C.E.

Ptolemy proclaims himself pharaoh of Egypt and founds the Ptolemaic dynasty.

95–66 B.C.E.

The Kingdom of Armenia reaches its greatest extent under Tigranes II (known as Tigranes the Great). Its territory extends from the Mediterranean coast in the west to the shores of the Caspian Sea in the east.

51–30 B.C.E.

The reign of Cleopatra VII, the last pharaoh of Egypt and the last of the Ptolemaic dynasty.

30 B.C.E.

Egypt becomes a Roman province.

First century

ca. 1 C.E.

Bantu-speaking peoples begin to disperse across Africa.

ca. 40

Christianity is introduced to Egypt.

64

Rome occupies Phoenicia, which becomes part of a new Roman colony called Syria.

66–73

A Jewish rebellion against the Romans ends in collapse with the destruction of Jerusalem and the Second Temple. This is the traditional date for the beginning of the Jewish Diaspora.

70

The Roman emperor Vespasian and his son Titus besiege Jerusalem and destroy the Jewish Second Temple.

Second century

ca. 100

The Axumite kingdom is established in present-day Ethiopia.

110

The Himyarite kingdom is founded in Arabia.

132–135

The Jewish leader Shimon Bar Kochba briefly ejects the Romans from Jerusalem and reestablishes a Jewish state but Roman forces reconquer Bar Kochba's state within three years. The new Roman name for the territory, "Palaestina," becomes standard over the coming centuries. Jerusalem is renamed Aelia Capitolina by the Romans, and Jewish people are prohibited from entering the city.

Third century

Bantu-speakers reach the north and southeast of present-day South Africa.

ca. 200

Greek records mention Jews in Ethiopia.

The Nok Culture of present-day Nigeria ends.

222

The rule of the Sassanian dynasty over the Persian Empire begins when the vassal king Ardashir revolts and captures the Persian capital, Ctesiphon.

285

The Romans abandon their African territories on the northwest coast.

FOURTH CENTURY

ca. 300

The Empire of Ghana emerges in present-day Mali.

ca. 301–314

Christianity becomes the state religion of the Kingdom of Armenia.

313

The Edict of Milan legalizes Christianity in the Roman Empire.

324

The Axumite kingdom conquers the Meroitic kingdom (present-day Sudan).

392

Christianity becomes the official religion of Roman Empire.

FIFTH CENTURY

428

The Kingdom of Armenia comes to an end following conquests by the Iranian Sassanian Empire and the Roman Empire.

429

The Vandals, an European people, begin their conquest of the north coast of Africa.

451

The Council of Chalcedon establishes the Coptic Church of Egypt as a distinct church body.

SIXTH CENTURY

510

The death of Hashim ibn Abd al-Manaf, the progenitor of the Hashemites.

533

Vandal territories in North Africa are conquered by the Byzantine Empire.

SEVENTH CENTURY

610

The prophet Muhammad receives the first revelations of the Quran, the principal religious text of Islam.

622

The *hijra*—the prophet Muhammad and his followers leave Mecca and flee to Medina. The Muslim calendar is counted from this year.

632

The death of the prophet Muhammad; Muslim conquests outside of Arabia begin.

632–661

The period of the Rashidun Caliphate, the first Arab caliphate, also known as the period of the rule of the Rightly Guided Caliphs or the Righteous Caliphs.

639–642

Muslim Arabs conquer Egypt.

640

Arab armies begin their conquest of North Africa bringing Islam to the region.

642

The Persian Sassanian dynasty comes to a decisive end with the Arab victory over Persia at Nehavand.

Islam is introduced to the Azeris by their Arab conquerors.

650–1300

Large, cattle-owning, Iron-Age "Toutswe tradition" communities in existence in present-day Botswana.

661

Ali, son-in-law and cousin of the prophet Muhammad, is assassinated in Kufa in present-day Iraq. He is buried in Najaf and his tomb later becomes the site of the Imam Ali Mosque.

661–750

The period of the Umayyad Caliphate; the second Arab caliphate.

680

The killing of Ali's son Husayn at Karbala in present-day Iraq.

691

The Dome of the Rock, an important Muslim site to the present day, is built in Jerusalem.

EIGHTH CENTURY

706–715

The Umayyad Mosque is built in Damascus.

ca. 750

The Kingdom of Kangaba, from which the powerful Empire of Mali emerges, is founded in present-day Mali. The Songhay state also emerges in present-day Mali.

750–1258

The period of the Abbasid Caliphate; the third Arab caliphate.

NINTH CENTURY

Muslim Arabs settle in the Horn of Africa.

The Takrur state is founded in present-day Senegal.

ca. 800

The Kingdom of Kanem emerges in the Lake Chad region.

873–874

The disappearance of the 12th Shii imam—the leader believed by the Shia to be the rightful successor to the prophet Muhammad.

TENTH CENTURY

Islamic Somali nomads begin to expand southward; Arab trading posts at Mogadishu (in present-day Somalia) and Kilwa (in present-day Tanzania) are established.

The Bambandyanalo-Mapungubwe trading center on the Limpopo River flourishes.

909–1171

The period of the Fatamid Caliphate; the fourth and final Arab caliphate.

945–1055

The period of the rule of the Iranian Buyid dynasty in Baghdad.

969

The city of Cairo is established in Egypt by the Fatimid dynasty as their capital.

990–1020

Oghuz Turks, including the clan of Seljuk, migrate southward from the Aral Sea and convert to Islam.

ELEVENTH CENTURY

Bantu-speakers migrate from mainland Africa to Madagascar.

The major Iron-Age settlement known as Leopard Kopje is built in present-day Zimbabwe.

1037–1194

The period of the Turkic Seljuk empire.

1040

The Seljuk leaders Tughril Beg and Chagri Beg lead a rebellion that defeats the forces of the Persian Ghaznavid dynasty at the Battle of Dandanqan.

ca. 1050

Islam is introduced to West Africa.

1054

The foundation of the Berber Almoravid dynasty in present-day Western Sahara.

1055

The Seljuk leader Tughril Beg captures Baghdad and is named "sultan of the east and west."

1063–72

The reign of the Seljuk sultan Alp Arslan.

1069

The Berber Almoravid dynasty conquers Morocco.

1071

The Battle of Manzikert; the Seljuk Turks under the leadership of Alp Arslan defeat the Byzantines and Turkic elements begin to populate the Anatolian peninsula (present-day Turkey). The Byzantine emperor Romanos IV Diogenesis is captured in the battle.

1077–1307

The period of the rule of the Seljuks of Rum on the Anatolian peninsula (present-day Turkey).

1080–1375

The period of the Armenian Kingdom of Cilicia. Armenians begin migrating into Cilicia, a region extending from the northeast coast of the Mediterranean Sea inland to the Taurus Mountains, around 1080 and establish a Christian state.

1092

The Seljuk sultan Malikshah I dies. The Seljuk empire is at its greatest extent stretching from the Hindu Kush to eastern Anatolia and from Central Asia to the Persian Gulf.

1099

European Crusaders capture Jerusalem and begin to establish Christian states in the Middle East.

1100–1300

The Bambandyanalo-Mapungubwe trading center (on the border of present-day South Africa and Zimbabwe) is at its height.

TWELFTH CENTURY

The Great Zimbabwe civilization develops in present-day Zimbabwe.

1117

The beginning of the rule of the Zagwe dynasty in Ethiopia.

1147

The Berber Almohad dynasty is founded in present-day Western Sahara.

ca. 1150

The Ghana Empire is at its height in West Africa.

1150

The Berber Almoravid Empire collapses and their territories come under the control of the Almohads.

1169

The Fatimid Empire collapses.

1169–1867

The semi-autonomous Kurdish Ardalan state flourishes in northwest Iran.

1171–1250

The rule of the Kurdish Ayyubid dynasty is founded by Saladin.

1187

Saladin, the founder of the Ayyubid dynasty, recaptures Jerusalem from European Crusaders.

1194

Togrul III, the last Seljuk sultan, is defeated by the Iranian Khwarezmian Empire.

1199–1300

The period of the greatest flourishing of the Cilician Kingdom of Armenia. Armenian culture experiences a golden age despite expansionist pressure from its Arab and Byzantine neighbors.

Thirteenth century

The kingdom of Benin emerges in present-day Nigeria. Mossi states begin to be established in present-day Ghana.

Mogadishu is the preeminent port in East Africa.

ca. 1230

The Kanem state in present-day Chad and Libya reaches its height.

1235

The Mali Empire is founded in present-day Mali.

1236–42

Mongol invaders rule over the Azeris.

ca. 1240

The Mali Empire absorbs the Ghana and Songhay states.

1243

The Seljuks become vassals of the Mongols.

ca. 1250

The Takrur state in present-day Senegal is absorbed by the empire of Mali.

1250

The rule of the Mamluk dynasty in Egypt begins; Egypt becomes the center of the eastern Arab world.

1258

The Mongols under Chenggis Khan sack Baghdad and kill the Abbasid caliph. This event marks the end of the Abbasid Caliphate.

1265

The death of Hulegu, grandson of the Mongol leader Chenggis Khan, and founder of the Ilkhanid dynasty.

1268

The Ethiopian Zagwe dynasty is overthrown and the Amharic Solomonic dynasty is established.

1269

The Almohad Empire collapses.

1285

The Muslim Afar are unified under the Caliphate of Ifat in present-day Ethiopia and Somalia.

1299

Osman I, founder of the Ottoman dynasty of the Ottoman Empire, declares independence from the Seljuks.

The Mongols under Ghazan Khan sack Damascus and conquer Syria.

ca. 1300

The Yoruba state of Oyo is established in present-day Nigeria. The Oyo Empire later becomes a major power in West Africa.

Fourteenth century

Kilwa is the most important trading port on the east coast of Africa.

The founding of the Kongo kingdom on the Congo River in present-day Angola and the Democratic Republic of the Congo.

The Great Zimbabwe civilization in present-day Zimbabwe reaches its height.

Muslim trading colonies and kingdoms are established on Madagascar.

Ingombe Ilede is a major Central African trading link with the east coast.

ca. 1325

The Mali Empire reaches its height.

1340s

The Songhay state becomes independent from the Mali Empire.

ca. 1350– ca. 1500

The Bachwezi dynasty rules over the Bunyoro-Kitara state (in present-day Uganda) and the Nyoro religion develops.

ca. 1350

The Hausa city-states emerge in present-day Nigeria.

1375

Levon V, the last king of the Armenian Kingdom of Cilicia, is deposed.

1381–1404

The Turkic leader Timur conquers Iran, Iraq, Syria, parts of India, and parts of the Ottoman Empire, enlarging his empire to a scale comparative with that of the Mongols of the previous century.

1382–1517

The rule of the dynasty of the Circassian Mamluks in Egypt and Syria.

1382–1399

Barquq, a Circassian Mamluk, declares himself sultan and rules the Mamluk lands of Egypt and Syria until his death.

1386

The State of Borno is established in the Lake Chad region.

1387

The Turkic leader Timur establishes the Timurid dynasty over Persia.

FIFTEENTH CENTURY

The Ndongo Kingdom is established to the south of the kingdom of Kongo in present-day Angola.

1415

The caliphate of Ifat is conquered by Ethiopia; the Ifat state is succeeded by the Adal state.

1443

Portugal establishes its first fort on the West African coast in present-day Mauritania.

1444–81

The reign of the Ottoman sultan Mehmed II the Conqueror.

1447–51

Wars between the Turkic Black Sheep and White Sheep tribal confederations in Anatolia (present-day Turkey).

1453

The Ottomans capture the Byzantine capital of Constantinople (present-day Istanbul); the city subsequently becomes the capital of the Ottoman Empire.

1482

Portuguese explorers reach the Congo River estuary and encounter the Kongo kingdom.

1484

Christianity is introduced to the Kongo kingdom.

ca. 1490

The Mali Empire is eclipsed by the expanding Songhay Empire.

1491

The Kongo king Nzinga Nkguwu and his court are converted to Christianity.

1492

Jews expelled from Spain are welcomed into the Ottoman Empire by Bayezid II.

1494

Pro- and anti-Portuguese factions develop within the Kongo kingdom.

1498

Portuguese Vasco da Gama visits cities on the East African coast.

SIXTEENTH CENTURY

by 1500

The site of Great Zimbabwe is abandoned; civilization moves north and the Mutapa Empire is established.

1500s–1700s

Successive Tsonga kingdoms, Nyaka, Tembe, and Maputo flourish in present-day Mozambique.

1501–1722

The period of the rule of the Safavid dynasty in Iran. Twelver Shia is established as the state's official faith.

1501

Shah Ismail founds the Safavid dynasty of Iran.

1502–1509

The Portuguese conquer much of the East African coast and gain control of trade.

1505

The Funj kingdom is founded in present-day Sudan.

1506

Civil war breaks out in the Kongo kingdom; Affonso I succeeds as king with Portuguese support; Affonso attempts to westernize the Kongo people.

1507

The Portuguese capture Muscat and establish forts along the northern coast of Oman.

ca. 1510

Start of the Atlantic slave trade.

1511

The Portuguese discover the uninhabited island of Mauritius.

1512–20

Reign of the Ottoman sultan Selim I.

ca. 1515

The Songhay Empire reaches its height in West Africa extending inland from the Atlantic coast along the course of the Niger River to the southern limits of the Sahara Desert.

1517

The Ottoman sultan Selim I defeats the last of the Mamluks and conquers Egypt.

1520–66

The reign of the Ottoman sultan Suleyman "the Magnificent."

1520s

The Kongo kingdom supplies slaves to the Portuguese on São Tomé.

1526

The Adal state declares Islamic holy war on Christian Ethiopia.

1526

The Borno state controls Kanem.

1543

Ethiopia conquers the Adal state.

ca. 1550

The Wolof Empire dissolves.

The Mali Empire ceases to exist.

A centralized Luba kingdom is in existence in the present-day Democratic Republic of the Congo.

ca. 1550s

The Bunyoro kingdom in present-day Uganda reaches its greatest extent.

Tutsi people found the kingdom of Ruanda (present-day Rwanda).

1551

The Ottomans conquer Tripoli in present-day Libya.

1556

War breaks out between the Kongo people and the Portuguese-backed Ndongo people to the south; the Ndongo ngola (ruler) is victorious; Portuguese slave trade with the Ndongo expands.

1557

The Suleymaniye Mosque in Istanbul is completed by the architect Sinan.

1571

Defeat of the Ottoman navy by a combined European fleet at the Battle of Lepanto.

1571

The Portuguese drive Jaga invaders from Kongo; the Kongo kingdom becomes a Portuguese vassal state.

1574

The Selimiye Mosque in Edirne is completed by the architect Sinan.

The Ottomans control most of North Africa except Morocco.

1576

An independent Portuguese fort is established at Luanda in present-day Angola; it becomes a major slave depot.

1587

The Portuguese take control of the Cape Verde Islands.

1590

The Songhay Empire is conquered by the Moroccans.

1590s

Dutch trading ships begin to stop for supplies at the future site of Cape Town (in present-day South Africa).

The Dutch occupy Mauritius. Dutch settlement of the island does not begin until the 1630s.

1591

The Muslim Kanem-Borno state in Central and West Africa reaches its greatest extent stretching across present-day Chad, Cameroon, and Nigeria.

SEVENTEENTH CENTURY

1600s

The Tutsi kingdom in Urundi (present-day Burundi) is established.

1619

The Portuguese and the Jaga people conquer the Ndongo kingdom.

1623

Nzinga Mbandi (also known as Anna) becomes the Ndongo queen and leads the Ndongo against Portuguese rule.

1625

The Dahomey state is established in present-day Benin.

1631

England establishes its first colonial post on the Gold Coast in present-day Ghana.

ca. 1640

Fante states emerge in present-day Ghana.

1641

The Dutch take Luanda from the Portuguese; Nzinga forces the Portuguese from Angola.

1648

The Angolans and the Dutch are defeated by Brazilian landowner Salvador de Sa restoring the colony to Portugal.

1649–1850

The semi-autonomous Kurdish Baban state flourishes in northern Iraq and eastern Turkey.

ca. 1650

The Bemba kingdom is founded in present-day Zambia.

The Sultanate of Wadai is founded in present-day Chad.

1650

The Portuguese are driven out of Oman by the Omanis. The Omanis begin to establish a maritime trading empire that eventually encompasses Zanzibar and Mombasa in East Africa as well as parts of India.

1652

Omani Arab traders begin to settle on the East African coast.

1657

Former Dutch East India Company soldiers and other groups of Europeans settle as farmers (Boers) in the Cape Town area (present-day South Africa).

1657–1677

Khoikhoi people and Boers in conflict in present-day South Africa.

1665–1670

The Portuguese invade and establish rule over the Kongo kingdom.

1670

The rule of the Alawid dynasty begins in Morocco.

1670s

Asante clans unify in present-day Ghana.

1699

The Omanis displace the Portuguese and control much of the East African coast.

EIGHTEENTH CENTURY

The emergence of the Lozi kingdom in present-day Zambia.

A centralized Lunda Empire emerges in present-day Democratic Republic of the Congo.

The Funj Sultanate of northern Sudan reaches its greatest extent.

ca. 1700

The kingdom of Kong emerges in present-day Ivory Coast.

1703–30

The reign of the Ottoman sultan Ahmed III.

1710

The Dutch abandon Mauritius.

1715

The French occupy Mauritius.

1718–30

The Tulip Period in Ottoman history; the Ottomans consolidate their territorial gains and enter a phase of cultural growth.

1722–36

The Safavid dynasty of Iran collapses under a series of invasions from Afghan, Russian, and Ottoman forces.

1727

The Dahomey state in present-day Benin reaches its greatest extent.

1740

The Segu state is founded in present-day Mali.

1744

The First Saudi state is founded by Prince Muhammad ibn Saud.

1748

The Dahomey state in present-day Benin is conquered by the nascent Oyo Empire.

1749

The Al Bu Said dynasty comes to power in Oman.

1756

Sabah I, the first emir of Kuwait, comes to power with the support of the Ottoman sultan.

1756

The Seychelles become a French territory.

ca. 1770

Umbundu kingdoms are established in present-day Angola.

1789

The Oyo Empire centered in present-day western Nigeria reaches its greatest extent.

1794

The Seychelles are captured by the British.

1795–1799

Several unsuccessful Boer rebellions against Cape authority take place.

1795–1925

The period of the rule of the Qajar dynasty in Iran.

by 1797

The Merina kingdom is established on Madagascar.

1798

The French general Napoleon invades Egypt.

1799–1878

A series of nine Cape-Xhosa wars between the Xhosa and the Boers and, later, the Xhosa and the British: the Xhosa are eventually defeated by the British.

NINETEENTH CENTURY

by 1800

The Kazembe state in present-day Zambia controls transcontinental trade routes.

19th century

Buganda supplants Bunyoro as most powerful kingdom in the region.

1801

Ottoman and British forces take Egypt from France.

1805

Muhammad Ali comes to power in Egypt.

1806

The British take control of the Cape from the Dutch.

The Cape and Mauritius become British colonies.

1807

The Ottoman sultan Selim III is deposed and imprisoned by members of the Janissary corps (the sultan's standing army). He is murdered by the Janissary the following year.

1808–39

The reign of the Ottoman sultan Mahmud II. The Ottomans lose control of Greece and Algeria during this period prompting the sultan to dismantle the Janissary corps and established a new military structure. These reforms lay the foundations for the later Tanzimar (or "reform") period.

1809

The Hausa states are overrun in the Fulani jihad (holy war). The Sokoto Caliphate is founded by the Fulani in present-day Nigeria.

1814

The Seychelles become a British colony.

by 1815

The Nguni kingdoms of Ndwandwe (ruled by Zwide), Ngwane (ruled by Sobhuza I), and Mthethwa (ruled by Dingiswayo) dominate the region east of the Drakensberg Mountains.

1816

The Fante state in present-day Ghana is defeated by the Asante.

1816

Shaka becomes the leader of the Zulu people. He rules until his death in 1828.

1818

Dahomey breaks away from the declining Oyo Empire.

1818–19

The Zulu-Ndwandwe war establishes Zulu supremacy in the region.

1819–39

The Mfecane period of mass migrations and wars in present-day South Africa.

1820

Britain concludes the first of a series of agreements with local rulers on the southern shore of the Persian Gulf intended to limit the activities of maritime raiders in the area. These states become known as the Trucial States.

1820s

Mzilikazi founds the Ndebele kingdom in present-day South Africa.

1821

The Egyptians destroy the Funj kingdom.

1821–29

The Greek War of Independence against Ottomans rule.

1822–1837

Much of the East African coast comes under Omani rule.

1824

Moshoeshoe founds the Basuto kingdom (present-day Lesotho).

The second Saudi state is founded by Turki ibn Abdallah ibn Muhammad.

1824–1874

Four major Anglo-Asante wars leave the Asante Empire in disarray.

1827

The Battle of Navarino; European forces supporting the Greek struggle for independence decisively defeat the Ottoman navy.

ca. 1830

The Muslim Sokoto state of present-day northern Nigeria reaches its greatest extent.

1830s

The Ngoni state of Gaza emerges in present-day Mozambique.

ca. 1830

The Babito prince of Bunyoro founds the independent Toro kingdom in present-day Uganda.

1831

The Sotho people defeat the invading Ndebele.

1832

Zanzibar becomes the capital of Oman.

ca. 1835

Arab and Swahili slave trading caravans begin to visit the interior of East Africa.

1836

The Oyo Empire dissolves and the Ibadan Empire emerges in present-day southern Nigeria.

1836

The Portuguese outlaw the slave trade in their territories.

1836–48

The Great Trek brings Boers into conflict with peoples across the interior of present-day South Africa.

1837

The Ndebele migrate north to Matebeleland in present-day Zimbabwe.

1838

The Zulus are defeated by the Boers at the Battle of Blood River.

1839

The Boer republic of Natalia is founded.

1839–65

The reign of Mswati I over the Ngwane and the creation of a powerful Swazi nation.

1839–76

The Tanzimat (or "reform") period in Ottoman history. Reforms of industry, military, and banking intended to modernize the state are instituted.

1840s–80s

Height of the Arab and Swahili slave trade in East Africa.

1841

Mayotte (one of the Comoros Islands) becomes a French colony.

1842

French rule in Algeria begins.

1843

The Boer republic of Natalia is seized by the British who rename it the colony of Natal.

1847

Liberia is established by freed American slaves.

1850s

The Oromo people begin to establish Muslim kingdoms in Ethiopia.

The Muslim Wadai state in present-day Chad reaches its greatest extent.

1852

The South African Republic (Transvaal) is founded by Boers.

The Muslim Tukolor Empire is established in present-day Mali.

1852–73

British explorer David Livingstone travels Central and East Africa.

1854

The Orange Free State is founded by Boers.

1856

Zanzibar becomes an independent sultanate.

1858

The Portuguese abolish slavery in their territories.

1859–70

War between the Bunyoro and Toro kingdoms in present-day Uganda.

1859–69

The Suez Canal is constructed in Egypt by a French company.

1860–67

The Venda and Sotho peoples drive the Boers out of lands north of the Olifants River.

1865–68

Basuto becomes the British colony of Basutoland after its defeat by the Orange Free State.

1867

The first diamonds are discovered in the Vaal Valley (in present-day South Africa).

1870s–80s

The Second Manding Empire is established in present-day Senegal as successor to the empire of Mali.

1873

The Zanzibar slave market closes.

1876

The Young Ottoman reformers introduce a new constitution that limits the power of the Ottoman sultan and establishes a parliament. Sultan Abdulhamid II later suspends this parliament.

1877

The British annex the Boer Transvaal republic.

1877–78

Russo-Turkish War; the Ottomans lose control of Cyprus.

1878

Circassian refugees arrive in Jordan, reviving the ancient city of Amman, which later becomes the country's capital. Circassians who had first been settled in the Balkans after their expulsion from the Caucasus also arrive in Syria and Israel.

1879

Rabih b. Fadl Allah begins to build an empire in present-day Chad and Nigeria.

1880s–1914

The "Scramble for Africa;" European states compete to establish colonial control over the majority of the African continent.

1880–81

The "Gun War"—an unsuccessful Sotho rebellion against British rule.

The Transvaal Boers rebel against British rule.

1881

French rule begins in Tunisia.

1882

British rule begins in Egypt.

An Anglo-Egyptian force conquers Sudan.

The Muslim leader known as the Mahdi begins campaigns against the British and Egyptians.

The first *aliya*, or "ascent," of Jewish immigrants fleeing persecution in Russia and Central Europe begins to arrive in Palestine.

1883–84

The Zulu Civil War follows the British partition of Zululand.

1884–85

At the Berlin Conference the European states reach a series of agreements assigning mutually recognized spheres of influence in Africa. European colonialism in Africa accelerates rapidly.

1884

French Somaliland (present-day Djibouti) and British Somaliland (present-day Somalia) are established as colonies.

The Germans colonize South West Africa (present-day Namibia).

1885

The British colony of Bechuanaland (present-day Botswana) is established in the territory of the Tswana people.

The Comoros become a French colony.

The Belgian king Leopold II establishes his personal colony—the Congo Free State—in the present-day Democratic Republic of the Congo.

The Spanish colony of Río de Oro is established in present-day Western Sahara.

1885–87

Zululand is divided between British Zululand and the Transvaal.

1886

Italian Somaliland (present-day Somalia) is established.

The city of Johannesburg is founded in present-day South Africa.

1889

The Mahdist State in present-day Sudan reaches its greatest extent.

1890

The Barotseland Treaty delivers the Lozi kingdom to the British South Africa Company (BSA) as Barotseland, part of BSA's colony of Northern Rhodesia.

The British South Africa Company colonizes Southern Rhodesia (present-day Zimbabwe).

1891

Britain declares a protectorate over Nyasaland (present-day Malawi).

The House of Al Rashid defeats the second Saudi state at the Battle of Mulayda.

1892

The Dahomey state is conquered by the French.

The Trucial States of the Persian Gulf become British protectorates.

1893

The Kanem-Borno state is defeated by Rabih b. Fadl.

The French conquer the Tukolor empire.

1894

Swaziland becomes a British colony.

1894–97

The Hamidan Massacres are carried out under the policies of the Ottoman sultan Abdulhamid II. As many as 200,000 Armenian are killed and many thousands more are forced to emigrate.

1895

Britain and Germany complete their partition of the territories of the Sultanate of Zanzibar. The British take control of Kenya.

France forms a federation of colonies that becomes French West Africa.

The French colonize Madagascar.

1896

The British found the Gold Coast colony on the territory of the defeated Asante Empire in present-day Ghana.

Italian forces are defeated by the Ethiopians at the Battle of Adowa; Ethiopia conquers the Oromo kingdoms.

The Bunyoro and Toro kingdoms in present-day Uganda become British protectorates.

1897

The Benin kingdom and the Ibadan Empire in present-day Nigeria are conquered by the British.

Urundi (present-day Burundi) comes under German rule.

Theodor Herzl, the founder of political Zionism, convenes the first World Zionist Congress in Basel, Switzerland, to promote the idea of a Jewish homeland in Israel.

1897–1900

The Bemba state is conquered by the British South Africa Company; it becomes part of Northern Rhodesia (present-day Zambia).

1898

Anglo-Egyptian forces conquer the Mahdist state.

The Second Mandinka Empire is conquered by the French.

1899

Kuwait becomes a British protectorate. Britain continues to recognize nominal Ottoman rule over Kuwait but deploys warships and troops to deter Ottoman occupation.

1899–1902

The Anglo-Boer War (also known as the Second Boer War) ends with the two independent Boer republics (the Orange Free State and the South African Republic) being defeated by the British.

Twentieth Century

1900

Buganda becomes a part of the British protectorate of Uganda.

1901

The French conquer the empire of Rabih az-Zubayr ibn Fadl Allah and the Mossi states in the Lake Chad area.

1902

Abd al Aziz al Saud recaptures the former Saudi capital of Riyahd from the Al Rashid.

The remaining Asante territories are annexed to the British colony of the Gold Coast (present-day Ghana).

1902–03

The Ovimbundu people engage in the failed Bailundo Revolt against the Portuguese colonization of present-day Angola.

1903

Mauritania becomes a French protectorate.

The Sokoto state in present-day Nigeria is conquered by the British.

1904–05

An uprising by the Herero people is suppressed by German forces in South West Africa.

1907

A new constitution limits the absolute power of the Iranian monarchy for the first time.

1908

The Belgian government takes control of the Congo Free State from the king renaming it the Belgian Congo (the present-day Democratic Republic of the Congo).

The Young Turk Revolution reestablishes the suspended 1876 Ottoman constitution and parliament. The Young Turks advocate limits to the power of the sultan. The revolution is a significant step towards the eventual dissolution of the empire.

1909

The Wadai state is conquered by the French.

1910

The Union of South Africa unites the British Cape and Natal with the Boer republics.

1911

Italy occupies Libya.

1912

The Afrikaner-based National Party and the South African Native National Congress (SANNC) are formed.

French rule begins in Morocco.

1912–13

The Balkan Wars; the Ottomans lose their territories in the Balkans to nationalist independence movements.

1913

A coup initiates the Rule of the Three Pashas (key government ministers) over the Ottoman state; the Ottomans form an alliance with Germany.

1914–18

World War I

1914

Egypt becomes a British protectorate.

1915

The Sykes-Picot agreement between France and Britain decides the future of territory within the Ottoman Empire.

1915–17

The Ottoman government deports hundreds of thousands of Armenians to Syria because of their suspected pro-Russian sympathies. Many thousands die as the result of violence or privation. Armenian historians refer to these events as the Armenian Genocide.

1916–18

The "Arab Revolt" against the Ottomans is encouraged and partly funded by the British.

1916

The German colonies of Togoland (present-day Togo and Ghana) and Kamerun (present-day Cameroon) are occupied by Britain and France.

Ruanda (present-day Rwanda) and Urundi (present-day Burundi) are occupied by Belgium.

Qatar becomes a British protectorate.

1917

Britain issues the Balfour Declaration in favor of the establishment of a Jewish state in Palestine.

1918

At the end of World War I the Ottoman Empire is defeated by Allied forces. The League of Nations grants Britain a mandate over the former Ottoman territories of Iraq, Palestine, and Transjordan, and the French gain control of Syria and Lebanon.

At the climax of the "Arab Revolt" an Arab army captures Damascus, ending four centuries of rule by the Ottoman Empire.

1920

The Syrian National Congress proclaims Faysal bin al-Hussein bin Ali el-Hashemi King Faysal I of Syria. He is swiftly deposed by French forces and France establishes the State of Greater Lebanon, including parts of the Lebanon Mountains and the Bekaa Valley traditionally regarded as part of Syria.

1921

Faysal I is installed by the British as the king of Iraq.

1922

Armenia is incorporated into the Union of Soviet Socialist Republics (USSR).

Britain grants self-government to Egypt.

The British government takes control of League of Nations' Mandate of Palestine.

Turkish nationalists abolish the Ottoman sultanate.

1922–24

The short-lived Kingdom of Kurdistan exists in northern Iraq.

1922–39

The Mandate period sees large-scale immigration of Jewish farmers, workers, and intellectuals from Europe to Palestine. Tel Aviv, Haifa, and Jerusalem grow substantially, and a culture develops with modern Hebrew as its language.

1923

The Republic of Turkey is declared with Mustafa Kemal as its first president.

Egypt becomes a constitutional monarchy.

The South African Native National Congress becomes the African National Congress (ANC).

1923–24

The British government takes control of the British South Africa Company territories of Southern and Northern Rhodesia (present-day Zimbabwe and Zambia); Africans in the Rhodesias begin to be forced into reserves and whites are encouraged to settle.

1925

Abd al Aziz al Saud captures the cities of Mecca and Medina.

The Iranian parliament appoints Reza Shah (also known as Reza Pahlavi) to the throne of Iranian.

Turkey adopts the western Gregorian calendar.

1927–31

The short-lived Kurdish Republic of Ararat exists in Turkey.

1928

Inkatha, the Zulu nationalist movement, is founded.

1930

Haile Selassie I becomes emperor of Ethiopia.

1932

The foundation of the modern Kingdom of Saudi Arabia with Abd al-Aziz Ibn Saud as king.

1932

Iraq becomes an independent state. Faysal I, crowned in 1921, is head of state.

1934

Mustafa Kemal is awarded the title "Atatürk" ("Father of the Turks").

1935–41

Italian forces invade and occupy Ethiopia.

1936–39

Arab protests against British rule and Jewish immigration in Palestine erupt into the Arab Uprising. In 1937 the Peel Commission recommends the partition of Palestine.

1937

Substantial oil reserves are discovered by the Kuwait Oil Company, which is partly owned by the British Anglo-Persian Oil Company (later British Petroleum).

1938

Death of Mustafa Kemal Atatürk, first president of the Republic of Turkey.

Oil is discovered in Saudi Arabia.

1939–45

World War II; many major battles are fought in North Africa between Allied and Axis forces.

1939

King Ghazi of Iraq dies and is succeeded by his son King Faysal II. As the new king is still a child, his uncle Abd al-ilah rules in his stead.

Oil is discovered on Qatari territory.

1941

British and Free French forces occupy Syria. The French undertake to grant Syrian independence.

Lebanon is occupied by British and Free French forces.

British and Russian forces invade Iran during World War II and depose Reza Shah because of his support for the Axis powers. Reza Shah's son, Muhammad Reza Pahlavi, is installed on the throne by the British.

1943

Lebanon becomes independent.

1945

The Arab League, an organization of Arab states, is founded.

1946

The last French forces leave Syria.

Transjordan becomes independent as the Hashemite Kingdom of Jordan.

1947

The Pan-Arabist Baath Party is founded.

1948

President David Ben-Gurion declares Israel's independence in Tel Aviv, in accordance with the United Nations partition plan.

The first Arab-Israeli War results in an influx of thousands of Palestinians into southern Lebanon.

Apartheid begins in South Africa.

1950s

The Kariba Dam is built on the Zambezi River displacing thousands of people.

Oil is discovered in the Trucial States, and foreign companies begin investing in oil extraction and production facilities.

1951

King Abdullah of Jordan is assassinated.

Libya becomes independent from Italy.

1952

A coup deposes the British-backed monarchy in Egypt; rise to power of Gamal Abdel Nasser.

Eritrea is federated to Ethiopia.

Hussein, the grandson of Abdullah, becomes king of Jordan and rules until his death in 1999.

Turkey joins the North Atlantic Treaty Organization (NATO).

1952–60

The Mau Mau rebellion in Kenya fights against British rule. The rebels are defeated militarily but numerous concessions are made by the colonial authorities.

1953

King Faysal II becomes king of Iraq.

Northern Rhodesia (present-day Zambia), Southern Rhodesia (present-day Zimbabwe), and Nyasaland (present-day Malawi) are combined to form the white-minority ruled Central African Federation (CAF).

1956

Gamel Abdel Nasser becomes president of Egypt. Nasser nationalizes the Suez Canal leading to the Suez Crisis; Israel, Britain, and France invade Egypt but are compelled to reach a peace settlement before achieving their military goals.

French Morocco and Spanish Morocco become independent as a single nation.

Sudan becomes independent from British and Egyptian rule.

Tunisia becomes independent from France.

1957

Gold Coast becomes independent from Britain as Ghana.

1958

A military coup in Iraq overthrows the monarchy and the country is declared a republic. One of the coup leaders, Abdel-Karim Qasim, becomes prime minister.

The Zambia Africa National Congress (ZANC) is formed in the Central African Federation with Kenneth Kaunda as president.

French Guinea becomes independent from France as Guinea.

1958–61

Egypt and Syrian unite to form the United Arab Republic. The Republic is dissolved after a military coup in Syria.

1959

Hutu elements overthrow the Tutsi monarchy in Ruanda (present-day Rwanda).

1960

Chad becomes independent from France.

Dahomey becomes independent from France.

French Cameroon becomes independent from France as Cameroon

French Sudan becomes independent from France as Mali.

Gabon becomes independent from France.

Ivory Coast becomes independent from France.

Madagascar becomes independent from France.

Mauritania becomes independent from France.

Middle, or French, Congo becomes independent from France as the Republic of the Congo.

Niger becomes independent from France.

Nigeria becomes independent from Britain.

Oubangui-Chari, a part of French Equatorial Africa, becomes independent from France as the Central African Republic.

Senegal becomes independent from France.

Somalia becomes independent from Britain.

The Belgian Congo becomes independent from Belgium as the Republic of the Congo (later renamed Zaire and currently named the Democratic Republic of the Congo).

Togoland becomes independent from France as Togo.

Upper Volta becomes independent from France as Burkina Faso.

The South West Africa People's Organization (SWAPO) is founded in South-West Africa (present-day Namibia).

The Organization of Petroleum Exporting Countries (OPEC) is formed.

The provinces of South Kasai and Katanga (now Shaba) announce their secession from the Democratic Republic of the Congo producing a civil war; a military coup follows.

1961–91

Eritrean War of Independence. The Eritrean People's Liberation Front (EPLF) and the Eritrean Liberation Front (ELF) fight a 30-year war to liberate Eritrea from Ethiopian rule. The war ends with the fall of the Ethiopian government and independence for Eritrea follows in 1993.

1961

Sierra Leone becomes independent from Britain.

South Cameroons becomes independent from Britain and unites with former French Cameroon to form the Federal Republic of Cameroon.

Tanganyika becomes independent from Britain.

The Angolan independence war begins.

Kuwait becomes fully independent from Britain and joins the Arab League. Iraq threatens to invade Kuwait but backs down after British forces are deployed to defend it.

1962

Algeria becomes independent from France.

Ruanda-Urundi becomes independent from Belgium as the separate nations of Rwanda and Burundi.

Uganda becomes independent from Britain.

The Front for the Liberation of Mozambique (Frelimo) is formed in Mozambique.

The Zimbabwe African People's Union (ZAPU) is formed in South Rhodesia (present-day Zimbabwe).

The royal family of North Yemen is overthrown in a military coup and the country is renamed the Yemen Arab Republic.

1963

Kenya becomes independent from Britain.

Zanzibar becomes independent from Britain.

The Organization of African Unity (OAU) is founded.

Government forces reunite the Democratic Republic of the Congo.

The Central African Federation is dissolved.

The Zimbabwe African National Union (ZANU) is formed in South Rhodesia (present-day Zimbabwe).

1964

Northern Rhodesia becomes independent from Britain as Zambia.

Nyasaland becomes independent from Britain as Malawi.

Tanganyika and Zanzibar unite to form Tanzania.

The African National Congress leader Nelson Mandela is imprisoned in South Africa.

Formation of the Palestine Liberation Organization (PLO), a political organization with the goal of eliminating the Jewish state of Israel and establishing an Arab Palestinian state in its stead.

1965

A military coup in Algeria brings Houari Boumedienne to power. The Algerian army is to remain the dominant force in Algerian politics for the next 40 years.

Gambia becomes independent from Britain.

Suleyman Demirel becomes prime minister of Turkey. He will hold the office six more times in the coming decades.

Tutsis purge many Hutus from the army and state bureaucracy in Rwanda.

1966

Basutoland becomes independent from Britain as Lesotho.

Bechuanaland becomes independent from Britain as Botswana

Antigovernment guerrilla activity begins in Chad.

South West Africa People's Organization rebels begin operations against South African forces in South West Africa (present-day Namibia).

1967–79

The period of guerrilla warfare against the white-minority government of Rhodesian carried out principally by the Zimbabwe National Liberation Army and the Zimbabwe People's Revolutionary Army.

1967

The Biafran (Nigerian Civil) War begins.

South Yemen gains independence from British rule as the People's Republic of South Yemen.

The Third Arab-Israeli (or Six-Day) War begins with a preemptive Israeli attack amid fears of an invasion by the combined forces of Egypt, Jordan, and Syria. After a rapid victory for Israeli forces, the war ends with a large gain in territory for Israel.

Uganda abolishes its traditional kingdoms.

French Somaliland becomes the French Territory of the Afars and the Issas.

1968

Equatorial Guinea becomes independent from Portugal.

Mauritius becomes independent from Britain.

Swaziland becomes independent from Britain

Britain announces its intention to withdraw from all protection agreements with states in the Persian Gulf. Bahrain, Qatar, and the seven emirates of the Trucial States begin negotiations for the formation of a union of Arab emirates.

Palestinian militants in southern Lebanon launch attacks against Israel. Israel responds by destroying 13 civilian airliners owned by Arab countries at Beirut airport.

1969

A military coup in Libya brings Muammar al Qaddafi to power.

The United Nations declares South Africa's occupation of South West Africa (present-day Namibia) illegal.

1970

Biafran secessionists are defeated in Nigeria.

Gamel Abdel Nasser dies and is succeeded by Anwar Sadat as Egypt's president.

In Jordan the PLO challenges King Hussein's authority and a civil war erupts. Syrian tanks enter the country in support of the PLO, and Hussein asks for military assistance from the United States. A peace treaty is signed and the PLO is forced out of Jordan.

South Yemen is renamed the People's Democratic Republic of South Yemen.

1971

Bahrain and Qatar withdraw from the union of Arab emirates. The emirates of Abu Dhabi, Dubai, Sharjah, Ajman, Umm al Qaiwain, and Fujairah form the United Arab Emirates (UAE).

Qatar becomes independent from Britain.

Idi Amin Dada seizes power in Uganda.

The Republic of the Congo is renamed Zaire as part of President Mobutu's "authenticity" drive to remove foreign influences.

Libya begins to nationalize foreign oil company holdings.

1972

Eighty thousand Asians are expelled from Uganda by Idi Amin Dada.

Armed conflict between North and South Yemen over border disputes.

Hutu people in Burundi revolt against the Tutsi ruling elite leading to a civil war in which over 100,000 Hutus are killed.

The first Sudanese civil war ends.

1973

The fourth Arab-Israeli (or Yom Kippur) War; Egypt and Syria launch a surprise military attack on Israel on the Jewish holiday of Yom Kippur, at first inflicting heavy losses on Israel but with little ultimate territorial gain.

Swaziland bans political parties and the king assumes absolute power.

1974–91

The Ethiopian Civil War. Several rebel groups in Ethiopia and Eritrea fight to overthrow the governments of Mengistu Haile Mariam. The war ends in victory for a coalition of rebel groups known as the Ethiopian People's Revolutionary Democratic Front (EPRDF).

1974

Portuguese Guinea becomes independent from Portugal as Guinea-Bissau.

Emperor Haile Selassie I is overthrown by the army in Ethiopia. Mengistu Haile Mariam comes to power as the head of the Derg government.

Turkey invades northern Cyprus following a period of political violence between Turkish and Greek inhabitants of the island.

The United Nations recognizes the PLO as representative of the Palestinian people and grants them permanent observer status. PLO chairman Yasir Arafat addresses the General Assembly of the UN.

1975–2002

The Angolan Civil War. A long-running conflict between the Soviet- and Cuban-backed Popular Movement for the Liberation of Angola (MPLA), the South African- and U.S.-backed National Union for the Total Independence of Angola (Unita), and the National Front for the Liberation of Angola (FNLA) ends with the MPLA forming a government.

1975

Angola becomes independent from Portugal

Cape Verde becomes independent from Portugal.

Mozambique becomes independent from Portugal.

São Tomé and Príncipe become independent from Portugal.

The Comoros become independent from France.

Dahomey is renamed Benin

King Faysal of Saudi Arabia is assassinated by his nephew. Faysal's brother, Khalid bin Abd al-Aziz Ibn Saud, takes the throne.

Start of the civil war in Lebanon; Christian militants ambush a bus carrying Palestinian in Beirut, killing 27.

Western Sahara is ceded to Morocco and Mauritania by Spain.

1976

In Angola the MPLA defeats the FNLA but conflict with Unita rebels continues.

The Economic Community of West African States (ECOWAS) is established.

In Rhodesia (present-day Zimbabwe) the Zimbabwe African People's Union and the Zimbabwe African National Union merge to form the Zimbabwe African National Union Patriotic Front (ZANU-PF) resistance movement.

The Seychelles becomes independent from Britain.

1977

First Shaba War in Zaire (present-day Democratic Republic of the Congo) as the Katanga province attempts to secede; Moroccan and French troops help quell the uprising.

Mengistu Haile Mariam takes power in Ethiopia and launches the "red terror" campaign of political oppression.

Fighting takes place between Somalia and Ethiopia over the Ogaden region.

The French Territory of the Afars and the Issas (formerly French Somaliland) becomes independent from France as Djibouti.

1978

Israel invades southern Lebanon in response to continuing PLO attacks. Israel withdraws after the United Nations calls for an end to hostilities but leaves control of southern Lebanon to a Christian pro-Israeli militia.

The U.S.-sponsored Camp David accords end the state of war between Egypt and Israel.

Uganda invades Tanzania.

Second Shaba War; a second unsuccessful Katangan rebellion takes place in Zaire (present-day Democratic Republic of the Congo).

1979

The shah of Iran Reza Pahlavi flees into exile. Senior religious leader Ayatollah Ruhollah Khomeini returns to Iran from exile and takes power. The country is declared to be an Islamic republic following a national referendum.

Fifty-two U.S. diplomats are taken hostage in Iran by a group of radical Islamist students. They are held for 444 days.

Ahmad Hasan al-Bakr resigns as president of Iraq and is succeeded by his vice president, Saddam Hussein.

Israel and Egypt sign a peace treaty following the Camp David accords in the United States.

President Amin of Uganda is ousted by Ugandan rebels aided by Tanzanian forces.

South Africa and Rhodesia (present-day Zimbabwe) escalate their military activities in Angola.

1980–88

The Iran-Iraq War results in hundreds of thousands of deaths on both sides without territorial gain.

1980

White-minority rule in Rhodesia ends; the new government renames Rhodesia as Zimbabwe.

A series of antigovernment demonstrations known as the Berber Spring brings unrest to Berber areas of Algeria.

The Israeli parliament officially annexes East Jerusalem to Israel.

1981

Egypt's president Anwar Sadat is assassinated by Muslim extremists; Hosni Mubarak becomes president.

Israel bombs an Iraqi nuclear research center.

1981–86

The Ugandan civil war; rebels led by Yoweri Museveni win power.

1982

Israel launches a second invasion of Lebanon and quickly advances to Beirut. Christian militias carry out massacres at Palestinian refugee camps in West Beirut.

Tens of thousands are killed in Syrian operations against the Muslim Brotherhood rebellion in the city of Hama.

Senegal and Gambia unite to form the Senegambia Confederation.

1983

Shii Muslim militants bomb the U.S. and French barracks in Lebanon, killing more than 300.

Sudan adopts Sharia (Islamic holy) law against the wishes of the non-Muslim majority in the south; civil war breaks out.

1984–85

In "Operation Moses" 8,000 refugee Falasha are airlifted from Sudan to Israel.

1984

The Kurdish Workers Party (PKK) begins a secessionist campaign in southeast Turkey.

Upper Volta is renamed Burkina Faso.

1985

Israel withdraws to a "security zone" in southern Lebanon.

The Organisation of African Unity (OAU) admits Western Saharan representatives; Morocco leaves the OAU in protest.

1986

Nigerian writer Wole Soyinka wins the Nobel Prize for Literature.

South Africa declares a state of emergency after escalating troubles in the townships.

The United States bombs Tripoli, Libya.

1987–93

First Palestinian Intifada

1988

Gassing of the Kurdish Iraqi village of Halabja by Iraqi government forces resulting in thousands of deaths.

Two competing governments are set up in Lebanon: a mainly Maronite Christian government in East Beirut led by Michel Aoun, and a mainly Muslim government in West Beirut led by Salim al Huss.

South African and Cuban forces begin to withdraw from Angola.

1989–96

The first Liberian Civil War. Conflict between the Liberian government, the National Patriotic Front of Liberia (NPFL), the Independent National Patriotic Front of Liberia (INPFL), the United Liberation Movement of Liberia for Democracy (ULIMO), and Economic Community of West African States Monitoring Group (ECOMOG) forces ends with 200,000 dead and millions displaced. Following peace agreements Charles Taylor is elected president in 1997.

1989

Ayatollah Khomeini, Supreme Leader of Iran, dies and President Ali Khamenei is appointed his successor.

The Senegambia Confederation is dissolved.

1990

Iraq invades and occupies Kuwait following accusations that Kuwait is stealing oil from Iraqi oil fields.

Nelson Mandela is released from prison in South Africa; the ANC ends its armed struggle; talks with the government begin and the state of emergency is ended.

The civil war in Lebanon ends. A government of national reconciliation is set up.

South West Africa becomes independent from South Africa as Namibia.

North and South Yemen are unified as the Republic of Yemen. Ali Abdallah Saleh, former president of North Yemen, become president of the new republic.

1990–91

The Persian (First) Gulf War; a U.S.-led coalition ejects Iraqi forces from Kuwait and liberates the country. Subsequent large-scale uprisings against Saddam Hussein's rule in the south and north of Iraq are suppressed with brutal military action. Retreating Iraqi forces cause billions of dollars worth of damage to the infrastructure of the Kuwaiti petroleum industry and ignite hundreds of oil wells, causing an environmental disaster.

1990–93

The Rwandan Civil War. An interethnic conflict between an invading force of exiled Tutsis under the banner of the Rwandan Patriotic Front (RPF) and the Hutu-dominated government of Juvenal Habyarimana results in the Arusha accords and a power-sharing government in Rwanda.

1991–2002

The Sierra Leone Civil War. Conflict between the government, Revolutionary United Front (RUF) rebels, and Economic Community of West African States Monitoring Group (ECOMOG) forces over control of Sierra Leone's mineral wealth results around 100,000 deaths and displaces more than a third of the population.

1991

Mengistu loses control of Ethiopia.

Civil war breaks out in Somalia as President Barre is ousted by rebel clan groups. Former British Somaliland declares its independence from Somalia as the Somaliland Republic.

Rebels launch an antigovernment offensive in Sierra Leone sparking a bloody civil war.

In South Africa all apartheid policies are officially abandoned following negotiations between the government and the ANC.

1992

King Fahd of Saudi Arabia adopts the Basic Law of Government in which the Quran is cited as the nation's constitution.

1993

The Oslo accords between the PLO and Israel; Israel recognizes the PLO as the legitimate representative of the Palestinian people and the PLO renounce terrorism and recognizes Israel.

Israel launches a major attack against Hezbollah in southern Lebanon.

Melchior Ndadaye becomes Burundi's first Hutu president. He is assassinated by Tutsi soldiers and the country is plunged into ethnic conflict in which as many as 300,000 people are killed.

Eritrea becomes independent from Ethiopia.

Tansu Ciller becomes Turkey's first female prime minister.

1994

The Rwandan Genocide. Rwandan president Juvenal Habyarimana and Burundian president Cyprien Ntaryamira, both Hutus, are killed when their plane is shot down by unknown assailants. In the three months following the assassinations Hutu militias and the Hutu-dominated Rwandan military massacre between 800,000 and 1 million Tutsis and Hutu moderates. Concurrently with the massacres the largely Tutsi Rwandan Patriotic Front (RPF) resumes its rebellion and overthrows the government bringing the killings to an end. About 2 million Hutus flee Rwanda after the overthrow of the government fearing violent Tutsi reprisals but none take place.

The ANC wins the first nonracial elections in South Africa; Nelson Mandela becomes the country's first black president.

Israeli prime minister Yitzhak Rabin, Israeli foreign minister Shimon Peres, and PLO chairman Yasir Arafat are jointly awarded the Nobel Peace Prize.

1995

In Qatar Prince Hamad bin Khalifa seizes power from his father and begins to institute liberal reforms.

1996–97

The First Congo War. In Zaire (the present-day Democratic Republic of the Congo) rebel forces backed by Uganda and Rwanda overthrow President Mobutu Sese Seko and Laurent Kabila takes power.

1996

The Al Jazeera satellite television station is launched in Qatar following the abolition of censorship laws.

1997

Zaire is renamed the Democratic Republic of the Congo following Laurent Kabila's seizure of power at the end of the First Congo War.

In Egypt 58 foreign tourists are murdered by gunmen; the government bans fundamentalist Islamic groups.

1998–99

The Guinea-Bissau Civil War. Separatists and rebel groups overthrow the government of Joao Bernardo Vieira.

1998–2000

The Eritrean-Ethiopian War. Tens of thousands are killed on both sides in a war that ends with minor border changes.

1998–2003

The Second Congo War, also referred to as Africa's World War or the Great War of Africa, is the most devastating conflict to occur in Africa since the end of Word War II. Eight African nations and dozens of militias become involved in fighting in the Democratic Republic of the Congo. More than 5 million people are killed in the fighting or as a result of malnutrition and displacement.

1999–2003

The Second Liberian Civil War. Liberians United for Reconciliation and Democracy (LURD) rebels overthrow the government of Charles Taylor.

1999

Abdullah, son of Hussein, is crowned king of Jordan as Abdullah II.

The first democratic elections in Qatar since 1971 take place. Female citizens are allowed to vote for the first time in the nation's history.

The PKK's leader Abdullah Ocalan is captured by Turkish security forces in Kenya leading to a major reduction in Kurdish separatist activities.

TWENTY-FIRST CENTURY

2000

Israel withdraws from southern Lebanon.

President Assad of Syria dies; Assad's son, Bashar al-Assad, is installed as president.

The Second Palestinian Intifada commences.

The U.S. naval vessel USS *Cole* is damaged in a suicide attack in Aden and the British embassy in Aden is bombed. Both attacks are blamed on Muslim extremists.

2002

Coptic Christmas is recognized as an official holiday in Egypt.

2003–08

The Darfur conflict in Sudan. A rebellion in the Darfur region against the Arab-dominated government is met with air attacks by government forces and a sustained campaign of ethnic violence carried out by government forces and the government-backed Janjaweed militia. An estimated 100,000 die in each year of the conflict and the United States and other governments accuse the Sudanese government of genocide. Combatants and refugees cross freely into neighboring Chad contributing to the civil war there.

2003

Invasion of Iraq (Second Gulf War). U.S., British, and allied forces invade Iraq, depose Saddam Hussein, and dismantle the Baath Party. An interim U.S. administration in Iraq is established.

PLO leader Yasir Arafat dies.

Oman's first female minister is appointed.

Shaykh Zayed bin Sultan al-Nuhayyan, who has served as president of the UAE for more than 30 years, dies and is succeeded by his son Shaykh Khalifa.

2005–07

In the Central African Republic rebel forces in the north of the country fight a bitter insurgency against the government. Thousands of lives are lost before a peace accord ends the fighting in 2007.

2005–08

The Civil War in Chad. Rebel groups forming the United Front for Democracy and Change (FUCD) oppose the government of Idriss Deby. Combatants and refugees from the Darfur conflict in neighboring Sudan are heavily involved in the war.

2005

An autonomous Kurdish region in the north of Iraq is declared. Massoud Barzani is elected as its first president.

The Transitional Iraqi Assembly is elected as a result of Iraq's first open and democratic elections for 50 years.

The conservative former mayor of Tehran, Mahmoud Ahmadinejad, is elected president of Iran. Many potential opponents are barred from standing by religious authorities.

The International Atomic Energy Agency (IAEA) accuses Iran of contravening the Nuclear Non-Proliferation Treaty by restarting its uranium enrichment program. The Iranian government insists the program is for peaceful purposes only.

Syria withdraws from Lebanon.

King Fahd of Saudi Arabia dies and is succeeded by Prince Abdullah bin Abd al-Aziz al-Saud.

Mahmoud Abbas is elected president of the Palestinian Authority.

Shaykh Khalifa announces the UAE's first democratic elections.

In Zimbabwe the government launches Operation Drive Out Trash (or Operation Murambatsvina) to clear slum areas. Hundred of thousands of urban and rural poor are made homeless.

2006

Elections bring Hamas, an Islamist party, to power for the first time in the Palestinian Authority. Western donor states cut off aid to the Palestinian Authority, declaring Hamas a terrorist organization.

Jalal Talabani, a leading Kurdish politician, is elected president of Iraq.

The July War or Second Lebanon War; Israel invades Lebanon and withdraws a month later. Thousands of Lebanese seek refuge in Syria during Israel's military operation against Hezbollah in the south of the country.

Former Iraqi president Saddam Hussein is found guilty of crimes against humanity by an Iraqi court and executed.

The Jordanian-born leader of al-Qaeda in Iraq, Abu Musab al-Zarqawi, is killed in an air strike.

2007

In Iraq the Kurdish regional government assumes responsibility for security in the autonomous northern Kurdish region.

Israel bombs a facility in Syria that it claims is being used for a nuclear weapons program.

The IAEA claims that Iran will be capable of producing nuclear weapons within three years. The United States imposes tough economic sanctions against Iran in protest at the country's developing nuclear program.

In Algeria an Islamist group calling itself al-Qaeda in the Islamic Maghreb launches a series of deadly bomb attacks against civilian and government targets.

United Nations African Union Mission in Darfur (UNAMID) troops begin arriving in the Darfur region of Sudan as a peacekeeping force.

2008

In Algeria 60 people are killed in bombings carried out by al-Qaeda in the Islamic Maghreb.

A Jewish woman is appointed Bahrain's ambassador to the United States. Houda Nonoo is believed to be the first Jewish person appointed as an ambassador for an Arab nation.

Four Copts are killed in gun attack on a Coptic-owned business in Cairo. Egyptian courts uphold the right of 12 Christians who had converted to Islam to reconvert to Christianity.

King Abdullah becomes the first head of an Arab nation to visit Iraq since the U.S.-led invasion of 2003.

Turkey's Constitutional Court finds the ruling Justice and Development Party guilty of becoming the focus of anti-secularist actions but narrowly avoids banning it as a political party.

The International Criminal Court (ICC) files 10 war crimes charges (including three of genocide) against Sudan's President Omar al-Bashir for his actions in the Darfur conflict.

An Israeli-built barrier seperating the Gaza Strip from Egypt is breached by Hamas militants. Hundreds of thousands of Palestinians cross into Egypt.

Israel launches air and ground attacks against Palestinian targets in the Gaza Strip in response to rocket attacks launched into Israel by militants

GLOSSARY OF CULTURAL TERMS

a cappella   Vocal music without instrumental accompaniment.

abarusura   The historic army of the Bunyoro kingdom.

abaya   A lose ankle-length over garment traditionally worn by women in Muslim societies.

abd   An Arabic word meaning "slave" or "servant." *Abd* is often used as part of name in Arabic culture; for example the name Abdullah means "servant of Allah."

Abuk   An important YATH in the Dinka religion. Abuk was the first woman and is associated with rivers.

adoimara   The "whites" (or lower class) in Afar society.

African Franc Zone   A group of African countries whose currencies are linked with the French franc at a fixed exchange rate. The currency that these countries use is called the CFA or CFA franc.

Afro-Beat   A form of popular West African music.

age-grades   The various social levels in certain societies. Each person belongs to a particular age-set that moves up through the various age-grades.

age-regiments   A largely historical feature common to many southern African peoples. Men or women were organized by age into these groups, which were usually used as mobile sources of labor or occasionally as a source of troops. Different societies structured or organized their age-regiments in various ways. The Zulu age-regiments under Shaka, for instance, were largely concerned with warfare and remained together for much longer than in other African societies. Age-regiments were an important way of providing social unity.

agora   An open public space in an ancient Greek city that served as a marketplace and public meeting place.

ahl al-bayt   An Arabic phrase meaning "people of the house" and used in the context of Islamic tradition to refer to the family of the prophet Muhammad.

ait   An Arabic term meaning "sons of" or "tribe." *See also* **Banu**.

akhet   The season of flooding in ancient Egypt.

akhnif   A long, embroidered cape once worn by Jewish men in North Africa.

akiwor   Initiation of Karamojong girls into adulthood.

akple   A mixture of corn and cassava flour used to make a food that is usually eaten with meat or vegetable stew.

Akuj   The supreme god of the Karamojong religion.

Ala   In the Igbo religion, Ala is generally considered to be the Earth goddess. Shrines are dedicated to Ala, and the Igbo's most important festival, the Yam Festival, is celebrated in her honor.

aliyah   A Hebrew term literally meaning "to ascend" and used to refer to the immigration of Jewish people to Israel or to Palestine before the establishment of Israel.

Allah   The Muslim name for God.

aloalo   A carved wooden pole on a Mahafaly tomb.

amaNdlozi   The revered ancestors of a Ndebele family, who are believed to be spirit guardians.

amelu   The ruling class of Sumerian society.

amenokal   In the past, the Tuareg were divided into seven main confederations. Each was led by an *amenokal*, or king.

Amma   The Dogon supreme god.

Amon   In ancient Eygpt, Amon was a local Theban god depicted with a ram's head and symbolizing life and fertility. Over time, Amon became identified with RE and eventually became known as Amon-Re.

Anansi   A spider character, known as a trickster, who features in many West African folktales.

ankh A T-shaped cross with a loop at the top. It is based on the ancient Egyptian hieroglyph for eternal life.

apartheid An Afrikaans word meaning "apartness" or "separateness." It is generally used to refer to the South African government's policy of racial and ethnic segregation and white domination. Officially, apartheid was in effect from 1948 to 1991, though racist policies had been in place before this date. The government definition of apartheid was "separate development of the races."

Apedemak An ancient Nubian god.

aperit An overnight Karamojong festival for elders.

apoikiai A form of ancient Greek colony with the status of an independent city state.

appliqué A decoration or trimming of one material sewn or fixed onto another.

arghul An ancient instrument from rural Egypt, a type of double clarinet.

ari An Afar house of flexible sticks covered with mats.

asaimara The politically dominant class in Afar society.

asantehene The Asante king.

asapan Initiation of Karamojong boys into adulthood.

ashough A traditional traveling entertainer in Armenian culture.

askari Africans who fought in the colonial armies of German East Africa during World War I.

Astarte The Phoenician Moon goddess, renamed "Tanit-Pene-Baal" (meaning "Tanit the Face of Baal") by the Carthaginians.

atabeg An honorific title originating during the Seljuk dynasty for a noble charged with raising the son of a ruler.

ataliqate A Circassian custom in which the children of nobles were raised and educated by their vassals.

auxilia Elements of the Roman army made up of noncitizens, principally men from the Roman provinces.

avant-gardistes A Congo (Democratic Republic) art movement of the 1970s that attempted to create a uniquely African art style unaffected by foreign influences.

awoamefia The *dukowo* head of the Anlo Ewe.

ayana A saint of the Oromo religion.

azat A part of the Armenian nobility.

Baal-Moloch The Phoenician Sun god, renamed Baal-Haman by the Carthaginians.

badgir A ventilation device used in traditional Iranian architecture.

badima Pedestal-based drums used at Tonga funerals.

badimo Offerings that Sotho people make to their ancestors to ask for assistance or in gratitude.

bakama A Bachwezi king.

balopwe A group of official ministers that helped the Luba king with certain duties.

banda In Herero society, a lineage of ancestors that is traced through a person's female relatives.

bandair A large Berber tambourine with an extra set of strings (snares) across its surface for added vibrations.

bani An Arabic term meaning "sons of" or "tribe." Arabic grammar requires that the word is sometimes written as BANU.

Bantustan An alternative name for a HOMELAND.

banu An Arabic term meaning "sons of" or "tribe." Arabic grammar requires that the word is sometimes written as BANI.

bany In the political structure of the Dinka, each group has a priestly or religious clan, called a *bany*, whose historical role was to control and safeguard the land.

bao kiswahili An East African version of MANKALA.

baraka A blessing bestowed by a MARABOUT or the spiritual power of a *marabout*.

basango Spirits in the Tonga belief system. They are associated with particular regions or neighborhoods.

Baswezi A Nyamwezi society devoted to SWEZI.

bataka The Ganda term for the head of a clan.

bavide In the Luba religion it is believed that these spirits exert a bad influence on people.

B.C.E. An abbreviation for "Before the Common Era," a

term used to refer to the time period preceding the first year of the revised Gregorian calendar.

bdeshkh   A powerful Armenian noble equivalent to a prince or viceroy.

bebtara   A Falasha religious official.

Bena Yanda   A Bemba clan. The name literally means "Crocodile Clan."

bendir   A traditional frame drum used in North Africa.

beng   The head of the BANY in Dinka society. The name means "Master of the Fishing Spear."

bet ha-knesset   The Hebrew term for a synagogue.

bey   A Turkish title for the governor or commander of a *beylik* (province or district) of the Ottoman Empire. The term remains in use today as a respectful title for a man.

beylerbey   A Turkish title for a senior BEY (governor or commander) in the Ottoman Empire; ranking higher than a bey in the hierarchy of the imperial government and the overall governor or commander of a BEYLERBEYLIK.

beylerbeylik   An administrative division of the Ottoman empire governed by a BEYLERBEY. A *beylerbeylik* usually consisted of several smaller BEYLIKS.

beylik   An administrative division of the Ottoman Empire governed by a BEY.

bieri   A form of ancestral reverence practiced by the Fang as part of the Fang religion.

Black Consciousness   A movement that emerged in the 1970s with medical student Steve Biko as one of its leading thinkers. Biko formed the South African Students Organization (SASO), which was based on the principles of Black Consciousness. The movement stressed pride in being black, emphasized black values and culture, and rejected white culture and white liberalism.

Boeremusiek   Light, danceable Afrikaner country music.

bokulaka   A Mongo village chief.

bolombato   A Manding gourd harp.

braaivleis   An Afrikaner barbecue.

bridewealth   A practice common among African people in which a marriage between a couple is sealed with a gift—often cattle, but it may be cash or other animals—from the groom

to the bride's family. The bride is not regarded as property. It is usually considered to be compensation to the bride's family for loss of a working member or a token of respect. Part of it may be used by the couple to set up home together.

brimbiri   A Nuba stringed musical instrument.

bugalli   A Nyamwezi porridgelike dish.

bulogi   Witchcraft as believed in by many Nyamwezi.

burka (*burqa*)   A lose-fitting over garment that covers the entire body and with a veiled opening for the eyes. Traditionally worn by women in some Muslim cultures.

burra   An Afar camp, usually comprising one or two ARI.

butala **granary**   A mud and grass granary with a thatched roof.

bwiti   A politico-religious movement practiced by the Fang, which has replaced BIERI as the main religious force. Bwiti combines aspects of both Christianity and *bieri*.

cahen   A Falasha religious official.

calabash   A type of gourd whose hollowed-out shell has a wide variety of uses from container to musical instrument. Calabashes often figure in African legends where the two halves are used, for example, to symbolize the union of heaven and earth, man and woman, or land and sky.

caliph   An historical title for the supreme ruler of an Islamic state. *Caliph* is an English transliteration of the Arabic term *khalifa*, meaning "successor." In early Islamic history the title of caliph was held by the political and spiritual successors of the prophet Muhammad as heads of the Arab Muslim polity. Subsequently the title was claimed by or attributed to the leaders of several different Muslim sects.

canopy   A layer in a forest formed by the crowns (branches and leaves) of trees. Rainforests have more than one canopy. The upper canopy occurs at a height of 90 to 150 feet, but this layer is pierced by occasional tall trees called emergents. One or two lower canopies occur at roughly 60 feet and 30 feet. The canopies are inhabited by tree-dwelling species such as birds, bats, and monkeys. The sunlight is strong and the vegetation is thick and virtually impenetrable. Below the canopies, relatively little sunlight penetrates down to ground level, where vegetation is more sparse.

caravan   A company of travelers journeying together, often with a train of animals loaded with goods.

Casamance-style music   A percussive style of music from the Casamance region of Senegal and Gambia.

caste A rigid class distinction generally based on birth, wealth, and occupation. The Hindu (Indian) caste system consists of four main castes, called *varnas*, into which a person is born. The top *varna* is occupied by Brahmans (religious leaders and scholars); the next consists of Kshatriyas (rulers, nobles, and warriors); then come the Vaisyas (bankers and other kinds of businesspeople); and the lowest varna comprises the Sudras (artisans and laborers). Besides the four varnas there is a fifth category of "outcastes," called *panchamas* (fifths), untouchables, or the "children of god". Many attempts have been made to eliminate the system, and laws and modern urban life have lessened its rigidity somewhat.

cataphract An armored cavalry soldier. *Cataphracts* originated among the nomadic peoples of eastern Iran but were later deployed by the armies of successive Persian dynasties, the Armenians, the Greeks, the Romans, and the Byzantines.

cataract An unnavigable or hazardous stretch of river, perhaps created by rapids, waterfalls, or a narrowing of the riverbanks. There are six major (numbered) cataracts on the Nile River between Aswan and Khartoum, some of which once formed political frontiers.

C.E. An abbreviation for "Common Era," a term used to refer used the time period that began with the first year of the revised Gregorian calendar.

CFA An abbreviation for "Communauté Financière Africaine," CFA is the currency used by the Central and West African countries that form the African Franc Zone. The CFA franc is on a fixed exchange rate with the French franc. The initials originally stood for "Colonies Français d'Afrique," but the term was changed after these territories became independent from colonial rule.

chaabi A form of popular music in Morocco; a mix of Arab, Berber, and contemporary Western styles, the lyrics tending to highlight political and social issues.

cheikhas Women musicians from rural Algeria from several centuries ago. The male equivalent is **cheikhs**.

chikha A female singer in Morocco. (Note: it can also have negative connotations; *chikha* can also mean "prostitute.")

chimurenga A contemporary African music based on the rhythms of the MBIRA. Created by Thomas Mapfumo, *chimurenga*—which means "liberation war"—played an important role in the struggle for majority rule in Zimbabwe (then Rhodesia).

Chitimukulu The name and title of the Bemba kings. It literally means "Chiti the Great" and refers to Chiti, the leader of the Bena Yanda, who founded the Bemba kingdom. All the following kings were named after him.

chiton A loose-fitting ankle-length garment worn by men and women in ancient Greece and later introduced to the Middle East and North Africa.

chleuh Professional Berber musician-dancers of the High Atlas Mountains of Morocco.

Chukwu A supreme being acknowledged by some Igbo groups. Chukwu is the creator of the visible universe.

chuppa The ceremonial canopy symbolizing the home under which a traditional Jewish wedding takes place.

cikunza A Chokwe mask used as part of the initiation of boys into adulthood.

ciondo A Kenyan bag made from sisal.

circumcision A relatively simple, if painful, procedure (removal of all or part of the foreskin) for males but a much more serious operation (ranging from minor to severe genital mutilation) with long-lasting consequences for females. This practice is highly controversial, however, and is opposed by many African women.

clan A group of people, usually several lineages, who claim descent from a common ancestor or ancestors.

clibanarii A heavily armored cavalry soldier deployed by various historical armies across the Middle East.

compound An enclosure containing living quarters. Compound is often used to refer to a group of buildings lived in by members of the same family or extended family. One compound may include several buildings.

confederation An alliance of political groupings.

congo A popular style of Central African music that developed in the Congo (Republic) and Congo (Democratic Republic). Also referred to as *soukous*.

copra The dried "meat" of the coconut. Copra is the source of coconut oil.

Coptic The word "Coptic" is derived from *aiguptios*, the Greek word for Egyptian, which comes from an Ancient Egyptian name for Memphis. Today, the word "Coptic" has acquired many different meanings. As a noun, it is the name of an Afroasiatic language written in the Greek alphabet that is now largely extinct. Used as an adjective, Coptic can refer to the Copts (the Christian minority in Egypt); the Coptic (Christian) churches of Egypt and Ethiopia; to a historical period in Egypt's history; and to certain artifacts. Not all Copts are members of the Egyptian Coptic Church; some are Roman Catholics or belong to various evangelical sects.

Those that are members of the Coptic Church are sometimes called Orthodox Copts. The historical Coptic Period is basically Egypt's Christian Era, which can be dated from either the 200s to 642 or from 451 to 642. "Coptic" is also used to refer to artifacts that were produced in Egypt during its Coptic Period, but not necessarily by Coptic artists. Finally, "Coptic" can be used to describe the Ethiopian Christian Church, which traces its origins to the Egyptian Coptic Church.

couscous A spicy dish originating in North Africa that consists of a steamed, coarse-ground grain such as semolina. Couscous is popular in the Sahel region of West Africa.

crux ansata A cross used from the fifth century onward in Egypt (during the **Coptic** Period), the shape of which is based on the Ancient Egyptian hieroglyph for "life" (the *ankh*). These crosses often decorated gravestones.

daff A large frame drum used extensively in the traditional music of various Middle Eastern cultures.

Dak The legendary son of NYIKANG.

darabouka A Moroccan clay drum.

dardar The head of an Afar sultanate.

davul A large double-headed drum used in traditional Turkish music.

deforestation The clearing of trees in a forest. In the African rainforests, huge tracts of land are being cleared of trees every year. The reasons are primarily economic. In poorer countries, where most rainforests are, their clearance is a way of raising much-needed cash to pay off debts to foreign banks and governments. Also, the growth of urban areas has led to the intensification and extensification of agriculture: More land is needed to farm, and this land is farmed more intensively, leaving it little time to recover. In forest areas, this can result in a permanent loss of forest if the land is not allowed time to recover from cultivation. Deforestation causes soil deterioration, which can lead to soil erosion. It can also indirectly lead to a decrease in rainfall as trees are an essential part of the climatic processes that produce rain.

delta An apron of land made from sediment deposited at the mouth of a river.

demotic A simplified system of ancient Egyptian hieroglyphic writing.

Deng An important YATH in the Dinka religion, Deng is associated with rain, thunder, and lightning.

derra A colored blouse once worn by Jewish women in North Africa.

dervishes Members of a branch of Islam called SUFISM. Dervishes are dedicated to a life of poverty and chastity.

desertification A process of land degradation in which previously fertile land can be turned into barren land or desert. It is usually caused by drought or the overuse of fragile lands. Desertification occurs only in drylands, which have low, infrequent, and irregular rainfall and high temperatures. This includes the SAHEL semidesert region in West Africa, where desertification has become an increasingly urgent problem in recent decades, and, in southern Africa the fringes of the Nambi Desert and the semidesert Kalahari.

devshirme A form of tax in the Ottoman Empire in which non-Muslim rural communities living within the empire were required to provide a number of young male slaves to the Ottoman government. These boys were converted to Islam and trained for military or religious occupations.

dhimmi A non-Muslim subject of a state governed according to SHARIA law. Historically the Muslim empires and states of the Middle East have recognized an obligation to protect the lives, property, and freedom of religion of *dhimmi* in return for their loyalty to the state and the payment of a poll tax known as the JIZYA.

dhow A cargo ship with a raised deck at the stern (rear end) and sails, which is used along Indian Ocean coasts.

diaspora A large-scale migration of a group of ethnically related people from their traditional homeland. From the Greek term meaning "dispersion" or "scattering."

diel The founding family of a Shilluk village.

Difaqane A Sotho-Tswana word meaning "scattering." It is used to refer to the period (1819–39) of mass migrations and wars in the southeastern half of southern Africa. The Difaqane was triggered by the rise of the Zulu kingdom. This period is known as the **Mfecane** by the Nguni peoples east of the Drakensberg Mountains.

disenfranchisement Depriving a person of the right to vote or other rights of citizenship.

dishdasha A long robe, usually white in color, traditionally worn by men in many Middle Eastern cultures. In some countries it is known as at THOB.

divination A common feature of many African religions, divination is practiced by diviners who use various tools (such as wooden figures, plants, bones, or seeds) to divine the spiritual cause of a specific problem such as illness, accident, or misfortune.

diviner A practitioner of DIVINATION.

diwani   A highly decorative form of calligraphic Arabic script developed by artists of the Ottoman courts in the 16th and 17th centuries.

Dja-gay   The first human according to the Nuer religion. Dja-gay is said to have emerged from a hole in the ground at a holy place called Duar.

domba   In Venda society, girls who have completed the VHUSHA initiation process attend a school known as the *domba* to learn the duties expected of wives and mothers. Domba can also refer to the process of initiation itself.

drahm   A unit of currency used in the Persian empire from the beginning of the Sassanian dynasty (third century C.E.).

drought   Water shortage caused by a prolonged period of inadequate rainfall. Drought can have a devastating affect on the land and people who make their living from the land, in particular reducing the number of nomads, for example, in the SAHEL region of western Africa in recent decades.

duduk   A traditional Armenian wind instrument.

dufia   The head of a village in Ewe society.

dukowo   A council of Ewe *dufias* who acted as advisors to the overall leader of a whole region.

durra   An alternative name for the cereal sorghum.

dyamu   A Malinke word for a group of people who share the same name, male ancestors, and taboos.

dyeli   A name for professional singers (bards) among the Bambara and Malinke. Dyeli are often involved in maintaining oral history as their songs retell and preserve Manding history.

Ehi   The people of the historic Kingdom of Benin believed that every human had a spirit of destiny, called an Ehi, which the soul created before birth in conversation with Osanobua.

Eid al-Fitr   A Muslim festival held on the first day of the 10th month of the Islamic calendar to mark then end of RAMADAN.

ekitela   Subsections of Karamojong society whose members gather for festivities relating to the seasons and the harvest. *Ekitela* is literally the name of a reddish soil.

electric *mbira*   A contemporary African style of music that translates the sounds of the *mbira* into guitar riffs accompanied by complicated drum patterns and vocals based on traditional singing styles.

emahiya   A brightly colored body wrap worn by Swazi men and women.

embalming   The treatment of a dead body, usually after removing the internal organs, with various chemicals to prevent it from decaying. The ancient Egyptians practiced embalming so that the dead could use their own bodies in the afterlife. Early embalmers used tarlike substances as embalming solutions, but better techniques using dry natron (a naturally occurring salt) were developed over time.

emir   A title of high nobility used throughout the Arab world and historically in some Turkic states. The precise rank of the title has varied considerably across time periods and geography.

emporia   A form of ancient Greek or Phoenician colony that was essentially a recognized trading post founded by one state in the territory of another state.

enkang   Maasai rainy-season homes.

Epiphany   A yearly festival held on January 6 in many Christian churches commemorating both the revealing of Jesus as Christ and the baptism of Jesus.

epiphytes   A plant that grows on another plant but is not a parasite—an epiphyte does not obtain its nourishment from its host or cause the host any harm; found particularly in rainforests.

erg   An area of shifting sand dunes in a desert.

erosion   Can be used to refer to the loss of soil cover, which has been eroded by the action of wind or rain.

Esu (Eshu)   A god of the historic Kingdom of Benin and of the Yoruba people. Often described as the "trickster god," Esu tells OLODUMARE of the activities of other ORISA and of people.

fama   A Bambara local leader.

feluccas   Small, narrow boats propelled by oar or wind that have been used on the Nile River for centuries.

fez   A brimless felt hat shaped like a truncated cone. Also known as a TARBUSH.

fiqh   The study of Islamic jurisprudence.

firman   A decree issued by the monarch of certain historical Muslim states including the sultans of the Ottoman Empire.

forest-foragers   Forest-dwelling peoples who are mainly hunter-gatherers.

fou-fou   Cassava root turned into flour and made into a kind of dough.

fusha   The standard written form of the Arabic language traditionally used in literature.

gadaa   The historic Oromo democratic system.

gandu   The basic unit of the cooperative system in which most Hausa agricultural work is carried out.

Garang   An important YATH in the Dinka religion. Garang was the first man and is associated with the sun. Garang is also a common Dinka family name.

garigue   Heath and poor scrub with patches of bare rock and soil.

Gaua   An evil god in some Khoisan religions, also called Gawama, who tries to disrupt the work of Nadi.

geerewol   A dance performed at a Fulani WORSO. These dances prove the ability of men to attract women.

Gelede   Festivals incorporating masked dancers held by the Yoruba at regular intervals. Now largely to entertain, they were once intended to appease local witches.

ger   The traditional Mongolian frame tent sometimes erroneously referred to as a yurt.

gerber   An Oromo water container made from a whole goatskin with the leg, tail, and neck openings tied.

ghaita   A Berber reed instrument.

ghana   The title—meaning "war-chief"—of the kings of the ancient empire of Wagadu. It later came to be used as the name for the medieval Empire of Ghana.

ghazal   An ancient and popular poetic form common across many Arabic-speaking and Persian-speaking cultures. Originating in sixth century C.E. pre-Islamic Arabic verse, the structural requirements for a *ghazal* are strict and demanding.

ghazi   A general term for a warrior engaged in a Muslim holy war.

Gikuyu   According to the Kikuyu religion, the Kikuyu are descended from Gikuyu, the son of Ngai.

ginna   The "great house," generally lived in by the male head of a Dogon village or clan.

gorfa   A Bedouin granary.

granary   A building or room in which grain is stored.

Great Vidye   The creator-god of the Luba religion.

griot   A general West African name for storytellers, singers, and musicians.

groundnut   A group of plants including the peanut, which are a cash crop and food item in many African countries.

guedra   A Moroccan drum made from a cooking pot with a skin stretched over its opening.

gum arabic   A gum exuded by certain acacia trees. It has many uses, including the manufacture of ink, food thickeners, and pills.

gumbri   A small, three-stringed Berber lute.

hadith   A general term for reports about the actions or words of the prophet Muhammad. Originally transmitted orally, *hadiths* were later evaluated by Muslim scholars and written down in collections. These collections continue to be important references in discussions of Islamic law or history to the present day.

haikal   A screen that separates the sanctuary from the choir in a Coptic church.

hajj   A pilgrimage to the city of Mecca, Saudi Arabia. Performing the hajj at least once is the duty of every Muslim who is physically able and can afford to do so.

hakpa   A session at a Ewe festival that is a general singing practice for everybody.

halal   An Arabic term meaning "permissible." The term is most frequently used in English to refer to food that has been prepared in accordance with Islamic dietary laws, but in Arab cultures it can be used to refer to anything that is permissible according to Islam.

hale   Societies to which many Mende belong. Among the most important *hale* are Poro and Sande. Others include Humui, Njayei, Yassi, and Kpa. Until recently the working of these societies was kept from noninitiates, so they are often referred to as "secret" societies.

halo   A feature of some Ewe festivals, it is an exchange of insulting songs between neighboring villages.

hammada   An area of rock platforms and boulders in a desert, covered with a thin layer of sand and pebbles.

Hanukkah   An annual eight-day Jewish festival that commemorates the reconsecration of the Second temple in

Jerusalem in 164 B.C.E. The date of the celebration is determined according to the Hebrew calendar and takes place between late November and late December according to the Gregorian calendar.

haratin Lower-class Berber oasis cultivators.

harayto A traditional top worn by rural Afar men.

harmattan A cool, dry, dusty wind from the Sahara Desert that blows toward the West African coast, especially from November through March. .

Hasidim A sect of Judaism founded in eastern Europe during the 18th century C.E. and characterized in the present day by devotion to the traditional precepts of the religion.

havalu A session at a Ewe festival in which the composer teaches a new song to his fellow drummers.

hazaj A poetic meter frequently used in the epic poetry of Middle Eastern cultures.

henna A reddish-orange dye made from plants and used as a paint with which to decorate skin or dye hair.

hieratic A simplified, handwritten form of ancient Egyptian hieroglyphics largely used by priests.

hieroglyph A picture symbol used in hieroglyphics.

hieroglyphics A form of writing, especially used in ancient Egypt and Nubia, that uses pictures and symbols to represent concepts, objects, or sounds.

highlife A dance music style that is often considered the national music of Ghana. Early forms of it originated in Ghana's southern Cape Coast area in the 1880s. The name "highlife" was coined during the 1920s in the context of Ghanaian ballroom dance orchestras. Highlife incorporates African guitar techniques brought from Liberia by Creole mariners in the beginning of the 20th century and has also been influenced by colonial military bands. It became very popular during and after World War II but had declined by the 1980s.

hijab An Arabic term referring to the convention of modest dress for Muslims. The term is commonly used to refer to women's dress only. Precise definitions vary between cultures, but the conventions for women's dress usually require the complete covering of the body except the face and hands.

Hijra An Arabic word meaning "migration" commonly used to refer to the emigration of the prophet Muhammad to the city of Medina in 622 C.E.

himation A heavy cloak usually worn over a CHITON in ancient Greece.

hogon The spiritual leader of the Dogon, responsible for, among other things, preserving myths.

homeland Usually meaning the land or country in which one lives or was born, it also refers to the South African BANTUSTANS. Created by the South African government during the **apartheid** era, these were artificial homelands in which black African peoples were forced to live. They often bore no relation to the areas with which groups had historically been associated. The 10 homelands were created from 260 "native reserves" that had been in existence since 1913. Homeland facilities and infrastructure were poor and their inhabitants suffered from overcrowding and poverty.

hoplite Originally the citizen soldiers of the ancient Greek city-states and, later, soldiers of other states that employed similar tactics and equipment.

horovel A traditional form of Armenian music.

Horus An ancient Egyptian Sun god, usually depicted with a falcon's head; the lord of heaven.

Humui A Mende HALE that helps to regulate sexual behavior. The rules of Humui prohibit certain kinds of sexual relationships, such as those with girls under the age of puberty or with nursing mothers.

hunter-gatherers People who live off food that can be hunted or collected from the wild and do not cultivate crops or raise livestock.

Ifijoku A god worshipped by the Igbo as the giver and protector of yams—a form of sweet potato that plays a central part in the village economy.

igikubge A Tutsi headdress worn by royals.

iklan The third and lowest class within the Tuareg social structure.

ikula A wooden Kuba knife. Introduced by the peace-loving Kuba king Shamba Bolongongo, the *ikula* replaced the SHONGO.

ilterekeyani The name of the most recent Maasai age-set to reach the age-grade of elder.

imajeghen The Tuareg nobility, one of whom is elected as the AMENOKAL of each confederation.

imam In Shii Islam the imams are historical figures believed to have been the rightful successors of the prophet

Muhammad. In Sunni Islam *imam* is used more generally to refer to religious leaders and teachers.

Imana   The benevolent god of the Hutu and Tutsi.

imdyazen   A traditional traveling entertainer in the Berber culture of North Africa.

imdyazn   A type of Berber band usually made up of four musicians, including a poet as leader.

imghad   A Tuareg social classification referring to the ordinary citizen.

imraguen   A Moorish social class of largely itinerant fisherman who live along the coast of Mauritania.

imwu   A rounded bunlike hairstyle worn—more commonly in the past—by Teke men of noble rank.

imzi   A Zulu homestead.

inabanza   The *inabanza*, one of the Luba BALOPWE, had charge of ritual matters concerning the *mulopwe's* sacred role.

inakulu   The principal wife of an Ovimbundu chief. They are believed to have supernatural powers in the Ovimbundu religion.

Incwala   A three-week-long period, also called the First Fruits Festival, when the king and nation of Swaziland reaffirm their relationship.

indigo   A deep blue dye usually made from certain plants.

indlu   The basic social unit in Swazi society is the *indlu* (a husband and wife and their children). Several *indlu* make up an UMUTI. The members of an *umuti* typically share agricultural tasks.

ingondo   Small Twa pots that were intended to contain love charms. Twa women would wear them tied around the waist to ensure their husband's affections.

injera   A pancakelike bread made from TEFF.

inkosi   Historically, the Xhosa's allegiance was to their clan, led by an *inkosi* whose status was gained through his mother. *Inkosi* (which means "thank-you") were obliged to be hospitable and generous, and their powers were limited by public opinion and counselors.

inselbergs   Isolated rocky hills rising abruptly from a flat plain or plateau. In southern central and southern Africa inselbergs are known as *kopje*.

intifada   An Arabic word meaning "shaking off" that is often loosely translated as "rebellion" or "uprising." The term has been used to refer to several rebellions or protracted periods of civil disturbance by Arabic-speaking communities in North Africa and the Middle East in the 20th and 21st centuries, most famously the First Intifada (1987–93) and the Second, or al-Aqsa Intifada, (beginning in 2000) of the Palestinians against Israeli rule.

iqta   A form of tax farming that developed during the Abbasid Caliphate period (750–1258). Tax farming is the practice of assigning the responsibility for collecting state taxation for a particular area to a local governor, military official, or other important figure.

iscathamiya   An A CAPPELLA Zulu singing style originally from the all-male workers' hostels of 1920s Natal.

Isis   An ancient Egyptian fertility goddess, usually depicted as a woman with cow's horns; wife and sister of OSIRIS and mother of HORUS.

itoom   A type of sculpture used in divination by the Kuba. A moistened disk would be rubbed on the back of the sculpture while the diviner recited certain phrases. The phrase at which the disk stuck would reveal the answers to the client's question.

iwan   An architectural feature consisting of a vaulted space walled on three sides and open on the fourth. Iwans were originally a feature of Persian architecture in the pre-Islamic period and later became a common feature of Islamic architecture and secular architecture across the Muslim world.

iwisa   A knobkerrie—a stick with a round knob at the end—used as a club or missile by Zulu warriors.

izar   Long, striped garment, usually red or white, once worn by Jewish women in North Africa.

jali   Manding term for GRIOT; the traditional caste of musician storytellers.

jambiya   An Arabic word for "dagger" commonly used to refer to a specific kind of dagger with a short curved blade associated with Yemeni culture.

jihad   An Arabic term meaning "to struggle" or "to strive." Historically the term has been used to describe the individual Muslim's duty to strive to improve the self and the society in which one lives. One part of the meaning of the term has always referred to a Muslim's duty to engage in warfare when required to do so under the terms of Islamic law. Precise definitions differ among Muslim denominations.

jile   An Afar dagger.

jinn   A supernatural creature, often described as being composed of fire, common in Arabian folklore and also referred to in the Quran.

Jit Jive   A term coined by the internationally successful Zimbabwean group, the Bhundu Boys. It is an energetic dance music featuring MBIRA-style guitars.

jizya   A poll tax traditionally levied on part of the non-Muslim community in states governed according to SHARIA law. Payment of the *jizya* symbolized a non-Muslim's acceptance of and loyalty to the Islamic state, and non-Muslims were accorded protection and the freedom to practice their religion from the state in return. According to tradition the *jizya* was introduced during the eighth century. Over time the details of the *jizya* varied greatly under different regimes and was still levied in Egypt in the mid-19th century.

juju   Yoruba urban music of Nigeria.

Juok   The god of the Shilluk people. Juok is an abstract divine being who is thought to have created the world.

ka   An ancient Egyptian concept defined as the "life force." According to ancient Egyptian philosophy the *ka* was the force that left the body on death.

Kaaba   An approximately cube-shaped building in the city of Mecca, Saudi Arabia. It is more than two thousand years old and is regarded as the most sacred site in Islam. All Muslims face towards the Kaaba during prayers.

kabaka   A Bugandan king.

kabosy   A Madagascan instrument similar to a guitar.

Kaddish   A Jewish prayer with numerous variations. The most widely known and commonly referred to version of the Kaddish is the Mourners' Kaddish, which forms part of traditional burial and memorial rituals in Judaism.

kaffir   An Arabic term used in an Islamic context to refer to non-Muslims.

kaffiya   A traditional Arabian male headdress.

kafu   A group of Malinke villages making up a distinct social unit, headed by a MANSA.

Kaikara   The Nyoro harvest goddess.

kalam   An Arabic term for the academic study of Islamic theology.

kalindula   A Zambian bass instrument and the very fast-paced form of music of the same name.

kalunga   A type of TALKING DRUM from Nigeria.

Kalunga   The supreme god of the Chokwe. Also known as Nzambi.

kamanja   A traditional Persian stringed instrument related to the violin.

Kanaga   The "Hand of God," the name of a Dogon mask worn by newly initiated young men.

kasbah   A fortress of defendable citadel in an Arab city or town.

kashrut   A Hebrew term referring to the dietary laws of Judaism.

kente   Colorful cloth generally made by Asante weavers and considered the national dress of Ghana. Kente cloth is famous for its complex patterns. The colors used in each cloth have established symbolic meanings.

keskes   A lidded pot in which couscous is steamed.

kess   A Falasha community priest, similar to a rabbi.

keta   Strip-woven cloth generally made by Ewe weavers that uses contrasting warp and weft colors with inlaid designs. It is similar to Asante KENTE cloth.

kettledrum   A drum made from a hollow metallic hemisphere with a flexible top that can be tightened or loosened to change the pitch.

kgotla   A Sotho-Tswana term that can be used to mean both meeting place and court.

khamsa (*hamsa*)   Arabic for "five." A symbol of the hand representing the five holy duties of Sunni Muslims commonly used in jewelry, amulets, and charms across the Arab world but particularly in North Africa.

khamsin   A strong local wind in Egypt.

khan   A title for a military or political leader that originated among the nomadic peoples of Central Asia and was later adopted by Turkic and Mongol peoples who introduced it to the Middle East.

khanate   The territory governed by a khan.

khanga   A rectangular cloth printed with a border and a design that includes a Swahili proverb.

khanjar   A short dagger with a curved blade associated with Omani culture and very similar to the Yemeni JAMBIYA.

kharaj A form of tax originally levied as a lump sum payment on newly conquered territories by the Arab rulers of the seventh century. Over time the tax evolved into a more general payment levied against agricultural land regardless of the faith of the owners.

khatchkar A carved memorial stone featuring a Christian cross commonly found in Armenian communities.

khums A form of tax levied under SHARIA law requiring the payment of one fifth of the value of specified assets. Originally the *khums* tax applied specifically to booty acquired in warfare.

kia A trancelike state that Kung healers usually achieve by performing a dance. This activates *num* (an energy from the gods), which is then used as a healing force.

kibbutz A collective community in Israeli society traditionally relying on agricultural production for their livelihood but increasingly employed in other enterprises as well. The first kibbutzim were founded in Palestine in the first decades of the 20th century by Jewish immigrants before the establishment of the modern state of Israel. Only about five percent of modern Israelis live on kibbutzim.

Kibuka The Ganda god of war, brother of Mukasa.

kidumu A mask worn by Tsaayi (eastern Teke) dancers at funerals and celebrations.

kinjal A traditional Circassian dagger.

Kintu The first man in the mythology of the Ganda.

kippah The traditional skullcap worn at all times by Orthodox Jewish men and sometimes by other Jewish men (and some women) during Judaic rituals. A *kippah* may also be worn by non-Jewish men as a mark of respect at Jewish rituals or Jewish holy sites.

kissar A Sudanese stringed instrument similar to a lyre.

kitumpa kya muchi One of the names a Luba diviner could call a MBOKO.

kize-uzi Fonio grain, the smallest cultivated seed. The Dogon call it "the little thing."

koine A form of the Greek language that became the lingua franca of the eastern Mediterranean from ca. 300 B.C.E. to 300 C.E.

Kongolo The Songye ruler of the Luba kingdom.

kontingo A three-stringed, Manding musical instrument.

kora A popular stringed musical instrument played widely throughout West Africa but thought to originate from Manding culture.

kosher The common English transliteration of the Hebrew term *kasher* denoting food that conforms to the dietary laws of Judaism.

kot A traditional Armenian female headdress.

Kowth The creator-god of the Nuer religion. The Nuer pray to Kowth for health and good fortune.

Kozo The name of a particular NKISI NKONDI used in matters concerning women's affairs.

Kpa A Mende HALE. Kpa members, who are largely men, are trained to use herbs to treat minor ailments.

kpegisu One of the oldest traditional Ewe drums, the *kpegisu* was probably originally a war drum.

kpezi A clay and raffia drum used at Fon funerals.

kufic A traditional form of calligraphic Arabic script. Kufic Arabic script was in use in parts of the Arabian Peninsula in the pre-Islamic era.

Kuomboka An annual Lozi festival centered on the rise and fall of the waters of the Zambezi River and the transfer of the king's capital from Lealui to Limulunga.

kuuarmuon A magistrate figure among the Nuer peoples; also known as the "leopard-skin chief" because, in the past, he would wear a leopard skin to indicate his status.

kwosso A fast ball game played by the Afar.

laibon A Maasai prophet or healer.

lamba A wraparound dress that is a very traditional style of Madagascan clothing rarely worn today.

language family A term used in linguistics to describe a group of languages, distinct but with elements in common and related historically in that they are descended from a common language. Examples of important language families in Africa and the Middle East include Afro-Asiatic, Niger-Congo, and Turkic.

leaven Any substance, such as yeast, that helps dough to rise.

Leza The creator god of the Tonga religion.

lifela Sotho songs describing the life of migrant laborers.

Likube The supreme god of the Nyamwezi religion, variously referred to as Limatunda (the Creator), Limi (the Sun), or Liwelelo (the Universe).

lineage An extended family that shares a common ancestor. If descent is traced through the male line, the lineage is patrilineal. If descent is traced through the female line, the lineage is matrilineal. Several related lineages make up a clan.

Lisa The Sun god of the Fon religion who represents strength and endurance and who causes day and heat. He is the son of MAWA.

lithoko Sotho poetry praising a noble person.

litunga A Lozi king.

lobola The name used by many Bantu-speaking people of Southern Africa for **bridewealth**.

lolwapa A low-walled courtyard that lies at the heart of a Tswana compound.

lost-wax (lost-beetle) A metal-casting method used by Asante goldsmiths and other metalworkers for centuries. A wax model of the object is made and encased in a clay mold. When the clay mold is heated, the wax melts and molten metal is poured into its place through a hole in the mold. The lost-beetle method, which may be even older, is similar but uses a real object such as a beetle or seed rather than a wax model.

Lukiko The council of ministers of a *KABAKA*.

Macardit A *YATH* in the Dinka religion. Macardit is the source of death and sterility.

madrasa An Arabic word meaning "school." A madrasa may be religious (Muslim or non-Muslim) or secular. Historically the role of madrasas was to teach the principles of Islam as well as many other subjects, and in the present day the great majority of madrasas continue this tradition.

Maghreb The Arabic name for the region comprising Morocco, Algeria, and Tunisia.

mahamba Chokwe ancestral and nature spirits that act as intermediaries with KALUNGA.

Mahdi In some interpretations of Islamic theology the Mahdi is a prophesized figure who will live on earth in the final years before the day of resurrection bringing truth, peace, and justice. Several Muslim leaders have claimed to be the incarnation of the Mahdi from the seventh to the 20th centuries but none have received wide recognition.

maina A male Kikuyu social division that shares political power with the *mwangi*.

makhzen A Moroccan Arabic term meaning "warehouse" originally used to refer to the centralized bureaucracy created by the Moroccan monarchy in the 16th century. In the present day the term is also used derogatively to refer to the governing elite of Morocco.

makossa A fast and popular style of Central African dance music that originated in Cameroon. It combines HIGHLIFE with elements of African American soul, jazz, funk, and rock.

Mamluks A military force in historical Muslim states that was controlled directly by the **caliph** or **sultan**. The first known Mamluk force served the Abbasid caliphs at the end of the ninth century C.E. Originally Mmluk soldiers were usually enslaved as children during raids into non-Muslim lands, converted to Islam, and then trained in dedicated military academies. Later the Mamluks became a hereditary class and acquired power in their own right.

mangrove forest (mangrove swamp) A forest of mangrove trees—tropical evergreen trees with intertwining roots that form a dense thicket. Mangrove forests generally occur along coasts and rivers, where their networks of roots help to anchor the soil. This can create areas of swampy land, hence their alternative name of mangrove swamps. Many West African mangrove forests have been cleared for rice cultivation. This DEFORESTATION is a threat to the great variety of animal and marine life that inhabits these areas.

mani The title of the Kongo king. Also, it is the name of an Azande initiation society that flourished in the early 20th century.

mankala An ancient game, played in many parts of the world, in which seeds are moved around a board.

mankuntu Cylindrical Tonga drums of varying pitch.

mansa A Malinke chief or king.

manyatta A camp in which, for their initiation into adulthood, young Maasai men of about 16 years of age live away from their village.

mapoto A beaded apron worn by a married Ndebele woman.

maqam A traditional Arab melody form.

maqama A traditional form in Arabic literature characterized by rhyming prose.

maquis Shrubby mostly evergreen vegetation.

marabi An early form of TOWNSHIP jazz based around three chords.

marabout An Islamic religious leader or teacher in West Africa or, historically, in North Africa. In the Berber language *marabout* means "saint."

marimba A type of xylophone, also called a balaphone. Its tuned wooden bars are played with sticks, and gourds below the bars act as resonators to amplify the sound.

masabe Spirits of the Tonga belief system. Masabe are considered to be invasive and are thought to attack and possess people. Also, the name of a Tonga drum.

mashta A female singer in Tunisia.

masquerade A festival at which masks and costumes are worn. Many African cultures have rich heritages that include masquerades, which when taken to the Americas by slaves became the ancestors of many modern carnivals.

matano Made from clay or wood, *matano* figures are used to illustrate the stories and *milayo* that are part of the teaching process of Venda girls undergoing initiation.

Mawa The creator god of the Fon religion. Mawa is the Moon god and has both male and female characteristics. Mawa is also associated with MAWU, the supreme god of the Ewe religion, which is related to the Fon religion.

mawali A collective Arabic term for the peoples of territories conquered by the Muslim Arab armies of the seventh century who subsequently converted to Islam.

mawe The basic Mende social and economic unit.

Mawu The supreme god of the Ewe religion. Mawu is usually only approached through the *trowo*. Mawu is associated with MAWA, the creator god of the Fon religion, which is closely related to the Ewe religion.

mbanje Long CALABASH pipes still occasionally smoked by some Tonga women. The *mbanje* used by men tended to be smaller and made from clay.

mbaqanga A vocal style that can be traced back to the four-part harmonies of 1950s African American bands. South African musicians at first copied these harmonies but then added an extra voice, creating a five-part harmony style reminiscent of African singing.

Mbar The first man according to Lunda legend.

mbari A political division in Kikuyu society, literally meaning "ridge"—of which Kikuyuland has many.

mbira An instrument used widely by many African peoples. It consists of tuned metal strips, attached to a resonating metal box, which are plucked with the thumbs. One of the most popular musical instruments in Central Africa, it is used in both traditional and modern music. Also called a *sansa* or thumb piano.

mboko A carved wooden figure used in Luba divination.

Mboli The all-powerful god of the Azande religion.

mbweci A Chokwe staff used by men on long journeys as a walking stick.

Mebere The one god of the Fang religion.

mesgid A Falasha synagogue.

mezonad A Tunisian musical instrument similar to a bagpipe.

Mfecane An Nguni word meaning "crushing." It is used to refer to the period (1819–39) of mass migrations and wars in the southeastern half of southern Africa. The Mfecane was triggered by the rise of the Zulu kingdom. It is known as the DIFAQANE by the Sotho-Tswana people west of the Drakensberg Mountains.

mfumu Nyamwezi diviners.

mhondoro In the Shona religion, the ancestral spirits of influential people. *Mhondoro* spirits provide the link between mortals and god.

mihrab A feature of Islamic architecture. A *mihrab* is a niche in the wall of a mosque that indicates the direction of the KAABA in the city of Mecca and, therefore, the direction Muslims should face in prayer.

mikisi mihasi Commemorative sculptures made by the Luba people that are named after certain ancestors.

milayo A Venda saying that expresses a wise or clever observation or a general truth or belief.

millet A historical term for a community sharing the same faith within the territory of the Ottoman Empire. The principal non-Muslim millets were Orthodox Christian, Armenian, Syrian Christian, and Jewish.

minaret A slender tower, topped by a platform and attached to or associated with a **mosque**.

minbar A flight of steps in a mosque, leading up to a seat from which the speaker can address the congregation.

minsereh Carved wooden female figures used by the Mende Yassi society for healing and divination.

minyan The minimum number of 10 adult Jewish males required for certain forms of communal worship in Judaism. Some Jewish communities allow women to form part of the *minyan.*

mishiki In the Luba religion, it is believed that these spirits control the supply of game and fish.

mizimo Spirits of dead ancestors revered by the Tonga. They are particular to certain families only.

Mkhulumnqande The creator-god of the Swazi religion.

mogho naba The supreme ruler, or king, of the Mossi.

Molimo The creator-god of the Tswana religion.

monoculture The continuous growing of one particular type of crop.

monogamy The practice of having only wife or husband.

Monophysite doctrine The Coptic Christian doctrine that asserts the unity of both the human and the divine in the nature of Christ.

monotheism The belief in a single, all-powerful god.

monotheistic The practice of believing in only one god.

monsoon A seasonal wind of the Indian Ocean, or the (rainy) period during which it blows from the southwest.

montane forest (cloud forest) "Montane" literally means from or inhabiting mountainous regions. A montane forest is made up of trees and vegetation that prefer the cool and moist conditions of highland areas. These forests are also sometimes known as mist or cloud forests.

Moombi In the Kikuyu religion, the wife of GIKUYU. According to legend she bore him nine daughters, the origin of the nine main clans of the Kikuyu.

moran After they have undergone circumcision, young Maasai men join the age-grade of *moran,* often translated as "warriors." Moran did act in the past as the Maasai army, but they mainly provide a flexible pool of labor for specific tasks such as herding.

mosque A Muslim place of worship.

mpsikidy A Madagascan diviner.

mud cloths Bambara mud cloths are woven by men but bear geometric designs applied by women. A pattern is painted onto a just dyed cloth using mud, then soap, then more mud. When the cloth is dry, the mud is scraped off, which removes the dye from the area beneath and leaves the pattern exposed. Usually, mud cloths are made with a pale pattern on a dark background.

mudzimo The ancestral spirit of an ordinary person according to the Shona religion.

muezzin A crier who calls the Muslim faithful to prayer. The muezzin may stand on the platform of a MINARET.

Mugizi The Bachwezi god of Lake Albert.

Muhingo The Bachwezi god of war.

Mukasa The great god of the Ganda religion.

mulena mukwae The princess chief of the Lozi kingdom, who was based in Nalolo.

mulopwe The Kunda ruler of the Luba kingdom. The *mulopwe* was the head of the government and the religious leader, and was believed to have supernatural powers.

murundu A circumcision ceremony for boys entering adulthood in Venda society.

Musang The first woman according to Lunda legend.

mushkinu The middle class of Sumerian society consisting of merchants, farmers, laborers and all nonslaves who were not part of the ruling AMELU class.

musimbo A type of Tonga drum.

musnad The script of the ancient South Arabian alphabet in use by the eighth century C.E.

muwahidun An Arabic term meaning "unitarians" used by followers of the Salafi branch of Sunni Islam (also known as Wahhabism) to refer to themselves.

mvet A stringed Fang instrument that is a cross between a zither (a musical instrument that has strings stretched over a resonating box) and a harp.

mwaash a mbooy Masks made from wood, beads, cowrie shells, and fibers that were used as a tool of royal justice by the Kuba. They were supposed to be able to assess the behavior of the king's subjects. When they appeared before their subjects, the king or chief wore the whole costume.

mwadi Made by the Tetela people, a Mongo subgroup, a *mwadi* is a mask that is part of a costume worn by dancers who performed at funerals and weddings.

Mwaku The son of MUSANG and MBAR.

mwami A Tutsi king.

mwana pwo The name for the mask and raffia (palm fiber) costume used by the Chokwe to represent the ideal wife and beautiful woman.

mwangi A male Kikuyu social division that shares political power with the MAINA.

Mwari The supreme god of the Shona religion, referred to as Murungu in historical documents.

mwata yamvo The title of the king of the Lunda Empire. It comes from an early Lunda ruler of the same name.

mwenge A beer brewed in Uganda from bananas.

n'anga Religious and medical practitioners of the Shona religion, who both heal illnesses with herbs and diagnose evil forces at work through divination.

naba A chief in Mossi society.

Nadi The supreme god of some Khoisan religions.

nakharar An historical title held by the leading caste of Armenian nobility.

nakomsé Literally meaning "the right and power to rule," the nakomsé is the Mossi ruling class, and was made up of chiefs, kings, and emperors in the past.

nalikwanda The royal barge of the Lozi LITUNGA.

Nambi A goddess of the Ganda religion; the daughter of the king of heaven, and wife of **Kintu**, the first man.

naqqara A kettledrum played by Berber musicians.

naskh A traditional form of calligraphic Arabic script. Printed Arabic texts typically use a version of *naskh*.

nastaliq A traditional form of calligraphic script developed in Iran in the 14th and 15th centuries.

nazir Leader of a Baggara group. The *nazir* acts as the official link with the Sudanese government.

ndilo A bowl used in the past for divination at the courts of Venda chiefs, in particular to identify witches.

ndlovukazi The title of the mother of the Swazi king; it literally means "Lady Elephant," a reference to her considerable influence and power.

ndop A series of wooden sculptures that represent Kuba kings. The statues were used to both commemorate a dead king and initiate a new one. *Ndop* were considered to be the receptacle of the king's spirit and would be placed by the king's bed. After his death, the statue would be placed next to the new king in order that the spirit could be passed on. Although over 100 Kuba kings were known, only 19 *ndop* have survived.

Nduala The Bachwezi god of pestilence.

Ngai The all-powerful god of the Kikuyu religion. Also, the name of the supreme god of the Maasai religion.

Ngewo The supreme god of the Mende religion.

ngikenoi Subsections of Karamojong society whose members gather for certain ceremonies. *Ngikenoi* literally means, "fireplace with three stones."

ngil A pre–20th century Fang society whose members had both political and judicial powers.

ngitela Social groupings of the Karamojong people of Uganda that celebrate religious and social events together. They are determined by geography.

ngoma A Venda drum played at a chief's court.

ngombo wa tshisuka A divination tool used by Chokwe diviners. It comprises a basket that contains over 60 carved wooden objects, each with a symbolic meaning.

ngoni A four-stringed lute, in the past played by Bambara musicians to inspire men to fight.

ngozi In the Shona religion, harmful ancestral spirits that are thought to cause evil; they can be the spirits of people who were murdered.

ngwenyama The title of the Swazi king or male ruler; it literally means "lion." The female equivalent given to the Queen Mother or senior queen is ndlovukati.

Nhialac A Dinka divinity or YATH, Nhialac can be several things: the sky; what is in the sky; an entity sometimes called "father" or "creator"; and also a power that can be possessed by any *yath* or even a particular man.

nizamiyya A form of institute of higher education founded in the 11th century C.E. in the Seljuk Empire by Nizam al-Mulk (1018–92).

Njayei   A Mende *hale*. Njayei initiates use herbs and other substances to cure mental illness, which is attributed to breaching this society's rules.

nkisi nkondi   The Kongo people make different figures out of wood, iron, and other materials they call *nkisi nkondi,* or "power figures." Nails, spikes, or blades would be embedded into the figure to mark an occasion or to deal with a particular problem, grievance, or other matter or to rouse the figure's magical or medicinal properties.

nomad   Used to describe a particular lifestyle followed by many desert-living peoples. Nomads are "wanderers" (the word derives from *nomas,* Latin for "wandering shepherd"), but they usually travel well-used paths, and their movements are dictated by the demands of trade or the needs of their herds for pasture and water.

nomori   A type of figurine made by Mende artisans.

nsikala   The *nsikala* acted as a temporary ruler when the reigning MULOPWE of the Luba kingdom died or was unwell.

ntemi   Self-governing Nyamwezi chiefdoms.

ntomos   Societies among the Bambara and Malinke whose responsibility it is to prepare young boys for circumcision and initiation into adulthood.

nubsa   The Fang term for a form of **bridewealth** that became due on the birth of a couple's first child.

nyamakala   Professional groups representing different craft workers among the Bambara and Malinke.

Nyambe   The supreme god of the Lozi religion.

Nyame   The supreme god of the Asante religion.

nyangas   Male herbalists in the Ndebele religion.

Nyikang   The hero-god of the Shilluk religion. He is thought to have founded the Shilluk and to be reincarnated in the figure of the RETH.

nyonyosé   A Mossi social class of ordinary civilians. *Nyonyosé* means "ancient ones" or "children of the earth."

Nzambi   The creator god of the Lunda religion.

Nziam   The creator god of the Teke religion.

oasis   A fertile pocket in an arid region where water from an underground source reaches the surface.

oba   A position held by a descendant of a town's founder in Yoruba society, passing in turn to princes from several ruling houses. Also, the title of the king of the historic Kingdom of Benin.

Obatala   The most important of the Yoruba ORISA, Obatala is the chief representative of **Olodumare** on earth. Obatala was taught to create the human form into which Olodumare then put life.

ocher   A yellow or reddish-brown clay. Many African people traditionally use ocher to color and style their hair or paint their bodies.

oding   A traditional flute from Cameroon usually played only by women. The *oding* is filled with water.

Ogun   A god of the historic Kingdom of Benin, Ogun was the god of farmers, hunters, and metalworkers. In the Yoruba religion, Ogun is the god associated with iron and is often shown respect by taxi drivers who have singled him out for protection while they drive their vehicles.

ohemmaa   Commonly referred to as the "queen mother" in some literature, the *ohemmaa* is actually the most senior Asante woman and not necessarily the mother of the **asantehene**.

Ohiguwu   A god of the historic Kingdom of Benin, Ohiguwu is the bringer of death.

olaiguenani   A chairman of Maasai age-grade meetings.

Olodumare   The supreme god (the owner of Heaven) in the Yoruba religion.

Olukon   A god of the historic Kingdom of Benin, son of Osanbua, who brought prosperity and long life.

omakipa   Ivory clasp buttons that were given by an Ovambo bridegroom to his bride in the past.

omda   An official of a Baggara group responsible for collecting taxes and settling disputes.

omukama   A king of the Bunyoro kingdom.

onigi   Meaning "sticks" in Yoruba, *onigi* refers to hairstyles in which the hair is wrapped to resemble sticks.

orinka   A Maasai ceremonial club.

orirembo   A Bachwezi royal enclosure.

orisa   Yoruba spirits or deities, each with its own cult, priests, temples, and shrines. There are more than 400 *orisa* in the Yoruba religion.

Orit The Falasha name for the TORAH.

oruzo In Herero society, a lineage that is traced through a person's male relatives.

Osanobua The creator-god of the historic Kingdom of Benin, Osanobua brought prosperity and long life.

Osiris An ancient Egyptian god, ruler of the underworld and judge of the dead.

oud A traditional stringed instrument commonly used in Middle Eastern music.

ozonganda A Herero compound.

Palearctic faunal realm A biogeographical zone that includes Africa north of the Sahara, Europe, and most of Asia north and west of the Himalayas.

paleontology The study of the fossil remains and ancient life-forms.

panku An advisory legislative council in the Hittite state.

papyrus A tall, reedlike water plant, or the writing material made from it by the ancient Egyptians. The ancient Egyptians also used papyrus to make boats.

Passover A Jewish festival that celebrates the deliverance of the Jews from slavery in Egypt.

pastoral Characteristic of, or like, pastoralists and their ways of life.

pastoralist A person who raises livestock.

peret A season in the ancient Egyptian calendar during which the Nile flood receded and planting took place.

pharaoh The title of the kings of ancient Egypt.

pir A Sufi teacher or master.

pitsos Sotho term for public meetings.

polis An ancient Greek city, city-state, or a collective term for the citizens of a city or city-state.

polity A general term that refers to a group with some form of cohesive political organization. It may refer to a loosely organized society, such as a tribe, but can also mean any politically organized group including a state or an empire.

polygamy The practice of having more than one wife or husband.

pongo A decorated and patterned bark cloth typical of the forager art of Congo (Democratic Republic).

Poro A Mende HALE for men. Initiates are taken to a camp in the forest where they live in seclusion for weeks. Poro teaches Mende ideals of manhood, settles local disputes, and regulates market trading.

protectorate A state or territory that is controlled by a usually stronger nation. In particular it is used to refer to the colonies established by Europeans in Africa.

Ptah An Ancient Egyptian god, worshipped as the creator of both gods and mortals.

pylon A monumental gateway, such as one at the entrance to an ancient Egyptian temple. Ancient Egyptian pylons often resembled shortened pyramids.

pyrethrum A plant of the chrysanthemum family, or the insecticide made from the dried heads of certain varieties.

qabiil The Somali clans.

qalittis Female religious leaders in the Oromo religion.

qanat A traditional water-management system used to deliver potable water and irrigation by the use of subterranean tunnels. Developed in Persia at an unknown date, the techniques later spread across the Middle East and to North Africa and southern Europe with the Arab conquests of the seventh century C.E.

qanoun A traditional stringed instrument similar to the zither used in Middle Eastern music.

qasida A traditional form of Middle Eastern poetry with origins in pre-Islamic Arabic literature and oral traditions.

qat A plant of the staff-tree family. The fresh leaf is chewed for its stimulating effects or used in tea.

quallus Hereditary Oromo religious leaders.

qumqum An Arabic perfume sprinkler.

Quran The central religious text of Islam.

rabab A bowed instrument, similar to a fiddle, largely used in the MAGHREB.

rabbi A scholar and teacher of Jewish law who is qualified to decide questions of law and ritual and to perform ceremonies such as marriages.

rai A hugely popular form of music in Algeria and Morocco, *rai* has its roots in the Algerian rural musicians of several centuries ago but has been adopted by a new generation of young, disaffected Algerians as a form of protest music.

rainforest Dense forest found in tropical areas with heavy rainfall. The trees are nearly all broadleaved evergreens. The crowns of these trees merge to form several canopies of leaves and branches. The upper canopy is pierced by even taller trees called emergents. The temperature is about 80°F throughout the year with 80 percent humidity. Up to 50 percent of the rain that falls on a rainforest consists of water released into the atmosphere by the forest itself, so without the forest, the rainfall in the region is greatly reduced. Also, rainforests are ecologically very rich and house a greater variety of flora and fauna than most other environments.

Ramadan The name of the ninth month of the Islamic calendar and the religious observances that Muslims undertake during this month. Muslims traditionally fast between dawn and sunset during Ramadan, say additional prayers, and are encouraged to read the Quran.

rebec A medieval fiddle and ancestor of the RABAB.

reg An area of gravel and pebbles in a desert.

reliquary figure A carved wooden statue designed to protect Fang ancestral relics.

reth A king who is the ruler of the Shilluk people of southern Sudan, believed by his subjects to be the incarnation of the legendary hero-god NYIKANG.

riika The Kikuyu name for an AGE-SET.

rumbira A contemporary style of Zimbabwean music that blends electric MBIRA with Congo (Democratic Republic) rumba rhythms.

rwais A group of professional Berber musicians who mix poetry, dance, and music in their performances.

Sabbath The Jewish holy day of rest, usually Saturday.

sadaqa A form of voluntary charity in Muslim culture (in contrast to the ZAKAT charity required of Muslims).

Sahel A semiarid belt of savanna extending across Africa from west to east that forms the transition zone between the Sahara Desert to the north and the more fertile region to the south.

salinization The buildup of salts in the soil that often occurs in poorly drained, irrigated drylands. As the water level rises, evaporation also increases, leaving behind the salts from the water. The concentration of salts in the soil impairs plant growth and causes crop yields to drop.

sanafil A traditional garment worn by the Afar; it is wrapped around the waist and tied on the right hip.

Sande A Mende HALE for women. Initiates are taken to a camp in the forest where they live in seclusion for weeks. Sande mostly teaches Mende ideals of womanhood, though it also provides health care and advice for women.

Sango The Yoruba ORISA associated with thunderstorms and the anger of OLODUMARE.

sangoma A Nguni word for a diviner or prophet. *Sangoma* literally means "people of the drum."

sanjak An administrative district of the early Ottoman Empire. By the end of the 14th century the *sanjaks* had become subdivisions of the larger BEYLERBEYLIKS.

sanza An Azande musical instrument made of wood or hollowed gourds and similar to a balaphone.

savanna Open grasslands, often with scattered bushes or trees, characteristic of parts of tropical Africa.

sayyid An honorific Arabic title afforded to males descended from the prophet Muhammad through his grandsons.

saz A long-necked stringed instrument used in traditional Turkish, Iranian, and Armenian music.

saza Historic provinces of the Bunyoro Kingdom.

scarification The practice of making scratches or shallow cuts to adorn the body or face. The scar formed when such a cut heals is called a cicatrix.

scribe A professional writer who copied manuscripts before the advent of printing.

scrub Dense vegetation consisting of stunted trees, bushes, and other plants. Also referred to as bush.

seder A ritual feast held on the first or second night of the Jewish festival of PASSOVER.

seminomadic pastoralism A form of PASTORALISM involving the seasonal movement of livestock.

seminomadic Used to describe lifestyles that involve a seasonal or regular movement from place to place.

sharia The system of Islamic law, which governs all aspects of a Muslim's life. The Arabic term means "the path to the water hole."

sharif A traditional Arabic title originally afforded to an individual who protects the tribe. Sunni Arabs use the term as an honorific title for the male descendents of the prophet Muhammad's grandson Husayn ibn Ali.

sharkan A traditional form of Armenian religious music.

shash A black, cloth headdress traditionally worn by a married Afar woman. Also known as a *mushal*.

shawm A musical instrument used in the Maghreb; an ancestor of the modern oboe.

shaykh A traditional honorific title typically used in the Arab world to refer to a senior and respected member of a tribe or to a prominent Islamic scholar. Among the Bedouin it is the traditional title of a tribal leader.

shemu A season in the ancient Egyptian calendar during which the waters of the Nile reached their lowest level and the harvest took place.

Shii A member of the SHIA denomination of Islam.

Shii Islam The second largest denomination of Islam.

shifting cultivation A land use system in which a patch of land is cleared and cultivated until its fertility diminishes, and then abandoned until restored naturally. This type of farming has long been practiced in Africa.

shikuki Ovambo reed baskets used for catching fish.

shiruba A women's hairstyle common in East Africa, composed of tiny braids worn close to the scalp at the roots and loose at the ends.

shongo A multibladed throwing knife. A deadly weapon, the *shongo* spins through the air when thrown, allowing it to inflict the maximum damage. *Shongo* were used by many people in East and Central Africa, the Azande and Kuba in particular.

sibhaca A Swazi dance performed by men.

Sigd A unique Falasha festival that celebrates the return of the exiles from Babylonia, led by Ezra and Nehemia.

sikidy A form divination practiced in Madagascar.

Silk Road A system of overland routes (not a constructed road) crossing nearly 4,000 miles of Asia and used for about 1,500 years for trade between the East and the West. It was named for silk, a valued commodity transported over it.

simoom A hot, violent, sand-laden wind of the desert.

sira An Arabic term for a biography of the prophet Muhammad.

sirata Designs on Maasai shields that indicate the AGE-GROUP and family of the shield's owner.

sirocco A hot, steady, oppressive wind that blows from the Libyan Desert (which is part of the Sahara Desert) across the Mediterranean into southern Europe, often accompanied by rain and dust.

sisal A strong durable fiber made from leaves of the sisal plant; it is used to make rope, baskets, and other goods.

sistrum A rattle-like musical instrument with bells.

siwa A Swahili brass horn used to announce ceremonies and religious events.

slash-and-burn A form of shifting cultivation practiced in forest regions. It is a short-term method of cultivation in which forest is cleared by cutting down and burning trees and other vegetation for temporary agricultural use. Although labor intensive, this method is ideally suited to the tropics. It allows the soil to recuperate, and the burning of vegetation fixes nutrients in the soil.

solidus A form of currency originally issued by the Romans in the fourth century C.E., which continued to be used throughout the Byzantine period.

soukous An African version of Cuban rumba music. Also a generic term for all Congo-Zairean dance music. It can also refer to a particular style of folk dancing.

steppe An extensive grassy plain, usually without trees.

subsistence agriculture A type of agriculture in which all or most of the crop is consumed by the farmer and his family, leaving little or nothing for other uses.

Sufism A mystical tradition in Islam.

sultan An Islamic title that has been used historically for many different offices of state. The title was first used by Mahmud of Ghazni, the founder of the Turkic Ghaznavid dynasty (975–1187) which ruled much of present-day Iran and Iraq, to distinguish his worldly authority from the spiritual authority of the CALIPH. Rulers of the Seljuk and Ottoman Empires typically held the title sultan, and the title is still in use in the present day by the monarchs of certain Muslim states such as Oman and Brunei.

sungu The *sungu*, one of the Luba BALOPWE, was a sort of prime minister who mediated between the people and the MULOPWE.

Sunni   A member of the Sunni denomination of Islam.

Sunni Islam   The largest denomination of Islam.

suq   The traditional commercial center or public market in an Arab city.

Swezi   A spirit in the Nyamwezi religion that is believed to influence people. Individuals who have been attacked or possessed by Swezi must join the BASWEZI society in order to obtain relief from its influence.

synagogue   A Jewish house of worship.

taboo   A social prohibition or restriction laid down by culture, tradition, or convention that forbids, for example, certain actions and helps to define acceptable behavior.

tafsir   The Arabic term for commentaries on the Quran.

tagelmust   A length of dyed cotton cloth (traditionally indigo in color) worn by Tuareg men to cover the head and face.

Tahi   A Chokwe diviner.

tajwid   The discipline of reading the Quran.

talking drum   A drum that can be used to mimic the tonal qualities of African languages. The pitch of talking drums can be adjusted by tightening the "waist" of these drums, which are often hourglass shaped. Talking drums probably originate from Wolof culture.

tallit   A Jewish prayer shawl worn by men and women during certain religious rituals. It has a knotted and twined fringe around its edge.

Talmud   From the Hebrew word for "learning," the Talmud is a collection of writings and instructions on the Jewish way of life (especially civil and religious law), based on oral teachings from the time of Moses.

tambour   A Nubian stringed musical instrument.

Tanzimat   A period of administrative reform and modernization in the Ottoman Empire during the 19th century C.E.

tarbush   A cylindrical red felt hat traditionally worn by various ethnic groups in the Ottoman empire. The tarbush is also known as the fez, particularly in Turkey.

tawhid   The Arabic word for the concept of monotheism in Islam.

tbeck   A large basket in which couscous grains, sorted according to size, are stored.

teff   A small, cultivated grain rich in iron and protein.

tefilla   A general Hebrew term for "prayer" and a small leather box containing verses from the Hebrew bible worn by Jewish men on the arm or the forehead during prayers.

tell   A mound of decayed building material built up over successive generations.

thob   A traditional ankle-length garment, usually with long sleeves, worn by men across the Arabian peninsula and in some other Arab countries. In some countries it is known as a *dishdasha*.

thuluth   A traditional form of calligraphic Arabic script that emerged in the 11th century C.E. and was later developed by Ottoman calligraphers.

timar   An area of land awarded by sultans of the Ottoman Empire to military commanders between the 14th and 16th centuries.

tinkhundla   Local authorities in Swaziland based on small groups of chieftaincies. In 1978, the Swazi king revived parliament (which he had previously dissolved in 1973) with a system of indirect, nonparty elections based on *tinkhundla*. This system allows the king to preserve his hold on power.

Tisiefa   In the Ewe religion, *Tisiefa* means the "Other World," which is where people go after death.

togu na   An open-sided building in the main square of a Dogon village. It is used for council meetings.

Torah   From the Hebrew "to instruct," Torah refers to the first five books of the Old Testament regarded collectively. It can also refer to the scroll on which this is written, as used in synagogue services, or the whole body of traditional Jewish teaching, including oral law.

Towahedo   The Orthodox Christian Church in Ethiopia, which has close links with the Egyptian Coptic Church.

township   Government-built towns in South Africa that were created during the APARTHEID era to house people evicted from "white" towns. Townships often had poor facilities and high population levels. As their inhabitants' labor was still needed in the "white" towns, however, the government developed "subsidized busing" to take people from the townships to their place of work. The journey could take up eight hours and could cost a person a quarter of their wages.

trekboer   A migrant Afrikaner farmer. *Trekboers* led the colonization of areas inland from the Cape in the 1700s.

tro   A spirit or deity in the Ewe religion.

tsetse fly   The Bantu word, "tsetse" literally means "the fly that kills." Tsetse flies carry organisms that can cause severe illnesses in both animals and humans. They flourish near rivers and in swamps, and their presence can make a region uninhabitable. The tsetse fly is particularly widespread in Central Africa.

tukl   A Nuba building with a thatched, cone-shaped roof.

tumba   A Kongo tomb sculpture.

tumellano   Sotho songs in which groups of people sing together in harmony.

Tyi-wara   A mythical half-man, half-antelope attributed with the introduction of cultivation to the Bambara.

tzedaka   The Judaic obligation to perform charitable and philanthropic acts.

ubuhake   A system whereby a Hutu could enter into a client relationship with a Tutsi, who would provide cattle to herd and general protection, in return for menial tasks.

ujamma   A rural village in Tanzania established as part of the villagization policies as set out in the Arusha Declaration in 1967, after which attempts were made to reorganize Tanzanian society along socialist lines.

ummah   An Arabic term for "community" or "nation." In the context of pan-Arabism it is used to refer collectively to all Arabic-speaking peoples or Arab nation-states. In the context of Islam it is used to refer collectively to all Muslims.

umnumzana   Each Swazi UMUTI has as its head an *umnumzana*, who is usually male but can be a woman. The *umnumzana* settles disputes, allocates land, and organizes workers.

umuti   A social unit made up of several Swazi families.

urbanization   The process of making a predominately rural area more industrialized and urban. This often involves the migration of rural people into towns.

ushr   A general tax levied on the Muslim inhabitants of territories conquered by the Arab Muslim armies of the seventh century.

vako-drazana   Traditional Madagascan songs.

vakojazzana   A contemporary Madagascan music style that combines jazz with VAKO-DRAZANA.

valiha   A Madagascan horn consisting of a long tube (in the past, it was usually of bamboo) with 20 or more strings stretched lengthwise around its circumference.

vhusha   In Venda society, girls who have reached puberty undergo this six-day initiation process.

villagization   The process of restructuring rural communities into planned, often state-controlled, villages.

vodu   A spirit or deity of the Fon religion. The plural of vodu is vodun (or vodoun, which is also an alternative name for the Fon religion). Vodun are very similar to the TROWO of the Ewe religion. *Vodu* is probably the origin of the word "voodoo," a term that embodies Western misunderstandings about the Fon religion—"voodoo" is often incorrectly described as involving "black magic," witchcraft, and the worship of fetishes (idols).

Voortrekker   An Afrikaner who took part in the Great Trek (1836–45).

wadi   A normally dry watercourse in the desert that is subject to flash flooding after heavy rain.

Waqaayo   The supreme god of the Oromo religion.

waqf   In Islam an endowment of property for charitable purposes.

warp   Lengthwise threads in a woven cloth.

wattle-and-daub   A building technique using a woven latticework of sticks thickly plastered with clay.

waya   A togalike garment worn by Oromo men.

weft   Threads that go across the warp in a woven cloth.

worso   A Wodaabe (Fulani) annual festival that celebrates marriages and births of the previous year.

yaake   A dance performed at a *WORSO* in which men are judged for charm, magnetism, and personality by elders.

yad   A hand indicator for use while reciting the TORAH.

Yanda   A carved wooden figure used in the Azande religion to represent the Yanda spirit.

Yassi   A Mende *HALE* that is devoted to the art of spiritual healing. Female Yassi diviners use *MINSEREH* figures.

yath   A divinity or power of the Dinka religion.

Yemoja   A female *ORISA,* associated with water, rivers, lakes, and streams.

yeshiva   A Judaic institute for the study of the Torah and the Talmud.

zakat   The Islamic obligation to give a percentage of one's earnings to charity.

zilin   A Fon singing technique similar to the blues.

zimbabwe   A dry-wall (without mortar) stone house or enclosure built by the Shona.

Zoroastrian   Characteristic of, or relating to, Zoroaster or Zoroastrianism; or a follower of Zoroastrianism—the religion of the Persians before their conversion to Islam. It was founded by Zoroaster (who probably lived in the 1200s), and it includes belief in an afterlife and in the continuous struggle between good and evil. Zoroastrians pray in the presence of fire, which is considered to be a symbol of order and justice.

BIBLIOGRAPHY ❧

Many of these books are reprints or revised editions. In general the most recent edition has been listed here.

GENERAL: THE MIDDLE EAST

Fawzia Afzal-Khan, ed. *Shattering the Stereotypes: Muslim Women Speak Out* (Northampton, Mass.: Olive Branch Press, 2005).

Lindsay Allen. *The Persian Empire* (Chicago: University of Chicago Press, 2005).

Mark Allen. *Arabs* (New York: Continuum, 2006).

Galal Amin. *The Illusion of Progress in the Arab World: A Critique of Western Misconstructions* (New York: American University in Cairo Press, 2006).

Yahya Armajani and Thomas Ricks. *Middle East Past and Present* (Englewood, N.J: Prentice-Hall, 1986).

Henry T. Azzam. *The Arab World Facing the Challenge of the New Millennium* (New York: I. B. Tauris, 2002).

Gawdat Bahgat. *American Oil Diplomacy in the Persian Gulf and the Caspian Sea* (Gainesville: University Press of Florida, 2003).

Shmuel Bar. *Warrant for Terror: Fatwas of Radical Islam and the Duty of Jihad* (Lanham, Md.: Rowman and Littlefield, 2006).

Roby C. Barrett. *The Greater Middle East and the Cold War: U.S. Foreign Policy under Eisenhower and Kennedy* (New York: I. B. Tauris, 2007).

Patrick Bascio. *Defeating Islamic Terrorism: The Wahhabi Factor* (Boston: Branden Publishing, 2007).

Jonathan P. Berkey. *The Formation of Islam: Religion and Society in the Near East, 600– 1800* (Cambridge, U.K.: Cambridge University Press, 2002).

Christopher Catherwood. *A Brief History of the Middle East: From Abraham to Arafat* (New York: Carroll and Graf, 2006).

Richard J. Chasdi. *Tapestry of Terror: A Portrait of Middle East Terrorism, 1994–1999* (New York: Lexington, 2002).

Youssef M. Choueiri. *Modern Arab Historiography: Historical Discourse and the Nation-State* (New York: Routledge Curzon Taylor and Francis Group, 2003).

William L. Cleveland. *A History of the Modern Middle East*, 3rd ed. (Boulder, Colo.: Westview Press, 2004).

Rodney Collomb. *The Rise and Fall of the Arab Empire and the Founding of Western Pre-Eminence* (Stroud, U.K.: Spellmount, 2006).

David Damrosch. *The Buried Book: The Loss and Recovery of the Great Epic of Gilgamesh* (New York: Henry Holt, 2007).

Joyce M. Davis. *Martyrs: Innocence, Vengeance, and Despair in the Middle East* (New York: Palgrave Macmillan, 2003).

Adeed Dawisha. *Arab Nationalism in the Twentieth Century: From Triumph to Despair* (Princeton, N.J.: Princeton University Press, 2003).

Dennis J. Deeb. *The Collapse of Middle East Peace: The Rise and Fall of the Oslo Peace Accords* (New York: iUniverse, 2003).

Toby Dodge. *Inventing Iraq: The Failure of Nation-building and a History Denied* (New York: Columbia University Press, 2003).

Kenneth R. Dombroski. *Peacekeeping in the Middle East as an International Regime* (New York: Routledge, 2007).

Sydney N. Fisher and William Ochsenwald. *The Middle East: A History.* 2 vols. (New York: McGraw Hill, 1997).

Ronald Florence. *Lawrence and Aaronsohn: T. E. Lawrence, Aaron Aaronsohn, and the Seeds of the Arab-Israeli Conflict* (New York: Viking, 2007).

Carolyn Fluehr-Lobban. *Islamic Societies in Practice* (Gainesville: University Press of Florida, 2004).

James Gelvin. *The Modern Middle East: A History* (New York: Oxford University Press, 2005).

Fawaz Gerges. *The Far Enemy: Why Jihad Went Global* (New York: Cambridge University Press, 2005).

Deborah J. Gerner and Jillian Schwedler, eds. *Understanding the Contemporary Middle East* (Boulder, Colo.: Lynne Rienner Publishers, 2004).

Joseph Ginat, ed. *The Middle East Peace Process: Vision Versus Reality* (Norman: University of Oklahoma Press, 2002).

Stephen J. Glain. *Mullahs, Merchants, and Militants: The Economic Collapse of the Arab World* (New York: Thomas Dunne, 2004).

Gary S. Gregg. *The Middle East: A Cultural Psychology* (New York: Oxford University Press, 2005).

Alain Gresh and Dominique Vidal. *The New A–Z of the Middle East* (New York: I. B. Tauris, 2004).

Peter L. Hahn. *Crisis and Crossfire: The United States and the Middle East since 1945* (Washington, D.C.: Potomac Books, 2005).

———. *Historical Dictionary of United States–Middle East Relations* (Lanham, Md.: Scarecrow Press, 2007).

Victor Davis Hanson. *Between War and Peace: Lessons from Afghanistan to Iraq* (New York: Random House, 2004).

Colbert C. Held. *Middle East Patterns: Places, Peoples, and Politics* (Boulder, Colo.: Westview Press, 2006).

Clement M. Henry and Robert Springborg. *Globalization and the Politics of Development in the Middle East* (New York: Cambridge University Press, 2001).

Dilip Hiro. *The Essential Middle East: A Comprehensive Guide* (New York: Carroll and Graf, 2003).

Albert Hourani. *A History of the Arab Peoples* (Cambridge, Mass.: Belknap Press of Harvard University Press, 1991).

Faleh A. Jabar and Hosham Dawod, eds. *Tribes and Power: Nationalism and Ethnicity in the Middle East* (London: Saqi, 2003).

Nikki Keddie. *Modern Iran: Roots and Results of Revolution* (New Haven, Conn.: Yale University Press, 2003).

Hugh Kennedy. *The Prophet and the Age of the Caliphates* (London: Longman, 1989).

———. *When Baghdad Ruled the World* (New York: Perseus, 2006).

Gilles Kepel. *Jihad: The Trail of Political Islam* (Cambridge, Mass.: Harvard University Press, 2003).

Rashid Khalidi. *Palestinian Identity: The Construction of Modern National Consciousness* (New York: Columbia University Press, 1997).

———. *Resurrecting Empire: Western Footprints and America's Perilous Path in the Middle East* (Boston: Beacon Press, 2004).

Michael G. Kort. *The Handbook of the Middle East* (Brookfield, Conn.: Twenty-First Century Books, 2002).

Neal Kozodoy, ed. *The Mideast Peace Process: An Autopsy: New and Expanded Edition from Oslo to Disengagement* (New York: Encounter Books, 2006).

David Leeming. *Jealous Gods and Chosen People: The Mythology of the Middle East* (New York: Oxford University Press, 2004).

Gwendolyn Leick. *Mesopotamia: The Invention of the City* (London: Penguin Books, 2001).

Bernard Lewis. *From Babel to Dragomans: Interpreting the Middle East* (New York: Oxford University Press, 2004).

———. *The Middle East: A Brief History of the Last 2,000 Years* (New York: Scribners, 1995).

———. *The Multiple Identities in the Middle East* (New York: Schoken Books, 1998).

Phebe Marr. *The Modern History of Iraq* (Boulder, Colo.: Westview Press, 2004).

Philip Mattar, ed. *Encyclopedia of the Modern Middle East and North Africa*. 4 vols. (New York: Thomson Gale, 2004).

Mark Matthews. *Lost Years: Bush, Sharon and Failure in the Middle East* (New York: Nation Books, 2007).

Melani McAlister. *Epic Encounters: Culture, Media, and U.S. Interests in the Middle East, 1945–2000* (Berkeley: University of California Press, 2001).

Hugh Miles. *Al-Jazeera: The Inside Story of the Arab News Channel That Is Challenging the West* (New York: Grove Press, 2005).

Jennifer Miller. *Inheriting the Holy Land: An American's Search for Hope in the Middle East* (New York: Ballantine Books, 2005).

Beverley Milton-Edwards and Peter Hinchcliffe. *Conflicts in the Middle East since 1945* (New York: Routledge, 2004).

Roy Mottahedeh. *The Mantle of the Prophet: Religion and Politics in Iran* (New York: Simon and Schuster, 1985).

Helen Nicholson and David Nicolle. *God's Warriors: Crusaders, Saracens and the Battle for Jerusalem* (New York: Osprey, 2005).

Oystein Noreng. *Oil and Islam: Social and Economic Issues* (New York: Wiley, 1997).

George Packer. *The Assassins' Gate: America in Iraq* (New York: Farrar, Straus and Giroux, 2005).

Marvin Perry and Frederick M. Schweitzer. *Antisemitism: Myth and Hate from Antiquity to the Present* (New York: Palgrave Macmillan, 2002).

James Peters. *The Arab World Handbook: Arabian Peninsula and Iraq Edition* (London: Stacey International, 2005).

Lawrence Pintak. *Seeds of Hate: How America's Flawed Middle East Policy Ignited the Jihad* (Sterling, Va.: Pluto Press, 2003).

Nicola Pratt. *Democracy and Authoritarianism in the Arab World* (Boulder, Colo.: Lynne Rienner Publishers, 2007).

David Pryce-Jones. *Betrayal: France, the Arabs, and the Jews* (New York: Encounter Books, 2006).

Donald Quataert. *The Ottoman Empire, 1700–1922*, 2nd ed. (Cambridge, U.K., New York: Cambridge University Press, 2005).

David Romano. *The Kurdish Nationalist Movement: Opportunity, Mobilization and Identity* (New York: Cambridge University Press, 2006).

Nir Rosen. *In the Belly of the Green Bird: The Triumph of the Martyrs in Iraq* (New York: Free Press, 2006).

Barry M. Rubin. *The Long War for Freedom: The Arab Struggle for Democracy in the Middle East* (Hoboken, N.J.: Wiley, 2006).

James A. Russell, ed. *Critical Issues Facing the Middle East: Security, Politics, and Economics* (New York: Palgrave Macmillan, 2006).

Anthony Shadid. *Night Draws Near: Iraq's People in the Shadow of America's War* (New York: Henry Holt, 2005).

Vaughn P. Shannon. *Balancing Act: U.S. Foreign Policy and the Arab-Israeli Conflict* (Burlington, Vt.: Ashgate, 2003).

Yaacov Shimoni. *Biographical Dictionary of the Middle East* (New York: Facts On File, 1991).

Avi Shlaim. *The Iron Wall: Israel and the Arab World* (New York: Norton, 2000).

Reeva Spector Simon, ed. *The Jews of the Middle East and North Africa in Modern Times* (New York: Columbia University Press, 2003).

Dan Smith. *The State of the Middle East: An Atlas of Conflict and Resolution* (Los Angeles: University of California Press, 2006).

Robert Spencer, ed. *The Myth of Islamic Tolerance: How Islamic Law Treats Non-Muslims* (Amherst, N.Y.: Prometheus Books, 2005).

Sandy Tolan. *The Lemon Tree: An Arab, a Jew, and the Heart of the Middle East* (New York: Bloomsbury, 2006).

Christopher Tyerman. *God's War: A New History of the Crusades* (Cambridge: Mass.: Belknap Press of Harvard University Press, 2006).

M. E. Yapp. *The Near East Since the First World War: A History to 1995* (London: Longman, 1996).

Salim Yaqub. *Containing Arab Nationalism: The Eisenhower Doctrine and the Middle East* (Chapel Hill: University of North Carolina Press, 2004).

GENERAL: AFRICA

J. Abbink, Mirjam de Bruijn, and Klaas van Walraven. *Rethinking Resistance: Revolt and Violence in African History* (Leiden, Netherlands: Brill, 2003).

Jean Marie Allman, Susan Geiger, and Nakanyike Musisi. *Women in African Colonial Histories* (Bloomington: Indiana University Press, 2002).

Molefi K. Asante. *The History of Africa: The Quest for Eternal Harmony* (New York: Routledge, 2007).

Robert H. Bates. *When Things Fell Apart: State Failure in Late-Century Africa* (New York: Cambridge University Press, 2008).

William Beinart and JoAnn McGregor. *Social History and African Environments* (Oxford, U.K.: James Currey, 2003).

A. Adu Boahen. *Africa Under Colonial Domination, 1880–1935* (London: J. Currey, 1990).

Edith Bruder. *The Black Jews of Africa: History, Religion, Identity* (Oxford, U.K.: Oxford University Press, 2008).

James T. Campbell. *Middle Passages: African American Journeys to Africa, 1787–2005* (New York: Penguin, 2006).

Jean-Pierre Chrétien. *The Great Lakes of Africa: Two Thousand Years of History* (New York: Zone Books, 2003).

Robert O. Collins. *Africa: A Short History* (Princeton, N.J.: Markus Wiener, 2006).

Frederick Cooper. *Africa Since 1940: The Past of the Present* (Cambridge, U.K.: Cambridge University Press, 2002).

Catherine Coquery-Vidrovitch. *African Women: A Modern History* (Boulder, Colo.: Westview Press, 1997).

David Coulson and Alec C. Campbell. *African Rock Art: Paintings and Engravings on Stone* (New York: Harry N. Abrams, 2001).

Basil Davidson. *Africa in History: Themes and Outlines* (New York: Collier, 1991).

———. *Modern Africa: A Social and Political History* (London: Longman, 1994).

Diagram Group. *African History on File* (New York: Facts On File, 1994).

Manthia Diawara. *African Cinema: Politics and Culture* (Bloomington: Indiana University Press, 1992).

Wayne Edge. *Africa* (Guilford, Conn.: McGraw-Hill/Dushkin, 2006).

Robert B. Edgerton. *The Troubled Heart of Africa: A History of the Congo* (New York: St. Martin's Press, 2002).

Christopher Ehret. *An African Classical Age: Eastern and Southern Africa in World History, 1000 B.C. to A.D. 400* (Charlottesville: University Press of Virginia, 1998).

J. D. Fage. *A History of Africa* (London: Routledge, 1995).

Toyin Falola and Christian Jennings. *Sources and Methods in African History: Spoken, Written, Unearthed* (Rochester, N.Y.: University of Rochester Press, 2003).

———. *Africa* (Durham, N.C.: Carolina Academic Press, 2000).

———. *Key Events in African History: A Reference Guide* (Westport, Conn.: Greenwood Press, 2002).

Bill Freund. *The African City: A History* (Cambridge U.K.: Cambridge University Press, 2007).

C. Magbaily Fyle. *Introduction to the History of African Civilization* (Lanham, Md.: University Press of America, 1999).

Stefan Goodwin. *Africa's Legacies of Urbanization: Unfolding Saga of a Continent* (Lanham, Md.: Lexington Books, 2006).

April A. Gordon and Donald L. Gordon. *Understanding Contemporary Africa* (Boulder, Colo.: Lynne Rienner Publishers, 1996).

Blaine Harden. *Africa: Dispatches from a Fragile Continent* (New York: Norton, 1990).

Robert W. Harms. *The Diligent: A Voyage Through the Worlds of the Slave Trade* (New York: Basic Books, 2002).

Susan S. Hunter. *Black Death: AIDS in Africa* (New York: Palgrave Macmillan, 2003).

John Iliffe. *Africans: The History of a Continent* (Cambridge, U.K.: Cambridge University Press, 1995).

———. *The African AIDS Epidemic: A History* (Athens: Ohio University Press, 2006).

Elizabeth Allo Isichei. *A History of Christianity in Africa: From Antiquity to the Present* (Grand Rapids, Mich: W.B. Eerdmans, 1995).

Tim Jeal. *Stanley: The Impossible Life of Africa's Greatest Explorer* (New Haven, Conn.: Yale University Press, 2007).

Robert William July. *A History of the African People* (Prospect Heights, Ill.: Waveland Press, 1992).

Vincent B. Khapoya. *The African Experience: An Introduction* (Upper Saddle River, N.J.: Prentice Hall, 1998).

Chima J. Korieh and Raphael Chijioke Njoku. *Missions, States, and European Expansion in Africa* (New York: Routledge, 2007).

Benjamin N. Lawrance, Emily Lynn Osborn, and Richard L. Roberts. *Intermediaries, Interpreters, and Clerks: African Employees in the Making of Colonial Africa* (Madison: University of Wisconsin Press, 2006).

Nehemia Levtzion and Randall Lee Pouwels. *The History of Islam in Africa* (Athens: Ohio University Press, 2000).

Paul E. Lovejoy. *Transformations in Slavery: A History of Slavery in Africa* (Cambridge, U.K.: Cambridge University Press, 2000).

Keith Lye. *Encyclopedia of African Nations and Civilizations* (New York: Facts On File, 2002).

John S. Mbiti. *African Religions and Philosophy* (Oxford, U.K.: Heinemann, 1990).

B. R. Mitchell. *International Historical Statistics: Africa, Asia and Oceania, 1750–1993* (London: Macmillan Reference, 1998).

Joyce Moss and Lorraine Valestuk. *African Literature and Its Times* (Detroit: Gale Group, 2000).

James L. Newman. *The Peopling of Africa: A Geographic Interpretation* (New Haven, Conn.: Yale University Press, 1995).

Beatrice Nicolini. *Studies in Witchcraft, Magic, War, and Peace in Africa* (Lewiston, N.Y.: Edwin Mellen Press, 2006).

Paul Nugent. *Africa Since Independence: A Comparative History* (Houndmills, Basingstoke, U.K.: Palgrave Macmillan, 2004).

Roland Anthony Oliver and Anthony Atmore. *Africa Since 1800* (Cambridge, U.K.: Cambridge University Press, 1994).

Roland Anthony Oliver. *The African Experience* (New York: Icon Editions, 1992).

Thomas Pakenham. *The Scramble for Africa, 1876–1912* (New York: Random House, 1991).

John Parker and Richard Rathbone. *African History: A Very Short Introduction* (Oxford, U.K.: Oxford University Press, 2007).

John Reader. *Africa: A Biography of the Continent* (New York: Knopf, 1998).

Marcus Rediker. *The Slave Ship: A Human History* (New York: Viking, 2007).

Barnaby Rogerson. *A Traveller's History of North Africa* (New York: Interlink Books, 1998).

Kevin Shillington. *Encyclopedia of African History* (New York: Fitzroy Dearborn, 2005).

Kevin Shillington. *History of Africa* (New York: St. Martin's Press, 1995).

John K. Thornton. *Africa and Africans in the Making of the Atlantic World, 1400–1680* (Cambridge, U.K.: Cambridge University Press, 1992).

James Walvin. *Atlas of Slavery* (Harlow, U.K.: Pearson Longman, 2006).

H. L. Wesseling. *Divide and Rule: The Partition of Africa, 1880–1914* (Westport, Conn.: Praeger, 1996).

Tiyambe Zeleza and Dickson Eyoh. *Encyclopedia of Twentieth-Century African History* (London: Routledge, 2003).

PREHISTORY AND GENERAL ANCIENT HISTORY: AFRICA AND THE MIDDLE EAST

Guillermo Algaze. *The Uruk World System: The Dynamics of Expansion of Early Mesopotamian Civilization* (Chicago: University of Chicago Press, 1993).

David W. Anthony. *The Horse, the Wheel, and Language: How Bronze-Age Riders from the Eurasian Steppes Shaped the Modern World* (Princeton, N.J.: Princeton University Press, 2007).

Richard E. Averbeck, Mark W. Chavalas, and David B. Weisberg. *Life and Culture in the Ancient Near East* (Potomac, Md.: CDL Press, 2003).

Lawrence Barham and Peter Mitchell. *The First Africans: African Archaeology from the Earliest Tool Makers to Most Recent Foragers* (Cambridge, U.K.: Cambridge University Press, 2008).

Robert L. Bettinger. *Hunter-Gatherers: Archaeological and Evolutionary Theory* (New York: Plenum Press, 1991).

Piotr Bienkowski and A. R. Millard. *Dictionary of the Ancient Near East* (Philadelphia: University of Pennsylvania Press, 2000).

Michael S. Bisson and Joseph O. Vogel. *Ancient African Metallurgy: The Socio-Cultural Context* (Walnut Creek, Calif.: AltaMira Press, 2000).

Jean Bottéro, Clarisse Herrenschmidt, and Jean Pierre Vernant. *Ancestor of the West: Writing, Reasoning, and Religion in Mesopotamia, Elam, and Greece* (Chicago: University of Chicago Press, 2000).

Stephen Bourke. *The Middle East: The Cradle of Civilization Revealed* (London: Thames and Hudson, 2008).

Graham Connah. *African Civilizations: Precolonial Cities and States in Tropical Africa: An Archaeological Perspective* (Cambridge, U.K.; Cambridge University Press, 1987).

Izak Cornelius and Pierre Jacques Venter. *From the Nile to the Euphrates: An Introduction to the Ancient Near East* (Stellenbosch, South Africa: MACU, 2002).

C. Wesley Cowan, Patty Jo Watson, and Nancy L. Benco. *The Origins of Agriculture: An International Perspective* (Washington, D.C.: Smithsonian Institution Press, 1992).

Eric Delson. *Encyclopedia of Human Evolution and Prehistory* (New York: Garland, 1999).

Fekri A. Hassan. *Droughts, Food, and Culture: Ecological Change and Food Security in Africa's Later Prehistory* (New York: Kluwer Academic/Plenum Publishers, 2002).

Jacquetta Hawkes. *The First Great Civilizations; Life in Mesopotamia, the Indus Valley, and Egypt* (New York: Knopf, 1973).

Michael A. Hoffman. *Egypt Before the Pharaohs: The Prehistoric Foundations of Egyptian Civilization* (Austin: University of Texas Press, 1991).

Donald C. Johanson, Lenora Johanson, and Blake Edgar. *Ancestors: In Search of Human Origins* (New York: Villard Books, 1994).

Chapurukha Makokha Kusimba and Sibel Barut Kusimba. *East African Archaeology: Foragers, Potters, Smiths, and Traders* (Philadelphia: University of Pennsylvania Museum of Archaeology and Anthropology, 2003).

David Lambert. *Encyclopedia of Prehistory* (New York: Facts On File, 2002).

Richard E. Leakey. *The Making of Mankind* (New York: Dutton, 1981).

Charles Keith Maisels. *The Emergence of Civilization: From Hunting and Gathering to Agriculture, Cities, and the State in the Near East* (London: Routledge, 1990).

———. *The Near East: Archaeology in the "Cradle of Civilization"* (London: Routledge, 1993).

Béatrix Midant-Reynes. *The Prehistory of Egypt from the First Egyptians to the First Pharaohs* (Oxford, U.K.: Blackwell, 2000).

Steven J. Mithen. *After the Ice: A Global Human History, 20,000–5000 BC* (Cambridge, Mass.: Harvard University Press, 2004).

P. R. S. Moorey. *Idols of the People: Miniature Images of Clay in the Ancient Near East* (Oxford, U.K.: Published for the British Academy by Oxford University Press, 2003).

Stephen Oppenheimer. *The Real Eve: Modern Man's Journey Out of Africa* (New York: Carroll and Graf, 2003).

Louis L. Orlin. *Life and Thought in the Ancient Near East* (Ann Arbor: University of Michigan Press, 2007).

David W. Phillipson. *African Archaeology* (Cambridge, U.K.: Cambridge University Press, 2002).

Michael Roaf. *Cultural Atlas of Mesopotamia and the Ancient Near East* (New York: Facts On File, 1990).

Renzo Rossi. *Cradles of Civilization: Ancient Egypt and Early Middle Eastern Civilizations* (Bath, U.K.: Cherrytree Books, 1995).

Georges Roux. *Ancient Iraq* (Harmondsworth, U.K.: Penguin, 1992).

H. W. F. Saggs. *Civilization Before Greece and Rome* (New Haven, Conn.: Yale University Press, 1989).

Jack M. Sasson. *Civilizations of the Ancient Near East* (New York: Scribner, 1995).

Thurstan Shaw. *The Archaeology of Africa: Food, Metals, and Towns* (London: Routledge, 1993).

Daniel C. Snell. *A Companion to the Ancient Near East* (Malden, Mass.: Blackwell, 2005).

Chester G. Starr. *A History of the Ancient World* (New York: Oxford University Press, 1991).

Bruce G. Trigger. *Understanding Early Civilizations: A Comparative Study* (Cambridge, U.K.: Cambridge University Press, 2003).

Trevor Watkins. *Origins of Agriculture in the Near East* (London: Routledge, 2000).

Robert J. Wenke. *Patterns in Prehistory: Humankind's First Three Million Years* (New York: Oxford University Press, 1990).

ANCIENT AND MEDIEVAL TEXTS IN TRANSLATION

Muhammad ibn Jarir al-Tabari. *History of Al-Tabari* (New York: State University of New York Press, 1985–2007).

Jim Colville, Muhammad ibn Abd al-Malik Ibn Tufayl, and Averroes. *Two Andalusian Philosophers* (London: Kegan Paul International, 1999).

Abolqasem Ferdowsi, Dick Davis, and Azar Nafisi. *Shahnameh: The Persian Book of Kings* (New York: Penguin, 2007).

Edward Fitzgerald. *Rubaiyat of Omar Khayyam: A Critical Edition* (Charlottesville: University Of Virginia Press, 2008).

A. R. George. *The Epic of Gilgamesh: The Babylonian Epic Poem and Other Texts in Akkadian and Sumerian* (London: Penguin, 2003).

Ghazzali and Michael E. Marmura. *The Incoherence of the Philosophers: A Parallel English-Arabic Text* (Provo, Utah: Brigham Young University Press, 2000).

Herodotus, Carolyn Dewald, and Robin Waterfield. *The Histories* (Oxford, U.K.: Oxford University Press, 1998).

Jalal al-Din Rumi, and J. A. Mojaddedi. *The Masnavi*, book one (Oxford, U.K.: Oxford University Press, 2004).

———. *The Masnavi*, book two (Oxford, U.K.: Oxford University Press, 2007).

Geoffrey Lewis. *The Book of Dede Korkut* (Harmondsworth, U.K.: Penguin, 1982).

Moses Khorenatsi and Robert W. Thomson. *History of the Armenians* (Cambridge, Mass.: Harvard University Press, 1978).

Nizam al-Mulk, and Hubert Darke. *The Book of Government or Rules for Kings* (London: Curzon, 2002).

Saadi and W. M. Thackston. *The Gulistan (Rose Garden) of Sa'di: Bilingual English and Persian Edition with Vocabulary* (Bethesda, Md.: Ibex, 2008).

Saadi. *The Orchard: The Bostan of Saadi of Shiraz* (London: Octagon, 1998).

INDEX